W9-BZI-180

"To Work for the Whole People"

John Ireland's Seminary in St. Paul

"To Work for the Whole People"

John Ireland's Seminary in St. Paul

Mary Christine Athans, B.V.M.

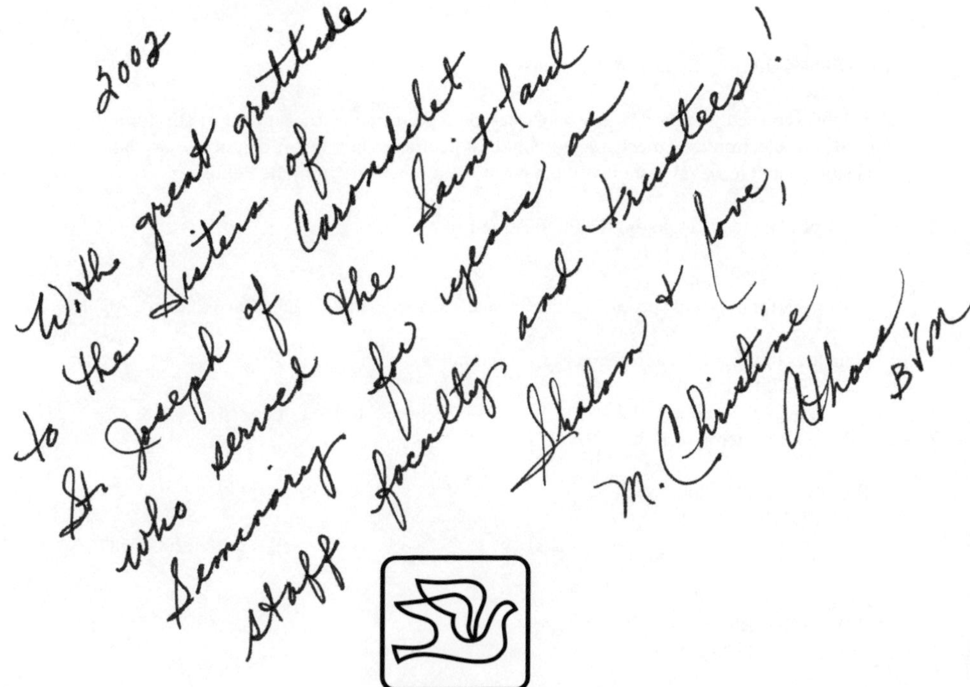
2002
With great gratitude
to the Sisters of
St. Joseph of Carondelet
who served the Saint Paul
Seminary for years as
staff, faculty and trustees!
Shalom & love,
M. Christine Athans BVM

PAULIST PRESS
New York / Mahwah, N.J.

Note: "To Work for the Whole People" is a quotation from the speech of Archbishop John Ireland at the dedication of the Saint Paul Seminary, September 4, 1895.

Jacket Photos (clockwise from top left): James J. and Mary Mehegan Hill (Courtesy of the James J. Hill Papers, James J. Hill Reference Library, St. Paul, Minnesota); Archbishop John Ireland (Courtesy of the Archives of the Archdiocese of St. Paul and Minneapolis); seminarians Henry Kolbeck, Joseph Vollmecke, William Nolan, and Thomas Flood in 1935 (Courtesy of the Archives of the Archdiocese of St. Paul and Minneapolis); and the new Saint Paul Seminary complex completed in 1989 (photo by Roger Rich).

All other photos in this volume are courtesy of the Archives of the Archdiocese of St. Paul and Minneapolis, the Archives of the Saint Paul Seminary, the Archives of the University of St. Thomas; and the James J. Hill Papers, James J. Hill Reference Library, St. Paul, Minnesota.

Jacket design by Lynn Else
Book design by Celine Allen

Library of Congress Cataloging-in-Publication Data

Athans, Mary Christine.
"To work for the whole people" : John Ireland's seminary in St. Paul / Mary Christine Athans.
p. cm.
Includes bibliographical references (p.) and index.
ISBN 0-8091-0545-4
1. Saint Paul Seminary (Saint Paul, Minn.)—History. 2. Ireland, John, 1838–1918.
3. Hill, James Jerome, 1838–1916. I. Title.

BX915.S52 A74 2002
230'.07'32776581—dc21

2001058763

Published by Paulist Press
997 Macarthur Boulevard
Mahwah, New Jersey 07430

www.paulistpress.com

Printed and bound in the
United States of America

Contents

Foreword: Archbishop Harry J. Flynn ix

Prologue: Mary Christine Athans, B.V.M. xiii

Introduction xv

Time Line xx

Abbreviations xxi

PART I: PROPHETS AND PIONEERS:
THE FOUNDERS OF THE SAINT PAUL SEMINARY (1850–1918)

1. Laying the Foundation: Joseph Cretin 3
2. Dreams for the Future: Thomas Langdon Grace, O.P. 16
3. From Vision to Reality: John Ireland 27
4. If It Hadn't Been for a Woman... 41
5. "The Hill Seminary" 53
6. The Dedication 63
7. The Saint Paul Seminary: The Early Years 73
8. Becoming Rooted in a Changing Church 103

PART II: THE SAINT PAUL SEMINARY:
FROM WORLD WAR I TO VATICAN II (1919–1961)

9. Austin Dowling: "The Rhetoric of Architecture" 135

10: John Gregory Murray:
Priesthood in the Era of "Catholic Action" 168

11. William O. Brady: Professor, Rector, Trustee, Archbishop 202

PART III: VATICAN II TO THE MILLENNIUM:
AFFILIATION, CLARIFICATION, CHALLENGES, AND GROWTH (1962–2000)

12. The Binz-Byrne Era:
Vatican II and a New Vision of Priesthood 233

13. John R. Roach:
Facing the Seminary Challenge (1975–1985) 270

14. The Seminary Within the University:
Crisis, Consolidation, Clarification (1985–1995) 312

15. Harry Joseph Flynn: Beginning the Second Century 359

16. "To Work for the Whole People" 386

Epilogue 433

Appendices

A. Rectors 437

B. Faculty 438

Notes 445

Bibliography 515

Index 533

DEDICATED TO

THE SAINT PAUL SEMINARY SCHOOL OF DIVINITY

COMMUNITY—

PAST, PRESENT, AND FUTURE

Foreword

The story of the Saint Paul Seminary is not easily or quickly told. It is rich and complex, filled with characters and events that go beyond the education of future priests. While that noble task has been at the heart of the seminary for now over a hundred years, as Sister Mary Christine Athans, B.V.M., demonstrates so ably in the following pages, the seminary has also functioned as a mirror for the life of this local church and for the greater universal Church.

My revered predecessor and founder of the Saint Paul Seminary, Archbishop John Ireland, conceived of the seminary as an instrument of service. Under its roof, in its classrooms, chapel, and library, students from the region would be challenged to make themselves worthy to be pastors of God's people. From the very foundation of this seminary formation was serious business, for Ireland took the role of religion in society very seriously. "His" priests would be equipped with the knowledge, character, and temperament to participate in that society and able to speak boldly and compellingly the vision the church offered the world. For Ireland, seminary formation required that candidates who presented themselves for Holy Orders be tested so that the people of God might benefit from the best pastoral leadership the church could provide.

In succeeding generations, the work of the seminary has gone on with quiet perseverance. As one reads this fine record of a theological school and seminary, one learns how institutions move from concept to reality. One discovers the strengths and weaknesses of those who populate them. Most important, the reader learns how this institution created structures and regularly changed or adapted them so that it might be more responsive to the needs of the church at a particular time. As one who was a seminary rector, I am well aware that seminarians experiencing seminary life may think it is hardly responsive enough to their needs and concerns. That is why this extensive telling of the story of The Saint Paul Seminary is so important, for it lays out the whole picture, identifying the circumstances, issues, and priorities that governed how the school and its faculty made their decisions always with a faithful eye to what the church requires.

In a hundred years, any institution shows notable change. The Saint Paul Seminary in its early years physically looked different from the way it does today. The large sprawling campus with six major buildings and a chapel has been consolidated into a single facility on a seven-acre corner of its original site. The faculty, once composed totally of priests, is now a wonderful blend of priests and religious women as well as laywomen and men. The once simple administrative structure of a single secretary and bursar has grown to include multiple staff professionals needed to support the expectations of contemporary higher education and the expanded requirements of seminary formation. Even the student population has changed as seminarians and others study together in common pursuit of their commitments to church service.

Over this one-hundred-year period, however, the seminary has not wavered in its central mission: the education of candidates for the priesthood. Each generation of faculty and administrators has weighed carefully how best to do that. Yet, the Saint Paul Seminary, as these pages narrate, has been faithful to its primary commitment. The quality of its spiritual formation program, the way its pastoral education program connects the seminary to the parishes of the archdiocese, and the affirmation it has received for the rigor and coherence of its academic training all reflect a deep awareness of the seminary staff about how important it is that the people of God have able and excellent pastors.

I am grateful for the diligent work of Sister Christine on what has become a labor of love. She has spent hours in the archives of the archdiocese pouring over more than a hundred years' worth of correspondence, reports, minutes of meetings, and other ways we humans keep a record of our lives. She has interviewed scores of people who know parts of the story and who could offer new angles and perspectives on what some might say is just a "simple fact." Sister Christine has exercised her discipline well, allowing the written and oral records to bear witness to what the Saint Paul Seminary has become for this local church and the region it serves. Read here the story of an institution that is in fact a story of faith—the faith of its founder, the faith of its episcopal leaders, the faith of generations of faculty, students, and staff, and the faith of the people whose prayers and support have given rise to this wonderful school and maintain it still today.

Archbishop Harry J. Flynn
Archdiocese of Saint Paul and Minneapolis

Mural in the apse of Saint Mary's Chapel by Bancel La Farge (ASPS)

Prologue

In the apse of Saint Mary's Chapel at the Saint Paul Seminary School of Divinity is a mural painted by the well-known artist Bancel La Farge. It depicts the post-resurrection appearance of Jesus on the shore of the Sea of Galilee to Peter and some of the other apostles. Surrounded by boat and nets, after an unexpected catch in the early morning hours, a startled Peter recognizes Jesus as the Risen Lord. Jesus invites Peter to respond to the question that challenges all who would follow Christ. He asks very simply: "Do you love Me?"

A mural can give the impression of a larger-than-life experience. Often, the combination of hues—some vivid, others muted—tell a story beyond the present depiction. The apse of Saint Mary's Chapel presents the images of Peter and Jesus. But it recalls the earlier experience of Jesus calling Peter to leave his boat and nets and follow Him. Peter did so with all his faults and all his gifts. This fisherman, then named Cephas, committed his life to the one he believed to be the Messiah.

Peter had learned from Jesus over the years. He had been with him when the multitude was fed, and when his mother-in-law and others were cured. He had heard the commission: "You are Peter and upon this rock I will build my church . . ."—though he may not have understood it very clearly. He was on the mountain at the Transfiguration, at the meal the night before Jesus died, and in the Garden of Gethsemane during the agony. He cut off the ear of a soldier in a show of bravado, and denied his Lord to a maidservant in the courtyard. And, most of all, he had heard the cock crow. . . .

After the crucifixion Peter must have been confused when he and John discovered that the tomb was empty. With the reports—first from the women, and then from the disciples who had been on the road to Emmaus—there was excitement and hope. The appearances of the Risen Lord in the upper room were both fearful and ecstatic. Throughout it all, Peter must have wondered how he could do *tshuvah*—repentance—how he could turn around and face the Lord after his betrayal. Certainly he was no longer worthy.

But there on the shore of the Sea of Galilee it happened. It must have seemed to Peter that there was no one else there but himself and the Lord—and the question was asked again and again: "Do you love Me?" And Peter could only answer, probably through his tears: "Lord, you know everything. You know that I love you!" (John 21:15–17).

For over one hundred years, the lives of thousands of people associated with the Saint Paul Seminary—now the School of Divinity of the University of St. Thomas—have been confronted with Peter's challenge. Students, faculty, staff, trustees, church leaders, benefactors, and friends—in chapels, classrooms, libraries, residence halls, administrative offices, board rooms, teaching parishes, and hospital wards—have heard the same question. Sometimes they have responded in joy and sometimes in pain. All have known the struggle of conversion as they have prepared or have helped others prepare for ministry in the church.

The life of an institution is like a mural. Often it lends itself to a panoramic view of the larger phenomenon. Although it has a focus, it can also present the whole *history* of an event or a relationship in addition to the moment being depicted.

The Saint Paul Seminary School of Divinity continues to respond to that question of the Risen Jesus. But it brings to each moment the history of all the events and relationships over the century that make it what it is today. That story—with its many hues and shades—is embodied in the joys and sorrows, the struggles and accomplishments, the holiness and frailty of the persons who have made up the community, both individually and collectively.

At the dedication of the Saint Paul Seminary on September 4, 1895, Archbishop John Ireland enjoined those connected to the school "to work for the whole people." It is in pursuing that goal, within the context of Jesus' question to Peter, that the present members of the Saint Paul Seminary School of Divinity community have embarked upon the next millennium.

Mary Christine Athans, B.V.M.
Professor of Church History
The Saint Paul Seminary School of Divinity
of the University of St. Thomas

Introduction

For a Methodist millionaire to contribute half a million dollars to build and endow a Catholic seminary in the United States in the 1890s was unthinkable. Yet James J. Hill, president of the Great Northern Railroad and philanthropist of the "Gilded Age," honored his devout and loving Catholic wife, Mary Theresa Mehegan Hill, by establishing the Saint Paul Seminary in St. Paul, Minnesota, in 1894. Hill's resources and practicality, coupled with Archbishop John Ireland's vision of the American Catholic Church and the education of priests necessary to serve within it, provided a new approach to seminary education at the end of the nineteenth century.

Ireland's vision of seminary had been cultivated through his own formative years as a seminarian in France, and it built on the dreams, hopes, and early efforts in seminary education of his predecessors, Bishop Joseph Cretin, and Bishop (later Archbishop) Thomas Langdon Grace, O.P. Both had seminaries attached to their episcopal residences and used their limited resources to educate young men for the priesthood. Perhaps more important, both had been models for a commitment to seminary education on the frontier. Ireland imbibed their views, all the while realizing that circumstances did not allow for grandiose development.

John Ireland's experience in promoting seminary education, both in the founding of the Saint Thomas Aquinas Seminary in St. Paul in 1885 and in serving on the committee for the establishment of the Catholic University of America in the 1880s, enhanced his desire to build a major seminary in his archdiocese which would serve as a regional seminary. Not even he could have expected that Hill's largesse would make that possible in 1894.

The history of the Saint Paul Seminary will be considered in three stages of development: Part I (1850–1918) will discuss the precursors and the founders, as well as the establishment and the life of the seminary until the deaths of James J. Hill and John Ireland; Part II (1919–1961) will focus on the period from the implementation of the Code of Canon Law in 1918, and its impact on seminaries, to the advent of Vatican II; Part III (1962–2000) will reflect on the changes in seminary life after Vatican II, and the affiliation of the seminary with the University of St. Thomas.

Although I did not plan to structure the seminary history in terms of the ordinaries of the archdiocese, it has evolved that way, and understandably so. The archbishop has the primary responsibility for education for ministry in his diocese, and his vision is a dominant factor in the formulation of programs of preparation for ministry. Part I, therefore, provides the historical context of the early years and focuses on the seminary through the vision and labors of Bishop Joseph Cretin, Archbishop Thomas Langdon Grace, O.P., and Archbishop John Ireland. Part II studies the seminary through the lenses of the three easterners who followed Ireland: Archbishop Austin Dowling, Archbishop John Gregory Murray, and Archbishop William O. Brady. Part III reflects on the period of Vatican II and after under the leadership of Archbishop Leo Binz and his coadjutor Archbishop Leo Byrne, Archbishop John R. Roach, and Archbishop Harry J. Flynn. If three is a "holy number" in the Christian tradition, we have several trinities here. My methodology has been primarily historical, with attention to theological issues and sociological data when needed.

Reverend Charles Froehle (rector 1980–1993) asked me to undertake this study in conjunction with the celebration of the centennial of the seminary. I am especially grateful to the three living rectors—Msgr. William L. Baumgaertner, Father Charles L. Froehle, and Father Phillip J. Rask—for their support, cooperation, and encouragement throughout this endeavor. I also appreciate the willingness of Archbishop Harry J. Flynn, Archbishop John R. Roach, and other major figures in the life of the seminary—past and present trustees, alumni/ae, faculty, staff, and students—to be interviewed, thus allowing for a "living" historical perspective. I have tried to balance the interviews by dialoguing with persons from different age groups and differing ecclesial perspectives. There are many I would have liked to have interviewed but time did not permit it.

The archival material in the James J. and Mary Hill Papers at the James J. Hill Reference Library in St. Paul was graciously made available to me by the director, Dr. Thomas White, and his able assistant, Eileen McCormack. The archives of the Archdiocese of St. Paul and Minneapolis contain a wealth of correspondence and other documents. I am grateful to the archivist, Stephen Granger, and to his assistant, Patrick Anzlac, for their assistance. I also appreciate the help of Lynn Conway at the archives of the Catholic University of America, the locus of the John A. Ryan Papers. The Minnesota History Center proved valuable for the Cass Gilbert Papers and additional material from newspapers and periodicals. The Archbishop Ireland Memorial Library of the University of St. Thomas holds a complete set of *The Saint Paul Seminary Register* (later *The Saint Paul Seminary Bulletin*) as well as many rare books important to the early life of the seminary. The rare book room was kindly opened to me by the director, Mary Martin, and the curator, Sheila Hague. I am also grateful to John Davenport, head of Special Collections in the University of St. Thomas Archives, and to Ann Kenne, University archivist/record manager.

Three scholars were extraordinarily generous in reading part or all of the manuscript and offering suggestions: Joseph P. Chinnici, O.F.M., Joseph P. Connors, and Joseph M. White. Without these "three Joes" I could easily have become discouraged with the challenge of the project. They are excellent scholars as well as kind and gentle persons to whom I am forever indebted. Others who read part or all of the manuscript and offered valuable suggestions were Bishop Raymond Lucker, Msgr. William Baumgaertner, Father Charles Froehle, Father Phillip Rask, Father Edward Flahavan, Dr. Victor Klimoski, Dr. Thomas Fisch, Thomas Keefe, Eileen McCormack, James Kellen, and Sister Jane McDonnell, B.V.M. The mistakes, of course, are my own. I am also grateful for the support and friendship of Dr. Anne Klejment who has been working on a parallel project. Our opportunities to discuss and share our material were extremely valuable to me.

Victor Klimoski, who was dean of the Saint Paul Seminary School of Divinity during the majority of this undertaking, was wonderfully supportive in allowing me lightened schedules to pursue this project. A Research Assistant Grant from the University of St. Thomas provided a free semester in the fall of 1994, and a sabbatical from the School of

Divinity in 1997–1998 allowed time for major work on this volume. I am also grateful to Dr. Jeanne McLean, the present academic dean, for her assistance and encouragement.

The competence and generosity of my research assistants Reverend Michael Cronin, Daniel Knaup, Reverend Robert Hart, Andrew McAlpin, and William Gerlach were helpful at every turn. I also appreciate the assistance of Janet Gould, secretary to the rector/vice-president, for providing me with copies of numerous documents, and Gerald Milske for transcribing the interviews. Will Winterer and Cal Meland offered valuable technical assistance. Thomas Keefe, associate vice-president for institutional advancement (1993–1999), afforded moral and institutional support and marvelous Irish cheer when the undertaking seemed to lag. William Hickey who succeeded him in that position energetically continued the tradition.

I am deeply indebted to Victor Klimoski for his remarkable guidance and advice in editing this manuscript. His knowledge and love of the school provided the context; his literary competence offered a loving critique. I am grateful for his support and his friendship. Johanna Baboukis and Janet Gould have once again assisted me in the production of a book. Their secretarial and technological skills, meticulous care in proof-reading, and advice in finalizing the text—as well as their generosity, good cheer, and perseverance in the face of challenge—were enormously helpful.

Last, but certainly not least, I appreciate the confidence which Lawrence Boadt, C.S.P., editor of Paulist Press, and assistant editor Joseph Scott, C.S.P. ("the fourth Joe"), have placed in me. Their encouragement and assistance have helped to bring this volume to publication.

This project has been a spiritual as well as an intellectual challenge. The prologue will, I hope, put the undertaking in perspective. Seminary education at the beginning of the new millennium is laden with many challenges. My years at the Saint Paul Seminary (1984 to the present) have been blessed and my experience of "trying to help educate the clergy *before* they are ordained" has been an exciting venture. I am grateful to the faculty, staff, and students who have enriched my life. I also appreciate the support of my family and my religious congregation, the Sisters of Charity of the Blessed Virgin Mary, for their encouragement during these years.

My hope and prayer is that this volume, in addition to telling the story of the Saint Paul Seminary, will contribute to an understanding of the growth of the Catholic Church in the United States, particularly in the Upper Midwest. May it also provide an appreciation of the creativity and stability of the founders of this institution, and all who have helped to carry out its mission of preparing people for ministry in the Catholic Church in the United States—and beyond.

Ordinaries of the (Arch)diocese of Saint Paul (and Minneapolis)*

Established 1850

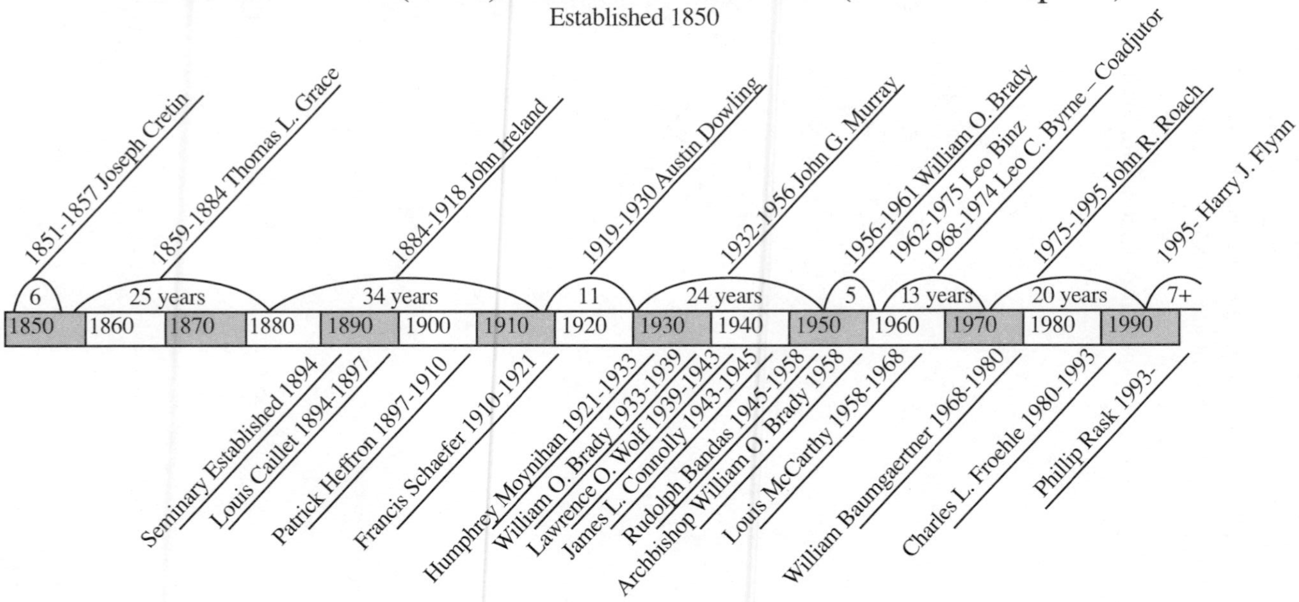

*The Diocese of Saint Paul became an archdiocese in 1888.
The name was changed to the Archdiocese of Saint Paul and Minneapolis in 1966.

Abbreviations

AASPM	Archives of the Archdiocese of St. Paul and Minneapolis
AATS	American Association of Theological Schools (The AATS name was changed to ATS in 1974.)
ACUA	Archives of the Catholic University of America
ASPM	Archdiocese of St. Paul and Minneapolis
ASPS	Archives of the Saint Paul Seminary
ATS	Association of Theological Schools of the United States and Canada
CGP	Cass Gilbert Papers, Minnesota Historical Society
CCD	Confraternity of Christian Doctrine
CUA	Catholic University of America
DP	Austin Dowling Papers, AASPM
ER	*Ecclesiastical Review* (Name was changed to *American Ecclesiastical Review* in 1944.)
JARP	John A. Ryan Papers, CUA
JGMP	John Gregory Murray Papers, AASPM
JIP	John Ireland Papers, AASPM; and MHS
JJHP	James J. Hill Papers, Hill Reference Library, St. Paul
LBP	Leo Binz Papers, AASPM
LCBP	Leo C. Byrne Papers, AASPM
MAPS	Master of Arts in Pastoral Studies
MARE	Master of Arts in Religious Education
MATS	Midwest Association of Theological Schools
MHS	Minnesota Historical Society

NC	*Northwestern Chronicle*
NCA	North Central Association of Colleges and Universities
NCCB	National Conference of Catholic Bishops
NCEA	National Catholic Educational Association
NCRLC	National Catholic Rural Life Conference
NCWC	National Catholic Welfare Conference
NPASPM	Necrology of the Priests of the Archdiocese of St. Paul and Minneapolis
PPF	Program of Priestly Formation
SPS	Saint Paul Seminary
SPSSOD	Saint Paul Seminary School of Divinity
USCC	United States Catholic Conference
WOBP	William O. Brady Papers, AASPM

I
Prophets and Pioneers
The Founders of the Saint Paul Seminary
(1850–1918)

CHAPTER 1

Laying the Foundation
Joseph Cretin

> Down into his school basement he went, and there chose two boys whom he had already admitted to serve in the sanctuary, and, leading them up stairs to the altar of the Blessed Virgin, he said: "My dear boys, let us kneel and say a prayer. I put you under the protection of God and of His Blessed Mother; you are the beginning of my diocesan Seminary, the first seminarians of St. Paul."[1]
>
> Bishop Joseph Cretin's Commissioning of John Ireland and Thomas O'Gorman, Cathedral of St. Paul, April 1853

The dream of a seminary for the Diocese of St. Paul was born with the appointment of Joseph Cretin as the first bishop to serve the newly-established Minnesota Territory. The United States Congress voted on March 3, 1849, for territorial status for that vast area bordered by Iowa to the south and the Canadian border to the north, by the Mississippi and St. Croix Rivers to the east, and the Missouri and White Rivers to the west. The Catholic bishops of the United States, meeting at the Seventh Provincial Council in Baltimore the following May, recommended that the 166,000-square-mile territory of Minnesota be constituted as a diocese with St. Paul as the see-city.

Events in Europe delayed the process. Revolutions had erupted throughout Europe in 1848. Pope Pius IX, initially perceived to be liberal and open to a united Italy at the time of his election to the papacy in 1846, became increasingly convinced that he needed to take a more conservative stance. A pivotal and traumatic event was the 1848 assassination of his chief minister, Pelegrino Rossi. Pius fled Rome in disguise on November 24, 1848, and took refuge in Neapolitan territory at Gaeta. He did not return to Rome until April 12, 1850.

The Gaeta experience had a permanent effect upon the pontiff. "Pio Nono"—as he was known by the Italians—became almost paranoid in identifying liberal principles proposed in any country affected by the French Revolution of 1789 with efforts to destroy the church. Not surprisingly, a new diocese in the United States was not a primary concern for Pius IX in the early years of his pontificate. Nonetheless, he eventually erected the new Diocese of St. Paul on July 19, 1850, despite the fact that the principles of the United States and its separation of church and state were a product of revolution and the Enlightenment. The next twenty-eight years of his pontificate became an exercise in defending an embattled church and attempting to solidify the authority of the papacy. The definition of the doctrine of the Immaculate Conception in 1854, the promulgation of the *Syllabus of Errors* in 1864, and the definition of papal infallibility at Vatican I in 1869–1870 were all efforts to build up the spiritual power of the papacy as its temporal power was slipping away.[2]

In its earliest years, the Minnesota area had been predominantly inhabited by French missionaries and fur traders. It seemed fitting, then, that a French priest would be the first bishop. That appointment was given to Joseph Cretin, who was born in Montluel in the Department of Ain on December 10, 1799, as Napoleon Bonaparte was becoming de facto dictator of France. Cretin was the youngest of four children of a devout Catholic bourgeois family which had suffered in the French Revolution. His grand-uncle, a Carthusian monk, was guillotined; his mother spent time in prison; his home was a shelter for priests and nuns during the Reign of Terror.[3] Certainly this atmosphere affected his sense of values and his deep devotion to the church. Joseph received his first Holy Communion on May 12, 1812, while Pope Pius VII was being held prisoner by Napoleon.

Cretin attended the *petit séminaire* at Meximieux from 1814 to 1817, but not specifically in the clerical program. He continued his study of philosophy at L'Argentière and Alix. After a time his parents became impatient with his indecision. They did not want to pressure him to be a priest, but his father strongly encouraged him to make up his mind. In 1820 he finally made a clear decision for priesthood and

Joseph Cretin, bishop of St. Paul from 1851 to 1857

began his theological studies at Saint-Sulpice in Paris as a student for the Archdiocese of Lyons. In October of that year he wrote to his family at Montluel: "At last I have put on the cassock, never to put it off. To tell you of my joy in exchanging the garb of the world for that of renunciation to its aims and promises, is beyond my power."[4]

The church to which Cretin committed his life in the post-Napoleonic age was recuperating from the pain of revolution and dictatorship which had caused it severe suffering. Napoleon had negotiated a compromise with the church in the Concordat of 1801, which provided relief from the fear and persecution of the previous decade. Under the Concordat the Catholic liturgy was restored, church property was returned to the clergy, and all bishops were to resign to allow Napoleon an opportunity to nominate a new hierarchy. The number of dioceses in France was limited to fifty and, to allow for greater state control, the dioceses were made coextensive with departments (provinces). In effect, public practice of the Catholic religion was permitted as long as it conformed to government regulations.

With the Concordat, Napoleon also published the "Organic Articles," a return to Gallicanism, in which the Roman Catholic Church in France understood itself as more or less free of the ecclesiastical power of the papacy. The Articles had not been approved by Pius VII, who protested vehemently. Clashes between the pontiff and the emperor were inevitable, culminating in the excommunication of the emperor by the pope, and the captivity and house arrest of Pius VII in France. Because he refused to succumb to Napoleon's imperial pressure even after imprisonment, Pope Pius VII emerged a hero in the waning days of the emperor. Moreover, the restoration of the Catholic Church under Napoleon, however controlled, did allow seeds to be planted for the religious revival of the nineteenth century.

Reaction against the Enlightenment and the French Revolution gathered momentum in the early nineteenth century as the people of Europe became convinced that so-called freedom had led only to anarchy and political control had resulted in religious distortion. Those who thirsted for stability and spirituality saw in Catholicism the religion of tradition and authority which would allow for peace and security again. In yearning for the joys of yesteryear, many idealized the past.

Nineteenth-century romanticism, born out of the trauma of the French Revolution and Napoleon, flourished with a new sense of the glories of the medieval world. The emotional, the sensate, and the mysterious become dominant themes in literature. Intuition substituted for reason. A neo-Platonic, neo-Augustinian dualistic vision of the human person with an emphasis on darkness, sin, and guilt replaced the more rationalistic Thomistic model of grace-building-on-nature that had been more acceptable in the era of the Enlightenment.

Romanticism's impact on the Catholic Church was enormous. It ratified the conviction of conservatives who decried liberal principles based on reason and who championed the values inherent in an authoritarian structure. The restoration of royalty to their thrones in 1815 by the Congress of Vienna was perceived by some as a kind of "resurrection" experience: the church had been given a new opportunity to reform and transform itself, to come back to life—a "second spring." The desire was not only to rebuild the church in Europe, but to carry the message of the Gospel to the far corners of the earth. Many religious orders were refounded, and new congregations were born. Devotionalism was rekindled. It was within that period of renewal and excitement in the church in France that Joseph Cretin arrived at the Seminary of Saint-Sulpice in Paris.

To understand Joseph Cretin and later bishops, rectors, and faculty members of the Saint Paul Seminary, it is important to have some knowledge of the Seminary of Saint-Sulpice. It was the mother institution of the Society of Saint Sulpice founded by Jean-Jacques Olier (1608–1657) in the seventeenth century. The reforms for seminaries from the Council of Trent (1545–1563) had been slow in coming to France. Key to French seminary reform was Père (later Cardinal) Pierre de Bérulle (1575–1629), who brought the Oratorians, founded by Philip Neri (1515–1595) in Italy, to France in 1611. He believed that the model of secular priests living in community without vows, grounded in a deeply christological spirituality, should be the basis for the development of a holy and zealous clergy so needed in post-Reformation France.

The French school of spirituality, in which Bérulle was a commanding presence, included Jean-Jacques Olier, John Eudes (1601–1680), founder of the Congregation of Jesus and Mary—the Eudists—and Mother Madeline de Saint-Joseph (1578–1637), twice prioress at the Great Carmel in Paris and friend and confidante of Bérulle.[5] Their writings emphasize *adoration*—which required an attitude of *abasement* before God; *adherence* to Jesus—the one who perfectly adored the Father; *annihilation* of all self-interest; and *abnegation*—as exemplified in Mary's perfect servanthood. These dispositions of the soul prepared one for the *apostolic duty* of spreading the message of Christ and building the kingdom of God.[6] This spirituality became foundational to the Sulpician model of education for priesthood.

Bérulle's successor as the leader of the Oratory movement was Charles de Condren (1588–1641). He laid great emphasis on the victimhood of Christ. Joseph M. White, in his study *The Diocesan Seminary in the United States,* summarized Condren's thought as follows:

> As a perfect victim, his [Christ's] sacrifice on the cross was the act of priestly mediation that made redemption possible. The resurrected Christ in heaven is the eternal victim and priest and therefore the source of grace. The ordained priest reproduces Christ and provides the means of grace to believers through the Mass and the sacraments.[7]

It was the identification of Christ and the priest, as espoused by the French School in the seventeenth century, that enhanced Sulpician spirituality. "The character of Holy Orders confers, as it were, a new nature, a new personality upon the priest. He is drawn by ordination into the personality of Christ, and with Him becomes by state, by an *ontological* reality, an official person."[8] The scholastic interpretation of priestly ministry within the category of ontology had been common since the Middle Ages, but was basically a metaphysical description. The French school proceeded to a psychological analysis. This theology and spirituality emphasized the separation between priest and laity, between ordained and non-ordained. To be identified with Christ the Eternal Victim required great self-discipline and self-denial.

Jean-Jacques Olier was influenced by Condren's vision of priesthood and incorporated his ideas into the retreats he gave to those preparing for ordination and to members of the diocesan clergy. After a series of experiments in which Olier and a group of priests living together established seminary programs at Chartres and at Vaugirard, they became convinced of the need to expand and search for a larger facility. The parish of Saint-Sulpice, in the Faubourg Saint-Germain district of Paris, was under the jurisdiction of the abbey of Saint-Germain which was a benefice of Henri de Bourbon. "With the latter's approval, the incumbent curé ceded the parish to Olier, who became pastor in August 1642."[9] Olier then established a community of priests and seminarians at Saint-Sulpice and the life of the most famous seminary in France began.

The decision of the archbishop of Lyons to send Cretin to Saint-Sulpice not only was pivotal for his own preparation for ministry but would also have a profound effect on the implementation of seminary education in the dioceses of Dubuque and St. Paul. Cretin took Sulpician spirituality and discipline seriously. Archbishop John Ireland, in his unfinished life of Bishop Cretin, describes a booklet which the young Cretin began writing while at Saint-Sulpice in 1821. He entitled it: "Method and Practice in order to sanctify all my actions and to spend the whole day in union with our Lord Jesus Christ." According to Ireland: "The booklet is precious. It unlocks the soul of Joseph Cretin, as he was, not only in the Seminary of Saint-Sulpice, but, no less, throughout his whole career, to the hour of his death in his missionary home in St. Paul."[10] A separate leaf with a summary of this "Rule" was found on the table next to Cretin's bed after his death.

One of the "General Means of Sanctification" that Cretin listed was: "To beg often from God that He make me more humble, more void of myself, that He extirpate within me all love of myself; to say often to Him, that I wish to do nothing that is not done through Him and for His greater glory." Ireland claimed:

> From early youth to the day of his death, Joseph Cretin aimed at being a saint—the saint of the old school of Christian sainthood, so remote alas! from the usual trend of modern thought and habit . . . totally immersed in the supernatural, seeing all else through its prisms . . . seizing upon all the uses and practices that authorized heroes of Christian saintship believed to be necessary or profitable in the subjugation of the body to the surer flights of the soul towards the All-Perfect God.[11]

Cretin was imbued with a love of priesthood and a desire to serve God grounded in a christologically-oriented spirituality and a strong sense of discipline which were the fabric of life at Saint-Sulpice. He had even hoped to give the last full measure and volunteer for the missions in China, but was dissuaded in his earlier years.

After his ordination for the reinstituted Diocese of Belly in 1823 by Bishop Alexander Raymund Devie, Cretin was assigned to the parish at Ferney, not far from the city of Geneva, a stronghold of Protestantism. Ferney had also been the home of Voltaire, the arch-critic of the Catholic Church. Building up the morale of Catholics who were frequently challenged by the *hérétiques* was one of Cretin's goals. As a young curate, he founded a school for altar boys that grew into a boarding school for secondary students.[12] He loved students, teaching, and the challenge of educational administration. Eventually he became the pastor of the parish and was beloved by the people. He had valuable friendships with other priests in towns nearby such as John Vianney, the Curé of Ars, and Peter Chanel, who later joined the Marist Fathers and became a missionary and martyr on the island of Futuna in Oceania. The dearest friend and confidant in his life was his sister Clemence to whom he wrote regularly and with whom he shared his inmost thoughts. During his years as pastor one chronicler stated: "All who know Monsieur Cretin spoke with admiration of his faith, his kindliness of heart, his zeal, his devotedness to youth, his great charity, his love of the ceremonies of the sanctuary."[13]

It was Bishop Mathias Loras of Dubuque, Cretin's former professor and friend at Meximieux, who, while on a recruitment trip in Europe in

1838, ignited again within the young French priest the challenge of the foreign missions. Loras invited Cretin to teach the Indians and immigrants in America, where there was enormous need. Cretin reflected painfully on the difficult question of leaving his beloved sister, his father who was near death, and a parish that he loved well. He became convinced, however, that this was a call he must heed. After receiving permission from the bishop of Belly for a temporary absence, he literally stole away from his family, students, and parishioners at Ferney on August 16, 1838, to join Bishop Loras and the other recruits at Le Havre for the trip to America.[14] In the same group were four subdeacons, including Lucien Galtier (1811–1866) and Augustin Ravoux (1815–1906), both of whom would be important figures in Minnesota history.

Before their arrival at Dubuque, Loras came to know and appreciate even more the gentle, creative, competent Cretin, and their friendship deepened.[15] Loras made Cretin his vicar-general, a lofty title for one who would be a missionary to the Native Americans, a circuit rider to the immigrants, and who, despite his shy and reserved demeanor, was eager to develop new approaches to evangelization. During Cretin's years in the Dubuque diocese, a major part of his ministry was centered in Prairie du Chien. It was there that Cretin brought a small printing press and printed pious tracts and holy cards for the spiritual development of his far-flung congregations. The press also became a resource for Father Augustin Ravoux, who spent two months with Cretin in 1843 and printed a book in the Sioux language entitled *Path to the House of God*.[16]

When St. Raphael's Seminary was established in 1840 in Dubuque, Cretin was appointed the first rector and served as rector, professor, and administrator for eleven years. This small enterprise was located on one floor of the episcopal residence and consisted of a few students studying classics, philosophy, and theology. Both Loras and Cretin dreamed of establishing a diocesan college which would also serve as a seminary. The 1848 report of Bishop Loras to the Lyons Society stated: "A college, which will serve as a seminary, is being prepared. We have 8 students, a few of them in Sacred Orders."[17] The present-day Loras College is the outgrowth of that plan.

No wonder, then, when the northern section of the Dubuque diocese was to be given independent status, Joseph Cretin was appointed the first bishop. His trip to France for discernment purposes culminated in a visit with his ordinary of earlier days, Bishop Devie, who urged him to put aside his scruples. Devie consecrated Cretin bishop on January 26, 1851, and also offered to educate prospective candidates for the priesthood for the newly-formed missionary diocese of St. Paul gratis at the *petit séminaire* at Meximieux. Cretin never forgot that promise.

The newly-consecrated bishop arrived in St. Paul on July 2, 1851, on the steamboat *Nominee*. The pilgrimage to France changed his life. In addition to being ordained to the episcopacy, he had embarked upon a journey of fundraising and recruitment, and in all he had been successful. Cretin was welcomed by Father Augustin Ravoux in St. Paul and given a tour of the area, including the simple log chapel built by Father Lucien Galtier in 1841 and expanded by Father Ravoux in 1847. In the summer of 1851 it became the first "cathedral." The thirty-six-year-old Ravoux was the only priest in the diocese with the exception of two missionaries near the Canadian border. In 1851, the Minnesota territory had about six thousand white settlers, of whom three thousand were Catholic, and a population of about thirty thousand Indians.

The far-sighted Ravoux, when he learned of the establishment of the diocese, had negotiated for property that would allow for a proper cathedral to be built. He put up a bond for twenty-one lots for the sum of $800 with Vetal Guerin.[18] He also made a down payment on the lot on the corner of Sixth Street and Wabasha Avenue where he believed the new cathedral should be built. The cost of that property was $100, but it included some lumber already on the ground for building, so Ravoux felt it was not an exorbitant price. Shortly after his arrival, Cretin paid for the twenty-two lots and received the deeds. Plans were made immediately to build a new cathedral which would also serve as rectory, seminary, boys' school, library, and parish center. It was completed by November 1851, at a total cost of $5,000.[19] That was the location of the first seminary of St. Paul.

During his years as vicar-general in Dubuque, Cretin had a warm relationship with the Sisters of Charity of the Blessed Virgin Mary. In January 1851, after accepting the episcopacy, he wrote from Lyons and requested "two or three of your good Sisters" to join him in St. Paul to begin a school in the new diocese.[20] Due to the lack of sisters to fulfill commitments already made, and the inability of this mostly Irish community to speak French, they did not accept Cretin's invitation. Following Bishop Loras's advice, Cretin then invited the Sisters of St. Joseph of Carondelet from the St. Louis area. They "responded with alacrity." Four of them traveled north on the Mississippi and arrived in St. Paul on November 3, 1851. They founded a girls' school in the old log cabin chapel which became St. Joseph's Academy, established St. Joseph's Hospital shortly thereafter, and from 1905 to 1987 served at the Saint Paul Seminary in various capacities, as will be discussed later.[21]

Cretin was now fifty-three years old. By this time he was described as short, corpulent, bespectacled, shy, a bit rigid, urbane, elegant in speech, and courageous.[22] He regularly taught catechism to the children and courses to the seminarians. With his musical accomplishments (he played the flute and the organ), Cretin brought a sense of *esprit* to the liturgy. He never tired of teaching hymns in French, English, and Latin to the congregations he visited. Father Anatole Oster recalled that even years later it was not uncommon to hear an Irish settler singing *"En ce jour, O bonne Madonne!"* as he walked the streets of St. Paul.[23]

According to the directives of the Council of Trent, every cathedral or metropolitan church was to erect a seminary for the education of "poor boys" as future priests, although the sons of the more affluent could attend if they paid their own expenses. Candidates were to be of legitimate birth and at least twelve years old. They were to be of good character and have a certain competence in their ability to read and write.[24] A major goal of Cretin early on was the building of a seminary for the diocese, probably not unlike St. Raphael's in Dubuque. In the meantime, he personally took charge of the completion of studies of the three seminarians who returned with him from France: John Fayolle, Edward Legendre, and Marcellin Peyragrosse.[25]

In the fall of 1851 Cretin began a school for boys on the first floor of the cathedral complex. His faculty, for several years, consisted of any priests or seminarians he could enlist. Most interesting are letters from a seminarian named Daniel J. Fisher who had come to St. Paul from New York at Bishop Cretin's invitation, hoping to convert Indians. Instead, Fisher found himself a teacher in a classroom—not nearly as glamorous and heroic as working among the Native Americans and possible martyrdom. He wrote to a New York seminarian: "My mission is among dirty little ragged Canadian and Irish boys. Every day, morning and afternoon, I practice patience with these wild little fellows—try to teach them who God is and then instruct them in the mysteries of the A.B.C." He found the adults, as well as the children, to be indifferent and irreligious. It was a great mortification "to take charge of these impudent and insulting children of unthankful parents."[26] Bishop Cretin ordained Daniel Fisher on the vigil of Pentecost in 1853; he was the first American to be ordained for the Diocese of St. Paul.[27] Fisher returned to the East a few years after his ordination. One of the "wild" little Irish fellows who may have attended his ordination was quite possibly John Ireland, the future archbishop of St. Paul.

The families of John Ireland and Thomas O'Gorman had arrived together in St. Paul in 1852 and the boys were enrolled as students at the cathedral school. Bishop Cretin's decision to begin a seminary for his diocese with the goal of attracting the sons of the immigrants who could eventually provide a native clergy for the area became embodied in these two Irish boys. John Ireland, age fourteen, and Thomas O'Gorman, age eleven, both showed academic promise. They must have been somewhat startled when, on an April morning in 1853, Bishop Cretin chose them as his first seminarians. Cretin was hardly non-directive in his vocational counseling when he dedicated them before the statue of Our Lady of Victory and said: "You are the beginning of my diocesan Seminary, the first seminarians of St. Paul."[28] Ireland wrote of the incident some sixty years after the fact, recalling that Bishop Cretin "spoke with ecstasied countenance of the sublimity of the priesthood, of the duties it imposes, of the holiness of thought and affection it requires."[29]

Father Ravoux escorted Ireland and O'Gorman to France where they would study at the *petit séminaire* at Meximieux as their patron had done many years before. They arrived in October 1853, foreigners in a strange but exciting land. Their "home away from home" during those vital teenage years was with Clemence Cretin, who mothered them and sometimes chastised them, but very clearly loved them as her own. They were, however, never to see Bishop Cretin again.

Before returning to St. Paul, Father Ravoux visited in France and also did some recruiting. He shared with potential missionaries stories of life in the Upper Midwest of the United States with its extraordinary need for priests to face the challenges of converting the Indians and ministering to the immigrants on the frontier. Ravoux returned to the United States with seven seminarians, among them Louis Caillet and Felix Tissot of Lyons, Claude Robert of Le Puy, Anatole Oster, George Keller, Francis Hurth, and Valentine Sommereisen of Strasbourg. They arrived in St. Paul on June 16, 1854.

What might Joseph Cretin have been like as a bishop and seminary rector? One of his seminarians, Louis Caillet, spent three years of study and preparation in the seminary at the cathedral residence. Bishop Cretin was a model for him and the other young men who arrived on the frontier to finish their program for priesthood. Accustomed as they were to aristocratic bishops who lived in palaces and consorted with royalty, it must have stunned them to see Bishop Cretin sweeping his own room, chopping wood, and working in the garden. He would wake one of them each morning to serve his 5:00 A.M. Mass. Sometimes they would accompany him as he visited the churches and missions in the diocese, often living in primitive conditions. They saw the bishop actively ministering to the sick and dying and responding to those in need, Catholic and non-Catholic alike. Anatole Oster, a classmate of Caillet and the last to be ordained a priest by Bishop Cretin before his death, was equally impressed with Cretin's simplicity and spirituality. Mostly, Oster remembered Cretin challenging him to preach well and his injunction: "If you wish to do good to your people love God above all things and also love your people with your whole heart."[30]

Cretin's health began to deteriorate in 1856. His final months of suffering were acute, and Caillet was one of two seminarians who attended him.[31] The only thing the bishop complained about was the fact that he was causing work and disruption for those who were caring for him. On one occasion when Caillet asked him the cause of his depression, he answered: "I am so long sick," then added, "not for myself do I speak so, but for yourselves, I feel that I (am) now uselessly ruining your health."[32] Louis Caillet was alone with Cretin when he died on February 22, 1857. Cretin had been bishop, rector, and mentor for him. When Caillet was appointed the first rector of the Saint Paul Seminary in 1894, he clearly had a superior model.

Cretin exemplified charity, humility, and simplicity. The spirituality he had learned at Saint-Sulpice had served him well and would influence Ireland, Caillet, and others who would establish the Saint Paul Seminary. Although, as Marvin O'Connell suggests, that spirituality was introspective, individualistic, somewhat self-indulgent, and with a hint of Jansenism, the personal austerity practiced in those early days as seminarians in France may explain how ordinary men were able to find the inner strength to endure the hardships of the frontier in America. Life on the missions took a physical and emotional toll. The idealism of the romantic era, and the discipline which aimed to sublimate worldly desires to higher spiritual goals, were foundational to the extraordinary lives of the French missionaries in the new world.[33] Joseph Cretin was an admirable example of this combination of gifts and imbued the members of his infant diocese with hopes and dreams for a vibrant church in America and for an institution that would educate those who would minister within it.

CHAPTER 2

Dreams for the Future

Thomas Langdon Grace, O.P.

> We had indulged the hope of being able to establish a seminary for the diocese with the faculty and Board of Directors from among our own clergy; but the pressing needs for the services of the clergy in other departments, together with our limited resources, has compelled us to postpone the undertaking until circumstances will be more favorable.[1]
>
> Pastoral Letter of Bishop Thomas Langdon Grace
> to the Clergy of the Diocese of St. Paul
> April 1867

St. Paul was without a bishop for more than two years following Cretin's death. This "interregnum" caused St. Paul to be described as "the widowed diocese." The indefatigable Father Augustin Ravoux served as administrator. During that time the new cathedral planned by Bishop Cretin was, for the most part, completed. Financial resources were especially tight due to the panic of 1857, so a scaled-back building resulted.

A vacancy in the episcopacy on the frontier was not easy to fill. The Diocese of St. Paul in the frigid Northwest, where challenges demanded heroic commitment, was not seen as a prime appointment. Father Anthony Pelamourgues of Davenport, vicar general to Bishop Loras, was appointed but went to Rome to return the documents and beg to be excused. Pope Pius IX finally agreed. Next, the Holy Father appointed Father Thomas Langdon Grace, O.P., who also returned the bulls of appointment to Rome by mail and asked that he be allowed to decline the assignment because of his "unworthiness." The pope proved more insistent this time and returned the documents to Grace with a positive command to accept. In a spirit of obedience the Dominican did so, and was consecrated bishop on July 24, 1859, by Archbishop Peter Richard Kenrick in the cathedral in St. Louis.

No one was more delighted to have an ordinary for St. Paul than the veteran missionary Augustin Ravoux, who was eager to be free of his administrative responsibilities. He felt compelled, however, to explain to the Society for the Propagation of the Faith in Paris why it had become so difficult to acquire a bishop for the diocese. He wrote: "In view of the great needs of a new diocese and of the small resources of it, it is a hard task to struggle against difficulties, so that the mitre has become an object of dread."[2] Among the challenges facing the new bishop which Ravoux mentioned was that "a seminary be opened." Another member of the St. Paul clergy, Father Johann Fayolle, wrote to his priest-brother in France regarding the situation of procuring a bishop, "Nothing is yet done for the erection of a seminary, the future is not very bright, the new bishop will have much to do. The episcopal sees in the United States are not *sine curis* and generally ambition leads [candidates] to refuse the mitre [rather] than accept it."[3]

Although Thomas Langdon Grace reluctantly accepted the challenge, his commitment to the diocese never wavered once he was installed. He was born on November 16, 1814, in Charleston, South Carolina. Baptized "Langdon Thomas," he was the eldest son of Irish immigrants, Pierce and Margaret Grace, who had been married in County Kilkenny in 1810. His parents both came from distinguished and educated families. His father was a teacher by profession and also served as an officer in the United States Army during the War of 1812. Pierce Grace always insisted on a good education for his children. The family moved for a time to Pennsylvania and finally settled in Ohio.[4]

In 1828, fifteen-year-old Langdon attended the minor seminary in Cincinnati which was under the direction of the Dominican Bishop Edward Fenwick. Within a year he decided to enter the Order of Preachers at St. Rose Priory in Springfield, Kentucky. He received the Dominican habit and took "Thomas" as his name in religion on June 10, 1830. One year later, on June 12, 1831, he made his religious profession and continued the formation program in Kentucky until 1838 when his superiors sent him to Rome for studies.[5]

Thomas Langdon Grace, O.P., bishop of St. Paul from 1859 to 1884. Named titular archbishop of Siunia in 1888.

His early years in Italy were spent at the Santa Maria Sopra Minerva in Rome. He was ordained to the priesthood on December 21, 1839. The following year he fell ill with smallpox and nearly died, and in 1842, for reasons of health, he was assigned to the Dominican House of Studies at Perugia. In 1843 he was sent to Santa Maria della Quercia near Viterbo, and, on September 20, 1844, received the degree of Lector of Philosophy and Theology.

Preparing for the priesthood in Rome and his further studies in Perugia fortified Grace to be a leader in education. He was in Europe between the revolutions of 1830 and 1848 when church and state, religion and society, were in flux. It is interesting to note that the famous French author Henri Dominique Lacordaire, well known for his preaching on political liberalism and ultramontane theology at Notre Dame in Paris in 1835, retired to Rome when controversy over his ideas became notable. In 1839 Lacordaire joined the Dominicans and established, at Nancy, the first Dominican house in France since the Revolution. The struggles of the church in France and the controversies surrounding Lammenais, Lacordaire, and Montalambert could not have been unknown to the American Dominican who arrived in Rome in the aftermath of Gregory XVI's encyclical *Mirari Vos* (1832), which condemned religious liberty and the separation of church and state. Whether Grace ever met Lacordaire is not known, but the contrast between ecclesiastical politics in Rome and life on the frontier in the United States could not have been more pronounced.

Upon his return to America, Grace was assigned to teach at St. Joseph College in Ohio and St. Rose Priory in Kentucky. His teaching career was brief. In 1846, his superior sent him as associate to Father Joseph Alemany, O.P. (later archbishop of San Francisco) at the parish of St. Peter in Memphis, Tennessee, due to the enormous need for priests in the area. He became pastor in 1849, and was the only priest in western Tennessee for a year.[6]

Grace loved his years in Tennessee. He was respected for his intelligence, prudence, and eloquence. Education was always a priority for him. He cared for the sick during the cholera epidemic in 1852, ministered to the immigrants, and was responsible for building what many considered to be "one of the most splendid edifices west of the Alleghanies"—the Church of Saints Peter and Paul in Memphis, dedicated on January 17, 1858.[7]

When Thomas Langdon Grace arrived in St. Paul in 1859, life in the community and the surrounding area had changed radically from its condition at the time of the arrival of his predecessor. By 1857 the *Metropolitan Directory* of the Diocese of St. Paul indicated that fifty new churches or stations had been established since Cretin's arrival, bringing the total to twenty-nine churches and thirty-five stations. Twenty priests ministered to a Catholic population of 50,000 (in a total white population of 150,000). There were two religious communities of men—the Benedictines and the Brothers of the Holy Family. Benedictine sisters established a priory in the diocese, joining the Sisters of St. Joseph as a second congregation of women religious.[8] Not only had St. Paul increased sizably, but Bishop Cretin's short tenure had seen a substantial increase in institutions and services for the Catholic population.

Grace was the first American-born episcopal leader in the Upper Midwest in the 1850s. In an area where the French clergy had been predominant for such a lengthy period, an Irish-American appointment was not altogether welcomed by some of the French priests. The fact that Grace asked Ravoux to be his vicar general was interpreted by some as an act to appease the French.

The bishop was proud of his Irish lineage, and the Irish immigrants were delighted to have him. But he denounced the Fenianism of the

1860s and saw danger in excessive nationalism.[9] He was also proud of his Dominican heritage. When he arrived in St. Paul there were no other members of the Order of Preachers in Minnesota. It must have been difficult to be separated from the religious congregation he had joined expecting a life of shared prayer, study, and apostolic work.

Thomas Langdon Grace had been born and educated in the South and had lived there or in the border states all of his life with the exception of his European experience. To find himself in the North on the brink of the Civil War was possibly the cultural shift that was the biggest challenge for him. Some citizens were hostile regarding the Union draft, and there were rumors that the bishop, being a southerner, sympathized with the Confederate cause. Grace spoke explicitly on this matter with a newspaper reporter and stated: "I have always encouraged my people to enlist in the defense of their country. I have discouraged them from trying to avoid the draft . . . and have always told them that they have enjoyed the protection of the Government and ought to be ready at all times to defend it."[10] His young curate, the recently returned and newly ordained Father John Ireland, was authorized to speak on the subject from the cathedral pulpit, and did so in March 1862 with great patriotic fervor. Possibly to alleviate any concerns regarding his loyalties during the war, Bishop Grace offered to supply a chaplain to care for the spiritual needs of the Catholic soldiers fighting in the Union Army. Although the officers of the Fifth Minnesota regiment had elected a Methodist minister, Governor Alexander Ramsey decided that a chaplain should be appointed to serve the Catholics in all of the Minnesota units. Father Ireland, back from France for less than a year, received that appointment.[11]

Grace was always appreciated as a man of intellectual acumen. In February and March of 1860 he gave a series of lectures that was very well received and reported in the press with accolades. He spoke on the subject of "Human Rights" at Mozart Hall on February 23, 1860, for the benefit of the St. Vincent de Paul Society. The hall was filled and the proceeds (between $200 and $300) were given to the poor. One newspaper reported as follows:

> A crowded audience listened to one of the most polished ethical dissertations of Human Rights, such as is seldom heard by the public. His liberal sentiments were such as no man of any de-

> nomination of Christians could object to; and while he did not in direct terms express his abhorrence of that great violation of Human Rights—the American system of slavery—it was evident from the whole tenor of his discussion, that the good bishop regarded the institution with sentiments of abhorrence, as at once a violation of the laws of God and of humanity.[12]

On March 13, 1860, Bishop Grace was invited to speak on "Civil Government and Human Laws Considered as External Defenses of Human Rights" at the state capitol. The proceeds were designated for the free hospital, the responsibility of the women of the Episcopal Church of St. Paul. Catholics and others were grateful for the relief given by the hospital to many of the poor Catholics in the area the previous winter. Protestant as well as Catholic clergy, professional people, and leading citizens attended the lecture, which gave Grace a platform for teaching and for ecumenical dialogue.[13]

In his quiet way Grace espoused an open-minded, energetic Catholicism as exemplified in the American Catholic converts and intellectuals of the time, Orestes Brownson and Isaac Hecker. He subscribed to Brownson's *Quarterly Review* and Hecker's *The Catholic World,* and was known to be one of three American bishops with whom Hecker was on particularly friendly terms. Like Hecker, Grace promoted a Catholic university in the United States long before most bishops saw it as a need or an option. As early as 1880 he was entreating others to consider founding a higher seminary for philosophy or theology. He is credited with encouraging Bishop John Lancaster Spalding to advocate the cause. Spalding's powerful sermon on education at the Third Plenary Council of Baltimore in 1884 ultimately persuaded the bishops to agree to the challenge.[14] This becomes particularly significant in light of the future relationship of the Saint Paul Seminary and the Catholic University of America.

Grace, a round-faced, balding bishop with a portly build and a placid demeanor, was a gentleman and a gentle man. He communicated to those with whom he associated a certain refinement and cosmopolitan spirit. He was never flamboyant or impetuous in his judgments, but always generous and measured in his speech. He was highly respected by priests and laity, Catholics and non-Catholics, and by other bishops. O'Connell comments insightfully:

> Above all, he possessed a serene appreciation of his own worth, which kept him preserved from the least pang of jealousy; the success of others did not threaten or trouble Thomas Grace. This quality proved crucial in his relationship with [John] Ireland. Grace was never a leader who initiated projects, but neither would he obstruct a subordinate who did. John Ireland's restless genius, with all its rough edges, thus found an ideal superior in Grace, who benevolently gave his gifted younger colleague free rein and always bestowed credit where credit was due.[15]

In 1862, while Ireland was serving as a chaplain in the Civil War, Bishop Grace set up the Ecclesiastical Preparatory Seminary of Saint Paul. Grace had great goals for seminary education in the diocese, but he was also realistic enough to know that the needs of the church in Minnesota, in terms of personnel and finances, did not allow for the kind of theological institution that he would have liked to build. He opened his small seminary on the second floor of the old cathedral building and employed William Markoe, a former Episcopalian minister, as headmaster and teacher. Father Anatole Oster soon joined Markoe as teacher and spiritual director, and trained the students to sing the chants at the liturgy and assist at services. Twenty-three boys were initially enrolled.[16]

Grace reevaluated the project after four years. In June 1866 the Benedictine monks who had established a monastery in the St. Cloud area were given the status of an abbey and decided to build a college/seminary. The Benedictine community invited Bishop Grace to lay the cornerstone at St. John's on July 19 of that year. It was a valuable addition to what was then the Diocese of Saint Paul. The seminary, which would open the following year, would train candidates for both the Benedictine Order and the diocesan priesthood. Grace decided to take advantage of the opportunity for seminary education within the diocese for at least some of the candidates. Five students who had been at the Ecclesiastical Preparatory Seminary of Saint Paul were among the first students at St. John's. Among them were John Shanley, later bishop of Fargo, and Joseph B. Cotter, the first bishop of Winona.[17]

In 1867, the Ecclesiastical Preparatory Seminary merged with the Cathedral School. Markoe continued as a "co-principal" working with

Sister Columba Auge, C.S.J., originally from Lotbiniere, Canada.[18] The school, which enrolled both boys and girls, was under the direction of Father John Ireland, the pastor of the cathedral, who invested great energy in revitalizing the institution.[19]

After assessing the demands of the diocese, Grace finally concluded, as he prepared for his first *ad limina* visit to Rome in 1867, that it was impossible to offer adequate seminary education in his own see without trained faculty and sufficient resources. With the widespread needs of Native Americans and the far-flung parishes of the immigrants, how could he send even a few clergy away for studies to establish a faculty? It was a grave disappointment, but Grace finally wrote a pastoral letter to the priests and people explaining why he was postponing his plans for building a seminary. In it he stated: "The pressing need for the services of the clergy in other departments, together with our limited resources, has compelled us to postpone this undertaking."[20] He had become convinced that it was best to send the more advanced students to seminaries in other dioceses where the developed curriculum and a full faculty would offer them better opportunities to pursue their studies. In addition to attending St. John's, seminarians from St. Paul attended St. Francis in Milwaukee, St. Vincent in Missouri, St. Bonaventure in New York, All Hallows in Dublin, the American College at Louvain in Belgium, and the College of Propaganda in Rome. For a Dominican who was as committed to education as Grace, this must have been a painful conclusion.

The bishop did explore another option. Although he had given up hope of staffing a diocesan seminary with priests from his own diocese, in 1879 he invited the German Jesuits who had founded Canisius College in Buffalo, New York, to consider sending a group to open a college in St. Paul. As a member of a religious order himself, Grace certainly understood that the emphasis on education in religious orders often produced priests with scholarly credentials for higher education; the availability of some such scholars might solve his problem. The Jesuits at Canisius had, however, received too many such requests, and declined the offer.[21]

This incident is noteworthy for several reasons. It seems unusual that Grace, a Dominican, would invite Jesuits and not Dominicans, considering the history of competitiveness between these two religious congregations. Second, one wonders if Grace was aware of Ireland's increasing antipathy toward the role that religious order clergy played in preparing men for diocesan priesthood. In addition, the friction between German Catholics in the United States who were resisting acculturation, and those English-speaking Catholics, many of them Irish, who espoused a kind of cultural Americanism, was beginning to emerge as a struggle for the soul of the American Catholic Church. It is fascinating to reflect on what might have happened had the German Jesuits of Buffalo accepted the invitation of Bishop Grace to establish a college/seminary in St. Paul.

Grace made two decisions, however, which had an enormous impact on seminary education in the future archdiocese of St. Paul. At the very time he was contemplating the pastoral letter explaining the postponement of the seminary project, he purchased forty acres of land on Lake Johanna north of St. Paul with the hope that one day a seminary would be established there. Ralston Markoe recalled that at age nine he was invited one day to go for a buggy ride with the bishop. When he inquired where they were going, the bishop told him that they were on their way to look at some property. The youngster questioned, "Why do you want to do that?" When the bishop responded that he might want to buy it, the boy persisted and asked why he wanted to buy a farm in the country. Markoe remembered that Bishop Grace responded, "Some day I hope to build a seminary here." The boy asked, "When are you going to build it?" Smiling, but with a hint of sadness, the bishop responded, "Oh, Rollie, that will be long after I am dead and gone."[22] This was the property that provided the nucleus of land chosen by Archbishop Austin Dowling for Nazareth Hall, the minor seminary of the archdiocese, which was finally built in the 1920s.

The second decision that Bishop Grace made which had a lasting impact on seminary education, in fact on all education in Minnesota and beyond, was the purchase of what was known as "the Finn Farm." This property became the eventual home of what is now the University of St. Thomas.[23] Finn, who was technically illiterate, accidentally shot off a finger from his right hand while cleaning his rifle at Fort Snelling on July 9, 1847. Because of his physical disability, he was discharged from the army on July 21, 1848, and two weeks later married a young widow named Elizabeth Reynolds. Although little information is available regarding Finn's war record, he did qualify under the Mexican Veteran Pension Law. He was also able to apply for a bounty land grant of 160 acres for soldiers who had served in the Mexican War under a U.S. Government Act of February 11, 1847. Finn selected land in the area of Shadow Falls, which was then part of the Fort Snelling military reservation. He bought an abandoned house and moved it to the property in order to stake his claim. With further acquisitions, Finn held most of the land between the Mississippi River and what is now Fairview Avenue, and from Marshall Avenue on the north to St. Clair Avenue on the south.

There is no information as to how Finn and his wife came to know John Ireland, but Joseph Connors comments: "It may be conjectured that these two Irish immigrants, each rather proud of his soldiering experience, had a good basis for congenial relationship."[24] In 1874, Finn—by this time in his fifties—learned that Bishop Grace was considering building a Catholic industrial school for boys, a proposal dear to the heart of Father Ireland. Finn offered to sell 452 acres of his farm for $125 an acre. The corporation established by Bishop Grace bought the land in May 1874.

The construction of the school and the engagement of staff proved to be a lengthy and complicated matter. In 1877 the Catholic Industrial School of Minnesota opened in a new building operated by Brothers of the Third Order of St. Francis. It was chiefly for orphans and wayward boys, those who lacked intellectual skills and might be led astray, and others who, as the *Northwestern Chronicle* stated, "under certain circumstances, might be sent to the Reform School."[25] Its success was short-lived, and in 1879 the project was moved out to Clontarf, Minnesota. The corporation found itself in need of money and sold 280 acres of the property in St. Paul to now Coadjutor Bishop John Ireland for $37,711.25.[26] By this time Ireland was making serious plans for a seminary and hoped to use that property. Finn apparently knew that, and on July 11, 1880, he canceled the remaining notes for $23,000 with the understanding that he would receive an annuity of $500 per year.

In September 1883 Finn sold Ireland forty more acres for $13,000, "and in his last will and testament, dated March 16, 1889, bequeathed all his property to Archbishop Ireland and made him executor with the concurrence of his wife for whom due provision had already been made."[27] William Finn died on March 24, 1889, and his wife Elizabeth died ten years later. Their legacy was important for the establishment of the St. Thomas Aquinas Seminary which became the College (now the University) of St. Thomas, St. Thomas Academy, and the Saint Paul Seminary.

Had it not been for Bishop Grace's initial negotiation, it is possible that these major institutions of the archdiocese would have been located elsewhere, or might not exist at all.

Events of 1875, however, did not allow Bishop Grace to concentrate on the Catholic Industrial School of Minnesota. On February 12, 1875, a papal brief was issued that established the Vicariate of Northern Minnesota, which consisted of almost two-thirds of the original diocese. The abbot of St. John's, Rupert Seidenbusch, O.S.B., was named vicar apostolic with residence at St. Cloud. The seminary at St. John's was, therefore, no longer in the diocese of St. Paul. Perhaps of even greater consequence for the future of Minnesota was the appointment, also on February 12, 1875, of John Ireland as vicar apostolic of Nebraska. Bishop Grace was stunned and left immediately for Rome to plead in person with Pope Pius IX to reconsider and appoint John Ireland coadjutor of the Diocese of St. Paul. Ireland, in the meantime, wrote to the pope and asked to be relieved of the appointment in Nebraska, and enclosed the letter and the papal documents in a packet with a cover letter to Bishop Grace in Rome. He wrote to Grace: "My consolation is that it is all in your hands and not in my own."[28]

An amazing turn of events occurred when the packet of mail and documents were lost in the wreck of the steam ship *Schiller* off the Scilly Islands near England. They were recovered some two months later and returned to Ireland the following June.[29] It was fortuitous that this occurred, because Bishop Grace had succeeded, possibly beyond his own expectations, to secure the appointment of Ireland to succeed him in St. Paul. On May 8, 1875, Pope Pius IX appointed John Ireland coadjutor bishop of St. Paul with the right of succession. The archdiocese, the Saint Paul Seminary, and indeed the entire Catholic Church in America would have had a very different imprint had not the energetic, creative John Ireland been consecrated coadjutor bishop of St. Paul on December 21, 1875. The major seminary that had continued to be a dream for Bishop Grace during his active years would become a reality for his successor.

Chapter 3

From Vision to Reality
John Ireland

> Taking into consideration the wondrous development of religion in the diocese of St. Paul, and also the urgent recommendations lately sent from Rome to the bishops of America that each diocese have at least the preparatory seminary, we propose with God's help to open in September, 1885, in St. Paul, a seminary in which the youth of the diocese whom God may inspire with a vocation to the priesthood, will be able to pursue at least their classical studies.... This diocesan seminary will be the principal work of our episcopate, and from it we expect the most fruitful results.
>
> Bishop John Ireland
> *Northwestern Chronicle*
> December 4, 1884

John Ireland had been groomed by two bishops to be a leader in the diocese that they all loved. His years as coadjutor (1875–1884) were an opportunity for him to become more comfortable with episcopal responsibilities. Having been blessed with an ordinary who allowed great latitude to the younger man's creativity, Ireland was able to promote various projects with Grace's blessing. Because the older bishop was convinced that substantial financial resources had to be forthcoming before the task of building the seminary should be undertaken, that project had to wait until Grace's resignation on July 31, 1884, when Ireland succeeded him as bishop of St. Paul.

In one sense it seemed as if everything in life had prepared John Ireland for episcopal office.[1] In another sense, it seemed almost incredible that the son who had been born on September 11, 1838, to Richard Ireland and Judith Naughton in Burnchurch, County Kilkenny, Ireland, would one day be an archbishop of the church—and of the Catholic Church in America at that.[2]

John Ireland, almost forty-six years old when he became bishop of St. Paul, inherited traits from both his parents. Richard Ireland has been described as "a stern disciplinarian, an unbending patriarch, who expected and received obedience from his extended family." He had a restless ambition, and some resentment at the lot dealt to him as an Irishman.[3] He was a widower with a three-year-old daughter, Mary Ann, when he married "Julia" (as Judith was known) in 1836. His second wife is portrayed as "a severely handsome woman with dark hair and a wide mouth, whose natural playfulness—so the family tradition had it—acted as a wholesome foil to her husband's often grim demeanor."[4] They had four children in addition to John—Ellen, Eliza, Richard, and Julia—born between 1842 and 1849 in the midst of the potato famine in Ireland.

John went to the local school in Burnchurch and learned the basics of reading, writing, and mathematics. The parish priest taught him some Latin—enough to serve Mass. As a boy he was profoundly influenced by Father Theobald Mathew, the Franciscan priest and temperance preacher. John served Mass for the friar and assisted him as he went about preaching and giving the pledge to abstain from liquor.

In the winter of 1848–1849, with the potato famine at its height, Richard Ireland decided he would join those who were emigrating to America. Richard's sister Anastasia and her husband James Howard had died in the famine, and their four children had become a part of the extended Ireland family. The eldest of these, Thomas Howard, and Richard's unmarried sister, Nancy, accompanied him on an exploratory voyage to the new world. They settled for a time in Burlington, Vermont, where Richard worked as a carpenter. Eventually he was able to send for Julia and the other nine children, who arrived in the late summer of 1849.

Life was not easy for the Ireland clan, and by 1851 they moved west to Chicago, where they stayed only a few months. John briefly attended the University of St. Mary of the Lake.[5] During the brief interim in Chicago, Richard Ireland met John O'Gorman, also from Kilkenny, and the two of them decided to join their families and resources and travel together to Minnesota in the hope of finding land and employ-

John Ireland, bishop (later archbishop) of St. Paul from 1884 to 1918. St. Paul was named an archdiocese in 1888.

ment for a new beginning. The nineteen of them traveled from Chicago to Galena and onto the Mississippi River where they took the steamer *Nominee* upstream, arriving in St. Paul on May 19, 1852. Although the date is variously given, the *Minnesota Democrat* briefly welcomed the two "respectable and intelligent Irish families" to the frontier town.[6] It was at this very time that Bishop Cretin was in the East attending the First Plenary Council of Baltimore.

The arrival of the Irelands and the O'Gormans less than a year after Bishop Cretin reflects the movement of the Irish into what had been a predominantly French fur trading area. The two families lived together in a hastily built camp-like dwelling (a long room without windows and with partitions made of bed sheets for privacy for the families), until lots were procured. Three houses were built for the Irelands, the O'Gormans, and Nancy Ireland who took care of the Howard children. Close relationships were formed in those circumstances. The long-standing friendships between John Ireland and Thomas O'Gorman, who spent their formative years studying together in France, and Ellen Ireland and Ellen Howard, who attended St. Joseph Academy and then entered the Sisters of St. Joseph of Carondelet together on September 8, 1858, were to have an enormous impact on the Catholic Church in Minnesota.

Little did the Irelands or the O'Gormans realize when they arrived in St. Paul in May 1852 that in April of the following year the bishop would invite two of their sons to prepare for the priesthood in France. These young boys were to become world travelers before age fifteen. Their excursion to France began on September 20, 1853, with Father Augustin Ravoux, the crusty, committed French missionary who had served the Minnesota area almost single-handedly since 1844. They boarded a steamer for Galena, Illinois, then went on to the east coast by train, and over the ocean again, just about four years after their families' initial voyage west to escape the famine. The boys occasionally delighted in playing tricks on Ravoux, and he was probably relieved to deposit them at the seminary at Meximieux in mid-October.[7]

Bishop Cretin had wasted no time in accepting the invitation of the bishop of Belly to send potential candidates for the priesthood to be educated at Meximieux gratis as a contribution of the French diocese and of Bishop Cretin's alma mater to the missions in America. Meximieux lay on the major post road about halfway between Lyons and Geneva. It was a large facility—a U-shaped building to which various additions had been made over the years, surrounded by terraces, gardens, and wooded areas.[8] With little or no understanding of French, the two young Irish boys must have experienced some fear and homesickness on reaching their destination.

To understand how Meximieux changed John Ireland's life, one must appreciate how he had lived before that time. Marvin O'Connell described the situation poignantly:

> It cannot be overemphasized, first of all, that he had begun life as a refugee, a displaced person, who as a child had fled from his homeland and from the unimaginable horrors of the Great Irish Famine of the 1840s. Once arrived in an America where help wanted signs had routinely appended to them the terse statement "Irish Need Not Apply," the Ireland family drifted from place to inhospitable place. . . . Typical of the masses of immigrants who crowded into the United States in the nineteenth century, John Ireland, his parents, and his siblings, were people nobody wanted, rootless, unsettled, insecure.[9]

It was at Meximieux that John Ireland found a life of stability, order, and predictability. He became fluent in French, which would be an enormous advantage in later years. He cultivated a taste for things French, and the orator Bossuet became one of his favorites. He discovered that he was a good student, possessed a keen mind, and had a passion for learning. The emphasis in the curriculum was on language and literature, which prepared students for theological study and canon law. He took courses in physics and mathematics, which may explain his later commitment to the study of science in seminary. This latter interest was not typical because of the alienation between religion and science in the nineteenth century.

John Ireland developed a sense of camaraderie with his classmates in the very masculine environment of about one hundred fifty seminarians and some seven priests who were their teachers and mentors. Early on he was inducted into the Sodality of the Blessed Virgin Mary, a select group of students with leadership qualities, from which he derived a certain piety which stayed with him through the years.

Bishop Cretin's sister, Clemence, who lived in nearby Montluel, provided reality therapy for the two young Americans on occasion. She was clearly the mother figure for them in their adolescent years, and did not hesitate to correct them when she deemed it necessary. She made certain they had warm clothes and were well cared for, and they spent vacations with her. Regarding John, O'Connell suggests that Clemence had a "nagging worry that her protégé's prowess as a student came at the expense of his piety," so she arranged a pilgrimage for him in her company to the Curé of Ars.[10] Marie Cretin, Clemence's niece, became a friend and confidante of John during those years.[11]

At Meximieux John Ireland learned that he was a leader, that he was an American, and that he was part of a universal church. It is not difficult to believe that even at that time he aspired to leadership *in* the American Catholic Church. Although he never denied his Irish roots, he was clearly *Jean Ireland des États-Unis*.[12] He was convinced that the United States was the greatest land on earth, and to be "American" and "Catholic" was the best of both worlds.

Ireland's love for Meximieux was in superlatives. In later years he would speak of it in rapturous terms, stating that it "awakens in my soul remembrance of peace and happiness; Meximieux speaks to me of virtue and truth." In his unfinished "Life of Bishop Cretin," Ireland reminisced about Meximieux in the third person:

> The writer of the present narrative refuses to pass over the name of Meximieux without a personal and fond salute.... The years of his residence at Meximieux were years of unalloyed happiness—years, too, of precious fruitage that has stood well by him in the long career of his priesthood. The influences of Meximieux have never faded from his mind and heart; his gratitude to Meximieux has never had a moment of interruption.[13]

From Meximieux, Ireland proceeded to do his theology at the *grand séminaire* at Montbel, the Marist scholasticate near Toulon. He had hoped to study philosophy at Strasbourg and to learn German, and then return to Belly for theology, but that was not to be. Very likely it was for economic reasons; by this time both Bishop Cretin and Bishop Devie were dead and the commitments to educate candidates for the priesthood from the American frontier may have been less clear.

Ireland never developed an affection for Montbel; in fact, he seemed to dislike it. O'Connell conjectures that the Marists conducted it primarily for their own candidates, and that this may be the reason for Ireland's later antipathy toward religious orders. He admits that it is an unanswered question and it could also be that later circumstances caused him to read an interpretation back into his earlier years.[14]

The Marists prepared their men for missionary work in the South Seas as well as other areas around the world. They provided a solid education based on a model not unlike the Sulpician model, which had become accepted in both Europe and America. Ireland worked diligently, as had been his pattern at Meximieux, and five 8-by-15-inch notebooks and a portion of a sixth illustrate not only some of what he studied, but a basic methodology he espoused for the rest of his life. Each of the notebooks is devoted to an area of theological discourse: revelation; the incarnation and grace; justice and rights; the place of the Virgin Mary in the economy of salvation; and the nature of the church. On the right-hand side of the notebook he would summarize what he had learned from one of the standard textbooks. On the page facing this Latin summary, he would include other statements in French, English, or Latin that would support or challenge the basic thesis, or provide an anecdote to illustrate the question. He quoted the prominent theologian Giovanni Perrone, S.J., frequently, and also referred to Bossuet, Orestes Brownson, the Protestant scholar William Paley, and the Jewish composer Mendelssohn.[15]

Among his theological reflections, notes, and clippings are comments and articles on the validity of secession from the American Union and the civilization of the Japanese. There is evidence that some of the material, such as clippings from the Boston Catholic newspaper, *The Pilot,* were added later. These notebooks were to become a rich resource of material for preaching and teaching in later years. When Ireland gave spiritual conferences to the students at the Saint Paul Seminary, he was fond of stating, "We must study and read and think with pen in hand, and keep neat notebooks as a summary of our work."[16] Clearly, he had done that as part of his preparation for priesthood.

Before returning to the United States in 1861, Ireland made a farewell visit to Meximieux where he was greeted warmly and presented with a medal of the Blessed Virgin Mary by the members of the seminary sodality. It was not easy to bid *adieu* to this French world where he had grown to manhood in eight important years. Returning to the United States on the brink of the Civil War was an adjustment. To be with his family once again involved both pain and joy. His brother Richard had died; his sister Ellen had joined the Sisters of St. Joseph. He was eager to meet his new bishop and begin a life of service as a priest. Twenty-three years old, handsome, well-educated, filled with zeal and enthusiasm, John Ireland embraced the challenge.

If the young candidate expected to be ordained to the priesthood immediately upon his return to St. Paul, he was mistaken. Bishop Grace preferred to have an opportunity to evaluate the young deacon. Ireland lived at the bishop's residence next to the cathedral and worked as Grace's part-time secretary. He was finally ordained to the priesthood on December 22, 1861, and assigned as an assistant pastor to the cathedral.

Emotions were volatile in those early months of the Civil War. The organization of the Fifth Regiment, Minnesota Volunteer Infantry, had begun on December 19, 1861, and was still in process in the spring. Bishop Grace, as mentioned above, inquired of Governor Alexander Ramsey regarding the status of spiritual ministry to Catholics in the ranks, and volunteered a priest for the pastoral care of the soldiers in the Minnesota Fifth. Ramsey accepted Grace's offer of John Ireland and appointed him state chaplain to the Catholics of all the Minnesota units serving in the western areas. Ireland "joined the Fifth Minnesota, at Camp Clear Creek, Mississippi, shortly after the Battle of Pittsburgh Landing [Shiloh] and began his ministry."[17] When the Methodist chaplain James F. Chaffee fell ill, Ireland succeeded him as U.S. Chaplain to the Fifth Minnesota and served in that capacity until March 19, 1863, less than ten months. Reminiscing in later years he stated, very likely with hyperbole: "My years of chaplaincy were the happiest and most fruitful years of my ministry."[18]

Ireland returned to St. Paul, was reassigned to the cathedral, and once again became Bishop Grace's secretary. He lived in the clergy residence on Sixth Street with Bishop Grace, the vicar general Father Augustin Ravoux, Father Louis Caillet, and Father Anatole Oster. The Ecclesiastical Preparatory Seminary of St. Paul, founded in his absence, was on tenuous grounds, and was discontinued in 1867. In that same year, Father Caillet was assigned to build a new parish, St. Mary's, in the Lowertown area of St. Paul. Father Ireland was appointed to succeed him as pastor of the cathedral and to supervise the newly combined cathedral school which would serve both boys and girls. Ireland's commitment to education found its first outlet in this project.

That was, however, only one of Ireland's several passions. Marvin O'Connell has admirably described Ireland's many involvements over the years. Only two will be briefly mentioned here before focusing on his ongoing engagement with seminary education. He was deeply committed to the temperance movement, from the founding of the Father Mathew Society of St. Paul in 1869, to the organization of the state Catholic Total Abstinence League, to the establishment of the Catholic Total Abstinence Union of America in 1872. Elected vice-president of the last organization in 1873, he suddenly found himself active in a national arena.[19]

A second passion for Ireland was his involvement in the Catholic colonization movement.[20] Ireland was convinced that the immigrants arriving from Europe could thrive best, both socially and spiritually, if they owned their own farms and imbibed rural rather than urban values. Ireland's goals, and the entrepreneur James J. Hill's desire to have communities for his ever-growing railroads, coincided at that point. The Catholic population of Minnesota grew, as did the St. Paul and Pacific Railroad, to the delight of *both* "empire-builders."

Ireland's appointment as coadjutor bishop following Grace's plea to Pope Pius IX gave the young bishop new prestige and the luxury of planning for the future while still not having to carry all the responsibility for the diocese. Bishop Grace, shortly after celebrating the twenty-fifth anniversary of his episcopal consecration on July 24, 1884, and about four months before his seventieth birthday, announced his resignation.[21] It was widely accepted that the reason for Grace's resignation at that time was that he wanted John Ireland to attend the Third Plenary Council of Baltimore as the ordinary of the diocese. Grace understood the importance of this council and appreciated the energy and intellect Ireland could bring to its debates.

The Catholic Church in the United States had been operating in a more or less collegial style of church government from the First Synod of Baltimore in 1791. The American bishops' seven provincial councils of Baltimore between 1829 and 1849, and the two plenary councils of Baltimore (1852, 1866), had presupposed a collegial ecclesiology. With the First Vatican Council (1869–1870), however, and its decree on papal infallibility, the emphasis on the centralization of authority in the papal curia did not appear to welcome a collegial approach. To the surprise of the American bishops, the Holy See decided to convoke a third national council of bishops at Baltimore. Because the United States was still considered mission territory, it was under the authority of the Sacred Congregation for the Propagation of the Faith, known by its Latin title *Propaganda*. Some suspected that the Holy See wanted to control the American Church, primarily by the appointment of an apostolic delegate. A council engineered largely by the Vatican appeared to be the first step in that process.[22]

The archbishops, or the senior suffragan from each ecclesiastical province of the United States, met with the cardinals of Propaganda in Rome in November 1883 to plan the council's agenda. Although the "Romanizing" of the church in America seemed to be the major thrust of the Propaganda officials, the American prelates were able to accept many agenda items proposed to them and reinterpret them in an American context. Most important, the Americans protested the appointment of an Italian, Archbishop Luigi Sepiaci, as apostolic delegate to preside over the council. Pope Leo XIII rescinded his earlier decision and named Archbishop James Gibbons of Baltimore to preside over the council as apostolic delegate.[23]

The council opened at the Cathedral of the Assumption in Baltimore, the remarkable basilica planned and built by John Carroll, the first bishop of the United States. Fourteen archbishops and coadjutor archbishops, fifty-seven bishops, seven abbots, and thirty-one superiors of religious orders of men processed into the cathedral in all their splendor.[24] The Catholic population of the United States had increased to more than six million, and the immigration of Catholics was increasing daily. Although Nativism was still a reality in the United States, and Catholics along with Jews and blacks were prime targets for its hostilities, the Catholic Church was nonetheless becoming a force with which to be reckoned.

Baltimore III was in session from November 9 to December 7, 1884. The bishops held their meetings at St. Mary's Seminary, about half a mile away from the cathedral. The schedule for the council included having the prelates gather in the late afternoon on Sundays for Vespers at the cathedral. During the week they assembled each evening for Benediction of the Blessed Sacrament, at which time a sermon was preached. John Ireland made his debut on the second evening of the council—Monday, November 10, 1884. He delivered a ninety-minute sermon on "The Church—The Support of Just Government." (In the published collection of his lectures it is titled "The Catholic Church and Civil Society.") His conviction that Catholicism and the United States of America were a perfect union was expressed in superlatives.

> Republic of America, receive from me the tribute of my love and my loyalty. I am proud to do thee homage, and I pray from my heart that thy glory will never be dimmed—*Esto perpetua!*...Believe me, no hearts love thee more ardently than Catholic hearts, no tongues speak more loudly thy praises than Catholic tongues, and no hands will be lifted up stronger and more willing to defend thy laws and thy institutions in peace and in war, than Catholic hands. Again—*Esto perpetua!*[25]

Ireland also attempted to reconcile the principles of liberty espoused by the United States and the tradition of authority proclaimed by the Catholic Church.

> Do not imagine a conflict between liberty and authority. License sacrilegiously calls itself liberty, "making liberty a cloak for malice;" despotism dares usurp the holy name of authority, and the conflict is between despotism and liberty. Liberty and authority are one. Liberty presupposes and follows from authority; authority has liberty for its object.[26]

Ireland never ceased believing that the wedding of liberty and authority were essential for the growth of the Catholic Church in the United States.

Education was a major agenda item at Baltimore III—in particular, clerical education. Bishop Grace had long hoped for the foundation of a Catholic university for philosophical and theological studies on a graduate level. Grace, knowing John Lancaster Spalding, bishop of Peoria, to be eminently suited for the task, encouraged him to become the advocate for the project. Spalding, a scholar educated at Louvain, gave a stirring speech to the council members on "University Education," reflecting with his brother bishops on the question, "Is not the love of excellence, which is the scholar's love, a part of the love of goodness which makes the saint?"[27] Later in the speech he challenged them:

> Let there be then an American Catholic university, where our young men, in the atmosphere of faith and purity, of high thinking and plain living, shall become more intimately conscious of the truth of their religion and of the genius of their country, where they shall learn the repose and dignity which belong to their ancient Catholic descent, and yet not lose the fire which glows in the blood of a new people.[28]

Spalding not only inspired the bishops to vote in favor of the founding of a Catholic university, but he had two donors in the wings, the Caldwell sisters, Mary Gwendoline and Mary Elizabeth, who became major benefactors for the endeavor.

Archbishop Gibbons chaired the governing committee of the new university, and John Ireland was one of seven (arch)bishops, along with several prominent lay people and one priest, appointed to the committee. The archbishop of St. Paul actively raised funds for the new university. He also played a key role in the decision to build the school in Washington, D.C., rather than elsewhere, and helped to shape and form the new institution in a variety of ways.

While Ireland was still in Baltimore immersed in the work of the council, an article appeared in the December 4, 1884, *Northwestern Chronicle,* the Catholic newspaper of the Diocese of St. Paul, which was a surprise to many people. Bishop Ireland announced that a preparatory seminary would be built in the diocese and be ready for occupancy by September 1885.[29] Ireland was not going to allow national commitments to impede his desire to develop a model seminary.

James Connors's remarkable history of the (then) College of St. Thomas, *Journey Toward Fulfillment,* describes in detail the early years of the St. Thomas Aquinas Seminary which opened on September 8, 1885.[30] The Industrial School building had been maintained well, but was renovated and a wing was added. The land upon which the new seminary stood was a personal gift from Ireland, and he also paid from his own savings $46,000 of the $72,000 required for the first buildings.[31]

Faculty and students were recruited. Ireland's friend Thomas O'Gorman was appointed rector. One variation was that the mission of the institution was broadened; publicity began to emphasize that seminary could be understood in a broad sense, as educating not just those who were preparing for priesthood but also those preparing for other professions such as law and medicine, or who just wanted a solid liberal arts education.

The first use of the new seminary was in August 1885 when Bishop Ireland scheduled the annual diocesan priests' retreat there and invited his friend Bishop John J. Keane of Richmond, Virginia (later the rector of the Catholic University of America) to be the retreat director. Ireland wanted his priests to have a sense of ownership in the new enterprise. This event underscored his conviction that the education of diocesan priests should be conducted by diocesan priests.

In the early days of the St. Thomas Aquinas Seminary, the student body was indeed a very unusual mix. From 1885 to 1894, it was several schools: a junior high school, a high school, a junior college, a minor seminary, and a theological seminary—all under one roof.[32] The Catholic Church in the United States, especially in the Middle West and West, was making valiant attempts to educate its own, but in those days of increasing immigration, resources had to be shared. From this variegated community several academic institutions developed: the College (now University) of St. Thomas, the St. Thomas Military Academy, the Saint Paul Seminary, and the preparatory seminary Nazareth Hall.

In November 1885 Bishop Ireland reported that there were thirty-eight pupils in the classical and preparatory department and twenty-four seminarians in philosophical or theological studies. That latter number grew to fifty-five in the 1893–1894 academic year, the last year in which the "major seminary" students were in residence on the college campus.[33] By 1894, John Ireland had ordained sixty-three seminarians for the diocese.

Assembling a faculty to teach in such an institution was a difficult challenge. Some distinguished figures from Europe and America were enlisted, but often they moved on after a few years. If it was difficult to retain faculty, it was not much easier to find individuals who were qualified and willing to be rector. Ireland's first choice, his classmate Thomas O'Gorman, lasted only two years (1885–1887), although he continued on the faculty teaching church history until 1890. He was then offered the chair of ecclesiastical history at the Catholic University of America, where he distinguished himself as an author and a lecturer. In 1896 he was appointed bishop of Sioux Falls, South Dakota. In the eight years in which St. Thomas had a combined seminary and college program, there were four rectors. Some of the faculty went on to become members of the faculty of the Saint Paul Seminary in 1894.

The challenges of a frontier seminary with enormous limitations in finances and personnel did not dampen Ireland's enthusiasm. There were great and good connections in the community on which he could rely. It was clear, however, that the multi-faceted institution which was known as the St. Thomas Aquinas Seminary was not a satisfactory arrangement for the future. Not even Ireland, however, could have dreamed that a major seminary would literally be built and given to the archdiocese before the end of the century.

Chapter 4

If It Hadn't Been for a Woman...

> For nearly thirty years I have lived in a Roman Catholic household, and daily have had before me and around me the earnest devotion, watchful care, and Christian example of a Roman Catholic wife, of whom it may be said, "Blessed are the pure of heart for they have seen God," and on whose behalf tonight I desire to present and turn over to the illustrious Archbishop of this diocese the seminary and its endowment as provided in the deeds and articles of trust covering the same.[1]
>
> James J. Hill
> Speech at Dedication of The Saint Paul Seminary
> September 4, 1895

That Catholic woman was Mary Theresa Mehegan Hill, wife of the Methodist millionaire and "empire builder" James Jerome Hill. Hill's statement at the dedication ceremony of the Saint Paul Seminary on September 4, 1895, was prefaced by the forthright comment: "Some of you may wonder why I, who am not a member of your church, should have undertaken the building and endowment of a Roman Catholic theological seminary."[2] He was very clear that the role of his wife was pivotal in his decision to make such an extraordinary contribution to a church that was not his own.

Who was the wife of this entrepreneur? Mary Theresa Mehegan was the daughter of Irish natives, Timothy Mehegan born in County Cork in 1812, and Mary McGowan born in County Leitrum in 1827.[3] They were part of the stream of Irish immigrants threatened by economic conditions in Ireland which culminated in the potato famine in the 1840s. Timothy and Mary were married at St. Joseph's Church on

Sixth Avenue in New York City and their first daughter, Mary Theresa, was born July 1, 1846. In 1847 they moved to Chicago where another daughter, Anna Eliza, was born in 1849.[4]

A year later, the young Mehegans decided to move north along the Mississippi and arrived in St. Paul on May 21, 1850. They bought a house at Minnesota and Bench Streets where their neighbors included pioneer priest Father Augustin Ravoux, and, eventually, the Ireland family, some of whom would become lifelong friends. It was not an easy transition for Mary McGowan Mehegan. She was not used to having Native Americans in war paint ride by her home uttering strange cries, or others who were inebriated throw bricks down the chimney. Timothy, however, took the new challenges in stride. He was never a successful businessman, but was described by a neighbor as "more refined than the average man in our small town, and his manners were dubbed by the envious as 'Mehegan airs.'"[5]

When Mary Theresa was only eight years old, her forty-two-year-old father, Timothy, whom she dearly loved, died unexpectedly on Christmas Eve in 1854. It was a painful time for a widow with two small children. With little in the way of financial support, Mary McGowan Mehegan remarried not long thereafter, but it was not a happy marriage. A twenty-two-year-old seminarian, Louis Caillet, who had been in the United States less than a year, ministered to the family in their difficult times. He prepared Mary Theresa for her first Holy Communion. Father Caillet became a friend, confidante, and mentor to her during her adolescent years.

When St. Joseph Academy was founded by the Sisters of St. Joseph of Carondelet in 1851, Mary Theresa Mehegan was among the first twelve girls enrolled in the school, along with the daughters of the Irelands and the Howards. Archbishop John Ireland's sister, Ellen Ireland (later Mother Seraphine, C.S.J., provincial of the Sisters of St. Joseph and a foundress of the College of St. Catherine), and Mary Theresa would reminisce in later years about their elementary and secondary school days.

Upon graduation from St. Joseph Academy in the waning days of the Civil War, Mary Theresa was employed as a waitress at the Merchants Hotel in St. Paul.[6] It was there that she met James J. Hill, who frequented the dining room with his bachelor business friends. Mary was an attractive and proper young woman, described by one biographer as "a sensible, high-principled girl."[7] The enterprising Jim Hill was impressed with Mary, particularly "her grave, dignified bearing . . . her fresh colleen beauty and fierce devotion to the strict precepts of the Roman Catholic upbringing which . . . made her one of the most attractive young women in St. Paul."[8]

Unable to join the Union Army because of an eye injury in his childhood, Hill decided to marry and settle down. In 1864 he proposed marriage to the lovely Irish colleen. Mary Theresa went to Father Caillet for advice. Although Hill was not a Catholic, the priest approved of the young man and thought that he had "unusual mental powers."[9] Father Caillet was a realist and possibly something of a "prophet." He advised Mary that if she decided to marry this young entrepreneur, she should further her education so as to be a companion to him in his career. Many years later Mary remembered the words of Father Caillet and shared them with her daughter Clara: "Your life may not be an easy one, but you must continue to educate yourself to be his companion."[10]

Mary Theresa took her spiritual father's advice. She became engaged to James Hill on June 8, 1864, when she was not quite eighteen and he was twenty-six. Shortly after, she matriculated, probably with financial assistance from her fiancé and other friends, at St. Mary's Institute in Milwaukee, Wisconsin, the newly established convent finishing school of the School Sisters of Notre Dame. Both practical training and "accomplishments" were offered: she learned French and studied music, natural philosophy, etiquette, letter writing, calisthenics, needlework, embroidery, tapestry, and beadwork. For economic reasons she stayed on through the summers to complete the program as quickly as possible.[11] The confidence and competence, character and religious devotion she acquired would serve her well in the years to come. Little did she realize that her education was preparing her to be not only a good wife and mother and an able family administrator, but also a gracious hostess who would welcome millionaires of the "Gilded Age," church dignitaries, and even a president of the United States into the Hill mansion on Summit Avenue.

During 1864–1865, James Hill worked extensively with the Northwest Packet Company out of Chicago. That proved fortuitous for the young couple. On Sundays James would come to Milwaukee and call for Mary at the convent. They would take walks by Lake Michigan, duly chaperoned by one of the lay sisters. At one point James asked Mary if she would consent to live in India if he were to organize a line of steam-

James J. Hill

Mary Theresa Mehegan Hill

boats on the Ganges River. There is no indication as to her answer, but she no doubt realized that she was marrying an adventurous man.

James set up a home in St. Paul so that when Mary completed her studies and returned they could get married. Because it was a "mixed marriage" of a Catholic and a Protestant, the Catholic Church law of the time did not permit the couple to be married in the church sanctuary. Therefore, the ceremony was scheduled in the bishop's house for Monday, August 19, 1867. They planned it for an early hour so that they could take the train to Milwaukee for their honeymoon.

Mary had asked that Father Caillet preside at the marriage ceremony when she made the arrangements with Father John Ireland. Unfortunately, the young curate failed to deliver the message. The bride was gravely disappointed that her longtime friend did not arrive to officiate. Father Ireland offered to substitute, but Mary declined and asked for Father Anatole Oster instead.[12] This is ironic considering the later relationship of the Hills with Archbishop Ireland.

After their honeymoon, the young couple began their life together in their modest house on Canada Street near the present Grove Street in St. Paul. In 1871, with their family expanding, they moved to a new home at Ninth and Canada, and when that grew too small (they had ten children, nine of whom lived), James Hill decided to build another enlarged home on the same site. The house at Ninth and Canada, where most of the children grew up, was a home which held loving remembrances for them.

James J. Hill's ancestors were also from Ireland, but were of Scotch Protestant ancestry. His paternal grandparents moved to Canada in 1829, and his maternal grandparents in 1832. It was in Rockwood, near present-day Guelph in eastern Ontario, that James Hill (father of James J. Hill) met Ann Dunbar. He was a Baptist and she a Methodist. They were married at Eramosa, Ontario, in 1833 and settled on fifty acres of wooded land "in the bush" a few miles outside of Rockwood where the land had to be cleared and a house built. They became the proud parents of four children. The first, who died as an infant, was named James. The next, Mary Eliza, was born in 1835. When another son was born on September 16, 1838, he, too, was named "James" in keeping with the family tradition. (As a teenager this James chose "Jerome" as a middle name for himself, probably due to his fascination with Napoleon Bonaparte, whose brother was named Jerome.)[13] A younger brother, Alexander Samuel Dunbar Hill, was born in 1839.

A boyhood accident, the result of an accidental stroke of an arrow, left James without the use of one eye. Although a traumatic experience, it did not impede his reading ability or his enthusiasm for learning in his growing years. In spite of his eye injury, Jim Hill was a voracious reader. Hill's biographer Albro Martin concludes: "It is possible that James could perceive shades of light and dark with the eye. Both eyes twinkled with humor or flashed with anger equally well, and it is unlikely that those who did not know ever suspected that the Empire Builder was blind in one eye."[14]

James's experiences at the district school in his earlier years were typical. His first teacher was John Harris, a Quaker born in Cork, Ireland. Hill did not find the classroom exciting, however, and one day when he was about ten years old he skipped school and went off into the woods to finish reading *Ivanhoe*. Although libraries were not typical on the frontier, the Hill home had works of Shakespeare, the poetry of Burns, a Bible, and a dictionary. All of this created a desire in Jim Hill to learn.

In 1849 the Reverend William Wetherald arrived in Eramosa Township. Frustrated with the public schools, the Quaker teacher decided to establish his own center of learning. He was convinced that some parents would pay for advanced instruction for their sons if he provided it. He realized his goal when Rockwood Academy opened in 1850. The tuition and fees were steep for the younger James Hill. In order to attend Rockwood he registered as a commuter student rather than a boarder, walking four miles to school each weekday. One winter, however, he was able to be a resident student because Wetherald found chores for him to do so that he could earn his room and board.

Perhaps no other person had such a profound influence on the young Hill as William Wetherald. Not only did the boy receive a solid foundation in Latin and English, mathematics and the classics, but he was trained in a certain mental discipline perhaps not uncharacteristic of the Quaker atmosphere of plain living and high thinking that were Wetherald's philosophy and spirituality. The impact of his Quaker teacher's training also proved fundamental, as is obvious when reading Hill's voluminous hand-written correspondence and diaries. Whether as a young entrepreneur or later as a railroad magnate, his rhetorical skill, carefully reasoned business and financial calculations, appreciation of art, literature, and music, and solid sense of values are clearly reflected.

Hill never forgot the enormous impact that Wetherald had on him. Years later he would invite Wetherald to visit him with the salutation

"My Dear Old Master," and then continued: "I have looked forward for some years to a time when I could have you pay us a visit and renew some of the days that were spent so pleasantly under your care."[15] In 1881 Wetherald accepted the invitation, which included gifts of train tickets and funds for a month-long visit to St. Paul and the surrounding area. Hill was delighted to share his lovely wife and family with his "dear old master."[16]

In his teenage years, James had had dreams of college and medical school. All of that changed, however, with the death of his father on Christmas day in 1852, a tragic coincidence he would share with his wife whose own father died on Christmas eve just two years later. He was only fourteen, and as the eldest son in the family he found himself with new responsibilities. In spite of the hopes of his mother and his teacher, there was no money for tuition, so his education at Rockwood Academy had to be terminated. The next two years spent as a clerk, however, in a general store in Rockwood were not lost. Learning about bookkeeping, distribution of goods, and the experience of relating to the agricultural community proved invaluable to him in the future.

By 1854 the family moved to Guelph, and James became a clerk at McElroy and Mitchell's grocery store. In 1856 at the age of seventeen he decided to strike out on his own. His sister was married and seemed well provided for, and his brother Alec was sixteen and able to care for their mother. His study under Wetherald had challenged him to look beyond the local scene. All of his life he had dreamed of going to the Orient.

Seventeen-year-old James left Canada and headed for New York where he did farm work near Syracuse. He then traveled on to Albany and eventually to New York City, hoping to book passage on a ship to the Orient. The expense was beyond his slender budget. After visiting Philadelphia, where he became intrigued with opera, and Richmond, Virginia, where he had his first taste of the culture of the South, he turned west.

The young adventurer traveled by railroad to Chicago and beyond. In Dubuque he boarded a steamboat to go north on the Mississippi River. Some of his friends from Rockwood Academy had been from the Red River area and had encouraged him to visit. He arrived in St. Paul on July 21, 1856, all of his funds gone, but with hope and excitement for a new life. While still on board, he had been offered a job on the levee by the steam packet officer.[17] Everyone came to know "Jim" Hill around the Saint Paul levees, and often pronounced his names as one—"Jimhill."[18]

The saga of the business adventures of James Hill is an important part of the history of the development of transportation in the United States in the second half of the nineteenth century. Briefly, from his work on the levee he became involved in freight forwarding, steamboats, and wholesale distribution. After the Civil War he went into business on his own, specializing in transporting wood and coal. He formed a partnership with the well-known fur trader Norman Kittson to purchase a string of steamboats which traversed the Red River to Winnipeg, Manitoba, in Canada. When it became clear that railroads were the wave of the future, he developed plans to take over the bankrupt St. Paul and Pacific Railroad that ran northwest from St. Paul to the Red River and then north to Canada.

Hill developed important relationships in that venture, and several of the associates of those days (George Stephen, Donald Smith, John S. Kennedy, and Norman Kittson) would be lifelong colleagues and friends. With capital investments from both Canada and New York, the group acquired the St. Paul and Pacific in 1879 and renamed it the St. Paul, Minneapolis and Manitoba Railway (often referred to as "the Manitoba"). Hill served as general manager until 1882 and thereafter as president.[19]

Hill's dream had always been for a transcontinental railroad with a base in St. Paul that would offer the possibility of opening up trade between the Upper Midwest and the Orient. At first he built a series of north-south lines to aid in developing the agriculture in the Red River Valley. He established a connection from St. Paul to Duluth, which gave him an alternate route to Chicago via Lake Michigan, and built lines in South Dakota and Iowa. By 1887 the Manitoba reached Helena, Montana, with the potential of transporting the wealth of that mining region.

During the years 1889–1893 Hill found himself developing transportation systems both east and west. He built and operated his own line of steamships on the Great Lakes to carry grain and flour to Buffalo, New York and other ports in the East. At the same time, his dream of a transcontinental railroad was approaching completion. The Manitoba was reorganized and renamed the Great Northern Railway, and despite all the challenges and obstacles of financing at home and abroad and of laying track through passes in the Rockies and the Cascades, the Great Northern reached Puget Sound in 1893—escaping the Panic of '93 by only a few months.

In 1890, in the midst of some of his most complicated business transactions, Hill announced that he would build a Catholic seminary for the

Archdiocese of St. Paul.[20] The projected date of completion was 1892. There was no doubt delight on the part of the Catholic community and astonishment from the Protestants. For a Methodist millionaire to contribute half a million dollars to build and endow a Catholic major seminary in the United States in the 1890s was beyond any Catholic dream.

The project got off to a slow start. Viewed from the vantage point of the seminary, the building enterprise seemed to be an extraordinarily lengthy undertaking. When one considers, however, that the announcement, planning, and construction of the seminary, about which Hill insisted on having every last word, was happening at the same time as some of Hill's most high-powered and pressured maneuvers, it is amazing that he considered committing himself to the seminary project.

Hill believed strongly in educational endeavors, and contributed to many religious schools in Minnesota, such as Macalester College (Presbyterian) and Hamline College (Methodist) in St. Paul—both Protestant institutions at that time. He donated $1,000 to Luther Seminary in 1886, and $10,000 each to Bethel Seminary and Swedish Baptist Seminary in the 1900s. Only personal motives—his love for his wife and his appreciation for Father Caillet—explain the extraordinary contribution of half a million dollars to build a Catholic seminary in the 1890s.

Father (later Monsignor) Louis Caillet is the third and lesser-known figure in the decision to build the Saint Paul Seminary. It is questionable whether the gift of the seminary by James J. Hill would have been made without this gentle French priest. Caillet's relationship to Mary Hill was pivotal. As noted earlier, Mary looked to Father Caillet for advice after the death of her father, and he genuinely became a "father figure" in her life.

Caillet was born in Lyons, France, on November 21, 1832, and baptized Louis Eugene. Father Augustin Ravoux's visit to the seminary at Lyons while Caillet was a student there awakened in the young seminarian the desire to work among the Native Americans and immigrants in Minnesota. Ravoux made it clear that life in the wilds of the Upper Midwest would not be easy but he clearly inspired the seminarians to consider a missionary vocation. Ravoux was apparently a very effective recruiter. He returned to St. Paul with seven seminarians, including Caillet, who continued their studies for the priesthood under the direction of Bishop Cretin.

Cretin died, however, before Caillet finished his preparation and, because a new ordinary was not appointed for two years, Louis Caillet was ordained a priest on August 21, 1857, by Bishop Clement Smyth, O.C.S.O., coadjutor bishop of Dubuque, who had been abbot of the Trappist Monastery at New Melleray in Iowa. Caillet was then assigned to the cathedral in St. Paul, and also served as missionary in the surrounding territory.

There was a need for new parishes when the Civil War ended in 1865. As noted above, Bishop Grace assigned Caillet to begin a new parish in Lowertown St. Paul to be called St. Mary's. This congregation, to which Mary Hill and the children later belonged, would become Caillet's love throughout his years of priesthood. Although he became vicar general of the archdiocese in 1893 and rector of the Saint Paul Seminary in 1894, his heart was always at St. Mary's. He stated: "It is my desire that I be buried from St. Mary's Church, the Church I loved so well and will love to the last."[21] His request was granted at the time of his death in 1897. Father Caillet's role as rector will be discussed in chapter 5. His relationship to the Hills, however, was foundational to the decision of James J. Hill to build the Saint Paul Seminary.

Caillet was a frequent guest in the Hills' homes, presided at baptisms and weddings, and became "the family chaplain." In 1869 James Hill wrote in his diary: "Father Caillet spent the evening at the house and presented me with a missal."[22] No doubt this was because Hill sometimes accompanied Mary and the children to Mass on Sundays, and Catholics would have been elated if this prestigious citizen had decided to join their church.

When James Hill decided that his children should be tutored at home for their early education, it was Caillet who, in 1879, recommended August N. Chemidlin. The priest had known Chemidlin and his wife since his ordination in 1857, and over the years they had developed a deep friendship. Chemidlin had been born in Lorraine in France and had been educated by the Jesuits at Nancy. He was an enthusiastic, free-spirited individual who attempted various business enterprises, but seems to have been best suited for work as a teacher and tutor. He was much beloved by the Hills and included in many family celebrations. During the summers he joined the family at Lake Elmo, at Lake Minnetonka, and at "the farm" in North Oaks. Caillet also spent part of his summer vacation with the Hills and the two Frenchmen would spend hours walking, conversing, and joking together.

After the death of his wife, Chemidlin moved to a house just two blocks away from St. Mary's. He and Caillet traveled to France in 1889

Louis Caillet, rector of the Saint Paul Seminary from 1894 to 1897

and again in 1895. The letters from each of them to the Hills and others give fascinating insights into the devout, gentle, somewhat shy Caillet, and the charming, flamboyant, jesting Chemidlin, both beloved friends of the Hills.[23] Their letters to the family, especially the children, are warm and often touching.

It is Chemidlin, however, who describes Caillet's affection for Mary Hill best in his letter to her at the time of the priest's death. Mary was in New York with her son Louis who was having surgery when Caillet died on November 28, 1897.[24] She was unable to attend his funeral. Chemidlin wrote: "I did not expect that he would leave us so soon, and I always hoped that he would bury me. He was more than a brother to me.... And your loss is as great as mine. *He could hardly have loved you any better if you had been his daughter, and he had an equal affection for Mr. Hill and the children.*"[25]

It is understandable, then, that in Hill's speech at the time of the dedication of the Saint Paul Seminary he singled out, in addition to his wife, this priest who was so beloved by the Hill family. Hill's tribute could not have been more specific or more public, with Caillet on the platform.

> To most of you I need hardly mention the name of Monsignor Louis Caillet, whose long life as a Catholic priest has been spent among you, and whose devotion to duty, whose broad Christian charity and whose unswerving zeal for the spiritual welfare and upright life of both young and old have endeared him in an unusual degree to the hearts of the people of St. Paul, both within and without the church which he has so dearly loved and so faithfully served. Over forty years of active service have left him somewhat impaired in health, but with a spirit as patient and devoted as when he first came among you so many years ago. I may say truthfully, that had it not been for my intimate knowledge of and admiration for his character as a Christian pastor and a personal friend, it is very probable I would never have thought of assuming the responsibility for the work which has been dedicated today.[26]

Although Hill never joined the Catholic Church, he continued to accompany Mary and the children to Mass on Sundays, and even took the children if Mary was ill. In later years he seems to have been more of a "generic" Protestant for whom Methodist, Baptist, and Quaker influences had been formative. Hill probably did more to perpetuate Catholicism in the Upper Midwest than many who were a part of that tradition. The Saint Paul Seminary would have been a very different institution if James Hill had not married Mary Theresa Mehegan in 1867.

CHAPTER 5

"The Hill Seminary"

> Our esteemed citizen, President James J. Hill, has consented to build and endow an institution of learning, costing at least $500,000, in the interests of higher education for the Catholic priesthood and the selection of the site is left to the Archbishop of St. Paul.
>
> *Northwestern Chronicle*
> November 5, 1890

James J. Hill's gift of $500,000 to build a Catholic theological school was first announced to the community in the *Midway News* (September 6, 1890).[1] The following month, when Archbishop Ireland issued his annual seminary appeal for St. Thomas Seminary, he stated that Hill's gift would be

> devoted to the erection of buildings for the exclusive use of the theological students and for the perpetual endowment of professorial chairs, the number of which in this manner will be increased beyond all that otherwise would have been possible for us and in the fullest compliance with the most advanced requirements of the Church in this country and in this age. The new theological seminary will be ready for use, it is expected, in the autumn of 1892.[2]

Ireland, who became archbishop with the erection of the ecclesiastical province of St. Paul in 1888, donated forty acres on the east bank of the Mississippi River adjacent to the St. Thomas Aquinas Seminary as the site for the new seminary.[3] The pristine wooded area near St. Thomas was conducive to a cloistered atmosphere, and seemed ideal for a major seminary.

Ireland had made another decision earlier which proved salutary for the projected seminary. In 1872, St. Paul's first system of horse-drawn trolley cars had been set up on Grand Avenue but ended well before the new seminary. In 1889, the archbishop joined with Thomas Cochrane, one of the founders of Macalester College (established, as St. Thomas was, in 1885), and contracted with the St. Paul City Railroad Company to build and equip an extension of the Grand Avenue streetcar to Cretin Avenue. The new electric streetcar extension was completed in February 1890, and Archbishop Ireland was one of those pictured up front on the first ceremonial run. Having the streetcar terminus at one of the entrances of the seminary and accessible to seminarians, particularly during the years they were not allowed to have cars, was a convenience for generations of students.

"The Hill Seminary," as it was commonly known in the early years, was slow in getting started. The building permit was not issued to Hill until September 13, 1892, shortly before the ground-breaking.[4] Archbishop Ireland was nervous about the delay. The previous spring he had written to Father Caillet from Rome: "I was most grateful to hear that Mr. Hill has given final orders to the architect. It will be the greatest relief to me to feel that the work will be going on by the time I return home. It is in one way fortunate that I am absent—so that any ideas I might have cannot interfere. What I want is that the work go on."[5]

In May 1892, Ireland wrote to Hill from Rome describing his recent audience with Pope Leo XIII and the Holy Father's comments regarding Hill's benevolence:

> You will permit me to tell you the great pleasure I enjoyed in my last audience with the Pope. He spoke to me at length of his high appreciation of your princely generosity in building our seminary, and of the great honor thereby conferred upon the church in America. He wished me to thank you most cordially in his name and present his complements to Mrs. Hill. He hopes that some time he may meet yourself or members of your family in Rome. He finished by telling me that on my departure from Rome I should have to take to you a token of his esteem and a letter from him.[6]

No doubt Vatican officials considered Hill's donation not only a magnanimous benefaction but quite extraordinary. That a Protestant would provide such a gift to the Catholic Church was astounding. The *Syllabus of Errors* (1864) had condemned religious liberty, freedom of the press, and the separation of church and state some thirty years earlier. The concrete experience of the church benefiting from such generosity in a religiously pluralistic system must have given some of the critics in the Vatican cause for reflection.

Ireland could not help but see the donation of the seminary in political terms, and was not hesitant to be explicit in describing the situation to Hill: "I may add that in the many controversies I had to settle in Rome regarding ecclesiastical matters in America, the knowledge of your generous gift to the Diocese of St. Paul was of no small aid to me in winning for my course the esteem of the authorities."[7]

When James Hill committed himself to a project, there was no question that he would bring it to completion. He was a micro-manager, however, who felt compelled to make every decision. The demands of the Great Northern in the early 1890s proved too time-consuming to allow him to turn his attention to the seminary. Because it was his intention to supervise all the details of the building complex, he felt it was better to delay the seminary rather than turn the direction of it over to those who might squander the money.

Hill's concern about the wise use of money on the part of the archbishop was solidly based. He was more than aware of Ireland's lack of financial acumen. He knew that the archbishop's valuable land was mortgaged to the maximum and that he lacked liquid assets. Ireland borrowed from Hill—even begged him for loans—on more than one occasion. According to O'Connell: "Ireland received from Hill at least $110,000 in cash over the five years after December 1892, not enough to deliver the archbishop from bankruptcy, but enough to keep the wolves from the door."[8]

In addition, Hill interceded with many of the top financiers of the Gilded Age such as John D. Rockefeller, William K. Vanderbilt, Michael Cudahy, Jacob Henry Schiff, Philip D. Armour, and Marshall Field to contribute money to Archbishop Ireland or join his property syndicate. O'Connell added: "Twice Ireland, with Hill's help, appealed for relief to these eastern money-men, almost all of whom were also powers in the Republican party. Though the figure cannot be determined with certainty, it would seem that the efforts of 1894 and 1897–1898 netted him about $500,000."[9] With an eye to the future, Hill determined that the financial arrangements for the seminary and the management of the endowment would be set up as a trusteeship which would last through the lifetime of his sons and for twenty-one years after.

Hill chose a young architect, Cass Gilbert, to design the buildings and oversee construction. Gilbert and his architect friend James K. Taylor had just completed the Endicott Building in downtown St. Paul (1888–1890). It was an extraordinary six-story L-shaped store and office building in Renaissance-revival style. This achievement, plus earlier work Gilbert had contributed to the construction of the Hill Mansion on Summit Avenue, seems to have caught James Hill's attention.

Gilbert's first prospectus submitted to Hill on December 31, 1891, described the basics for seven buildings including the chapel. It indicated that the total cost should not exceed $200,000. The contract for construction was awarded to James Carlisle and Sons of Minneapolis on August 8, 1892, for $141,950.[10] The final product was not dissimilar to what was proposed, with the exception of the fact that building a separate chapel was postponed.

The relationship between Hill and Gilbert was strained from beginning to end. As early as April 1892, Gilbert received a memo from Hill's secretary that read as follows:

> Mr. Hill called in regard to the drawings for the seminary. He said that they should have been sent down to his office for him to look over and see if they were correct. He said that he doubted very much if they were.
>
> Also said that if you could not attend to this he must look for someone else. Expects to go away the latter part of the week and must see sketches before then.[11]

Gilbert complied, but the young architect—who admitted to his own "audacious egotism"[12]—collided frequently with the "Empire Builder."

If there was any doubt in Gilbert's mind that Hill insisted on making all the decisions, the following letter allowed for no ambiguity. Hill wrote to Gilbert:

> I have a number of letters from you, referring to different matters. Among others, I notice some omissions and changes in the

> plans. I do not desire any change to be made without its first being submitted to me. Even if you have made an error in the plan, as submitted, you must, before making any change, resubmit it. Two or three things have already crept in that have apparently increased the cost, and I am not willing that this should occur again, under any conditions. . . . I would rather stop the work rather than have any uncertainty. You know what difficulty we had in arriving at a conclusion in regard to these plans, and I do not want to go to sea again.[13]

Lest there be any misinterpretation, Hill's private secretary, W. A. Stephens, wrote to Gilbert only a week later:

> Mr. Hill directs me to write you that, in connection with the construction of the new Theological Seminary buildings, he does not want you to furnish any plans, specifications, sketches or data of any kind to contractors, or others, for the purpose of making estimates, or otherwise, for either heating, lighting or plumbing work, or of any other matters pertaining to the construction of said buildings, without first submitting all such plans and data to him and receiving his approval thereof. . . . Kindly acknowledge receipt of this letter.[14]

Gilbert submitted all the bids for contracts to Hill as requested, and letters in both the Hill and Gilbert Papers indicate that Hill made the most minute decisions—even regarding the locks on the doors and the style of doorknobs in the various buildings.[15]

When the seminary was completed in December 1894, and the contractors' accounts had been audited and certified, Gilbert wrote to Hill with some pride. The total amount for construction of the six buildings was $184,268.13. In conclusion, he added: "As you may remember the original proposed cost was placed at a limit of $200,000.00. I take pleasure in calling your attention to the foregoing figures confident that they will meet with your approval."[16]

Gilbert's confidence was ill-placed. In February he received a letter from Hill's private secretary at the Great Northern Railway Building which stated: "It is impossible in view of the objections made by Mr. Hill to some of the extra items on which you charge commission, to close your account. I hand you herewith a check for $500.00 as payment on account, which practically closes the matter up, outside of the extra items questioned by Mr. Hill. These I see no way of settling before his return."[17]

Gilbert responded the following day with his most candid missive. He made it clear that the bill was based on the schedule of changes that had been submitted to Hill prior to the construction, and that where it varied it was "materially less" than what had been agreed upon. He was upset because the bill was in Hill's possession in sufficient time for him to state his concerns, if he had any, before leaving town. The architect was left to ruminate about some vague and undefined "objections." Gilbert's concluding paragraph stated unabashedly that he had been ill-treated, and he was no longer hesitant to say so:

> The circumstances would seem to me to have justified a less arbitrary treatment and it is due me that I should know what the objections are founded on. After learning what they are if I can reasonably concede them I certainly will do so; for I am anxious to get the matter adjusted even if it is necessary to do so by making a compromise on the balance due me, though in view of all the circumstances I do not think I should be placed in such a position.[18]

Designing and overseeing the construction of the Minnesota State Capitol, or even the United States Supreme Court Building in Washington, D.C.—edifices for which Cass Gilbert is acclaimed—probably did not compare with the challenge he endured dealing with a St. Paul railroad magnate who was building a Catholic seminary.

The character of seminary education will be discussed in chapter 7, but it is important to note here that one of the major criticisms of U.S. seminaries in the nineteenth century was that they were often thought to be injurious to the health of the candidates: buildings were cold and drafty, food was poor, and there was rarely an opportunity for exercise. Perhaps no one was more outspoken about this matter than John Talbot Smith in *Our Seminaries: An Essay on Clerical Training,* published in 1896. Smith had attended St. Michael's Seminary in Toronto and was ordained in 1881 for the Diocese of Ogdensberg, New York. He was active as a writer in a variety of areas, but turned his attention to seminaries in the 1890s. He articulated his concerns graphically:

> What are our seminaries but homes for hypochondriacs, where dyspepsia, headache, constipation, biliousness live riotously and drive many students to the grave, or bring on scrupulousness and other forms of insanity, or send them into the world with lowered vitality and enfeebled constitutions. The mere change from the active life of the world, where vitality is fed by air and physical exercise, to the quiet, dreamy, physically inactive life of the seminary is enough to deprive the vigorous youth of physical and mental vitality within the year.[19]

Several other seminaries were also established in the United States during this era, notably Saint Bernard's in Rochester, New York, completed in 1893, and Kenrick Seminary in St. Louis, Missouri, which opened in the same year, but in old buildings. St. Joseph's Seminary at Dunwoodie, the major seminary for the Archdiocese of New York, was completed in 1896. St. Patrick's Seminary, Menlo Park, opened as a minor seminary in 1898 and expanded to include a major seminary by 1904. These seminaries, and most others of the period, were huge institutional complexes consisting of a central section and main entrance, with wings extending from either side. Usually those who were studying philosophy would be housed in one wing, and the theology students in the other. The chapel, faculty quarters, library, kitchen, and dining area were often in the central section. The result was that all of seminary life could be lived under one roof.

The Saint Paul Seminary was decidedly different from any of the seminaries being built in that era. Archbishop Ireland believed that the young men should get vigorous exercise in the brisk Minnesota climate if they were going to be healthy, hearty priests. Therefore, separate buildings would require that they move outdoors from dormitory to classroom to refectory to chapel (originally housed in the administration building), or to the gymnasium, allowing them to be invigorated by fresh air and exercise.

The six red-brick buildings were comfortably situated on a bluff overlooking the Mississippi River at the terminus of Grand Avenue. An article entitled "The New Seminary of St. Paul," published in *The Catholic University Bulletin* (April 1895), offered the following description: "The buildings are in the North Italian style, simple, solid and impressive." The author, Reverend Patrick Danehy, professor of scrip-

The Saint Paul Seminary administration building in the 1890s

ture, Hebrew, and homiletics at the seminary, pointed out the distinctiveness of having separate buildings, and included a diagram of the layout. He added:

> They are all built of red pressed brick, have either plain gable or hip roofs, and by the solidity of their walls remind one strongly of the monastic edifices of a bygone age. The partitions are fireproof throughout, while the stairs and the landings on each floor are of iron. The buildings are heated by steam, lighted by gas, supplied with hot and cold water.... The corridors are laid with thick matting and thus the footfall of the passerby does not break in upon the quiet of the student.[20]

During the years when silence was a major expectation in seminary life, the quiet was, no doubt, appreciated.

The final cost of the seminary was $260,000, according to the *Register* (catalogue) of the Saint Paul Seminary in 1896.[21] (The article in

The Catholic University Bulletin stated $200,000, but it is likely that that did not include the furnishings.)[22] The administration building contained a fireproof library at the south end and a private chapel on the north as well as parlors and offices, and the living apartments and reading room of the professors. The classroom building had four lecture rooms on the first floor, one of which was the science laboratory. The second floor was the auditorium (the *aula maxima*) which seated about five hundred people and was used for classes, public lectures, and all-school liturgies until St. Mary's Chapel was erected.

Most unusual was that, in the five-story dormitories, each student had *two* rooms—one for sleeping and one for study. The *Register* added: "On all the floors there are lavatories and bath rooms supplied with hot and cold water. Each residence has on the first floor a large chapel for the daily devotions of the students, and a well appointed infirmary."[23]

Two other buildings important to the students' needs were the refectory and the gymnasium. The refectory was replete with kitchen in the basement, a dining hall with a highly polished wood ceiling and large fireplace, and servants' quarters on the second floor. Danehy noted: "The kitchen, I am credibly informed, is supplied with all the appliances and means required by the culinary artist in making his most delicate experiments."[24]

The gymnasium building, which was also the heating plant for the complex, was identifiable from afar by a tall smokestack with borbelled brick crosses etched in the stone on the top. This remarkable edifice, a gem among Gilbert's accomplishments, had a main hall which opened to a wood-paneled ceiling, and an elegant truss system for roof support. Greek crosses abound as punctuation marks in the wrought-iron ornamentation.[25] The height and style almost evoke a cathedral atmosphere. With the noise of competitive sports echoing through the gym, however, one would not normally make that association. Not only was the gym fully equipped, but the heating plant was written up in an illustrated article in the *Engineer's Journal* (February 1895) as "one of the most perfect in the land."[26] In addition to the gym and the heating facility, there were four additional rooms to be used for quieter recreation—one supplied with newspapers and journals from around the world.

James J. Hill may not have been aware of the criticism of seminaries current at that time, but he had a clear vision of what he thought was useful and appropriate. At one point, Archbishop Ireland was said to have questioned the need for two rooms for each seminarian; Hill replied that it would be two or none![27] The emphasis, therefore, on the excellence of the facility, and the provision of a healthy and vigorous educational environment was a tradition built into the very walls of the seminary.

The vision of preparation for priesthood was Ireland's, but the buildings were clearly a monument to Hill. No one arriving on the campus could avoid the comparison. The administration building looked like an impressive railroad depot. The dormitories were referred to as "Jim Hill's boxcars." The classroom building was "the roundhouse." The tall smokestack of the gymnasium/heating plant ("the engine") hovered congenially nearby.[28] It was indeed—even visually—"the Hill Seminary."

CHAPTER 6

The Dedication

The smart carriages that swept down Summit Avenue toward the river that late summer day... were carrying the *creme de la creme* of Twin Cities' society. When they crossed Lexington and particularly after they passed Snelling Avenue, the sleek horses that drew them stepped a bit higher and tossed their heads expectantly as they caught a whiff of country air. Meanwhile, a few blocks away, humbler folk, making their way to the same destination, hung to the straps of the electric trolley cars which had begun recently to bump noisily along Grand Avenue. So they all eventually arrived, the elite and the commonality, at the great sweep of green lawns perched above the lordly Mississippi and adorned with shrubbery and handsome trees whose bright leaves seemed to have defied the rigors of a long, hot summer, lawns upon which now stood a collection of six, shining-new, red-brick buildings, themselves decked out in flags and bunting. So it was that top hats and fur tippets mingled indiscriminately with shiny blue serge suits and simple frocks, the elegantly coifed and manicured with those whose hands were red and deeply calloused. It was all very Catholic, it was all very American. Everybody—whether hailing from the mansions atop St. Anthony's Hill or from the mean little houses of the Connemara Patch beneath Dayton's Bluff—everybody had come to celebrate the dedication of what everybody called Mr. Hill's seminary.[1]

Marvin R. O'Connell
"Meximieux and Mr. Hill: John Ireland's Dream Come True"
Saint Paul Seminary Centennial Address
September 8, 1994

The year 1894–1895 was clearly one of settling in and preparing for the formal dedication.[2] The students moved into the new buildings September 6, 1894. A headline in the St. Paul *Pioneer Press* read: "Hill Seminary Opens To-Day" with the subtitle: "Another Great Educational Institution in St. Paul."[3] It took almost a year, however, to complete the buildings, put the program in place, and prepare for the dedicatory ceremonies scheduled for September 1895.

One event that first year which led to an established tradition was the celebration of the feast of the Conversion of Saint Paul. On February 2, 1895, Ireland wrote to James J. Hill with letters and instructions regarding "the Empire Builder's" proposed trip to Rome. The archbishop added: "We celebrated the feast of the patron Saint, Jan. 25th, and sixty-five priests attended. They were amazed at all that they saw."[4]

The excitement of preparation for the dedication, the anticipation of the guests, and the physical arrangements for the enormous number of persons to be accommodated provided a challenge to all involved. Hill's secretary wired him in New York on August 20, 1895, "Do you wish free transportation issued Buffalo and Cleveland to St. Paul and return, in favor of Monsigneur Satolli and prelates attending dedication St. Paul Seminary. Are rooms to be furnished free."[5] On August 28, Hill sent the following telegram to John Gordon of the Northern Steamship Company, Buffalo, New York—part of Hill's Great Northern enterprise:

> Rev. Dr. O'Gorman will call on you for transportation for Monsigneur Satolli and a party of priests not over thirteen in number, who wish to leave Buffalo on Steamship Northwest Friday next for Duluth. Please furnish tickets Buffalo to Duluth and return, and arrange to make bill on Archbishop Ireland here for rooms and meals furnished the party. I have issued ticket H925 Sault Ste. Marie to Duluth and return for Bishop Vertin who will join the party at the Soo [sic]. Please make same arrangements for berth and meals for the balance of party.[6]

In another telegram, September 2, 1895, to W. C. Parrington in Duluth, Hill wrote: "Archbishop Ireland cannot leave St. Paul this morning to meet Monsigneur Satolli and party. Will you please do whatever is necessary for their comfort, and see that they are equipped with the necessary transportation to come to St. Paul. Sleeping car accommodations should be provided and bill made on Archbishop Ireland for it."[7] Hill was accommodating, but his largesse did not extend to picking up all the bills for the visiting clergy.

The arrival of the dignitaries from the East on the Great Northern's steamship to Duluth and the subsequent railroad trip to St. Paul contributed to the atmosphere of celebration. Father Thomas O'Gorman, Ireland's boyhood friend, now a professor of church history at the Catholic University of America, personally escorted the apostolic delegate, Archbishop Francesco Satolli. Also in the party were Msgr. Nugent of Liverpool, England; Msgr. McMahon of Washington, D.C.; and the Reverends Doctor Pace, Bouquillon, Dumont, and Shahan of the Catholic University of America, with which the Saint Paul Seminary was to be affiliated. Monsignor O'Brien traveled from Rome, and others who attended were from New York, Chicago, and the University of Notre Dame. There were, in addition to the apostolic delegate, four archbishops, ten bishops, and over four hundred priests in attendance.

On September 4, 1895, a bright balmy autumn day, there was excitement in the air as almost 20,000 people arrived to witness the dedication ceremonies at the Saint Paul Seminary. An altar was erected on an elevated platform on the east side of the administration building (with a canopy to protect the dignitaries from the sun), so that the throng of participants could see the liturgy. The Stars and Stripes floated above the group on a newly-erected 150-foot flagpole, a gift from Mrs. James J. Hill.[8] Chairs were provided only for the clergy and distinguished guests; others had to stand.[9] Considering the length of the Pontifical Mass and the sermon that followed, that was noble indeed.

The events of the dedication day were reported in various newspapers—Catholic and secular—throughout the United States. The headline in the *Chicago Times* read "Hill Seminary Open" and exhibited a large photograph of Msgr. Satolli. It described the procession of "high dignitaries and churchmen" in detail, stating that it began in the administration building led by the crossbearer and "accompanied by the little acolytes swinging their censers." It also reported: "As this is the feast of St. Rose of Vitalbo, the clergy were attired in white."[10]

Msgr. Satolli celebrated the Pontifical High Mass with various members of the seminary faculty assisting him. Mr. and Mrs. Hill and their family occupied the front seats in the congregation. A separate platform had been erected for the choir—a group of two hundred members from various church choirs in St. Paul accompanied by the Danz Orchestra under the direction of Mr. John F. Gehan, choirmaster at the cathedral. They sang Gounod's *Messe Solennelle of St. Cecilia.*[11] It was a moving and impressive event and the liturgy was concluded with a solemn benediction imparted by Msgr. Satolli.

Reverend Dr. Thomas O'Gorman delivered an extended sermon after the Mass. In his reflections he quoted St. Francis de Sales: "I declare with emphasis that ignorance in a priest is more to be dreaded than sin, because it does not merely lead to his ruin, but dishonors and degrades the Sacerdotal character. For the priest knowledge is the eighth sacrament, and the greatest misfortunes have come upon the church wherever the Ark of Science has been permitted to fall from the hands of the Levites."[12]

O'Gorman was a historian who shared Archbishop Ireland's conviction that although religious truth does not change, it must not fear to enter into a relationship with the scientific world and learn from it. The speaker identified three remarkable changes in society which were affecting the life of the church in its mission in the late nineteenth century. The transformations were in the political realm, in experimental and applied science, and in the sphere of social economics. "The seminary of this day and this land cannot ignore the civil, natural and social sciences, while it holds on to the theological science as its chief and professional subject."[13]

But Thomas O'Gorman could not conclude his sermon without sharing with the assembled throng what would always be for John Ireland and himself a pivotal moment in their lives. He described, with some nostalgia, Bishop Cretin's selection of the two young Irish boys forty-three years before, especially Cretin's declaration: "You are the beginning of the diocesan seminary of St. Paul." Taking note of the venerable retired Archbishop Grace, and of his classmate John Ireland, both behind him on the platform, O'Gorman added: "A diocesan seminary! Such was his dream and his prophecy and such too was even the hope of his beloved and venerable successor, who is still, thank God, with us. The dream has been realized, the prophecy accomplished and the hope fulfilled by one of those boys, now your archbishop."[14]

O'Gorman then described another young man who arrived in St. Paul not many years after that who had a "keen brain and indomitable energy" and who "kept mind and heart open to the needs and aspirations of the age." It was the vision and generosity of the other young man—James J. Hill—and his "princely donation," which allowed for the building of the Saint Paul Seminary. With God's blessings and with the approval of Pope Leo XIII through his representative Msgr. Satolli, O'Gorman predicted that the seminary would be among "the great schools of the church, the world renowned nurseries of saints and scholars."[15]

Following the sermon, a procession of prelates, priests, and seminarians formed and visited the six buildings, each being solemnly dedicated by Msgr. Satolli. Luncheon followed in the refectory where some two thousand persons were served. Thousands of people toured the new buildings during the afternoon, spirited on by the First Regiment Band from Fort Snelling, which provided both sacred and patriotic music for the visitors.[16]

The evening event was for invited guests only and began at 7:30 P.M. in the *aula maxima,* which was full to overflowing. Among those in attendance were college presidents, professors from the University of Minnesota, members of the city and state governments and the board of education, and officers from the Department of Dakota accompanied by their wives. Mary Theresa Mehegan Hill and her daughters sat in the front row of the audience. The elite of the Northwest were all present for this auspicious occasion.

Archbishop Ireland presided over the event, with the apostolic delegate on his right, and the benefactor, James J. Hill, on his left. Other members of the hierarchy, rectors of other Catholic colleges and universities, professors of the Catholic University of America, and prominent citizens—Catholic and non-Catholic—occupied the stage. The seminary choir offered musical renditions. Before delivering his address to the assembly, Archbishop Ireland read two telegrams of special significance. The first was a congratulatory message from Pope Leo XIII extended by Cardinal Rampolla, Papal Secretary of State: "Rome, September 2, 1895.—Msgr. Ireland, Archbishop of St. Paul, St. Paul, Minn.: The holy father offers you his heartfelt felicitations on the dedication of your Seminary. He invokes affectionately the blessing of God upon yourself, upon the founder of the Seminary, Mr. James J. Hill, and upon his family."[17] Ireland probably beamed at this statement of approval from the Vatican for all that had been accomplished.

The second telegram, whatever its formality, had personal meaning for Ireland. It was from James Cardinal Gibbons of Baltimore, the ecclesiastical figure with whom Ireland had fought side by side to defend many causes of the American Catholic Church. Gibbons, the gentle, moderate pastor, often tempered the archbishop's zeal and wrote many letters to Ireland in St. Paul that always began: "My reverend and dear friend . . ."[18] On September 4 the message over the wires read: "I regret my unavoidable absence. Hearty congratulations on dedication of Seminary, a nursery of religion and science and a splendid monument to the munificent zeal of its princely benefactor, Mr. James J. Hill."[19] The absence of Gibbons, unofficial primate of the Catholic Church in the United States and dear friend of Archbishop Ireland, was the one missing element on that day of remarkable celebration.

Having communicated the congratulations of the pope and Cardinal Gibbons, Ireland—in his usual exuberant style—set forth his hopes and dreams for this institution which he had said early on would be the primary work of his episcopate. He announced: "St. Paul's Seminary is the school of the Catholic priesthood of the Northwest." James J. Hill had built an "empire"; it sounded as if Ireland would like to do the same in another sphere. With added vigor he stated: "St. Paul's Seminary proclaims to-night [sic] its solemn pledge that the education given within its walls shall be at all times the best and the highest. Nothing short of the best and the highest is worthy of the priesthood, worthy of the cause which the priesthood represents and of the interests which it is to serve."[20] Possibly to the discomfort of the seminary faculty present—as well as those who would occupy those positions in years to come—Ireland declared: "Should St. Paul's Seminary ever in days to come fall below this evening's ideal, be it publicly anathematized as faithless to its baptismal promises, faithless to the just demands of the founder, faithless to the inspirations and orders of its sponsor and first archbishop."[21]

Ireland continued with O'Gorman's theme of the morning sermon: the need for science, political economy and sociology, and literature to be studied side by side in the seminary. "Culture, refinement, scholarship must ever be the characteristics of Christ's priesthood."[22] The archbishop's love for the United States, so evident on every occasion, was not absent here. With his characteristic hyperbole he stated: "America, be thine this seminary—thine in imperishable love; thine in sacred devotion to thy life and weal. We consecrate it to thee this evening. The stars and stripes will never be lifted above hearts more American than the hearts of the masters and students of St. Paul's Seminary."[23] Though he may have been an Irish immigrant educated in France, there was no doubt that America claimed his allegiance forever. He reminded his audience: "Patriotism is a religious virtue; good citizenship is the practical application through life of Christian ethics." He was a loyal son of the church and a fiery patriot to the end.

Ireland's expansive view was always integrated into his hopes and dreams. The Catholic community must have been almost giddy with this new "ecumenical" experience. Catholics were not accustomed to enjoying any benefits in a predominantly Protestant culture, much less having a Methodist millionaire build a Catholic seminary. In the past, some of Ireland's experiences with Protestants had not always been positive. Still, he had spoken at the World's Parliament of Religion in Chicago in 1893—just two years before. Therefore, the inclusive tenor of the following statement should not be dismissed:

> The influence radiating from this seminary will reach more immediately the people of its own religious faith. They are a large part of the general population of the Northwest. Beyond them, however, must our influence go. Its spirit will be *to work for the whole people,* offering its strength to uphold every noble cause, and willing to cooperate with all men who labor to serve God, humanity, and country. No narrowing lines, holding back from doing good wherever.... Allies will always be here to unite with those who heal the wounds of suffering humanity, or strengthen the social bonds, and the institutions of the country. Allies will always be here to extend the hand of friendship to all who war for the living God of the universe, and for Christ Jesus the Saviour of men.

His final challenge was delivered with passion: "In God's name, I bid thee, go forth, and do thy work."[24]

Ireland concluded his speech with a tribute to Hill. He stated clearly: "The merit of the whole project—from the first to the present moment is all his own." The archbishop pointed out that "The highest use of wealth is in the service of humanity." Later, "Wealth, under the control of a noble soul, is a great social blessing." He thanked Hill "with all the warmth of which hearts are capable." And he thanked Mrs. Mary Hill as well.[25]

Then followed addresses by Professors Joseph Sontgerath and Patrick Danehy, a dedication ode by Reverend W. H. Sheran, and music by the seminary choir. The second half of the program included the addresses of Professor Humphrey Moynihan, Bishop John J. Keane, the rector of the Catholic University of America, and finally the apostolic delegate. Father O'Gorman read the apostolic delegate's speech.

The moment for which everyone had been waiting, however, was Hill's concluding address. He stated: "I earnestly join with you all in the hope that its work in the future will merit and receive the divine blessing, and that its sons will take their places in the religious world as intelligent, worthy and devoted followers of their Divine Master."[26] Hill paid an admiring tribute to Msgr. Louis Caillet, who had been both a pastor and a personal friend to him. Without the priest's example, Hill questioned whether he would have thought to undertake the project. (See chapter 4, p. 52.)

Hill then addressed the question which many had: why had one who was not a Catholic made such a substantial donation to build a Catholic seminary? We know the answer. His Irish Catholic wife of almost thirty years had been a loving, devoted Christian. What higher praise than to attribute to her the verse from the Beatitudes: "Blessed are the pure in heart, for they will see God" (Matt 5:8; see chapter 4, p. 41). Michael P. Malone, in his recent biography of Hill, described the relationship of James and Mary Hill: "They formed an exceptionally close bond, and the couple remained harmoniously dedicated to one another throughout their long life together. Both of them held strongly traditional views about marriage and family, and no scandal or even accusation ever arose about their relationship."[27] Hill then stated that it was on her behalf that he was turning over the seminary and its endowment as provided in the deeds and articles of trust to the archbishop of St. Paul.

Before concluding, however, Hill added that he was aware that most other denominations had members who were able to be supportive of their congregations in a material way. Because of the "large number of [Catholic] workingmen and women, coming from almost every nation and clime" who were not able to provide for places of worship and the education of those who would lead them, Hill decided that this would be a worthy cause. He agreed with Archbishop Ireland's vision that there was no conflict between science and divine revelation. Although unspoken, he also admired Ireland's uniquely American vision of the Catholic Church which certainly was congenial to his way of thinking and working. He, therefore, decided to devote a portion of his world's goods "to the work of educating for the priesthood men who would be able to preach down the spirit of unbelief and to stand as shining lights along the pathway that leads to heaven."[28]

Ireland and Hill were two extraordinary men, both born in the same year—born, in fact, in the same month, the very month that Joseph Cretin was sailing to America to begin his life as a missionary. The Catholic Church in the Upper Midwest developed uniquely because of these men. At certain periods in their lives Ireland and Hill had been "competitors"; at other times they had been somewhat dependent on each other. Now they were enjoying the successes of their late fifties. As they grew older, possibly they were able to share each other's joy. Ireland and Hill in a certain way became symbols of church and society on the frontier—competing, yet supporting each other in an effort to achieve the American ideal.

Hill received letters of congratulation from a variety of sources in the weeks following the dedication. J. R. B. Kelley, editor of *The Catholic Recorder* of Manchester, New Hampshire, wrote in gratitude for Hill's gift to the Catholic Church. He admitted to being an admirer of Archbishop Ireland and the following letter provides evidence that Ireland's reputation was alive and thriving on the East Coast.

> I believe if Archbishop Ireland could be placed in absolute controll [sic] of the affairs of the church in the U.S. he would in the few years of life yet remaining to him, Americanize Catholicism and catholicize America and the dawning of a new century would disclose to the world a reformation in the western continent surpassing any similar event in the eastern world since the morning of the Christian era.[29]

More touching, however, was a letter from his friend, confidante, and fellow director in various enterprises over the years—D. Willis James. After thanking Hill for the newspaper he had received describing the dedication of the seminary, and noting how impressed he was with the addresses of Msgr. Satolli and Archbishop Ireland, he added a more personal note:

> But you will allow me to say that what delighted and interested me most was your own address, and its beautifully true reference to Mrs. Hill, in every word of which I most cordially unite. To you the day must have been a happy one, the consummation of so many plans and hopes, and especially as a recognition of God's goodness in the gift of a wife of whom we all know it can truthfully be said that the "Pure in heart shall see God."[30]

D. Willis James was an influential New York businessman and conservative financier who often thought that Hill took on more debt than was wise in his creative ventures. Malone described James as one of the "hardheaded financial types";[31] yet he clearly had enormous respect and appreciation for Mary Hill.

D. Willis James also shared Hill's vision regarding the relationship of religion to the growth and development of the United States. He reflected:

> I am in heartiest sympathy with the broad outlook into the unseen future, which has influenced you to make this generous gift. That the Roman Catholic Church is bound to have a most potent influence on the future of the United States is certain, and that an educated priesthood, educated in America, and in touch with the life of Americans, will be a factor for good I do not doubt. Your work, then, becomes of great national importance, and in connection with the vast work Archbishop Ireland is accomplishing, will have a bearing on the future history of the United States.[32]

He concluded with additional congratulations and sentiments of trust that "when the labor of earth shall cease" his friend and colleague "will hear the welcome 'Well done, good and faithful servant.'"[33]

CHAPTER 7

The Saint Paul Seminary

The Early Years

> The seminary is a place of probation and experiment. What you are in the seminary you will be for time and eternity. Keep three things constantly before your mind's eye: You must be a *saint*, a *scholar*, and a *gentleman*. The seminary is not so much a place where you pick up a little knowledge of philosophy or theology. It is established to prepare your character in piety and holiness principally for your future career.[1]
>
> Archbishop John Ireland
> Conference to Seminarians, 1895

John Ireland's Vision of Seminary Formation

Although James J. Hill was responsible for the financial and physical arrangements of the Saint Paul Seminary, he never made any effort to control the academic or spiritual life of the institution.[2] That was the province of John Ireland. And few were more enthusiastic about a solid seminary program than John Ireland. As noted above, it was while he was still at the Third Plenary Council of Baltimore in 1884 that he announced the establishment of the St. Thomas Aquinas Seminary. With Baltimore III, the need for dialogue and critique regarding seminary development in the United States became more acceptable and was enhanced with the founding of the *American Ecclesiastical Review* by Reverend Herman Heuser at St. Charles Seminary, Philadelphia, in 1889. Although the goal of this journal was continuing education for the Catholic clergy, the role of the seminary in the preparation of candidates was also a topic for discussion.

In addition, a variety of published volumes on seminary education became available in the early years of the Saint Paul Seminary, many of which corroborated Archbishop Ireland's vision. In 1896 Cardinal Gibbons published the largely irenic volume *Ambassadors of Christ.*[3] More critical of the system was *Our Seminaries: An Essay on Clerical Training* (1896) by the New York priest, John Talbot Smith.[4] In 1898 the Sulpician John Hogan published *Clerical Studies,* a series of essays some of which had been previously published in the *American Ecclesiastical Review.*[5]

Each adopted a particular typology for reflecting upon the education necessary for the future priest in the United States. Cardinal Gibbons stated:

> In fact, the priest embodies in his own person the threefold profession of judge, of advocate, and of physician. As judge, he is called upon to decide doctrinal and moral questions—which requires a knowledge of the divine and ecclesiastical law; as advocate, he must plead the cause of God before the people—which demands a well-furnished and disciplined mind; as physician, he has to prescribe the remedies for spiritual maladies—which presupposes a deep insight into the human heart, and study of its complex distempers.[6]

John Talbot Smith's "practical standard" was sixfold. His description was of the priest as: (1) a gentleman; (2) an educated gentleman; (3) an educated gentleman fitted for public life; (4) physically sound; (5) acquainted and in sympathy with his environment; (6) imbued with the true missionary spirit.[7] Although not involved in seminary education himself, Smith had many creative ideas about preparing students for the pastoral tasks awaiting them. He particularly questioned the situation of isolating candidates in seminaries, separating them from normal society during the years of their preparation.

Hogan's volume analyzed the various courses in the seminary curriculum. In the preface he stated that the outcome of such study would be that "ever-growing, varied knowledge will become one of the happy necessities of their [priestly] existence, bringing with it inexhaustible enjoyment, perennial freshness of mind, dignity of life, and a power every day greater to be useful to others."[8] In a letter to Hogan in early 1897, Patrick Heffron, then vice-rector of the Saint Paul Seminary, mentioned that Hogan's book was being read aloud during meals in the refectory. Students identified with it in terms of their own experience and some of them were known to reflect: "The author must have had Saint Paul Seminary in mind when he wrote his book."[9]

Archbishop Ireland's vision of the church in America conditioned his model of priesthood and his ideals for the education of both priest and laity. Fortunately for future generations, a student named John F. Duggan copied almost verbatim some of Ireland's conferences with his seminarians in 1895. Duggan wrote that the talks included a rich variety of subjects of an inspirational nature on the intellectual and spiritual development of the future priest. He reflected, "The energetic Archbishop was full of his subject, and delighted in addressing his students, and spurring them on to high achievement in their chosen vocation." These transcriptions were finally published in 1939 in *The Ecclesiastical Review.*[10] In the vast literature today about the education of seminarians, it is difficult to discover any description superior to Ireland's vision of the priest as *saint, scholar,* and *gentleman.*

Ireland never underestimated the ability of people to judge the authenticity of church leaders, and a priest who was not desirous of being holy could easily be disregarded, although he might be a capable administrator and a poignant preacher. Ireland admonished the students time and again:

> The three necessary qualities of a seminarian are sanctity, scholarship, and gentlemanliness. As the seminarian is, so is the priest. The priest must be a holy man. Knowledge without sanctity is merely a great weed which produces nothing. Sanctity is the fundamental requisite of the priestly life. If you do not make an effort to be holy men you have not in you the stuff of which priests must be made.[11]

Holiness, however, was no substitute for knowledge. The priest had a responsibility to the people he would serve to teach and preach well, neither of which would be possible without a solid grounding in theology and the other sciences. Ireland stated: "The priest must have a thirst for knowledge and be a scholar. Your professors stand ready to give you an example in all things, and you must cooperate. Pay attention to your masters, absorb and assimilate what they give you."[12]

The archbishop frequently told the students that they should think with a pen in hand. He encouraged them to be independent thinkers:

> Your years in the seminary are not entirely for accumulation of knowledge, but to think. Thinking is education. When a subject is presented to you, examine it for yourself, do not dismiss it from your mind until you are able to say you understand it. Do not think a certain statement or proposition is true merely because your professor says so. Know the reason of it in your own mind. When the subject is presented, revolve it in your own intellect, analyze it, create objections, make it your own. Do not pass over any matter with a half knowledge of it. It is better to do one subject well than to pass over twenty in a slipshod manner. After this process use your pen and ink; write down your thoughts. This will help you to preserve them in your memory. I recently came across a striking passage in St. Augustine. It is this: "Whatever I learned I have learned by writing."[13]

In no area was Ireland as clear and as specific as when directing the students to learn how to be gentlemen. The archbishop knew that many of those he was instructing were immigrants or the children of immigrants and often came from the non-affluent segments of society. If they were to be leaders in the American Catholic Church, they needed to be able to operate on a par with those who enjoyed the benefits of wealth without bowing to them. Once again, authenticity should reign supreme:

> The priest must be a gentleman. Manners are but the reflection of the interior man, and a criterion of it. You must learn gentlemanly deportment. Even table manners indicate your breeding and betray whether you are a gentleman or not. There is nothing more disgusting than to behold a slovenly man. The priest must have proper deportment, keep clean and dress well. Students

should keep their clothes neat and clean, teeth brushed, hair combed, shoes polished, and keep shaven. *The priest must be able to enter with equal ease and politeness the cottage of the poor and the palace of the prince.*[14]

Ireland's directives to the seminarians and his enthusiasm for learning grew out of his ecclesiology. Influenced by Isaac Hecker and Orestes Brownson, Ireland was more concerned about the church's mission than with the institution. His focus was more on what the church "does" than on what it "is." Function over structure; action over nature.[15]

Ireland was comfortable with the authoritarian structures of the church—but it was more than that for him. He saw the church in terms of incarnation and organism. For John Ireland,

> The Church is the incarnation of divine love and mercy, and, as such, she cannot but concern herself with all things that make for the betterment of man, for the happiness of man, wherever he is, in whatsoever relationship he is found to exist. . . . Nothing, then, that is of service to man, either as the individual or as the member of society can be alien to the heart and the work of the church. Her charity must be catholic, embracing all human interests, compassionating and remedying every ill, blessing and furthering every human good. God is the author of the natural as well as the supernatural order, and He cares for both. Over both, in the name of God's love and mercy, the church must extend her maternal beneficence.[16]

The church continues the incarnation; therefore, the church must somehow be identified with Christ, or perhaps even be Christ. Through the unity of Christ's divinity and humanity in the "Word made flesh," the secular and the spiritual are united and harmonized.[17]

The incarnation continues in the life of humanity in the church as an active living organism. Ireland stated:

> There was needed this other act—the institution of the Church, the creation of an ever-living, ever-quickening organism, through which the fruits of the inscrutable mysteries of the Incarnation

> and Redemption were continued through the ages.... An organism of communication was needed, wide-spread over earth, abiding there until the end of time, so long as humanity itself is predestined there to abide.[18]

The archbishop was unabashed in his joy in the attainment of an archdiocesan seminary which, in effect, was a regional seminary. He was not, however, just a "brick and mortar man." Ireland's conviction regarding the necessity of a diocesan seminary was grounded in his ecclesiology and in his belief in the unique role of the diocesan clergy.

Ireland perceived distinctions between diocesan priests and religious order priests, and articulated them in the sermon he delivered at the consecration of his childhood friend and confrere, Thomas O'Gorman, as bishop of Sioux Falls, South Dakota, April 19, 1896. He stated, perhaps to the distress of some: "The priesthood which I commend with all my earnestness to the care of the episcopate is the diocesan priesthood." The archbishop admitted that there was room in the church for religious orders of priests, and sufficient work for them to do. He recognized the value of their labors. But he saw that their organization and purpose was to meet extraordinary emergencies, to do special work, "to obey directly the behests of the Supreme Pontiff." This removed them from the bishop's jurisdiction. Ireland concluded: "When we talk of the Bishop's priests in his diocese, they fall outside this enumeration. He cannot depend upon them for the work of his diocese; nor is his care required or allowed, in the formation of their priesthood. The orders attend to their own growth and choose their own work."[19]

Ireland made it very clear that it was the diocesan clergy upon whom the bishop could count for fidelity in good times and bad. He continued:

> I think it may be said with some truth that the diocesan clergy have been underestimated and neglected. The rough and ready work fell largely to their lot, and leisure for study was not afforded them. The notion, too, most false and pernicious, was spread that less growth of mind and soul was expected from them than from the order clergy; that perfection attached rather to vows and ecclesiastical ordinances than to the intrinsic sa-

> credness of the priesthood, and the dignity of the ministry of saving souls.[20]

John Ireland was going to see to it that the training of diocesan priests was second to none. His seminary would not only help to form priests who were gentlemen, scholars, and saints, but men who could take pride in the fraternity to which they belonged as diocesan clergy. The future of the Catholic Church in America, Ireland was convinced, depended on it. He concluded that portion of his sermon as follows:

> The Church will not have a widespread, regular and well-sustained growth unless the diocesan priests are fully conscious of the dignity of their state and ministry, and are fully equipped by all the qualities of mind and heart for their great work. It must never be forgotten that the normal clergy for a diocese are its own incardinated priests; as they grow and work, so will the diocese expand and prosper.[21]

Ireland's ecclesiology was indeed hierarchical, and the phenomenon of the religious orders did not seem to fit into his scheme. He saw them as semi-autonomous bodies within the Catholic Church and beyond his control. Ireland's policies did not allow for the expansion of the religious orders in the archdiocese, and he allowed few priests from orders permission to enter.[22] His conviction regarding the unique role of the diocesan priesthood led him to establish a major seminary staffed and administered by diocesan priests rather than Sulpicians, Vincentians, or Jesuits.

It was no secret that Ireland had little appreciation for the Jesuits. In 1892 he had written to Caillet from Rome: "Our enemies—the Germans and the Jesuits—watch all details and send word at once to Roman authorities, so as to prejudice them against us."[23] A month later Ireland again wrote to his vicar general: "The Germans and the Jesuits have done all that they could to misrepresent our school ideas. The Jesuit papers in Italy keep up the fight but to no purpose."[24] If there was no place for religious order priests, especially Jesuits, in the archdiocese, there was certainly no place for them as faculty members in his seminary. Ireland was convinced that the role of diocesan priests would be enhanced within the diocese if those who taught seminarians were themselves diocesan priests.

Early Faculty of the Seminary

The archbishop appointed all officials and members of the faculty. The curriculum and guidelines for discipline were all at Ireland's direction. The government of the institution was entrusted to the rector, the vice-rector, the spiritual director, the deans, and the counselors. These officials, together with two professors chosen by the archbishop, constituted the council of the seminary, which met monthly. Their responsibility was to vote for the promotion of students to orders, or in some instances to vote for dismissal or other extraordinary punishment. They also made recommendations regarding examinations and the general welfare of the seminary. Meetings of the faculty and other officials were held at the beginning of the semester, and before ordinations and examinations. Matters of concern were referred to the council.[25]

The appointment of Msgr. Louis Caillet as rector was certainly an acknowledgment of the unique role the gentle French priest had played in the establishment of the seminary. Caillet accepted the position, but certainly not because he had any desire for administration. On September 9, 1896, Archbishop Ireland appointed Father Patrick Heffron vice-rector with wide powers, especially in financial matters. In October Caillet confided to Mary Hill with some sense of relief: "Although I cannot say that I like Seminary life, I feel much better contented under the altered circumstances than I did last year. Father Heffron seems to take an earnest interest in his new work and do it in an intelligent manner. The rest of the faculty are working well and are in very good spirits."[26] Because of Caillet's frail condition, however, he was rector for only three years until his death on November 28, 1897, serving also as vicar general of the archdiocese from 1893 to 1897.

Humphrey Moynihan, one of the priest faculty who later became rector, stated that Caillet's "very presence among the students was an exalting influence. His gentle gravity, his priestly piety, his mellow wisdom silently made themselves felt in the lives of the young men entrusted to his paternal care." Most impressive was his calm bearing and simple trust in God as he prepared to die.[27]

Archbishop Ireland was determined to enlist an excellent seminary faculty. Although he believed that diocesan priests should be taught by diocesan priests, preferably Americans who knew and understood the culture, he was realistic enough to know that he would have to rely mostly on "imports" for his faculty at the beginning. Early on he contacted his friend Msgr. Denis O'Connell at the American College in Rome requesting suggestions for recruits for the faculty. O'Connell made several recommendations, perhaps the most famous a French biblical scholar named Alfred Loisy. O'Connell wrote: "If you could only get Loisy of Paris for Scripture. He is the best biblical scholar in the Church."[28] The archbishop had correspondence with Loisy, but there is no evidence that an appointment was specifically offered.[29] Considering Loisy's role in the Modernism crisis and his later condemnation, it is fascinating to speculate on what might have happened had Loisy been offered and accepted the position.

Those selected to staff the new seminary were broadly trained at some of the best European Catholic universities. Reverend John Soentgerath was one of Denis O'Connell's recruits. A native of Cologne, Germany, he completed his doctorate at the Gregorian University in Rome and in 1890 came to teach dogma and canon law at St. Thomas.[30] In 1896, however, he moved to the Pontifical College Josephinum, which served mostly German candidates, and was rector there from 1899 to 1923. Reverend Alessandro Cestelli, a native of Tuscany, was appointed professor of moral theology in 1894 after completing doctoral work at the University of Pisa. He joined Father Soentgerath two years later in transferring to the Josephinum.[31] Father John Chareyre, a member of the Academy of St. Thomas in Paris and a priest in the Marist Order, came to the United States at the request of Archbishop Ireland, who was familiar with the work of the Marists because of his own experience of studying theology at Montbel.[32]

Father Humphrey Moynihan came from County Limerick in Ireland where he had studied under the Jesuits and taught with them at Mungret College near Limerick City. He was highly recommended to Ireland when the archbishop was visiting Limerick. Archbishop Ireland made arrangements for his advanced study at the American College in Rome under the direction of Denis O'Connell. After completing his studies in September 1892, Moynihan traveled to Minnesota expecting that he would begin teaching at the Saint Paul Seminary. With the delay in the construction of the seminary, Ireland appointed Moynihan as his secretary, allowing them to develop a bond that would be important in years to come. Moynihan succeeded far beyond expectations, leading Ireland to write to O'Connell in 1894: "Moynihan is a remarkable man."[33]

Moynihan taught apologetics and was prefect of studies. With Caillet in ill health, Moynihan was virtually the rector during that period, according to James Reardon, who began studies at the Saint Paul Seminary in the fall of 1895.[34] However, with Heffron's appointment as vice-rector in 1896 and his accession to rector after Caillet's death in November 1897, Moynihan seems to have been limited to the classroom. When Father John F. Dolphin resigned the presidency of St. Thomas due to fragile health, Humphrey Moynihan was appointed to that position and served from 1903 to 1921. In 1921 he returned to the Saint Paul Seminary as rector.[35]

Another European to serve on the first faculty and eventually become rector of the seminary was Francis J. Schaefer. Born in Kuellstedt, Sachsen, Germany, he had been invited by Archbishop Ireland to become a student for the archdiocese while a seminarian at the Propaganda College in Rome. He completed his doctorate at the Institut Catholique in Paris. Assigned in 1894 as the first professor of church history at the Saint Paul Seminary, "Germany Schaefer," as he was known, later served as rector from 1910 to 1921.[36]

The first scripture professor was one of the few Americans and the only one from the Midwest—Reverend Patrick Danehy. He was born in Waupun, Wisconsin, attended college at St. John's in Collegeville, Minnesota, studied classics at St. Francis Seminary in Milwaukee and philosophy and theology at the Grand Seminary in Montreal, Canada. After ordination for the Archdiocese of Saint Paul in 1881, he served in parishes for about eight years. Archbishop Ireland assigned him to study at the newly opened Catholic University of America in Washington, D.C. (1889–1891). He later pursued biblical studies at the University of Louvain in Belgium (1891–1893).[37] Danehy taught scripture at the Saint Paul Seminary from 1894 to 1901. Subsequent to that he became pastor of St. Stephen's Parish in Minneapolis (1901–1904) and also served as spiritual director to the Catholic students at the University of Minnesota until his death in 1904.[38]

Two other priests, both from New York, served on the first faculty but stayed only one year each: Father Anthony Joseph Gerhard and Father Nathaniel McCaffrey. The only lay member of the faculty was Professor John A. Hartigan, who was appointed to the St. Thomas Aquinas faculty in the early 1890s as a science teacher. In 1894 he became professor of chemistry and physics at the Saint Paul Seminary and continued in a shared appointment between the college and the seminary. Hartigan, bright and efficient in the classroom, was appreciated by most students.[39]

The original faculty was clearly international in character. One of the first seminarians who moved into the new building in the fall of 1894 was John Augustine Ryan. Later to become one of the outstanding moral theologians in the United States, Ryan's early experiences at the Saint Paul Seminary appear to be typical of the seminarian of his time. Reflecting almost fifty years later on the faculty of the seminary in the early years, he wrote:

> The teaching staff which Archbishop Ireland assembled for his new institution was well above the average of American ecclesiastical seminaries in 1894. Most of the faculty members had been trained with specific reference to the chairs which they were respectively to occupy. Almost without exception they were comparatively young men, but only one of them is now living.[40]

Student Life

Although the buildings were not quite complete, sixty-five students moved across the street from St. Thomas on September 6, 1894. The staircases had not yet been installed in the residence halls. There was no water in the residences for some time. The seminarians had to use outdoor toilets for the first few months and had a basin and pitcher in their rooms and a commode under their beds.[41] The kitchen and dining room were also unfinished, so the seminarians returned to St. Thomas three times daily for their meals until December 8, 1894.[42]

Despite the inconveniences, there was an air of excitement about being part of the new venture. The spacious dormitories with two rooms for every student were extraordinary for those who had lived in the crowded conditions at St. Thomas. When the students were finally able to occupy both of their rooms in November 1894, John A. Ryan wrote in his diary:

> At last the longed for condition of our student life has been realized; we have just been directed to occupy our study room. We find ourselves at length in possession of two rooms each which will be sacred from every intrusion except that of the irrepressible superior, and of the chamberlain. How much better we shall study remains to be seen; but one thing is certain, we have now no reasonable excuse for losing our time.[43]

Attired in cassocks as the normal garb for classes, meals, and general activities on campus, students followed the monastic horarium common to most seminaries of the day. Liturgies during the week were held in the smaller chapels in the residence halls. Sundays and special feasts were celebrated in the *aula maxima,* the auditorium on the second floor of the classroom building, until St. Mary's Chapel was completed in 1905. For Sunday liturgies and special feasts the seminarians would wear cassocks, surplices, and birettas. The older seminarians anticipated with a certain glee the first Sunday liturgy after the arrival of the new members. Often the "novices" would forget their new birettas on the seats behind them. When they sat down at the appropriate time, a loud crunch was usually heard, and an expensive portion of their new wardrobe sometimes had to be replaced.[44]

The spiritual life of the students was closely tied to the horarium.[45] From the rising bell at 5:25 A.M. when an assigned student knocked on each door and called out "Benedicamus Domino" (Let us bless the Lord!) there were few surprises. If the response "Deo Gratias" (Thanks be to God!) was not forthcoming, the responsible student made other efforts to rouse the occupant of the room. Morning prayer and meditation (5:50–6:20 A.M.) were preparation for Mass. Classes began at 8:00 A.M., after breakfast and a brief recreation and study period.

Time was set aside at 11:45 A.M. for the "particular examen"—examination of a fault or imperfection which one was trying to erase. Dinner at noon, during which there was spiritual reading, was followed by a period of recreation until 1:55 P.M. Classes and study periods consumed the period from 2:00 to 5:00 P.M., followed by a brief period of recreation, with the exception of the Wednesday afternoon time off. At 5:25 P.M. students assembled for rosary, and spiritual reading or a conference.

After supper at 6:00 P.M. there was recreation until 7:30 P.M., followed by two hours of study time or seminars. Night Prayer included a general examination of conscience. Students retired at 10:00 P.M. and the "Grand Silence" was observed from night prayer until after Mass and breakfast the following morning.

The 1908 *Rules of the Saint Paul Seminary* were very direct in describing expectations: "When young men enter the seminary it is presumed that they have that spirit of honor and of piety that allows no breach of order or of discipline." Even more explicitly it states: "If the rules of the seminary are considered irksome, students will please, of their own accord, withdraw from the seminary."[46] The rule of silence during the day, although not as stringent as the "Grand Silence," was to be strictly observed "at all times within the residences and class buildings, on the stairs and in the hallways." Students could talk between exercises outside the buildings, but not when going to or from High Mass, Vespers, or Benediction.[47] Other directives regarding dress, curtailing activities off campus, and general behavior were explicit. Seminarians should not be "guilty of buffoonery," nor were nicknames to be used. "Students shall address a companion as Mr. and not merely by his given name or surname. A student who permits familiarity of address shows a lack of self-respect."[48]

Rules for recreation were specific. A student was expected to go for walks with his own *camerata*—a system in the Roman colleges where students were grouped, usually under a prefect. They were "not allowed to pay visits, enter shops, stores or offices without the express permission of the Dean." To leave the campus after nightfall without the express permission of the dean, or to enter at any time a place where intoxicating drink was sold, or to bring liquor onto the seminary premises, or to visit theatres or other unbecoming places were to be punished by immediate dismissal.[49] A cloistered environment was considered the norm for most seminaries in that era.

Protecting seminarians from temptations and "worldliness" meant an altered schedule: Wednesday afternoons free when their non-seminarian friends were at work or school. Summers were a time to work outside the school, to be at home and reconnect with family, but life at the seminary was generally cloistered; there were few opportunities for contacts with the "outside world," except monthly family visits on campus.

On Wednesday afternoons seminarians were free to take walks on or adjacent to the campus. The forty-acre tract of land on a bluff overlooking the Mississippi River provided natural beauty and tranquility even after the "river boulevard"—a gentle, winding road—was constructed in 1907.[50] Proximity to the streetcar on Grand Avenue on the east side of the campus allowed ready transportation for special events at the cathedral. Recreation in the gymnasium and playing fields was encouraged. The gymnasium was fully equipped and offered ample opportunity for healthful exercise.

In such a closed community, extracurricular activities were important. The Lacordaire Society and the Hill Literary and Debating Society were two of the first and most popular on campus. Eventually certain ethnically oriented organizations began to develop. In 1899 the seminary welcomed visitors from the German Catholic Central Society. Shortly after, the *Paulus Verein,* the St. Adelbert Bohemian Literary Society, the Baraga Society (a Slavic organization), and the St. Stanislaus Kostka (Polish) Literary Society were formed. By 1919 there was a St. Vaclav Czech Literary Society.[51]

As with most seminaries and novitiates, entertainment was dependent on the creativity of the students. On the eve of Thanksgiving Day, 1897, the Lacordaire Society prepared an entertainment which included an overture by the "Seminary Orchestra" and a march by the Mandolin Club. A piano solo as well as recitations and declamations were included. The Choral Society was a popular area for involvement. The faculty and students of the College of St. Thomas were sometimes invited to these special programs.[52] Ireland's vision of the priest as a cultured gentleman included offering the students opportunities in music and drama.

On March 27, 1900, the St. Paul Clerical Total Abstinence Society was founded, also a group dear to Archbishop Ireland's heart.[53] Its aim was a study of the liquor problem, and strategies for encouraging abstinence among priests and in society at large.

The Seminary Curriculum and Academic Life

The seminary curriculum in the United States had been proposed just ten years previously at the Third Plenary Council of Baltimore. The Catholic bishops of the United States made it clear that there was a need "to lengthen and widen" the course of studies for the priesthood over the previous short program. They mandated a minor seminary course of six years, equivalent to high school and junior college. Courses required in the minor seminary were to provide a strong base in classical languages and classical studies, courses in the humanities, and a formation program to prepare students for the spiritual life of a cleric.

The major seminary program would also consist of six years—two of philosophy and four of theology. No longer could a student be rushed along with only two years of philosophy and one or two of theology, as was common in most American seminaries. With the increase in the size of the Catholic population in America and added expectations for the clergy, the bishops committed themselves to improving the quality of seminary education in this major reform.

The curriculum at the Saint Paul Seminary followed the basic "Plan of Studies" which grew out of Baltimore III.[54] Although four years of theology were prescribed, pressure from bishops whose dioceses were in need of priests sometimes took precedence, and the program was abbreviated at some U.S. seminaries to three or three and a half years for their students. That trend was halted with a letter from the Sacred Congrega-

The Saint Paul Seminary Orchestra in the early 1900s

tion of Propaganda that Cardinal Gibbons read to the assembled archbishops at their annual meeting on April 25, 1906. In it, the cardinal prefect of Propaganda, Cardinal Girolamo Gotti, expressed his regret that some American seminaries were not abiding by the prescription for six years of major seminary. The bishops and superiors of seminaries were told that no exceptions were to be allowed. The 1906–1907 *Register* informed students of this requirement and added:

> The St. Paul Seminary always mapped out its programme for a full term of six years. Occasionally, however, for special reasons, students have been promoted to the holy priesthood who had not gone beyond three, or three and a half years of theology. Henceforth, as in the past the Seminary will try to carry out in good faith the instruction of the Holy Father.[55]

The "theologians" studied dogma, moral, scripture, canon law, liturgy, church history, and homiletics. Those in philosophy took courses in logic, metaphysics, the history of philosophy, and cosmology as well as biology, physics, and chemistry. In 1902 the program of studies was divided into departments of theology, philosophy (which included the sciences), and the arts (language and literature).

All of the students were obliged to study English and German; Hebrew, Greek, and French were electives. Despite Ireland's many conflicts with "the Germans," the requirement in that language would seem to be an acknowledgment of the need for communication with the many German-speaking communities in the Upper Midwest.

The admissions requirement in Latin was demanding, but it was not until 1908 that a course in "Patristic and Ecclesiastical Latin" was offered.[56] Latin was the language in the seminary for those who came from Europe and had not yet mastered English.[57] Latin textbooks were in use. According to Emmet Henry Weber, "Latin had become the only language used in lectures, discussions and written essays in the classes of dogma, moral, canon law, logic and metaphysics."[58] That statement has been disputed. Despite various directives over the years from the Congregation of Seminaries and Universities, formed in 1915, that seminarians be taught in Latin, that practice was never completely adopted at the Saint Paul Seminary.[59]

By 1902 textbooks for courses were listed in the catalogue by surnames of the authors, e.g., Hurter for dogmatics, Bouquillon for moral theology, Cornely for scripture, Brueck for church history, and Vecchiotti for canon law.[60] In 1908 the manuals of Adolphe Tanqueray in dogmatic and moral theology were adopted. Tanqueray, a French Sulpician with doctorates in theology and canon law, taught dogmatic and moral theology at St. Mary's Seminary in Baltimore from 1887 to 1902. Teaching mostly second-generation Irish-Americans, he realized the need for Latin textbooks which were accessible to the student with limited Latin skills. His volumes continued in use at the Saint Paul Seminary into the 1960s.[61]

Publications by faculty and former faculty members were used by the seminarians, e.g., *The History of Philosophy* by Father William Turner, *A Living Wage* by Father John A. Ryan, *A Textbook of Literary Criticism* by Father William Sheran, and Father Bernard Feeney's books on the spiritual life. The text for special lectures on the Catholic Church in the United States was *A History of the Catholic Church in America* by Thomas O'Gorman, then professor of church history at the Catholic University of America.[62]

Patrick Danehy, professor of scripture, in his description of "The New Seminary at St. Paul" in *The Catholic University of America Bulletin* (April 1895), expounded on the curriculum:

> Holy Scripture and Church History are not secondary studies in this course, but take equal rank with the others. In connection with the classes in Scripture, lessons are given in Hebrew and in New Testament Greek. Next year an advanced course in English literature will be added to the curriculum, another in biology, and a series of lectures on Sociology and Political Economy will be given in the winter months. It is not expected that every student will follow all the courses. That is a matter which will be decided for each one by the faculty. But all will be taught the sciences as thoroughly as may be.[63]

Danehy echoed the convictions of John Ireland, Thomas O'Gorman, John J. Keane, John Lancaster Spalding, and other more liberal figures in the Catholic Church in that era that the priest must be knowledgeable about progress in the physical sciences and the use of the inductive method, as well as aware of the developments in sociology and political economy.[64]

John A. Ryan concluded years later: "The courses given at St. Paul Seminary were as good as those presented in any other training school for priests in the United States, and probably somewhat better than in the majority." As a future faculty member, Ryan's field of study would be moral theology, but scripture—offered four periods a week—seemed to be an area of fascination for him in his student days:

> My academic life at the St. Paul Seminary (1894–1898) was devoid of events or experiences that could be accounted either exceptional or noteworthy. I did not find any of the courses in the theological curriculum tedious or uninteresting, although I naturally had preferences among them. For example, I devoted an exceptional amount of time to the theories then current on the inspiration of Scripture and to the different opinions concerning the effects of original sin.[65]

As motivation, students were encouraged to compete for prizes in the various academic areas for each year of study, and the recipients were listed in the *Register* the year following. Those who participated in seminars, open only to students who had an average above 85 percent, were also listed. In these seminars, professors and students would meet once a week, and twice each month public "academies" were held at which the best papers were read and discussed. Archbishop Ireland, the faculty, and some of the clergy of the diocese were often in attendance.[66] These presentations were also listed in the annual catalogue.

The subjects of the academies offer clues as to the intellectual life of the school. John A. Ryan's academy presentation in 1897 was: "The Influence of Jewish Theories of Inspiration on Christian Exegesis." Other papers during that year included: "The Relations of Evolution to the Theistic Problem" by Mr. William Shanahan, "The Mode of Christ's Presence in the Holy Eucharist, and the Constitution of Matter" by Mr. John Seliskar, "The Origin of the Episcopate" by Mr. Andrew Rindie, and "Family, Church and State" by Mr. James Reardon.[67] In future years, Ryan, Shanahan, Seliskar, and Reardon were all to be assigned to the seminary faculty.

Ryan offered an interesting reflection on the freedom of opinion allowed students within the required courses:

> In passing, I would emphasize the fact that the student of theology is allowed a much greater freedom of opinion than the average person assumes. The official Catholic doctrines of faith and morals are, of course, binding upon all Catholics, lay and clerical, but there are a great number of related questions concerning which even the authoritative specialists are not in full agreement. In this broad field of theological opinion there are very few views for which a student cannot invoke the authority of a distinguished theologian. Indeed, the student is occasionally tempted to wish that the area of disputed and free questions was not quite so comprehensive, and that the area of obligatory doctrine and theological unanimity was somewhat wider.[68]

Ryan was probably not atypical of many seminarians who desire a kind of certitude that would allow them fewer questions when they encounter pastoral issues on the parish scene.

Although the seminarians were not allowed to leave the campus for lectures except on rare occasions, notable dignitaries and lecturers frequently visited. In addition to the apostolic delegate and archbishops and bishops from the dioceses that sent students, others came to see the impressive institution. Despite their many differences regarding church and culture in America, Bishop Bernard McQuaid of Rochester, New York, shared with Archbishop Ireland a similar vision of seminary education. McQuaid, who had built a model seminary in New York, visited the Saint Paul Seminary on two occasions in the summer of 1904.[69]

In the Saint Paul Seminary *Register* (later *Bulletin*) even into the 1970s there was a section titled "Chronicle of the Year" listing visiting dignitaries, guest lecturers, and special events of the previous year. The following sample provides a glimpse of this aspect of campus life in the Ireland era.[70] In 1898, Albert, Prince of Flanders and heir to the throne of Belgium, visited the campus in the company of Archbishop Ireland and Louis Hill. Dr. De Costa of New York spoke to the students on the present condition of the Protestant Episcopal Church—providing an ecumenical dimension. Reverend Edward A. Pace, professor of psychology at the Catholic University of America, delivered three lectures before the students of philosophy on the scope and method of psychology. The Abbé Felix Klein, a friend of Ireland's who wrote the preface to the French translation of the life of Father Isaac Hecker which occasioned the Americanism controversy, was also a guest at the seminary. On one of his several visits, Ireland's colleague among the Americanists, the Right Reverend Msgr. Denis J. O'Connell, who had been rector of the American College in Rome, made a presentation to the students on the legal status of the pope in the city of Rome. Dr. James J. Walsh, author of *The Thirteenth—the Greatest of Centuries,* lectured almost every year from 1912 to 1923. John Ireland saw to it that if the students could not go out to "the world," he would import stimulating speakers who would keep the seminarians abreast of intellectual and cultural currents that would be helpful to them in their future ministry.

Spiritual Formation

Father Anatole Oster, one of the first seminarians recruited by Father Ravoux for the diocese in 1854, was appointed spiritual director in 1898.[71] The role of spiritual director was not clearly defined in that period, but the selection of Oster with his long white beard, symbolic of his age and wisdom, probably balanced the youth and comparative inexperience of the newly-appointed rector, Patrick Heffron.

Oster had completed his studies for priesthood under Bishop Cretin and had served in the diocese for almost fifty years. He was a revered and holy man who by his prayerful example and listening ear was available to students and brought a sense of history and tradition to their preparation for priesthood. He was also on the faculty as professor of ascetic and pastoral theology. The following year he was listed as vice-rector and as one of the deans of the residence halls.[72] He had, however, little formal training for the tasks to which he was assigned.

Father Oster provided inspiration for the development of a grotto about the turn of the century. He set up a small statue of Mary in a ravine in the woods west of what is now Cretin Residence; it became the locus for a grotto in honor of Our Lady. By 1917 funds were collected from students and alumni, and the main part of the grotto was constructed that year at the cost of $800. The students built the retaining wall and the stone steps. Eventually a stone bridge was constructed over the creek, and a wooden bridge farther downstream. Due to lack of funds, the life-sized statue was not added until 1930.[73] The popes encouraged devotion to Mary, especially in the months of May and October. Marian exercises, so popular in the church in that era, found ready and willing participants at the Saint Paul Seminary.

In 1902 Father Bernard Feeney joined the faculty after a full life as a pastor and served as professor and spiritual director until 1917. In 1911 he had a series of articles published in the *American Ecclesiastical Review,* later republished posthumously in a small volume titled *The Ideal Seminary*.[74] Many of his insights prefigure the structures of spiritual formation and field education programs that have evolved since Vatican II. He believed in "keeping the spiritual department in the first place, not only nominally but in reality, and of spreading responsibility for it over the whole faculty, instead of confining it to a spiritual director."[75] He understood the four essential elements of the seminary to be: (1) living with Jesus; (2) studying His life and work; (3) learning His teachings; and (4) training in the habits and practices in which He trained the apostles. In this fourth element he emphasized training for pastoral work and in moral habits "that are the chief constituents of priestly character."[76]

One of the major opportunities for spiritual growth for seminarians each year was the annual retreat. In 1904 Abbot Francis Aidan Gasquet of the English Congregation of Benedictines visited the United States. Archbishop Ireland, upon learning of his plans, invited him to preach a retreat to the students at the Saint Paul Seminary. Gasquet found the task demanding:

> I say nothing about the retreat, except that, as in America they look for conferences of an hour in length, in place of our accustomed thirty minutes, it is by no means an easy time for the retreat-giver. What with these conferences, the hearing of confessions and the necessary private talks with those who came to give me their confidence and ask my advice, I was kept fully occupied.[77]

The experience, however, was an impressive one for him. His assessment of the students must have made Archbishop Ireland proud.

> I will only say that of the intimate experience I gained during my week at St. Paul's Seminary, that I found the students earnest, devout and zealously anxious to fit themselves in every way during the years of their training for the work of the sacred ministry. I should be glad to think that I made as favourable an impression upon them and their professors as they made upon me.[78]

The annual retreat was an important part of the spiritual program. Sometimes it was given by a member of the faculty, and on other occasions by a priest from outside the seminary. Interestingly, on September 16, 1918, shortly before John Ireland's death, the retreat was directed by the Reverend John J. Donoher, S.J., a Jesuit from Campion College, Prairie du Chien, Wisconsin, who preached the fall retreat to the seminarians. This suggests that Ireland may even have mellowed in his harsh feelings toward the Jesuits.[79]

The Role of the Library in Seminary Life

To enable professors and students to achieve their academic goals, Ireland knew that a solid library was a necessity. Although the books were housed in various rooms in the administration building until the Archbishop Ireland Memorial Library was completed in 1950, the quality of the volumes was substantive. The first catalogue of the seminary, published in 1896, stated: "The library contains at present four thousand volumes. These include all the classical authorities on philosophy and theology. The library receives regularly sixty magazines, theological, philosophical and scientific, in the English, French, German and Italian languages."[80]

The purchase of books was a priority, and the princely sum of $2,000 was budgeted annually for that purpose. The rector or vice-rector regularly presented to the board of trustees a list of books for purchase and the money was allocated accordingly. In the minutes of the board meeting of May 12, 1897, it was recorded: "Rev. P. R. Heffron reported a list of books that had been purchased and paid for during the year ending 1896 amounting to two thousand dollars. The list was approved and ordered."[81] Subsequent references indicate that the list of books was presented prior to acquisition.[82] It might well have been that the archbishop and other members of the board wanted to approve the books before purchase!

In a related area, on July 14, 1897, the board "authorized [the rector] to procure 30 book cases for use in the rooms of the advanced students."[83] They were purchased for $5.00 each. Clearly the board desired that the books be put to good use both in and out of the library. On January 10, 1900, in addition to the motion to approve the purchase of books, it was stated: "A motion to authorize the librarian to catalogue the library at the cost of $200 which sum to be taken from the library fund was made and passed."[84]

When Abbot Gasquet was on campus preaching the retreat for the seminarians in 1904, he had an opportunity to inspect the library. He was duly impressed and attributed the library's excellence to the special care of Archbishop Ireland who collected volumes, often on his excursions to Europe, which increased the library substantially. Gasquet remarked: "It was a source of wonder to me to find already on the shelves almost every book of any value for the purpose he had in view. I tested the collection in various ways, by looking for works I hardly supposed could be found there, but in most instances they were in their places."[85]

The Saint Paul Seminary was heir to the private collections of both clergy and laity that it holds in its Rare Book Room today. Under the label "EX LIBRIS—J. Cretin" are volumes including *Genie de Christianisme ou Beautés de la Religion Chrétienne* by François-August Chateaubriand (2 vols.), published in Paris in 1808. Written in the front of both volumes is "Cretin—1815." Very likely these were sources for his course work at Meximieux. Five volumes of Chateaubriand, published in 1809, contain bookplates which read "Rev. A. Ravoux, St. Paul, Minn."

A copy of the Latin Vulgate, *Biblia Sacra,* published in Antwerp in 1590 indicates that it was part of the library of Bishop Grace. Perhaps one of the greatest historical treasures is a Bible, published in 1647, inscribed successively by Bishop Loras, Bishop Cretin, and Bishop Grace, who presented it to the Saint Paul Seminary Library before his death in 1897. It is bound in dark green leather with gold trim depicting urns and flowers in Italian style, with gold leaf on the edge of the pages. That small volume, and the history of its ownership, provides a tangible link to the early history of the Catholic Church in the Upper Midwest.[86]

Bishop James McGolrick of Duluth, an early member of the board of trustees, not only donated books such as a well-marked copy of John Locke's *Essay Concerning Human Understanding* with his name in the front cover, but also a rare volume entitled *De Universali Methodo Philosophandi* by Cesar de Horatius. An illuminated bookplate in the front cover states: "This book was in the private library of Pius VI." On the lower part of the page is handwritten: "257th Pope 1775–1799." Bishop McGolrick also presented to the seminary his collection of geological specimens. At the board of trustees meeting July 14, 1897, the treasurer was authorized to pay the expenses for transporting them and for building shelves and cases for keeping them in the science laboratory in the classroom building.[87]

Another extraordinary contributor to the library was William James Onahan, a Chicago businessman and political leader committed to Catholic causes. He became a close friend of Ireland's in the Catholic colonization movement, and later joined with Henry Brownson, son of the famous convert Orestes Brownson, to organize the First Lay Congress in Baltimore in 1889, at which Ireland had a prominent role.[88] Between September 1896 and April 1897 Onahan donated five hundred volumes—books and periodicals—to the seminary library. The contributions of all benefactors were listed by name each year in the *Register*. In that same issue, reviewing the major events of the past year, reference is made to: "November 12, 1896—the Hon. William J. Onahan of Chicago, read before the seminarians his scholarly lecture on Lacordaire." At that time John A. Ryan was president of the Lacordaire Literary and Debating Club.[89]

Both James J. Hill and Mary Hill are listed as ongoing contributors to the library. James J. Hill donated books, pamphlets, Civil War records, and proceedings from the Republican Party Convention. Mary Hill regularly contributed copies of the *North American Review* and the *Popular Science Monthly.* In 1898, Archbishop Ireland gave the library his copies of Isaac Hecker's *The Catholic World* from April 1865 through March 1889, although three volumes were missing. Ireland's love of books was never in doubt.

Relationship with the Catholic University of America

Archbishop Ireland's heart was always with education. Whether it was the Cathedral School in St. Paul, the Catholic Industrial School, the St. Thomas Aquinas Seminary, the Catholic University of America, the Faribault-Stillwater Plan, the Saint Paul Seminary, or the College of St. Catherine—education was a priority for him. When he envisioned two of these projects in special relationship to each other, it very likely gave him special satisfaction.

Ireland had been heavily involved in the decisions and fundraising surrounding the building of the Catholic University of America. It was his hope that that institution would be a hub for Catholic thought and—located in the nation's capital—a symbol that American Catholicism had come of age. Ireland's close friend John J. Keane was appointed the first rector of the Catholic University on September 7, 1887, and one of his initial organizational responsibilities was to draw up the university constitutions. When they were finally approved by Pope Leo XIII on March 7, 1889, one of the sections read:

> Colleges and seminaries, without prejudice to their autonomy, may by authority of the Board of Trustees be affiliated to the University. When this has been done the diplomas conferred by such colleges as evidence of the acquirements of their students shall be accepted in lieu of an examination for admission to the University.[90]

After the Catholic University opened on November 13, 1889, it became clear that two distinct forms of affiliation were possible: the establishment of religious houses in the vicinity, where students could live while taking courses at the university; or affiliation with seminaries at a distance. Many religious communities chose to establish houses of study near the university (Paulists, Dominicans, Marists, and Holy Cross Fathers). It was to their advantage to be able to send their candidates to study at the Catholic University and yet retain responsibility for the spiritual and pastoral formation of the students.

In the fall of 1894, Archbishop Ireland entered into negotiations with the Catholic University. The Saint Paul Seminary became the first seminary located at any distance from Washington, D.C., to affiliate. In his annual report, Bishop Keane stated:

> An admirable example has been given to the Seminaries and Colleges of the country by the affiliation to the University of the Seminary of St. Paul, at St. Paul, Minnesota. In virtue of this affiliation, the University has the right to preside over and pass upon the examinations for degrees held in the Seminary; and the Seminary has the privilege of having the Baccalaureate of the University conferred on students who pass said examinations satisfactorily. The advantages of such an arrangement, both for the University and for the seminaries, are manifest.[91]

For Ireland, this was the wedding of two institutions that he loved. For Keane, it represented hope that other seminaries would follow the same course.

The affiliation with the Catholic University allowed the Saint Paul seminarians, upon completion of their four-year program of theology, to take the required examinations and earn the S.T.B. (bachelor of sacred theology) degree from the Catholic University of America. They were then able to enroll in the university and, after only one year of study, earn an S.T.L. (licentiate in sacred theology). Patrick Danehy wrote enthusiastically about the new arrangement in 1895:

> But now that the seminary is affiliated to the Catholic University and in common with other seminaries in the land which are to be affiliated likewise, will have its program for examination sent down from the University, even better results may be looked for.... A member of the University faculty will be present at those examinations, and no doubt the bachelor's degree may thus be obtained before going to Washington.[92]

In the 1898 *Register* there was a notation regarding the fact that a student could present himself for the baccalaureate degree from the Catholic University; however, there is no evidence in the early years that any did. In September 1905 the new rector of the Catholic University, Ireland's longtime friend Denis O'Connell, visited the seminary in an effort to clarify the specifics of the arrangement with the rector, Father Patrick Heffron. The affiliation was active from 1906 to 1931. In the 1912 *Register* three students (Joseph T. Barron, Francis J. Rakowski, and Vincent J. Ryan) were listed as having "successfully passed the University Examinations for the Degree of Baccalaureate in Theology."[93] Two or three students were regularly listed in succeeding years until 1931. Until 1912, however, the Saint Paul Seminary was the only seminary at a distance that was affiliated to the Catholic University in Washington, D.C.

The Continuing Presence of Archbishop Ireland

The archbishop visited the seminary frequently—on an average of once a week when he was in the city—"and took a personal interest in every detail of management."[94] He presided at examinations twice a year as an active participant. In a letter to James J. Hill in 1895 he reported: "We have just finished the semi-annual examinations, in which the students really distinguished themselves."[95] The examination consisted of three hours of written response to questions and forty minutes of oral interrogation each half year.[96]

With the turn of the century Ireland invited his brother bishops who were sponsoring students in the seminary to join him in administering the oral examinations. When semester exams began on January 11, 1901, Archbishop John J. Keane of Dubuque, Bishop Richard Scannell of Omaha, and Bishops Thomas O'Gorman, James McGolrick, Joseph Cotter, John Shanley, and James Trobec from the Province of St. Paul were all present.[97] Ireland presided at the examinations in both philosophy and theology, and the bishops assisted, which gave them the opportunity to observe the priesthood candidates from their dioceses at close range—possibly too close for some of the students! The *Register* noted that some of the clergy from the Twin Cities were also in attendance and all were satisfied with the results: "In the matter of talent and application, the students of the Saint Paul Seminary compare very favorably with the best scholarship of America and Europe. This opinion was expressed by the visitors, who congratulated the Rector and the Faculty upon the excellent work done in the Seminary."[98]

When the final grades were recorded, the custom was to announce them to an assembly of faculty and students. On June 13, 1904, Archbishop Ireland made the following remarks after the reports were distributed:

> The marks just read are full of music and poetry to some of you, but to others they must be reproach. It must be admitted that there are differences of talent, but it must also be conceded that there are differences of energy. There is latent talent in all men, but it must be dug up. It won't do to let it remain latent. There must be work, hard work, and conscientious application, if you would achieve anything. You must bring out every talent you possess to win the prize.[99]

Ireland expected nothing but the best from his seminarians and he was not shy about challenging them.

As noted above, Ireland gave a half-hour conference to the student body whenever he visited. On these occasions he would join the faculty and students for supper. As was the custom, unless it was a special feast day, there was spiritual reading at the noon dinner, and a student was assigned to preach a sermon at the evening meal. Ireland listened carefully to the readings and sermons in the refectory, often commenting on the content and delivery of the students.

Edwin Vincent O'Hara, later archbishop of Kansas City, was ordained a priest by Archbishop Ireland from the Saint Paul Seminary in 1905 for the Archdiocese of Oregon City. Ireland profoundly influenced him in his seminary years, as he later recalled: "When I entered the seminary, the archbishop was at his prime; his personality radiated through the halls. His frequent visits and his presence at oral examinations—to which he often brought visiting prelates—left upon us an indelible impression of intellectual power, strength of conviction, and apostolic purpose."[100]

After supper Ireland would meet with the faculty for an hour or more. All were expected to be present. Reardon described these sessions in glowing terms:

> The discussion covered a wide range of subjects, theological, philosophical, scientific, literary, with all of which he showed an astounding familiarity. It was a pleasure to listen to his sparkling conversation, a steady stream of fascinating talk, interspersed

> with witty sallies that were never flippant. There was a personal magnetism about him that held the undivided attention of his listeners who could not help admire his remarkable versatility.[101]

Ireland's high standards applied not only to the students but also to the faculty. Members of the faculty were to give good example, not only by solid preparation of their course work but also by regular attendance at spiritual exercises on Sundays and holy days of obligation. As a result, the priest faculty were forbidden to accept outside liturgical assignments whereby they would be absent from Solemn Mass and Vespers on those days. According to Reardon: "Rather would he allow a parish to go without Mass on Sunday than permit a faculty member to be absent from his accustomed place on that day. The professors were inclined to regard this regulation as rather stringent."[102] The faculty members were to be role models for the students, not only in their adherence to spiritual practices but also in providing a solid academic base for the development of priesthood candidates.

Ireland always exuded a certain joy and optimism when reflecting on his seminaries. When he announced plans to build the St. Thomas Aquinas Seminary he had stated: "The diocesan seminary will be the principal work of our episcopate, and from it we expect the most fruitful result." In 1895 he reiterated his goal, this time in reference to the new theologate: "The seminary is the chief object of concern in my ministry. My heart and soul are wrapped up in it, and I always visit it with intense pleasure."[103]

One might assume mistakenly that Ireland's commitment to the seminary was largely an administrative necessity. His devotion, however, was genuinely personal. Father Patrick Keany, who was a seminarian from 1916 to 1923, recalled a speech which Archbishop Ireland gave to visiting bishops and seminarians. He told the story of a group of Roman matrons who were displaying their best jewelry. One woman, however, was not wearing her best jewels. She informed the others that she would bring hers later. When she returned she was accompanied by her five sons—handsome young men. She said: "Here are my jewels." Archbishop Ireland then turned to the section of seminarians in the audience and said to the bishops, "And these are my jewels."[104]

As the twentieth century began, Ireland's role as a leader of the episcopacy in the United States was curtailed. With the promulgation of

Testem Benevolentiae, the Americanists—despite protestations to the contrary—felt chastised. His foray into international diplomacy, as a liaison between the Vatican and President McKinley in the wake of the Spanish-American War, had failed. The cardinal's red hat continued to elude him. At the turn of the century, at the age of sixty-two, John Ireland set his sights back in St. Paul: a chapel and a new residence hall at the Saint Paul Seminary, a magnificent cathedral in St. Paul, and a "co-cathedral"—now the Basilica of St. Mary in Minneapolis. Ireland's legacy would be set in both words and stone.

CHAPTER 8

Becoming Rooted in a Changing Church

Rev. dear Father:

Your letter enclosing $59.00 for the seminary fund from Mendota has been received by the Rev. Secretary. You will permit me to say that this sum is not sufficient. The maintenance of the Seminary Fund to a certain figure is of vital importance to the spiritual interests of the diocese, and it must be maintained. For past years there has been an annual deficit; that cannot be allowed for the present or the future years. Nor would there have been a deficit at any time if all parishes, or the greater portion of them, made responsible contributions. With the advice of the counselors of the Diocese I have put the minimum contribution to be received from each parish at a sum averaging *75 cents for each family in the parish.* The average I am determined to demand. It is a positive tax on the parishes, which the bishop has a right to impose, and the parishes must be made to understand their duty in the matter.[1]

Archbishop John Ireland
January 13, 1895

The Board of Trustees and Mr. Hill

Despite the generous gift of $500,000 for six buildings and an endowment from James J. Hill, the Saint Paul Seminary was expected to sustain itself financially on a day-to-day basis through tuition, room and board, and the generosity of members of the parishes of the archdiocese. Ireland made it very clear that although the buildings were a contribution of one major benefactor, the ongoing donations should be from parishioners on the local level.[2] This fiduciary responsibility set the agenda for the board of trustees and signaled that the movement from a "grand idea" to a lived reality had begun.

Archbishop Ireland, as chair of the board, presided over the first meeting, which was held on September 17, 1895. Other members of the board included the rector, Msgr. Louis Caillet, Bishop James McGolrick of Duluth, Bishop Joseph B. Cotter of Winona, the archdiocesan chancellor Reverend John Stariha, and two laymen, Anthony Kelly of Minneapolis and John D. O'Brien of St. Paul.[3]

The cost of the seminary buildings with furnishings had been $240,000. James J. Hill, desiring to keep the seminary financially viable, established a seminary trust for the $260,000 balance with the Minneapolis Trust Company. This trusteeship was to last through the lifetime of his three sons and for twenty-one years thereafter.[4] Because the endowment was not operative until September 1895, finances in the 1894–1895 academic year were subsidized in part by the College of St. Thomas, and by a loan from the archdiocese. In January 1895, James J. Hill advanced the seminary $12,000. These amounts were repaid within a few years.[5]

At the first meeting of the board, which would meet monthly, Anthony Kelly was requested to procure from the Minneapolis Trust Company "a detailed list and description of the securities held by it for the benefit of the St. Paul Seminary in the trust agreement, showing the rates of interest or other income yielded by said securities."[6] The board was challenged to understand its options and learned very quickly that it was expected to be strictly accountable to the trustee and to James J. Hill himself. Hill's stringent oversight, which was built into the arrangement for the administration of the endowment, allowed few independent decisions where money was concerned.

Other clarifications were required. Ten faculty salaries were to be paid by the trust. Caillet emphasized the necessity of designating which professors would be included in that group because there were additional members on the faculty.[7] The list of books requested for purchase for the library from the trust fund was an annual submission for which exactitude was also expected.

Even the hiring of a bookkeeper had been under Hill's watchful eye as attested to by a file of letters of application in the Hill Papers, of which the following was probably the most creative. Answering an advertisement in *The Pioneer Press* on December 18, 1894, and writing on stationery from the Merchants Hotel, T. J. Fortune stated that he was a practical bookkeeper of more than twelve years' experience and held high references for character and ability from such well-known citizens as the Hon. H. F. Stevens, Judges Willis and Twohy, Pierce Butler, and others. He then confessed:

> Though I am unmarried I cannot say that I would object, if at any time, some good looking Irish girl would be so blind as to become infatuated by my many personal attractions and become a Mrs. or Mis-Fortune; for, of course, the latter would of necessity follow the former.
>
> My religious persuasion is such that when I shuffle off this mortal coil I hope to greet St. Patrick in the mansions of eternal bliss through the gates of my Irish Catholicism.
>
> Awaiting your reply which may never come, and if it does I fear the surprise will be the death of me.[8]

There is no indication that Mr. Fortune received a response to his application. Mr. E. A. Nolan was hired. In 1897 his salary was increased from $40.00 to $50.00 per month, and by 1908 was $100.00 per month. He served as secretary and steward of the seminary until January 1, 1917 when he resigned. His successor, Louis A. Hastings, was hired for $60.00 per month plus board.[9]

Beginning with the 1896 *Register,* a list of all donors and amounts was published. Titles of volumes donated to the library were included. As of 1898 a "Legal Form for Bequest to the Saint Paul Seminary" was included on the back of the title page for anyone who might want to include the seminary in his/her will.[10]

On March 11, 1896, Anthony Kelly offered a resolution that "the present pension of students is insufficient to meet the current expenses" and recommended a raise in tuition. Although the board seemed to agree, it was decided that the decision be postponed until the following meeting, very likely because Archbishop Ireland was not in attendance. On May 20, 1896, Bishop Cotter moved that the pension of the students be raised from $150 to $175. It passed, but not unanimously, and remained at that level until 1902.[11] The *Register* was very explicit in terms of coverage: "The cost of tuition per year, including rooms, board, text books, laundry, the use of library, laboratories and medical attendance, is $175.00."[12]

Accountability in financial matters to both the board and the Minneapolis Trust Company was a major challenge for Caillet, who never saw himself as an administrator and who was by then in failing health. Caillet resigned as treasurer of the board at the September 9, 1896, meeting, but remained rector until his death about a year later. As mentioned above, in the fall of 1896 Archbishop Ireland appointed the Reverend Patrick Heffron as vice-rector of the seminary with broad powers of governance. Bishop McGolrick offered a resolution that Heffron be "authorized to sign all drafts, orders, and vouchers." In addition he was commissioned "to do any and all things provided for or required by the trust deed between James J. Hill and the Minneapolis Trust Company as fully and completely as the Rector might do personally." The resolution was adopted unanimously.[13] Even Heffron, for all his organizational skills, felt the scrutiny of Hill and the Minneapolis Trust Company. After Caillet's death on November 28, 1897, Heffron was appointed rector.

Patrick Heffron had been one of the members of the original faculty of the St. Thomas Aquinas Seminary. Born in New York City on June 1,

Patrick R. Heffron, rector of the Saint Paul Seminary from 1897 to1910

1860, he moved with his family to Ripon, Wisconsin, where he attended elementary school. After completing high school in Mantorville, Minnesota, he proceeded to business college and law school in Rochester, Minnesota, where he came to know Father Thomas O'Gorman. Heffron did his early preparation for the priesthood at St. John's in Collegeville, and his last six years at the Grand Seminary in Montreal where he received an S.T.L. degree in 1883 and was ordained to the priesthood in December 1884.[14]

As a newly-ordained priest, Heffron taught dogmatic theology at St. Thomas for two years. Archbishop Ireland then sent him to Rome to study at the Santa Maria Sopra Minerva, where he earned doctoral degrees in theology and canon law in 1889. When he returned to St. Paul, Ireland did not assign him to the seminary but appointed him pastor of the cathedral parish.[15] Heffron's appointment as vice-rector and later rector may have been perceived by some as the invasion of an "outsider" because he was not a member of the first faculty. There were those who would have preferred Humphrey Moynihan, but Archbishop Ireland thought otherwise.

Heffron was fortunate to have Anthony Kelly as financial advisor on the seminary board; Kelly's death in 1899 was a genuine loss to the seminary. William C. Toomey replaced Kelly and was "granted all the powers and functions exercised by Mr. Anthony Kelly as financial director and otherwise."[16] This included negotiating with the Minneapolis Trust Company on stock transactions.

Surveillance would not be too strong a word to describe Hill's oversight of the seminary. In the Great Northern Railway Building in St. Paul at Rosabel and Third Street, Hill housed not only the offices of the Great Northern, but also another office staffed by seven employees under the supervision of John J. Toomey, brother of William C. Toomey, which looked after Hill's many personal investments—national and international.[17] That office also had responsibility for oversight of the Saint Paul Seminary finances.

John J. Toomey allowed no detail to escape his inspection. A memo to his brother regarding the statement of operation of the seminary for the ten months ending June 30, 1903, was very specific. He was particularly concerned about salaries and wages, and the increase for provisions:

> The statement of cost of meals for the month of June shows an increase of nearly 3 cents per day per head, the whole of which apparently is attributable to increased cost of "groceries and vegetables". I do not know that provisions are more expensive this year than last, and with a larger number of students to take care of the cost per day per head should be rather under than over last years figures.[18]

The following month J. J. Toomey sent another memo, this time questioning the "Salaries of Professors Extra" which, he said, showed "a glaring increase of over 150%." He added: "There are also other items of expense which are open to criticism and require explanations." He complained further:

> The statement of "Cost of Meals" is not complete in that it does not give the number of Professors, Students, etc., to whom meals were furnished during that month. A memorandum at the foot of the statement shows that 1540 meals were furnished during the month at a cost of 23 cents per meal which is high. Allowing 93 meals per day for the month for one individual it would appear that the average number furnished with meals daily was 16, and I think the statement referred to should be returned to the Seminary for particulars in this respect.[19]

The following summer John J. Toomey wrote directly to the rector, Reverend P. R. Heffron, questioning why extraordinarily large sums were due from students as indicated in the statement at the end of June. "The indebtedness referred to aggregates to $1,155.00 divided between eight students five of whom owe from $180.00 to $280.00 each. I should like to know from you the necessity for allowing this indebtedness to accumulate and what the prospects are of making collection of same."[20] Toomey also asked for an explanation regarding "Professors Board Unpaid."

Regarding the new chapel, about which more will be said later, J. J. Toomey stated bluntly:

> We have not had from you the information requested in our letter of June 10th last in regard to the expenditures made in con-

> nection with the new chapel, and will thank you to furnish same, showing total expenditures to date, and the total amount outstanding and particulars of same.
>
> If Mr. Hill should desire information from us in regard to the Seminary accounts and matters generally it may be awkward to have to present these figures without having information from you to enable us to readily explain the necessity for the accumulation of indebtedness referred to. I trust it will be convenient for you to give an early reply to these inquiries.[21]

On August 17, 1904, Heffron replied in a brief letter sending a report of the chapel account, and indicating that the amount due from the students and the professors' board had been balanced with the exception of $50.00 and $55.00 respectively. He concluded: "I beg to acknowledge at this time your esteemed favor of an earlier date enclosing a forecast of the revenues of the endowment for which please accept thanks."[22] Clearly, the finances of the seminary were being analyzed to the last penny.

Day-to-day administration and domestic responsibilities were a challenge for the rector as well. It was difficult to get good help and to provide proper supervision. Father Heffron asked that a community of Sisters of St. Joseph of Carondelet be established at the Saint Paul Seminary and be put in charge of the domestic affairs. He was aware that in 1901 Archbishop Ireland had approached his sister, Mother Seraphine, and requested that a community of sisters be established at the College of St. Thomas to manage the housekeeping department and supervise the work in the residence halls and dining room. According to Sister Clara Graham, C.S.J., "After prayerful consideration and consultation with her Council, Mother Seraphine reluctantly consented to ask Sisters to give the work a trial."[23]

Five sisters were assigned to the Saint Paul Seminary in 1903, with Mother Sebastian Cronin, C.S.J. as superior. Sister Martina Waldron was in charge of the sewing, assisted by Sister Mary Francis Quinn. Sister Felicia McGinnis supervised the dining room, while Sister Ludmilla Lally took over the culinary department. Sister Sebastian recalled in later years that "the students' laundry was taken to the Sisters of the Good Shepherd (and later to the Elk Laundry), and brought back in individual bundles, each of which had to be checked for sewing."[24]

The new seminary with its attractive campus overlooking the river was not an uncongenial environment. However, the sisters, as well as about twenty maids, lived on the second floor of the refectory service building. Sister Clara Graham, C.S.J., reflected:

> Since the architect was a man, and plans for the building had been supervised by men, there was much to be desired in the way of privacy for the Sisters, and of comfort and convenience for the girls. Mother Sebastian and her little band of co-workers soon knew how things should be, but they did not ask to change them. The ideal they set for themselves was that work done at the Seminary, domestic or otherwise, was primarily to advance vocations to the priesthood.[25]

Although many would consider that the sisters were doing only "menial tasks"—cooking the meals, caring for the altar linens, sewing, cleaning, and eventually serving as nurses in the infirmary and assistants in the library—they became an integral part of the seminary community. Their contacts with the students were limited, but they brought a prayerful element, as well as organization on the practical level, to the all-male environment.

Saint Mary's Chapel

Seminary enrollment grew consistently in the early years. Sixty-five students had moved into the new buildings in 1894. By 1898 there were 110; by 1900 the student body had increased to 118, fourteen of whom were from San Francisco. Although the Saint Paul Seminary described itself as a provincial seminary serving the Upper Midwest, students came from the Far West as well.

The *aula maxima* served as a chapel through those early years, but the plan for a separate chapel was never forgotten. An appropriate chapel for the seminary, dedicated to Mary, became one of Ireland's goals as the new century began. It had long been held that "just as the seminary is the soul of the diocese, so too is the chapel the soul of the seminary."[26] What better day to lay the cornerstone for the new chapel than at the celebration of the golden jubilee of the arrival of Bishop Cretin?

The jubilee commemoration should have taken place on July 19, 1900, the date of the establishment of the diocese, but Archbishop Ireland was in Europe, so it was postponed to coincide with the fiftieth anniversary of the arrival of Bishop Joseph Cretin on July 2, 1901. Bishop McGolrick celebrated a Pontifical Mass on the seminary grounds, and Archbishop Ireland preached. At 4:00 P.M. Bishop James Trobec of St. Cloud laid the cornerstone, and Ireland's childhood friend, Bishop Thomas O'Gorman, preached the sermon. Once again the bishop of Sioux Falls reiterated how Bishop Cretin had chosen John Ireland and himself as "the beginning of my diocesan Seminary, the first seminarians of St. Paul."[27]

One of the significant persons unable to attend that day due to illness was Mary Theresa Mehegan Hill. She wrote in her diary: "I shall have to be content to stay in my room today and will have to miss the Cretin celebration at the Seminary in remembrance of Bishop Cretin's arrival in St. Paul fifty years ago today. I am of the few who were here before he came."[28] The description of the jubilee celebration in the St. Paul *Dispatch* on Tuesday, July 2, 1901, under a sub-heading "New Seminary Chapel" states, "To be built with a $40,000 donation by Mrs. James J. Hill." Mary Hill was present in spirit at the laying of the cornerstone, and her generosity continued over the years.[29]

On September 26, 1901, the seminary board met with Clarence E. Johnston (1859–1936), a well-known but less flamboyant architect than Cass Gilbert, to discuss a design for the chapel. Known later as "the quiet man of Minnesota architecture, Johnston was a tremendously versatile and prolific designer."[30] According to Paul Larson's description, Johnston seems to have been the antithesis of Gilbert: "Johnston was a man of extraordinarily broad sympathies, with a tolerance for the most fractious of clients, an uncanny ability to see his way through the most politically entangled commissions, and above all an abiding sense of how much of the value of his work stemmed from its service to other people's needs and aspirations."[31] Johnston had submitted a design for the Minnesota State Capitol in 1895 but lost to Cass Gilbert. By 1901, however, Johnston had established himself as a leading institutional architect and the state put him on its payroll.[32]

Johnston submitted plans for the proposed chapel basement. At the trustees' meeting, Johnston was authorized to procure a landscape survey of the ground for the chapel and "authorized to receive bids for the construction of the foundation of the proposed chapel as shown by the plans presented."[33] On October 16, 1901, a special meeting of the trustees was held and the contract was awarded to the lowest bidder, P. M. Hennessy, for $3,232.00. By May 31, 1902, Johnston was empowered to secure bids for the work necessary for enclosing the new building.[34] At the board meeting on July 26, 1902, the bid of Lauer Brothers was accepted for $30,242.00.

William C. Toomey was "authorized to sell and dispose of such amounts of the stock of the St. Paul Company, held by the St. Paul Seminary" to procure funds for the payment of the contract.[35] He negotiated the agreement, signed on October 1, 1902, between James J. Hill and The Saint Paul Seminary Corporation, whereby the original trust agreement was modified so that a portion of the principal of the trust fund in an amount not exceeding $32,000.00 could be used for the building of the chapel. The Minneapolis Trust Company was thereby empowered to sell bonds of the St. Paul Gas and Light Company for that purpose.[36] By January 23, 1903, the board had instructed the rector to procure estimates from Johnston for the chapel interior.

The Minneapolis Trust Company's officials were not happy with the process and wrote to John J. Toomey in Hill's office affirming the agreement of October 1, 1902, to sell bonds in the amount of $32,000.00. The letter stated: "These bonds have been sold through your brother, Mr. W. C. Toomey, and the proceeds have been paid out by us to the joint order of the Lauer Brothers, the contractors and the St. Paul Seminary." Clearly unhappy with the procedure, the officials concluded their letter: "We are under the impression that the construction of the chapel was begun without asking any authority for the erection of the same from the trustee. No authority has been granted by the trustee other than that the money from the sale of said bonds has been paid out as above stated, on the request of Mr. Hill and the St. Paul Seminary."[37]

It would seem that there were turf wars as to who could appropriately make decisions regarding money from the trust. Other than being involved in the financial agreement, Hill had little to do with the building of the chapel, a situation very different from his micro-management in the construction of the original buildings.

St. Mary's Chapel, on a high plot of ground about one hundred feet north of the administration building, provided a striking contrast to "Hill's boxcars" and the other seminary buildings. The outer walls were constructed of Kettle River sandstone with Bedford stone trimmings. The interior, basilica style, had a long nave ending in a deep circular apse at the sanctuary. The description in the *Northwestern Chronicle* was in Johnstonesque language: "The dominant idea was to be serviceability. Hence there was no useless display; all was useful, humble, simple, solid and impressive. The style is that known as North Italian."[38]

At the time of the dedication, the *Chronicle* stated that the chapel was patterned on the Roman Church of St. Paul Outside the Walls.[39] Stone columns and arches were not yet carved nor was the apse decorated until the 1920s, when Archbishop Dowling undertook an elaborate remodeling of the interior. Even in the early stage, however, pews were arranged in choir style to facilitate antiphonal singing.[40] The minimal decoration resembles the restored chapel as it exists today.

On May 24, 1905, Bishop Cotter of Winona consecrated St. Mary's Chapel. Bishop McGolrick celebrated the Pontifical Mass, and Bishop O'Gorman of Sioux Falls preached the sermon. O'Gorman acknowledged that, with the erection of the chapel, the seminary was now "complete." His primary reflection, however, was on worship and grace and how they find their synthesis in the Eucharist. The chapel as the center for eucharistic celebration was pivotal for priestly formation. O'Gorman concluded: "If a material building can be said to be a soul—and I believe it can—capitol, soul of the nation, of state; cathedral, soul of a diocese; Vatican Basilica, soul of Christendom; then this seminary is the soul of our province, this chapel is the soul of our seminary; for here is the source of life, hence flows out life, here is conceived and hence is born the priest."[41] Bishop O'Gorman, faithful friend of Archbishop Ireland and of the seminary, was elected to the board in the fall of 1905.

While the chapel was being built, the board received a request for "the proposed taking of a portion of the Seminary grounds for boulevard by the Park Board along the river bank."[42] With the addition of the chapel and the construction of the river boulevard,[43] the seminary established itself as the "anchor" at the end of Summit Avenue. In a dozen years the seminary had evolved from "Mr. Hill's Seminary at the end of Grand Avenue," to an impressive institution on the corner of Summit Avenue and Mississippi River Boulevard.

Six Bishops Consecrated in Seminary Chapel

The most noteworthy event in the early history of the seminary was the consecration of six bishops, all for the Province of St. Paul, in St. Mary's Chapel on May 19, 1910. The unexpected deaths of Bishop Cotter of Winona and Bishop Shanley of Fargo, and the resignation of Bishop Stariha of Lead, South Dakota, all in 1909, were followed by the erection of two new dioceses—Crookston in northern Minnesota and Bismarck in North Dakota—plus the assignment of an auxiliary bishop to St. Paul in 1910. The seminary community was especially delighted with the appointment of their rector, the Reverend Patrick R. Heffron, as the bishop of Winona.[44]

It was an extraordinary two-day celebration beginning with "First Vespers," at which the *consecrandi* took their episcopal oaths and received the blessed insignias for the next day's ceremony. The students hosted a luncheon for the bishops-elect following this event, which included presentations and the singing of the "Ecce Sacerdos Magnus."

The day of consecration was radiant with sunshine and the blossoms of spring. Approximately 550 priests assembled in the *aula maxima* and at 9:40 A.M. processed to the chapel followed by the dignitaries and bishops-elect who had gathered in the administration building. Fourteen (arch)bishops, two abbots, and ten monsignori joined the apostolic delegate, Diomede Falconio, O.F.M., and Archbishop Ireland, the officiant of the rites. Governor Adolph Olson Eberhardt and other dignitaries were escorted by an honor guard of the first battalion corps of cadets of St. Thomas College at the entrance of the chapel.[45]

The chapel was filled to capacity and beyond. Twelve hundred invitations were extended, and although the numbers vary, it was estimated that about one thousand people crowded into the limited space. The congregation was described as follows: "Even before the clergy had entered, St. Mary's Chapel had filled rapidly. Relatives and friends of the *consecrandi* occupied seats in the ambulatoria on either side of the edi-face [sic]. The nave, from which the choir had been removed, was well nigh filled with priests. The gallery was given over to the chanters of the Mass, and the visiting sisters."[46] Once again, Bishop O'Gorman was the preacher, and used his historical talents to relate the present event to the growth of the Catholic Church in the United States beginning with

Bishop John Carroll.[47] The solemn consecration and investiture was impressive. The chronicler of the event for the *Register* did not hesitate to commend the seminary: "It was generally agreed by all present that a high level of rubrical perfection had been attained in the services, and that the last word in the realm of ceremony had been spoken very probably for many a year to come."[48]

The ceremony did not conclude until 2:30 P.M. The priests of the archdiocese hosted a banquet under a large tent overlooking Grand Avenue. Under the canopy, 628 places were set for the newly-consecrated bishops and the distinguished visitors. The archbishop read a cablegram of congratulations from the Holy Father, and the party adjourned until an evening reception.

The six newly-consecrated bishops hosted a reception from 8:00 to 10:00 P.M. on the veranda of the administration building and received the congratulations of large representations of the various parishes of the Twin Cities.[49] It was a day of great significance which acknowledged the growth of the Catholic Church in the Upper Midwest. The Saint Paul Seminary in a relatively brief time had become a symbol for that emergence.

Bishop Patrick Heffron must have had added joy to be one of the six ordained to the episcopacy in St. Mary's Chapel that day. He had presided over the seminary in its formative years and the chapel was one of the most notable achievements of his rectorship. It had not always been easy, however. Father Francis A. Missia, who was appointed chairman of the music department of the seminary in 1907, stated in an interview in the 1950s that some professors were greatly disappointed with Heffron's appointment as rector in 1897, and "they would have preferred someone who had been born and received his entire education in Ireland or in Europe. For this and for other reasons, Heffron experienced a certain amount of opposition to his policies from the faculty members."[50] The early years of the seminary were apparently not devoid of complicated relationships and fractious politics.

The pressure of responsibility wore on Patrick Heffron during his tenure as rector (1897–1910), and apparently he had a nervous breakdown in 1904.[51] Happily, he recovered, and six years later was appointed to the See of Winona. His work as rector, while clearly challenging, won recognition for its genuine depth of pastoral concern for students. As one tribute for Heffron's years of dedication noted: "A distinct factor in the success of his career has been his positive genius in dealing with students. . . . He ruled most where he seemed to rule least; and the strongest rebuke attached to any infringement of the seminary discipline came from the simple realization that the lofty confidence of the rector had been violated."[52]

Early Expansion

Seminary enrollment had increased to 168 by 1904, fluctuated somewhat, and by 1911 was 166. The board had authorized Archbishop Ireland to have plans prepared for a separate library building,[53] but with the rise in the number of students, it became clear that the priority was an additional residence hall. That discussion began on May 17, 1911, just one month after Reverend Francis J. Schaefer, one of the first faculty members, was appointed rector to replace Bishop Heffron. (See chapter 7, p. 82.)

James J. Hill's financial genius was of great benefit to the seminary. The $260,000 invested in 1895 had blossomed, and a "Statement of Endowment Funds June 1, 1911" indicated that that sum had grown to $474,300. Hill, therefore, agreed to selling stock (and he designated exactly which ones) to provide funds for the new dormitory.[54] In the 1911–1912 academic year the enrollment reached 182, including twenty-two students from Dubuque and twenty-three from Chicago. Crowded conditions confirmed the fact that the decision to build a new residence hall was indeed necessary.

Francis J. Schaefer, rector of the Saint Paul Seminary from 1910 to1921

The archbishop turned to his friend Emmanuel Louis Masqueray, the highly-respected French artist who was the chief architect for both the Cathedral of St. Paul (1906–1915) and the Co-Cathedral of the Immaculate Conception (1906–1914)—renamed the Basilica of St. Mary in 1926—as well as many other houses of worship in the midwestern United States.[55] Ireland's French connection, love of history, and admiration for the great cathedrals of Europe found a kindred spirit in Masqueray.

With these two extraordinary commissions, Masqueray decided to settle in St. Paul, although he maintained an office in New York as well. Partly through Ireland's influence, Masqueray received over twenty church commissions and designed three more cathedrals.[56] In 1912 he agreed to divert his attention from magnificent houses of worship to become the chief architect for the new residence hall at the Saint Paul Seminary. At the board meeting on January 17, he presented sketches and estimates, and was authorized to accept bids. Work began in the spring with Hoy and Elzy as contractors.

The building was the same style as the other two residences, but larger. It had seventy-six student rooms, a large infirmary, an oratory, and two spacious recreation rooms on the lower level.[57] By mistake, the rooms had sinks with hot and cold running water! Father Schaefer reported to the board that "the roughing in for sinks (pipes bringing hot and cold water as well as water pipes) in the students' rooms, placed there by mistaken order of the architect, Mr. E. L. Masqueray" was an additional expense to be dealt with. The board agreed to use the piping at some future time and then to reimburse Mr. Masqueray for the outlay in the amount of $1,286.55.[58] In the spring of 1914, however, Archbishop Ireland paid the plumber $1,980.55 for the hot and cold water in the students' rooms, which amount was to have been paid by Masqueray. For the students who were to live there in the future, it was indeed a *felix culpa*—a luxury the seminarians who lived in the other residence halls did not enjoy.

James J. Hill's commitment to the seminary was evident again in an unexpected donation. The completion of a substantial part of the new residence was anticipated by summer 1913. However, the plan had been to leave the infirmary and the fourth and fifth floors unfinished until further funds were available. On October 7, 1912, Father Schaefer paid a visit to James J. Hill in his office in the Great Northern Building and extended an invitation to a reception at the seminary in honor of his seventy-fifth birthday. In addition to accepting the invitation, "an offer was made by Mr. Hill that the entire building now in course of construction should be completed and that he, Mr. Hill, would cover the deficiency in the funds at the disposal of the Seminary for that purpose." Masqueray was commissioned to get exact figures for Hill so that the entire building could be completed.[59]

Hill's additional donation of almost $15,000 made possible the completion of the new residence hall in time for the priests' retreat in August of 1913, and for the occupancy of students the following fall when the enrollment reached 221.[60] By 1915 there were 219 students—54 from St. Paul and 53 from Chicago; the enrollment remained at that level for several years thereafter. The 1914 *Register* described the new residence and expressed gratitude to Hill:

"The generosity of our honoured founder, Mr. James J. Hill, who gave a substantial donation towards it, made its early completion possible; and the thanks of the Seminary go out to him for this new pledge of his interest in the work of educating the Catholic priesthood."[61] The ongoing generosity of the Protestant entrepreneur to the Catholic seminary continued to be a source of amazement to the community.

The addition of a well-equipped infirmary was a genuine asset in a period when many seminaries were criticized for unhealthy conditions and a lack of nutritional diets and opportunities for exercise. From 1898, the *Register* had included the requirement that "All applicants for admission are made to undergo a medical examination under the hand of an experienced physician."[62] In 1901, the board appointed Father Heffron and Father Stariha "to arrange with hospitals and physicians for the care of sick students."[63] Beginning in the 1902–1903 academic year, James C. Markoe, M.D., was listed in the *Register* after the faculty as "attending physician." A substantial infirmary on campus from 1913 certainly made Dr. Markoe's task easier. Prior to that it had been necessary for him to go to the room of each student who was sick.[64] The 1913 *Register* offered the following description: "In the new residence there is an infirmary with all modern appliances for the care of the sick; it is in charge of a trained nurse."[65] One would presume that, as in later years, the nurse was one of the Sisters of St. Joseph of Carondelet.

With the completion of the new dormitory, Bishop James McGolrick recommended to the board that the three residence halls be named "in honor of the first three bishops who exercised direct and actual jurisdiction in the territory that became and is the Diocese of St. Paul." Accordingly, the residence farthest north was named "Loras"; what had been the South Residence became "Cretin"; and the new building was named "Grace" in honor of the recently deceased archbishop. Stone tablets with the new names were procured and affixed to the buildings and are there to this day.[66]

A fire broke out in the refectory on September 22, 1915, evidently caused by a defective fuse, resulting in serious damage to the roof. Other than that, the seminary had been remarkably free from crises of a material nature. The seminary buildings were adequately insured, and it was decided to replace the shingle roof on the refectory with a new slate one. The trustees and administrators voted for "two additional water-mains for better water service in the buildings and for protection against fire." The repairs and improvements over the summer just past had included replacing gas lights with electricity in the administration building, the chapel, and the gymnasium. After the fire, the need to wire Loras, Cretin, and the refectory for electricity seemed imperative.[67] It was fortunate that more damage had not occurred.

Faculty Recruited by Catholic University

Ireland worked diligently to establish a stable faculty, sending younger priests to study, but always wrestling with losing them—often to the Catholic University of America. His boyhood friend, Thomas O'Gorman, the first rector of Saint Thomas Aquinas Seminary (1885–1887), and a member of the faculty there, was the precursor. He was invited to assume the chair of ecclesiastical history at the Catholic University of America in 1890. His principal literary work, *A History of the Roman Catholic Church in the United States,* was published in 1895 and was used as a text at the Saint Paul Seminary for many years. O'Gorman, a scholar at heart, considered his years at the Catholic University among his happiest.[68]

Thomas Edward Shields, who had been ordained from Saint Thomas Aquinas Seminary in 1891, received his doctorate in biology from Johns Hopkins University in Baltimore in 1895, and then taught that subject at the Saint Paul Seminary from 1895 to 1898. In 1902 he became professor of physiological psychology at the Catholic University about which more will be said later. John A. Ryan, as mentioned above, received his S.T.D. from the Catholic University in moral theology in 1905, and returned there to teach in 1915.

Joseph T. Barron, the youngest priest (as of 1912) to be ordained from the Saint Paul Seminary, was one of the first three students to receive the S.T.B. from the Catholic University of America in 1912. He then studied at the Catholic University from 1915 to 1917 and was assigned to teach philosophy at Saint Paul Seminary. In 1926 he returned to Catholic University where he taught philosophy and served as acting dean prior to his premature death in 1939. He authored the book *The Elements of Epistemology,* which was translated into several languages.

During his years on the faculty in St. Paul, Barron became a good friend of F. Scott Fitzgerald who came to visit him regularly at the seminary during the winter of 1919 when he stayed home from Princeton and lived with his parents on Summit Avenue.[69] According to Andrew Turnbull, he consulted the priest about his writing:

> Leaning back in his deep leather chair with his cassock wrapped around his legs against the cold, Father Joe would hold forth on all manner of subjects, sacred and profane. His darting, journalistic mind appealed to Fitzgerald; he was witty and sociable yet inflexible on matters of religion.

Barron would listen to Fitzgerald's iconoclasms, and then say softly, "Scott, quit being a damn fool."[70]

In 1921, after Scott's marriage to Zelda and a trip abroad, they returned to St. Paul for the birth of their child. Once again, Scott continued to visit with Barron. He claimed to have nothing to do with the church after his marriage, but his daughter was baptized a Catholic with Barron as her "godfather."[71] Barron's relationship to Fitzgerald continued after his appointment to Catholic University. The Fitzgeralds moved to Baltimore in 1933, and Zelda had a nervous breakdown shortly after. Scott came to see Barron in Washington, but it proved sad for both of them.[72]

Barron's years at Catholic University were successful. It was while returning to St. Paul for his mother's funeral in November 1938 that he suffered a heart attack. He died April 13, 1939, in St. Joseph's Hospital and was buried from the Saint Paul Cathedral.[73] O'Gorman, Shields, Ryan, Barron, and more recently Michael Patrick O'Connor and Dominic Serra—the Saint Paul Seminary has regularly provided faculty for the Catholic University of America.

Characteristics of the Student Body

Although it is impossible to identify the ethnic composition of the student body or of the alumni—unless one guesses from the surnames—a study of the St. Paul diocesan clergy from 1884 to 1918 by Daniel Patrick O'Neill provides a fascinating vantage point from which to reflect on a particular group who were, for the most part, graduates of the Saint Paul Seminary. O'Neill studied the St. Paul priests in ten-year cohorts. (Priests who arrived in the U.S. as infants or young children were considered to be native sons.)[74]

O'Neill's table on the "Ethnic Stock of Minnesota Natives Between 1861 and 1930" includes the number and percent of Irish-Americans, German-Americans, Bohemian-Americans, Polish-Americans, and "Other" according to decades. It is interesting to note that the period 1861–1870 has a total of two Irish-Americans ordained—obviously John Ireland and Thomas O'Gorman. In the decade 1881–1890 there were 21 native sons ordained (15 Irish-Americans, 3 German-Americans, 1 Polish-American, and 1 Other). In the first decade of the twentieth century, the total was 36 (12 Irish-Americans, 7 German-Americans, 11 Bohemian-Americans, 3 Polish-Americans, and 3 Other). In the period 1911–1920 there were 61 native clergy ordained (28 Irish-Americans, 18 German-Americans, 4 Bohemian-Americans, 7 Polish-Americans, and 4 Other). O'Neill notes: "Between 1881 and 1910, two-thirds of the recruit cohorts were foreign in origin. From half to three-fifths of them completed seminary in the United States. Thus, the Saint Paul diocese had a clergy which was American educated, at least in part, before it had an American-born clergy."[75]

If Ireland's goal was to develop a native clergy for the diocese, the establishment of the Saint Paul Seminary was the major reason for his success. He believed that families were more likely to encourage their sons in a vocation to priesthood if they could study in the near geographical area. The initial impact, according to O'Neill, was the increase in the number of candidates from farm backgrounds. As America became more urbanized, so did the Catholic population and the candidates for priesthood. "In the 1890s, only a tenth of the native sons were from white collar families; in the 1911–1920 cohort, their proportion increased to a fourth."[76]

Better screening of candidates was another value of a local seminary. It eliminated relying on European bishops and rectors for recommendations which might result in less desirable students being encouraged to study for missionary dioceses. Ireland required that seminarians from outside the diocese spend at least two years at the school before ordination.

O'Neill suggests that the reason for the comparative lag in the number of German-American vocations was twofold: (1) Ireland's strong views on Americanization and his conflict with leaders of the German community; (2) the presence of the German Benedictines at St. John's Abbey and their staffing of several parishes in the Twin Cities. By 1930, however, the ethnic background of local candidates had stabilized at 40 percent Irish-American, 30 percent German-American, 10 percent Polish-American, 10 percent Bohemian-American, and 10 percent Other. In the final analysis:

> The recruitment and formation of the St. Paul diocesan clergy was the work of many individuals: parents, priests, religious, friends and bishops all had a role in fostering vocations and in encouraging clerical candidates to affiliate with the St. Paul diocese. The major figure in the transformation of the diocesan clergy from a foreign to an American group was Archbishop John Ireland. Policies that he adopted in the 1880s led to the Americanization of the St. Paul diocesan clergy after World War I.[77]

The Issue of Race

Ireland was also a leader in the area of civil rights for African-Americans, and exercised that leadership in regard to educating "negroes" for the priesthood. Perhaps his concern for this issue emanated from the fact that when his family arrived in St. Paul in 1852 and settled in an area known as Lowertown, several families in the area—in fact, one next door to them—were black.[78]

The Catholic Church had been slow to respond to the question of morality in racial questions. Even at the time of the Civil War in the United States, the Holy See had condemned the slave trade, but not *slavery.* Many Catholics, especially in the South, continued to reject vehemently the possibility of integrated worship and religious education, much less a black clergy. Some religious orders had accepted black candidates for priesthood, and a few were ordained, but the only black diocesan priest in ministry in the United States, Augustine Tolton, was educated and ordained in Rome in 1886.[79]

Ireland frequently spoke out against "the color line." He gave passionate speeches. In 1890 at St. Augustine's Church in Washington, D.C., he proclaimed:

> And they who order and compel a man because he is colored to betake himself to a corner marked off for his race, practically contradict the principles of justice and of equal rights established by the God of mercy who lives on the altar. The color line must go and soon, too. The line will be drawn at personal merit. The shame and scandal of putting colored people in corners and lofts in Catholic churches must be wiped out. The doors of all Catholic institutions must be opened to colored Catholics.[80]

Ireland not only spoke out for integration, but actively sought black candidates for priesthood.[81] On one occasion Archbishop Ireland was asked if he would admit a "colored student" into his seminary. After a resounding "Yes!" he was asked what he would do if others would object to or even "embarrass this student for the priesthood because of his color." The archbishop responded: "I would expel all such students, for their act would prove conclusively to me that they were unworthy of the high office to which they aspire. There is no room in the Catholic Church for racial prejudice."[82]

Father John R. Slattery of the Mill Hill Fathers of St. Joseph (which became an independent congregation in 1893—St. Joseph's Society of the Sacred Heart in the United States), an ardent advocate of the concerns of blacks in the Catholic Church and a friend of Ireland's and Denis O'Connell's, stated in an article that he wrote in the *Catholic World* in 1888 that he knew of no Catholic college in the United States that accepted African-Americans. The *Northwestern Chronicle* responded: "True, it is rather far toward the Arctic Circle, and may not be called on to accept colored students; but if they apply they will find, we are confident, that their complexion... will not cause any difference in their reception nor in treatment at St. Thomas Seminary, St. Paul."[83]

The following fall, with the assistance of John Ireland, John Henry (Harry) Dorsey—a fourteen-year-old candidate for the Mill Hill Fathers—was accepted at St. Thomas seminary to begin his studies for the priesthood. In attendance only one year until the Mill Hill Epiphany Apostolic College was completed, Dorsey was ordained to the priesthood as a Josephite in 1902.[84] Although his time at St. Thomas was brief, Dorsey was the first black student at the school, "and at that time possibly the only black seminarian in the United States." When Dorsey went out to the missions he was one of two black priests in the United States and the only one who received his entire seminary training in America.[85]

The first black to attend seminary and be ordained as a diocesan priest in the United States was Father Stephen Theobald. In 1906, Archbishop Ireland received a letter from a young black lawyer from British Guiana in South America who believed that he had a vocation to the priesthood. Ireland sent him the examinations and applications. Theobald was not only accepted at the Saint Paul Seminary in 1907, but proved to be a brilliant student. He was ordained for the Archdiocese of St. Paul in 1910. Theobald served briefly at the cathedral and also assisted with matters of canon law until he was appointed pastor of St. Peter Claver Parish which had been established by Ireland for "Colored Catholics" in 1892.

Theobald's influence was felt far beyond the upper Mississippi. With the encouragement of Archbishop Ireland he became active in national movements for black Catholics on the American scene. In 1932 he presented a report, prepared in conjunction with notable leaders—black and white—such as John La Farge, S.J., and Thomas Turner, to the National Catholic Welfare Conference urging the hierarchy to allow capable black Catholics the opportunity for Catholic education. Theobald's death from

Reverend Stephen Theobald, ordained from the Saint Paul Seminary in 1906

appendicitis on July 8, 1932, "deprived black Catholics of an articulate spokesman and served to dramatize the depressing prospects for black diocesan clergy in the early 1930s."[86]

The Americanist Crisis and the Effects of Modernism

The Saint Paul Seminary was thriving in the pre-World War I period: enrollment was up, faculty had stabilized, new buildings had been added, the spirit was high. The nation was in the midst of the Progressive Era—an optimistic period exuding the enthusiasm of President "Teddy" Roosevelt and others. The country was convinced that the unique "melting pot" of the United States could make life better for all Americans, and the "muckrakers" were on hand to remind the nation that improvements were necessary.

Directives emanating from Rome, however, were not as positive, particularly for those who had espoused an "Americanist" perspective. The 1899 promulgation of *Testem Benevolentiae*—the letter of Pope Leo XIII to James Cardinal Gibbons that condemned certain beliefs in the Catholic Church associated with Isaac Hecker—dashed the hopes of many of the more progressive Catholics in the United States. The results of this "phantom heresy," which centered more on French church-state relations than on conditions in America, were the curtailing of enthusiasm for matters theological and the burden of defending one's orthodoxy in turn-of-the-century church politics. The optimism of the previous decade seemed to evaporate.

The election to the papal throne of Giuseppe Sarto as Pope Pius X in 1903 initiated one of the most conservative periods in modern Catholic history. He presided over the Modernist crisis in the Catholic Church in the early twentieth century.[87] Its effect upon seminaries was experienced particularly by the faculty. The July 3, 1907, decree *Lamentabili* condemned sixty-five theological propositions labeled "Modernism." Two months later, on September 8, 1907, Pius X promulgated the encyclical *Pascendi Dominici Gregis*. The document condemned an amalgam of doctrines often taken out of context. Particular targets were the philosophy of immanentism and the historical-critical method in interpreting scripture. The writings of St. Thomas Aquinas were again mandated as the foundation for all philosophical and theological study in Catholic institutions.[88]

Concern for Modernism in seminaries resulted in the decree *Praestantia* issued *motu proprio* on November 18, 1907, which stated "bishops should refuse to ordain to the priesthood young men who give the slightest reason for thinking that they are attached to condemned doctrines and dangerous novelties."[89] St. Joseph's Seminary or "Dunwoodie" in New York, led by a group of progressive Sulpicians who had founded a journal, *New York Review,* in which two of the accused Modernists George Tyrell and Alfred Loisy had published articles, was under particular scrutiny.[90] *Acta et Dicta,* the journal of the St. Paul Catholic Historical Society, which was housed at the Saint Paul Seminary, provided no such threat.[91]

As leader of the American Catholic hierarchy, Cardinal Gibbons wrote to the Holy Father agreeing with the condemnation of the stated errors, and pledged obedience to the regulations. Archbishop Ireland and other members of the board of trustees of the Catholic University of America did the same and "asserted their determination to make a survey of its library for modernistic books and a recommendation in regard to them."[92]

In April 1908, Ireland published an article in the *North American Review* on "The Dogmatic Authority of the Papacy." The archbishop of St. Paul stated: "The starting-point of Modernism is the assumption that, of itself, human reason is powerless to establish either the existence of God as a transcendent reality, or the divinity of the mission and person of Christ." After discussing the theories of various philosophers, he concluded:

> The radical mistake of Modernism and of its methods of apologetics is that it excludes or, at least, minimizes overmuch the functions of the intellect, thereby unduly reducing its theodicy to sentiment—to mere subjectivism. Against this subjectivism Pius X appeals to the reasoning faculty in man, to the intellect, whose rights and convincing force he valiantly defends.[93]

It was, according to Ireland, necessary for the pope as the official guardian of the deposit of faith to defend Christian doctrine.

In an unpublished article entitled "The New Theology—Modernism," Ireland praised the twentieth century with its many discoveries and inventions, not because they were "modern" but "because they mirror the goodness and power of God whose existence the Modernists deny." The Holy Father was simply "restoring God to His rightful place in the universe."[94] Ireland felt obliged to support the papal statements, but he could not deny his own progressive spirit.

If Catholics in the United States overreacted to the Modernism crisis, it was because the wounds of the accusations of "Americanism" were still fresh. According to Gerald P. Fogarty, S.J.: "With the condemnation of Modernism following so closely on the condemnation of Americanism, the American Catholic Church lapsed into an intellectual slumber from which it did not awaken until the 1940s."[95] The question of the relationship between Americanism and Modernism continues to be explored,[96] but in the early twentieth century Catholic intellectual life in the United States was still in its adolescence. There were few scholars who had the luxury to become immersed in the questions that were consuming European Catholics at that time. After 1908 none were encouraged to explore theological questions apart from a Thomistic orientation. One can only speculate about lost potential and stunted growth. Except in the area of social justice affirmed by the encyclical *Rerum Novarum,* intellectual exploration was discouraged or simply not allowed in the seminary.[97]

On September 1, 1910, Pius X issued the decree *Sacrorum Antistitum* in which the decrees condemning Modernism were applied to diocesan seminaries. Although the pope acknowledged the importance of learning in seminary life, he stated: "It is proper, therefore, that enthusiasm for learning should be kept under control." He encouraged the study of the assigned subjects but added:

> Lest the young students should waste their time on other questions and be distracted from their principal study, we absolutely forbid them to read newspapers and reviews, however excellent these may be, and we make it a matter of conscience for superiors who fail to take precautions to prevent such reading.[98]

According to the Vatican, the reading room adjacent to the gymnasium at the Saint Paul Seminary which contained reviews, periodicals, and newspapers from around the world was only a distraction to the seminarians' preparation for priesthood.

The best-known requirement of the document, however, was the profession of faith and oath against Modernism. It was imposed on all entering ecclesiastical office (bishops, priests, deacons). Seminary faculty were required to take the oath in public at the beginning of each academic year. Not only must this have been a trying experience for some individuals, but Joseph M. White concludes: "With these unprecedented provisions, the Holy See made a decisive advance in exerting control over the seminary and by doing so reversed the Tridentine tradition that assigned the ordinary responsibility for determining the content of clerical training to bishops."[99]

From 1910 until 1960 the diocesan seminary in the United States experienced few changes in form or curriculum. The stringent restrictions placed on theological inquiry discouraged innovative intellectual activity. No doubt, Archbishop Ireland and individual professors continued to provide encouragement and stimulation for the students, but the seminary became a place for learning general knowledge and preparing for the profession of ministry, not a center for creative intellectual thought.

The Passing of the Seminary's Founders

At the celebration of James J. Hill's seventy-fifth birthday at the seminary on November 18, 1912, Archbishop Ireland announced that there were 399 alumni—104 in Minnesota, 20 in California, 12 in Illinois, 32 in North Dakota, 28 in South Dakota, 26 in Nebraska, and others in Montana, Oregon, Michigan, Wisconsin, Ohio, and other places east.[100] Hill's gift to the seminary had yielded remarkable fruits for the Catholic Church in America.

When the founder came to the seminary periodically for receptions at which the students and faculty expressed their gratitude, his message was often one of spiritual inspiration. One might have thought the following words were Ireland's and not Hill's. In 1896 James J. Hill challenged the future priests:

> You are fitting yourselves to be messengers of Christ to the world. Your vocation is the highest and the best that is allotted to man. Nothing but the truths and graces of Christ will save humanity. Wherever throughout the history of the last nineteen hundred years a bright spot is visible, there the light of Christianity has shone. You are to be bearers of salvation to human society upon earth, as well as to souls for life to come. As your friend, as one interested in your success and in the work that lies before you, I entreat you to work well in the Seminary. Professors of merit are here to teach you. Material comforts surround you to lessen the difficulties of your labors. Make good use of your opportunities.[101]

At the celebration in 1912 his reflection was similar, but he added: "No life is more beautiful than his [the priest's] since his days are passed in doing his duty conscientiously. The responsibility that rests upon him is great, but as long as he does that faithfully all is well."[102] Hill shared not only his money but also his wisdom and spirituality.

It was, therefore, with genuine sadness that the seminary mourned the death of its founder on May 29, 1916. James J. Hill had been a larger-than-life personality with a ferocious work ethic. According to his biographer Michael P. Malone, "his hand reached into every aspect of building the regional economy and the social order, from transportation to agriculture, mining, lumbering, maritime trade, and, not to be forgotten, town and city building." But even Malone acknowledged that, of all his philanthropic ventures, "His favorite project became the Saint Paul Seminary."[103] He had been an "empire builder" in more than one world.

John Ireland, born the same year as Hill, lived to celebrate his eightieth birthday September 11, 1918, but died two weeks later. On January 5, 1915, in the fortieth year of his episcopal ordination, the seminary had held a special reception and dinner in his honor. It was also twenty years after the dedication of the institution that he said would be the major work of his episcopacy, and he had every reason to feel joy and satisfaction.

The address given on the occasion by the Reverend James H. O'Neill of the Diocese of Helena recounted the archbishop's extraordinary life and his accomplishments. Apart from the rhetoric of the evening, it was clear that the seminary was indeed the "child of his predilection." Ironically, it had evolved from the unusual yoking of two dynamic, great-hearted, sometimes irascible men who changed the face of the church and society in the Upper Midwest and beyond. O'Neill's speech described the gratitude of the seminary for the commitment of both men to its cause:

> Oh happy St. Paul Seminary! Blessed beyond thy compeers in that thou hast associated with thy foundation and early history *two of the most illustrious names* on this broad continent—James J. Hill, the Empire Builder of the fertile and opulent Northwest and *John Ireland* the distinguished spokesman and mighty champion of the Catholic Church beneath the free folds of the Star Spangled Banner.[104]

The "fresh air" of Ireland's ecclesiology, reflected in the open spaces of Hill's seminary, became a symbol that to be American and to be Catholic was more than compatible; it was the hope for the future of the Catholic Church in the United States. Hill's and Ireland's cooperation in the establishment and ongoing support of the seminary provided a stability that allowed for creativity in preparation for priesthood matched by few seminaries in the United States at that time. That the development of this institution should have taken place on "the frontier" was even more remarkable.

In the waning days of World War I, the people of the Archdiocese of St. Paul, the Twin Cities, the state of Minnesota, the nation, and others at great distances greeted the news of the death of John Ireland on September 25, 1918, as the end of an era. The archbishop was the great Americanizer who had been affectionately dubbed "the Consecrated Blizzard of the Northwest." He was the giant of a churchman whom Cardinal Gibbons described as "the Lion of the fold of Juda."[105] Catholics and others mourned him throughout the world, but none more than the priests and seminarians of the archdiocese. His vision of church and priesthood and seminary had changed their lives.

The last of the "founders" of the seminary to depart this world was Mary Theresa Mehegan Hill. Mary was a remarkable woman—detectable in the diary she kept quite regularly from 1891.[106] Although many of the entries do not seem personal, her actions speak louder than her words. She spent the largest part of her time raising her children, administering her household, caring for the sick and the poor, and devoting time to Catholic educational and charitable institutions. Her family was foremost in her priorities, and frequent references to "Papa" indicate that Mary and James stayed in close touch even when he was traveling. Sometimes she joined him, as on a trip to England and Scotland in 1894, when she described the beauties of the country as well as her enjoyment of the cultural opportunities. She loved reading (especially books about the Far East), crocheting, and quiet time at North Oaks.

Part of her seems to have "died" with her husband. On Saturday, May 29, 1920, Mary wrote in her diary: "Four years ago today, Papa left us—this is a sad world now." Ten days later she reflected: "A lonely feeling stays with me today and I am alone, too. This is the anniversary of our engagement on June 8, 1864. How much has happened since then." Clearly, he had been a focal point in her life.[107]

Even after the death of James J. Hill, Mary continued her interest in and support of the Saint Paul Seminary in a very concrete way. In August 1920 she made a "splendid gift" of $200,000 to the seminary endowment fund. On August 2, 1920, the board, in crafting a resolution of appreciation, stated that they were offering Mrs. Hill gratitude not only from the archdiocese, but also from the other dioceses whose students were also the beneficiaries of her generosity.[108]

Mary Hill died on November 22, 1921. The seminary mourned her and paid her tribute:

> The hundreds of young men who were raised to the priesthood in St. Mary's Chapel, and who saw in Mrs. Hill's simple dignity, unaffected piety, and generosity of soul the exemplar of Catholic womanhood, were stirred to fresh admiration and gratitude on learning of her great gifts to religion two years ago, notably the gift to the Seminary crowning the endowment established by Mr. Hill. The name of Mrs. Hill will never be forgotten in the prayers of the priests and students of St. Paul Seminary.[109]

Indeed, if it hadn't been for a woman—Mary Theresa Mehegan Hill—the Saint Paul Seminary would not have come into existence at the time and place that it did. Without her influence and generosity, the "Empire Builder" and the "Consecrated Blizzard" might have put their financial contributions and energies elsewhere. The quiet example of a gentle but firm woman set their priorities straight. She was the link between the millionaire entrepreneur and the ecclesiastical leader of the process of Americanization in the Catholic Church, and became the "mother" responsible for bringing to birth the Saint Paul Seminary, which changed the face of the Catholic Church in the Upper Midwest and beyond.

II
The Saint Paul Seminary
From World War I to Vatican II
(1919–1961)

CHAPTER 9

Austin Dowling

"The Rhetoric of Architecture"

> The thoughts of a people are as manifestly revealed in the rhetoric of its architecture as in the resounding periods of its spoken or its written word. Our streets live. They have a language. The stones cry out. Every quarter has its message which he who runs may hear and understand. Commerce, industry, business, culture, art, play, religion—all have their symbols, familiar and easily recognized, on street and thoroughfare, on road and highway, throughout the land.... Thus, the story of the Church's planting in this country, of her sudden and prodigious growth, and of her high hopes today, may readily be deciphered in the large alphabet of her buildings.[1]
>
> Archbishop Austin Dowling
> Consecration of the Seminary Chapel
> Cleveland, Ohio, October 28, 1925

John Ireland had been a dominant figure in the Catholic Church in the Upper Midwest for the fifty-seven years of his priesthood. It was difficult to imagine life in Minnesota without him. To succeed Ireland was an unenviable challenge, but that was the fate of Austin Dowling. Both were the sons of Irish immigrants but had little else in common.

Dowling was an easterner to the core. He was born in New York City on April 6, 1868, to Daniel and Mary Teresa Santry Dowling, and on April 19 was baptized Daniel Austin. The family moved soon after to Newport, Rhode Island, where he became a student at the Academy of the Sisters of Mercy. His sister and only sibling joined the Sisters of

Mercy of Providence, Rhode Island. Austin attended the Christian Brothers' Manhattan College in New York City from which he received an A.B. degree with high honors in 1887.[2]

That same year Dowling began his preparation for the priesthood at St. John's Seminary in Brighton, Massachusetts, and completed his studies at the Catholic University of America. After ordination to the priesthood on June 24, 1891, in the Cathedral of Saints Peter and Paul in Providence, he was assigned to the Catholic University for one more year to earn the licentiate in sacred theology, doing graduate studies in theology and church history. Interestingly, one of his professors was Father Thomas O'Gorman, first rector of St. Thomas Aquinas Seminary in St. Paul.[3]

After a year of pastoral work in Providence, Dowling became professor of church history at St. John's Seminary in Brighton for two and a half years. History was always his passion. Marvin O'Connell claims that he was "a man who was by taste, habit and profession an historian; he could not set about finding solutions to problems facing him until he examined those problems in the light of the past."[4] Even as archbishop, Dowling delivered two series of public lectures on church history at the College of St. Thomas in 1922 and 1923.[5] His love for history permeated his sermons and other presentations.

In 1896, Dowling was recalled to his diocese and for two years served as editor of the *Providence Visitor,* becoming one of the better known Catholic editors in the United States. Subsequently he resumed pastoral work and in 1905 was appointed rector of the cathedral in Providence. Seven years later the Holy See chose Austin Dowling to be the first bishop of Des Moines, Iowa.[6] Receiving the news on January 13, 1912, he believed that he was being sent into "exile" in the West.

Dowling had a fine intellect and excellent organizational skills. In Iowa he was appreciated for his courage, simplicity, and kindness. Above all he had a deep commitment to education and founded a Catholic college in Des Moines to help develop an educated laity. He never envisaged himself, however, as a successor to "the Consecrated Blizzard of the Northwest." In fact Dowling described himself in his address at his installation in the Cathedral of St. Paul on March 25, 1919, as "the unknown, the unexpected, the undistinguished successor of the great Archbishop Ireland."[7] According to Reverend T. Kenneth Ryan,

Austin Dowling, archbishop of St. Paul from 1919 to 1931

who attended the Saint Paul Seminary from 1924 to 1930 and who was ordained by Dowling, "there was a fierce loyalty to John Ireland—absolutely fierce. Priests who had been reprimanded and bossed and pushed around still held him as their idol. Archbishop Dowling never quite came up to that. A different type entirely."[8]

The contrast between Ireland and Dowling was in both physical appearance and personality. Ireland was tall and broad-shouldered. He had craggy features and commanding voice, always projecting strength and dynamism. In his later years he had a mane of white hair which distinguished him from others in a crowd.[9] A French newspaper had described him during an 1892 lecture tour in Paris:

> Tall, well-built, his face a mixture of energy and sweetness, frank and refined, his look clear and penetrating, his voice warm, sonorous as brass, his speech fluent, at times familiar, at times lofty. Simply dressed, he wears no pectoral cross or evidence of his dignity, not even a watch chain. His old-fashioned trousers and large hob-nailed shoes reveal a gentleman who does not frequent the best New York clothiers.[10]

Dowling, however, was "a short, plump man with scanty, thin grey hair, and a fair complexion" who had a soft-spoken manner, shy demeanor, and gentle approach. Those who first met him would be "aware of the delicate features of his oval face, the round chin, the Roman nose, and the blue eyes brightly reflecting his warm smile."[11] Despite his more retiring approach, he was an impressive orator and a competent administrator, committed to education no matter what the cost.

By the time the new archbishop arrived, the Saint Paul Seminary was approaching its twenty-fifth year. In that quarter century, the expectations for seminary education had changed from the Americanizing focus mandated by the 1884 Third Plenary Council of Baltimore and were moving toward a vision in which conformity to the Vatican's view of the world was predominant. In 1908 the Catholic Church in the United States was removed from the jurisdiction of the Sacred Congregation of Propaganda and was no longer considered mission territory. This curtailed some of its frontier "privileges." The Sacred Congregation of Seminaries and Universities, created November 4, 1915, became the overseer of seminary education, mandating a new era of centralization in Rome. The congregation, and the new Code of Canon Law that became effective May 19, 1918, encouraged conformity and stifled creativity in seminary education—even for a bishop.

Dowling wanted the Saint Paul Seminary to flourish, but he did not want to compete with Ireland whose affection for the major seminary was uncamouflaged. This post-World War I period of the "roarin' 20s" which witnessed the closure of immigration and the stabilization of the churches in the United States was a time for brick-and-mortar bishops, and Dowling was to be one of them.

Dowling's View of the Church in America

The vision of the new archbishop of St. Paul for the church in the United States and the education of priests was no less American than that of John Ireland. Dowling described the challenge for Catholics in the post-World War I era as follows:

> The old order passeth, giving place to the new. Immigration has all but ceased, and when revived—if it is ever permitted to

> revive—it is not likely to attain the proportions of former days. . . . Language, customs, memories, pass with a generation. So far, the Church in this country has been singularly sustained by the momentum of spiritual agencies that were derived from other lands and other times. In the new day there will be no such powerful auxiliary to supplement our own normal activity. *It will be the American Catholic Church or it will be nothing.*[12]

Dowling analyzed the challenge for American Catholics in the 1920s as the predicament of those who were immigrants or children of immigrants—until recently, poor and disadvantaged—who associated their religion with "the old country," as well as with their poverty and second-class status. Ethnicity and religion were intertwined. For some immigrants, religion was a casualty as they rose on the economic scale and became more "American." In an experience not unlike that of Jews and others from Eastern Europe, "as they progress in wealth and station, they frequently strive to hide their origins, to change their names and affect manners that do not belong to them. Even when they keep up the practice of their religion, they are frequently ashamed of it."[13]

The solution, Dowling believed, was to convince people that "foreignism" and Catholicism were not intimately linked. The anti-immigrant sentiment of the 1920s, plus the activities of the Ku Klux Klan vis-à-vis Jews, Catholics, and blacks, and the association of Catholics with anti-prohibition movements contributed to the "siege mentality" that many Catholics experienced in that period. With the 1928 defeat of Governor Alfred E. Smith, the first Catholic to run for the presidency on a major party ticket, the fears and concerns of Catholics that they would never be more than second-class citizens were underscored.

The goal of developing an American Catholic Church could be achieved only by education, according to Dowling, and his vision was national as well as parochial. One of the beneficial by-products of World War I had been the establishment of the National Catholic War Council. It provided an opportunity for the Catholic bishops of the United States to assemble, coordinate programs for chaplains and refugees, and develop ecumenical and interfaith relations by working with the Federal Council of Churches and the Joint Distribution Committee which coordinated Jewish relief programs. It was also an opportunity to coordinate efforts with the federal government and to prove that Catholics could be just as "American" as other Americans. The bishops had not been convening regularly since the Third Plenary Council of Baltimore and found the experience helpful in fostering a spirit of cooperation and Catholic unity.

In the postwar period, the Catholic hierarchy had a desire to capitalize on the new sense of unity. Cardinal Gibbons, the unofficial "patriarch" of the American Catholic Church who had only recently celebrated the golden jubilee of his ordination to the episcopacy, wrote to the American bishops on May 24, 1919: "I beg to announce that the First Annual Meeting of the American Hierarchy will convene on September twenty-four, in Divinity Hall, Catholic University of America."[14] At that meeting in 1919 the National Catholic Welfare Council (later National Catholic Welfare Conference) was established, and Dowling was very involved in it.[15] An administrative board of seven prelates was elected to prepare a program. Five departments were organized: Education, Social Work, Press and Literature, Lay Societies, and Home and Foreign Missions. In addition to being elected to the board, Dowling was also named treasurer and chairman of the Department of Education. He filled those positions conscientiously for nearly ten years until ill health required him to relinquish the responsibilities.

The Establishment of Nazareth Hall as the Minor Seminary

Closer to home, Dowling's first major project was to establish the Archbishop Ireland Educational Fund. On the first anniversary of the death of his predecessor, Dowling commended the late archbishop for his commitment to education and the many achievements of his era. He stated, however, that what was needed in the present decade was "to develop, coordinate and consolidate this educational system to provide for greater efficiency." Among his goals were the erection of a preparatory seminary, a school for the training of the sister-teachers of all the religious congregations engaged in school work in the diocese, high schools at strategic locations, a system of complete supervision for all educational institutions, and a permanent fund. To do this he announced a campaign for $5,000,000.[16]

Early enthusiasm for the archbishop's campaign led 45,551 people to pledge a total of $4,392,872.50. However, unpaid pledges in the following year amounted to $1,700,000. In the summer of 1923, seminarians were assigned to call upon delinquent subscribers to encourage them to continue payments.[17] The largest allocation of the fund was $1,280,000 for the construction and partial endowment of the new minor seminary.[18]

Pope Pius XI, on August 1, 1922, had written an apostolic letter entitled *Officiorum Omnium* regarding the recruitment and training of priests. The pontiff enjoined parish priests "to preserve from the contagion of the world boys who showed signs of an ecclesiastical vocation."[19] In a letter to the archdiocese regarding the opening of Nazareth Hall, Dowling referred to this document as well as the new Code of Canon Law and its mandates for seminaries: "The words of the Holy Father are a strong commendation of the plan which the diocese is following in erecting Nazareth Hall." The atmosphere would not only provide an environment for growth in spirituality, but "in the teaching and the study of the Latin language 'which we can almost call a Catholic tongue.'"[20] It would also provide "the means for poor boys of good talent and from good homes to study in preparatory seminaries, either from their own resources or by direct solicitation from the charitably disposed laity."[21]

Dowling had decided to build the preparatory seminary on property on Lake Johanna, north of St. Paul, forty acres of which had been purchased for $800 in 1866 by Ireland's predecessor, Archbishop Thomas Langdon Grace.[22] The institution, which became known as Nazareth Hall, was Dowling's pride and joy. It opened on September 12, 1923, and was an impressive structure with an imposing square tower providing accommodations for two hundred students. Over three hundred could worship in the artistically designed chapel. Reardon described Dowling's relationship to the school:

> Nazareth Hall was the apple of his eye and woe betide the priest or layman who dared to utter an uncomplimentary syllable about the institution, its architecture, location, purpose, faculty, or product. Every other institution in the diocese was a step-child, seldom visited except officially. At Nazareth Hall a suite of well-furnished rooms was set apart for him to which he retired from time to time to rest and recuperate and breathe the invigorating suburban air.[23]

The impact of the establishment of Nazareth Hall was felt no place more than at the College of St. Thomas. The college found it difficult to sustain the effects of the withdrawal of the minor seminary from its campus on enrollment, scholarship funds, physical resources, and even alumni support.[24] Nazareth Hall received the largest portion from the Archbishop Ireland fund, and the college's hopes to construct needed new buildings were dashed.

St. Thomas fell on hard times in the 1920s,[25] but in the eyes of many priests in the archdiocese nothing warranted Dowling's invitation to the Holy Cross Congregation of Notre Dame, Indiana, to take over the administration of the College of St. Thomas for a five-year period beginning in 1928. Archbishop Ireland had specifically stipulated in a letter of August 30, 1894, which had been included in the minutes of the board of trustees of the College of St. Thomas, that the college should never come under the control of a religious order.[26] From the presumed perspective of the deceased archbishop, the only thing that would have made Dowling's decision worse would have been had he invited the Jesuits!

Dowling's rationale was that there simply were not enough priests to staff the Saint Paul Seminary, Nazareth Hall, and the College of St. Thomas. The fact that the transfer to a Holy Cross administration had been effected with great secrecy added salt to the wounds of many of the priests of the archdiocese who were alumni of the college. The archbishop clearly saw the decision as a matter of life or death for St. Thomas.[27]

Dowling's Influence on the Saint Paul Seminary

The establishment of Nazareth Hall certainly had an impact on the Saint Paul Seminary. Thereafter, the majority of the students would be prepared in a cloistered environment, which Dowling believed was more appropriate than a college campus. In his sermon at the Sulpician Seminary in 1919 Dowling had stated:

> The foundation-stone of the seminary, then, is the upbuilding of the spiritual life in the long novitiate and under the semi-monastic regimen of the Tridentine regulations.... The priest of the future... should be armed as never before to meet the errors

> and to overcome the temptations of the times. He should, first, be grounded on the firm foundation of the interior life and schooled in the practice of priestly virtues.

Dowling admitted that courses of study had changed to meet the needs of the day, but regarding seminaries, he underscored, "their spirit has not changed. They are still, as in the beginning, *the walled garden in which the heavenly Sower sows the seeds of priestly virtue, of divine truth, of pastoral zeal.*"[28]

Dowling, the educator, was not satisfied, however, that those preparing for priesthood would imbibe only piety and devotionalism. He also believed in the rigors of academic challenge. Just as Ireland's experience at Meximieux had colored his vision of seminary training, so, too, Dowling's years at Brighton had influenced his vision of education for priesthood as intellectually rigorous and demanding scholarly seriousness. No one had an impact on his training comparable to that of the famous Sulpician John B. Hogan, the first rector of St. John's. Shortly after Hogan's death, Dowling wrote a tribute which, perhaps, says as much about Dowling and his vision of seminary education as it does about Hogan. It is worthy of the following lengthy quotation:

> He was forever whetting the appetite for knowledge, challenging the impatient, prodding the slow. His method was the same, whether we met him in class or on a walk or in his room. It was his business to set us thinking—an occupation which he would never admit was highly superfluous in the life of a priest. Often he would seem to go to the very limit of daring in the vigor with which he plied us with objections, annihilated all our arguments and then walked off without vouchsafing an answer to our difficulties.
>
> But, sure of his own faith, he had no fear for ours, while he did fear the vicious effect of smug satisfaction which a boy may feel—and never afterwards lose—in dealing flippantly with the grave problem of thought....
>
> No doubt, at times, this fine temper of his mind left him open to misunderstanding and exposed him to the suspicion of being a "liberal," and liberal he was if by liberty we mean freedom from narrowness and pettiness and the fussiness of those

> who are always in terror, nor did he think that truth had anything to fear from investigation. It was, perhaps, his childlike faith so serene, so secure, so full of charity that made him so absolutely fearless of error that he always met it, not with strategy, but in faith and open fight.
>
> Not his least attractive feature was his characteristically youthful mind. It never aged. His experience widened; his knowledge increased; his powers were developed, but he still confronted the field of science with the frank curiosity of a child. His mind, like his heart, was always wide open.[29]

Accordingly, the archbishop was committed to a strong theological faculty. To accomplish that, he needed solid administrative leadership. In the summer of 1921 Dowling was ready to make some changes.

Humphrey Moynihan had left the Saint Paul Seminary faculty in 1903 to become rector/president of the College of St. Thomas. By 1919 Moynihan had encountered both personal and administrative difficulties, including salary disputes with lay faculty when only oral contracts were the order of the day. Also, Archbishop Ireland had apparently promoted Moynihan unsuccessfully to succeed Bishop McGolrick of Duluth who had died January 23, 1918. Ireland had been Moynihan's great mentor, and the archbishop's death soon thereafter was particularly painful for him. According to Connors, Humphrey Moynihan was, in the years after 1919, "a deeply fatigued man."[30]

The Reverend Francis J. Schaefer, who had spent almost eleven years as rector and twenty-seven years on the Saint Paul Seminary faculty, resigned his position in the summer of 1921. Archbishop Dowling, desirous of making a change at St. Thomas, appointed Humphrey Moynihan as rector of the Saint Paul Seminary, a role the priest would probably have cherished in earlier years. At the age of fifty-seven, he moved across the street to take on the challenge of administering the major seminary.

Humphrey Moynihan as rector is remembered by students as a quiet, gentle, white-haired individual, a priest of the "old school," a scholar who emphasized culture and refinement. According to some, his concept of being a good priest was to be a gentleman, aware of table manners and precise about language. The portrait presented is that of a dignified "old man" who critiqued the students' sermons before they preached them in the dining room at the evening meal.[31] One wonders how differently he would have approached the task twenty-five years earlier when he was passed over for vice-rector in 1896, and rector in 1897.

Tradition holds that Dowling's greatest contribution to the Saint Paul Seminary faculty was his invitation to "the three wise men from the East"—seminarians from Fall River, Massachusetts, studying in Washington, D.C. All three "followed the star" to St. Paul after ordination to join the major seminary faculty: William O. Brady taught moral theology from 1926 to 1933, was rector from 1933 to 1939, and was archbishop of St. Paul from 1956 to 1961; James L. Connolly, professor and spiritual director from 1929 to 1943, and rector from 1943 to 1945, was named coadjutor bishop of Fall River, Massachusetts, in 1945; and Francis J. Gilligan, who taught moral theology from 1928 to 1957, was nationally known for his efforts to eradicate racial prejudice and mediate labor disputes.

All three of these men had been trained by the Sulpicians at St. Mary's Seminary in Baltimore (philosophy) and the Sulpician Seminary in Washington, D.C. (theology). That tradition, which was known to be rather rigorous, became dominant at the Saint Paul Seminary. The impression of some of the students, including T. Kenneth Ryan, was that "the easterners" thought of themselves as socially superior. Charles Eg-

Humphrey Moynihan, rector of the Saint Paul Seminary from 1921 to 1933

gert is more pointed, noting that there were times when he felt the students were treated like "theological hillbillies."[32]

Other faculty in the Dowling era included Father William Busch, who had excellent insights regarding the liturgy and who encouraged T. K. Ryan to write some articles for the newly founded journal *Orate Fratres* published at St. John's University in Collegeville;[33] and Father Jeremiah C. Harrington, a follower of Msgr. John A. Ryan. Father Harrington was apparently at the eye of a storm in the spring of 1926. A memo in the chancery archives signed by five students stated:

> We the undersigned students of Father Harrington's class deny the truth of the charge that Father Harrington denounced the Archbishop in class. We on the contrary have heard Father Harrington time and again read and refer to the Archbishop's public utterances in terms of highest praise. The specific charge that Father Harrington said that the Archbishop had not read a theology book in ten years is a pure fabrication.[34]

Rumors regarding faculty orthodoxy and/or appropriate commentary were apparently not uncommon in the 1920s, or in any period in seminary history.

Archbishop Dowling's personal interest in the seminarians was obvious from early on. Msgr. Humphrey Moynihan, while rector of the Saint Paul Seminary, wrote to a friend in 1927: "The Archbishop . . . has a keen eye for every promising candidate for the priesthood." He claimed that Dowling knew many of the boys at Nazareth Hall as well as their teachers knew them, and the relationships he established continued to influence their lives at Saint Paul Seminary, to ordination and beyond.[35]

Moynihan wrote of the archbishop's many visits to the Saint Paul Seminary. Frequently on Sundays he would join the seminary community for a meeting of the Thomas L. Grace Literary Society or some other group in the *aula maxima,* listen to papers prepared by the students, and offer his comments. His gentle, kindly approach was appreciated.[36] Moynihan commented: "He was casting around for promising young men and sending them to the best universities."[37]

Student Life after a Quarter Century

T. Kenneth Ryan's recollections of student life were vivid, even at the age of ninety-three. He remembered Father "Billy" Busch trying to counteract the cultural vacuum at the seminary by announcing that there would be a "concert" after supper. They would gather to hear some classical music on the Victrola. However, because it was immediately after supper, many would fall asleep. In his second year, Kenneth Ryan was sacristan. One of his tasks was to turn off the master switch at 10:00 P.M. so that all the lights in the residence hall would be extinguished until he turned the switch on again at 5:25 A.M. when the rising bell was rung. However, as sacristan he would save the old candle stubs and get a big bowl and a wick that he would light, so he could read another hour after lights out. In retrospect, he wondered whatever would have happened had there been a fire and no lights to allow them to exit the buildings.[38]

Daily Mass was in the oratories in each residence hall. Seminarians wore cassocks and surplices to the Eucharist. There was silence for breakfast with a brief break after, followed typically by four classes in the morning and two in the afternoon. Ryan's recollection was that it was like being in the army. The classes were straight lectures, rarely in Latin—although textbooks were in Latin. Students took notes, but never asked questions. Extreme deference toward professors was the order of the day. One rarely got advice on how to study or develop one's own gifts or talents. Dinner was served at noon, and after a brief reading from *The Imitation of Christ,* a book was selected for table reading. Ryan particularly remembers a volume entitled *Now I See* by the famous British convert Arnold Lunn.

The spiritual life of the seminary followed the pattern set in previous years—regular prayers at morning and night, Particular Examen just before noon, rosary every day in the *aula* after the spiritual director's conference. Father James H. ("Harry") Prendergast was named spiritual director by Dowling on August 9, 1921, and the impression was that the archbishop appointed him because he was loyal and supportive in terms of the financial needs of the archdiocese.[39] Interestingly, Dowling wrote to Prendergast in December 1920 to thank him for his zeal and cooperation "which has brought it about that St. Canice's is the first parish which as a parish has pledged itself to provide the fund for a Burse in the Preparatory Seminary."[40]

The following August, Dowling wrote to Prendergast stating that "it is about time for the change of which we have already spoken to take place." He added:

> The work you are about to undertake in the Seminary is most important and will require considerable preparation. You will find I think in Dr. Moynihan a sympathetic counsellor and of course my door and my heart are always open to you. The conferences are only a part of your work. I think you can gain the confidence of the young men and become an inspiration to them.[41]

Prendergast is remembered as cordial and friendly, but not very adept when it came to spiritual direction.[42] James L. Connelly, one of "the wise men from the East," succeeded him as spiritual director in 1929.

May devotions included the opportunity for the seminarians to honor Mary in the ever-developing grotto. One of the seminarians, Pius Mutter, with the help of his friends built a stone bridge across the stream in the grotto area.[43] The seminarians gathered after dinner in May and on special feast days to sing the "Salve Regina" or an appropriate liturgical hymn.

Off-campus days continued to be Wednesday and Saturday from after dinner to 3:00 P.M.—and once a month it was extended to 4:00 P.M. Archbishop Ireland's 1908 "Rules of the Seminary" were still in effect in the 1920s. They expressly stated that "visiting theatres or unbecoming places, will be punished with immediate dismissal."[44] T. Kenneth Ryan confessed, however, that on one occasion he risked his future at the seminary by attending "The Beggar's Opera" in downtown St. Paul. He got someone to sign in for him and was back by 5:00 P.M. He was thrilled by the production and recalled it as "a wonderful piece of knowledge."[45]

As in previous years, the rector invited notable lecturers to the seminary to share their insights with the students, who were not allowed to go even across the street to a lecture at St. Thomas. Among these invited lecturers was Cardinal Michael Faulhaber, archbishop of Munich, who visited the seminary on May 17, 1923.[46] Other luminaries who lectured at the seminary in the decade of the 1920s included Eamon De Valera, president-elect of the Irish Republic, and such scholars as Theodore Maynard, Frank J. Sheed, and James J. Walsh. In addition, seminary alumni John A. Ryan and Edwin O'Hara presented lectures to the students, usually on topics of social concern.[47]

These lectures were not without practical consequences. One of the most important groups at the seminary in the 1920s and 1930s was the Mission Society. Seminarians taught catechism at Twin City mission churches on Sundays of the academic year. They received special preparation for their work, including a course in catechetics. Some 750 children were taught in four missions. In 1925 the Mission Society became involved with the Summer Vacation School Movement—a project of alumnus Edwin O'Hara, founder of the National Catholic Rural Life Conference. As of 1930, four students were Summer Vacation School Catechists and taught in eight states.[48] Moderator of the Mission Society was the Reverend Rudolph Bandas, future rector, and an authority on catechetics.

For many years the seminarians went home for the Christmas holidays, but in 1928 the faculty decided that the students should stay at the seminary during that time to celebrate the feasts in the more cloistered environment. Instead they were given two weeks off at the end of the semester, beginning January 25, the feast of the Conversion of Saint Paul. At noon on that day, after the liturgical celebration, they could breathe the air of the outside world for a fortnight.[49] Likewise, summers were a time to live at home and be temporarily employed. Most important, it was an opportunity to connect again with one's family.

The Changing Climate of Seminary Formation

Pius XI, who became pope in 1922, was a scholar himself and was concerned about the quality of seminary education. In 1923, in the encyclical *Studiorum Ducem,* he reaffirmed the importance of Thomistic philosophy and theology, especially in the seminary. In 1924, in the *motu proprio Bibliorum scientiam,* he required that all scripture professors in major seminaries have degrees from the Pontifical Biblical Institute or the Pontifical Biblical Commission. The Sacred Congregation of Seminaries and Universities issued a letter entitled *Ad Regnum* in 1926, which mandated that a course in catechetics be taught in the seminary. All of these directives strengthened the seminary curriculum, but they also tightened the authority of the Holy See over diocesan seminaries.[50]

Most specific to this oversight was the decree *Quo Uberiore* of the Sacred Congregation of Seminaries and Universities issued on February 2, 1924. This required that all bishops submit triennial reports on seminaries within their dioceses. Printed questionnaires were sent out and seminary officials were expected to provide information on enrollment, course offerings, textbooks, the faculty and their qualifications, and the extracurricular activities of seminarians. The timetable for submission of reports was designated by continents. Triennial reports from the United States were due in 1927. The completed information was sent to the apostolic delegate, Archbishop Pietro Fumasoni-Biondi.[51]

It was the task of the apostolic delegate to compose a report on the seminaries of the United States from the questionnaires and from his five years of observation of the institutions. The report, together with the questionnaires, was sent to the Sacred Congregation of Seminaries and Universities. The Cardinals of the congregation issued a letter May 26, 1928, "expressing their reactions and making recommendations" over the signature of Archbishop Fumasoni-Biondi.[52]

The letter was specific in its concerns: (1) Minor seminaries that operated as day schools were to become boarding schools "where students resided day and night under the watchful care of responsible Superiors." (2) The role of the spiritual director was to be enhanced. (3) Rectors were to be selected who possessed the qualifications set down in Canon 1360. (4) Exaggerated importance should not be given to athletics, especially games with other schools. (5) Christian modesty should be observed in matters of hygiene, especially in bathing arrangements. (6) The whole deposit of faith must be presented in a scientific and orderly manner. (7) Latin, the "Catholic language," must be taught, learned, used, and studied with particular zeal. "Their Eminences . . . insist that the lectures on philosophy, theology, and canon law, as well as the recitations in the same subjects, be held in the Latin language." In addition, all examinations must be held in Latin. (8) The study of canon law should be given a more important place in the curriculum.[53]

Archbishop Dowling was no stranger to the apostolic delegate and knew that Archbishop Fumasoni-Biondi had an appreciation of his vision of education for priesthood. In fact, after the dedication of the new seminary in Cleveland at which Dowling gave the sermon, the apostolic delegate wrote:

> Your Grace's clear delineation of the essential requirements in the priest of our day and your emphasis of the seminary's obligation to provide the Church in America with priests of piety, culture and zeal merit the highest commendation and command the attention of all who are charged with responsibility for the priest of tomorrow.[54]

Dowling, however, differed with the Sacred Congregation in their requirements regarding the teaching of classes in Latin. That had not been the practice since the opening of the Saint Paul Seminary. It was not Archbishop Ireland's Americanist approach, nor did it serve Dowling's vision. When Dowling learned of a visit from Fumasoni-Biondi in the fall of 1928, he must have realized this point of vulnerability.

Father T. Kenneth Ryan remembers Fumasoni-Biondi's visit well. As a student Ryan was in charge of reading at meals. Part of the assignment was to choose a brief scripture text and check it with Msgr. Moynihan ahead of time. On the special occasion of the dinner with the apostolic delegate Ryan selected: "Be ye therefore perfect..." (Matthew 5:48). When he approached the rector for approval, Moynihan laughed out loud, something he did only on rare occasions.[55]

After dinner, Archbishop Dowling, Archbishop Fumasoni-Biondi, Msgr. Moynihan, and some of the faculty gathered in the rector's office before the evening's activities began. According to Father Lawrence O. Wolf, a faculty member at the time, the question of teaching classes in Latin was raised. Fumasoni-Biondi was surprised that such was not the case at the Saint Paul Seminary. Archbishop Dowling stated very directly, to the surprise of many in the room, that it would happen only over his dead body![56]

After dinner, a reception was held in the *aula maxima* at which the Reverend Alphonse J. Schladweiler greeted the apostolic delegate in the name of the seminary in a *Latin* address. Archbishop Dowling then welcomed the delegate in the name of the priests of the archdiocese. A paper on the history of the seminary was presented by one of the students, Thomas J. Shanahan. His Excellency's response "dwelt on the possibilities of America as a mission field, on the place of the Latin tongue as the language of the Church and of her prayer, and on the need of piety as well as learning in a seminary."[57] Dowling had his way, however; courses continued to be taught in English at the Saint Paul Seminary.

Enrollment at the seminary varied only slightly. The decade began (1919–1920) with 214 students, and ended (1929–1930) with 224. Humphrey Moynihan wrote to Clara Hill Lindley, daughter of James J. and Mary Hill, in 1927: "You will be pleased to hear that we have had a very good year at the Seminary. I think the standard is rising year after year. Next September we shall not be able to accommodate all who will apply."[58] On June 26, 1928, he reported to Mrs. Lindley that thirty-seven priests had been recently ordained, and added: "The number of ordinations in the Saint Paul Seminary will soon reach a thousand—that is, since its foundation."[59]

The Role of the Board of Trustees under Dowling

The role of the board became increasingly less important. As chair of the board, Dowling attended his first meeting on May 14, 1919. The principal areas of business were the listing of the faculty who would receive their salaries from the trust, the approval of the financial report for the past year, the election or re-election of board members, and raising the price of room, board, and tuition. Some meetings were called and not held for lack of a quorum. The most extraordinary business was the receipt of $200,000 for the seminary endowment from Mary T. Hill as discussed on August 2, 1920, but other than that the most noteworthy item was the allocation of funds to build "a garage for six cars for such Professors as have automobiles."[60]

The time between board meetings became more lengthy. There were only two meetings in 1922 and two in 1923. At the meeting on June 23, 1923, it was decided to hand over to the Archbishop Ireland Educational Fund a legacy of $6,000 bequeathed to the Saint Paul Seminary. It specified: "In making the transfer the trustees were influenced by the consideration that this action carried out the intention of the testator."[61] One wonders if it did not also comply with the wishes of the archbishop who was eager to complete Nazareth Hall for the coming fall semester.

With the opening of Nazareth Hall in 1923, the construction of a new chancery building at 244 Dayton Avenue in the same year, the preparation of the *Ad Limina* report,[62] plus other responsibilities, the Saint Paul Seminary does not seem to have been a priority for Dowling during this period. No board meeting was held between September 17, 1923, and November 19, 1924; there was another hiatus until October 7, 1925. At the one and only board of trustees meeting held in 1924, money was allocated for building a fire escape in the classroom building at a cost of $363.80.

The Establishment of a Sisters' College

Another event of the mid-1920s that involved the seminary and had a substantial effect on education in the archdiocese was the establishment of a "Sisters' College." With the death of Mary Hill, a variety of financial complications ensued for the Hill heirs. On August 4, 1925, the James J. Hill mansion at 240 Summit, across from the cathedral, was sold at public auction for approximately $100,000, a relatively small amount considering its worth of $500,000. It was purchased by Alvin Greenman, vice-president of Northwestern Trust Company—the organization that was the administrator of Hill's investments and properties.[63] The following day it was announced that the purchase had been made for four daughters of James J. Hill (Rachel Hill Boeckmann, Gertrude Hill Gavin, Clara Hill Lindley, and Ruth Hill Beard) who were transferring ownership "to the St. Paul archdiocese of the Catholic church."[64] There was speculation that it would become a center for social welfare work of the archdiocese.

Two weeks later it was announced: "The James J. Hill home, when renovated, will be converted into a normal training school for nuns."[65] This fulfilled another of Dowling's goals for education in the archdiocese. It was explained that the need to educate sisters teaching in the schools was usually met by sending them to summer school at secular universities, or Catholic colleges or universities at a distance.

The St. Paul Diocesan Normal Institute, as it would be known, opened on January 19, 1927, with three hundred nuns at the opening classes. It provided for "guest faculty"—mostly members of the seminary faculty—who would teach courses both during the summer and on

Saturdays during the academic year. In late 1926, Archbishop Dowling wrote to Clara Hill Lindley: "I am about to install two hundred desk chairs in the various rooms for a Saturday class which I intend to open shortly after the New Years. Several of the professors of the Seminary have consented to give these courses."[66]

The St. Paul *Dispatch* announced: "The institute will in time be affiliated with one of the regular archdiocesan colleges and degrees will be conferred." Dowling added that, although this venture was experimental, a fully equipped normal school was essential "because sisters are the empire builders of today."[67]

Father Humphrey Moynihan, who also corresponded with Clara Hill Lindley, reported on the "promising start" of "the Normal School." He wrote:

> Saturday classes have been in operation now for some weeks and six professors from the Seminary have been lecturing to three hundred Sisters. While we had no misgivings as to the spirit with which the nuns would enter upon their work, we had no idea of the eagerness and enthusiasm they have been showing. Even with the few courses now being given one can see what a blessing the school will be.[68]

Without the cooperation of Moynihan and the seminary faculty, the development of the Normal School would have been impossible.

The Completion of the Interior of St. Mary's Chapel

While Dowling, "the builder," seems to have neglected the Saint Paul Seminary in the earlier years, by 1925 his attention began to shift to St. Mary's Chapel. On June 2, 1925, Maginnis and Walsh, the Boston architects who were coordinating the decorations of the interior of Nazareth Hall and the Cathedral of St. Paul, wrote to Clarence H. Johnston, architect of St. Mary's Chapel: "We have been invited by Archbishop Dowling of St. Paul, for whom, as you know, we have done considerable professional work, to design certain furniture and appointments for the chapel of the major Seminary on Summit Avenue." The Boston architects stated: "We are solicitous not to come in conflict with your professional interest"—so they wished some word that they were not impinging on his territory.[69] This would appear to be the first indication of Dowling's desire to move ahead with the decoration of St. Mary's Chapel.

The chapel needed not only a beautiful interior, but beautiful music as well. The major business of the board of trustees meeting on December 15, 1925, was the procurement of a substantial organ for the Saint Paul Seminary Chapel. The minutes read: "His Grace Archbishop Dowling and the Rector of the seminary were requested to act as a committee for the selection of the organ for the seminary chapel at a cost not to exceed ten thousand dollars."[70]

There was another lapse of a year in meetings until December 26, 1926—again at 8:00 P.M. at the chancery. It would seem unusual to have a meeting the day after Christmas, but one can suppose that it was the annual meeting of the corporation and had to take place within the calendar year. The minutes of the meeting are prosaic; no mention is made of the chapel, nor is there any request for funds. However, the archbishop was moving ahead with improvements in the interior decoration. On December 11, 1926, he had written to Clara Hill Lindley:

> Doubtless you have heard of the work being done in the Seminary chapel. We are having the capitals carved and afterwards we shall put in new stalls and benches for the Professors and students. That with the installation of a new organ will be a great improvement. But you no sooner begin one thing than you need to do another. Already critical eyes are discovering the need of decoration while another derides the idea of doing anything before painting the building. As we have raised the pension of the students to $400 a year we are enabled to do these things better than formerly—a little every year.[71]

Humphrey Moynihan also wrote to Mrs. Lindley a week later describing "an old-fashioned Minnesota winter that swooped in some days ago, sending the mercury galloping down to nearly twenty below zero, and piling up enough snow for any ordinary winter." He then reported on the chapel—about half the capitals carved, the contract for the stalls in place. He wrote with delight: "Six months from now St. Mary's will be a real seminary chapel. You can imagine what it means to us. The

Archbishop with his fine ideas and good taste is leaving his impress upon everything."[72]

By March 29, 1927, the carving of the capitals was completed by Frank Leirich.[73] Dowling was eager to proceed further but admitted in December 1927: "The Seminary has the ambition to do something for its sanctuary but it will not begin to do anything until next summer."[74] However, on the Feast of the Conversion of St. Paul, January 25, 1928, Dowling could not contain himself any longer. He wrote to Maginnis and Walsh:

> Will you at this time, if you have not before, take up the matter of the St. Paul Seminary chapel and undertake such studies as will determine the development of the sanctuary along the lines of our previous conversation, and also the rest of the chapel. My wish is that, by June, everything will be decided, contracts let, and immediate operations begun as soon as the school year is over so that much may be done before school is resumed in early September.[75]

The necessity for raising money for the venture did not escape Dowling. In the spring of 1928 he wrote to the priests of the archdiocese, reminding them that he had discussed with them at the annual retreat the previous June the likelihood of decorating the interior of the seminary chapel. His request was very specific:

> As the diocesan Seminary chapel is peculiarly the possession of the priests and seminarians, for whom it is all but exclusively used, I feel that many of our priests would like to make a contribution to the cost of the erection of the altars. Roughly, we have placed that at about $20,000.[76]

He then added the suggestion that they send no less than $25.00 each, and if they couldn't send it immediately, they should notify him and send it in June.

At the annual retreat in June 1928, Dowling reminded the priests of their indebtedness for their seminary education. He reiterated this in a letter in July, hoping to dispel the notion that life insurance policies would satisfy the debt unless "this insurance is ample enough to include the interest charges over a long period of years." More ominous was his statement: "On the occasion of the last retreat, I called your attention to the prejudice which a neglect of this obligation might cause in the advancement of priests to occupations involving administrative capacity."[77] One wonders if Dowling's desire to finish the chapel decor did not enhance the pressure he was putting on the priests, most of whom were alumni of the Saint Paul Seminary.

A special meeting of the board of trustees was finally called for July 13, 1928, at which the archbishop explained his plans "to complete the adornment of St. Mary's Chapel." Plans were submitted for the painting of the chapel and the installation of stained-glass windows. The estimates were $11,600 for the decorative painting and $12,500 for the windows. "It was resolved that contracts for the decoration of the chapel be left in the hands of Archbishop Dowling and Messrs. Maginnis and Walsh of Boston."[78]

James J. Hill had been notorious for micro-managing the construction of the first six buildings of the Saint Paul Seminary, but he might have found a rival in Austin Dowling, whose oversight of the decoration of St. Mary's Chapel was meticulous. The archbishop kept track of minute details and made decisions regarding every item under consideration. If the arrangement between James J. Hill and Cass Gilbert had often been antagonistic, Dowling's relationship to Bancel La Farge—the artistic designer for the chapel—was just the opposite.

Dowling and La Farge had known each other from childhood. The La Farges were a wealthy New England family who counted among their ancestors Benjamin Franklin and Commodore Oliver Hazard Perry, famous naval officer in the War of 1812. In the spring of 1859 in Newport, Rhode Island, William and Henry James introduced Perry's granddaughter—Margaret Mason Perry—to their friend John La Farge. Although she was from a prestigious Protestant family and he was a Catholic, their relationship blossomed and they were married on October 15, 1860. She was received into the Catholic Church shortly thereafter by Father Isaac Hecker, founder of the Paulist Fathers and a frequent visitor in the La Farge home.

Both John La Farge and his son Bancel were trained in France and Italy for their artistic careers, and—in addition to working in oils, mosaics, watercolors, and pastels—made significant contributions in the area of stained glass. Henry Adams wrote of his friend John: "La Farge alone could use glass like a thirteenth-century artist."[79] Both father and son were meticulous craftsmen.

Bancel's brother, John, joined the Jesuits and was well known in literary circles as well as for his commitment to social justice.[80] John La Farge, S.J., reflected in his later years on the relationship of Archbishop Dowling and his brother Bancel:

> Dowling . . . as a child had been a next-door neighbor of ours in Newport. Archbishop Dowling took a great interest in my brother Bancel, the mural painter, and invited him out to Saint Paul where he did some work, along with his son Tom, on the Cathedral and on the chapel of Saint Paul Seminary.
>
> Bancel became extremely fond of Archbishop Dowling, and the Archbishop's influence had much to do in strengthening Bancel's faith and enlightening him as to the liturgical program of the Church.[81]

What the Jesuit failed to mention was that Austin Dowling was the son of the butler in the mansion next door and as a youth had been befriended by Bancel, the young gentleman of means.[82] In later years, it was the archbishop who opened his home to Bancel and his son Tom on their trips to St. Paul.

The extensive correspondence of Archbishop Dowling, Maginnis and Walsh, and Bancel La Farge on the decoration of the chapel offers a blow-by-blow description of the progress. It is clear that Dowling wanted the very best, and he wanted it done immediately. He discovered it would take longer than anticipated. At one point he reflected: "I find myself faced with problems that have suddenly become actual. We are backing into the job like a cat that is being brought in by the tail!"[83]

There was dialogue with the faculty. Dowling admitted that he was "trying to induce the Seminary faculty to do away with the organ console on the floor and to make use of the console in the loft. To retain the console in the aisle will mar the finished decoration."[84] One suspects that Father Missia, the choir director, was especially concerned about this issue.

In a letter the following November, Dowling referred to "your reactions to Father Ziskovsky's criticisms of the altar plans." Almost defensively Dowling stated: "I am most anxious that this altar, situated in a major Seminary and therefore a typical altar, should be above criticism and I have invited suggestions from the gentlemen at the Seminary not now for the first time but rather for some months back."[85] Concessions were made to lengthen the predella and to enlarge the altar table by two inches.

A concern was the covering of the crucifix during benediction. Dowling stated: "I am disposed not to lay much stress on the elevated throne for Benediction. When it is sufficiently elevated then the complaint is made that the Sanctuary lamp conceals the exposition." In discussing the tabernacle, Dowling reminded them that there must be some kind of a cover over it, "perhaps partly hiding and partly displaying its workmanship." It was clear that the archbishop felt reprimanded regarding the tabernacle at his beloved minor seminary. "The absence of a cover at Nazareth qualified the Apostolic Delegate's full satisfaction with our lovely altar. Some of these things make me sick."[86] One of the more blunt comments of his episcopate.

It was the rector who gave the suggestions for the dedications for the four side oratories: St. Lawrence the Deacon, St. Thomas Aquinas, St. Francis de Sales, and St. John Vianney.[87] The subject for the stone carving over the main entrance, however, was Dowling's choice: the Annunciation.[88] Dowling was very pleased with the carving on the front portal, but was surprised when he saw the "two models for the tympana" over the side doors. "One of those models is a cartouche of the Pope's coat of arms sustained by two adoring angels. Our reputation as idolators would be maintained if we permitted this to be executed."[89] When the papal coat of arms does appear it is without the adoring angels.

The stations of the cross became a major area of dispute. Dowling asked Humphrey Moynihan to discuss them with the faculty, who suggested "a modelled design sunk into the wall" as at Nazareth Hall. Dowling explained why he thought that could not be done.[90] In May 1929, Moynihan reported that the faculty liked the Rambusch station design and the suggestion of enamel "but do not like the location, for they wish to have the stations on the side walls rather than on the columns." He explained that when the students make the stations as a group they turn toward each station. "Nobody could see the face of the station if it is attached to the column."[91] Apparently the original proposal was that they be on the inside of the columns facing the windows.

Rambusch, after a visit to the chapel, proposed that the stations be hung ten feet high on the sides of the columns above the choir stalls in full view of everybody. The rector had no objection, nor did Dowling, so the matter was finally settled.[92] A few weeks later Dowling wrote to Maginnis and Walsh and stated: "I am glad that the Stations will hang their escutcheons in the very vizards of the critics. I am in no hurry about them."[93]

T. Kenneth Ryan remembered "the altar crisis" and the fact that after it was installed it was discovered to be the wrong marble and had to be replaced.[94] Dowling said in a letter to La Farge in June 1929: "The altar that was installed was in fact red Morocco instead of Algerian onyx. Seeing it, I was surprised that so vivid a red should be juxtaposed to the red Numidian and set upon so delicate a floor. On discovering their error the marble people undertook to supply the correct marble."[95]

One of the most striking areas of the chapel design was the plan for the windows. La Farge's stained glass was particularly creative. He "refined the practice of deep-toned opalescence introduced by his father." This phenomenon has been described as follows: "The opaque particles in opalescent glass scatter the light, so as to create different levels of transparency within the same pane of glass. The resulting three-dimensional effect, though subtle, is quite real and highly dramatic."[96] In a letter to Dowling, La Farge explains: "In the clerestory windows I expect to eliminate some of the crosses shown in the present designs, but I would like to keep the one in the lower window (#2 from the left). The lower windows would be very rich and upper ones quite light in color."[97] The effect of lightness in the upper portion of the chapel, and the depth of the hues of the lower windows, especially when the sun illuminates them from the east in the morning and the west in the afternoon, provides a sense of radiance in St. Mary's Chapel to this day.[98] These, in addition to the rose window on the north end of the nave, create a warmth and richness of color conducive to prayer.

The other area in which La Farge distinguished himself in the chapel decor was in the paintings of the side altars and in the semidome of the apse, originally over the high altar. La Farge did these paintings on canvas in his studio in New Haven, Connecticut and then shipped them to St. Paul to be affixed to the walls. Dialogue with Dowling on the nature of the paintings was accomplished largely by correspondence. In these areas, Dowling's theology comes to the fore. In discussing the chapels of the Blessed Virgin and St. Joseph, the archbishop wrote:

> These shallow chapels . . . , you have seen by the architect's drawing, have no tabernacles or pedestals but have left an adequate space for paintings. The purpose of the chapel is entirely devotional—the treatment of that painting must be quite the same. It is to be the Regina Cleri, the Queen of the Clergy, that the students' thought must turn. Her function was as theirs, the guardian of the Body and Blood of Christ. For them she is not in the tragic mood of Calvary but Christ's familiar, elate [sic], mystic, so one with her Divine Son that she has love and pity and prayer for men as priests should have.

He then describes his vision for the painting of Joseph, and adds: "In both chapels development of the theme lends itself to a deeply religious and I was going to say emotional appeal to young fervors."[99]

By the end of March, La Farge had sent "the two cartoons of Our Blessed Lady and St. Joseph, designed for the Altarpieces of the Seminary." Dowling's response to Maginnis and Walsh is perceptive: "I do not see much the matter with them, save in details. I feel like tempering the trancelike gaze of Our Lady. The act of blessing is perfectly correct theologically but very unusual in art. It represents authority priesthood [sic] which I think is what Mr. L. had in mind. The hand & rosary are hard for me to swallow." Dowling adds: "St. Joseph's posture seems to be too graceful. . . . Should he face his clients or seem to walk away from them? I leave the matter in your capable hands." He concludes by stating that he agrees to pay $1,500 apiece for the two paintings.[100] The painting of Mary as finally affixed to the chapel wall presents her in quiet meditation, eyes closed, hand over her heart. She wears a flowing gown and her head is surrounded by a halo. The rosary is missing!

The most extraordinary challenge for La Farge was painting the apse—the semi-dome over the altar.[101] Instinctively, the artist knew that project required reflection and meditation. He wrote to Dowling on February 13, 1929: "There is much to say about the painting for the tympanum which I won't undertake now. As it is a serious undertaking I have wished to put all the other work off my hands before starting very definitely on it."[102]

Earlier La Farge had received an inspirational letter from Dowling in which the archbishop described the theme he had chosen for this central mural—the post-resurrection appearance of Jesus to the apostles on the seashore as described in John 21: the famous question, "Do you love me?" and Peter's answer, "Lord, You know everything. You know that I love You," followed by the commission of the Risen Christ: "Feed my lambs. Feed my sheep." Dowling described the scene further:

> To read the chapter is to get the "compositio loce." The grey dawn on the seashore, the seven fishermen and Christ asking for food. Their empty nets which Christ fills and filling, reveals himself. They find Him in their daily food. They come to shore, Peter the first, half clad and Christ feeds them—the glowing embers, the fish, the bread and when they are fed, the remembered words he spoke. No vengeance for his death, no reproach for Peter's treason, the only echo of the trial room in the thrice repeated question, Lovest thou me? Thrice he confessed and this time did not deny that he loved Christ and thus received his charge to feed the lambs, to feed the sheep.

Why did Dowling think this the most important theme for a mural over the high altar in the seminary chapel?

> So priests become Christ's men not because they are stainless, not because they are wise but because they have grace to love Christ and in the love of Christ they feed—not shear—the sheep. Is this then paintable? I know it has been painted but can it be done to carry to others the meaning it has for me?[103]

La Farge took Dowling's reflections seriously. "Your splendid letter giving me your conception of the subject remains as the basis of my ideas for its treatment. So I am proceeding in that direction."[104] About three weeks later on February 13, 1929, La Farge informed the archbishop that he was taking a hurried trip to Munich, but the painting for the apse of St. Mary's Chapel would not be far from his thoughts. He wrote: "I keep rereading your splendid conception of the subject and with this in my pocket I hope to refresh my... jaded artistic spirit in this short time I will have on the other side."[105]

Dowling was not the only one with inspirational thoughts regarding the apse. In a letter to Maginnis and Walsh on May 11, 1929, Dowling wrote: "Yesterday I trembled listening to a proposition of Father Busch to deal with this surface from the point of view of abstract art. Please God if that should ever be done, I may not be around to see it."[106] In somewhat more restrained terms he shared the following with Bancel La Farge:

> I wrote Mr. Maginnis recently that one of the gentlemen of the Seminary faculty had spoken to me in the interest of treating the apsidal half dome surface with a design along the lines of abstract art. As I gathered from his presentation of it, it found its expression in some glorified hoops with mystic woods at strategic points giving a key to the offertory consecration and communion of the Mass. I probably did not give the plan the consideration it deserved.[107]

La Farge came to St. Paul in August 1929 to supervise the installation of the canvases for the face and soffit of the great arch, and to inspect the placement of the windows. Upon his return, La Farge wrote to express his gratitude: "My delightful stay with you was most beneficial, so that I feel I have profited very much by it. The calm of mind and spirit which I always experience when I am with you means much to me. For this and for your lavish hospitality I am deeply grateful."[108]

Dowling preferred to make decisions regarding the artistic decor of the seminary chapel, but the stock market crash of October 1929 had its repercussions. The seminarians were largely oblivious to it. Most of the families of the seminarians were not wealthy, so it seemed to have little direct impact. However, at five board meetings in 1930 the major discussion was dealing with real estate "acquired for the Seminary account through mortgage foreclosure." The Northwestern Trust Company as trustee for the seminary was requested to take over the responsibility.[109] At the last meeting of the trustees at which Dowling was present, September 19, 1930, the primary conversation was on the "proposals from the Northwestern Trust Company for the sale of the Coulter farm and the Henry Linn farm on which the mortgages had been foreclosed." The proposals were declined as "not sufficiently favorable." At the same meeting "William H. Egan reported on the results of his investigation of six farms on which mortgages held by the Seminary had been foreclosed."[110] The contrast between the life of the seminary and Dowling's immersion in the almost ethereal decor of the chapel and his involvement with the painful processes of mortgage foreclosure during the Great Depression is striking.

Bancel La Farge returned to St. Paul in May 1930 to oversee the installation of more canvases and further work with the decor. On August 9, 1930, La Farge wrote to Dowling regarding the apse: "I am sending you some tentative sketches for the half-dome of St. Paul's Seminary." He explained that he had done other sketches but found them unsatisfactory. The sketches included different color schemes, some with the central figure of Christ in different positions.[111] He was eager for a response from the archbishop.

Archbishop Dowling's Final Days

Dowling never saw the completion of the great painting for the semidome for which he had provided the inspiration. In the fall of 1930 he had what was described as "a very severe crisis of the heart."[112] But La Farge and his task were never far from his thoughts. On November 13, 1930, two weeks before he died, the archbishop had his secretary, Father Francis Schenck, write to La Farge about the financial arrangements regarding the chapel:

> In such a frame of mind his thoughts are constantly bent upon the things that he has left unfinished. Naturally his mind turns to the Seminary Chapel and the great painting you are preparing for the Sanctuary. He has not the least idea of disturbing you in your work or asking you to hasten or to qualify in any way the things he considers you are doing so satisfactorily. The burden of his thoughts, however, turn [sic] to a more prosaic phase of the situation and he wanted me to say how deeply interested he is in being able to complete the financial side of this work in his lifetime. He does not wish you to be exposed to any misunderstanding or any questioning as to the payment of the work.

Dowling, probably not realizing that his death was imminent, hoped it would be possible for La Farge to accelerate his work so that it could be completed in the archbishop's lifetime. Acknowledging the labor of love which the chapel had been for La Farge, the secretary added:

St. Mary's Chapel in the 1930s

> He does not wish to convey to you that there would be any disposition on the part of anybody to quarrel with the situation as it is *but he realizes that both you and he are perhaps less exacting about business methods than good judgment requires.* And your work at the Seminary has been so satisfactory that he does not wish you to be exposed to the slightest annoyance.[113]

Dowling died on November 29, 1930. The mural was finally affixed to the wall of the apse in the 1932–1933 academic year. Despite all the changes in the renovation of the chapel in the 1980s and 1990s, the mural continues to be the one artistic piece that all members of the seminary community since 1932 can use as a reference point in reflecting on their relationship to the institution and their commitment to ministry.

Dowling's health had been failing for some time. The most explicit admission of his illness was in a long letter to Clara Hill Lindley on

March 15, 1928. He was in residence at the Kahler Hotel in Rochester, having tests and receiving treatment at the Mayo Clinic for high blood pressure and a heart condition.[114] Lindley, who had been very generous to the seminary[115] and was close to the archbishop over the years, was apparently one of his few confidantes. Dowling wrote to her on April 11, 1928: "Many thanks for the lovely roses which came to me from you for Easter. They are still flourishing and inviting me to think of your precious friendship."[116] He continued to attend meetings in Washington, D.C., and announced that he would visit her in New York. In December 1928 he wrote: "I plod along, slipping into old age with as much grace or as little disgrace as I can manage."[117]

After Dowling's death his childhood friend, Bancel La Farge, who would ultimately fulfill Dowling's goal of a completed St. Mary's Chapel, wrote: "Besides being the great personality by which he was distinguished, he was the dearest friend one could have, so that I treasure now the memory of my ties with him."[118]

Humphrey Moynihan's letters to Clara Hill Lindley at the time of Dowling's death perhaps best describe the archbishop's relationship to the seminary. The rector stated: "In his own quiet way he did a great deal for the seminary in particular."[119] Later he wrote: "The Archbishop almost made himself one of us—we almost forgot that he was our Archbishop when he was in the midst of us."[120]

The obituary in the *Register*, probably written by the rector based on the eulogy given at one of the funeral liturgies, referred to Dowling's spiritual conferences to the seminarians. It stated: "By them he sought to mould in the souls of seminarians priestly convictions, priestly attitudes, priestly sympathies, unmasking with rare deftness the folly of worldliness and instilling a repugnance for softness into those who aspired to follow in the footsteps of Christ." Dowling's love for education and the intellectual life was not forgotten. The obituary continued:

> And while the Archbishop strove to deepen and enrich the spirit of holiness in the seminarians he strove with no less zeal to foster in them a love of learning.... Spiritual leadership, he always held, must be enhanced by intellectual leadership, if the Church is to be truly effective in its great mission to teach and sanctify the world.[121]

The last ordination at which Archbishop Dowling officiated less than six months before his death was held on June 9, 1930, not in St. Mary's Chapel on the Saint Paul Seminary campus, but in the Cathedral of St. Paul. Twenty young men were ordained priests, thirteen for the Archdiocese of St. Paul. Among them were members of the first graduating class of Nazareth Hall. Ordinations, he believed, should be a cause for celebration not just for families, faculty, and friends, but for the entire archdiocese. He saw preparation for priesthood, and training of religious and lay persons for teaching and social work, as part of the larger educational challenge. Dowling believed solid education for priesthood was crucial and a strong Saint Paul Seminary would ensure a vibrant faith in the Midwest for years to come.

Chapter 10

John Gregory Murray

Priesthood in the Era of "Catholic Action"

> The subject of the clergy conference for the week of May 12–19 in the usual deanery centers will be "Catholic Action" as set forth in the encyclicals of the last four popes. That each of the priests in the Archdiocese may have at least one treatise that attempts to make practical application of the principles contained in the encyclicals I am sending you by mail a copy of "Catholic Social Action" by Father Crofts, the Dominican.... The conference will not be limited to this particular treatment of the theme but will embrace the whole subject of Catholic Action in its application to the individual, the parish, and society at large.[1]
>
> Archbishop John Gregory Murray
> December 14, 1937

On October 29, 1931, exactly eleven months after the death of Archbishop Dowling, John Gregory Murray, "the popular, dynamic little bishop of Portland, Maine,"[2] was appointed to the See of St. Paul. Msgr. James C. Byrne, archdiocesan administrator, and Msgr. Humphrey Moynihan, rector of the Saint Paul Seminary, traveled to Portland to welcome their new ordinary to the West.

The January 27, 1932, issue of *Time* magazine described the installation of the new archbishop with its pomp and ceremony. The journalist reported that "three flights of pigeons encircled the Cathedral dome in bright sunlight during the episcopal procession and installation." Murray was described as "a genial prelate who was once a newsboy on the streets of Waterbury, Conn." He is reported to have said at the ceremony: "My feeble words fail to express the profound gratitude of my soul. I am as the great apostle himself, stricken dumb and blind on the way to Damascus.... I am dismayed at my own helplessness. I can only cry out with the Apostle of the Gentiles: 'Lord, what wilt thou have me do?'" On a personal note, Murray confided to the *Time* reporter that he preferred walking or trolley-riding to automobiling and added: "I do only the things I'm supposed to do, and then only at the last minute."[3]

Murray, like his three predecessors, was the son of Irish immigrants. He was born in Waterbury, Connecticut, on February 26, 1877, the son of William Murray of Carrickmacross, County Monaghan, and Mary Ellen Connor Murray of Maryborough, County Leix. He was educated in the Waterbury public schools, and always had a deep commitment to his home town, his parish, and his diocese. Upon graduation from Waterbury High School in 1895, John Gregory entered the Jesuit College of the Holy Cross in Worcester, Massachusetts, and graduated with a bachelor of arts in 1897. He was then sent to the American College in Louvain, Belgium, to complete his studies for the priesthood.[4] He was ordained a priest of the Hartford Diocese on April 11, 1900, and his love for Hartford never left him. According to James P. Shannon: "To the end he remained convinced that God had stood in the middle of Hartford and created the world."[5]

Murray's first assignment was as chaplain to the Hartford County Jail and professor of Greek, Latin, and German at St. Thomas Preparatory Seminary. The comparisons and contrasts between the two institutions must have proved instructive. One can conjecture as to whether his experience in Hartford impacted his attitude toward seminary education in later years.

In 1903 Murray was appointed chancellor of the diocese and resided in the bishop's house—even after he was consecrated auxiliary bishop in 1920. In 1922 he became pastor of St. Patrick's Church in Hartford and lived there, his only parish experience in fifty-six years of priesthood. In 1925 he was appointed bishop of Portland, Maine. Murray was an organizer and a builder, as were many of his brother bishops in that era. Thirty-one new parishes were organized during his episcopate in Maine. He was particularly committed to education. New schools were built, a superintendent of schools was appointed, a diocesan weekly newspaper was established.

On a national level, Murray was a founding member of the Catholic Historical Society (1919), and was active in the National Catholic Welfare Conference. His intelligence and capability were acknowledged in 1927 when he received an honorary doctor of sacred theology degree from his alma mater, the Catholic University of Louvain.[6]

The Depression of the 1930s had a significant impact on Catholic communities throughout the United States. There was a severe financial crisis in the diocese of Portland in 1931, and because it was a corporation sole with all the diocesan property held in the name of the bishop, the result was a diocese that was virtually bankrupt. John Gregory Murray phoned his friend, the Catholic millionairess Genevieve Brady, in New York, and asked her for financial assistance. She replied, "Bishop, I can't get you out of debt, but I can get you out of Portland." He was appointed archbishop of St. Paul shortly thereafter. "If it hadn't been for a woman. . . !"[7]

Murray arrived in St. Paul at one of the lowest points of the Great Depression. He was clearly aware of the needs of the people, as illustrated in the following letter to the priests in the archdiocese requesting that they announce at all the Masses the need for contributions to the Community Chest. He referred to the "unusual burden upon the welfare agencies of the entire nation" and added: "Not only must they provide for all those who even in normal conditions depend upon them for assistance but they must assume the task of caring for thousands who have never felt the suffering of destitution at any time in the past." In appealing for contributions to this worthy cause, he was very specific:

> Not from a surplus which most of us enjoy no longer but from the resources which we consider necessary for ourselves it is our duty to share with those who have nothing. Let every wage earner give at the rate of one day's pay a month and let every school child endeavor to deny himself to give at least five cents a month, making the contribution on that basis for twelve months.[8]

It is noteworthy that this request was not for a Catholic organization, but for a civic group which was endeavoring to help the community in a time of crisis.

John Gregory Murray, archbishop of St. Paul from 1932 to 1956

Murray's First Challenge

The Depression was the major national concern, but the most weighty challenge for Murray on the local scene was the question of the continuance of the Holy Cross Fathers at the College of St. Thomas. Their five-year contract would expire in 1933, and although the Holy Cross Congregation's expectation had been for a more permanent arrangement, many priests were adamant that St. Thomas be returned to archdiocesan control. Humphrey Moynihan, shortly after the death of Archbishop Dowling, wrote to Clara Hill Lindley: "The St. Thomas College situation is a very grave one and only a man who knows his way around in the field of education can deal with it wisely and prudently."[9]

Murray proved that he was equal to the challenge. After hearing every side of the issue and facilitating the process with relative equanimity, the new archbishop—when learning of Ireland's letter that St. Thomas never be given over to a religious congregation—made the courageous decision not to renew the Holy Cross contract. Father James H. Moynihan, brother of Msgr. Humphrey Moynihan, was appointed president in the summer of 1933. Not only had a problematic experience been concluded, but the year that followed brought new life to the campus.[10]

The situation at St. Thomas solidified Murray's relationship with the priests of the archdiocese. Connors described Murray as follows: "With his buoyant personality, his sparkling intelligence, and his simplicity of manners, he had swiftly developed excellent rapport with the priests of the diocese, from veteran disciples of John Ireland to young men recently ordained by Austin Dowling."[11] With new enthusiasm at St. Thomas, the archbishop's credibility was enhanced.

Murray Appoints a New Seminary Rector: William O. Brady

Saint Paul Seminary was not a focal point of the archbishop's concern during his early years in St. Paul. Although Murray had arrived in January 1932, and had visited the Saint Paul Seminary to preside at liturgies on special occasions, almost seventeen months passed before he called the first meeting of the board of trustees for June 19, 1933. Preoccupied with St. Thomas and other pressing concerns, the archbishop was probably grateful that there was no crisis at the major seminary.

Murray had, however, decided to make some changes. Humphrey Moynihan had been rector for twelve years, and at the age of sixty-nine, after years of administration at both St. Thomas and the Saint Paul Seminary, deserved a respite from responsibility. The oral tradition provides the following story regarding the appointment of the new rector. One day Archbishop Murray arrived at the seminary, walked down to one end of the hall where the resident faculty lived and knocked on the door of Father Rudolph Bandas. He said: "Father, I am considering appointing you rector of this seminary." Bandas replied with great deference: "Archbishop, I am honored that you would consider me. I will pray about it and give it great consideration." Archbishop Murray then went to the other end of the hall and knocked on the door of Father William O. Brady, and indicated that he was considering appointing him the rector of Saint Paul Seminary. Brady replied: "I'll take it!"[12] Brady was appointed and, as rector (1933–1939), as a member of the board of trustees while bishop of Sioux Falls (1939–1956), and as archbishop of St. Paul and chair of the board of trustees until his death (1956–1961), had a strong and enduring influence on the seminary.

Brady was highly respected as a moral theology teacher. Father Edward Grzeskowiak, a student at Saint Paul Seminary from 1930 to 1936, remembers Brady as "easy to talk to, frank and forward, and concrete in teaching pastoral theology."[13] Msgr. John Sweeney, a seminarian from 1935 to 1941, recalls: "I think in many ways Brady was excellent. He allowed lots of questions, but he didn't allow enough speculation. He was a little narrow by today's standards. But he was very good and clear. . . . Some would have said he never had a doubt in his life, and it showed in his teaching."[14]

Several priests reported this quality of certitude in Brady—the man who was later to become their archbishop. Even Msgr. Francis Gilligan, one of the "three wise men from the East" who came with Brady and Connelly to St. Paul in their early years, concurred. Msgr. Ambrose Hayden used to reminisce with Gilligan when the latter was in his nineties and in frail condition at a nursing home. Hayden would jog Gilligan's memory: "Father Gilligan, I remember when you and Archbishop Brady used to walk along the grotto and make bets on when the lilacs would bloom—and Archbishop Brady always won." Gilligan replied thoughtfully: "You know—there was one thing about Archbishop Brady. He was never unsure of anything!"[15]

This same quality held true when Brady was rector. He was definite and well organized. Things were either right or wrong. He had strong organizational skills. It was not easy to be head of an institution during the Depression, but Brady's efficiency allowed him to do well in untoward circumstances. He gave a "new look" to the catalogue.[16] His reputation for "cleaning house" of students whom he did not feel were suitable for priesthood continues to this day.[17]

Brady reorganized the class schedule so that the four periods in the morning were devoted to the more academic theological courses. In the afternoon, students attended what were considered less intensive classes, e.g., Gregorian Chant, Hebrew, Canon Law, Breviary, and later Business Administration. Pedagogically, this proved beneficial for the students. It also allowed for a welcome change in the horarium. Instead of rising at 5:25 A.M., students were allowed to sleep until 5:50 A.M.—very likely a popular adjustment.[18]

During Brady's years as rector, his friend James L. Connolly was appointed spiritual director. As was the custom, Connolly gave a half-hour spiritual conference daily in the period before dinner. Brady instituted a weekly rector's conference and took over the Monday evening period for his purposes. Connolly's conferences were remembered as dull, so Brady's appearance very likely added some energy to the schedule.

The rector also rearranged the liturgical schedule of the house. Meditation, morning prayer and Eucharist had usually been held in the oratories in the three residence halls, but Brady directed that the main chapel be used for everything.[19] With Brady and Connolly at the helm, and Gilligan on the faculty, "the three wise men" seemed to be in control. Sulpician spirituality with an eastern flavor was in the ascendancy.

Pope Pius XI, always interested in seminary education, promulgated an encyclical on priesthood, *Ad Catholicii Sacerdotii,* on December 20, 1935. The apostolic delegate to the United States, Amleto Cicognani, described it as "a veritable 'Summa' of all that has been said and written on priesthood, its dignity and duties, and on the preparation for the priesthood."[20] Archbishop Cicognani wrote to the American bishops requesting that the document be read and studied in all the seminaries. An extended quotation from the encyclical was included on the second page of the two editions of *The Rules of the Saint Paul Seminary* which received the imprimatur of John Gregory Murray.[21]

The First Vatican Visitation

In 1937, the eighty-year-old Pius XI ordered an apostolic visitation of all the Catholic seminaries in the world to take place in 1938 and 1939. Archbishop Cicognani was appointed "Apostolic Visitator" for the United States, with seven American bishops as "Associate Visitators." Questionnaires were sent out before the visitation requesting basic information. The visitors usually stayed only a day or two.

Archbishop Edward Mooney was the apostolic visitator assigned to the Saint Paul Seminary. He was accompanied by the Rev. A. M. Stitt as secretary and the canonical visitation was held November 10-11, 1938. The anticipated thorny issue was teaching classes in Latin. Father Charles Eggert remembers the visitation largely because it was the one time that Father Brady gave a talk in Latin at dinner![22] After the community Mass on November 11, which Mooney celebrated, he addressed the faculty and students "explaining the nature and purpose of the Apostolic Visitation and bringing to all the blessing of the Holy Father."[23]

Although no summary letter was issued to the American bishops as had been done in 1928, a collection of seminary-related documents titled *Enchiridion Clericorum* was published in 1938 which spelled out in detail the mandates and expectations for seminaries. With the death of Pius XI on February 10, 1939, however, and the advent of the war in Europe, extensive Vatican oversight of seminaries was at least temporarily halted.[24]

The Appointment of Lawrence O. Wolf as Rector

The following summer, William O. Brady was appointed bishop of Sioux Falls, South Dakota. During Murray's tenure as archbishop the pattern had been established of only one meeting of the seminary board and the corporation each year in October. A special meeting was called, however, on August 24, 1939, at which the new rector, the Very Reverend Lawrence O. Wolf, was present. He became ex officio a member of the board. Wolf was the first alumnus of the Saint Paul Seminary to be appointed to that office. He was also the first native of the archdiocese to become rector. Born in Minneapolis, he converted to Catholicism as a young person, attended the College of St. Thomas for his classical studies, and then took his philosophy and theology at the Saint Paul Seminary. After his ordination to the priesthood on June 14, 1924, he went to Louvain for further studies. In 1926 he was assigned to the seminary as professor of philosophy, but in 1928 returned to Louvain to study for a doctorate. After completing his Ph.D. in philosophy in 1929,

Lawrence O. Wolf, rector of the Saint Paul Seminary from 1939 to 1943

he resumed his position at the seminary for a decade before being appointed to succeed Brady in 1939.[25]

Wolf was a good teacher, appreciated by the students. Father Vincent A. Yzermans, a seminarian from 1946 to 1951, who was highly critical of the academic education he received at the Saint Paul Seminary, considered Wolf one of the two good professors he had. "He was a refined, highly intelligent man, a former rector of the institution who was forced to restrict his activities because of ill health."[26]

Archbishop John R. Roach, at the Saint Paul Seminary from 1941 to 1946, remembered Wolf's rector's conferences as well researched and solid.[27] Msgr. Terrence Murphy, Roach's classmate, recalled that as a seminarian he had been inspired by Wolf's zeal, but in retrospect realized that "he was so rigid he was unrealistic."[28] Wolf was edifying in his own way and was probably a very holy man, but Roach and others found him incredibly literal and inflexible as rector. One Wednesday afternoon in the summer during the war years when the seminarians were out for a walk in almost 100-degree heat, several of them were carrying their hats instead of wearing them. Father Wolf happened to be driving by and saw this. He stopped to instruct the students to put their hats on immediately! Wolf, a convert with no parish experience before coming to the seminary, was not as understanding and pastoral as students might have hoped.[29]

James P. Shannon also remembered discussing with Father Wolf, at the suggestion of his mentor at St. Thomas, Father Frederic Beiter, that possibly the required course in elementary Latin at the seminary could be waived because he had been a Latin major. Wolf proceeded to tell him "in a kindly but earnest fashion" that the course could not be waived and added "that my request smacked of pride, and that the purpose of seminary training was to help candidates for the priesthood learn the virtue of humility." Apparently, the rector shared the incident with the teacher of the Latin course, Father Francis Missia, who—in the course of two semesters—never called on Shannon, never returned any of the four written examinations for the course, and gave him an "F" for both semesters.[30]

Shannon was not the only "victim." Archbishop Roach remembered that Missia didn't appreciate anyone from Nazareth Hall or St. Thomas, and that he, and several of his friends who were also good students, got "D's" or "F's" from Father Missia in Latin. In turn they were called before Wolf who, according to Roach, was "much less understanding than he should have been." When Roach and others in later years applied to the University of Minnesota for graduate courses, the "D's" and "F's" on their transcripts were a problem. They went back to Father George Ziskovsky, who was registrar, and he changed their grades to "B's."[31]

With the advent of World War II, the face of the College of St. Thomas changed. As a result of the draft, enrollment plummeted. St. Thomas, in an effort to retain its faculty and programs, negotiated a contract with the government to train naval personnel under the V-12 program. The goal was to provide two years of college background to sailors who would then enter the naval officer candidate schools. One of the results of this arrangement was the need to take over Ireland Hall, and to request that the St. Thomas Academy boarding students move over to Loras Hall on the Saint Paul Seminary campus. The program was in effect at St. Thomas from 1943 to 1945.[32]

Wolf was adamantly against the use of the seminary buildings for anyone other than seminarians. He believed that it was in conflict with the intention of the founder of the seminary, James J. Hill. To complicate matters, Archbishop Murray agreed to allow St. Thomas to use Loras Hall without having told the rector beforehand.[33] Wolf resigned rather than agree to the arrangement and returned to his appointment in the philosophy department. Father Thomas Conroy remembers that shortly after Wolf resumed his teaching position, he stated: "Gentlemen, I can now look you in the eye."[34] Wolf apparently felt that he could not carry out the wishes of those in authority on that matter, and was apprehensive of any "outside group" which might invade the campus or exert pressure. According to Msgr. William Baumgaertner, Wolf was not in favor of the efforts to acquire accreditation in the 1940s for those very reasons.[35] Unfortunately, he contracted tuberculosis and became sickly, although he did not die until 1972.

James Connolly Becomes Rector

Another of "the wise men from the East," James L. Connolly, became Wolf's successor. Like Brady, he was born in Fall River, Massachusetts and did his entire seminary preparation under the Sulpicians. He was or-

James L. Connolly, rector of the Saint Paul Seminary from 1943 to 1945

dained for the Fall River diocese in 1923, but in 1924 incardinated into the Archdiocese of St. Paul. Archbishop Dowling sent him to Louvain for further studies where he received his doctorate in church history in 1928; he joined the faculty at the Saint Paul Seminary that same year. Connolly was appointed spiritual director during Brady's term as rector, and in 1940 became rector of Nazareth Hall.

With Wolf's resignation in 1943, however, Murray called upon Connolly to take the rectorship of the Saint Paul Seminary, a position he was to hold for only two years. Connelly, known to the students as "Gentleman Jim" or as "Blitz" (because he threw so many students out of Nazareth Hall), was remembered in a variety of ways by former seminarians. By some, such as Archbishop Roach, he was remembered as a gracious person whose relaxed approach was welcomed after Wolf, but who had limited impact on the seminary. Others saw him as an authority figure who was *not* understanding in time of family crisis. To still others he appeared as a self-promoter with the desire to be elevated to the episcopacy. Terrence Murphy appreciated his willingness to allow him to take two courses (in sociology and economics) at the University of Minnesota, one in the summer and one during the school year, at the recommendation of Father Gilligan.[36]

The war years were complicated by the question of exemption of seminarians from the draft. In 1942 Archbishop Murray wrote to all the priests of the archdiocese explaining that the status of seminarians was precarious, and that the Board of Bishops of the National Catholic Welfare Conference (NCWC) had recommended that there be continuous class sessions throughout the year so that there would be no question that the seminarians were trying to evade the draft. While acknowledging the problem, and giving directives that seminarians should "avoid public places of recreation as well as employment to avoid exciting criticism and insidious propaganda by the irreligious," the archbishop concluded: "As the strain of seminary life has already taken a heavy toll on the health of both seminarians and teachers I have decided not to adopt such extreme measures in this jurisdiction."[37]

By 1943–1944, however, the strong recommendation from the NCWC became almost a mandate. Summer schools were established that allowed for an accelerated program of three "semesters" a year. This program commenced at the Saint Paul Seminary on June 27, 1944.[38] According to Father Thomas Conroy, Father Francis Missia described it most accurately as "the damnable accelerated course." Conroy said: "Everything was condensed. It was kind of like instant theology . . . log-water theology."[39] The result was that the work normally accomplished in a nine-month academic year was conflated into six months. With the exception of brief holidays in June and January, classes were held year-round.

Students were very conscious of the war, however, and that put many things into perspective. In some instances, former classmates or neighbors were killed in battle. On the home front, there were sacrifices to be made. The heating in the buildings was minimal, and Msgr. William Baumgaertner, a student at the Saint Paul Seminary from 1941 to 1946, remembers that the students wore every bit of clothing they had to keep warm in the winter. Because of rationing the food was not great, but the complaints were minimal.[40]

Thomas Conroy, a seminarian from 1943 to 1948, recalled: "We were in SPS most of WWII. We were not allowed radios. Thus we depended on others to tell us of the defeat of the Nazis. We also needed them to tell us of that mysterious atomic bomb."[41] One of Conroy's classmates, Father Alfred Wagner, remembers that not only were there no radios, but neither did they have access to newspapers or magazines unless one could sneak a look at the daily paper outside the door of the dean of the residence hall before he took it in in the morning. Listening to the news during recreation was permitted, but the noise in the recreation room was such that one could hear very little. Wagner described Saint Paul Seminary during those years as "a blend between a medium security prison and a retreat house."[42] John Roach recalls that his father would clip important articles out of the newspaper and bring them to him on visiting days so that he could stay in touch with the momentous events of the war.[43]

The Saint Paul Seminary celebrated its golden jubilee in the midst of the war. At a board meeting in May 1944, Father Connolly "requested approval for necessary expenses to be incurred during the summer of 1944 as part of the preparation for the Golden Jubilee Commemoration, October 12, 1944."[44] Archbishop Murray offered a Pontifical Mass in St. Mary's Chapel on what would have typically been Alumni Day and the Most Reverend Edward D. Howard, archbishop of Portland, the only alumnus as of that time to have been made an archbishop, preached the sermon.[45]

After the liturgy a festive dinner was held, followed by a meeting in the *aula maxima.* This enthusiastic gathering, with the rector, Father Connolly, presiding, was the beginning of a campaign to raise funds for "a modern, fireproof library adapted to present and future needs" to be named the "Archbishop Ireland Memorial Library."[46] Details of the campaign to raise funds and the construction of the library will be considered later, but it is significant that, despite the war, alumni and friends gave generously toward a significant addition to the seminary in honor of its jubilee.

In the spring of 1945, Connolly was appointed coadjutor bishop of his home diocese, Fall River, Massachusetts. He was invited to return for Alumni Day, October 19, 1950, and preach the sermon on the occasion of the dedication of the Archbishop Ireland Memorial Library, the project for which he had been a major catalyst during his time as rector. Several sources indicate that being a bishop was a time of loneliness and trial for him. He died September 12, 1986, in Fall River. [47]

A Belated Appointment: The Rectorship of Rudolph Bandas

When the war drew to a close, the Saint Paul Seminary was once again looking toward the appointment of a new rector. As Murray had done once before in 1933, he offered the position to Father Rudolph Bandas. This time the offer was accepted. Bandas had been passed over three times before. The turnover of rectors—four within six years—added to the sense of instability in the complicated war era.

Bandas, who was of Bohemian heritage, was born near Silver Lake, Minnesota on April 18, 1896. He had studied classics at the University of Minnesota and the College of St. Thomas before entering the Saint Paul Seminary in 1915. Ordained a priest by Archbishop Dowling in 1921, he was soon after sent to England for further studies at Oxford and Cambridge. From there he went to the Angelicum University in Rome where he received a doctorate in philosophy. Bandas also studied at Louvain where he earned the degrees of S.T.D. et M. in 1925.[48]

As professor of dogmatic theology and catechetics, Bandas's specialty was the apostle Paul's teaching on redemption. He was the author of several books including *The Master Idea of Saint Paul's Epistles* and *Contemporary Philosophy and Thomistic Principles.* Msgr. John Sweeney recalls that Bandas was considered a good teacher in his early years. He was a dean and he was of the younger crowd. In later years, however, he simplified material too much and was not willing to explore new ideas in theology. He stuck with what he had learned in Rome and Louvain in the 1920s.[49] Archbishop Roach recalled that Bandas was not a bad teacher but offered very limited content. There was not much opportunity to expand one's theology. However, he admired Bandas from afar for the work he was doing with youth ministry.[50]

Rudolph Bandas, rector of the Saint Paul Seminary from 1945 to 1958

Prior to his appointment as rector, Bandas had served as archdiocesan director of the Confraternity of Christian Doctrine (CCD) while meeting his responsibilities on the seminary faculty. In August 1934, Murray wrote a lengthy letter to the priests regarding the necessity of adequate training in catechetics for both priests and lay people so as to teach Christian doctrine in the parishes. He reminded them that the Sacred Congregation of Seminaries and Universities in 1926 required that every seminary offer "a special course in pedagogy designed to set forth the method of teaching religion, developed not only by proper principles but also by practical experience." Murray continued:

> For that reason most of the seminarians under our jurisdiction have given much of their free time week-ends and throughout the vacation period to the fulfillment of this law wherever there was need and opportunity for their services. They have worked under the professor of catechetics in our major seminary at St. Paul, the Reverend Rudolph G. Bandas, Ph.D., S.T.D., S.T.M., who has had supervision of their work both in the classroom and in the missionary field. This experience of Reverend Dr. Bandas has prompted us to request him to take over the duties of the office of Diocesan Director of the Confraternity of Christian Doctrine while continuing the very important work of teaching at the seminary so that the program within the classroom may be coordinated with the activities initiated in every parish of the archdiocese for a more orderly, sustained and comprehensive course of Christian training in the ranks of the young and old.[51]

For Murray, the CCD—and the Catholic Youth Centers that grew from it—were part of the commitment to Catholic Action, and he believed that the seminarians should be involved. Father Eugene Abbott, at the Saint Paul Seminary from 1951 to 1957, recalled his experience of teaching CCD classes at Our Lady of Guadalupe Parish, and the opportunity it provided to broaden one's vision of church and ministry.[52] Father Richard Wolter, however, remembers trying to teach students from Central High School at St. Peter Claver Parish in the released time program, and feeling unprepared for the challenge.[53] Bandas, however, became internationally famous for his publications in catechetics. He was invited to teach a course on catechetical methods for high-school teachers at the Catholic University of America in the summer of 1947.

Bandas was known to be well connected at the Vatican. Therefore, the notification on June 26, 1954, that he had been appointed by Pope Pius XII as a consultor to the Sacred Congregation of Seminaries and Universities was not a complete surprise.[54] On January 15, 1955, he learned that he had received the rank of Domestic Prelate. Archbishop Murray presided at the ceremony conferring this honor on March 12, and extended his felicitations to Msgr. Bandas, although he made it clear that Bandas's appointment had come directly from the Vatican and not through his intercession.[55]

For all the mixed interpretations of Bandas's style of leadership from both former faculty and students, there are two areas of special accomplishment for which he is always praised: the accreditation of the seminary, and the construction of the new library building.

First Seminary to Receive North Central Accreditation

The necessity of accreditation was a sometimes contentious issue among bishops and seminary educators in the period between the world wars. There were those who believed that it would be dangerous if seminaries starting conforming to secular standards. The sacrament of Orders should be sufficient. An emphasis on grades and degrees could erode the need for humility among those to be ordained, and "ambitions to earn degrees would harm the fraternal charity in the seminary community."[56] Former rector Lawrence O. Wolf believed strongly that the seminary had accountability only to the church. "It starts with the church and ends with the church."[57] Bandas, however, believed that accreditation would contribute to the credibility of the seminary as an educational institution.

In the 1920s representatives of the most prestigious of the regional associations offering accreditation, the North Central Association of Colleges and Universities (NCA), opened a dialogue with leading Catholic educators. At the annual meeting of the minor seminary department of the National Catholic Educational Association (NCEA) in 1928, a resolution was passed "to take steps to become standardized." In the 1930s the college departments of several Catholic seminaries were accredited.[58]

New issues were forced upon the major seminaries as a result of World War II. The 1944 "G.I. Bill" offered veterans of the armed forces substantial financial assistance for higher education and professional training. The veteran, however, had to choose from among a list of "approved" institutions. Seminaries of the Catholic Church in the United States were on no such approved list.[59]

Rudolph Bandas, who was deeply devoted to education, saw the value of establishing accreditation. His active leadership in the first year of his rectorship led to the North Central Association accrediting, at their annual meeting in Chicago March 25–30, 1946, the six-year course of studies of the Saint Paul Seminary, the first major seminary of any denomination in the United States to receive accreditation. It was a test case that paved the way for other seminaries, Catholic and Protestant, to apply for accreditation.

When Bishop William Mulloy of Covington addressed the NCEA seminary departments in 1946, he challenged members to come "out of their isolation" and held up the recent accreditation of the Saint Paul Seminary "as a positive relationship with the educational world."[60] His statements contained echoes of the vision of Archbishop Ireland. Mulloy, an alumnus of the Saint Paul Seminary (1916), preached the sermon on Alumni Day at the seminary on October 12, 1946. At that time he stated with pride in regard to the accreditation: "Ever the leader in the field of progress, deeply appreciating the immediate and mediate needs of the Church, the St. Paul Seminary blazed the trail in her efforts to equip men for the future."[61]

Other accreditations and approvals followed:

> On April 18, 1946, Mr. Malcolm M. Willey, Vice President of the University of Minnesota, informed the Seminary authorities that the University of Minnesota automatically accepts the accrediting by the North Central Association and that as far as the University of Minnesota is concerned the Saint Paul Seminary is "now fully accredited."[62]

A month later, May 14, 1946, the seminary was approved as an institution for the education of veterans under Public Law 346—the Servicemen's Readjustment Act of 1944. In the following month, June 7, 1946, the State of Minnesota's Department of Education approved the Saint

Paul Seminary "as an agency for the education of teachers for accredited Catholic High Schools." It also "authorized the granting of a High School Standard General Certificate to any Seminarian who has obtained a B.A. degree and 15 semester credits in Education."[63]

In the 1952 *Register,* Vatican documents were used to provide support for the accreditation process:

> The accreditation of the St. Paul Seminary by recognized accrediting agencies was sought in conformity with the prescription of the Congregation of Bishops and Regulars, May 10, 1947 (*Acta Sanctae Sedis,* Vol. XL, p. 336) and the Instruction of the Congregation of Seminaries and University Studies of August 28, 1948 which recommended the granting of legal academic degrees for the safeguarding of the liberty of choice of state, for the utility of priests, and for the prestige of Catholic education.[64]

It is noteworthy, however, that the accreditation of the Saint Paul Seminary by the North Central Association and the University of Minnesota both took place in 1946, preceding the statements from the Vatican.

At the board meeting of January 8, 1947, the trustees passed resolutions regarding the conferring of the B.A. and M.A. degrees. These had to be rescinded at the meeting the following April 9. The following clarification was written into the minutes:

> The secretary recalled that the St. Paul Seminary was accredited for the granting of B.A. degrees by the North Central Association on April 3, 1946 and by the University of Minnesota on April 18, 1946. He announced that the Seminary was now also accredited for the granting of M.A. degrees. The M.A. accreditation was extended to the Seminary by the N.C.A. Board of Review on February 28, 1947 and by the accrediting Board of the U. of M. on April 1, 1947.[65]

The board then passed a series of resolutions regarding the proper procedures involved in application and fulfillment of requirements for as well as conferral of degrees. B.A. degrees would be granted at the end of the second year of philosophy to those students who had fulfilled the requirements. All other students were encouraged to qualify for the B.A. at the conclusion of Theology IV. Bishop Brady moved, and Father Bandas seconded, a resolution which stated: "The requirements for the B.A. and M.A. degrees at the Seminary shall be the equivalent of the requirements demanded by the University of Minnesota or colleges approved by the N.C.A."[66]

The *Register* for 1946 described conditions for eligibility for the B.A. degree, and specified that the major field of study would be philosophy. The 1947 *Register* was the first to set forth the requirements for the M.A. degree and the two possible plans for fulfilling the program. Students applying for the M.A. had to have a "B" average in college and a reading knowledge of French or German in addition to Latin and Greek. The only M.A. degree to be offered for many years was in church history.

The Saint Paul Seminary had been the first major seminary at a distance to affiliate with the Catholic University of America in 1895 to offer the pontifical degree—the S.T.B.—to those students who chose to take the required examinations.[67] In becoming the first major seminary to be accredited by the North Central Association in 1946, the Saint Paul Seminary was maintaining the tradition that Archbishop Ireland had outlined for it.

The Archbishop Ireland Memorial Library

What became very clear as a result of the accreditation process was that a new library facility was absolutely necessary. The fact that the jubilee campaign was under way to raise money for the new building probably convinced the accreditors that it would materialize in the near future. The library was originally housed on the south end of the first floor of the administration building which had been constructed in 1893. The room was arranged in alcove fashion with wooden stacks twelve shelves high accommodating about twelve thousand books. With the growth of the collection over the years, the periodicals and volumes seldom used were shelved in rooms on the fourth floor. The Catholic Historical Society of St. Paul museum and book collection were also housed on the fourth floor. As early as 1903, the seminary library published a 122-page catalogue listing all its books. The pamphlet was available for twenty-five cents upon application to the secretary of the seminary.[68]

In 1922 Father Humphrey Moynihan set up a separate collection of books which were for spiritual reading and *belles-lettres* in two rooms at the south end of the first floor of Loras Residence. When Saint Thomas Academy students took over Loras Residence in 1943, the collection (by that time approximately five thousand books) was moved to the north end of the power house/gymnasium building, where—as Father Bandas later noted—"the books are exposed to all the soot, dirt and dust which emanates from the boiler room as well as to the danger of fire."[69]

Because of the enormous crowding, there was little or no space for the students to use books in the library. By 1948 the collection numbered over thirty-one thousand accessioned volumes; unprocessed and miscellaneous volumes brought the number closer to forty thousand.[70] With the crowded conditions, the environment for research was very limited. Archbishop Ireland, at the time of his death, had designated a sum of money in his will to be used for the library. This became the seedbed for the campaign that Father Connolly initiated. In November 1944, after the seminary's golden jubilee celebration, Connolly sent out a letter of appeal and received $21,000 from alumni and friends.

With the accession of Father Rudolph Bandas to the rectorship in 1945, plans were advanced for the new library structure. Austin Lang, of the firm of Lang and Raugland of Minneapolis, was hired as the architect. Father Bandas, along with Father Ambrose Hayden, librarian, and Father Thomas J. Shanahan, served as the committee for planning the new structure.[71] Father Hayden was assigned to the seminary as librarian shortly after his ordination, and during the summers studied for his B.S. degree in library science at the University of Michigan. In the 1948–1949 academic year, Father Shanahan, who was one of the first two priests to receive an M.A. in library science from the University of Michigan, was appointed librarian and professor of homiletics. Father Hayden continued on the faculty and as a member of the library board until 1951.[72]

At a meeting of the seminary board on January 8, 1947, Father Bandas announced that the Archbishop Ireland Library Fund amounted to $81,008.95; the John Ireland Memorial Library Fund, $30,776.91; unpaid pledges were approximately $2,000. He also explained that the architect's plans for the new library building were almost complete. The record states: "The Trustees decided that the building of a new library should be postponed until conditions have changed, and that the question of the location of the new library be given additional consideration."[73]

The "change of conditions" apparently referred to the lack of adequate funds. At the board meeting the following October it was stated explicitly that "according to the Articles of Incorporation the new library building could not be started until all necessary funds were on hand."[74] The Saint Paul Seminary Corporation was prohibited by its statutes from incurring indebtedness for any purpose.

In October 1948 Archbishop Murray, probably understanding that the fundraising for the library was moving too slowly, decided to make it a "diocesan project."[75] The ground-breaking took place December 13, 1948. A letter from Murray to Bandas evoked the following response from the rector on December 18:

> In the name of the faculty and students of the St. Paul Seminary I wish to express to Your Excellency our most profound gratitude for assuming this additional burden of providing a library for the Seminary. You will understand better the sincerity and depth of our appreciation if I describe briefly the present condition of our library.[76]

Bandas then outlined his major concerns: fear of fire; exposed and unprotected books inaccessible to both faculty and students in the many locations where they were stored; no study areas for faculty or students; reference books in the guest parlors where it was impossible for students to do research if the rooms were otherwise occupied; no work space for ordering, cataloguing, and repair of books.

The rector made his case well. "Serious investigations of any question on the part of our B.A. and M.A. candidates—by consulting the main stock of books—is [sic] still practically out of the question because of a lack of a study area." Bandas concluded: "To us, who have struggled under these intolerable conditions for so many years, the noise of the excavating machines is indeed music to our ears, an assurance that 'redemption is at hand.'"[77] He then reiterated his gratitude to the archbishop.

In a letter of February 10, 1949, Murray wrote to the seminary alumni and gave a financial accounting of the efforts to raise funds for the library. The estimate, however, was that the library, fully equipped, would cost $400,000 or more. Therefore, "it would be necessary for the 450 priests of the Archdiocese and the 900 in active service in other dioceses to contribute an average of $250 each."[78]

Donations were received, but ultimately, the archbishop assumed personal responsibility for funds which eventually had to be borrowed for the library.[79] Steenberg Construction Company of St. Paul received the contract. The St. Paul *Dispatch* announced that the library would be a "completely 'scientific' home for the seminary's 100,000 volumes, hundreds of which are ancient tomes." It added: "Space for 60 reference workers will be provided but there will also be 'carrells' or closed cells, sound-proof, in which students may work with typewriters"[80]—a far cry from the conditions to which they had become accustomed.

The cornerstone was laid on May 19, 1949, without ceremony.[81] The building was basically completed and the books were moved into the new Archbishop Ireland Memorial Library under the direction of Father Shanahan on January 23–24, 1950.[82] Winter in Minnesota was hardly the ideal season for the transfer, but it was a time of excitement for students and faculty alike.

The dedication of the new library, however, was to have special significance in the history of the church in St. Paul. It was the final event of the archdiocese's centennial celebration.[83] Archbishop Murray celebrated a Pontifical Mass on October 19, 1950, in Saint Mary's Chapel; Bishop James L. Connolly preached the sermon. Afterward all processed to the new library for the appropriate rituals. Then, in the spacious reading room, the archbishop conferred for the first time in the seminary's history the degree of master of arts on five recently ordained priests.[84] With a new building and a new program, the Saint Paul Seminary entered the second half of the twentieth century. Twenty-five master of arts degrees were conferred by the end of the Murray era.[85]

Repaying the archdiocese for the funds "loaned" for the library construction was an ongoing challenge. The board authorized the payment of $10,000 to the Archdiocese of St. Paul for that purpose in 1952, 1953 (two payments of $10,000 each), and 1954. The final chapter on the library debt was written in the board minutes for October 12, 1955:

> The Board voted that the Seminary should pay out of its own funds the balance of the indebtedness on the new John Ireland Memorial Library. The treasurer and rector of the Seminary immediately presented the Most Reverend Archbishop a check for $24,051.70. The Archbishop, however, declined the suggestion that the Seminary pay part of the interest on the debt. Since the

> construction and payment for the new library was undertaken solely in the name of the Most Reverend Archbishop of St. Paul, the Archbishop stated that he would issue a written statement transferring the Library to the Seminary.[86]

This was the last meeting of the board of trustees at which John Gregory Murray presided. In a certain sense, the library was a monument to him as well as to Archbishop Ireland.

Students from the 1950s remember the newness of the library, and the accessibility of the books. Father Eugene Abbott recalls helping Msgr. Shanahan in the library by painting the Dewey decimal numbers on the spines of books recently purchased or donated.[87] With the M.A. program available, there was no substitute for a modern library facility.

A Convent for the Sisters

One other building was erected on the seminary campus during Murray's episcopate—a new convent for the Sisters of St. Joseph of Carondelet. At the October 18, 1950, board meeting, on the day before the dedication of the library, mention was made of bequests from the late Nellie Bell and the late Clara Hill Lindley.[88]

At the board meeting the following December, the rector informed the members that when the mother general of the Sisters of St. Joseph, Sister Killian, came for her visitation in November she "complained to the rector that the Sisters at the seminary were unable to keep the required enclosure and that the Sisters' chapel was situated under the domestics' general dormitory."[89] The living quarters of the sisters were overcrowded and subject to much noise.

For years, almost twenty maids lived on the second floor of the refectory adjacent to the sisters' quarters. Their dormitory was above the sisters' chapel which was on the first floor. They did not have a rule of silence and were not expected to live as in a cloister. Hattie Klisch, who worked at the seminary in the early 1940s, remembers that there were seven sisters living on the second floor in private rooms. There were two double rooms for girls, and a dorm for fourteen to sixteen others. Hattie and her sister Helen worked in the administration building clean-

Sisters of St. Joseph of Carondelet on staff at the Saint Paul Seminary in the 1930s (left to right): Sisters Boniface Zeimetz, Cortona Bettinger, Martha Muhs, Justa Cullen, Theophane Hogan, and Demetrius Basta

ing the rooms of the professors and also helped in the refectory. In the summer, all three residence halls were thoroughly cleaned. The girls could attend Sunday Mass in St. Mary's Chapel, but had to sit in the choir loft. Hattie recalls the organ booming out, and wondered if the loft would fall. She was impressed by many of the faculty: Father McCarthy—neat as a pin; Father Bandas—very conservative; Father Busch—the walking encyclopedia; and Father Missia—eccentric, funny, and good at music. In many ways it was a spiritual experience, and some of the friendships she made with the other girls endured.[90] The situation of the sisters, however, was not conducive to the spiritual life.

The rector then announced that a donor in St. Paul "who wished her name to be withheld" offered to build a convent and chapel. The board voted unanimously to set aside a piece of property adjacent to the refectory for a separate sisters' dwelling.[91] On October 17, 1951, the trustees announced that Miss Minnie Bell had donated $133,662 to the seminary for the construction of the convent. An additional $11,328 was contributed for furnishings.[92] A further description in the 1951 *Register* stated that the convent was a memorial in honor of the John Bell family.

The dedication of the sisters' chapel and convent took place after a Pontifical High Mass celebrated by Archbishop John Gregory Murray on October 12, 1951—Alumni Day.[93] The chapel, with stained glass windows celebrating the glorious mysteries of the rosary, had a seating capacity of thirty-two.[94] The new environment must clearly have been "glorious" after the almost fifty years of crowded community living.

From the early years of the seminary, a Solemn Requiem Mass was offered each November "for deceased professors, alumni, friends, and benefactors." In the 1949–1950 *Register* the event was described with the list enlarged. After "professors and alumni" and before "benefactors," two other important groups were added: "students" and "Sisters."[95]

The sisters' contributions were gradually recognized. On November 1, 1953, after a special presentation of Cardinal Newman's "Dream of Gerontius" by the Seminary Dramatics Guild, a special welcome was extended on behalf of the student body to Mother Marie Modeste, C.S.J., the recently appointed superior of the new convent.[96] The sisters' assignments changed over the years, but the convent continued to be an integral part of the seminary community until 1987. Many priests fondly remember the spirit of the sisters and saw them as models of generosity and service.

Structuring Itself for the Business of Education

Student enrollment during the Murray era reflected something of the socio-cultural and political situations of the day. Despite the Depression, 232 students attended in the 1932–1933 academic year. However, from 1935 to 1942, the student body (with the exception of the year 1940–1941) was under 200. From 1942–1943 to 1949–1950, during World War II and its immediate aftermath, the number was well into the 200s (265 in 1950).

The 1950s saw a religious revival in the United States. The popularity of Bishop Fulton J. Sheen, the power of positive thinking of Norman Vincent Peale, the evangelical zeal of Billy Graham all brought a "new shape" to American religion—both Catholic and Protestant.[97] There was a vocation explosion in the Catholic Church. Thomas Merton's *Seven*

Storey Mountain became an inspiration for some in the post-World War II period. Seminaries and novitiates were bursting at the seams. The crowded conditions of that decade created a false sense that the church would never again want for laborers in the vineyard. From 1951 to 1961 the numbers at the Saint Paul Seminary never fell below 300, and for the years 1953 to 1955 reached the all-time high of 371. The two-room suites that James J. Hill had designed for sleeping and study for one student were occupied by two seminarians who lived in close proximity.

More efficient business methods became imperative in the administration of the seminary. Frank Schlick, who had served on the board of trustees for forty years, died in the fall of 1945. In 1946 Archbishop Murray appointed Ignatius Aloysius O'Shaughnessy to fill out Schlick's unexpired term. At the board meeting in October, on motion of Bishop Brady, O'Shaughnessy was elected for a term of five years. At the same meeting, Roman Sevenich, professor of parish business administration at the seminary from 1942 to 1959, was asked to prepare a study of the seminary's monthly expenses to help in determining the rate of board and tuition to be charged.[98]

The construction of the new library offered the possibility for much-needed expansion for business offices. In October 1949, Father Bandas read a letter to the board from E. J. Murphy, business manager at the College of St. Thomas, to I. A. O'Shaughnessy who had appointed him to do an assessment of the bookkeeping and business methods at the seminary. Murphy wrote: "The matter of the proper space for this type of work is probably as acute as the actual records." He suggested that "the library space in the Administration Building be made available for a business office as soon as the new library is completed." A motion passed, apparently with little discussion, by which the rector was directed to proceed at once—in consultation with O'Shaughnessy, Murphy, and Sevenich—"to draw up plans for the transformation of the old library into business offices."[99]

This redesign was particularly necessary due to the recent accreditation by the North Central Association. The NCA criteria made it imperative for the seminary to have clarity in its procedures.[100] In addition, the question of social security for seminary employees required protocols which far exceeded what had been acceptable in an earlier era. At the board meeting on December 15, 1950, the rector was authorized "to prepare the necessary ballot to be submitted to the employees at the Seminary." If two-thirds of the employees voted in the affirmative, "the rector was authorized to procure the necessary forms from the Internal Revenue Office and set up this system of Social Security at the St. Paul Seminary."[101]

Tuition continued to be raised periodically. In October 1949 the annual charge per student was raised from $500 to $600 per year. To make it look less formidable, students were charged $300 per semester, one half for tuition, the other half for room, board, and various fees. The *Register* in 1950–1951 described these in detail. The following year, the *Register* articulated its refund policy.[102] Father Bandas initiated and implemented significant changes, especially of a practical nature, during his tenure as rector.

Intellectual Life at the Seminary in the Murray Era

Although the latitude allowed seminarians for external interaction with the "world" varied considerably from 1932 to 1956, in many ways it was significantly the same. The possibility of going off campus to hear lectures or attend programs was rare. One such occasion was the attendance of seminarians at the convention of the Catholic Rural Life Conference and the Confraternity of Christian Doctrine at the Lowry Hotel in St. Paul on November 6, 7, 8, 1934. Archbishop Murray's enthusiastic letter inviting everyone in the archdiocese[103] and Rudolph Bandas' pivotal role in the establishment of the CCD while maintaining his faculty appointment in the seminary were probably responsible for this unusual departure from a more cloistered existence.

The array of speakers who made presentations at the seminary—some of them on more than one occasion—was impressive.[104] Among the outstanding lecturers were English author F. J. Sheed; Dorothy Day, founder of the Catholic Worker Movement; Father John La Farge, S.J., author and associate editor of *America;* Father Gerald Ellard, S.J., liturgical scholar; artist and Catholic Worker Ade Bethune; British author Theodore Maynard; Professor Mortimer Adler of the University of Chicago; Walter Farrell, O.P.; and the Russian Baroness Catherine de Hueck.

Other presenters in the post-World War II period were Cardinal Conrad Von Preysing, archbishop of Berlin; Cardinal Eugene Tisserant of the Vatican Library; Dietrich von Hildebrand; Father James Keller who spoke of the Christopher Movement; and the Baroness von Trapp who gave one lecture on family, and later a musical presentation with her family in the *aula*. Political leaders were sometimes at the podium. The Archduke Otto von Habsburg of Austria-Hungary and Dr. Kurt von Schuschnigg, former chancellor of Austria were among the most famous. Douglas Hyde spoke on "Communism as a Spiritual Problem."

The lesser-known included Father Peter Crumbley, O.F.M., who—beginning about 1917—gave occasional spiritual conferences at the Saint Paul Seminary on subjects such as "The Dignity of the Priesthood." In April 1942 he gave a retreat to the seminarians. Father Crumbley was a kind and gentle figure with a fine sense of humor who was the Catholic chaplain of the Illinois State Penitentiary in Joliet, Illinois, for many years.

Interestingly, a series of medical doctors, some from the University of Minnesota, lectured the seminarians regularly on good health care and various diseases. Sister Mary Suzanne of Maryknoll gave a slide presentation about her thirty years of work with lepers in the Fiji Islands. In January 1954, Daniel Mackay made a presentation on "Alcoholics Anonymous." This is only a partial listing that gives some indication of the variety to which the seminarians were exposed during their years of preparation. Whether they imbibed the wisdom shared with them may be questionable in some instances, but—for those who were interested—the opportunity was at hand.

The faculty were involved in a variety of professional groups. Father William Busch was a leader in the liturgical movement and often on the planning committees for the National Liturgical Week.[105] In August 1947, Busch, along with Father Lawrence Ryan, Father George Ziskovsky, and Father Richard Doherty attended the Liturgical Convention in Portland, Oregon.[106] Father Doherty was elected to the board of directors of the Catholic Theological Society of America in 1946, and was later elected president in 1963–1964.[107] In 1947, Doherty and Father John Sweeney attended the 5th Annual Week of Catholic Action Study for Priests at the University of Notre Dame.[108] The post-war period gave the faculty opportunities for development; some of them took advantage of these opportunities.

Spiritual Life in the Maturing Seminary

Following Connolly as spiritual director was Father Louis McCarthy. He had been a student at St. Thomas Academy, Nazareth Hall, and the Saint Paul Seminary before his ordination in 1932. He was sent to the University of Louvain for studies and received his Ph.D. in philosophy in 1936. McCarthy then taught at the Saint Paul Seminary from 1936 to 1940 before being appointed spiritual director. "Big Lou," as he was known to the seminarians, was a tall, impressive figure. Thomas Conroy remembered McCarthy both as a spiritual director in his student days and as rector during his teaching years at Nazareth Hall. According to Conroy:

> Lou was a very sensitive guy. A wonderful man to work for. . . . I think the students [at Nazareth Hall] were probably scared of him. . . . I remember him standing on the stage, all six foot four with a cassock making him look like about seven feet tall, saying, "I'm not as formidable as I look!"[109]

McCarthy's spiritual conferences were pivotal for James Shannon. The spiritual director presented commentaries on the Psalms which, Shannon stated, "opened new vistas of light and understanding for me as I came to see that God deserves worship from a person because God is." The conclusion that resulted from his reflections on McCarthy's conferences gave a new substance to his spiritual life: "Persons climb mountains because mountains are there. Persons worship God purely, and with no other motive, once they grasp that God is God." Shannon added: "This insight made an enormous difference in my life."[110] Shannon's classmate, John Roach, agreed that McCarthy's spiritual conferences were excellent, and that to this day he has yet to hear anything better on the Psalms.[111]

The spiritual director with the longest tenure in the history of the school was Father Lawrence Ryan. He was appointed in 1945, the same year that Bandas became rector. Ryan remained in that office until 1964. Lawrence was the younger brother of John A. Ryan, though very different from him. While he was a student at the Saint Paul Seminary from 1904 to 1910, John A. was one of his professors. Following ordination, Lawrence Ryan became an assistant at the Cathedral of Saint Paul and served there for thirty years—six as assistant and twenty-four as pastor.[112] He resigned in 1940 due to ill health, and served from 1940 to 1945 at St. Mary of the Lake in White Bear Lake.

In June 1945, at the age of sixty-five, Ryan was appointed spiritual director of the Saint Paul Seminary. To the seminarians of that time he seemed like a distant figure—"one-half of a God."[113] He gave four spiritual conferences a week to an auditorium of sometimes 350 or more students, was available for private counseling, and gave the six-day retreat in preparation for the deacon ordination.[114] With his somber spirit, somewhat inaccessible demeanor, and bald pate, he was in fact the opposite of the nickname given to him by the students—"Curly" Ryan. He was not a warm and fuzzy personality. According to Thomas Conroy, "his conferences were very good. Very solid stuff. And he had a pretty good idea of liturgical piety. He was a good friend of Father William Busch."[115] John Roach went to Larry Ryan for spiritual direction and found him helpful. In fact, Roach invited him to preach at his first Mass.[116] By the late 1950s and early 1960s, however, he was even more removed from the students. John Kinney, at the seminary from 1957 to 1963, did not find Ryan understanding or compassionate at the time of his father's death.[117]

Formation for priesthood and religious life from World War II to Vatican II was somewhat overwhelming to some of those in charge. The number of candidates was enormous, so the possibility of coming to know some 350 students individually was minimal. Many seminarians went informally to priest advisors on the faculty for direction in lieu of the possibility of contact with the spiritual director. The adage in religious life—"You keep the Rule and the Rule will keep you"—seemed to apply in the seminary as well. As long as one kept the rules, did not make "waves," and got decent grades, promotion to the next rank of orders was likely. As Vincent A. Yzermans attests, if one did speak out, one's future could be precarious.[118]

Complicating the problem of not always having spiritual direction available, the ethos of the seminary was such that the formation of close friendships was not encouraged. Students were warned against "particular friendships"—the euphemism for homosexual relationships. In many ways one was cut off from family and friends. If the four components of formation were then as they are now—human, spiritual, academic, and pastoral—many would agree that it was the area of human formation that was slighted. Father Fred Mertz claims that the picture of seminary life in St. Paul in his novel *The Ore and the Dross* is fiction, but many who were his classmates in the 1940s have no difficulty identifying the characters he portrayed.[119]

Concerns for family were sometimes considered "attachments" by those forming seminarians and novices in the pre-Vatican II church. The Gospel challenge was to leave father, mother, brother, and sister. Unfortunately, families often suffered as a result of insensitivities to the real needs of the moment. One priest, ordained in the 1940s, recalled a painful time when his sister, married to a service man overseas during World War II, was pregnant and expecting her baby. Because her husband was far away, she asked her brother to be with her when the time came for delivery. He received a message after breakfast one day that she had been taken to the hospital, so he went to the rector for permission. The response was, "No." When asked why, the rector responded, "Because there is no sign on you that you are her brother."

The seminarian went to his room devastated. After some reflection he returned to the rector's office and stated that even though he knew his future at the seminary would be in jeopardy, he felt that he had to go to his sister in her time of need. He stated, "I have decided to go to my sister—with your permission if possible, without it if necessary." The rector told him to go ahead, but offered no transportation. It took three buses to get to the hospital in Minneapolis. When he arrived he discovered that the baby had been born dead.[120] Seminary life has had painful moments as well as joyful ones in every era.

Student Life: Continuing the Cloister

The seminary rule books approved by Archbishop Murray in 1945 and 1954, while basically the same in structure and substance, offer a few additions in the 1954 edition. Under "Exercises of Piety" it states that students who leave the grounds on a free day without attending Mass and morning prayer will be dismissed from the seminary. It also notes that "Students are not to use the Sisters' Chapel." Most unusual in this category was the prohibition that "the students will not cross the lawn but always use the sidewalks; this rule is a matter of special observance by the students of Grace Building going to the Class Building."[121]

Seminarians were not allowed to use the house phones. Permission to use the pay phone for outgoing calls had to be obtained from the rector, or in his absence, the respective dean. Telephones were not to be used for social calls; incoming calls would not be accepted unless the matter was urgent—the importance of which had to be explained by the caller. Urgent messages would be delivered to students after dinner and supper.[122]

Regarding the matter of dress, seminarians were expected to wear a black suit and a black felt hat or straw hat whenever they rode on buses, in taxis, went downtown or appeared in public—even when on vacation! Garb while on campus, with the exception of times when one was doing manual labor or involved in athletic activities, was the black cassock. The 1954 version added: "Students are to wear a shirt and black trousers under their cassock. They are not to remove their cassock in the refectory while helping with the dishes. They are to keep their hands out of their pockets at all times."[123]

The offenses which brought about immediate dismissal from the seminary included the usual ones prohibiting the use of liquor, visiting saloons or taverns, bringing objectionable literature to campus, indulging in vulgar jokes and stories, leaving the seminary grounds without permission, and visiting theaters. One addition to the rule books approved by Murray, the breaking of which would result in dismissal, was: "Corresponding by mail or communicating in any way or at any time—except in cases of necessity—with members of the opposite sex other than immediate relatives."[124] In the post-World War II period, with some older candidates at the seminary, proscriptions were spelled out very explicitly.

Murray's Relationship to the Seminary

The Saint Paul Seminary benefited from Archbishop Murray's penchant for building, but—according to some—he did not seem to have a particular fondness for the major seminary. Archbishop Roach recalls interviews with Murray before sub-diaconate and before priesthood ordinations.[125] Father Thomas Conroy, who was ordained a few years later, claims: "He never really talked to us that I can remember. Ever. He came to these orders meetings in the spring. He was supposed to do that, I guess. And that was it. We didn't see much of Murray out here."[126] Msgr. William Baumgaertner, on the seminary faculty from 1949, corroborated the fact that they saw little of John Gregory Murray at the seminary—only on special occasions.[127]

The archbishop dutifully sent out letters to the archdiocese in early July announcing the seminary collection on the third Sunday of the month, and he wrote to the priests reminding them to pay whatever indebtedness they had on their seminary tuition. Murray wanted an effective seminary system, but remained aloof. He is best remembered by some priests as walking around the campus during the priests' retreats in June handing out assignments. Father T. Kenneth Ryan suggested that Murray had more priests than he knew what to do with—one reason why some were sent off to study or permitted to develop new projects.[128]

Murray, for all his intelligence and remarkable memory which intimidated some, had a simplicity which made him very attractive to the lay people. He walked everywhere, or else rode the "trolley car" or bus, which gave him an opportunity for contact with the ordinary people. In that he was a role model for the seminarians. According to Father Eugene Abbott, "he did extraordinary things in ordinary ways."[129] It seems particularly appropriate that one of the present vehicles for educating lay people in the Catholic schools—a program of the Saint Paul Seminary School of Divinity and the School of Education of the University of St. Thomas and the Archdiocese of St. Paul and Minneapolis—is titled "The Murray Institute."

On March 31, 1947, about 9:00 P.M., Archbishop Murray, returning from a St. Thomas board meeting, was struck by a car at Summit Avenue and Selby Avenue. He was alone and on foot, having assured the board member who had driven him home that he would be fine walking the short distance to the cathedral rectory. The accident was severe and he nearly died.[130] On May 14, 1947, the Reverend James J. Byrne, professor of dogmatic theology at the Saint Paul Seminary, was appointed auxiliary bishop. Although Murray continued to function, many of his activities were curtailed. He never presided at ordinations after that. Bishop Byrne was the ordaining bishop in subsequent years.

By 1956 Murray's health was deteriorating, and in April he was diagnosed with a granular cancer in the throat, which physicians declared inoperable. He continued confirmations and was present at the clergy retreat in June at the Saint Paul Seminary. According to Msgr. James Reardon, "a long and painful series of deep therapy x-ray treatments failed to bring relief, much less hope of a permanent cure. The archbishop walked from the Chancery to St. Joseph's Hospital and returned every day, refusing the offer of a ride on the plea that he needed the exercise."[131] On October 11, 1956, he succumbed to cancer—four months after Bishop William O. Brady was appointed coadjutor with the right of succession to the archbishop of St. Paul.

The seminary mourned the death of the archbishop, although he was a remote figure for many. Murray is not remembered in the history of the seminary for the enthusiastic vision of Ireland, or the artistic flair of Dowling. However, his concrete contributions—the library and the convent—tell us something of his life. He was an intellectual with great simplicity who was committed to education and "Catholic Action." The Saint Paul Seminary was a key institution in the archdiocese, which allowed him to carry out his unified plan. It grew and benefited from his benign but reticent oversight.

CHAPTER 11

William O. Brady

Professor, Rector, Trustee, Archbishop

> ...make evident to the priests of tomorrow how much can be done for the Church if the principles of a seminary textbook and the guidance of the papal letters are made to live in thoughtful action.[1]
>
> Bishop William O. Brady
> February 1950

John Gregory Murray's tenure was one of the longest of any archbishop of St. Paul; William O. Brady's was the shortest.[2] Yet, Brady's influence at the Saint Paul Seminary was not limited to his five years as ordinary. It began the day of his arrival as a new faculty member in 1926 and extended for thirty-five years until his death on October 1, 1961.

William Otterwell Brady was born February 1, 1899, in Fall River, Massachusetts, the second son of John J. and Gladys Davol Brady. He had an older brother, Louis, and a younger sister, Leonora. He attended the public schools in Fall River including Durfee High School where, as a senior in 1915–1916, he was editor of the yearbook, *The Durfee Record.* Part of the caption under his picture states:

> "Bill" is our Editor-in-Chief, and as such deserves much praise for the zeal and enthusiasm which have characterized his work. His famous sentence in the debate against Tech brings to our minds the saying "Who says too much says nothing;" but we doubt if this holds true in "Bill's" case.... Suffice it to say that

> "Bill" is an excellent scholar and one whom we hope success awaits in his every undertaking.[3]

Brady's seminary education was strictly Sulpician. He attended St. Charles College in Catonsville, Maryland (1916–1918) for his study of classics, Saint Mary's Seminary in Baltimore (1918–1920) for philosophy, and the Sulpician Seminary in Washington, D.C. for theology. His preparation for priesthood, however, took a somewhat unexpected turn in December 1922. Archbishop Dowling, while in Washington—very likely for business with the National Conference of Catholic Bishops (NCCB)—visited the Sulpician Seminary. Brady described the event in a letter to Dowling on February 11, 1923:

William O. Brady, archbishop of St. Paul from 1956 to 1961. He served as rector of the Saint Paul Seminary from 1933 to 1939 and again while he was archbishop in 1958.

> You will probably remember me as one of the four young men of the Fall River Diocese whom you approached on December 12th last at the Sulpician Seminary with the proposition that we should come and teach for you in your diocese in the event that there would be no opening for us at home at the time of ordination. This latter seems certain. There will be no place.[4]

Brady then shared with his future ordinary that—after thought, prayer, and advice—"I can honestly say that I feel ready to accept your offer." The young seminarian then laid out—in typical Brady style—his several questions: "In preparation, then, for acceptance of your offer, I would like—hoping not to appear bold or forward or out of place—to ask your Grace the solution of several questions that have proposed themselves."

The first question was whether Dowling would allow him to be ordained in the cathedral in Fall River so that his parents "who have sacrificed so much for me" could be present. Second, he inquired who would bear the expenses for the university course that would prepare him for teaching. Again, he did not feel that he could lay a further burden on his parents. Third, Brady asked what his area of specialization would be; he indicated that his preference would be dogmatic or moral theology. Lastly, in the event of acceptance, Brady wondered what the process of adoption would entail:

> I am in the last half of my third year in theology, ready for subdiaconate. Will it be necessary for me to come to Saint Paul and establish domicile before the dimissorials for orders can be signed, or will it be enough that my Bishop of origin call me with the understanding between himself and your Grace that I am to come to you after ordination?[5]

In April 1923, Dowling again visited the Sulpician Seminary, at which time Brady hoped to receive the answers to his questions. One senses the air of frustration in Brady's subsequent letter to Dowling: "As our meeting came to rather an abrupt end during your call here, I feel that there still remain some things that need a definite and decisive answer." First and foremost he mentions "ordination at home." He states: "May I presume that because the Bishop of Fall River will continue to call us, that we will be ordained there?"

The seminarian then reiterated his concerns about an area of specialization. "Am I right in drawing from your talk a wish that I work along the lines of methods in teaching religion? Such would please me greatly, for as I told you, I hope to be first a priest and secondly a teacher, with the teaching entirely subordinate to the priesthood." Brady reiterated more fully his concerns about monetary issues, referring to the fact that he had not been brought up in luxury, and that his father, an ordinary workingman, and his mother were both over sixty years of age. He did not want to ask them for further assistance. Brady concluded his letter by stating: "I trust that your Grace will understand me in this matter and not think me forward or impudent or mercenary." He added a reminder: "If I remember rightly, your Grace promised to send a letter of details of what you planned to do with us next year, of studies, ordination, etc. I await any wish of yours."[6]

Brady wrote to Dowling regularly during his years as a student. The concerns were often the same: the particulars of excardination/incardination; need for funds; where to pursue his studies; what specialization; what he would teach when he arrived in St. Paul. The correspondence reflects the sort of focused approach Brady would always take to any assignment he received, including that of archbishop.

William Otterwell Ignatius Brady was ordained to the priesthood December 21, 1923, for the Fall River diocese. The document of incardination into the Archdiocese of St. Paul is dated August 6, 1924. He had spent the academic year 1923–1924 at the Catholic University of America living at Caldwell Hall; he received the S.T.B. and M.A. degrees at the end of the year. He concluded, however, that to continue at the Catholic University was not feasible, and in a letter to Dowling in May he stated that he would take the archbishop's advice and brush up on his Latin and French with an eye to Louvain.

What followed was the great debate as to whether he should study at Louvain or at "the Angelico" in Rome. Dowling recommended that he confer by mail with Father Rudolph Bandas who had studied at both places. The pendulum moved back and forth, a state of life that Brady did not find comfortable. In a letter to Dowling August 6, 1924, Brady stated: "The double statement of your letter —'prepare to go to Louvain and confer with Bandas' and 'if Bandas thinks the Angelico would be better for you, you may go there instead'—leave me a little at sea still as well as yourself." He then described his further discernment with others, and concluded that his hope was that Father Bandas's recommendation would be "the Angelico." Brady added: "But no matter about this personal feeling. I do not care to make the choice. If your Grace would take the responsibility of saying definitely one place or the other, I will be glad to follow obediently."[7]

On August 20, 1924, he finally received word from the archbishop that he would go to Rome. In his response to Dowling, tucked in among the phrases of appreciation and "whatever you wish me to do," is a statement in which "Bill" Brady gave himself away. He wrote: "The state of indecision always irritates me."[8] This seemed to be true all through his life.

Living in Italy for two years gave him an opportunity to experience a Mediterranean culture, to learn Italian, and to become knowledgeable about ecclesiastical affairs. As early as December 1925, Brady wrote to Dowling regarding his future assignment. "I shall be ready to take any work you have for me. Please don't think I'm prying for information, but there are details to be arranged and a little foresight is much easier on the nerves than mad rushing at the end."[9] He pointed out the necessity of sending his books in sufficient time so that they would be there for his class preparation. He hoped to know what courses he would be teaching. In the spring of 1926 his doctoral dissertation *De gratiae reviviscentia in sacramentis ficte susceptis* was accepted summa cum laude, the only one so approved that year.[10]

After some traveling in Europe, Brady returned to Fall River for vacation time with his family. In a letter to Dowling July 13, 1926, it is apparent that he still did not know his specific assignment. After describing his departure from Rome and other ventures, he stated—in an effort to sound casual—"So 'there you are' as the current English phrase has it. And here I am, awaiting your wishes."[11]

It must have come to him as more than a surprise that after doing doctoral studies in dogmatic theology he would be assigned to teach moral theology. Although he was aware of the death of Father Jeremiah C. Harrington, professor of moral theology at the Saint Paul Seminary, on June 5, 1926, it seems not to have dawned on Brady that he would be the replacement. He wrote to Dowling on July 24, 1926: "Many thanks for your letter that came early this week. I shall need to brush up somewhat on the moral theology, but be assured that I shall put all there is in me into the work."[12]

The letters of Brady the seminarian and Brady the young student priest offer some insight into Brady as professor, rector, trustee, and ordinary. In his later years he was perceived as someone who made snap judgments, possibly because of his eagerness for decisions. He was not a patient person, even in his youth. As he acquired new and powerful roles he was even less accepting of those who did not conform to his expectations.

Brady was remembered as an excellent teacher. He had an attractive personality, was easy to talk to, and gave concrete examples when teaching both moral and pastoral theology. Some have suggested that it was in that capacity that he really had the greatest influence in the church—training future priests for the archdiocese and beyond. Moreover, that influence was extended beyond the campus. In 1932, Archbishop Murray appointed Brady "Master of Conferences," which made him responsible for deanery meetings held twice each year for the priests in the archdiocese. Brady determined the subjects for discussion, assigned papers to be read, and chaired the sessions. Finally, Brady was also named *officialis* of the archdiocesan tribunal.[13]

Minnesota was very far from Massachusetts, and a desire to maintain family connections was very real. When Brady's father died in 1928, William returned to Fall River for the funeral. He suggested to his sister Leonora, who had attended Bridgewater Normal School for two years, that she might benefit from coming west and completing her academic work at the College of St. Catherine. She came in 1930, completed one year of course work, and graduated from St. Catherine's with a bachelor's degree in English. After a year of teaching at Derham Hall, the secondary school of the Sisters of St. Joseph on the campus at St. Catherine's, she entered the novitiate of the Sisters of St. Joseph of Carondelet in St. Paul. As "Sister Mary William Brady, C.S.J.," she would be a strong supporter of and collaborator with her brother in years to come.[14] When Leonora was a novice, her mother came to Minnesota, settling not far from the seminary, and was supportive of her son during his rectorship at the Saint Paul Seminary.[15]

Brady as Seminary Rector

Brady's appointment as rector of the Saint Paul Seminary, and the stories connected to it, have been discussed above. In the letter of appointment June 26, 1933, Archbishop Murray stated: "On the feast of your patron I am asking you to take over the responsibility for the office of rector of St. Paul's Seminary in the hope that you may find this post an opportunity to realize the aims which you have entertained for the most fruitful service in training apostles for the vineyard of our Divine Master."[16]

At the age of thirty-four, Brady had grown in self-confidence and decisiveness. As rector, he continued to teach moral theology, pastoral theology to the deacons, and a class in Italian. He became well known as a preacher and lecturer. In addition to teaching at the seminary, he offered classes at the College of St. Catherine, at the Diocesan Teachers' College, and at St. Joseph's Academy. He wrote a weekly column under the general title of "Faith and Practice" for the *Catholic Bulletin* that many—both clergy and laity—found thoughtful and stimulating.

Not all of Brady's work was within the Catholic community. In 1928 he presented an address to the Minnesota Protestant ministers at Carleton College on "Catholic Education."[17] On November 23, 1933, he was invited to give an address at the Methodist Episcopal Church in Red Wing, Minnesota, on "Why I Am A Catholic."[18]

In 1934, Brady, still a newly-appointed rector, gave one of the addresses at the meeting of the Seminary Department of the National Catholic Educational Association Convention in Chicago.[19] His topic was "The Seminarians Vacation." In the introduction he discussed related statements from the Council of Trent, and pronouncements in the nineteenth and twentieth centuries (including Baltimore III and Leo XIII) which, he noted, were directive but not normative in regard to the question. He then set forth five approaches, from the strict villa system to a vacation spent completely at the will of the seminarian with little or no supervision, and the advantages and disadvantages of each.

Brady's evaluation of the five approaches are measured and realistic. Although he does not make a specific recommendation, he was most enthusiastic about the fifth option. He concluded:

> Finally there is the vacation now growing in the seminaries in the United States where seminarians spend a short time with their parents and the remainder in the care of some priest—usually away from home—by whom he is instructed in the practical work of the ministry, catechetics, street preaching, work among the underprivileged, etc. and by whom he is initiated in the work of Church, school and club, and from whom, also, the seminarian receives his first initiation into priestly work.

Brady saw this as a "genuine opportunity for seminarians' service," but acknowledged that there needed to be "a campaign to enlist the cooperation and sympathy of the parish priest in the work of the seminary." The cooperation of the clergy should be requested in taking seminarians with them on parish calls, sick calls, census taking, and other activities of the parish.

The involvement of the seminary in such summer projects was also required. Some sort of library service needed to be inaugurated if the expectation was that students would do some quality reading in the summer. Also "the assignment of seminarians to religious summer work should have some supervision by the seminary authorities (or by the ordinaries) so that the priests in turn to whom they are assigned could be given their responsibilities." Some form of public recognition of the seminarian would also enhance the solidarity between the priest and the seminarian and the relationship to the parish community.

Brady's vision of what would be described today as "field education" was broad and creative. In addition to his internal initiatives at the Saint Paul Seminary to restructure the schedule, offer a rector's conference weekly, provide a new format for the catalogue, etc., he also initiated proposals nationally to enhance seminary education. He was twice elected president of the Seminary Department of the National Catholic Educational Association and was serving in that capacity when appointed bishop in 1939. This, in turn, had its effects on the Saint Paul Seminary that was perceived as creative, progressive, and stable in an era when the country was suffering from economic crisis.

Although Brady made efforts to open up new vistas for the seminarians, his expectations of their behavior were exacting. He was not above checking on the students to see if they were obeying the rules. Gerald O'Keefe, a seminarian from 1938 to 1944, described one incident in the 1930s when Brady indicated that he was going to check the residence halls to make certain that the students were in their rooms. Apparently someone overheard this in the administration building and knew that some seminarians had decided to sneak off to attend a movie at a nearby theater. That person phoned the theater and asked the manager to relay an important message to the audience: "Mr. Tanqueray—please come home!" The name of the well-known author of seminary textbooks signaled a "crisis." The seminarians left the theater in great haste and were back in their rooms studying when the rector checked on them later in the evening.[20]

James P. Shannon, seminarian from 1941 to 1946, mused on the comments of priests who had known Brady as rector. "They often joked about his cockiness and omniscience. You could never tell him any news that would surprise him. He would act as though he had already heard it long before you did."[21] But he was clearly a "people-person" and students appreciated his energy and vitality.

Brady's Transition from Rector to Archbishop

Brady's time as bishop of Sioux Falls made him more sensitive to a rural environment. He arrived there when the diocese was in horrendous financial condition as a result of the Depression. As a good administrator he was able to negotiate unpaid loans and eventually returned the diocese to a sound financial base.[22] He liked the priests and the people, and became more at home with the rural and Native American members of the church in Sioux Falls.[23] However, it was unlikely that, even after two decades of living in the Upper Midwest, one could entirely "take the city (and the easterner) out of the boy."

Brady was named a trustee of the seminary in the years following his rectorship. In an unusual situation, Bishop Brady was present in 1939 to offer his resignation as secretary and treasurer of the board that he had held ex officio as rector. He received a vote of commendation for his years of service. Whether done spontaneously or preplanned is not known, but Brady's continuance as a member of the board was then moved, seconded, and approved. The minutes read: "On motion of Mr. Schlick and second of Bishop Lawlor, Bishop Brady was elected to the Corporation of the Seminary to fill out the unexpired term of Bishop Mahoney, deceased, said term to expire at the annual meeting of 1940 or until a successor be elected."[24] It would appear that Bishop Brady wanted to continue to be involved in the Saint Paul Seminary; one might ask to what degree he used his influence to effect the vote. One might also wonder about Father Wolf's response, knowing that his predecessor would be forever looking over his shoulder.

It took only a little more than a year for Brady to reap the benefit of his appointment to the board. The Sioux Falls Diocese owed a debt of $24,040 to the Saint Paul Seminary, a burden that Brady inherited when he became ordinary. He brokered a very beneficial deal. At the trustees meeting on October 28, 1940, it was moved and seconded that "the Board go on record as willing to accept a settlement of $5,000 in lieu of $24,040. All present, except Bishop Brady who did not vote, approved the proposal. Bishop Brady then expressed his satisfaction and thanked the Board for its action." At the same meeting, Brady was unanimously elected to the board of trustees for a full term, which he accepted.[25]

When Brady returned to St. Paul as coadjutor in the summer of 1956, with Murray's health in severe decline, it was clear that he would be taking over all of the responsibility in the near future. In fact, Murray was so ill that he was unable to attend Brady's installation ceremony in the cathedral August 21, 1956. Brady preached an impressive sermon—mostly a reflection of what he thought Murray would have said had he been present.[26] Brady's time as coadjutor was brief. Murray died October 11, 1956.

By 1955, Sister Mary William Brady, C.S.J., had become president of the College of St. Catherine.[27] This gave rise to the appellation "the reign of William and Mary" regarding the years 1956–1961 in the Archdiocese of St. Paul. Murray had lived in the cathedral rectory, but Brady was not eager to live in rooms on the third floor of that building. In a letter to Murray in June 1956, Brady discussed possibilities for his living arrangements. He suggested that he accept the invitation of the Sisters of St. Joseph to live on the second floor of the guest house at St. Catherine's. He specified that this would be temporary but would "allow a breathing spell in which to think out a proper archepiscopal house."[28] In early 1958 he moved to the Saint Paul Seminary.

Brady's Influence on the Saint Paul Seminary as Archbishop

There had been significant changes in the seminary in those seventeen years Brady was in Sioux Falls. When he left in 1939 the enrollment was 171; when he returned in 1956 it was 365. St. Mary's Chapel was so crowded that weekday Masses were celebrated for the philosophy students in Cretin Oratory, and "the philosophers" joined the theology students only for the Solemn High Mass on Sunday. On those occasions the choir loft was filled, bleachers were erected on the back wall, an extension was added to the stately choir stalls, and chairs and kneelers were placed in the ambulatories behind the choir stalls where one could not even see the liturgy in progress.[29]

Life in the seminary during the years Brady was archbishop was not only crowded but demanding—still lived under the old regime. Father Ladislaus Sledz, who was dean of Cretin Residence where the philosophy students lived, is remembered as a tough taskmaster.[30] Sledz, who had been a prisoner of war, was both scrupulous and authoritarian. The general interpretation was that if you could get through the first two years with Father Sledz, you certainly had a vocation![31]

Conditions were so crowded that two students continued to occupy the two-room suites in the residence halls originally planned for one. The theology students ate in the main dining room of the refectory with the faculty who were on a raised platform at one end. The philosophy students, however, had their meals in three smaller rooms—two downstairs, and one upstairs adjacent to the main dining room. The upper room, although separate from the main dining room, had windows through which students could view the faculty eating on the dais; this was labeled "heaven"—interpreted as such (in jest) because they had a view of the "beatific vision." The two lower rooms were less desirable. The one supervised by Father Sledz was named "hell." The other room was "purgatory."[32]

Most important for the seminary's future, Brady realized that the faculty had changed very little from the time he had been rector and most of the senior members were past their prime. He was convinced that changes needed to be made and fresh ideas sought. According to many who were students in the 1950s, the quality of teaching left something to be desired. Classes were taught from the manuals or from lecture notes passed along over the years. John F. Kinney, at the Saint Paul Seminary from 1957 to 1963, told of the entrepreneurial endeavor known as "the Kentucky Press." Two seminarians from Covington, Kentucky, started the enterprise and named it. The task was to mimeograph official class notes and sell them to class members. There were no textbooks for most classes, including scripture. It was all legitimate, and an opportunity to earn some pocket money. John and his classmate Robert E. Burke bought "the Kentucky Press" from the previous operators. What they discovered was that an "underground press" was also in operation; this included mimeographing and selling questions and answers for dogma exams—all, of course, *sub secreto.* They sold "the Kentucky Press" a few years later at exactly the right time. When Jerome Quinn arrived to teach scripture in the fall of 1961, "the Kentucky Press" became obsolete.[33] With the exception of Father David Dillon, who was academically and pedagogically the "shining light," most professors did not stimulate intellectual excitement among the students. Many were described as boring. This was a common concern in many Catholic seminaries, colleges, and universities in that era.

It was Msgr. John Tracy Ellis, in his ground-breaking lecture on "American Catholics and the Intellectual Life" at the Catholic Commission on Intellectual and Cultural Affairs in St. Louis in 1955, who candidly described the deficiencies in Catholic higher education and the absence of an intellectual tradition among Catholics in the United States.[34] His challenge was accepted by Father Gustave Weigel, S.J., who made a presentation to the same commission in 1957 on "American Catholic Intellectualism—A Theologian's Reflection." Weigel believed that the emphasis on apologetics had usurped the possibilities for genuine scholarship, and that the isolation of the seminary was a contributing factor.[35]

The most in-depth analysis of the situation was offered by Dr. Thomas F. O'Dea, sociology professor at Fordham University in New York, in 1958. His volume, *American Catholic Dilemma: An Inquiry into the Intellectual Life,* raised many questions, particularly about the role that authority played in Catholic education, especially in the seminary. O'Dea concluded that the basic characteristics of the American Catholic milieu that inhibited the development of mature intellectual activity were: formalism, authoritarianism, clericalism, moralism, and defensiveness. These five factors were operative on both manifest and latent levels.[36]

O'Dea pleaded for the necessity of research, for coming to grips with Catholic history, and for a break with formalism. He acknowledged that the post-World War II religious revival was in many ways superficial, but referred to the fact that at the root of such developments (e.g., large number of vocations, popularity of the liturgical movement, the Christian Family Movement, etc.) was "a serious search for a deeper spiritual life." He concluded: "For our God is also a God of history, and as intelligent creatures of God, men must give an account of themselves in history. Our duty to God, to the Church, to the Republic and to ourselves demands that the present critical reconsideration of ourselves should be carried forward."[37]

Whether or not Brady read the essays by Ellis and Weigel, or the volume by O'Dea, is not known, but he certainly would have been familiar with the conversation. In his address of welcome to the Catholic Theological Society of America Convention in St. Paul on June 24, 1958, he referred to the question, however obliquely: "Your annual meetings and continued twelvemonth exchanges are proof enough that there does exist an intellectual elite among us. Indeed, if we do not have an elite here, it would seem that current critics speak with double-barreled force."[38] Brady urged the theologians to consider as important "a synthesis between our theological thinking and our dusty-shoe area of practical action." Issues pressing for adequate explanation, he noted, were church-state relations, moral questions, and Mariology. Mostly, he pleaded for a simplicity of language: "The missionary message of the Church is hardly clarified by refuge in words like 'kerygmatic.'"[39] Brady reminded his audience that he had been a seminary professor before becoming a bishop some nineteen years before. He challenged them: "To you, our theologians, we want to turn, and to you we must turn, not for what our critics call the dry bones of theological argumentation but for that living and consoling inspiration which the theological sciences can give to a fuller understanding of God and a firmer union of all His creatures with Him."[40]

Brady's Re-Organizing of the Seminary

Brady's vision of the seminary—past, present, and future—and that of the rector, Msgr. Rudolph Bandas, could not have been more different. It must have been clear to Brady shortly after his arrival in St. Paul in 1956 that Bandas would have to be replaced. Even from their early years as young faculty members in the 1920s, Brady and Bandas seemed to have been incompatible. One commentator noted: "They were not on the same wavelength." Brady—the energetic, decisive, sometimes authoritarian personality—wanted to be in control; Bandas—the intelligent but enigmatic rector who never quite fit in—seemed aloof, rigid, above the crowd, sometimes suspicious, a disaffected person.[41] Father Gerald Baskfield was quoted as having said about the rector: "The trouble with Bandas is that he thinks the faculty is following him. What he doesn't know is that we're *after him*."[42] Both Brady and Bandas had gifts and liabilities; their relationship had been strained for a long time.[43]

The polarization of the faculty contributed to the unrest. Father Lawrence Ryan, Father William Busch, and Father Lawrence Wolf, it has been suggested, were a kind of troika more or less organized against the administration. It is possible that one or all of these complained to Brady about Bandas and suggested that he had had a sufficiently lengthy time as rector. Because the archbishop had been a colleague of Bandas from years past, he probably moved cautiously.

Replacing Bandas was more complicated than just reappointing him. Bandas was known to have friends in high places in Rome—especially Cardinal Joseph Pizzardo, prefect of the Sacred Congregation on Seminaries and Universities. As mentioned above, Bandas had been appointed a consultor to that congregation by Pope Pius XII on June 26, 1954, and elevated to the rank of Domestic Prelate a year later. To remove Bandas and replace him with a priest possibly less qualified might cause some consternation at the Vatican. Brady had to have an appointment for Bandas "which he couldn't refuse."

With the erection of the diocese of New Ulm in 1957, the perfect opportunity was provided. The pastor of St. Agnes Parish in St. Paul, Alphonse Schladweiler, was appointed the first bishop of New Ulm. Saint Agnes was a prestigious parish that had had outstanding pastors—

some of whom had become bishops. It was—in the context of the old "benefice" system—a worthy appointment.[44]

It is unclear when Brady informed Bandas of his appointment to St. Agnes. On January 2 the rector left the seminary to attend meetings in Rome. It was not until the students returned in February to begin the second semester that they learned that Msgr. Bandas had been appointed pastor of St. Agnes Church in St. Paul effective February 10, 1958. The first clue, according to David McCauley, seminarian from 1957 to 1963, was the big black Lincoln parked in the driveway in front of the administration building. No one ever parked there except the archbishop.[45] No formal announcement was made in assembly; the seminary learned the startling news by reading a note on the bulletin board. No farewell festivities were ever held for Msgr. Bandas. According to Charles Froehle, a classmate of McCauley's, it was very unceremonious.[46] The impression was that, after twelve and a half years as rector, Bandas had been "fired."[47]

The accompanying information was even more extraordinary. Msgr. Gerald O'Keefe, chancellor of the archdiocese, announced in *The Catholic Bulletin* (February 8, 1958) several appointments, including Bandas's assignment to St. Agnes. Most significant was the final statement: "The Archbishop reserves to himself the rectorship of the St. Paul Seminary."[48] A few weeks later the chancellor announced that effective February 22, 1958, the archbishop had appointed Msgr. Lawrence O. Wolf vice-rector of the seminary, and Father David Dillon administrative assistant to the rector. The statement reiterated that Archbishop Brady was "reserving to himself the rectorship of the seminary."[49] This unusual situation has been explained by some as Brady's effort to avoid complications in Rome. Had he appointed someone who did not seem as qualified as Bandas, there might have been repercussions from Cardinal Pizzardo. When Brady made himself the rector, the Vatican could hardly complain.

Dillon, although his title was administrative assistant, was in charge of the internal affairs of the seminary and was considered the "acting rector." He gave rector's conferences, sat in the rector's place in the dining room, and was the final authority—with the exception of the archbishop—for permissions and decisions. He was listed as secretary-treasurer of the board of trustees, although no board meetings were held during his tenure. The students liked Dillon; he was a breath of fresh air. He seemed to be euphoric about being "acting rector" although he didn't have the specific title.[50] Many, and very possibly Dillon himself, thought that he would be appointed rector when the dust settled.[51]

Brady moved into the seminary in February 1958, used the rector's office, and lived in the rector's quarters. On February 23, 1958, the deacons for the Archdiocese of St. Paul were ordained to the priesthood. Although they were still students finishing their programs, they could then help in the parishes on weekends. James Whalen remembers that Brady called the newly-ordained deacons into the rector's office one-by-one to give them their assignments.[52]

The archbishop was not particularly visible on campus, but he did give a few rector's conferences. David McCauley recalled one on the subject of authority. Brady was very clear about the fact that he did not want "Yes" men. If they disagreed with him, they should let him know. It was all right to challenge him. However, once a decision was made, he expected that it would be accepted and carried out.[53] In some ways, McCauley thought that Brady fashioned himself a kind of "John Ireland." He never sent a seminarian to the North American College in Rome, because he thought students should be prepared for priesthood in an American environment. When in Rome, he refused to walk the streets in a cassock; American bishops wore black suits in public, and he believed they should do the same in Europe. On one occasion when an elderly couple began to genuflect to kiss his ring, Brady was supposed to have said: "You're too old to be doing that. I don't want to be picking you up."[54] Brady was outgoing, had energy and flair, and probably wanted to be an inspiration and role model for seminarians as John Ireland had been.

In many ways, Brady as archbishop-rector enjoyed the camaraderie of his old colleagues—Baskfield, Busch, Doherty, and Wolf. He sometimes came for liturgy and for meals in the faculty dining room where the faculty ate breakfast and sometimes lunch. Dinner was still in the main dining room in the refectory where the faculty sat on the dais according to seniority in terms of year of ordination. Dillon sat next to Brady—a clear sign of his authority. Raymond Lucker, one of the youngest faculty members at the time, does not remember Brady's presence as intimidating. Instead, he recalls that he seemed to enjoy being back with his old cronies.[55]

Possibly Brady's greatest contribution was in appointing new members to the faculty and sending younger priests away to study for future assignments at the seminary. In 1957 Father John O'Sullivan was appointed professor of moral theology, sociology, and economics to succeed Msgr. Gilligan who was appointed pastor of St. Mark's parish in St. Paul. Father Raymond Lucker was appointed professor of catechetics, an area in which Msgr. Bandas had been deeply involved. They joined Father Jack Sweeney, Father William Baumgaertner, and Father Patrick Ahern as the "younger" members of the faculty.

Archbishop Murray had sent a select group of seminarians to do their theological studies at his alma mater in Louvain in the early 1950s. These included Mark Dosh, John Gilbert, James Moudry, and Patrick Ryan. Murray also assigned Ellsworth Kneal to the marriage tribunal—arriving on a Saturday afternoon at St. Helena's Parish and knocking on the door of Kneal's confessional to inform him of the assignment.[56] All of these priests would become members of the seminary faculty in the 1960s.

It was Brady, however, who sent Dosh, Moudry, and Ryan to the Angelicum, and Jerome Quinn to the Biblicum, for doctoral studies in Rome after ordination. In 1961, shortly before Archbishop Brady died, Father Mark Dosh took up his assignment as professor of metaphysics and ethics, Father James Moudry became professor of moral theology and sacramental theology, and Father Jerome Quinn was appointed professor of Old Testament and Hebrew. These teachers brought to the students new methods and a spirit of excitement for the exploration of scripture and theology in the immediate pre-Vatican II period. The manualist tradition was clearly on the wane.

Although Brady's original intent for sending Ellsworth Kneal to the Catholic University of America in 1958 for a licentiate in canon law was to develop the marriage tribunal, Kneal's life was changed, as was Brady's, with a faculty death. On June 7, 1960, as Kneal was driving back from Catholic University having completed his program, the gentle, much-beloved Msgr. Eugene J. Moriarity, who had been professor of canon law since 1937, died. Father Kneal found himself with an unexpected assignment. In addition to developing the tribunal, he was appointed professor of canon law and economics. A new perspective on canon law became a reality at the seminary. Later, Archbishop Binz sent Kneal to Rome (1965–1966) for his doctorate.[57]

The almost twenty-year reign of Pope Pius XII from 1939 to 1958 had seen the ascendancy of "cultural Catholicism" in the United States. In the post-World War II period, with vocations at an all-time high, it was difficult to think of the church as anything but growing in numbers and becoming more of the "establishment" in America. Pope Pius XII's death, in retrospect, was indeed the end of an era. The surprising announcement of the new pope, John XXIII, on January 25, 1959, that he was calling an ecumenical council was met with a variety of reactions. Initially, seminarians, as well as others in the church, were unclear about its import.

As preparations for the council ensued, exciting literature became available to Catholics who knew little about what a council could mean for the church. Perhaps one of the most influential volumes was *The Council, Reform and Reunion* by Hans Küng, the controversial priest-professor from Switzerland. The writings of European theologians such as Yves Congar, Karl Rahner, Edward Schillebeeckx, Jean Daniélou, Henri de Lubac, and others became available in English. The study of theology took on new life for priests, religious, lay people—and seminarians.

The Jesuit paleontologist-theologian-mystic Pierre Teilhard de Chardin, whose controversial writings on original sin were left unpublished because of the threat of censure from the Holy Office, died in 1955. Shortly after, some French friends published his work. In 1960 his volume *The Phenomenon of Man* appeared in English. These and other writings such as *The Divine Milieu, Hymn of the Universe,* and *The Future of Man* brought to many in the church—especially those in religious houses and seminaries—an exciting, expansive vision of God's world "moving ever onward in a stream of universal becoming."[58] Teilhard's impact, which contributed to the new appreciation of historical consciousness among Catholics, cannot be underestimated in terms of moving from a static to a dynamic understanding of truth as it was being interpreted in the church in the early 1960s.

"Dynamic" was also a word used to describe Brady. The seminarians liked his energy. He spoke well, his weekly column for the *Catholic Bulletin* was very popular, and he was appointed to one of the pre-conciliar commissions, which made them proud. He brought excellent skills in administration and leadership to the archdiocese after Murray's illness and lengthy reign. In a contagious way, his activity affected the seminary. John F. Kinney, ordained in 1963, recalled a time in the pre-council days when changes in the liturgy were being discussed. A seminarian asked Archbishop Brady if he thought that the liturgy would ever be in English. Brady replied: "Not in my lifetime!" Ironically, Brady's death not too long thereafter made that pronouncement only too true.[59]

Louis McCarthy Becomes Rector

One morning at breakfast in August 1958, "between mouthfuls of cereal," Archbishop Brady announced: "Father Dillon, I think you should know that I have appointed Msgr. McCarthy [then rector of Nazareth Hall minor seminary] as the new rector of the seminary." There was silence. Many have conjectured that Dillon was very disappointed. He never said that, but several of his colleagues intuited it. The lack of sensitivity of Brady's announcement was obvious to all. No gratitude was extended to Dillon for all that he had done. It was a painful moment for more than the "acting rector."[60] In later years, Father Mark Dosh remembers Dillon saying: "Never accept a position without the authority to go with it." In retrospect, Dosh believed Dillon was referring to his painful experience as "acting rector."[61]

One interpretation of McCarthy's appointment was that Brady was aware of the division in the faculty between younger and older members. Dillon had been more in the middle and therefore had been a good choice for the interim. Perhaps Brady wanted a rector familiar with the system, but who had some distance from the current challenges. McCarthy knew the Saint Paul Seminary well from his experience as spiritual director and professor of philosophy before becoming rector of Nazareth Hall, but had not been intimately involved with the seminary's internal life for ten years.

Many students knew Msgr. Louis J. McCarthy from their minor seminary days. They appreciated and respected him but were clearly surprised by his appointment. They liked Dillon and had hoped that he would stay on. There was no ill feeling for McCarthy, but not a lot of enthusiasm.[62] Many seminarians, having had McCarthy as a rector at Nazareth Hall for six years, felt, perhaps, that he knew them "too well," or that they had already heard much of what he had to say.

Msgr. Louis McCarthy had a challenging experience as rector of the seminary from 1958 to 1968. His early years under Archbishop Brady were difficult. Because of the way he had been appointed, there were those who thought that McCarthy felt subservient to Brady who continued to dominate the scene. One example of this was Brady's disapproval of the students out on the campus in their old clothes playing sports on Sunday. McCarthy knew that the students needed the air and exercise.[63] At the

Louis J. McCarthy, rector of the Saint Paul Seminary from 1958 to 1968

opening Mass of the school year in 1958, the archbishop announced that, in the future, Sundays would be observed as a day of rest and prayer. It was expected that the seminarians would wear their cassocks all day. For exercise they could walk around the perimeter of the campus.[64]

Some have suggested that this mandate, and other Brady directives (e.g., the priest must always wear a hat—straw in the summer, but black after Labor Day), were part of his New England background. The "Blue Laws" were still effective in those years, especially in the East, and Brady's vision of the priest had been instilled in him there.[65]

Campus Life in the Pre–Vatican II Era

The spiritual life of the seminarians revolved around the prayer and liturgical exercises of the day, not dissimilar to years past. One devotional experience remembered by many former seminarians was the long-standing tradition from the 1930s or before, of going to the grotto after dinner every evening in May (weather permitting) to pray the Litany of the Blessed Virgin Mary and sing an appropriate hymn to the Mother of God.[66] In the 1950s and 1960s, seminarians would gather at the grotto in both May and October. The rosary would be recited and the anthem of the season sung—in October the "Salve Regina," and in May—usually the Easter season—the "Regina Coeli."[67]

May devotions at the seminary grotto in the 1950s

In the period of the late 1950s and early 1960s, prayer to Our Lady to save the world from communism, and for the salvation of Russia, was common. Devotion to Our Lady of Fatima was at its height. Father Peyton, director of the Family Rosary Crusade, spoke to the students on more than one occasion. In the late 1950s Archbishop Brady allowed Father Peyton to conduct his Rosary Crusade in St. Paul. Father Richard Doherty organized it, with the music under the direction of Father John Sweeney. Rather than at the cathedral, it was held on the approach to the state capitol and developed into the largest religious gathering in the state of Minnesota up to that time.[68]

Every First Friday was an afternoon of recollection at the seminary, which concluded with a Holy Hour. Father John Sweeney was there to direct the music, and remembers fine talks given by the spiritual director, Father Lawrence Ryan. The devotional life of the students was not dissimilar to that of the Catholic Church at large in the pre-Vatican II era.

Guest lecturers were brought in to enrich the life of the students.[69] Among those who spoke in the *aula* from September 1956 to October 1961 were previous guests such as Fulton J. Sheen, alumnus, by then auxiliary bishop of New York, and the artist Ade Bethune. Msgr. Reynold Hillenbrand spoke on "The Layman's Role in the Church," and Father William Lynch, S.J., from Georgetown University lectured on "Psychological Implications in the Use of Mass Media." Msgr. Martin Hellreigel, deeply involved in the liturgical movement, offered a demonstration of low Mass and Canon Joseph Cardijn of Malines, Belgium, spoke about the Young Christian Workers and other movements that he had helped to found. The Jesuit scripture scholar Father Roderick A. F. MacKenzie made presentations on "The Psalms," "Literary Forms in the Old Testament," and "'Origins' in the Book of Genesis." These and other outstanding lectures became an important preparation for the seminarians in raising their consciousness on issues that would be crucial at Vatican II.

Movies were presented in the *aula* about once a month, except during Advent and Lent. These included well-recognized films such as "The Keys of the Kingdom," "East of Eden," "Death of a Salesman," "Tight Little Island," "The Student Prince," "The Ox Bow Incident," and "Great Expectations." Father James Whalen recalled one occasion when Father Lawrence Ryan discovered that the film for the evening was "The Naked City." He was outraged and interpreted the title at its worst, not realizing that the movie with Barry Fitzgerald was a police drama about the murder of a young girl and the manhunt which ensued![70] In May 1959, several students attended the Metropolitan Opera presentation of *Die Fledermaus* at Northrup Auditorium in Minneapolis.

The Saint Paul Seminary Drama Society offered some substantive presentations such as "Murder in the Cathedral," "The Little World of Dom Camillo," "Inherit the Wind," "Arsenic and Old Lace," and Henrik Ibsen's "The Enemy of the People." Music, under the direction of Father John Sweeney, was also an important dimension of seminary life, and concerts were given periodically.

The Board of Trustees under Brady

The financial condition of the seminary and its future well-being were of paramount concern to Brady, the businessman, who always expected that tasks would be carried out with efficiency. James Shannon, when president of the College of St. Thomas, portrayed his dealings with the archbishop as follows: "He prized brevity. I would lay out the problem, survey the available options, pick the one I favored, and offer my evidence. He would usually decide on the spot."[71] Raymond Lucker, who, while on the seminary faculty, was also assigned as archdiocesan director of the Confraternity of Christian Doctrine by Brady, described his interactions with the archbishop similarly. "He dealt with matters expeditiously. Sometimes meetings lasted only seven or eight minutes."[72]

This decisiveness applied to Brady's dealings with the seminary board of trustees. The regular annual board meeting in 1956 was scheduled for October 12, the day after Archbishop Murray died. At this meeting, Brady presided for the first time as chair and president of the corporation. After members passed resolutions of sympathy to members of Murray's family, finances were the order of the day. Archbishop Brady noted that the debt on the new library had been paid in full—the funds received totaling $362,727.31. It was noted that:

> Beginning in September, 1953, the Chancery Office of the Archdiocese of St. Paul, without any notification, began deducting 20% from the monthly bills presented to it by the St. Paul Seminary for the board and tuition of students affiliated with the St. Paul Archdiocese. These deductions were made monthly up to June, 1956, inclusive.... On September 1, 1956 the accumulated debt of the St. Paul Archdiocese to the St. Paul Seminary stood at $46,904.00.[73]

The final payments for the library were described the previous year in the minutes of the last meeting at which Archbishop Murray presided on October 12, 1955. No mention was made at that time of deductions from tuition and board to help in the repayment of the library debt.

Archbishop Brady's recommendation as recorded in the minutes of the board meeting is as follows: "The St. Paul Seminary is to issue a check to the Diocese of St. Paul for $46,904.00 as reimbursement for funds advanced by the Diocese for payment of debt on the new Library. The Diocese will in turn issue a check for the same amount to the St. Paul Seminary to liquidate its debt to the Seminary. The board took no stand on similar deductions in the future."[74] It is unclear as to the origin of this debt in the breakdown of figures given, if the arrangement as described at the 1955 meeting was final.

At the same meeting the board voted unanimously to set up a finance committee which would make a thorough study of the seminary's investments. One presumes that this was Brady's suggestion, as no other name is given. Msgr. Bandas moved, the archbishop seconded, and the board approved compensation of $50.00 for trustees coming from outside the Twin Cities. The allocation of funds for building repairs and determining the location for the new garage for professors' cars concluded the business.[75] Brady was known for his financial acumen;[76] with the seminary he was going to "hit the ground running."

When the board met October 15, 1958, the archbishop announced that Msgr. McCarthy had been appointed rector. In addition to the usual matters, the members discussed the policy regarding the seminary bank accounts and the safety deposit box. The minutes stated clearly: "No monies may be borrowed by any member of the Board of Trustees." It is interesting that those empowered to sign checks included Archbishop Brady, Msgr. McCarthy, and Father David Dillon. The same three, plus Miss Marie Berres, the bookkeeper, were authorized to open the safety deposit box.

Board member Bishop Schenck urged an examination of securities held by the seminary. A bequest of $52,000 from Miss Minnie Bell whose generosity had built a convent for the sisters was gratefully noted, as was a $40,000 gift from I. A. O'Shaughnessy.

One of the few non-financial items recorded was as follows: "Archbishop Brady instructed the Rector to ask the faculty members to consider whether this seminary should be exclusively a theological seminary or have both philosophy and theology. Should there be a new H.S. for divinity students?"[77] With an anticipated enrollment in the 1958–1959 academic year at 358, it is understandable that new arrangements for configuring the program for priesthood education would be under consideration.

The business of the board, however, continued to revolve around finances. At the October 14, 1959, meeting Archbishop Brady was happy to report that the financial condition of the seminary was good particularly "because of two large bequests from the Clara Hill Lindley Estate and the Clara H. Lindley Trust for Erasmus C. Lindley." The Hill largesse continued to benefit the seminary.

In the fall of 1960, at Archbishop Brady's last board meeting, in addition to the usual voting for the ten professors whose salaries would be paid out of the trust fund and approving the candidates for M.A. and B.A. degrees, it was announced that the previous spring the archbishop had approved an increase in tuition and board from $700.00 to $800.00 per year effective in 1960. Lastly, the question of granting an M.A. degree in theology was discussed and approved with the mandate: "The seminary faculty members are to look to the necessary steps in carrying out the plan."[78]

Brady's Death and Legacy

Archbishop Brady, at the age of sixty-two, appeared to those who knew him as vibrant and energetic. In fact, rumor had it he might be appointed archbishop of San Francisco. As a member of one of the preparatory commissions of Vatican II, he anticipated traveling to Rome for meetings. His sister, Sister Mary William, who had just completed her term as president of the College of Saint Catherine, was asked by her congregation to study theology at the Regina Mundi in Rome. Although she was not too eager to take on a new challenge at that time, her brother encouraged her to go. He expected to be in Rome before and during the council, and he suggested that on occasion he could extend his visit and they could enjoy some of Italy together.[79]

Little did anyone anticipate that on his flight to Rome on September 23, 1961, Archbishop Brady would suffer a severe heart attack. A cable from Archbishop Martin O'Connor, rector of the North American College, to Bishop Gerald O'Keefe on September 23 stated: *"Archbishop Brady Suffered Coronary Thrombosis During Flight Minimum Two Months Hospitalization Required Responding Medication Salvator Mundi Hospital."*[80] According to Sister Mary William, when the flight crew realized the seriousness of Brady's condition, they phoned ahead to Rome for an ambulance to meet the plane. Brady, however, refused to be taken off on a stretcher and sat in the front seat of the ambulance with the driver for the long ride from the airport to the hospital. That further complicated his condition.[81]

Dr. Charles Rea and Msgr. Francis Gilligan flew to Rome immediately and were a great source of support to Sister Mary William who lived at the hospital during that traumatic week. A lengthy letter from Dr. Rea in Rome to "Your Excellency" (probably Bishop O'Keefe) on the day after Brady's death described the archbishop's condition in detail. It was clear that he had had four, possibly five heart attacks within nine days. "Death was due to a massive coronary thrombosis with myocardial infarction" on October 1, 1961. Rea concluded: "If he had lived it would have meant a long convalescence and probably a life of semi-invalidism or certainly reduced activity as long as he lived."[82] Anyone who knew Brady could appreciate the fact that such a life would have been a great trial for him.

Messages came from every source when people learned of Brady's illness, and even more at the time of his death. Minnesotans—Catholics, Protestants and Jews—were stunned.[83] The seminarians were among those who felt stricken. Brady's body was returned to St. Paul by plane and lay in state at the cathedral. Members of the seminary faculty and student body were involved in singing the Office of the Dead on Sunday, October 8, 1961, and in the funeral liturgy on the following day. As the sun streamed radiantly through the fall leaves, an enormous crowd assembled—both state and church dignitaries—for the Solemn Requiem Mass for Archbishop William O. Brady.

Bishop Leonard Cowley was appointed administrator of the archdiocese. At a later time he shared the fact that after Archbishop Brady's death "I went through the file 'unfinished business' and there was nothing in there."[84] To some degree this represented the archbishop's compulsive nature—his desire to have everything completed expeditiously. From another perspective, perhaps he was anticipating a journey—but it was not to be a journey to Rome or to San Francisco. . . .

The seminary was the focal point for Brady from the day of his incardination into the archdiocese. One undated manuscript in the Brady Papers entitled "Spiritual Opportunities for a Seminary Faculty" offers some valuable insights into Brady and his standards for a seminary faculty. There is no indication as to which seminary faculty he was ad-

Faculty with Apostolic Delegate Egidio Vagnozzi in 1959. Front left to right: Rector Msgr. Louis J. McCarthy, Msgr. Lawrence O. Wolf, the Most Reverend Egidio Vagnozzi, Msgr. Lawrence F. Ryan, Msgr. William Busch. Standing: Reverend John A. Sweeney, Reverend William L. Baumgaertner, Msgr. George J. Ziskovsky, Reverend Raymond A. Lucker, Msgr. Thomas J. Shanahan, Reverend Eugene Moriarity, Msgr. Gerald T. Baskfield, Reverend Richard T. Doherty, Reverend John O'Sullivan

dressing, but from the text it is clear that, while he was a bishop, he was invited to give a conference to a seminary faculty with which he was not familiar.

In the conference Brady stated: "There is, or there should be, in the life of any priest assigned to the preparation of candidates to the priesthood, a special distinction, a special romance, a special spiritual opportunity for themselves." His reflections, however, were not totally idealistic. He referred to the problem of seminarians being in fear of their superiors, which could lead to concealment; he described the line of cleavage between professors and students; he pleaded for a sense of unity among the professors themselves; he challenged them to be role models. Lastly, he remarked:

> You need extraordinary natural virtue and equally extraordinary supernatural grace. You have decisions to make which will affect the church of God for a generation... or more. Have you ever made a decision or followed a policy on the basis of personality—your own, or the rector's or the student affected by your choice? Twice I have witnessed such in seminary life... once a decision pushed and pushed, but not for the good of the church, simply to embarrass the rector; once a decision pushed not for the good of the church, but made simply on the basis of blood and race... and the man who made it was a prominent author of a book on the Mystical Body.[85]

Although Brady's remarks above are to an unknown seminary, it is not difficult to read into his reflections his feelings about his time as rector of the Saint Paul Seminary. Some moments had obviously been painful, but he never lost his sense of being a member of a seminary community, whether as professor or rector or trustee—or as archbishop. It was a treasured part of his priestly ministry.

Ironically, when the Saint Paul Seminary board of trustees met on October 12, 1961, with Bishop Leonard Cowley presiding, only eleven days after the death of Archbishop Brady, and three days after his funeral, there was no mention whatsoever in the minutes of Brady's death, there were no resolutions of sympathy to his family, and there was no reflection on his many contributions to the seminary over the years.[86] William Otterwell Ignatius Brady, archbishop of St. Paul, who had seemed like a larger-than-life figure in the history of the seminary, suddenly appeared to vanish from sight.

Archbishop Brady's old friend, Msgr. William Busch, wrote a memorial in the winter issue of *Worship* that reminded the readers of Brady's commitment to the liturgical movement. He quoted from Brady's address at the second Liturgical Week in St. Paul in 1941 on "Liturgy and Christian Peace."

> Grouped about God's altar, we shall not be disturbed; for we well realize that true and lasting peace must be of God's own granting. Through the liturgy of the Church we still draw down God's grace, the basis of peace; through the liturgy we may still fortify the will of men to deserve peace; through the liturgy we may still manifest unity and practice concord, justice and charity. Through the liturgy we may still approach the God of Peace, who shall in His own good time share both His love and His peace with those who seek it confidently and with perseverance.[87]

The peace described above was very likely a welcome experience for the impatient, creative, energetic, and outgoing archbishop who for thirty-five years left his mark on the Saint Paul Seminary.

III

Vatican II to the Millennium

Affiliation, Clarification, Challenges, and Growth

(1962–2000)

CHAPTER 12

The Binz-Byrne Era

Vatican II and a New Vision of Priesthood

> Learn your facts and basic principles so that you can proceed later with certainty. We shall need well-trained men to help in the implementation of all that the Second Vatican Council has decreed for us. And while you study, *cultivate a sound spiritual life*. Without this we risk having priests who hand our people a stone when they ask for bread.[1]
>
> Archbishop Leo Binz
> The Saint Paul Seminary
> March 9, 1966

Even though Brady was one of "the three wise men from the East," he had "grown up" as a priest in St. Paul. His thirty-five years of association with the Saint Paul Seminary made him almost "a home town boy." He knew the political and religious terrain.

His successor could not have been more different. With the exception of Bishop Cretin, all of the archbishops of St. Paul for over one hundred years (1859–1961) had been Irish, or Irish-Americans. The appointment of a German-American must have gladdened the hearts of many who for years felt dominated by the Irish in the hierarchy. In addition, as *The Catholic Bulletin* pointed out, Leo Binz was the first Midwest native to be named archbishop.[2]

Binz was not an unknown quantity by any means. He was a friend of William O. Brady, with whom he studied at the Sulpician Seminary in Washington, D.C., and later in Rome. Their relationship endured, and it was Binz who celebrated the Pontifical Requiem Mass in the

Saint Paul Cathedral for Brady's funeral.[3] Little did he realize that he would be installed in that same cathedral some four months later as Brady's successor.

The seventh ordinary of St. Paul came from strong German roots. Leo Binz was born on October 31, 1900, the third child of Michael and Thecla Reible Binz of Stockton, Illinois. They lived on a small 160-acre farm near the Mississippi River east of Dubuque, Iowa. According to Leo's older sister, Josephine, he grew up as a typical farm boy, instilled with a lifelong appreciation for the importance of hard work.[4]

Binz had a close relationship with his pastor, Father Alfred Heinzler, who encouraged him in his discernment of a priestly vocation. During the reception following his confirmation, the young Leo rather boldly declared to the bishop of Rockford, Illinois: "I'm going to be a bishop!" He clearly felt confident of God's call to ministry.[5] Shortly before his fourteenth birthday in 1914, Leo departed for Loras College in Dubuque, where he began his preparatory studies for priesthood.[6] In 1918 he transferred to St. Mary's Seminary in Baltimore, where he received an A.B. degree in 1919 and an M.A. degree in 1920. From 1920 to 1921 he studied theology at the Sulpician Seminary in Washington, D.C., but was sent to the North American College in Rome from 1921 to 1924 to complete his preparation for priesthood and do further studies. He was ordained as a presbyter in the Basilica of St. John Lateran, March 15, 1924; he received the S.T.D. degree that same year from the University de Propaganda Fide in Rome.

The young Father Binz, however, did not return to Illinois immediately but was assigned to pursue a second doctorate at the Gregorian University in Rome. From 1924 to 1926, while he was immersed in doctoral studies, he was also an instructor at the North American College. Despite the demands of teaching, he completed his Ph.D. in philosophy in 1926.

After five eventful years in Rome, Binz was assigned as assistant pastor at St. Mary's Church in Sterling, Illinois. One year later he was appointed secretary to Bishop Edward F. Hoban of Rockford, and the year following he became the chancellor of the diocese for three years. From 1932 to 1936 he served in three pastorates and was also a diocesan consultor. Due to Bishop Hoban's influence, Binz was appointed secretary to the apostolic delegate, Archbishop Amleto Cicognani, in Washington, D.C., where he served from 1936 to 1942. He had already

Leo Binz, archbishop of St. Paul and Minneapolis from 1962 to 1975

been named a papal chamberlain by Pope Pius XI in 1934. He was renamed by Pope Pius XII on March 3, 1939, and appointed a Domestic Prelate the following August. At the time of Hoban's death Binz reflected: "He was the Architect of the program of life I have followed. I have often enough wished he had left me pastor in Belvidere, Illinois; but more spiritually I have gone forward in the confidence that he was the instrument of God's will in my regard."[7]

With impressive academic credentials and wide ecclesiastical experience, Binz was on the fast track for episcopal appointment. He was named coadjutor bishop and apostolic administrator to Bishop Francis M. Kelly of the Diocese of Winona and was ordained to the episcopacy in St. James Pro-Cathedral in Rockford, Illinois, on December 21, 1942. In his seven years in Winona, he reorganized the chancery, played an active role in education and administration, and perhaps is best remembered for being instrumental in the founding of Immaculate Heart of

Mary College Seminary. In 1949, Binz was appointed coadjutor with the right of succession to Archbishop Henry P. Rohlman of Dubuque. He succeeded to the see with Rohlman's resignation in 1954, and for seven years distinguished himself particularly in his commitment to Catholic education.

On December 16, 1961, Leo Binz was named archbishop of St. Paul. He was installed at the Saint Paul Cathedral on February 28, 1962. On that bitterly cold last day of February, some 84 bishops, 665 priests, and thousands of lay Catholics, plus dignitaries of city and state, assembled for the impressive occasion.[8] Binz knew that in seven months he would be leaving for the Second Vatican Council. He had little time to obtain even a superficial grasp of the problems that faced him.[9]

The archdiocese, however, was flourishing. A report to the Vatican titled "Information to the International Catholic Documentary" in early 1963 listed, among other statistics, 441 diocesan priests, 162 religious priests, 148 lay brothers, and 2,370 nuns and sisters. The number of schools, the Catholic press, the confraternities, pious unions, and Catholic action organizations involving the laity all indicated that he had come to a thriving local church.[10]

The new archbishop of St. Paul was familiar with bureaucratic procedures, and possessed the background and intelligence that allowed him to deal deftly with political and ecclesiastical issues at the Second Vatican Council. In an episcopal letter written to the archdiocese in January 1964, however, he stated that the success of the council "is ultimately more in the hands of the people than in those of the bishops."[11]

Msgr. Ambrose Hayden suggested that throughout his ministerial life Binz was "very conscious of being obedient to Rome," and "in that sense he was conservative." He had a formalistic approach to matters and a sincere love for "proper procedure."[12] Because of these qualities Binz looked to the Vatican for guidance on most issues. He took the council's mandate for change seriously, and established commissions to implement those changes. He often used the seminary faculty to provide workshops for priests to acquaint them with new approaches and procedures.[13] Binz was not a charismatic leader, and was described by some as preoccupied with detail. He seems, however, to have sincerely tried to find the middle path regarding the issues related to Vatican II. He customarily quoted Alexander Pope's phrase: "Be not the first by whom the new are tried,/Nor yet the last to lay the old aside."[14]

Binz and the Seminary

On March 2, 1962, two days after his installation, Archbishop Binz visited the Saint Paul Seminary officially. Faculty and students alike were eager to become acquainted with the tall, friendly leader who came to them with impressive credentials. Whereas Brady had a "forceful and aggressive style,"[15] Binz was described by some as basically shy—a person who made sincere efforts "not to create an image of a man, but rather an image of an office."[16]

Because of the Second Vatican Council, the regular annual October meetings of the Saint Paul Seminary board had to be re-scheduled for the four-year period 1962–1965. Binz never missed a trustees' meeting from 1962 to 1968. Even before his installation as ordinary of the Archdiocese of St. Paul, the board of trustees of the major seminary was "specially summoned"—presumably by the new archbishop.[17] Members assembled at the chancery on February 15, 1962, for a meeting which Binz chaired. The previous meeting—shortly after Archbishop Brady's funeral—had been the regular annual meeting on October 12, 1961, with Bishop Leonard Cowley, administrator of the archdiocese, presiding. Apparently Archbishop Brady's unexpected demise had raised concerns regarding the legal authority of the corporation.

What became apparent was that "a complete amendment of the Articles of Incorporation" was needed. Vincent O'Connor, lawyer for the corporation, and Paul Daggett were to be asked to draft the needed revisions and/or amendments.[18] In addition, Archbishop Binz directed that every auxiliary bishop of the Archdiocese of St. Paul have membership on the seminary board of trustees. Binz's organizational skills demanded that there be clear guidelines which would become operational in the event of any contingency.

The growth and development of the Saint Paul Seminary in the Binz era can be divided into two segments: (1) from 1962 to 1968 when Archbishop Binz was more involved in seminary affairs and Msgr. Louis McCarthy was rector; (2) from 1968 to 1974 when Archbishop Leo C. Byrne, coadjutor, was the primary contact with the chancery regarding seminary business, and Msgr. William Baumgaertner was rector.

Louis McCarthy had been appointed rector by Brady under the complicated circumstances involving Msgr. Rudolph Bandas and Father David Dillon. There were some who thought McCarthy was not altogether comfortable with Brady; the archbishop seemed to want to continue running the seminary.[19] With the arrival of Binz, with "Lou" McCarthy at the helm, and with the challenges of Vatican II, opportunities for new ventures were on the horizon. The enrollment in the 1961–1962 academic year was 281—the first time it was below 300 in several years—but there was still a sense of "bulging at the seams."

The "old guard" who had been at the seminary for many years (William Busch since 1913, Lawrence Wolf since 1926, Thomas Shanahan—librarian and homiletics professor—since 1931, scripture professor George Ziskovsky since 1932, and dogma professors Gerald Baskfield since 1933 and Richard T. Doherty since 1938) continued to dominate the seminary. However, as mentioned above, the three new faculty members who were added that fall—Dosh in metaphysics and ethics, Moudry in moral and sacramental theology, and Jerome Quinn in biblical studies and Hebrew—brought new personalities and contemporary methods welcomed by the students. James Moudry recalled his first day of teaching after returning from studies in Rome. Thirty-one years old, not that much older than some of the students, garbed in his cassock and nervous about his first lecture, he approached the lectern and before he could say anything the entire *aula* broke into applause. There was gratitude for the "new blood" that was being infused into the faculty. According to Moudry, Jerome Quinn was "turning the world upside down" in sacred scripture.[20]

Outstanding speakers made presentations in the 1961–1962 academic year, among them Dr. William F. Allbright, who spoke on "Archaeology and Biblical Studies," and the Reverend Raymond Brown, S.S., who lectured on "The Sacraments and John's Gospel." Father Joseph Gremillion of Catholic Relief Services spoke to the seminarians on "The Church's Needs in Latin America," and Elizabeth Grey of the Grail addressed the student body on "Africa in Evolution: A World Awakening."[21] There was a new emphasis on looking to the *écumené*—"the whole inhabited earth." All of these events contributed to an air of anticipation—a wonderment about what the Vatican Council would really mean for the future of the church and the priesthood.

A new archbishop and the commencement of the Second Vatican Council were not the only factors affecting seminarians in the early 1960s. With the election of John F. Kennedy as the first Catholic president of the United States, there was a renewed pride in Catholic identity. Moreover, the president's enthusiasm for active involvement in social concerns such as the Peace Corps, civil rights, and poverty issues encouraged the need to be actively involved in social justice.

Seminary Life in Transition

Academic life, according to students of that period, was not strong. John Malone, ordained in 1967, believed that this was due in large part to the horarium. Students were in class (mostly lectures) all day, were expected to be present for all spiritual exercises and meals, and were mandated to observe lights out and "strict silence" at 10:00 P.M. There was little time for research and creative intellectual activities.[22]

As late as the mid-1960s, many courses in the curriculum were still taught in "cycles." Although the students in Theology I usually had introductory courses in dogma and moral, it was possible for the *aula* to be filled with all of the Theology II, III, and IV students taking whatever course in dogmatic theology was being offered for that semester. In scripture and church history all four years took the same classes.

It was a radical departure, therefore, when that approach changed. The 1964–1965 Annual Report submitted to Archbishop Binz and the board of trustees specifically stated in regard to theology:

> First steps have been taken to realign the theology courses along the recommendation of the 1964 report. Dogma courses will no longer be taught in cycles. Moral courses will no longer be taught in cycles. A series in sacramental theology has been started. The Seminary will have to explore the further need of specialization in highly complex areas of current moral theology. The availability of personnel trained in ecumenism, Protestant theology, mystical and ascetical theology, patrology, religion, freedom and toleration, is highly to be desired.[23]

Historical studies were dealt a blow with the unexpected death of the Reverend Patrick J. Ahern, professor of church history and director of the M.A. program in American church history, on February 1, 1965, in the Canary Islands at the age of forty-nine. He was there recuperating from a heart attack he had suffered the previous October. Ahern had earned his doctorate from the Catholic University of America in 1952 and was the author of three well-respected volumes including the life of Archbishop John J. Keane.[24] The M.A. program in American church history was temporarily suspended due to lack of personnel. Msgr. John Sankowitz was appointed to the faculty and began his studies toward a Ph.D. in history at the University of Minnesota.[25]

For many years, European church history at the Saint Paul Seminary was associated solely with Msgr. William Busch. He had been appointed professor of church history in 1913 and served in that role until 1968, with a hiatus of seven years (1938–1945), part of which time he served as pastor at St. Mary of the Lake in White Bear Lake.[26] In 1968 he was named "Professor Emeritus" and was listed in that capacity until his death in 1971. Therefore, from 1913 to 1971, with a brief interlude, "Billy Busch" was a fixture at the Saint Paul Seminary. His outstanding contribution to the liturgical movement will be discussed in chapter 16.

As professor of church history, Busch is recalled as less than scintillating, easily led off on tangents, with an imitable style, and clearly unable to manage hundreds of students in the *aula* for class just before the noon meal. Ronald Bowers, ordained in 1964, recalled the one event that captured the nature of the "Busch classroom." Two of Bowers's classmates were playing cards, another was experimenting with paper airplanes, those with culinary skill were on the fire escape cooking hot dogs and passing them around to friends. Bowers himself was looking out the window, not particularly attentive to the lecture. Busch focused on him, apparently oblivious to the mayhem that was in progress, and said that if he was not going to pay attention he should report to the rector.[27] For some, church history was never boring.

On June 3, 1964, Msgr. McCarthy announced to the board of trustees that in cooperation with the College of St. Thomas a master of arts in teaching (MAT) was available to seminarians who had been recommended by the faculty and approved by their bishops. This was important to many of the Iowa bishops who expected their young priests to teach, usually on the high-school level, for several years after ordination.[28] The program, directed by Dr. James Byrne, chair of the Department of Education at the college, allowed for some classes to be taken at the seminary and some at the college leading to lifetime certification.[29] This program offered some of the better students the opportunity to acquire a master's degree. It was fortuitous that the degree was in place when the M.A. in church history had to be suspended.

Perhaps one of the outward signs of a new appreciation of the academic in the life of the seminary was the approval of the trustees on June 3, 1964, for an office space for the dean of studies to be placed on the porch of the administration building.[30] Students knew who the deans of the residence halls were; they were deans of discipline and held "real" authority in the seminarians' lives, granting permissions, checking them in on return to campus. The dean of studies seemed to the students to be inconsequential—largely because of the prescriptive nature of the program.

In the late 1950s and early 1960s the position of dean of studies was held by Msgr. Eugene Moriarity, Msgr. Gerald Baskfield, and Father David Dillon. In the spring of 1964, Dillon announced to the rector that he had decided to relinquish the role. Msgr. McCarthy either forgot this notification or did not take it seriously. The day before the fall semester started, McCarthy inquired of Dillon as to the status of curriculum, schedules, and faculty assignments. Dillon reminded him of his "resignation." With a sense of urgency the rector approached Father William Baumgaertner and asked him to take on the responsibility.[31] Baumgaertner became dean of studies at a significant time in the history of the seminary as post-conciliar challenges prompted reorganization of the seminary curriculum.

Baumgaertner had worked with the archbishop on various committees and was aware of Binz's desire for detailed information. He suggested to Msgr. McCarthy that an annual report of the academic year just completed be drawn up each year for the board of trustees. It would include not only a report on faculty, curriculum, programs, student statistics and finances, but also recommendations for the future. The dean had the major responsibility for organizing the data, and it became the vehicle for reflecting on the past and planning for the future.[32] This was especially important because the seminary was scheduled for a visit of the North Central Association in 1967 for its twenty-year reaffirmation of accreditation.

In addition, an institutional survey, initiated under the leadership of David Dillon during his deanship (1962–1964) and coordinated thereafter by William Baumgaertner, became an invaluable source for planning for the future. All faculty members were involved. Every professor was expected to produce a syllabus for each course he taught.[33] The

Committee on the Program of Graduate Studies was asked to develop an M.A. degree in theology that would, hopefully, receive preliminary affirmation from the NCA at the time of the twenty-year review. The Saint Paul Seminary "Institutional Survey" was completed in October 1967.[34]

A faculty handbook had been drawn up and approved in August 1966. It defined responsibilities and included statements on tenure, termination, and academic freedom. The Annual Report for 1966–1967 stated: "The full-time faculty was defined in such a way as to admit of the possible membership of laymen, something which has since become fact with the advent of Mr. William Curtis."[35] Curtis, who had been teaching public speaking at the seminary since 1951, was finally listed among "The Faculty," and not as a "Visiting Instructor," in the catalogue.

A team of examiners from the North Central Association visited the Saint Paul Seminary in December 1967. It reviewed the original accreditation given in 1947 and also recommended preliminary approval for the Master of Arts in theology program. The revision of the total curriculum was affirmed. The new curriculum and the Master of Arts in theology program were fully approved by NCA and instituted in the fall of 1968.[36]

Field education was not yet a requirement. On Wednesday afternoons, however, many seminarians taught in the Confraternity of Christian Doctrine (CCD) program in various parishes, largely to public-school students after regular school hours. John Malone recalled that each year a group of students would go to Our Lady of Guadalupe Parish as part of an informal arrangement. At the end of their time at Guadalupe, the seminarians would line up replacements for the following year. Michael Arms remembered that some taught at Totem Town, a facility for delinquent boys.[37]

The two-month summer deacon internship was inaugurated in 1963 for those to be ordained to the priesthood in 1964. Deacons were given faculties to exercise certain sacramental and related actions in their assigned parishes. The deacon was to wear a Roman collar and rabat and go by the title of "Father" to avoid confusion, but a short explanation of his special role was given on the first Sunday after he arrived.

McCarthy presented the goal of the program as follows: "We hope that this time of initiation into parish work this summer, together with the exercise of the priesthood on weekends after his ordination next spring, will prepare him as fully as possible for the work of the ministry when he receives his parochial appointment next June." He expressed his appreciation to the pastors for their cooperation in the effort "to give a still fuller and richer preparation to our future priests."[38] Msgr. McCarthy was in charge of the program for the deacons and also taught a two-credit course in pastoral theology for two semesters. By 1966 Msgr. John Sweeney was given broader responsibility for developing the pastoral formation program.[39]

Spiritual formation was less than personal in the early Binz era. Since the days of Archbishop Ireland, all seminarians were expected to report to the *aula* each weekday from 5:30 to 6:00 P.M. for a spiritual conference. The exception was the day confessions were heard. Conferences were given by the spiritual director on three days (Monday, Wednesday, and Friday) and by the rector on Thursday. This time slot late in the day before dinner could not have been less inviting to students already saturated by seven lectures during the day.

Msgr. Lawrence ("Curly") Ryan finally retired in 1963 at the age of eighty-four. He was replaced by Reverend Stanley Srnec, who was considered "a breath of fresh air" in his early years. Srnec recognized the fact that the students in philosophy (the last two years of college) and those in theology had very different needs, so he divided the group for spiritual conferences. In time, therefore, students attended only two conferences a week. Srnec is remembered as being kind and well prepared for the conferences, although he held the typical views regarding life and sexuality usually taught in seminaries prior to Vatican II.[40]

There was very little personal exchange between faculty and students. Relationships were very formal. Students knew they were being evaluated by faculty, and sometimes wondered if some members of the faculty knew their names. John Malone recalled one faculty member who frequently called him by the name of one of his classmates.[41] With the large enrollment and the class sizes in the hundreds, the main goal seemed to be to escape detection if one was not following all the rules completely.

Students were free to go to any priest on the faculty for spiritual direction. Each student, however, was expected to "check in" with the official spiritual director once a semester and discuss any major concerns. The spiritual director, as was the tradition, gave a conference during the monthly First Friday afternoon of recollection that concluded with

Benediction. Daily eucharistic liturgies and the early Sunday liturgy at which students received Communion were celebrated in the oratories in the residence halls. Due to the fasting regulations for Communion at that time, students attended an early Mass on Sunday and received the Eucharist. This was followed by breakfast and then a Solemn High Mass on Sunday at mid-morning in St. Mary's Chapel at which only the main celebrant received Communion. Cassocks and surplices were the garb for the liturgy, and birettas for solemn liturgies.

Vatican II began to affect the liturgical life of the seminary in 1964. Msgr. John Sweeney recalls receiving a handwritten letter from Archbishop Binz from Rome in the fall of that year informing him that the request of the U.S. bishops for liturgy in the vernacular had been approved. Binz asked Sweeney, chair of the music commission of the archdiocese, if enough good music was available in English. If so, the archbishop would issue a directive that the English liturgy could be implemented in the archdiocese on the First Sunday of Advent 1964. With much effort and practice, Sweeney prepared the seminarians for the Advent liturgies. The "new" liturgy was broadcast on the radio from the seminary on Christmas eve.[42]

With the changes in the liturgy came the call for more freedom. By 1966, change was in the air, and the students decided to "boycott the biretta." Gerald Milske, who entered Saint Paul Seminary in 1965, recalls: "For some reason the students decided that they would no longer wear birettas. So that Sunday [second Sunday in October 1966] for morning High Mass everyone came in to Saint Mary's Chapel without them. I remember because I was the organist—not one student out of 325 wore a biretta!"[43] There was little the faculty could do to enforce the rule.[44]

Msgr. John O'Sullivan, dean of Cretin Residence, frequently celebrated the morning Eucharist in that dorm. Former students recall that he usually gave at least three homilies at each Mass: one before and one after the Gospel, one after Communion, and sometimes one at the end! O'Sullivan, a good sociologist who also taught the marriage course, is remembered as dynamic and practical, but often repetitious. No one forgets his aphorisms, such as: "A priest is the only person who gets up at 5:00—twice a day!"[45]

By 1966, due to the liturgical changes initiated at the Vatican Council, there was only one community eucharistic celebration on Sundays, and weekday liturgies were moved to St. Mary's Chapel. Although the liturgy was in the process of changing into the vernacular, John Malone, ordained in 1967, recalled that the rector stated firmly: "Without doubt—you will not be saying the breviary in English!"[46]

Student Life

Many students survived the closed conditions of seminary life by antics, practical jokes, and mimicking the faculty. *Gaudeamus* was the one formal occasion when faculty could be mimicked. John Malone recalls directing one program that was a combination of "Fiddler on the Roof" and "Li'l Abner." Not all was spoofing, however. Malone also recalls the Drama Club doing a dramatic reading of "The Dream of Gerontius" with organ accompaniment.[47]

Students did not escape practical jokes. Thomas Hunstiger, ordained in 1963, recalled that at one point he found himself concerned about losing his hair. He confided this to some of his classmates who assured him that the solution was to use "bear grease," and that they could get him some from Canada. They had a special label made for a bottle of "lotion" they concocted containing a variety of substances including Johnson's paste wax and Elmer's glue. It was mailed to him from Ontario, Canada.

Tom decided to use this "miracle product" before the ceremony of tonsure, one of the "minor orders," admitting one to the clerical state and symbolized by clipping or shaving of the hair as a outward sign of one's commitment. Clearly, the lotion did not have the results for which he had hoped. Not only did Tom's hair become filled with glue and stick together, but—because of the terrible smell—he found himself using more after-shave lotion to cover the odor.

Bishop Leonard Cowley presided at the ceremony. His task of clipping Tom's hair provided more than the usual challenge. As he repeated the Latin phrase "Dominus pars hereditatis meae" (the Lord is the portion of the inheritance that falls to me), the white gloves he wore for the occasion became stuck to Tom's hair and he had difficulty extricating himself from it. Tom never heard anything from the rector or the faculty, but many students in the chapel knew exactly what had happened.[48]

Seminarians in this period were not allowed to read the entire newspaper lest they be led astray. One professor told them that newspapers were inundated with advertisements for women's underwear—hardly something for them to see. Sometimes the sports page was available to them. Not until after the Council did the entire paper begin to appear.[49]

In the middle to later 1960s there was an effort to initiate better dialogue between faculty and students. Stephen Adrian, ordained in 1968, was one who helped to compose the "Saint Paul Seminary Faculty-Student Conference Constitution." He believes that it was partly modeled on the movement for priests' senates in dioceses which was developing at that time. Although the conference had no legislative powers, it was an effort aimed at getting faculty and students together to negotiate solutions to student unrest revolving around rules which were no longer viable.[50]

The Decree on Priestly Formation

Optatam Totius, "The Decree on Priestly Formation," was voted upon by the bishops at Vatican II in October 1965 and passed 2,196 to 15. It was approved by the pope and bishops on November 28, 1965. There was a general assumption that seminary education had to be overhauled, but the implementation would be challenging. The Sacred Congregation for Seminaries and Universities was still headed by the aged and conservative Cardinal Pizzardo.

In 1966 Pope Paul VI appointed Archbishop Gabriel-Marie Garrone "pro-prefect" of the congregation to assist Pizzardo. Together they issued a letter in October 1966 "authorizing seminaries to experiment with seminary reform according to the principles of *Optatam Totius.*" The instruction directed that this should be done in relationship to the episcopal conference and reforms were to be of such a nature that they could be reversed. This document was the *magna carta* for seminary educators. To specify that each nation or rite should draw up its own "Program of Priestly Formation" (PPF) under the direction of the episcopal conference was a radical change and illustrative of the subsidiarity espoused by the council. Pizzardo was persuaded to resign in January 1968 at the age of ninety, and Garrone, who had been made a cardinal in 1967, became prefect of the newly-named Sacred Congregation for Catholic Education.[51]

In November 1966, the National Conference of Catholic Bishops (NCCB) established the Committee on Priestly Formation which began working on interim guidelines for American seminaries. The following year, Cardinal Garrone established a committee to draft the Basic Plan for Priestly Formation (*Ratio Fundamentalis*) which was approved by Paul VI in December 1969. In the United States, the Program of Priestly Formation—essentially an adaptation of *Ratio Fundamentalis* to the American scene—was approved by the NCCB in November 1969, and ratified by the Sacred Congregation on April 6, 1970, subject to some minor changes. After the final corrections and the addition of a section on ecumenism, the program was approved by the Sacred Congregation in January 1971 for a five-year period.[52] This approval for experimentation contributed to the spirit of *aggiornamento* in seminary education.

The Practical Realities of Seminary Life

On a practical level, it was clear that finances, maintenance and building expansion were major items on the seminary agenda in the 1960s. The Trust Department of the First National Bank of Minneapolis continued to administer the James J. Hill Trust. They requested a change in the agreement that would give them broader powers for investment. Board member I. A. O'Shaughnessy noted that the conditions of the trust would expire in April 1969; at that time "the entire amount will automatically be given to the St. Paul Seminary with no further conditions or restrictions of any kind."[53] This factor, in conjunction with the fact that interest rates were high, resulted in the vote of the board not to change the agreement.[54]

What became apparent was that the needs of the institution were far greater than ordinary maintenance. In a letter to Archbishop Binz on June 2, 1964, Msgr. McCarthy submitted points for the agenda for the next board meeting. Under finances he listed: "$25,000.00 debt to the archdiocese" and "$15,000.00 in the red for this year with four months still to be counted." The following item stated:

> Despite the above situation we are short of class-room space, office space, and a combination garage and storage building. North Central is to come to inspect the Seminary in the spring

> of 1967 and we must be as prepared as possible for this visit. Besides this reason, we urgently need space for class-rooms and offices for the Dean and Registrar.[55]

The only items mentioned in the minutes of this meeting were approval for an office for the dean of studies, and for a twelve-car garage for the faculty.[56]

The 1964–1965 Annual Report, however, stated clearly that in March 1965 the architectural firm of Bettenburg, Townsend, Stolte and Comb had been engaged to start work on three new buildings at the Saint Paul Seminary that would be built with the support of the *Opus Sancti Petri* fund. This predecessor to the Annual Catholic Appeal had been established by Archbishop Brady to raise money to build badly needed new high schools in the archdiocese. With four new secondary schools constructed, the Saint Paul Seminary became the next beneficiary. The need was apparent because the majority of the seminary buildings were more than seventy years old.

The new structures would include a classroom building, an auditorium, and a gymnasium.[57] On March 9, 1966, Archbishop Binz delivered an address at the seminary to a meeting of the district chairmen of the *Opus Sancti Petri* at which the faculty and students were also present. Binz spoke thoughtfully and enthusiastically about a new approach to seminary education. He affirmed that buildings were necessary, but that new methods were also in order. In referring to *The Decree on Priestly Formation* he reminded them:

> That same decree when speaking of seminaries states that "teaching methods (in seminaries) are to be revised both as regards lectures, discussions, and seminars and also the development of study on the part of the students, whether done privately or in small groups." I feel strongly that the new classroom facilities will help the faculty to implement these new teaching methods. After all I don't think much was heard about a seminar room in 1894 when this seminary was built. Neither was much heard about visual aids.[58]

The facilities would also be available for continuing study for priests, another major responsibility of the bishop.

In the spirit of John Ireland, Binz believed that the students needed to cultivate sound bodies as well as sound minds. A new gymnasium for recreation and enjoyment was in order. Binz felt strongly, however, that the plan for a swimming pool, which he highly approved of, should not be paid for out of the *Opus Sancti Petri*. He explained:

> The Opus Sancti Petri funds collected as they are in small donations represent sacrifices of hundreds, even thousands, of very poor people. In 42 years as a priest I have heard much criticism of spending the money of the poor for what can be judged a luxury; and hence I shall not subject the Church, the Archbishop or Opus Sancti Petri to that criticism.[59]

A separate fund to collect private donations for the swimming pool was established and Binz invited donors to contribute.[60] As he said in his speech, "If money can be found for that development I shall be a happy man indeed." With a sense of realism he added: "As sensitive to criticism as some people like myself can get, I am certain that no one can rightly accuse the St. Paul Seminary of having over-spent itself on athletic facilities in its first 72 years of existence."[61]

Binz was fully aware, however, that "brick and mortar do not make a first rate seminary program." Most important was a well-trained staff. He then listed the five priests in studies who would be returning in the near future—four of them to teach at the Saint Paul Seminary. He reflected: "I am thoroughly and absolutely convinced that before we can undertake any programs of worth here or anywhere else in the diocese we must have men who are competently trained in the various fields."[62] Binz then reminded the students of their responsibilities. His vision was broader than the seminary or the archdiocese: "Adequate facilities, trained staffs, and seminarians who know the value of study and prayer will build up a good Church in the northwest."[63]

Although Binz was informed of the progress on the buildings, and provided input when appropriate and made decisions when necessary, he did not attempt to micro-manage the project as had James J. Hill or Austin Dowling. Msgr. McCarthy had the major responsibility. In the spring of 1967 contracts were signed and the announcement was made that a one-and-one-half-million-dollar addition was planned at the Saint Paul Seminary—the first addition to the complex since 1951. A more welcoming entrance was constructed that necessitated a new address: 2260 Summit Avenue—a sign of openness to a new era.

The architecture was evidence of the "new look" in seminary education. The two-level classroom building in the southwest area of the campus would have six large classrooms, two seminar rooms, speech and music practice rooms, and a faculty lounge. It would be linked to the auditorium by a spacious foyer. The new *aula maxima* would have seating capacity for about four hundred, would be used for lectures and music, and would have a stage fully equipped for dramatic productions. There was also provision for projection facilities, closed-circuit television for teaching, and sound reproduction.

The gymnasium, on the east side of the campus, would contain a basketball court, four handball courts, an exercise room, locker rooms, and a swimming pool. It was specified that the gym would also be open to priests in the area. The buildings, although contemporary in style, would be red brick to blend with the already existing structures. The scheduled date for completion was March 1, 1968. Although finances plagued McCarthy during his rectorship, as will be discussed later, the *Opus Sancti Petri* made it possible for the seminary to build state-of-the-art buildings of which students and faculty were very proud.

One arrangement which provided ongoing difficulties for the seminary in financial affairs was that, since 1953, the Archdiocese of St. Paul took a 20 percent reduction in its room and board payments for the St. Paul seminarians. By 1967, this amounted to $222,012. In the same years, the seminary had to borrow $213,000 from the chancery to continue to operate. Deficits in the budget had become a regular problem. The minutes of the board of trustees on October 13, 1967 read:

> In order to make a completely new start, the Archdiocese canceled the entire debt of $213,000.00 and began as of September 1967, to pay the full board and tuition for all of its seminarians. The cancellation of the $213,000.00 debt is a *contingent* payment in as much as the Archdiocese is currently engaged in providing the seminary with three new buildings at the cost of more than one and a half million dollars. Accordingly, when the Father Francis Benz estate is paid to the seminary, the latter is to repay to the Archdiocese the principal and interest of this debt ($213,000.00), "unless it be the judgment of the Archbishop at

that time that the seminary has greater need." (Letter of Archbishop Binz, August 19, 1967.)[64]

Msgr. McCarthy expressed profound gratitude to Archbishop Binz for his intervention on behalf of the seminary.

The word "contingent," however, invited the interpretation that it was not really a cancellation. It was not forgotten in the succeeding years when Archbishop Byrne became acting chair of the board of trustees. Although a substantial Ford Foundation grant in the 1950s had allowed for upgrading faculty salaries and employing more adjuncts, Msgr. Baumgaertner recalled that the financial difficulties that resulted from the falling enrollment and inadequate tuition and board always left the seminary in need of requesting loans from the chancery.[65] It was not until January 19, 1972, that the debt of $213,000 that the seminary owed to the archdiocese as a contingent payment upon the receipt of the Benz Estate was "graciously canceled" with the repayment by the seminary of the cumulative interest.[66]

A New Archbishop and a New Rector

Two events had particular impact on the seminary in the 1967–1968 academic year: the appointment of Archbishop Leo Byrne as coadjutor

Leo C. Byrne, coadjutor from 1968 to 1974

William L. Baumgaertner, rector of the Saint Paul Seminary from 1968 to 1980

with the right of succession to Archbishop Binz; and the resignation of Msgr. Louis McCarthy and appointment of Msgr. William Baumgaertner as rector at the end of the academic year.

Leo C. Byrne was born on March 19, 1908, in St. Louis, Missouri, and spent most of his life there.[67] He was the youngest of ten children, attended Kenrick Seminary, and was ordained a priest on June 10, 1933. He served as executive director of Catholic Charities in St. Louis in the 1940s, and during that decade earned a master's degree in sociology (1942) and a master's degree in social work (1947) from St. Louis University. In 1954 he was consecrated bishop and appointed auxiliary to the archbishop of St. Louis. Seven years later he was appointed coadjutor bishop of Wichita, Kansas.

Archbishop Binz's health began to fail in the years after the council. Along with other health problems he had diabetes. He was responsible for chairing the Birth Control Commission established by Pope Paul VI to deal with that very controversial issue. Preparing to celebrate his silver jubilee as bishop in December, he asked the Holy See for a coadjutor. On August 2, 1967, Pope Paul VI appointed Leo C. Byrne as coadjutor with the right of succession.

Archbishop Byrne brought a concern for social justice and ecumenism as well as administrative skills. He was also committed to involving lay people in the post-conciliar church by establishing an Archdiocesan Pastoral Council, a Board of Education, and an Office of Urban Affairs. He was fearless on controversial issues, spoke out against the Vietnam War, and supported the United Farm Workers in their boycotts. He took a leadership role in the interfaith dialogue in Minnesota.[68]

Byrne was also conscious of internal justice issues and introduced a pension plan for the two thousand lay employees of the archdiocese and a due-process system for handling complaints within the archdiocese. He established a personnel board to advise him on the appointment of priests, and in January 1969 announced the first Archbishops' Appeal to raise funds for education, the Office of Urban Affairs, the Catholic Youth Centers, a priests' retirement fund, and care of the aged.[69]

Archbishop Byrne was one of the first bishops to call upon the church to study an expanded role for women.[70] At a board of trustees meeting of the seminary in October 1972, he made the suggestion that, when considering candidates for the board of trustees of the seminary, "the advice of women as members of the Board would be valuable."[71]

The coadjutor archbishop of St. Paul was recognized by his brothers in the hierarchy who elected him as one of the four American bishops to participate in the 1971 World Synod of Bishops. Later that year he was elected vice-president of the National Conference of Catholic Bishops. Although Byrne was considered by some a prophet and a visionary, he never became ordinary. Binz never relinquished his authority. It was an enormous shock to all when Byrne was found dead in bed of a heart attack on October 21, 1974.

Byrne's seven years as coadjutor were considered by some to be problematic for the seminary. Binz—for all practical purposes—"delegated" the major responsibility for the seminary to Byrne. Byrne's approach to seminary education was not what had been typical of previous archbishops. His experience in St. Louis was with seminaries administered and staffed by a religious order of priests who accomplished the task very well. Both Kenrick Seminary and Cardinal Glennon College Seminary were staffed by the Vincentians. The Jesuits had their philosophate in the Archdiocese of St. Louis. It was expensive both in dollars and in personnel for an archdiocese to operate a seminary.

In his early years in St. Paul, Byrne was known to bring up the issue at the beginning of board meetings by asking, "Why do we need a seminary at all?" Was it really worthwhile to continue to have an archdiocesan seminary when students could be sent to other seminaries?[72] Msgr. John Sweeney, when he was vice-rector, director of field education, and in charge of the music at the seminary, recalls meeting with Archbishop Byrne who wanted to make him pastor of a large parish. When Sweeney inquired who would take over his responsibilities at the seminary, he was told not to worry.[73] Sweeney stayed at the seminary. Such was not the case with William Hunt. Having completed his doctorate at Catholic University of America, he had taught dogmatic theology at the seminary for only three years when Byrne appointed him director of the Newman Center of the University of Minnesota in 1970. Personnel problems were paramount for Byrne during those difficult years when priests were leaving ministry in large numbers. There was the perception, however, that the archbishop wanted to "steal" seminary faculty for other purposes.

On May 31, 1968, when Archbishop Byrne was at the seminary meeting with Msgr. McCarthy, the rector requested that his resignation be accepted. William Baumgaertner remembers being called to the rector's office. Archbishop Byrne informed him that Msgr. McCarthy wanted to retire—a worthy request after his many years of service at the seminary. He then asked Msgr. Baumgaertner to become rector and assume the responsibilities within two weeks.[74] Msgr. McCarthy was appointed pastor of St. Luke's Parish in St. Paul.

Baumgaertner had grown up in St. Paul in a strong German family. His father was manager of *The Wanderer,* which was then published in German and English editions. Baumgaertner attended St. Thomas Academy (1935–1939) and, after two years at the College of St. Thomas, enrolled at the Saint Paul Seminary in the fall of 1941. During the war years, the six-year seminary program was condensed into five, as described above. With his classmates John Roach, Terrence Murphy, James Shannon, and others, William Baumgaertner was ordained to the priesthood on June 8, 1946.

Two weeks later Baumgaertner was on a train to Canada. He had not anticipated going off to studies, but was asked to do so and was offered the option of either Louvain or Laval. He chose the latter. In 1949, after three years in Quebec, he returned to teach at the Saint Paul Seminary with a Ph.D. in philosophy—and was the youngest member of the faculty for ten years. Baumgaertner's nineteen years on the faculty, and his experiences both as dean of Loras Residence and as dean of studies, were valuable in preparing him to be rector. Probably nothing could adequately prepare one for the rectorship in 1968–1969—a complicated period in American Catholic history and in the life of the seminary.

One of the first challenges for the new rector was at the dedication of the new buildings on Alumni Day, October 10, 1968. A group of protesters assembled to make a statement that the archdiocese should redirect its efforts toward the poor and not be investing in new buildings for seminary education. Archbishop Binz was prepared to defend the rationale for the new buildings, but on the advice of Msgr. Baumgaertner, he "refrained from mentioning the protesters."[75] To counteract any negative activity that was planned, Baumgaertner spoke to the seminarians and suggested that they go out, welcome the "protesters," and invite them to the ceremony. Most of them accepted the invitation, and the event proceeded without incident. There were about 210 persons present, including the contingent of "non-protesters."[76] An Open House was sponsored by the seminary on Sunday, October 20, to honor the district chairmen

The Brady Educational Center, dedicated in 1968

of the *Opus Sancti Petri,* board members and benefactors. People from all of the parishes were invited, and about fifteen hundred arrived on a beautiful fall day to admire the new buildings.[77]

As early as 1959, Archbishop Brady had requested that Msgr. James P. Shannon, president of the College of St. Thomas, undertake a study on the feasibility of the 4-4-4 plan for seminary education: four years of high-school seminary at Nazareth Hall; four years of college seminary at the College of St. Thomas; and four years of theology at the Saint Paul Seminary.[78] With student enrollment at an all-time high, even the construction of St. Austin's House for commuter students on the campus of Nazareth Hall failed to accommodate the needs of the seminarians.

With Archbishop Brady's death, and the convocation of Vatican II, decisions regarding changes in seminary education were put on hold. A Seminary Planning Commission was established, however, and on May 21, 1963, it recommended that the 4-4-4 plan of seminary education be adopted with the four years of college academically affiliated with the College of St. Thomas.[79]

Various plans were recommended, including locating the college seminary at the site of the Saint Paul Seminary and building a new theologate in North Oaks, on property that had previously belonged to the Hill family. Legal questions were raised regarding such a move. Would the intent of James J. Hill be violated, since the deed clearly stated that the purpose of his gift of buildings was for a *theological seminary?*[80] Although the Hill grandchildren agreed to the move, the last surviving child of James J. and Mary Hill, Rachel Hill Boeckmann, was not amenable to the idea. She wrote to Archbishop Binz December 26, 1963: "I think it must have been my father's wish when he said that the Seminary should not be moved away from St. Paul, that it remain where it is."[81] In retrospect, considering the affiliation of the Saint Paul Seminary with the College of St. Thomas some twenty years later, it is fortuitous that the theologate did not move that distance away. Again, if it hadn't been for a woman . . . !

Another approach in the revisioning of seminaries was cooperation and possible union with other theologates. The Conventual Franciscans operated Assumption Seminary in Chaska, Minnesota, and periodically sent some students to study at the Saint Paul Seminary. Some of their faculty occasionally taught a course as well. In the 1965–66 academic year, Father Juniper Cummings, O.F.M. Conv., wrote to Archbishop Binz regarding a "joint effort" between the two institutions. Archbishop Binz shared the letter and his reply with Msgr. McCarthy. McCarthy's answer to Binz discussed the "legal obstacles that may exist as to any joining of forces by us with the Franciscans." He enclosed pertinent articles from the Articles of Incorporation which "stress the freedom from control by any society or order of the Church." McCarthy added: "As you know, this is said to have been insisted on by His Excellency, Archbishop Ireland, so that the Jesuits would never be able to take over the Seminary. Whether this is true or not, I cannot say, but the conditions are there in any case."[82]

Father Jerome Dittberner was among those who taught as part of a faculty exchange. When it became clear that Assumption Seminary would close in 1970, Msgr. Baumgaertner approached the faculty at Chaska and invited them to consider positions at Saint Paul Seminary. Three Franciscans accepted: Father Peter Nichols in scripture, Father Jerome Dittberner in dogma, and church historian Father Eugene ("Adam") Bunnell. Dittberner was incardinated into the archdiocese in 1982.[83] John Ireland's vision of a seminary for diocesan priests run primarily by diocesan priests was not lost.

Saint John Vianney College Seminary

By the fall of 1967 it was clear that a decision was required regarding the feasibility of the 4-4-4 plan for seminary education. A questionnaire was sent to all the priests of the archdiocese by the Pre and Post-Ordination Committee chaired by Msgr. William Baumgaertner. The report on the results was issued February 12, 1968. There was a 79 percent response from the diocesan clergy and a 76.5 percent response from the religious clergy for a total of 486 votes. The results were overwhelmingly in favor of the 4-4-4 system. To the question: "Do you favor a four year integrated program at St. Thomas College?" the response was 459 affirmative and only 15 negative.[84]

The result was that St. John Vianney, the new college seminary, was born in the fall of 1968 with Msgr. John R. Roach as rector. It was agreed that the college seminarians would temporarily occupy Loras Hall and part of Cretin Residence, but would eventually move over to the College of St. Thomas. This necessitated the refurbishing of Loras Residence and the renovation of the oratory to adapt it for Mass and conferences, at a cost of $27,600.[85] Timothy Nolan, ordained in 1967, served on the St. John Vianney staff from 1968 to 1977. He recalled that the early years of sharing the campus were not easy. Initially the college students had a "package deal" on meals: breakfast at the Saint Paul Seminary, and lunch and dinner at the College of St. Thomas.[86] The campus was changing not only physically but also demographically, a situation which was not clarified until 1971.

The theology faculty was not happy with the younger college seminarians invading their premises. In June 1969 they voted against the continuation of college and theology students sharing Cretin Residence. Deacons and college students had different lifestyles. College and theologate programs had different educational goals. There was "the danger of compromising the separation of college and theology departments."[87] A special meeting of the board of trustees of the Saint Paul Seminary was called for June 17, 1970. Msgr. Roach provided historical background and then read the text of the resolution of the St. John Vianney Board that, instead of moving to the St. Thomas campus, St. John Vianney be allowed to expand Loras Residence. Despite Msgr. Baumgaertner's strong words regarding the problems that would likely occur as a result of that arrangement, the board thought it agreeable, probably for financial reasons. A resolution approving the leasing of Loras Residence and certain adjacent properties plus construction of additional facilities received preliminary approval and was confirmed in October 1970.[88]

The arrangement was not palatable to the Saint Paul Seminary faculty. A lengthy letter to Msgr. Baumgaertner from Msgr. John A. Sweeney, vice-rector, the Reverend Jerome D. Quinn, graduate academic dean, and the Reverend Patrick J. Ryan, academic dean, described why the presence of the college seminarians on the Saint Paul Seminary campus would not be helpful to either institution. They noted that "the St. Paul Seminary faculty was unanimous in its rejection of a permanent presence of St. John Vianney Seminary on the St. Paul Seminary campus." This was not meant as a lack of respect and appreciation for the college seminary, but "does indicate that the Faculty considered the future of the St. Paul Seminary would be seriously compromised by this presence."[89]

A special joint meeting of the board of trustees of the Saint Paul Seminary and the board of directors of Saint John Vianney Seminary was called by Archbishop Leo C. Byrne on January 27, 1971. The purpose was to review the present and future relationship of the two seminaries, and to "address themselves to the question of construction of additional facilities by Saint John Vianney Seminary on the Saint Paul Seminary campus." The faculty of the Saint Paul Seminary was "fearful that the two seminaries will not be able to obtain a separate identity and that there will be a confusion of goals at the two levels."[90]

Both rectors offered descriptions of the effects on their students of the two seminaries co-existing on one campus. After a lengthy discussion, Archbishop Byrne proposed: (1) that the board of trustees of the Saint Paul Seminary meet with the faculty of the Saint Paul Seminary to discuss the problem at hand; and (2) that Msgr. Roach and the board of directors of St. John Vianney Seminary present a case for added facilities that would be sent to the priests of the archdiocese. After both steps had been accomplished, a decision would be announced to the community at large.[91] When the board of trustees met with the Saint Paul Seminary faculty on March 1, 1971, a major concern pervaded the discussion that "the *lower* level of students sets the spirit of the whole institution." It was noted that this was the experience at Nazareth Hall.[92]

A complex of events affected the final decision. Nazareth Hall closed in 1971. At a meeting of the priests of the archdiocese "strong opposition was voiced to any building in this connection at the present time, and opposition to building a structure on the present campus of the St. Paul Seminary."[93] On July 20, 1971, John R. Roach was appointed auxiliary bishop of the archdiocese and was ordained to the episcopacy the following September. Father Kenneth Pierre was appointed rector of St. John Vianney Seminary. Archbishop Byrne announced that a decision had been made in August 1971 to relocate the college seminary in June 1972 to Brady Hall on the campus of the College of St. Thomas. Nolan reflected that this was in keeping with Shannon's original vision.[94] Archbishop Roach believes that was always the plan.[95] The result was that the Saint Paul Seminary became a theologate exclusively, and many there breathed a sigh of relief.

Seminary Education Reshapes Itself

The 1960s was a unique decade in American history, and seminaries were not excluded from the unrest that permeated the milieu: the Cuban missile crisis, civil-rights protests, the assassinations of John F. Kennedy, Robert F. Kennedy, and Martin Luther King, Jr. that stunned the nation, campus sit-ins, race riots, protests against the war in Vietnam, situation ethics, the sexual revolution. Educational approaches changed from "the old math" to "the new math," from "the old theology" to "the new theology." John Glenn had circumnavigated the globe in orbit in 1962. By the end of the decade—in 1969—men had landed on the moon! Change became the order of the day.

The mission to understand the *Church in the Modern World* had expanded to include sociology, psychology, politics, and ecumenism. The changes in the liturgy, especially from Latin to the vernacular, affected every person in the pew. The traditional model of the priest was being challenged. Education of future priests became a key area for renovation. The "new breed" of seminarians in the 1960s was asking questions unheard of in earlier times. As in the titles of the popular booklets by

Father Charles Froehle with seminarians in the early 1970s

John Powell, S.J., everyone was reflecting on *Why Am I Afraid to Love?* and *Why Am I Afraid to Tell You Who I Am?* Existentialism was in the air. Some were having identity crises.

It became clear to seminary educators that strict rules and required obedience had, in many ways, not served the priesthood well. Bishops were questioning seminary education. Bishop John K. Mussio wrote in 1965 of the seminarian: "If he is so secluded from his world that he becomes a stranger to it, then he has been successfully trained in uselessness."[96] Future priests needed to make decisions and take responsibility for their own lives.

Sociological and psychological studies supported these assessments. In April, 1967, the bishops of the United States directed that a "complete, professional, and objective study of the life and ministry of priests be undertaken." This resulted in the publication in the early 1970s of volumes such as *The Catholic Priest in the United States: Historical Investigations,* edited by John Tracy Ellis,[97] and *The Catholic Priest in the United States: Sociological Investigations,* a study of the National Opinion Research Center of the University of Chicago directed by Andrew Greeley.[98] Sociologists such as Joseph Fichter, S.J. and Andrew Greeley, and psychologists such as George Hagmeier and Eugene Kennedy, not only did substantive studies but also published and lectured extensively. Other volumes such as *Secular Priest in the New Church,*[99] edited by Gerard S. Sloyan, and the more sensationalistic *A Modern Priest Looks at His Outdated Church*[100] by James Kavanaugh brought these concerns closer to the people. The departure of priests and nuns from ministry in the late 1960s and early 1970s caused the further examination of formation programs.

The cry was for fewer rules and more freedom. By 1968 cassocks were no longer worn in the classroom at the Saint Paul Seminary. Some wore the Roman collar in class. Off campus, the black suit and white shirt were the order of the day for those who were not deacons. Cassocks were still worn to liturgical assemblies. The seminary was not unaffected by the long hair styles and beards which were common in the late 1960s and 1970s. When a student returned from the summer with a beard, Father Charles Froehle, dean of Cretin Residence, was asked by Msgr. Baumgaertner to tell him that "we do not allow facial hair." Froehle was reminded of that some years later when, as a faculty member and rector, he sported a beard himself.[101]

Although cars were not allowed, some seminarians had them and rented garages in the neighborhood so that they could use them "for social activities." It was not uncommon for seminarians to sneak off campus. Some were dating; others just wanted to be with friends. One of the favorite places to gather was the basement of "Casey's"—a local pub. Father Patrick Ryan, then dean of Cretin Residence, got wind of one particular event there, a farewell party for one of the seminarians. He checked all the rooms and discovered that about 85 percent of the seminarians were missing. He was furious, locked the doors of the dorm in an effort to "catch" the latecomers, and patrolled the building. The students went up the fire escapes, however, and eluded him at every point.

To "memorialize" the event, at the end of the year the whole class dressed in their black suits, white shirts, and black ties and went down to Casey's on a Saturday morning to have a class picture taken in front of the establishment. While the photographic session was taking place, a police van drove by slowly, curious as to what was happening. They convinced the police officer to allow them to take some "mock" pictures of him throwing them into the "paddy wagon." Eugene Tiffany recalls presenting the pictures to Ryan at the end of the academic year. By then the dean responded with a wry sense of humor.[102]

During this period when the Vietnam War was raging, there was concern that some seminarians had enrolled to avoid the draft. A number of students took part in anti-Vietnam demonstrations. In faculty discussions the question was occasionally raised as to whether certain students had a long-term commitment, or were only in seminary to avoid the war. If so, the consensus was that the number was very small.[103]

The Shannon Departure

The church was polarized over the reforms of Vatican II, and the promulgation of *Humanae Vitae* in the summer of 1968 added to the authority crisis. The announcement of the departure of Auxiliary Bishop James P. Shannon on a "leave" to New Mexico in January 1969 took place when the deacon class of the Saint Paul Seminary was having a day of recollection. The question that seemed to haunt the students was: "If Shannon can't handle it, how can we?"[104] Shannon, a bright, attractive, and dynamic individual, who had earned a Ph.D. at Yale, had successfully led the College of St. Thomas as president from 1956 to 1965. For many of the progressive clergy, he was a beacon of light in the American Catholic hierarchy. Priests, sisters, and brothers had been leaving active ministry in droves, but his departure cast a special pall over the archdiocese.

On May 28, 1969, the Minneapolis *Star* alleged that Shannon had submitted his resignation as pastor and bishop before leaving Minnesota for New Mexico. The publicity caused a storm, especially when the Chancery denied the resignation in the May 30, 1969, *Catholic Bulletin.* The confusion, Archbishop Binz stated, resulted from the fact that he had not shared Shannon's letter with the chancellor, Msgr. Terrance Berntson. Shannon wrote to the Minneapolis *Star* on June 4 confirming that his resignation had been submitted November 23, 1968.[105]

An open meeting of the Priests' Senate chaired by Father Roger Carroll took place at the Saint Paul Seminary on June 6, 1969. Archbishop Byrne was present. Shannon had requested that the priests make no statement about his decision. The majority finally agreed that a prayer service should be held on Sunday, June 8, 1969, at the cathedral as a show of unity and an opportunity for healing.

A separate group organized a march from the cathedral to the Mississippi River with the banner "SOS—Save Our Shannon." Some of the local clergy were angry; others saw the situation as an opportunity to cry out for openness in the church. The rally culminated with a prayer service on the mall across from the seminary on Summit Avenue. Msgr. Baumgaertner was delegated to represent Archbishop Byrne and offered a prayer which stated in part:

> For Bishop Shannon, with whom I have been associated for years as a classmate in schooling and as a fellow priest of this diocese for these twenty-three years, I beg the strength of heart that is born of suffering. With all here this afternoon, I too hope that the distress we have suffered will be fruitful in Christ. The forebearance [sic], the understanding, the love that this will require are gifts of God. God grant us that peace of Christ deep in our hearts that will be required to bear the burden of coming years. Without this, our efforts will be scattered by the winds.

Baumgaertner reiterated "the deep anguish" which Archbishop Byrne had expressed to the priests the previous Friday, and conveyed that message to those gathered on the mall. The rector added, "The events of the past few weeks dramatize again for us not only the need for leadership but also the great demands made on those who bear the responsibility."[106]

When the news broke six weeks later that Shannon had been married on August 2, 1969, his many friends and followers were devastated. It continued to impact the seminarians. Paul LaFontaine, ordained in 1972, saw it as a Greek tragedy. He remembers being confused by the turmoil, talking in a group with Father Froehle, sitting down with his spiritual director, Msgr. Ellsworth Kneal, about how to deal with *Humanae Vitae.*[107] Other questions which the situation evoked were priestly celibacy, and the possibility of a married clergy in the future.

This atmosphere was reflected in the Annual Report of 1968–1969:

> Our student body manifests at present the serious questioning and the uneasiness about priestly ministry that characterizes so large a percentage of our younger priests today. The influence of the departures from ministry are felt in their unsureness about what they are entering. There is a need for close contact not only with the faculty but with priests who are active in parish ministry, with priests also who are doing the planning, the thinking for the future of the priestly ministry in our and neighboring dioceses. There is real danger this year that the young men will lose heart.

The report added that there were good signs as well—a responsiveness to the need for prayer and a greater degree of responsibility.[108]

Program Changes

Spiritual formation was a major challenge in these years. Msgr. Stanley Srnec believed that in the upheaval after Vatican II what was needed was a balancing act—allowing some freedom, but not permitting the students to "go wild." In the years 1968 to 1970, however, Srnec believed that seminarians had gone beyond that. He perceived a rejection of church teaching and a rebellion against the papacy. In the last two years of his tenure he held almost no conferences. And it wasn't just the students for whom he was concerned. He believed that some of the faculty wanted "the new" immediately as well. By the spring of 1970 he asked Archbishop Byrne to be moved.[109]

The new spiritual director, Father Gerald Keefe, had spent twenty-three years in parish ministry. He had a very different approach to spiritual formation. Initially he gave some spiritual conferences but he decided to inaugurate formation teams where students would gather weekly. It was modeled on the style of Jesus meeting with his disciples. Keefe tried to meet with each group twice a month and worked out a plan for the group with the leader. He was conscious that the "in" thing was encounter groups and did not want the formation teams to imitate that approach. But he genuinely believed the students needed to share their humanity as well as their theology.

Keefe also believed that he should model the priest's need to go to the people, so he would go to the students' rooms for spiritual direction instead of having them come to him. He genuinely liked the students and sensed a need for healing in the community in the early 1970s. In his own words: "I took to the students naturally because I liked them."[110] He encouraged them to try dyad praying, contemplation, meditation, devotions, the *Prayer of Christians,* the Jesus Prayer, meditative writing. There was a clear emphasis on scripture and the liturgy. Social justice was not forgotten. In 1973, the publication *Formation Models in a Seminary Community* by Gerald Keefe was made available to every student. The major themes were word, sacrament, and community. This valuable book provided seminarians with guidelines and an inspirational text for grounding an in-depth development in spirituality.[111]

Every student still had to have a spiritual director. It could be any priest on the faculty except the dean of the residence hall in which the seminarian lived. Charles Froehle, on the faculty from 1968, remembers that most of the students went to "Jerry" Keefe because he was "very pastoral, apolitical, sensitive and understanding." According to Froehle, Keefe also complemented what Baumgaertner was trying to do as rector. "With Jerry Keefe—his gentle spirit and holiness—there was a good fit."[112] The commendations of the *Report of the Bishops' Committee on Priestly Formation* which resulted from the visitation of the committee to the Saint Paul Seminary on March 25–27, 1974, were appreciative of both the program and the director.[113]

The academic program began to change as well. Although there was satisfaction in the preliminary accreditation of the seminary to offer the M.A. in theology, only a limited number of students took advantage of the opportunity. It became clear that the master of divinity degree should be considered as an option. In August 1970, Msgr. Baumgaertner and Father Ryan visited in Chicago with Thomas J. Coffey, Assistant Executive Secretary of the North Central Association (NCA). They learned that the NCA did not as yet approve professional degrees, so accreditation by the American Association of Theological Schools (AATS) would be required. A document describing the M.Div. degree and the process for accreditation, as well as the pros and cons of being accredited by both the NCA and the AATS, was presented to the faculty and the trustees by the dean, Father Patrick Ryan, on September 8, 1970. Because the NCA would be returning for a visit for the final approval of the M.A. in theology in 1973, it was suggested that the M.Div. also be evaluated at that time. The NCA/AATS team visited the Saint Paul Seminary on November 4–6, 1973. The major recommendation from the report read: "It is the opinion of the Accreditation Team that St. Paul Seminary should be given full accreditation for the degrees Master of Arts and Master of Divinity without notation."[114]

The only institutional area of concern in the NCA/AATS report was: "undue burden on chief administrator in the area of financial management." Among the recommendations was "increasing the staff by the addition of a financial officer or business manager." The seminary was also encouraged to stress the "integration" of the "academic" and the "practical." The report noted that field education was not fully integrated into the life of the school, and that it would be helpful to utilize the pastoral supervisors in the total life of the school. The accreditors also recommended that "more elective opportunities" be available to students. "The present program is tighter than it needs to be in terms of required courses."[115]

When a team came the following March (1974) to conduct a visit on behalf of the NCCB Committee for Priestly Formation, they lauded the rector, the spiritual director, and the field education director, Msgr. John Sweeney, as well as "an extremely well-qualified and dedicated faculty, with a good spread of years of experience." The recommendations of the Bishops' Committee included the suggestion that "a greater effort be made to involve students in the decision-making process in the academic area." They concurred with the NCA/AATS recommendation that a Long-Range Planning Committee of the Board of Trustees be established. They also suggested that the various seminary departments be involved with their own departmental budgets. Their conclusion: "In short, the administrative facets of the seminary seem to be in excellent condition and very much in harmony with the *Program of Priestly Formation*."[116]

A new deacon internship program had been implemented for those who were ordained in 1971. After being ordained deacons in May, they attended a six-week summer school to prepare them for the parish experience which lasted from August 1 until Thanksgiving. Between Thanksgiving and Christmas, they did an internship in a Catholic school. After Christmas they returned to the seminary for the spring semester. According to Thomas Sieg, many in his class suffered from "deaconitis" in that last year.[117]

In 1972, the Interim Term had been inaugurated that allowed the month of January to be used for an intensive spiritual life program for Theology I, and other courses of a more practical nature that did not fit the more structured system of the regular semester. Sister Kathleen Marie Shields, C.S.J., director of elementary religious education for the archdiocese, helped to establish a supervised teaching program for the second-year theology students. As an adjunct faculty member, she conducted a course on Catholic education, part of which was a teaching practicum in which students were assigned to teach in one of the archdiocesan schools. This gave the seminarians first-hand knowledge of the role parish priests could play in the Catholic schools.[118]

Third-year seminarians worked in a hospital setting, and fourth-year theologians assisted with the archdiocesan Catholic Charities on social service projects—with the aged, children with emotional problems, unmarried mothers, alcoholics, and addicts. The broader aspects of field education were gradually developed in the 1970s. According to Msgr. John Sweeney, the interims "give seminarians a chance to use the theology and counseling techniques they have learned in class."[119]

With the M.A. in theology and the M.Div. approved, and the NCA/AATS and Bishops' Committee visitations completed, Father Patrick Ryan decided to relinquish his position as academic dean after five years. Ryan did not always seem to agree with the directions the seminary was taking at that time, but he made a substantial contribution in terms of preparing for the visitations and accreditations. He stayed on for one more year as professor of dogmatic theology, but then was assigned as a pastor in St. Paul.

In 1974 Msgr. Baumgaertner asked Father Charles Froehle to serve as dean. Froehle had thought that James Moudry, who had worked intensively on the M.Div. program, would have been the likely candidate. Froehle served as dean until 1980, at which time he became rector.

The End of the Binz-Byrne Era

The unexpected death of Archbishop Leo C. Byrne was a shock to all, and affected the seminary as well as the archdiocese. Archbishop Binz had been effectively in semi-retirement since 1967. After Byrne's death, Binz offered his resignation almost immediately. On May 21, 1975, Bishop John R. Roach was appointed archbishop. Binz continued to serve as apostolic administrator until June 10, 1975, when Roach took canonical possession of the archdiocese.

Archbishop Binz eventually moved to Maywood, Illinois, where he lived with his sister, Hazel. Msgr. William Baumgaertner recalls visiting Binz in Illinois when his health was failing, to tell him that the new Binz Refectory would be named for him. The archbishop expressed his pleasure and quipped: "I never denied that I enjoyed a good meal."[120]

Bishop John Kinney remembers joining Archbishop Roach for a visit with Archbishop Binz when he was dying of cancer. Binz was pensive and pained about some of the decisions he had made. Bishop Kinney reflected: "Archbishop Roach and I stopped and visited him in Illinois in his last months, and he was in tears through part of it because I really think he felt himself responsible, and that maybe what he was suffering was because of that." When asked if he was referring to the Shannon episode, Kinney replied: "Yes. . . . He took great personal responsibility. He was never able to say that publicly, but in his last months he kept going back over that, I think."[121] Archbishop Binz died of cancer on October 9, 1979, in Maywood, and was buried from the St. Paul Cathedral on October 16, 1979.

Archbishop Roach eulogized Binz at the funeral liturgy, noting that "there was a phenomenal predictability about him. What he did was done with great deliberateness and always only after prayer." Roach stated that he had the sense that Binz internally did not always appreciate some of the things he would be asked to do in the years after Vatican II. "The Church, however, had spoken and that was enough for him." The new archbishop stated, "There was a healthy optimism about him and even a boldness in doing the work of the Lord." He had "a remarkable combination of gentleness and fortitude." Lastly, Roach reflected: "He was an intensely human person who could suffer and know pain, who could be almost frivolous in his humor, but I think above all we could agree that he was a man of the Church. He passed among us and we are better for it."[122]

Although the image of Leo C. Byrne is writ large in the later years of the Binz era, it was well known that Byrne checked major decisions with Binz.[123] Had Byrne become the ordinary in 1967 or soon thereafter, would the future of the Saint Paul Seminary have been different? Would it have continued to exist? Byrne seems to have been less than enthusiastic about the seminary. Binz's support was never in question.

Chapter 13

John R. Roach

Facing the Seminary Challenge (1975–1985)

> As we begin these sensitive discussions, let us keep in mind the fact that we, as two archdiocesan institutions, are at a point in history where we share a joint *responsibility* to the Church.
>
> Archbishop John Roach
> Meeting of the Representatives of the Boards of Trustees of the College of St. Thomas and the Saint Paul Seminary
> December 16, 1983[1]

The first native son to become archbishop of St. Paul and Minneapolis was John Robert Roach. In 1987, only four archbishops in the United States had been auxiliaries in the archdiocese in which they were then serving. In that same year, only six archbishops were priests of the archdiocese in which they were the ordinary. Roach was one of them, and the people of Minnesota were proud.[2]

John Roach was born in Prior Lake, Minnesota, on July 31, 1921, the oldest of three children of Simon and Mary V. Roach. He had two sisters—Virginia, who was close to him in age, and Mona, who was much younger. As a teenager he worked in his father's general store on the Main Street of Prior Lake, a small town southwest of Minneapolis. His father was also part owner of the local bank. Both his parents had a profound influence on his life. His mother had been a schoolteacher before getting married. "She was a reader and taught me to love learning," Roach stated. "She also had a very deep respect for order. I'm a clean desk person, and I got that from my mother."[3] Simon Roach died unexpectedly of a heart attack in 1964 when Father Roach was headmaster

John R. Roach, archbishop of St. Paul and Minneapolis from 1975 to 1995

of St. Thomas Academy. After many years, the archbishop reflected, "He still has an influence in my life."[4]

Roach attended public elementary school in Prior Lake, and studied for two years at Shakopee High School. In his junior year he transferred to Nazareth Hall and began his studies for the priesthood. He proceeded to the Saint Paul Seminary in 1941 for philosophy and theology. Due to the accelerated program during the war, he was ordained to the priesthood on June 8, 1946.

Archbishop Murray assigned Roach to St. Stephen's Parish in Minneapolis for the summer, and Roach credits Father Rudolph Nolan with teaching him how to be a priest. That fall he was sent to St. Thomas Academy, where he taught Latin and religion. His mentor was Father Vincent Flynn, later president of the College of St. Thomas. Roach earned a master's degree in education from the University of Minnesota and served as headmaster of the academy from 1951 to 1968. During that period the school moved from the campus of the then College of St. Thomas to Mendota Heights. Roach's love for teaching and administration, and his commitment to education on every level, began there. He had a reputation as a stern disciplinarian—"a hard nose"—but was also appreciated by the students.[5]

In 1965, Roach was named a monsignor, and two years later Archbishop Binz appointed him the founding rector of the new college seminary named for Saint John Vianney. The years of residence in Loras Hall on the Saint Paul Seminary campus have been discussed in chapter 12. In the summer of 1971 Msgr. Roach learned that he and Msgr. Raymond Lucker had been appointed auxiliary bishops for the archdiocese. As auxiliary bishop from 1971 to 1975, Roach automatically became a member of the seminary board of trustees.

Roach: First Alumnus-Ordinary and Chair of the Board

In the spring of 1975 Pope Paul VI appointed John R. Roach archbishop of St. Paul and Minneapolis. He was installed in the Cathedral of St. Paul on July 16, 1975. After the experience of having two archbishops, the shock of Archbishop Byrne's death, and the resignation of Archbishop Binz, the archdiocese was happy to welcome a native Minnesotan to the helm. Roach's installation coincided with the 125th anniversary of the diocese, and was a celebratory event for the almost fifty-four-year-old prelate and the entire local church.[6]

Archbishop John R. Roach chaired his first meeting of the Saint Paul Seminary board of trustees on October 7, 1975. Once again, he was a first—the first alumnus of the Saint Paul Seminary to become ordinary and chair of the board. Several significant items were approved. The seminary board elected its first woman—Rose (Mrs. Richard) Palen—who served with insight and competence for many years.[7]

Rose (Mrs. Richard) Palen, first woman appointed to the Saint Paul Seminary board of trustees in 1975

On the agenda of that first meeting was action on constructing a new refectory. It had been proposed the previous year but with the untimely death of Archbishop Byrne the decision had been deferred. The old refectory building was no longer functional and was even unsanitary. Rebuilding it was clearly cost-prohibitive. "Archbishop Roach indicated that within the next 18 months sufficient funds would become available from the sale of Nazareth Hall to enable the archdiocese to underwrite a new building." The board voted unanimously for the project and empowered the rector to bring in plans for a new dining room.[8]

The new refectory, designed by Voight and Fourré, was completed on a site near Goodrich Avenue, and had a warm and welcoming atmosphere. W. Charles "Chuck" Henry, a graduate of the New York Institute of Dietetics who had become director of the food service in August 1973, brought experience and expertise to the position and supervised the transition. The move to the new building was scheduled for Christmas vacation 1977 and the old refectory building was demolished in late spring 1978. The much-loved Chuck Henry, an African-American, son of a Methodist minister, came to the seminary for what he expected would be a brief period and stayed for twenty-eight years.[9]

The second major building constructed on the campus in the late 1970s was a priests' retirement residence. Although the latter was not really a part of the seminary, because the plan was to build it on seminary property, legal questions arose as to whether such a facility would be compatible with the intention of James J. Hill. The advice of Timothy P. Quinn of Meier, Kennedy and Quinn, was:

> If the Archdiocese of St. Paul and Minneapolis and the Board of Trustees of the corporation make a determination that it is in the best interests of the seminary and the proper education of candidates for the priesthood that elderly and retired priests reside on the seminary premises so that the candidates for priesthood will grow in the knowledge of what is necessary and useful for the proper and efficient ministry of the church, then the building and maintaining of a retirement home for priests on the seminary property is well within the precatory language used in the trust instrument as the purpose for which the property should be used.[10]

James J. Hill was never far away!

Public Relations, Development, and Finances

The rector, Msgr. Baumgaertner, had been contending with the drain on capital reserves that resulted from the budget deficits over the years. He knew that the constant borrowing from the archdiocese and paying it back out of the endowment was a dangerous practice. J. Thomas Simonet, president of First Trust Company in St. Paul that managed the Hill funds, had been elected to the seminary board in October 1968. In his regular financial reports, he warned against using the endowment, which he described as "eating our seed corn."[11] In 1978 a committee was established to "review and detail the relationship of the seminary to the Archdiocese of St. Paul and Minneapolis, something which has not been done in twenty years."[12]

In 1979 the Saint Paul Seminary was selected to participate in the Lilly Endowment program for development officers in seminaries. James Fennell was hired as full-time director of development and received on-the-job training through the Lilly program.[13] Fennell would build on the initial groundwork laid by John Sondag, hired in 1973 as public relations director. With his background in journalism, Sondag, a former seminarian, created brochures, worked with alumni, and did public relations. He set up a schedule for visiting colleges in the region for recruitment.[14] During those years about twenty-four dioceses were represented at the seminary.[15] Fennell was responsible for both development and public relations.

Seminarians in the '70s

The 1970s were a traumatic time in the nation—the Vietnam War, Watergate and Nixon's eventual resignation, continued civil rights controversies, long hair, and "pot." It was a time of adjustment for the seminary as well. A glance through the seminary directories in the mid-1970s with smiling faces adorned with beards, mustaches, sideburns, and some very long hair offers real contrast to the pictures just a decade before.[16] The demolition of the old classroom building in the summer of 1972 may have represented the end of the old, and "open space" in more ways than one for pursuing new programs.

One such venture was the "Special Theology Program" begun in the fall of 1973—a five-year program for candidates who had college degrees but who did not have adequate background in philosophical or theological studies. The program drew on the resources of St. Thomas. Students lived at the Saint Paul Seminary and received their spiritual and liturgical formation there.[17] This was the forerunner of the Introduction to Priestly Ministry program (IPM) of the 1980s, and the present two-year pre-theology program.

Those who were seminarians in the late 1970s recall a stimulating and challenging environment. Kevin McDonough, at the Saint Paul Seminary from 1976 to 1980, reminisced that he and his classmates, Frederick Campbell, Jan Michael Joncas, Thomas Kommers, Michael Skluzacek, and others, came into an exciting institution. McDonough admits his bias in claiming that he had an exceptional ordination class, but added:

> Although I had been to good schools before I came to the Saint Paul Seminary, and been in some very competitive environments, I found that the seminary did not lag in that regard. Some view [the] seminary as a whole, as a sort of romper-room catechism class. But that was certainly not the atmosphere that I came into.

McDonough reflected further:

> It was a relatively new faculty, but it was a faculty which understood itself, and an institution that understood its continuity with a great history. So I came into a pretty exciting institution, both in terms of the peers that I had the honor of going to school with and the faculty and staff leadership as bearers of an institutional memory.[18]

It was not just McDonough who recalled those days glowingly. James Moudry, professor of sacramental theology and liturgy, stated that his experience of the student body at that time was very positive:

> Especially in the late '70s and early '80s I thought we were getting good people, and they were forward-looking people who were interested in the new reformed church.... McDonough,

> Joncas, Kommers, Paul Feela and a whole slug of people who gave you a lot of encouragement and a lot of hope. The guys from Dubuque, the guys from Omaha . . . [19]

The enrollment during the 1970s ranged from a high of 137 in 1977 to 109 in 1979.[20] John Bauer, ordained in 1979, noted that he discontinued his studies for priesthood after finishing St. John Vianney in 1971 because of the unsettled conditions in ministry. "In the '60s and early '70s there were so many people leaving and there was so much experimentation going on and a lack of clarity about what ministry was going to be all about. Everything was up in the air." By 1974, when he decided to resume his studies for the priesthood at Saint Paul Seminary, "things were beginning to settle down and in fact beginning to swing in the other direction."[21]

Transition to a New Rector

In 1980, after twelve years as rector in the challenging post-Vatican II era, Msgr. Baumgaertner concluded that it was time to seek new ways to serve the church's educational mission. Baumgaertner believed that both he and his classmate Msgr. Terrence Murphy, who had become president of the College of St. Thomas in 1966, knew that collaboration between the seminary and the college would be required for the good of both institutions. Baumgaertner confessed that he did not know when or how it would happen. He wanted the Saint Paul Seminary to be strong enough not to lose its identity if some kind of "merger" occurred and believed it was important to proceed only at the opportune time.[22]

At a special meeting of the seminary board on January 21, 1980, Archbishop Roach announced the resignation of Msgr. Baumgaertner effective July 1. The archbishop and the board expressed their gratitude for his twelve years as rector and thirty-one years on the seminary faculty. Baumgaertner had also served as president of the Midwest Association of Theological Schools in 1969 and was a founding member of the Minnesota Consortium of Theological Faculties and its president from 1977 to 1979. After retiring as rector, he continued to share his expertise as executive director of the Seminary Department of the National Catholic Educational Association (1980–1984), and as associate director for accreditation of the Association of Theological Schools (1984–1990).

The archbishop then announced that, according to the by-laws, it was his task "to appoint the rector with the approval of the Board." He had taken counsel with board members and announced that he wished to appoint Father Charles Froehle, currently vice-rector and dean of studies. In its approval, the board unanimously agreed that Father Froehle was "eminently qualified for the position which he will assume."[23]

Froehle was born in St. Cloud, Minnesota in 1937. His family moved to St. Paul in 1943 where he attended elementary school and one year of high school at St. Matthew's Parish. In 1952 he enrolled at Nazareth Hall, and proceeded to the Saint Paul Seminary in 1957. He was ordained on February 2, 1963, and assigned to the Basilica of St. Mary in Minneapolis in June, where ninety-five-year-old Msgr. James Reardon, a seminary faculty member from 1899 to 1909, was pastor. Froehle sometimes told the seminarians that when he was a newly-ordained priest his first pastor was seventy years older than he was![24]

In 1965, Archbishop Binz, on the recommendation of Msgr. McCarthy, asked Father Froehle to pursue studies toward a doctorate in sacramental theology and liturgy at the Angelicum in Rome.[25] Froehle began his studies in 1965 and was excited to be present for the closing session of Vatican II. After three years he successfully defended his doctoral dissertation, *The Idea of Sacred Sign According to Abbot Anscar Vonier* and returned to St. Paul to begin his work on the seminary faculty in the spring of 1968.[26]

As a young faculty member during those contentious days in the church, Froehle recalled the challenge of students' questions, efforts to liberalize the living situation, and—most of all—implementing the changes in the liturgy. In 1974 he became dean of studies and in 1977 was also appointed vice-rector. He was well prepared but never could have imagined the changes that would take place during his tenure as rector.

Seminary Board Expanded and Activated

At Froehle's first board meeting as rector in October 1980 the budget proposal indicated a $50,000 deficit which, it was hoped, would be compensated for by the Friends of the Seminary fund drive. If not, it would have to come from the endowment. Board members were reminded that the endowment principal had decreased over $500,000 in the past five years. Auxiliary Bishop John F. Kinney moved that a special meeting of the board be held in the near future "to discuss the possibilities for establishing a sound financial base for the seminary with the consideration of a program for endowment." The motion was approved. Archbishop Roach appointed an ad hoc committee which Bishop Kinney was asked to convene. Msgr. Terrence J. Murphy, a member of the seminary board since 1971, asked that an assessment be prepared as to the needs of the seminary for the next five years.[27]

Roach reflected that as late as 1980 the seminary board of trustees was really not a functioning board. Unless a special meeting was called, the board met only once a year for legal purposes and budget review.[28] Ironically, the original by-laws indicated that regular meetings of the board of trustees would be held on the second Wednesday of each alternate month.[29] In Archbishop Ireland's years, the board attempted to keep that schedule. Archbishop Dowling did likewise, although the business done was negligible and some meetings did not take place for lack of a quorum. It was while Archbishop Murray was chair that the board meeting became an annual event. For almost fifty years, the involvement of most trustees was minimal. With the financial situation worsening, that would change. Meetings became more frequent, but it was not until January 28, 1983, that it was agreed that there should be three meetings each year.[30]

It is important to note that in November 1980, Archbishop Roach was elected to a three-year term as president of the National Conference of Catholic Bishops and the United States Catholic Conference, having served the previous three years as vice-president. His responsibilities included representing the American hierarchy at the Vatican, and various other national and international obligations. During his tenure, the bishops completed the peace pastoral and began work on the economic pastoral. The archbishop had wide-ranging responsibilities during those years, but never missed a seminary board meeting.

The Process of Affiliation

Ultimately, the process of the affiliation of the seminary with the College of St. Thomas developed on two levels, as will be described in this chapter and the next. The first level regarding institutions included "battles" over property, buildings, financial arrangements, and governing power. There were confrontations between members of the boards of the seminary and the college, between members of the presbytery with competing views, between the seminary, the "neighbors," and the City Council. The challenges of this phase were basically resolved between 1983 and 1987.

The second level of the affiliation was the "battle over vision." This included differing perspectives on the question of priestly identity and the relationship of the priesthood to the laity. One view emphasized the value of education for ordained and lay ministry in the same setting. Others believed that priestly identity would be better achieved by maintaining separateness—a position held by some bishops, and indeed recommended by the Vatican itself. Discussion over the degree to which this separation needed to be implemented resulted in a process known as "program clarification" from 1986 to 1991. The separation of the School of Divinity into two divisions, written into the Affiliation Handbook in 1991, offered one solution to the ongoing question of preparation for ministry—ordained and lay.

The following story describes the remarkable achievement whereby a free-standing seminary became affiliated with a coeducational archdiocesan college, retaining its identity, and benefiting both. Such success resulted because a process developed whereby trust was established, a variety of perspectives were heard allowing most everyone a sense of investment in the project, and power was wisely negotiated by the archbishop and other principal players. Although *need* initially drove everyone to negotiate, ultimately it was the good of the institutions and the commitment to the archdiocese that convinced one and all that there was no alternative to cooperation. The story that follows describes the "battles" and the struggles for power, as well as the trust and commitment involved in the second founding of the Saint Paul Seminary.

First Suggestion of a "Merger"

At the board meeting in October 1981, Bishop Kinney presented a report of the Subcommittee on Financial Support for the Saint Paul Seminary. The hope for a drive for funds for Saint Paul Seminary was complicated by the fact that St. John Vianney Seminary had to vacate Brady Hall on the St. Thomas campus. The result was a decision to "build a new residence or otherwise provide for housing" for the college seminary. The committee presented several options for consideration regarding the Saint Paul Seminary. Archbishop Roach indicated that two of the options were unacceptable—the outright sale of the seminary property, or operating as in the manner of the past. Msgr. Murphy stated St. Thomas's openness to any arrangements for cooperation with the seminary. One phrase is conspicuous in the minutes: "Such information would be important if any consideration of *merger* with St. Thomas were to be considered." This was the first mention of a "merger" in any of the formal documents.[31]

The word "merger" was very threatening to the seminary faculty. Froehle reflected:

> Any consideration of merger at that early point was really anathema. . . . I don't know of anyone who thought it was a good idea. Peter Nickels, O.F.M. Conv. [dean of studies, 1980–1981], would use the scripture parable of the king who coveted the vineyard of the poor man. Ultimately the king killed him and took the vineyard. That was his image of what was going on.[32]

Others recall Nichols's comments on the "enemy from the North," referring to the College of St. Thomas.[33]

The faculty of the seminary was made minimally aware of the board discussions. The minutes of the November faculty meetings state that the board options did not address the programmatic objectives of the institutions, but rather were concerned with the use of the physical plant, energy efficiency, and such operational matters. James Moudry recalls the great reluctance on the part of the seminary staff, who had difficulty imagining the seminary related to the college.

> The tradition was so strong—[the seminary] was a self-contained operation. There was this fear or anxiety about what would happen. It was unspoken a lot, but my feeling was that it was pretty deep down. And it took some adventuresome spirit to say it's time to fix some of these things and here's a way to do it.[34]

A special board meeting held in December 1981 focused on four proposals of the Subcommittee on Financial Support. Because Bishop

Kinney was not able to attend, Thomas Dolan, vice-president for strategic planning for Norwest Corporation, and chair of the seminary Long-Range Planning Committee, presented the report. The proposal approved by the board with the most far-reaching effects provided for "the establishment of a committee to study possible *merger* of the Saint Paul Seminary with the College of St. Thomas." Before the end of the meeting, Father Froehle raised the question of the regionalization of the seminary. Should the board consider looking to the support of bishops in the area to help solve the problems under consideration?[35] The board did not respond to that suggestion.

Archbishop Roach reminisced on the early days of discussion regarding cooperation of the seminary and the college, and of the need which existed for both of them:

> I think what's important to understand is this. Msgr. Murphy and I are classmates. Very close friends. Both realists. St. Thomas had a lot of money, potentially a lot of money, and the Saint Paul Seminary had a lot of property. And the Saint Paul Seminary needed money but not as much property. St. Thomas needed property. It became a very logical, and to my mind, easy solution. In the meantime I know there was a lot of anxiety. ...But it became so clear that if the seminary were to have a future it would need to be in a highly cooperative endeavor with St. Thomas. At the time that we got to the resolution, to my mind it was pretty easy.

Roach added: "I wanted a strong seminary desperately. And the seminary was in trouble. And while we had an endowment, it was very modest. The endowment that the seminary had was primarily property. St. Thomas needed expansion."[36]

On January 13, 1982, Archbishop Roach met with Monsignor Terrence Murphy, Father Charles Froehle, and Monsignor Richard Pates, rector of St. John Vianney Seminary, to discuss the construction of a new building for St. John Vianney. The publication of the plan "would also announce that a second phase would include a program to provide for the long-range needs of the St. Paul Seminary." The summary of the meeting indicates that the archbishop had a clear direction in mind: "Working toward a situation in which the St. Paul Seminary would be incorporated into the St. Thomas structure while retaining its title and a certain unique identity." Even more specifically, participants in the January 13 meeting agreed that there be a study of "long-range feasibility of merger between St. Paul Seminary and the College of St. Thomas with St. Paul Seminary retaining as much of its identity as possible." The archbishop then proposed that a special committee be established which would concern itself with these long-range objectives.[37]

Minor test cases for cooperation between the college and the seminary were the leasing of Loras Residence and the lease or rental of land on the seminary campus for tennis courts displaced by the construction of Saint John Vianney Seminary. The Saint Paul Seminary had commissioned a study on land and building use of its campus known as the Dober Study which became a valuable resource for further discussions.

The Faculty Revises the Curriculum

In the meantime, life at the seminary was not standing still. A faculty workshop May 30–June 1, 1977, facilitated by Father Roman Vanasse, O.Praem., of the Catholic Theological Union in Chicago, began the process of writing a mission statement by identifying seminary goals and objectives. From that point forward, regular faculty workshops were scheduled each fall and spring.[38]

In the fall of 1981 a long-range planning process was set in place. In November a questionnaire was sent to alumni, pastors, and others in the archdiocese and beyond to ascertain what recommendations the broader church would have for the Saint Paul Seminary, what they looked for in seminary programs, and reactions to present programs as well as possibilities for the future. Although many of the faculty were excited about the process, there were some priest faculty who were not sure that input from the broader church was what was really needed in the renewal of seminary programs.[39]

At the faculty workshop in January 1982, Robert J. Burke, director of the Office of Pastoral Planning for the archdiocese, reviewed the data generated by the survey. Key areas were: (1) the curriculum, including field education; (2) personal growth issues; and (3) spiritual/liturgical formation. Questions were raised about a better connection to the Minnesota Consortium of Theological Schools, a relationship to St.

Thomas's M.A. in Catechetics program, and cooperative efforts with archdiocesan programs such as the Center for the Permanent Diaconate and the Center for Growth in Priestly Ministry.[40]

"The New Program"

The faculty worked diligently throughout the semester to develop four separate goals with objectives and action plans. At the June 8, 1982, board meeting, Father Froehle presented an eleven-page document to the board of trustees that included the goals and action plans to implement them, plus a revised version of the mission statement. The four goals stated that the seminary would: (1) improve the pastoral focus in its academic program and promote intense theological reflection in its field education; (2) improve its program of priestly formation and prepare seminarians for spiritual leadership; (3) initiate new programs of personal growth with a focus on commitment to celibacy, simplicity of lifestyle, and personal maturity; and (4) provide ministerial training programs for ordained and non-ordained ministers and for candidates for professional ministry within the church.[41] This last goal was the occasion for the revision of the mission statement.

The board discussed at length the proposed mission statement that "allowed for broadening the seminary programs beyond the education of future priests." Some felt it was too restrictive and did not allow for those who were interested in taking courses for enrichment alone. It was recommended that the statement be resubmitted with broader terminology. Two other questions were raised: Should the Saint Paul Seminary expand its programs in this direction? If it were to do so, how would it relate to the College of St. Thomas in this regard? Board member John Burke moved that a professional group be hired to do a feasibility study. The board approved. Msgr. Murphy then moved that "It is a position of the board of trustees of the Saint Paul Seminary that it is a good idea for the seminary to provide programs of this type for the local church." The board voted unanimously in favor of that motion, and then approved the whole action plan.[42]

A new revision of the mission statement was presented to the board on October 5, 1982. The statement maintained the focus on priesthood studies: "The Saint Paul Seminary prepares candidates for ordination to the ministerial priesthood of Jesus Christ, a ministry exercised in the service of the pastoral mission of the Catholic Church." The board, however, then approved the following secondary focus: "In addition it provides programs of preparation and enrichment for those involved in Church ministry, as well as programs of theological and pastoral education for others within the Church." Although the new mission statement was not approved by the board until January 28, 1983, the direction for a more inclusive program was clear.[43]

Implementing the Program: New Dean, New Faculty

Although intense faculty discussion and long-range planning were dominant, there was difficulty in filling the role of dean of studies after Father Froehle became rector. Scripture professor Father Peter Nickels, O.F.M. Conv., served in that position from 1980 to 1981, and was replaced by church historian Father Eugene "Adam" Bunnell, O.F.M. Conv., as interim dean for one year. In the fall of 1982, Victor Klimoski, who, among other administrative roles, had been director of graduate students at the School of Theology at St. John's University in Collegeville, was hired as the first full-time dean at the Saint Paul Seminary. A former seminarian, he had master's degrees in theology and education and was a Ph.D. candidate at the University of Minnesota, writing his dissertation on continuing education for the clergy. Stabilizing the position of academic dean was important, and Klimoski took the results of the self-study and the strategic plan and brought energy and administrative skill to implementing them.[44]

Board member and former faculty member Bishop Raymond A. Lucker and Dean Victor Klimoski

Sister Mary Daniel Hartnett, C.S.J., associate director and director of field education from 1976 to 1987

The "face" of the faculty was changing. For many years William Curtis, speech instructor, had been the only full-time lay person on the faculty. Sister Mary Daniel Hartnett, C.S.J., became the first woman full-time faculty member when she was appointed associate director of field education in 1976, and director in 1978. In that same year, Elizabeth Stodola became part-time music director. It was clear that, with the shortage of priests, religious and lay men and women would have to be considered for faculty positions. Former seminarian Thomas Fisch, who had already earned three master's degrees, taught as an adjunct for a year and then was sent by the seminary for doctoral studies in liturgy at the University of Notre Dame in 1980. His first year as a full-time faculty member was 1981.[45] In 1982 Sue Seid-Martin and her husband Larry Martin were hired to jointly fill the position of director of liturgical music.

There were also new challenges for the priest faculty. Father Dennis Dease was appointed spiritual director in 1979. In 1982, Father Ronald Bowers joined the faculty to teach canon law. Father Paul Feela was assigned to the faculty with a view to future teaching in liturgy, and Fathers Phillip Rask and Thomas McKenna returned from studies to teach scripture and pastoral studies respectively.[46] Father Froehle was selected to participate in a special program for chief executive officers of theological schools of the United States and Canada in July 1982 in West Point, New York, sponsored by the Association of Theological Schools. The seminary was moving ahead to implement its vision.

Bishop Bullock Chairs "Future Directions Committee"

In 1982 Archbishop Roach established an "Advisory Committee for Future Directions of the Saint Paul Seminary, Saint John Vianney Seminary, and the College of St. Thomas" and appointed his auxiliary William Bullock as chair. At the October meeting of the board of trustees Bishop Bullock explained that "the committee was meant to facilitate the communication of information between the respective institutions and boards of trustees."[47] Its membership included representatives of the three boards. The committee first met on December 3, 1982, to begin to identify key issues for discussion among the three institutions. Msgr. Murphy believed that undergraduate enrollment had leveled off, and the future of St. Thomas was more in the direction of expanded programs—one possibility being a downtown Minneapolis campus offering a degree in business administration. He indicated, however, that the college was interested in its relationship to the Saint Paul Seminary "although its profit and loss picture is less appealing."[48] The topic for the next meeting, scheduled for January 18, 1983, was space and programs.

The priests of the archdiocese did not want to be left out of the conversation. On December 1, 1982, Father John Gilbert, president of the Priests' Senate, wrote to Father Froehle with an invitation: "The steering committee thought it would be a good idea to hear from you about the Seminary and its future. I sense support for you in what many feel is probably the most difficult job in the diocese." He then raised questions for discussion, e.g., how much subsidy is received by the seminary from the archdiocese, should bishops consider regional seminaries, is it possible to continue the program with only eighty or eighty-five students?[49]

Land Use: Cooperation Between Seminary and College

In January 1983 the seminary board approved a resolution accepting the "land use zones" as determined by the Dober Study, and approved in principle the use of seminary land for the construction of tennis courts by the College of St. Thomas. There was extended correspondence on the tennis courts among several of the principals involved regarding legal issues, financial responsibilities, access to the courts by members of the seminary community, management, maintenance, and parking. In retrospect, although the tennis courts seem minor in the total affiliation agreement, they were the occasion for dialogue on the many ramifications involved in St. Thomas's use of seminary land.[50] Father Froehle wrote to Msgr. Murphy on March 18, 1983, prior to the formal signing of the tennis court agreement: "I have been pleased with past cooperative ventures between our institutions. Our present discussions of future cooperation look very promising. I have no doubt that the tennis courts will be yet another sign of our mutual support for each other's mission in this Archdiocese."[51]

By April 1983, a staff committee had been created "to actively explore all possibilities of cooperation between the college and the seminary." Members of the committee were Father Charles Froehle and James Fennell from the seminary, and Dr. Charles Keffer, provost, and Donald Leyden, vice-president for administration, from St. Thomas. In a letter to seminary board member J. Thomas Simonet, Fennell described the four key areas of study: (1) continuation of present efforts of cooperation; (2) acceleration of new efforts of cooperation; (3) acquisition of Saint Paul Seminary property by the College of St. Thomas; and (4) merger or affiliation of Saint Paul Seminary and the College of St. Thomas. Fennell felt that the first two areas were being successfully implemented but still did not deal with the issue of the long-term financial stability of the seminary. He admitted that "acquisition of land, at first seemed a remote possibility but now has received a serious second look." He described the situation as follows:

> Thus, it may be time to seriously look at a larger sale/lease purchase of land and buildings. It is clear that SPS is "land and building rich" (a strength and a weakness) and that CST is "student rich and land poor." At this point in our history, it may be time for a bolder decision. One possible scenario has been suggested to sell 20 acres of land and the buildings on these designated acres. Possible projected income is estimated at 7 to 9 million. Such a scenario leaves the seminary adequate building space, 10 acres of property, a sizable addition to endowment and funds for building renovation.

Fennell concluded his letter by stating that the fourth area of study, the merger of the two institutions, was also in process. "Father Froehle and

Msgr. Terrence J. Murphy, president of the College of St. Thomas

Msgr. Murphy have already traveled to Catholic University to study their model of merger. Thus, active interest and study of merger has begun."[52]

On April 26, 1983, E. Vincent Dolan, a realtor and appraiser, joined James Fennell and Donald Leyden for a confidential meeting to establish guidelines for appraisal of the Saint Paul Seminary campus. There were various options if the seminary were to choose to sell some or all of its property: sell land as a package on the open market; sell land for multiple dwellings such as condominiums; or sell lots along the River Road for private homes. Dolan was commissioned by the College of St. Thomas to begin work on the appraisal at once with a report available by July 1, 1983.

On June 9, 1983, *The Catholic Bulletin* published an article entitled "Committee to Study Integration of Seminaries, College" which was one of the first public descriptions of the plans under consideration. An interview with Bishop William Bullock offered the graphic description of five thousand St. Thomas students on a fifty-acre campus, and one hundred seminarians on a thirty-four-acre campus. Bullock stated: "The college needs to expand and the seminary, in some ways, needs to contract. They really are the answers to each other's problems.... It would be good for the seminary because they could concentrate more on preparing men for the priesthood rather than on how to fill the halls and pay the heat bill."[53] He noted that the committee had studied other institutions where a college and a seminary were under one administration, such as Seton Hall University, South Orange, New Jersey, the Catholic University of America, Washington, D.C., and St. John's University, Collegeville, Minnesota.

Bishop Bullock, Msgr. Murphy, Father Froehle, and Msgr. Pates met with Vincent Dolan to receive the results of his appraisal on June 24, 1983. Although the official twenty-one-page report was not sent to Msgr. Murphy until July 11, 1983, Dolan shared his appraisal that the "value in use" of the seminary campus was $12,000,000, and the "market value" was $4,400,000. Msgr. Murphy made it clear that St. Thomas was more interested in the land than in the buildings, and that "it is necessary for the St. Paul Seminary to determine what it wants to do and make a proposal to the College. The College would then respond." After Dolan departed, the group agreed that the appraisal should be presented to the entire Future Directions Committee. They also agreed that the presbytery ought to be involved in the discussion regarding the future of the Saint Paul Seminary, and Father John Gilbert was invited to join the Future Directions Committee meeting to help in planning presbytery participation.[54]

The Long-Range Planning Committee of the seminary board of trustees met on July 18, 1983. Daniel Dolan indicated that he believed that the appraisal reflected the possibility of only one buyer—the College of St. Thomas. The committee also felt that "value in use" should be clarified and possibly changed to "going concern use." The discussion included the fact that selling/leasing were not the only alternatives. A capital building and endowment campaign was a definite possibility. The committee concluded that the seminary would be in favor of leasing designated buildings and lands to the college, but it would not be in favor of selling land or buildings. Financial stability could be achieved by raising additional endowment funds.[55]

Beginning the Hard Negotiations

The Future Directions Committee met on July 22, 1983.[56] Thomas Dolan shared the report of the seminary Long-Range Planning Committee that it preferred to lease land and buildings rather than sell. He stated clearly that "SPS feels the need to retain the land for security because once the land is gone, SPS loses control over any future direction." David Koch believed there were only two viable options: the seminary could become a unique part of the college, or the college would acquire seminary properties, while the Saint Paul Seminary remained completely independent. Msgr. Murphy noted that he felt the college board would prefer the affiliation proposal. He also believed, "based on informal conversations with individual STC [St. Thomas College] trustees, that their preference is the 'purchase of the whole' of SPS." He would not, however, close the door to other possibilities. Another consideration was the seminary selling the land to the college and then leasing back on a long-term basis the facilities it needed.

Msgr. Murphy described the advantages that he believed affiliation would bring to the college, particularly in the acquisition of a graduate theology program. Msgr. Pates observed that, in his judgment, the majority of the priests would see affiliation as the best solution. Father Gilbert stated that the priests "almost unanimously recognize the value of a strong theological presence" but he felt there would be "amazing support" for an affiliation. He added: "The priests would reject outright just closing SPS down." He believed that the present situation should be communicated to the presbytery. Bishop Bullock asked the key question: "What exactly is the seminary looking at and is it being totally realistic in terms of—its financial resources?—its future theological program?" Msgr. Murphy added that "SPS must come up with a future plan and be very specific." This meeting, which appears to have been replete with frank exchanges, ended with Bishop Bullock's announcement that he would be in Rome for a time of study, and therefore another meeting was not being scheduled.[57]

Implementing the New Curriculum

While the Long-Range Planning Committee continued its complicated task of devising proposals for the board of trustees, new seminary programs were put in place in the fall of 1983 beginning with the Theology I students. The curriculum was totally revised with an emphasis on the relationship of academic study to parish life. One of the key elements was the "Teaching Parish" program under the direction of Sister Mary Daniel Hartnett, C.S.J. It linked work in the classroom and regular participation in a local parish for four years, an ongoing experience equivalent to an internship. This would allow students to integrate their academic work with their pastoral practice. The "Growth in Life and Ministry" (GLM) program, under the direction of Father Dennis Dease, was developed to provide for a more focused spiritual and personal formation. The "Introduction to Priestly Ministry" (IPM) program, an evolution from the "Special Theology Program," allowed candidates who needed additional philosophy and theology before beginning formal studies for the priesthood to study at the Saint Paul Seminary, with a priest-teacher specially assigned for that program. The "Evening Semester" program made courses available to priests and other ministers in the church who hoped to be enriched or to pursue a degree. An air of excitement permeated these ventures.[58]

Students' Intuition Confirmed

Students were not informed of the negotiations at hand, but the article in the *Catholic Bulletin* the previous June must have given rise to speculation. In preparation for the fall 1983 *Gaudeamus* program, which served to open each school year, the Theology II class had been warned not to focus their satire too strongly on the faculty. So they decided to select a theme, and what better than the relationship of the seminary to St. Thomas? The satire, performed for the entire seminary community, was framed around "Saturday Night Live," and one segment was a large weather map indicating that a "Murphy Clipper" was approaching the seminary campus and bringing foul weather. Throughout the program, someone portraying Msgr. Murphy was quietly moving around the campus with a tape measure—measuring the property while trying to look inconspicuous.

Thomas Brioschi (ordained in 1986), a member of the *Gaudeamus* Committee, recalls being called into the rector's office the next day with several of his classmates. Father Froehle and James Fennell asked them where they got their ideas and information. Finally convinced that the students really did not know what was in process, the administration realized it was mostly a coincidence, and information had not been leaked to them from any source.

Ironically, the following spring, while assisting in a major xeroxing project for the liturgy program, Brioschi, and his classmates John Estrem, Timothy Dornfeld, and Steven Broderson arrived in the administration building one evening to begin work and discovered that someone had accidentally left a draft of the "Affiliation Agreement: The Saint Paul Seminary, the College of St. Thomas, and the Archdiocese of St. Paul and Minneapolis" marked CONFIDENTIAL in the copy machine. They claim they did not read it, but the title was enough to indicate that the theme of their *Gaudeamus* program had not been totally fiction. They delivered the material to Father James Moudry, vice-rector and director of worship. Speculation abounded![59]

Preparing for Evaluation and Reaccreditation

As the affiliation drama unfolded, the seminary was also preparing for a formal review by the Vatican. A visitation and review of seminary programs in the United States had been mandated by Pope John Paul II in 1981. Archbishop Roach, as president of the NCCB/United States Catholic Conference (USCC), had been involved in the planning for the Vatican Study of American Seminaries, which was under the direction of Bishop John Marshall of Burlington, Vermont. The archbishop indicated that the Holy Father was concerned about the definition of priesthood that was being taught in seminaries, as well as the teaching of moral theology and allied questions.[60] Father Froehle, as president of the Midwest Association of Theological Schools (MATS) from 1982 to 1984, also had input into the process as spokesperson for the nineteen seminaries represented in MATS.

The final form of visitation and the visitation instrument were published in August 1983. Therefore, in addition to implementing the new curriculum and new programs and preparing a proposal for St. Thomas, the seminary readied itself for the Vatican visitation scheduled for the week of February 13–17, 1984. The visit preceded by only one month the reaccreditation visit of the North Central Association/Association of Theological Schools on March 12–14, 1984.[61]

Long-Range Planning Proposal to the Seminary Board

Due to the archbishop's participation in the Synod in Rome on Reconciliation, the fall board meeting was rescheduled for November 29,

1983. This allowed the Long-Range Planning Committee to reach a consensus in October, which stated that "the basic concept of retaining certain buildings and land for SPS and leasing the remaining property to St. Thomas College was agreed upon." It noted, however, that "sale of building [sic] and property can be an alternative." Safeguarding the interests of the seminary was the primary goal.[62]

Bishop Bullock wrote to the Committee on Future Directions October 28, 1983, to inform them that two scenarios would be presented to the seminary board on November 29, 1983—either a lease of land and buildings or a sale of part of the buildings and land.[63] However, as late as November 7, 1983, Thomas Dolan made the following statement in a letter to Father Froehle: "I think we should avoid the words 'cooperation, relationship and integration' in our proposal so we make it clear we are proposing keeping the two institutions separate."[64]

On November 16, 1983, the Long-Range Planning Committee reviewed the various drafts of proposals and made every effort to put them in historical context. The presuppositions included the following elements to ensure the future of the seminary: (1) an autonomous, self-determined, free-standing seminary and school of theology that can offer the appropriate programs; (2) adequate physical facilities; (3) financial security. They finally agreed on the following two proposals to be presented to the board of trustees.

According to Proposal I, the seminary would retain ownership of the entire thirty-eight acres of land, and would lease to the College of St. Thomas all the seminary land except the western border: from the River Road on the west to the Summit Avenue entrance road on the east, and from Goodrich Avenue on the south to Summit Avenue on the north. The lease would be for ninety-nine years. The seminary would give the College of St. Thomas sole ownership of the nine buildings on that land.[65]

In exchange, the college would provide the seminary with the use of McCarthy Recreation Building; first priority use of Baumgaertner Auditorium; year-round maintenance of all grounds currently owned by the seminary; heat, electricity, water and building maintenance for the seminary buildings at cost; one hundred parking places; renovation of the present administration building; construction of a new building that would provide living quarters for seminarians and priest faculty, dining room facilities, an oratory for 135 people, and an infirmary. The Saint Paul Seminary would retain ownership of the John Ireland Library,

St. Mary's Chapel, the administration building, the new residence building (located somewhere on the western border of the property), and land on the western border of the property as described above. The Saint Paul Seminary would begin a capital fund campaign in 1984 to renovate St. Mary's Chapel and the library as well as provide for an increased permanent endowment.

Proposal II was basically the same in terms of the seminary retaining ownership of land on the western boundary of the campus. The major difference was that "The seminary will transfer title and ownership of the remaining land (with the exception of the land and building associated with Byrne Residence) to the College of St. Thomas." It was also stated: "The sale price to the College of St. Thomas will be an amount of money to be negotiated by the Saint Paul Seminary with the College of St. Thomas on the basis of comparative real estate estimates of the value of the property."[66]

At the November 29, 1983, board meeting, one of the most important in the history of the seminary, Thomas Dolan presented the report of the Long-Range Planning Committee by means of a slide presentation of the mission of the seminary, projections regarding long-term financial viability, and the committee's preference for the future development of the Saint Paul Seminary land and buildings. According to Dolan's notes, Proposal II had become the preferred position of the committee. Both the seminary and the college had agreed that outright sale would be preferable to leasing—"a cleaner way of doing business." Archbishop Roach pointed out that "it was a canonical matter that in the alienation of property one must have two appraisals." A resolution to that effect was moved, seconded, and passed.

The board then voted to accept the proposal of its Long-Range Planning Committee "as its preference for the future development of the seminary" with the understanding that "the concept described in Proposal Two was being approved as the basis for negotiation with the College of St. Thomas." In approving the concept of sale rather than lease, it was "agreed that the dollar figure must be high enough to meet Seminary needs, i.e., in the neighborhood of $8,000,000." An ad hoc committee formed by the archbishop "with a view to formulating a final proposal for acceptance by both boards" consisted of John Burke, Patrick Barrett, Thomas Dolan, Thomas Simonet, Daniel Dolan, Reverend James Moudry, Reverend Mr. Lee Piche, and Reverend Charles Froehle. Bishop Bullock would also be a participant.[67]

Joint Meeting with Trustee Representatives

If November 29 was the most important board meeting for the future of the seminary, the joint meeting of representatives of the boards of trustees of the Saint Paul Seminary and the College of St. Thomas on December 16, 1983, with Archbishop Roach as chair was pivotal. Father Froehle offered initial comments and described recent events leading up to the meeting. Thomas Dolan made the formal slide presentation, including the proposal for the sale of some of the property and buildings to the college for $8,000,000.[68]

Msgr. Murphy also made a formal presentation. He believed that the undergraduate enrollment had stabilized and housing pressure was off. However, he saw the institution in a "growth mode." He stated:

> We see that the next few years will be years for this college to seriously consider the concept of the university, thus providing graduate schools in different areas. A graduate theology school would fit into these plans. With regard to the Theology School, we see this as a possible way of attracting more students to the seminary program because the student would then be part of a larger institution, the St. Thomas University.

Three models of affiliation were discussed. In the first, "the SPS could maintain its identity and formation program while in affiliation with the college." Various benefits were listed, including the obvious, that a merger was a better use of resources and would provide a living endowment for the Saint Paul Seminary through the college's success. The second option involved funding the seminary endowment with payment for land and buildings over a specified number of years. St. Thomas was clear that it was not interested in borrowing a large sum of money at commercial rates, and that the seminary's land and buildings represented a low priority in the immediate future of the college. One of the ongoing issues had been that it would cost in excess of three million dollars to bring the three almost ninety-year-old residence halls into compliance with the building code.[69]

It is interesting to note that the St. Thomas board had only recently approved a loan for $2,555,030 for remodeling, refurbishing buildings, and a new faculty/staff/student computerized identification system for the college. Conversations were also in process regarding the establishment of an engineering school, as well as dialogue regarding a relationship with the William Mitchell College of Law.[70] St. Thomas was, indeed, in a "growth mode."

The presentations were followed by frank and open discussion regarding finances, enrollment, endowment, and buildings. St. Thomas representatives said that the $8,000,000 price tag was too much and offered $3,000,000. Dr. Patrick Barrett suggested that they compromise at $5,000,000. Msgr. Murphy felt that the decision was too important not to take time and probe all of the possibilities.[71] Both groups then met separately to consider the questions raised. They came together for a final discussion and summary. There was common agreement on many issues: all wanted to do what was best for the church in this archdiocese; all wanted excellence in theological education; all agreed that the Saint Paul Seminary had more land and buildings than it needed; all agreed that autonomy was important for the seminary. The last item of agreement was the most focused:

> That we should proceed with further discussion focusing on the question of how SPS can remain autonomous and self-directed while affiliated with the College of St. Thomas. Both institutions must: (1) Explore a detailed structure of affiliation design. (2) Recognize the serious apprehension SPS has with such an affiliation. (3) Recognize that autonomy and self-direction are of the utmost importance.

Archbishop Roach concluded that the College of St. Thomas should "provide guarantees and discuss identity and autonomy of SPS with its own mission." He also suggested that some retention of physical buildings would be required for the Saint Paul Seminary.

Key questions remained: Can the college guarantee the Saint Paul Seminary its identity and autonomy? What does it mean to have program independence and financial independence? How much autonomy is possible if one entity is dependent on another for financial viability? Father Froehle made the following summary remarks: "It is clear that the College of St. Thomas has rejected the seminary's proposal of dividing land and buildings because of financial limitations. It is also clear that SPS needs to be convinced of what this affiliation will look like." It was agreed that at the next meeting "SPS would outline those things needed to define its autonomy, and St. Thomas would outline specifically what they envision affiliation to mean including land, buildings, programs, and outline also their guarantees to SPS." It was also agreed that the discussions had to remain confidential.[72] The meeting adjourned to prepare for Christmas and a new year that would offer the challenge of defining what "affiliation" really meant.

A second real-estate appraisal of the Saint Paul Seminary had been commissioned in accord with the archbishop's request. E. F. LaFond Company, Inc., submitted its appraisal on December 21, 1983, and its figures were considerably higher than E. V. Dolan's. The firm concluded that the "value by cost" would be $12,570,000, and the "market value" would be $9,200,000.[73] This gave the seminary additional bargaining power.

Father Froehle wrote to the seminary board members in January to report on the meeting of December 16, 1983: "At this point the College of St. Thomas says it is not in a financial position to assume the kind of debt that would be involved. They are very interested, however, in continuing the discussion and seeing what possibilities there are for accomplishing the same goals with different means." Father Froehle reminded the board members that the next meeting of the negotiating committee of representatives of the college and the seminary boards was scheduled for March 9, 1984. He also invited them to luncheon on February 14, 1984, to meet with the representatives of the "Roman Study" to be chaired by Bishop John McDowell, auxiliary bishop of Pittsburgh, during their visitation of the seminary.[74]

Vatican Visitation and NCA/ATS Reaccreditation

A single self-study was prepared by the faculty under the leadership of Dean Klimoski for both the Vatican visitation (February 13–17, 1984) and the reaccreditation visit of the NCA/ATS (March 12–14, 1984). (The AATS name had been changed to ATS—Association of Theological Schools of the United States and Canada—in 1974.) Shortly before the date of the Vatican visitation, Father Froehle received word that Bishop McDowell would not be able to chair the committee due to a death in the family, and Bishop Matthew H. Clark of the Diocese of

Rochester, New York, would lead the visitation team. The visit was thorough and productive, and remembered by those involved as a positive experience. An oral report was presented on the last day of the visit, and copies of the completed report of the papal visitation team were sent to the Sacred Congregation for Catholic Education, Bishop Marshall, Archbishop Roach, and Father Froehle in September 1984.[75]

In a cover letter to Archbishop Roach, Bishop Clark stated: "Due to your own close attention to the seminary and the leadership of a competent Rector and dedicated faculty, we believe that St. Paul Seminary has in place a sound program of priestly formation."[76] Commendations were reported at great length, particularly regarding the energy and vision exhibited by the faculty and administration in restructuring the programs and broadening the mission statement. The seminary was commended for "courage in facing its future."[77]

Recommendations included: a more active participation of the trustees in the governance of the school; a procedure for the selection of a rector; the recruitment of seminarians as a priority with leadership from the board; greater contact of faculty with seminarians; greater responsibility of the seminary in the admissions process with more specific policies and criteria rather than depending on the vocation offices of the dioceses sponsoring candidates.

Members of the faculty who were doctoral candidates were encouraged to complete their degrees, and additional teaching staff was needed especially in moral theology, church history, social justice, ecumenism, and theological reflection. It is noteworthy that searches were already in process for appointments in scripture and church history. The establishment of the position of a dean of students was encouraged.[78]

The question of a possible affiliation was not specifically discussed. Father Froehle noted that it had been agreed that the meetings between St. Thomas and the seminary would be confidential, and at the time of the Vatican visitation the situation was still too undefined and the possibility of a "merger" or affiliation did not seem imminent. Discussions touching on the topic were always in the context of the question: "If an affiliation were to take place, what would it look like?" No commitments had been made.[79] The Report states:

> The visiting team offers its encouragement to St. Paul Seminary to continue its planning activity, especially with neighboring

> St. Thomas College, St. John's Seminary, and other institutions, in matters of use and improvement of facilities, academic collaboration, and any other steps that will impact favorably upon the seminary's ability to carry out its goals (PPF #234, 289, 290).[80]

Cooperation with St. Thomas was viewed positively as long as the requirements of the Program of Priestly Formation were upheld.

The NCA/ATS team, chaired by Father James Coriden from the Washington Theological Union, offered commendations and recommendations not dissimilar to those in the evaluation of the Vatican team. One of the commendations noted the liturgical life of the community as being "of admirable quality (perhaps unparalleled in Catholic theologates today), including its unique and impressive musical components."[81] It recommended a full ten-year reaccreditation of both the M.Div. and the M.A. degree programs with no notations. It did, however, recommend that the seminary submit a written report in five years' time in reference to three areas of concern: (1) faculty upgrading; (2) library budget and staff; and (3) the progress of the redesigned degree programs and their new components.[82]

Between mid-February and mid-March substantial progress was made in the dialogue regarding affiliation of the seminary and the college. This is evident in the NCA/ATS report which states:

> One other very significant development must be noted: serious and substantial negotiations with the neighboring College of St. Thomas which may result in some form of closer relationship or affiliation. Both the college and the Seminary are sponsored by the Archdiocese; the Archbishop is president of both boards. They have engaged in various forms of cooperation and mutual assistance for many years; they are friendly neighbors who occasionally collaborate. For nearly three years the leadership of both schools has been exploring a variety of mutually beneficial arrangements, and a decision seems to be near at hand. Whatever the extent and outcome of these negotiations, the future of the Seminary seems secure from every point of view.[83]

How could the process have progressed so quickly?

"Those Breakfast Meetings"

The real action on affiliation was transferred to a subcommittee of the negotiating team that began a series of regular early-morning breakfast meetings in February 1984. This group, consisting of Thomas Dolan, Thomas Simonet, Father James Moudry, and Father Charles Froehle from the seminary, and Thomas Holloran, John McHugh, Dr. Charles Keffer, and Msgr. Terrence Murphy from the college, offered proposals, faced the difficult questions, built trust, and made the affiliation a reality. They met a total of eight times between February 7, 1984, and May 1, 1984. James Moudry recalled "those breakfast meetings":

> I was always impressed with the seriousness of the conversation and the way it went forward without a great deal of rancor, but with a good deal of frankness. And it often seemed to happen that someone like Holloran was able to summarize and articulate positions and do it with a great deal of smoothness to where we were in the conversation. I was very impressed with him....I felt that the seminary was being wooed by St. Thomas because they wanted it to work. We needed the money. They needed the land. I had the feeling that they really wanted this to work and that they were willing to make the concessions.[84]

When asked when he believed the affiliation would really work, Father Froehle responded: "When we began the small group breakfast meetings in February and March of '84. That's when we began to build trust. We began to see that we could work out an agreement which would allow us to retain some independence and our identity."[85]

Thomas Holloran reflected that the subcommittee began with the overarching conviction that they could make it work. The relationships of committee members helped. Holloran, McHugh, and Simonet had all been in law school together at the University of Minnesota. McHugh and Dolan had worked together at the Norwest Bank of St. Paul. Holloran had done some legal work for the Moudry Apothecary in St. Paul. According to Holloran, "Everyone felt the need for a strong seminary."[86]

St. Thomas presented an initial proposal at the first small group meeting on February 7, 1984, dealing with areas such as budget, largely the work of Dr. Charles J. Keffer. A second proposal was presented, written by Father Froehle. There was also an outline of the mutual advantages of affiliation for the college and the seminary.[87] These documents were the beginning of an effort to describe affiliation. The meeting of the larger negotiating team on March 9 was rescheduled for April 13, 1984, so that the proposal brought forth would be closer to final form. The areas for consideration were: (1) governance and administration; (2) matters of finance; and (3) physical resources.[88] Multiple memoranda of clarification were exchanged over the months in which the specifics were articulated. There was give and take on both sides. Msgr. Murphy and Father Froehle met with Archbishop Roach March 9 to brief him.

An extraordinary evolution occurred between February 7 and May 1, 1984. In an early proposal, all of the buildings on the seminary campus with the exception of the priests' retirement residence would be deeded to St. Thomas. One of the options was that the college would construct a new seminary residence that would then become the property of the Saint Paul Seminary. By April 9, 1984, however, a confidential memo of clarification on seminary stationery not only indicated that the Saint Paul Seminary would retain ownership of St. Mary's Chapel and the administration building, but the oft-described property boundaries seem to have changed at the April 9 meeting. The typed version states that the seminary would retain ownership of the land on the western boundary from the river to the west entrance road on Summit, and from Goodrich on the south to Summit Avenue on the north. However, Tom Dolan pencilled out Goodrich Avenue and wrote "Library." This key decision specified that the seminary would retain only the northwest quadrant of its property and the buildings thereon.[89]

By April the College of St. Thomas agreed that they would provide the seminary with the following as part of the affiliation agreement: seminary classes would be held in Brady Center; the Ireland Library would continue to serve as the theological library for the School of Divinity programs; food service would be provided in Binz Refectory; faculty, staff, and students could use McCarthy Recreation Building; Baumgaertner Auditorium would be available for seminary programs; the college would maintain all grounds on the seminary campus year-round, and allocate 120 parking places.[90]

The memo of clarification on "Governance and Administration" of the same date made a distinction between the "Ministerial Studies Program"—all classroom theological course work, field education, and Teaching Parish programs—under the direction of the College of St. Thomas, the degree-granting institution, and the "Ministerial Formation Program"—all programs of spiritual and personal growth and evaluation for ministry—under the direction of a separate seminary department. It provided for a Saint Paul Seminary Board of Trustees with specific responsibilities for the seminary per se. It was agreed that three members of the Saint Paul Seminary board (one of whom would be the rector) would sit on the board of trustees of the College of St. Thomas, and three members of the St. Thomas board would sit on the board of the seminary.

At that point in the negotiation, the rector of the seminary would become the "Dean of the Ministerial Studies Program of the College of St. Thomas." He would be responsible only to the president of the college, not to the vice-president for academic affairs, and only in matters that related directly to the studies program. Eventually it was agreed that the seminary would become a "school of divinity" of the college, and not simply another department.[91] The rector's other responsibilities, and those of the academic dean and the faculty, were also articulated.

Budget projections and financial arrangements abounded. After much dialogue, it was agreed that the College of St. Thomas would pay $2,500,000 for the land and buildings so designated in the agreement, and that "the College shall annually provide to the Divinity School the sum of Two Hundred and Fifty Thousand and no/100 Dollars ($250,000)."[92] The purpose of this annual payment was "to maintain and improve the quality of the School of Divinity."[93] Initially the $250,000 payment per year was only for ten years; the change later to payments in perpetuity was significant.

It was also agreed that the permanent employees of the seminary (current staff) would be retained in the same or similar positions. In a letter to members of the seminary board on May 1, 1984, Father Froehle described the work of the small negotiating team: "Today that group finally came to agreement on what such an affiliation would look like and decided to present their findings to the Boards of Trustees of the two institutions."[94]

Agreement in Principle Approved

The agreement in principle was approved by the St. Thomas board on May 16, and by the seminary board on May 23, 1984. At the latter meeting, the affiliation agreement was described in detail. Thomas Dolan stated that the small committee "has hammered out a strategic resolution to the Seminary's financial problem." He added:

> I believe what we have here as well is the issue of *stewardship,* stewardship of this land and these buildings. Stewardship to do what is good for the St. Paul Seminary, for the College of St. Thomas, for *this* Archdiocese and all the Archdioceses who send men here. The college's desire is simply to make this the best, most attractive seminary program any place in the United States plus acquire land and buildings for expansion of its programs over the next 100 years. We share their enthusiasm. We feel that their aim very closely matches the original charter given to us by John Ireland. So, today after a great deal of work and a great deal of prayer and thoughtful reflection, I can enthusiastically recommend to you approval of Resolution A.[95]

Three resolutions were presented to the seminary board: (1) preliminary approval of the affiliation; (2) a capital campaign to supplement the $2,500,000 from St. Thomas and the $1,100,000 from the sale of Nazareth Hall in order to construct a new dormitory and renovate St. Mary's Chapel and the administration building; and (3) the establishment of a building committee for the three structures mentioned above. All were approved. At the meeting Archbishop Roach noted that "the discussions had been long, thorough, and creative." He indicated his satisfaction with the process which had been employed and the documentation that was prepared. At the conclusion of the meeting he reminded the board members that he would be meeting with the priests of the archdiocese in June to receive their ideas and input, and that final action would have to be taken at the next board meeting.[96]

Although it was not mentioned in the minutes, in a confidential memo that Father Froehle wrote summarizing the May 23, 1984 meeting, he stated:

> In due course the program of pastoral studies at the College of St. Thomas, which currently offers M.A. degrees in theology, will be integrated into the seminary program. This will reduce duplication and enrich the lay program as well as the seminary programs. The separate dormitory will be an assurance for bishops who send their students here that there is a unique program for seminary students even within the context of the larger college.[97]

Although conversation regarding the desire not to duplicate the programs at the college and the seminary was mentioned in earlier discussions, the actual integration of the M.A. in pastoral studies and the continuing education program seems to be something of a late addition to the agreement. This may account for the fact that the difficulties that emerged in the years after the affiliation were not in the areas of administration and governance, land and buildings, or finances, but in programs, which led to the "battle" over vision. It is significant, however, that Father Froehle ended his memo with the statement:

> While no decision of this magnitude is without risk, it appears to offer some very strong advantages for the future direction of the Saint Paul Seminary. While no one seemed to be inclined in this direction in November, discussions have led us to believe that it is possible to do our task even better under this new umbrella.[98]

Presbytery Meeting—June 12, 1984

On May 21, 1984, Archbishop Roach wrote to the priests of the archdiocese announcing a presbytery meeting on June 12, 1984, to discuss the affiliation. Msgr. Murphy and Father Froehle prepared substantive materials that were sent to all the priests. Approximately 120 priests were present at the meeting which included presentations and discussion. The priests were then asked to complete a brief questionnaire. Priests who were not present were also invited to express their views through a questionnaire, and 140 responded. The results indicated that over 70 percent in both groups were in favor of affiliation, while close to 15 percent were opposed.[99] Others had mixed feelings regarding the arrangement.

In a memo to the planning committee, Father Froehle summarized some of the comments on the questionnaires: concern about the autonomy and self-direction of the seminary under the affiliation; questioning whether the seminary was receiving adequate money in return for what it was giving; and anxiety about what another fund drive would mean for the parishes. A minority of priests raised issues regarding how affiliation might impact the priesthood itself. In Froehle's summary of the meeting he notes the nature of those issues.

> Throughout there were a number of people who suggested that the seminary should close or be dramatically changed because of the lack of confidence that the writers had in the orthodoxy of the seminary's program. Some noted that they believe the seminary does not allow anyone except "liberals or left wing" students to be promoted. Others thought that this might be a subtle way to open the door to the ordination of women or the promotion of some dissolution of the priesthood. There was some fear that it would make it much more difficult for students to make a celibate commitment because of the presence of women.[100]

As these remarks indicate, a small element within the clergy was not supportive of the seminary or its programs—with or without the affiliation.

"The Two Charlies"

The preliminary affiliation agreement had to be fine-tuned, clarifications were necessary in the most minute areas, and a final document had to be written. This was the work of "the two Charlies"—Froehle and Keffer. Archbishop Roach stated: "I think we were very fortunate that we had people like Charlie Froehle, and people like Terry Murphy, and I realize that Charlie Keffer did much with it."[101] According to Father Michael O'Connell, who was vicar general and moderator of the curia of the archdiocese during this period, "the two Charlies" were "smart, capable, humble people who were without guile, and were also servants in the best sense of that word. The objective of the affiliation was more important to them than their own self-aggrandizement." O'Connell believes that Archbishop Roach and Msgr. Murphy needed "the two Char-

Charles L. Froehle, rector of the Saint Paul Seminary from 1980 to 1993

lies," and that they were "hugely determinative" in the success of the affiliation. As a result, "the seminary survived when lots of others were going down in flames."[102]

Father Froehle and Dr. Keffer also made presentations to the neighbors, some of whom were fearful that the expansion of the undergraduates onto the seminary campus would cause disruption. Information was sent to the publics of the two institutions, especially bishops who sponsored students at the Saint Paul Seminary, donors, and vocation directors.[103]

Dr. Charles Keffer, provost of the College of St. Thomas

Agreement for Affiliation

When the seminary board met on October 2, 1984, Thomas Dolan presented the Agreement for Affiliation, a nineteen-page document, which culminated in the resolution:

> Be it resolved that the Saint Paul Seminary Board of Trustees approve the agreement of affiliation between the College of St. Thomas and the Saint Paul Seminary effective July 1, 1985. This approval is subject to the formulation of a final written document of affiliation to be entered into by the Saint Paul Seminary, the College of St. Thomas and the Archdiocese of Saint Paul and Minneapolis, embodying all of the agreements between the parties regarding the affiliation including but not limited to the following: administration and governance, land and buildings, and financial arrangements.

In this document, under administration, the title "Rector/Dean" was changed to "Rector/Vice-President," which more aptly described the role of the head of the School of Divinity.[104]

The seminary board asked that the agreement be clear that if the archbishop of St. Paul and Minneapolis was no longer ex-officio chair of the St. Thomas board, the seminary could withdraw from the agreement. "This was meant to protect the Church from having its seminary under the jurisdiction of someone other than the bishop who has the responsibility for preparing men for priesthood." It was clear from the Saint Paul Seminary By-Laws that if the seminary should be dissolved or cease to exist, "all of the remaining real and personal property shall vest in and be transferred to the diocese of St. Paul." The new title "School of Divinity" was discussed. Some board members thought that "The Saint Paul Seminary" should be included and be sufficient. Other suggestions were made, but no action was taken. Archbishop Roach put the question to the board for approval of the affiliation and it passed unanimously.[105]

Resolutions were also passed to conduct a capital campaign and to authorize the development committee to initiate a feasibility study and contract for financing of the study. Both motions passed. The archbishop "noted that he had rarely seen the good of the Church placed in such prominence in similar negotiations. He thanked all who had been a part of the process."[106] By every measure it seemed that the affiliation was on the road to completion.

Enthusiasm High in Seminary Community

The 1984–1985 academic year began with enthusiasm. The first year of the "new program" had proved successful. The results of the Roman visitation and the NCA/ATS reaccreditation had been very positive. Affiliation negotiations were in their final stages. There were eighty ordination candidates, and eight non-ordination candidates enrolled in graduate programs. An additional 148 students were involved in the Evening Semester program and continuing education courses, bringing the total enrollment to 236.[107]

There were new faculty members on the scene. The diversity of backgrounds and of institutions from which these new faculty came contributed to a broadening of the vision of the seminary. Mark Smith, completing his dissertation at Yale University, became instructor in Old Testament. Sister M. Christine Athans, B.V.M., with a Ph.D. from the Graduate Theological Union at Berkeley, was appointed assistant professor of church history—the first woman hired for a full-time tenure-track academic position. Stephen Pope, a doctoral student at the University of Chicago Divinity School, replaced Father Bernard Yetzer for a year while the latter completed his dissertation in systematic theology at the Catholic University of America. Pope returned to the seminary faculty in 1986 to teach moral theology.

In 1984 Father Patrick Kennedy was appointed the first dean of students, replacing the deans of the residence halls, and also worked in field education and recruitment. With the death of long-time faculty member William Curtis, Carole Kastigar was hired as part-time instructor in communications and speech. Other staff additions included Sister Marion Riley, C.S.J., promoted to registrar in 1983, and Janet Gould as secretary in the field education department in 1984. Leonard Rogge, comptroller of the seminary through January of 1983, put into place stronger and more efficient methods of fiscal management. He was followed by Lois Nyman as the first business administrator. Former seminarian Gerald Anderley, who had worked at the seminary since 1975,

Sister M. Christine Athans, B.V.M., teaching church history to M.Div. students

became the new director of maintenance in 1980. In May 1983 Patricia McGrade, the first full-time secretary hired by the seminary in 1967, died of cancer. Elaine Marty became secretary to the rector. Dr. James Giefer was appointed seminary physician and Sister Margaret Mary Radaich, C.S.J., served as nurse in the seminary infirmary.

Student life was also vibrant. From *Gaudeamus* in September to *Jubilemus* in May, there was evidence of remarkable creativity. Some students brought imitating certain faculty members to a level of perfection. There were costume parties for Mardi Gras and Halloween. The vacant fifth floor of Grace Residence was a perfect place for a "haunted house" enhanced by the presence of a coffin, cobwebs, scary noises, and muted lights. One room showed evidence of despair. A "bloody arm" emerged from between two mattresses at the end of which was a copy of the book *Blessed Rage for Order* by David Tracey, S.J., a text assigned by Father Jerome Dittberner for his "Foundations" class, plus remnants of notes from that course. For "one"—it had been just too much![108]

Although the old residence halls were in poor condition, they were "home" to the students. Thomas Brioschi recalls that students were allowed to paint their rooms and decorate them as they wished. Seminarians also had a sense of ownership of the campus. They did maintenance chores, kept classrooms clean, raked leaves, and otherwise tended the campus. Someone was appointed "Pop Prefect" to keep the pop machine

Spiritual formation faculty in 1985 (left to right): Father Ronald Bowers, spiritual director and dean of spiritual formation Father Dennis Dease, Sister Paul Therese Saiko, S.S.N.D., Father Robert Schwartz, and Father Robert Moosbrugger, O.M.I.

full. A group served on the "Rat Patrol" to check the grounds at night and be sure that no one was destroying the grotto or other property. There was a spirit of fun and generosity often tied to the liturgy of the house.[109]

Students and faculty met bi-weekly for liturgy planning—an opportunity to follow a process of preparation for both weekday and Sunday liturgies. Some students participated in reader's theater productions directed by Carole Kastigar. The presentation in the fall of 1984 was "The Gospel of Mark." Sue Martin's extraordinary contributions to liturgical music brought a sense of *joie de vivre* to the liturgy. Evening Prayer at dinner every Thursday night was a bonding community experience as well as an opportunity to share announcements, humor, and a reflection from the rector.

Another opportunity for students and faculty to share was in monthly ministerial reflection sessions coordinated by Sister Mary Daniel Hartnett, C.S.J., and her successor Sister Diane Kennedy, O.P. Seminarians from different classes, plus one faculty member and one

Teaching Parish supervisor, would gather to reflect on a case study. The purpose was to assist students in integrating the academic, pastoral, and spiritual dimensions of their ministry preparation. This exercise also contributed to a sense of community.

If in the beginning of 1984 the future of the seminary was in question, by the end of that year it seemed assured. At the November 12, 1984, faculty meeting, Father Froehle announced that final decisions regarding the affiliation would be worked out in the coming winter, and the affiliation was projected for July 1, 1985. Father Froehle had already asked people, including faculty, to serve on the building committees. He stated that the seminary was in the process of hiring a firm for the capital campaign, a decision that would be in place soon.[110] The year 1984 concluded with a sense of accomplishment and well-being. The affiliation of the seminary with the College of St. Thomas seemed destined for completion in a matter of months. Events, however, were to prove otherwise.

Chapter 14

The Seminary Within the University

Crisis, Consolidation, Clarification (1985–1995)

> The seminary cannot remain static; it must be flexible if it is to continue to exist. I was deeply moved by those who talked about the need to fulfill our commitment to reach out to others and ask them to priesthood. The support of a priest who is willing to share his ministry is one of the most effective means of forming vocations. What is our level of commitment involving young people in ordained ministry?[1]
>
> Archbishop John R. Roach
> Presbytery Day
> September 18, 1985

At the first board meeting of 1985, Archbishop Roach welcomed new board members Bishop Lawrence Soens of Sioux City, Iowa; Patricia Gries, director of ministry for the archdiocese; and Sister Karen Kennelly, C.S.J., province director of the Sisters of St. Joseph of Carondelet. Thomas Dolan presented clarifications in regard to the affiliation. One was that the title of the institution would be "The Saint Paul Seminary School of Divinity of the College of St. Thomas." While lengthy, the title included both the mission and relationships now bound together in the new institution. There were questions about the use of the $250,000 that St. Thomas would pay to the seminary annually—an item for ongoing discussion and negotiation. Archbishop Roach saw the need for greater clarification about "the canons of Church law regarding the 'mandate' to teach at the seminary." Lastly, Patrick Moughan of the Community Counseling Services Company, Inc., reviewed the feasibility study that had taken place under David Agee and that indicated that the seminary could raise $3,750,000 during a one-year program. The board voted to conduct a four million dollar capital campaign beginning in the year 1985.[2]

What the board was unaware of was that the previous night, February 21, 1985, the archbishop had been arrested for driving while intoxicated in rural Chisago County where he has a cabin near Lindstrom, and had spent the night in jail. Father Michael O'Connell, vicar-general and moderator of the curia, recalls calling the archbishop out of the seminary board meeting on February 22 to inform him that word had come out on the wire services that the archbishop had been arrested. News organizations would probably be broadcasting it in the evening and it would certainly be in the morning papers.[3]

The next day the archbishop was scheduled to speak at an archdiocesan assembly and spoke of how he had "acted very imprudently" and was embarrassed. "Embarrassed, of course, for myself, but even more so for my family, for my friends, for you and the people of this archdiocese, the church I love very deeply." He asked for prayers and pledged himself to serve in a renewed way. He concluded: "I love this church and I love to serve it. I feel unimpaired in that service, but I need your prayers and I need your support."[4]

The regular Presbyteral Council meeting was scheduled for February 26, 1985. Once again the archbishop admitted his imprudence and embarrassment. Council member Father Ronald Bowers read a joint resolution co-sponsored with Msgr. Francis Gilligan that was unanimously passed by the council. It extended "our firm support and genuine understanding to our archbishop, John." It commended him as chief shepherd, spiritual leader, and "a pastor who has shown compassion and understanding to the Christian faithful." The conclusion stated:

> We know that he, like us, brings his human personality to ministry in this local church, and we wish to affirm both him and that ministry. He has extended a firm supporting hand to many in time of trouble. Reflecting on his pastoral care, we pledge our loyalty to him as we continue to walk with him promoting the cause of Christ and the welfare of the church.[5]

A standing ovation of the priests followed, and a copy of the statement was sent to the papal nuncio, Archbishop Pio Laghi, in Washington, D.C.[6] Calls and letters of support poured into the chancery not only from the archdiocese, but from around the nation. Archbishop Roach weathered the storm well. It never seemed to affect his ability to do the task at hand.[7] His friends would say that he changed and grew as a result of that experience and become more empathetic.[8] The homily he preached at the Cathedral of St. Paul on Good Friday 1985 testified to that.

Presbyteral Council Challenge

When the Presbyteral Council met in March, however, some members raised questions about the seminary capital campaign and how it would affect the parishes. Was it necessary to tax the parishes to construct another seminary building? Should the seminary continue to exist and what was its place within the archdiocese? Council member Father Edward Flahavan was aware that the Jesuits were downsizing their theologates from five to two. Should the archdiocese consider closing the seminary? With the enrollment lower, why not send archdiocesan students to other seminaries, free up priest faculty for the parishes, and spend the money on worthy social justice projects? Flahavan reflected later: "Why is the shadow of John Ireland so untouchable in this diocese?"[9]

Father Stephen Adrian moved that "within the next six weeks a meeting of the entire presbytery be convened to ascertain the level of commitment needed to maintain a program of local seminary training and the implication of that commitment (degree, resources, dollars, personnel, etc.)." Father Timothy Powers seconded the motion and it passed. The archbishop said that he would support such a meeting but asked that a representative of the seminary participate in its planning.[10]

The Presbyteral Council was a relatively new structure resulting from the 1983 revision of the Code of Canon Law. Prior to that, the Priests' Senate had been the representative vehicle for the priests in a diocese. The Priests' Senate and the entire presbytery in the Archdiocese of St. Paul and Minneapolis had always been active, vocal, and sometimes polarized, particularly at the time of the departure of Bishop Shannon. That polarization lingered; some wonder if it was ever really healed.

By the April 1985 meeting of the Presbyteral Council, it seemed that the seminary had become the focal point for those who wanted to challenge the system. The archbishop was concerned that the resolution passed in March would complicate the seminary capital campaign. The minutes state:

> In reflecting upon the resolution, the archbishop feels that, while he supports the resolution, the timing of such a meeting when the drive is already in place with consultants hired, would not be wise. He would ask the presbytery council to either withdraw their motion for the moment or seek some other action to defer the calling of a meeting. His perception is that if the motion is not withdrawn it would cause confusion. He would support a later meeting.[11]

There was, however, strong sentiment that the meeting had to go forward. Some members had been hearing on the deanery level that there were great questions concerning the seminary's future. According to Edward Flahavan, "We were hurting for numbers, hurting for dollars, dipping into the principal and planning a capital campaign without consultation or discussion with the priests." Most priests had little recollection of the earlier presbytery consultation. They felt the issues had not been discussed, and suddenly they were being asked to accept a tax for a new building at the seminary when "we're scrimping around here, and we're cutting jobs, and we're delaying the roof on a building."[12]

The archbishop felt that "there must have been some misunderstanding." All the priests had been sent substantial material prior to the June 1984 presbytery meeting and had been asked to respond. Over 70 percent of the 260 priests who had returned questionnaires had approved of the affiliation, suggesting that they understood what it entailed. It was really the proposed fund drive that caused the uproar. The priests claimed that they did not realize that the parishes would be solicited. Father Stephen Adrian moved, and Father Edward Flahavan seconded, a resolution that the "Presbyteral Council take ownership for consultation over the commitment to Saint Paul Seminary and that such consultation be completed and a recommendation be made to the archbishop by October 15, 1985."[13]

Father Froehle recalls sitting behind Archbishop Roach as one of the guests at the meeting. At one point the archbishop turned back to him and said, "I think we are going to have to do this."[14] The archbishop admitted to being perplexed. He thought the question of the affiliation had been decided. However, he "would not want to begin a capital fund drive without the support of the Presbyteral Council and the priests of the archdiocese." He admitted that it would involve "radical changes," but he was willing to call a meeting of the full presbytery. The meeting was to be conducted so that there would be genuine response to the questions and concerns that were raised.[15]

Father Frederick Campbell, who would be named auxiliary bishop in 1999, was secretary of the council at that time. He described three groups that had concerns: (1) the group that feared the assessment levied on parishes; (2) those who doubted that the seminary would have appropriate independence if the affiliation took place and feared that the relationship to the archbishop would be blurred; and (3) those who felt that St. Thomas was getting too powerful and was getting too good of a deal.[16] Campbell also noted that the affiliation stirred up deep feelings about the sale of the archdiocesan minor seminary, Nazareth Hall. For some priests, Nazareth Hall had been "given away" by the archdiocese. Edward Flahavan reflected that the minor seminary had been "home" for them when they were "little kids." Selling it was like giving away the family homestead. Some thought St. Thomas's "taking over" of the seminary was another kind of sellout. There were many raw emotions involved.[17]

In searching for reasons why this development occurred, some have conjectured that the archbishop's recent DWI arrest may have affected the situation. Neither Stephen Adrian nor Edward Flahavan felt that was the case. In fact, the majority of the priests wanted to be especially supportive of Roach at that time lest the Vatican decide he should be moved elsewhere. They did not want to lose him. But the impression of some people—including members of the seminary faculty and staff who were searching for an explanation for this turnaround—was that if priests wanted to be heard on an issue, this was the time to do it. The seminary became the lightning rod.[18]

When Archbishop Roach was asked if he felt that his personal situation had had any negative impact on the decision of the Presbyteral Council to have the consultation, he answered thoughtfully, "I really have no way to measure that. I suppose it could have with some, but I really have no way to measure that." He agreed that the priests had been marvelously supportive of him at that time. He also knew realistically that the capital campaign could not go forward without their support.[19]

With the passage of the April resolution at the Presbyteral Council, the affiliation was put on hold and the capital campaign was shut down. This left many of the seminary faculty and staff in a state of shock. The juxtaposition of the stability associated with finally reaching agreement on an affiliation with St. Thomas and the sudden insecurity that the seminary might close was mind-boggling. Priest faculty, some of whom had been there for many years, found it hard to fathom. The question for lay faculty, particularly those with children, was whether there would be a job in the coming year. Some seminarians considered transferring in case the Saint Paul Seminary were to close. It was an anxious time.

An expanded steering committee[20] engaged the services of Father Donald Bargen as facilitator for the Presbytery Day scheduled for September 18, 1985. A letter went out to all of the priests from Father Michael Kennedy, executive director of the Presbyteral Council, announcing the meeting and providing fact sheets and a questionnaire to be returned by July 10. He stated: "Very simply, the questions before the Presbytery are two: (1) Are you committed to maintaining our tradition of a local major seminary? (2) Are you committed to the program of priestly formation in our local seminary?" The responses to the questionnaire were analyzed by Dr. Donald La Magdeleine of the College of St. Thomas in a report of July 12, 1985.[21]

Local deanery meetings surfaced additional comments regarding what priests liked about the seminary as well as concerns they had about the program. Reports from the deaneries were due to Father Stephen Adrian by August 26, 1985. Minutes of the Presbyteral Council of July 23, 1985, state specifically:

> The archbishop was very explicit about what he wanted the September meeting to accomplish and each priest should be given ample opportunity for input into the questions raised. Therefore, if a priest is unable to attend the meeting at his deanery level, the dean from that deanery is asked to contact him.[22]

The archbishop did not want a repeat of the meeting of the presbytery in June 1984.

Drawing on the questionnaires and the reports from the deaneries, the committee planned the agenda for the day. The original intention had been to invite only the priests. Bishop John Kinney presented a motion at the seminary board meeting on May 29, 1985, that members of the Saint Paul Seminary Board of Trustees be present at the Presbytery Day and that there be time for some form of board presentation.[23] It was finally agreed by the planning committee that board members and non-priest faculty would be invited as observers. Father Michael Kennedy wrote:

> Because you are so vitally connected with the Seminary, I take this opportunity to invite you to join us on September 18th. I am enclosing a copy of the schedule and invite you to be our guest. Lunch and dinner will be provided. You are most welcome to be with us and I hope you will be able to do so.[24]

Two weeks before the Presbytery Day, Msgr. Richard Schuler, pastor of St. Agnes Parish, sent a proposal to the archbishop and priests of the archdiocese which he had largely composed. The names of twenty-one priests were listed at the end of the accompanying letter[25] which stated: "Seminaries are Tridentine in origin, development, functioning and methodology. They should be abandoned as we have known them." The proposal had two components: academic formation based on the "new theological synthesis of Pope John Paul II which employs the phenomenology of the Lublin/Cracow school" with a strong grounding in the Augustinian and Thomistic traditions; and spiritual and professional formation in which each student would have a freely chosen priest as a spiritual director and would then reside in a parish where his professional training would take place. Father John M. Bauer remembers a discussion of the proposal at a deanery meeting. Among others, he agreed to having his name appended, but his understanding was that this proposal was being placed on the table with others for discussion. He does not recall seeing the proposal in its final form. It is noteworthy that the letter does not have signatures, but a typed list of names.[26]

Others, such as Father Kenneth Pierre, former rector of Saint John Vianney Seminary, were not happy with a possible affiliation with St. Thomas. He had chaired the Commission on Ministry and had been instrumental in establishing the Office of Ministry in the archdiocese. His dream was for a "University of Ministries" on the Saint Paul Seminary Campus—a working megamall of ministry groups. He was not opposed to the perimeter of the campus being used by St. Thomas, but believed that a school of ministries, which included the seminary, would function better as an independent entity within the archdiocese.[27] Critics of the affiliation, therefore, came from both the conservative and the liberal ends of the spectrum.

Presbytery Day 1985: Deciding the Future

On September 18, 1985, a bright and beautiful autumn morning, over three hundred priests met in Baumgaertner Auditorium in Brady Educational Center on the seminary campus. Morning Prayer, with Msgr. Ambrose Hayden as presider, set the tone for the day. Great care had been put into the schedule and agenda. There were four issues for discussion framed as questions. Each was introduced by a priest who offered a ten- to fifteen-minute summary of the responses from the surveys and the deanery reports. Approximately forty minutes were allocated for floor discussion of each question. The four questions and those who introduced them are as follows:

> Given the criteria for the academic program of priestly formation, how adequately does the Saint Paul Seminary meet those criteria? (Msgr. John Sweeney)
>
> Given the criteria for the spiritual formation program of priestly formation, how adequately does the Saint Paul Seminary meet those criteria? (Father Arnold Weber)
>
> What are the implications of the affiliation of the Saint Paul Seminary and the College of St. Thomas with respect to program and costs? (Father Maynard Kegler)
>
> Are we committed to maintaining a theological seminary in the archdiocese of St. Paul and Minneapolis? (Father Timothy Wozniak)

A written vote was taken after each question was discussed. For each issue one could respond: Strongly Agree; Moderately Agree; Neither Agree nor Disagree; Moderately Disagree; Strongly Disagree; No Response.

As the day progressed, the discussion reached a deeper level. It became clear that spiritual formation and the challenge of celibacy were not just concerns for seminarians. One priest remarked, "If there is a problem regarding spiritual formation, we must look to ourselves." Another observed that "blame cannot be put on the seminary for the lack of vocations; it rests with all of us." Part of the problem, someone else noted, was that "we do not invite vocations; we need a more positive attitude."[28] Questions about priestly identity and how to communicate it surfaced. Amidst the sharing, sometimes laced with good humor, there seemed to be a growing sense of ownership for the future of priestly formation in the archdiocese. Most of the priests stayed for the entire day.

Father Kenneth Pierre, who was proposing a University of Ministries, reflected later that day in his journal:

> I spoke often during the day. I supported the academics of the seminary, but felt that the faculty was half the needed size. I said I was probably the person in the room who was most opposed to the affiliation because the diocese and not the College should take ultimate responsibility for ministry development. ...My final 90 seconds was used to remind the 200 [sic] priests who were there that we represented just one slice, one wedge of the ministry pie in the church today. I said that a question this far reaching should not, could not be made without a full consultation with the other 90% of the ministers of the archdiocese and with the people of the church.[29]

The archbishop offered summary remarks before Evening Prayer which was followed by a social hour and dinner. He was pleased about the size of the group and reflected that "although there are strong differences of opinion and that is understandable, there was a high level of good spirit." They had begun to share their notions about seminary—present and future. He also perceived a "strong sense of devotion to the seminary." He noted that his experience in the NCCB had given him a good perspective; many of the same questions were being asked across the United States. He concluded:

> I heard today what is in your heart about Church and priesthood, and I feel very good about that. Questions were raised that we did not have time to address about celibacy and models of ministry that we can at another time pursue without worry-

> ing for we have the respect of one another. It was a good day for me to hear things shared in the public arena about love for Church, priesthood, and how we train priests.

The archbishop expressed his gratitude to the Presbyteral Council, and added: "I needed to hear from all of you. We will decide how the monies can best be used. Nothing is being written in concrete and we will be open to the Spirit of God for the good of this diocese and the good of this Church."[30]

After dinner, an exhausted faculty adjourned to the porch of the old administration building. There, Father Stephen Adrian, chair of the steering committee, and a few other committee members were tallying the results of the written ballots. Although the specific percentages were not available until later, the answers were clear. For the first two questions the number of those who moderately or strongly agreed that the criteria for seminary formation were being met registered 60.2 percent (academic) and 56.1 percent (spiritual formation). The affiliation with St. Thomas was deemed strongly or moderately desirable from the program point of view by 61.5 percent of the priests, and from a financial point of view by 63.8 percent. The result in the final crucial issue involving maintaining a theological seminary in the archdiocese was strongly or moderately supported by 76 percent. Only 10.8 percent of the priests were strongly or moderately uncommitted. The others were "Neither Committed nor Uncommitted" or checked "No Response."[31]

The sense of relief among faculty was overwhelming as the anxiety of the previous six months began to evaporate. Father James Motl, O.P., who had joined the faculty as assistant professor of homiletics just a month before, had been astounded to learn when he arrived that there was the possibility that the seminary would close. He recalls being relieved that he would not have to pack his bags again.[32] The new academic year could truly begin with a sense of joy.

The Boards Approve

The Saint Paul Seminary board met on October 10, 1985, and approved the affiliation agreement to become effective July 1, 1986, having been assured that the Presbyteral Council, which would assemble on October 15, would present positive proposals to the archbishop. Five days later the Presbyteral Council recommended:

> That the affiliation of the College of St. Thomas and the Saint Paul Seminary take place as proposed. That the drive to build the seminary residence, renovate the administration building and St. Mary's Chapel, and establish an endowment for the seminary be undertaken with the support of the priests of the archdiocese.

In the light of the issues raised at the Presbytery Day regarding the academic and spiritual life of the seminary, vocation recruitment, sexuality and celibacy, the council proposed: "That the Council steering committee, the seminary administration, the office for priestly life and continuing education for priests meet to determine the best way to address these issues and report back to the archbishop and the council." That recommendation was amended to include: representatives from the Commission on Ministry, the Center for Ministry, the vocation office, and the permanent deacons. All of the above were approved by voice vote without dissent.[33] Archbishop Roach, probably with some relief and gratitude, accepted the recommendations.

At the College of St. Thomas board of trustees meeting on October 29, 1985, a motion for approval of the affiliation agreement, the affiliation handbook, and the amendments to the land use agreement for the Byrne Residence was passed without dissent. It was agreed that the executive committee would approve any modifications in these documents.[34]

On October 16, 1985, an article in the *Pioneer Press* by Clark Morphew described the recommendations to the archbishop and the affiliation. He concluded by stating that the Reverend Charles Froehle "believes that the affiliation would mean that the seminary would survive and become one of the centers for priestly formation in the U.S. Catholic Church." He then quoted Froehle directly: "I feel very good because we've gone a long journey and we've involved the priests like we never have before. And to have their support is worth every bit of effort."[35]

Continuing the Journey: Challenge from the Neighbors

If the complexity of matters of "church and state" are common in the United States, the affiliation of the college and the seminary would not be without a challenge in terms of the latter, albeit on a municipal level. The problems evolved largely because of the concerns of people in the neighborhood around the seminary. Father Froehle and Dr. Keffer had met with some of the neighbors on June 19, 1984, to explain the plans for the affiliation. Their reaction was one of "fear regarding the possible implications of an expanded College of St. Thomas on the Saint Paul Seminary campus."[36]

Once the Presbyteral Council made its recommendation to the archbishop and he approved it, the hope was that the affiliation would become effective July 1, 1986. The seminary was experiencing financial difficulties because it had planned its budget assuming that the affiliation would take place July 1, 1985. With the unexpected delay because of the presbyteral consultation, the seminary was again in the position of borrowing money from the archdiocese.[37]

An additional problem emerged that prevented final approval. In the overall plan for the City of St. Paul, an area had been designated along the Mississippi River as "the river corridor." This was an area approximately one city block deep from the East Mississippi River Road with special restrictions. No building could be constructed higher than forty feet in that area. The Annual Report of the seminary explained:

> If the river corridor plan had been consistent it would have included the western third of the seminary campus in the river corridor designation. Because this section was not surveyed, the city simply included the whole seminary campus in the river corridor designation. Thus the whole campus would be restricted in its building height. It is clear from conversation with city officials that this was done for convenience sake and did not literally follow the guidelines.[38]

These restrictions were clearly prohibitive to the college, which was unwilling to sign off on the affiliation until a special use permit could be obtained from the city which would supersede the river corridor restriction.

In addition, some of the neighbors protested the fact that the new seminary residence hall would include two towers that would exceed the forty-foot limit. Although the city attorney gave his opinion in May 1987 that those height limitations did not apply, when the site plan was submitted for review and approval, Neighborhood Districts 13 and 14 recommended to the City Planning Commission that the site not be approved. The City Planning Commission also had an open hearing and voted to send the matter back to the Zoning Committee, which—by a narrow vote—recommended that the city approve the project. The Planning Commission reviewed the matter again and approved the project with the fifty-six-foot towers.

The staff and students were not unaware of the frustrations involved in the negotiations with the city. Father Kenneth Pierre, adjunct faculty, recalled the *Gaudeamus* program September 5, 1987, in which one skit depicted

> Charlie Froehle, the rector, interviewing a student. The skit turned into an interview of Charlie as he would leap out of his chair at any mention of words like "zone," "council," "neighbor," "permit," etc. The point was that Charlie is so afraid of these words because the building plans for the new School of Divinity complex are being held up pending the resolution of several legal and zoning questions.... Charlie is always in control of himself and calm. The humor in the skit was that he was pushed over the threshold of his tolerance and became hysterical whenever normal conversation touched the raw nerve of his dealings with the city. Humor reveals reality in its own way. ...I'm glad the community can laugh. The sense of humor in the students is a delight. The stress that the administration and the students are under ought not to be happening. The community is becoming as jumpy as the rector in the skit.[39]

But some of the neighbors would not give up, and District 14 appealed to the City Council. Father Froehle, Father Moudry, and Sister M. Christine Athans, B.V.M., met with City Council member Mary "Kiki" Sonnen, who had been a student of Sister Christine's at Our Lady of Peace High School some years before. They asked her to explore options as to how the building could go forward. At the City Council hearing on October 8, 1987, Sonnen offered the following compromise: that the height limitation does apply but that the seminary be given a variance from that forty-foot height limitation. The plan was passed by the City Council.[40]

Father Froehle felt that the neighbors were not inherently against the seminary, which had been a good neighbor to them for many years. They were, however, using the seminary as a "weapon" to prevent the expansion of St. Thomas. Some were convinced that the noise and parking problems associated with undergraduate students would devalue their property. They also knew that the college was trying to designate other land for future expansion. The seminary became a lightning rod for their concerns. Once again, after many tedious meetings and negotiations, the situation was settled. The affiliation could proceed.[41]

Affiliation—*De Facto* and *De Jure*

It was two long years from the recommendation of the Presbyteral Council October 15, 1985 to the granting of a variance by the St. Paul City Council on October 8, 1987. During that time negotiations had continued between the seminary and the college. As mentioned above, the seminary budget had been constructed with the anticipation of the affiliation occurring July 1, 1985. St. Thomas was not eager to finalize the agreement because of the problems with the city, but it became clear that the seminary could not remain in limbo with its finances drained and its debts increasing.

In the spring of 1986 Father Froehle met with Msgr. Murphy to discuss this issue. Both knew that the affiliation would happen, but not until all the delicate detail had been worked out. They agreed that a Declaration of Intent would be signed on July 1, 1986, and at that time the affiliation would be activated *de facto.* Msgr. Murphy also agreed to advance the seminary $1,000,000. Father Froehle recalls that about a week later he went over to St. Thomas and walked back across the campus with a check for $1,000,000 in his pocket—a sure cause for optimism.[42]

Faculty and staff were likewise aware of the changes. There were meetings with the Human Resources Department of the College of St.

Thomas to arrange for insurance, pensions, and other benefits. Paychecks, as of July 1986, were issued by the College of St. Thomas. All functions and programs were integrated, even though there had not yet been any transfer of property. The college honored the seminary employees' years of service. Gerald Anderley, a former seminarian who had become director of maintenance at the seminary about 1980, and who is now associate vice-president for facilities of the University of St. Thomas, recalls that the seminary employees were treated well in the transition.[43] Among those with the greatest longevity was Leroy Mulcahey who had joined the maintenance staff June 10, 1966, and who continues to serve the school to this day.

The completion of the affiliation was celebrated on May 3, 1987. The affiliation ceremony took place in Saint Mary's Chapel at an Evening Prayer service presided over by Archbishop Roach. The archbishop spoke of the importance of the affiliation for the archdiocese; he was sure that John Ireland would be pleased. Msgr. Murphy described the implications for the College of St. Thomas. Father Froehle reflected on the new reality from the perspective of the seminary. Members of the boards of trustees of both the college and the seminary, and the majority of the Saint Paul Seminary School of Divinity community, were present. The signing of the parchment documents was followed by a festive celebration. As a result of the formal affiliation, the transfer of property from the seminary to the college was effective. The seminary retained the 7.1 acres of land in the northwest quadrant. All buildings except the administration building and the chapel were also transferred. The seminary received its final payment of $1,500,000.

Although Saint Paul Seminary faculty and students had been included in the various activities of St. Thomas from July 1986, perhaps the most significant evidence of the "marriage" was graduation in May 1987. The master's-level degrees of the Saint Paul Seminary School of Divinity were awarded at the College of St. Thomas commencement ceremony in Schoenecker Arena. The seminary had never had a formal graduation; ordination was typically the sign of the completion of one's seminary studies. The Annual Report stated: "It was a significant moment in the history of the seminary since it was the first group to have been involved in the graduation ceremony of the college since the affiliation."[44]

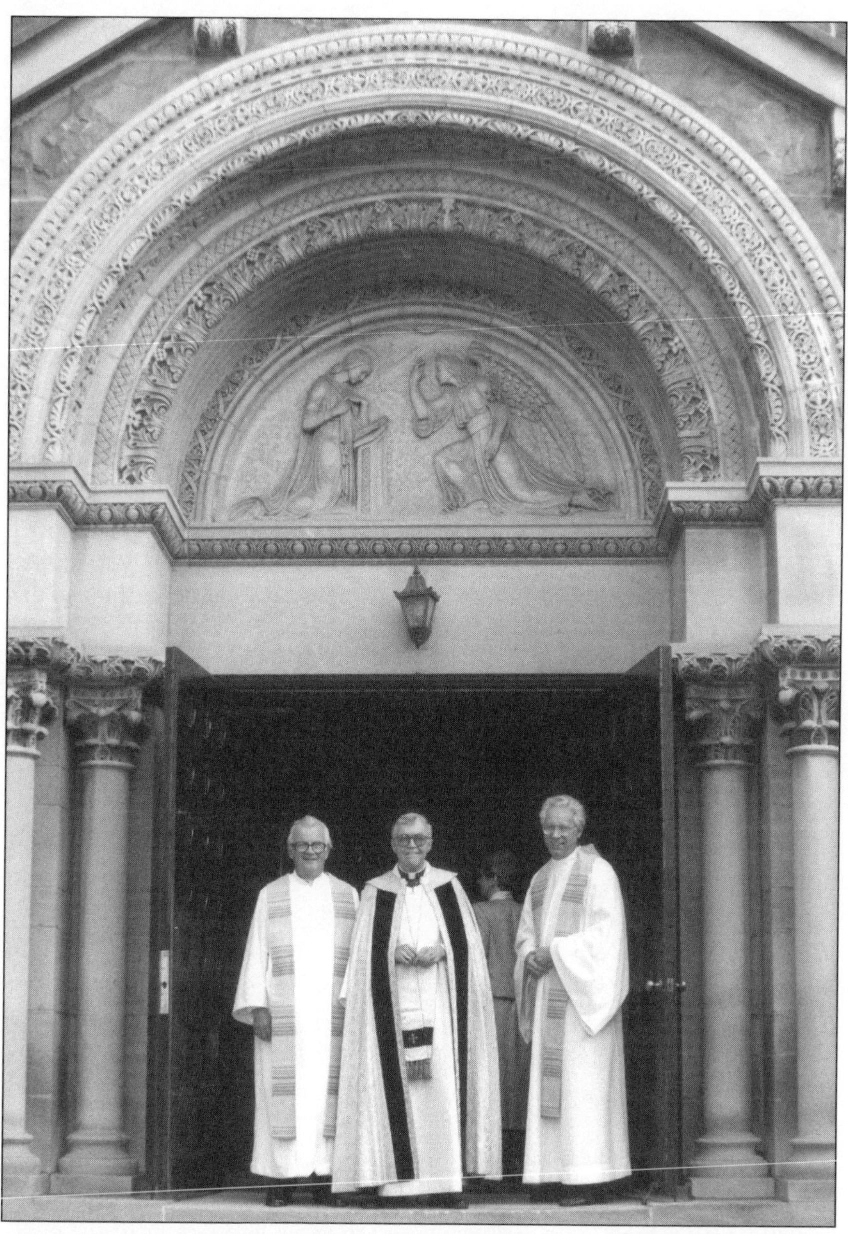

Msgr. Terrence J. Murphy, Archbishop John R. Roach, and the Reverend Charles L. Froehle in front of St. Mary's Chapel after signing the documents of affiliation, May 3, 1987

Capital Campaign

Shortly after it became evident that the seminary would continue to exist and the affiliation would go forward, Auxiliary Bishop Robert Carlson announced that a $1,000,000 life insurance policy had been taken out on him for which the Saint Paul Seminary would be the owner and beneficiary. Bishop Carlson, then forty-one years old, designated the gift to the seminary from which he had been ordained. Bishop Carlson and a group of twelve other individuals agreed to pay the premiums. Father Froehle characterized the gift as "overwhelmingly magnanimous" and said: "While we hope that it will be many years before the seminary prospers because of Bishop Carlson's generosity, we rejoice immediately for the confidence Bishop Carlson has expressed in this institution and its mission in the church in preparing future priests."[45]

While this gift offered support and encouragement for the future, there would be no building renovation or new residence hall unless the capital campaign was activated. At the board meeting on April 29, 1986, Archbishop Roach announced that Bishop Bullock had agreed to co-chair the campaign along with Joseph Lapensky of Northwest Airlines. Edward Fury of Community Counseling Services presented an update. The unsettled conditions with the city regarding height restrictions and the delay in the affiliation clearly did not help in fundraising. By late summer, Joseph Lapensky indicated that he was significantly involved in a project with Northwest Airlines and unable to continue with the campaign. Norbert Berg of Control Data agreed to be general chairman. With Bullock and Berg at the helm, the campaign moved ahead with the goal of raising $6.7 million dollars by August 31, 1987, in cash and pledges. That included the $2.5 million from St. Thomas and the $1.1 million from the Archdiocese of St. Paul and Minneapolis from the sale of Nazareth Hall.[46] Later, the board would agree to increase the goal to $9.1 million.

In February 1987, Bishop Bullock was named bishop of Des Moines, Iowa. Shortly thereafter, Msgr. Pates was appointed vicar for seminaries, as will be discussed later, and was asked to serve as co-chair of the capital campaign, replacing Bishop Bullock. Pates reflected regarding the capital campaign:

> Bishop Bullock had done a really good job. Father [Francis] Fleming had also been involved. Money had come from many different sources, but they still needed about three or four million dollars. When you hit that point it's kind of hard to get it running again. Archbishop Roach, Father Froehle, Norbert Berg, Thomas Simonet, Thomas Dolan, Bernice Johnson and director of development Donald Taylor had all worked tirelessly on the campaign.[47]

Msgr. Pates's leadership was important and on October 1989, with a $200,000 challenge grant from an anonymous donor, the campaign goal of $9.1 million was finally reached.[48]

Building Committees

Preparation for the new or renovated buildings had been set in motion on November 12, 1984, when Father Froehle sent letters inviting a cross section of persons to serve on one of the three sub-committees that would plan the seminary renovation. Faculty, staff, students, board members, representatives of those groups that were housed at the seminary, and others who would bring insight and expertise to the endeavor were included. Sub-committees would provide the grassroots assessment of needs and possibilities. The first meeting was held on November 19, 1984.[49] The sub-committees gathered as a whole for some introductory remarks by Father Froehle, and the chairpersons were introduced: Father James Moudry (St. Mary's Chapel renovation); John Burke, Jr. (administration building renovation); and Father Patrick Lannan (new residence hall). These sub-committees served through 1985 despite the delay due to the presbyteral consultation. The sub-committees gathered significant information and made preliminary recommendations. The seminary board voted at its April 29, 1986, meeting that the new residential facility for students and priest faculty be given first priority. Second would be the administration building. The chapel renovation would follow.

An organizational chart for the building project was established May 5, 1986. Under the leadership of Father Froehle as rector/vice-president, the Building Committee consisted of Richard Clements, chair, Gerald Anderley, Paul Cummings, Father James Moudry, and Clifford Olson. The seminary administration decided that the next phase of the project would be served best if representatives of the three subcommittees were formed into a Program Design Committee consisting of fourteen members.[50] Father Moudry, serving as chair, indicated that the three tasks of the committee would be:

> a) to review and update the program needs for each building so that what we want is clearly understood by the architect;
>
> b) to review the designs presented by the architect to evaluate their adequacy for our needs;
>
> c) to make whatever compromises between needs and designs may be required by budgetary considerations.

Archbishop John R. Roach comments on the model for the renovated chapel to Msgr. Richard E. Pates, surrounded by rector Father Charles Froehle (center) and board members (left to right) Bernice Johnson, Thomas Dolan, and Thomas Simonet.

Father Moudry also announced that the seminary board had approved the selection of an architect, John Rauma from the firm of Griswold Rauma Egge and Olson.[51] Shortly thereafter, Frank Kaczmarcik was hired as liturgical consultant.

The Program Design Committee met for three days of intense meetings with the architect May 27–29, 1986. One of the major issues requiring a decision had to do with the administration building: should the old building be renovated or a new facility constructed? In a memo to the Building Committee, James Moudry summarized the architect's first recommendation:

> Specifically, at issue is whether to renovate the existing structure which, to accommodate the office needs of the Divinity School and the archdiocese, would require putting an addition on the building, or to raze the existing structure and replace it with a new building. After presenting the case for both positions, Mr. Rauma's recommendation is to raze the existing structure and build a new office building.

After discussion, the Program Design Committee concurred without dissent.[52]

The Program Design Committee met almost weekly during that summer and into the fall. The administration building was originally designed as two floors and a "garden level" that also had offices. One of the key decisions was to link the three buildings together with the addition of a "commons" outside of the chapel which would serve as a gathering space and connect the residence hall, the new administration building and the chapel.[53] Richard Clements believed this would provide a more home-like atmosphere so that seminarians in the evening could go from their rooms to the chapel "in their slippers."[54] The "commons" would become the main entrance to the School of Divinity and provide a welcoming reception area for residents and visitors alike.

The initial plan had been to remove the apse and open an entrance at the south end of the chapel. The altar would be moved to the north under the rose window. These changes would establish the chapel as the central axis of the school. The possible removal of the apse occasioned strong feelings on the part of some of the alumni who wanted to retain the mural in the apse by Bancel La Farge (see Prologue). Archbishop

Roach mandated that it remain, and the south entrance of the chapel into the commons was redesigned to incorporate the apse.

On November 19, 1986, the trustees accepted the direction of the new architectural concept for the building project "with the understanding that the concept can be carried out in stages according to the availability of funds." In light of the nature and scope of the building project, Thomas Simonet recommended that the goal of the Capital Campaign be raised to $9.1 million. It was agreed that the increase from $6 million might be confusing to the public and would have to be clearly explained. Some board members were concerned that the $800,000 allocated for endowment was being eliminated in that proposal. Ultimately the board authorized a $9.1 million goal for the Capital Campaign, but stated that $800,000 be set aside for endowment.[55] Father Froehle, in a memo to the Building Committee and the Program Design Committee, explained the action of the board, stating that $8.3 million would be available to accomplish the task. He added: "If the plans are costed out at a higher figure, we will have to readjust the plans to fit the money available."[56] A most generous gift from Thomas Coughlan on behalf of the Coughlan family was the Mankato stone needed for the exteriors of the buildings that helped to tie the new structure visually to the St. Thomas campus.

By the April 14, 1987, board meeting, a few weeks before the official affiliation agreement was signed, adjustments were being made. The administration building was reduced from a three-story to a two-story building, but expanded in width to allow for the same square footage. There was an indication, however, that the archdiocese was backing off of its plan to house its ministry offices at the seminary. The minutes state that "the archdiocese is studying the feasibility of using other facilities instead of the seminary administration building for its offices."[57] Shortly thereafter that very decision was made. It clearly impacted the design of the administration building, and sent the Program Design Committee back to the drawing board.

An adjusted design for a single-story administration building was forthcoming over the summer. In September 1987, Father Froehle wrote letters to the Program Design Committee thanking them for their work over the past two years. He particularly expressed gratitude to Father Moudry for his leadership, and noted that because Moudry also served on the Building Committee "he will continue to represent [the Design Committee's] vision."[58]

Dislocation

In anticipation of the razing of the old administration building, arrangements had to be made for a new location for the administrative offices and living quarters of the priest faculty who were housed in the building about to be demolished. With space at a premium, there was little choice other than to move the seminary administrative offices to the convent. The Sisters of St. Joseph of Carondelet, who had served in many capacities at the seminary for over eighty years, had expected—as a result of the affiliation agreement—to vacate the convent July 1, 1988. Father Froehle asked if they could "anticipate their departure from the seminary by one year." Sister Ellen Joseph Hurley, Sister Bernadetta Kritzberger, Sister Martha Checka, and Sister Rita Costello moved out in late May 1987. The Annual Report stated:

> Thus ended a long and positive relationship of the Sisters living on the campus of the seminary. Their presence on the campus is missed because of the splendid example and witness they were to the vowed life. They were honored at a dinner toward the end of the school year for their many years of service.[59]

The temporary administrative center was named the Bell Building in honor of the family which had donated the money to build the convent in the early 1950s.

Not all of the offices could fit in the Bell Building. The Center for Ministry moved to Grace Residence adjoining the Vocations Office and the Office of the Permanent Diaconate. The Center for Priestly Ministry was relocated to Cretin Residence. Music and liturgy offices moved to Brady Center. The priests who had been living in the administration building moved to other facilities at the seminary or into housing owned by St. Thomas.

In addition, the Center for Continuing Education, the Master of Arts in Pastoral Studies (MAPS) program, and the BeFriender Ministry moved from their location in the Christ Child Center on the main campus to the Bell Building. Space was limited, and forging new relationships with faculty and staff from the Center was not always easy. In some ways, it was a "marriage"; in other ways, it was the merging of two families—an effort to achieve a "blended family"—each with its own traditions and expectations. The members of the eight-person staff of the Center had all been directly involved in planning and decision-making for Center programs. In the new School of Divinity, it was the twenty-two or more members of the faculty under the direction of the rector who were primarily responsible for those tasks. This more hierarchical approach caused frustration and a measure of pain for some.

Faculty had no place to gather except the dining room. Access to the Bell Building was limited, and complications sometimes ensued. St. Thomas began building an additional twelve new classrooms (six on each level) at the southwest corner of Brady Center. Jackhammers seemed to be constant, especially when classes were in session. This was the era popularly known as "The Saint Paul Seminary School of Divinity of the College of St. Thomas—Temporarily Under Construction!"

Changes in Faculty

At the end of the spring semester 1985, three priests on the faculty had moved on: Fathers Dennis Dease and Thomas Sieg became pastors, and Thomas McKenna left to complete his doctoral dissertation. Along with the appointment of Father James Motl, O.P., as associate professor of homiletics in the fall of 1985, Jan Viktora joined the faculty as assistant director of field education and instructor in pastoral studies, and Father John Szarke was appointed to the formation faculty.

With the transfer of the M.A. in Pastoral Studies and the Continuing Education programs to the School of Divinity in 1986, Dean Gene Scapanski, Arthur Zannoni, associate professor of Old Testament, and Sister Carol Rennie, O.S.B., instructor in pastoral ministry, became part of the faculty. Zannoni served as acting dean of the MAPS program from 1986 to 1988 while Scapanski was in Rome writing his doctoral dissertation at the Angelicum. Father Patrick Quinn, T.O.R., with a licentiate in spiritual theology from the Gregorian University in Rome, joined the formation faculty, and Sister Paul Therese Saiko, S.S.N.D., who had been part-time on the staff of both Saint John Vianney and Saint Paul Seminary, moved to the theologate full-time as spiritual formation advisor and adjunct instructor in scripture.

At the end of the 1986–1987 academic year, Sister Mary Daniel Hartnett, C.S.J., decided to retire. Her twelve years at the Saint Paul

Seminary (1975–1987) included her unique contribution as founder of the Teaching Parish program, which was commended by Sister Katarina Schuth, O.S.F, in her book *Reason for the Hope: The Futures of Roman Catholic Theologates.* In describing models of field education Schuth wrote, "One of the best examples of such a model is 'The Teaching Parish,' the program of the St. Paul [Seminary] School of Divinity, where each student's pastoral experience is based in one parish and student responsibility increases each year."[60] Sister Mary Daniel had a reputation for careful supervision, a remarkable ability to work with the pastors, a marvelous sense of humor, and a loving concern for the students.

Also departing the faculty that year was Father Merle Kollasch, a priest of the Diocese of Sioux City who had agreed to a two-year appointment as spiritual director and dean of formation. Father Patrick Kennedy was appointed pastor of Saint Joan of Arc Parish in Minneapolis, and Father Leo Tibesar, director of the Archbishop Ireland Memorial Library since 1976, became a hospital chaplain.

Sister Diane Kennedy, O.P., with a D.Min. from the Pacific School of Religion in Berkeley, was appointed director of Supervised Ministry in 1987. She had responsibility for supervised ministry in the three degree programs, working with Jan Viktora, director of the Teaching

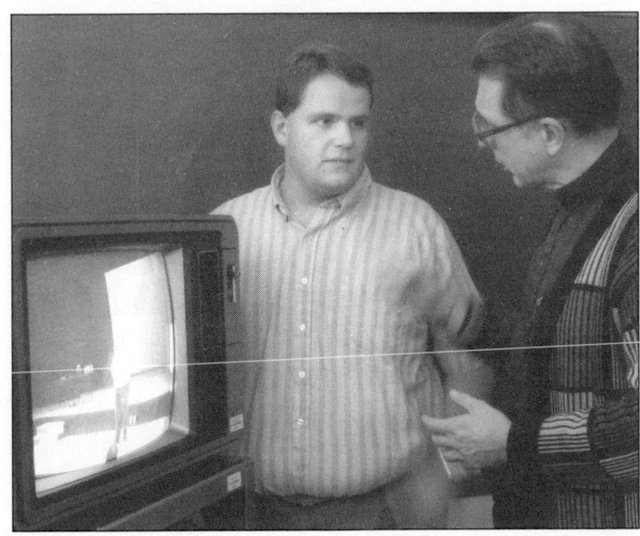

Father James Motl, O.P., discussing a videotaped homily with seminarian Michael Seis

Parish program, and Mary Robinson, director of BeFriender Ministry as well as supervising of students in Clinical Pastoral Education. Mary Martin, who had master's degrees in both library and theology, was appointed theological librarian, and Father Samuel Torvend, O.P., completing his doctoral work at St. Louis University, became instructor in pastoral theology with responsibility for teaching in the area of liturgy.

Father Robert Schwartz returned from Rome with his S.T.D. from the Gregorian University to become spiritual director and dean of spiritual formation. His doctoral dissertation, *Servant Leaders of the People of God: An Ecclesial Spirituality for American Priests,* was published by Paulist Press the following year. Monsignor John Sweeney, who had served on the seminary faculty for thirty years, and who had recently retired as pastor, returned to serve part-time on the formation faculty, sharing his joyful spirit and the wisdom of his years. Barbara Bohrer was appointed the first coordinator of Lay Spiritual Formation in 1988 enhancing the commitment of the School of Divinity to lay students.

Dislocation in terms of space, the many changes in the faculty, the addition of a new degree and new programs, an increase in the number of staff, and the growth of the student body led to the need for clarity in terms of lines of authority and relationship of programs. Although there was excitement about the new challenges, there was also some high-level tension among the faculty. The unsettled conditions contributed to the problematic of "program clarification" which the archbishop would require shortly thereafter.

Changes in Student Life

Since the early 1970s there had been some lay persons and religious enrolled in occasional courses at the seminary. In 1972, Robert G. Kennedy began studies for the M.A. in theology and in 1980 was the first layman to receive that degree. He recalls that after his final oral examination, Msgr. Baumgaertner, the rector, bought him a Coke, and Father Jerome Dittberner, director of the M.A. program, informed him that there would be a $15.00 "graduation fee." There was, however, no graduation; he received his diploma in the mail.[61] Dr. Kennedy is now on the University of St. Thomas faculty in the department of management.

In the fall of 1974 Jan Viktora became the first woman enrolled in the M.A. in Theology program. She is the only woman to have received a degree from the Saint Paul Seminary before the affiliation, after which all degrees were awarded by St. Thomas.[62] In 1984, however, three lay women enrolled in the M.Div. program and joined the class of Theology I. This was the first group in which the presence of lay women seemed to have a special impact, in part because of the musical and liturgical talents that some of those women brought to the community.

With the affiliation in 1986, the MAPS program—composed largely of women (lay and religious) and some men (mostly lay, but a few religious and priests)—became part of the School of Divinity. This added a large lay student population, many of them women,[63] but did not result in major integration of lay students and seminarians. Courses in the MAPS program were offered mostly in the evenings and in summer sessions, the first of which was held on the School of Divinity campus in 1987. M.Div. courses remained largely for seminarians with a few exceptions. Elective courses offered in the evenings, frequently taken by seminarians in the joint M.Div./M.A. program, were mixed groups and offered opportunities for interaction, but the number of seminarians in the joint degree program was minimal. All students, however, were invited to participate in liturgical opportunities, including Chorale.

The ordination class of 1987 was the first to have spent four years with the new curriculum including the Teaching Parish. For most it had been an opportunity to integrate the academic, pastoral, and spiritual components of the program. A new formation evaluation process had been inaugurated as well. Although faculty continued to comment and offer recommendations on each student, the faculty as a whole did not vote on the seminarians. The review boards that were instituted included specified persons from the faculty as well as the student's supervisor from the Teaching Parish. The boards made the final recommendation to the rector. Participation by the parish supervisor allowed input of a pastoral nature to be included in the student's evaluation. This valued addition to the seminarian's preparation is made explicit in the ordination ceremony when the rector specifies that the student not only has the approval of the seminary faculty, but also the approval of the particular parish that walks through the preparation period with the seminarian —challenging and encouraging him along the way.

Dealing with Sensitive Sexual Issues

Perhaps one of the more difficult events for the seminarians in this period was the announcement published in the local newspapers in February 1987 of the lawsuit against the Archdiocese of St. Paul and Minneapolis, the Diocese of Winona, and the Reverend Thomas Adamson regarding alleged sexual abuse.[64] There had been cases of sexual abuse in the archdiocese before, but Adamson had transferred from Winona to the archdiocese, and there were questions of how much people knew of his history, and why incidents had not been reported. It was eventually alleged that Adamson had abused at least nine boys over a seventeen- to eighteen-year period. Most devastating were the headlines: "Suit says church hid sex abuses by priest"[65] and "2 dioceses disclaim negligence in boys' alleged sexual abuse."[66] For some, worse than the alleged sexual abuse was the allegation of a cover-up.

"Pedophilia" was a word with which most people were unfamiliar in the early 1980s. Suddenly problems of that nature were being raised in day care centers, schools, and families. The church was not exempt. In the past, allegations and factual data regarding this crime by members of the clergy had often been handled as "in-house" matters in the chancery. Some bishops thought pedophilia was "curable" and sent priests away for treatment, and/or transferred them to another parish.

The mood at the seminary was somber the afternoon that the news broke. It was decided that morning classes would be canceled the following day. The students assembled and Father Froehle shared his concerns that students keep the situation in perspective, but also learn from such challenges, both individually and as a church. Many of the faculty were present and after the rector's conference, students and faculty moved into small groups to share their feelings and concerns.

The Adamson case challenged the seminary as well as the church at large to be conscious of the need for evaluation of candidates regarding these issues and for education regarding sexual abuse of any kind. Father Froehle and Father Michael O'Connell were interviewed on local television that evening. The rector was asked to explain what programs the seminary had in place to deal with such issues. The Growth in Life and Ministry (Spiritual Formation) program on celibacy and sexuality had been functioning for some years, but further efforts were made to include education regarding sexual abuse issues in its curriculum.

In 1988, Father Kevin McDonough, rector of Saint John Vianney Seminary and chancellor, and later vicar general and moderator of the curia, provided leadership in developing guidelines for the archdiocese to follow when faced with charges of sexual abuse. This was the first comprehensive policy to be produced by a Catholic diocese in the United States on sexual misconduct and it became a model for other dioceses.[67] With his brother, Father William McDonough, moral theology professor at the Saint Paul Seminary from 1990–1998, Father Kevin McDonough developed a unit on sexual abuse/misconduct titled "Boundary Issues in Ministry" in 1991; this unit was included as part of the M.Div. course on sexual morality.[68] The McDonoughs taught from a draft that was eventually published by Archbishop Roach in 1992 titled "Understanding Sexual Issues in Ministry."[69]

Bishops from the United States were challenged to develop a coherent approach for dealing with sexual abuse cases when they erupted. Saint Paul Seminary alumnus Bishop John F. Kinney, then bishop of Bismarck, North Dakota, was appointed chair of the NCCB Ad Hoc Committee on Sexual Abuse in June 1993.[70] Membership on the committee included Archbishop John R. Roach and Bishop Harry J. Flynn of Lafayette, Louisiana. Father Kevin McDonough served as a consultant. A committee report and suggestions on sexual abuse policies was published in 1994.

In the fall of 1990 the court ruled that the archdiocese and the Diocese of Winona had been willfully negligent in the Adamson case, and would have to pay $855,000 in compensatory damages and $2.7 million in punitive damages.[71] Once again Father Froehle addressed the seminarians at a rector's conference. He described the pain of the archbishop, of the priests, and of the people. He admitted, "You may feel confused and hurt, and even betrayed by some of what happened.... That leads to a kind of helplessness and frustration in knowing what to do." He offered three suggestions: "First of all, it is important to be willing to talk about these matters. We must never hide such things and pretend that they are not there. To act as though nothing has happened is to bury something that needs to be brought up, looked at, and then dealt with as best we can before moving on."

Father Froehle then reminded them to have deep compassion for the victims—think of them first. "The victim's rights must be primary and their needs must be met. We are a church which proclaims that the little ones are important." He then urged the students to recommit themselves to what they were doing. This included recognizing that:

> We live as a people of faith. We believe that we are the people of God as a church and because we are a people we are all too human. We will sin, we may even sin seriously and harm the lives of people. We may make bad judgments. . . . But we are people of faith who believe that God can raise us above our sinfulness and our failures. We believe that God can bring life out of death. We believe that there is resurrection after there is suffering. If we do not believe, then these are dark days indeed.

Father Froehle concluded,

> In a word, we are people who recognize where we have failed and we commit ourselves to change our ways so that we can be more faithful to the Gospel. That is how we want to live and that is how we want to lead the people. May these painful events be a reminder to us of what is most fundamental and most important—our relationship with God.[72]

Campus Life in a Time of Change

The challenge of these years did not overshadow student creativity about campus life. One of the most celebrative events was St. Patrick's Day, March 17, 1988. Thomas McDonough, third-year seminarian, planned and directed "McDonough's 1st Annual St. Patrick's Day 1K Run." It was a spoof on the many marathons that were enjoying popularity at that time. After Evening Prayer at community dinner the night before the event, he described—with the assistance of an overhead projector—the particulars of the event with maps, charts, and directions. Part way through, he explained, there would be beverages so the participants did not get dehydrated. At one station there would be an opportunity for psychological counseling if the challenge was evoking anxiety.

Green T-shirts with the name of the event on a large shamrock, and the name of the school, were available for a fee. All met at the Bell Building the next afternoon for the start of the race. Although it was a cold day, there was a warm spirit and a genuine sense of community. Television cameras were on hand and the event made the evening news.

Groundbreaking—Spring 1988

In December of 1987 the old administration building was razed to make room for the new construction. On December 14 there was a prayer service for faculty, staff, students, and guests on the cold empty porch with the Advent sky already dark. Father Froehle concluded his remarks:

> We are grateful for the vision and dreams of James Hill and John Ireland who built this structure, and to those who subsequently lived and worked within it. But our generation also has its vision and its dream built upon that earlier one. May future generations look back and thank God for our vision, and may they, too, have a new vision and new dreams—so that what happens here may always be the best service of God's people.[73]

News photographers and television cameras were present to capture the sight as the gold cross that had stood atop the building for ninety-three years was gently removed by the crane and delivered to Father Froehle. It would be stored for possible future use. Then the wrecking balls began the task of attacking the building.

For some this was a moment of nostalgia. For others, it denoted death and resurrection. Father Stephen Adrian believes that the new building that replaced the old

> opened the door for diocesan seminary education in the twenty-first century to happen. And it did that because the Saint Paul Seminary ceased to exist. At least the Saint Paul Seminary that priests knew. Once the administration building and the gold cross on top of that administration building came crashing down, it was as if the Saint Paul Seminary had been dissolved. Something died, and something new was born. The brilliance of

re-orienting the chapel was, if you will, a snapshot of that. The four walls stand but we're looking in a far different direction.[74]

That new direction was symbolized by the groundbreaking for the planned complex on March 30, 1988. Archbishop Roach presided over the ceremony during which representatives of various groups in the seminary community and the building committee turned over a shovelful of dirt—symbolic of the new beginning.[75] It was a cold day, but there was a hint of spring in the air. The general contractor for the project was McGough Construction Company, which began work the following week and moved rapidly because of favorable weather conditions.[76] No one dreamed that the buildings, with the exception of the chapel, would be completed in less than a year.

Moving In

Construction continued apace. When it became clear that the new residence hall and the administration building would be completed by spring 1989, Father John Forliti, vice-president for student affairs at the College of St. Thomas, came to Thursday night Evening Prayer and dinner and asked the students if they would consider moving into the new buildings in March instead of waiting until the end of May as had been previously planned. The college could then begin renovations on Cretin and Grace Residences early, allowing them to be available to the college students in the fall. The seminarians, of course, agreed.

Planning the move to the new residence was a major undertaking directed by the students themselves. The administrative skills and good humor of seminarians such as Mark McCormick, David Korth, David Beckman, and others resulted in a well-organized operation. Moving day was March 17, 1989—cold and windy, but not raining. Everyone pitched in, and the move was completed in four hours. Faculty offices and faculty residences moved within the next week.[77]

The last Eucharist to be celebrated in the oratory in Grace Residence, with Father Froehle as presider, was at 5:30 that evening. Almost the whole community crowded in. The departure from this chapel which had been a center for the prayer of seminarians for over seventy-five years was carefully planned. After the Eucharist, a procession formed—

cross bearer and acolytes with candles at the front. The icon of Mary was held aloft. Father Froehle was at the end of the procession, still vested and holding the Blessed Sacrament under the humeral veil, preceded by the incense bearer and more acolytes holding candles.

The procession moved outdoors where a light snow was falling. As the group wended its way toward the new illuminated buildings, a bell in a tower of the new residence hall began to ring out, beckoning the community to its new home. Unbeknownst to most, Gerald Milske, former seminarian and faculty secretary, and a few students had taken the old railroad bell that had been a gift from James J. Hill and installed it in the new tower. The sound of the bell on that chilly and snowy night represented the continuity in the history of the seminary that would not be lost. Of greater symbolic meaning was the Blessed Sacrament which Father Froehle brought to a resting place in Saint Mary's Chapel.

In this day of rejoicing, there was also a glitch. A special dinner had been planned for the students to celebrate a job well done. However, because the liturgy had taken so long, the staff at Binz Refectory thought there must have been some mistake. Therefore they closed at the usual time and when the starving students and faculty arrived there was no food! Crisis management, coordinated by Sister Carol Rennie, O.S.B., director of campus life, came to the rescue. Pizza and beverages were ordered and the party continued for the tired community in the new recreation room on the lower level of the residence hall. A new "tradition" of having pizza for supper on St. Patrick's Day to commemorate the move was born.

The Dedication

A series of dedication events was scheduled from September 19 to 24, 1989, to christen the new buildings. Tours and receptions were held for seminary alumni, Master of Arts in Pastoral Studies students and alumni, the board of trustees, the College of St. Thomas community, the archdiocesan staff, Serra Clubs, the Knights of Columbus, religious and deacons, parishioners from the archdiocese, and—of course—the neighbors.

Archbishop Roach presided at the dedicatory Eucharist on Saturday afternoon, September 23, 1989. The bell choir led the procession, and, accompanied by organ and trumpets, the congregation sang in joy and gratitude.[78] The chapel renovation was not complete, but the choir stalls had been removed, a new granite floor installed, and the altar placed at the opposite end of the building under the rose window. Ironically, the result of this reorientation and change was a space that resembled the chapel in its earliest days. Archbishop Roach commented that he hardly knew that the beautiful stained glass windows existed behind the choir stalls where they had been hidden for so many years. Suddenly new light was streaming into the chapel.

After the Eucharist the archbishop walked through parts of the new buildings blessing them with holy water. The congregation gathered in the quadrangle outside. God's blessing was asked on the new buildings and all who would work and study therein. Special plaques of recognition were given to those who had labored long and hard to make the new buildings a reality: Norbert Berg, Richard Clements, Thomas Dolan, Bernice Johnson, James Moudry, Clifford Olson, and Thomas Simonet. Only a few months before, James Moudry, who enjoyed a well-deserved sabbatical in the 1988–1989 academic year, had announced that he would resign from active ministry. His presence was welcomed by those who knew how much he had contributed to the affiliation and to building the new complex, but it was also a bittersweet moment for him and for his former colleagues as well.[79]

The event concluded with a reception in a festive spirit, perhaps not unlike the original day of dedication, September 4, 1895. Students, faculty, and staff had all contributed to the week's festivities. A genuine sense of community was in the air. The general consensus was: "We certainly do know how to give a party!"

A Bifurcated Vision

As mentioned earlier, the affiliation agreement delineated the particulars regarding governance, land and buildings, and finances. In retrospect, the same clarity was absent regarding programs. There were two different visions of how the seminary program and the graduate programs in pastoral ministry would interrelate. On April 10, 1985, the committee for the renovation of the administration building included the following in a draft of a statement to the board of trustees that is indicative of one vision:

> We also recognize that by Archdiocesan decision, the School of Divinity is becoming a "ministry center" for the Archdiocese. This direction is welcomed by the seminary. Such a center will address its resources to the broader ministerial needs of the local and regional Church. Increasingly, more and more people will turn to The Saint Paul Seminary School of Divinity to seek nourishment for their lives as Church ministers.[80]

This view had been the hope of the majority of the seminary faculty as well as the faculty and staff of the Center for Religious Education. Collaboration in ministry between clergy and laity would be a practical reality if future clergy and lay ministers studied and prepared together for their tasks in the parish. Trustee Rose Palen spoke vehemently in favor of this vision. She noted that when seminarians were ordained they would be ministering to and working with a substantial number of women. It would, therefore, be an advantage for them to study with women.[81] Most of the faculty saw the affiliation as a remarkable opportunity for that to occur.

The decision in the spring of 1987 not to locate the archdiocesan ministry offices at the School of Divinity seemed to some as symbolic of a distancing from that vision. Archbishop Roach was clear that the decision was not made for monetary reasons.[82] He had communicated the decision to Father Froehle when he was on campus for an event, but gave no detailed explanation. However, Patricia Gries, director of ministry personnel for the archdiocese, remembers that there was fear on the part of some that "if we let things get too connected, identities will be lost. . . . There were also fears that the seminary program would be tainted or watered down if lay people were involved."[83]

Archbishop Roach articulated his concern years later:

> I was very much in favor of a strong preparation for lay ministry. But to make that program so integral to the program for priestly formation that there was some ambiguity about it, I thought was a great mistake. We had to keep the program of priestly formation not totally distinct but focused enough and clear enough so that there would not be so much confusion that we lost that strong preparation.

Roach then told of having read an article about the Catholic Church in the Netherlands, which had been in the forefront of renewal, yet by the early 1980s seemed to be going to pieces. There were almost no seminarians in Holland at that time.

> And the answer was that they had totally lost the distinction between lay ministry and priestly ministry. And I didn't want that to happen here. I wanted to maintain a strong program of lay ministry. But I didn't want that to become so intertwined that we lost our sense of priestly ministry. That's why I decided to tilt on the side to the very formal kind of priestly ministry.[84]

Father Kenneth Pierre recalls that the imprint of the Dutch church on Archbishop Roach had been long-standing. In July 1976, Archbishop Roach had hosted a dinner for Cardinal Jan Willebrands when he came to address an ecumenical gathering at St. Olaf's College in Northfield, Minnesota. Pierre, as rector of St. John Vianney Seminary, was invited and later wrote in his journal:

> Archbishop Roach has referred to that evening often because of a question which he asked the cardinal after dinner. He asked what happened to vocations to the priesthood in the Dutch church. Archbishop Roach had remembered the Dutch church with admiration, but now it seemed without seminarians and almost without new ordinations to the priesthood. The cardinal answered that the people had lost their respect for the ordained priesthood. Archbishop evidently resolved that evening that he would not let that happen to this archdiocese and to prevent it he would hold the ordained priesthood in a position of preeminence.

Pierre remembered this incident at the ordination to priesthood in the Cathedral of St. Paul on May 25, 1985, when Roach in his homily discussed once again his conversation with Willebrands. However, the archbishop recalled asking the cardinal not what happened to vocations in Holland, but what happened to the church in Holland. Roach concluded that neglecting the ordained could have disastrous results for the church.[85]

The tension between these two views for the future of the Saint Paul Seminary School of Divinity escalated when bishops who sent seminarians to the seminary began questioning the focus of the "new" institution. Archbishop Roach recalled:

> I urged Charlie Froehle to go around and visit with the bishops and to get it clear. They were really afraid of what was happening... that we would no longer be a seminary. That bothered a lot of bishops because they didn't know what was happening. And they had no reason to know. We got through that, thank God. That was touchy.[86]

Vicar for Seminaries

Conversations about restructuring the administration of the two seminaries had been in process for some months. On August 6, 1986, Archbishop Roach met with Father Froehle and Msgr. Pates to discuss the possibility of a "Super Rector" who would be rector of both Saint Paul Seminary and Saint John Vianney Seminary and have the responsibility for development and recruitment. The perception was that the "on the job" responsibilities of the present two rectors were so great that it was difficult for them to give adequate time to some of the external issues.[87] The in-house responsibilities would then be handled by a vice-rector in each institution.

By April 1987, however, Archbishop Roach decided to institute a "vicar for seminaries" instead and appointed Msgr. Richard Pates to that position. The job description was not finalized for some weeks, and the announcement was not made until summer when Father Kevin McDonough replaced Msgr. Pates as rector of St. John Vianney Seminary. When Archbishop Roach was asked why he instituted that position, he stated: "I'm still not quite clear why I did that." There were the demands of the capital campaign, the complexity of the affiliation, and concern for clarity with the bishops.

> I didn't want to assign that to the Vicar General, and I trusted Pates on this question. So I did assign him, and he became a kind of convener of dialogue with both sides of the issue. I'm not sure if it really worked. But I was satisfied that I was hearing the kind of things the archbishop should know.[88]

Prior to his appointment as rector of Saint John Vianney, Pates had served as secretary to the apostolic delegate, Archbishop Jean Jadot, in Washington, D.C., from 1975 to 1981. In 1985, while rector of Saint John Vianney, he was also appointed to replace Donald Wuerl as executive secretary to Bishop John Marshall, the papal representative and director of the "Vatican Visitation" process instituted in 1981. Wuerl had just received the controversial appointment of auxiliary bishop to Archbishop Raymond Hunthausen of Seattle with special powers of oversight. From 1985 to 1988, Pates visited seminaries in the United States, established visitation teams, assessed the reports on seminaries against the objective criteria for seminary formation, sent the reports off to Rome, and met with Pope John Paul II on three occasions to report on the state of seminary education in the United States. To have this national perspective was helpful. Pates was very clear that what the Saint Paul Seminary School of Divinity was experiencing was not unlike the challenges which other seminaries were facing.[89]

The impression of some of the faculty, however, was that the appointment of a vicar for seminaries was adding one more layer to the bureaucracy. More to the point, some felt it was a strategy to dismantle the programmatic part of the affiliation fostering collaboration in preparation for ministry, and to make the seminary program into a separate entity again. A public relations brochure distributed in the fall of 1987 focused the consternation. It included a photo of two women and four men on the front steps of Saint Mary's Chapel. There were three seminarians—J. Michael Byron, Daniel Conlin, and Jeffrey Schleisman; one pastoral-studies student—Catherine Donovan; and two faculty members—theological librarian Mary Martin, and Father Samuel Torvend, O.P., attired in a suit and tie.[90] The absence of any Roman collar seemed to validate the concerns of those who feared that the identity of the seminary was being lost in the affiliation. The absence of even one Roman collar seemed to suggest that collaboration in ministry preparation was going too far.

Roach reiterated, however, that he was supportive of lay ministry but wanted clarity:

> People like Scapanski I had great respect for. But on the other hand I saw what happened in Milwaukee . . . places were losing

> their focus on priestly formation. And I didn't want that to happen here. I wanted both, but I wanted to be very clear that there was enough distinction so that there was not a total blur.[91]

In the winter of 1988 Archbishop Roach called a meeting of Auxiliary Bishop Richard Ham, Msgr. Terrence J. Murphy, Father Charles Froehle, and Msgr. Richard Pates. The archbishop voiced his concerns about the publication and the effect it was having on the bishops. He emphasized that the identity of the seminary had to be reinforced. The result of that meeting was a mandate that there should be two separate programs at the School of Divinity, one for seminarians and one for all others. Father Froehle was commissioned to see that this was accomplished.[92]

Program Clarification

Father Froehle began working with Vice-Rector Father Moudry, Dean Victor Klimoski and members of the administrative staff to provide for the clarity which the archbishop required. That challenge, together with the stress of other responsibilities, coupled with a family history of heart disease, resulted in symptoms that prompted Father Froehle to have an angiogram on April 19, 1988. He was told that he would need quadruple heart bypass surgery. While awaiting a date for the surgery, he prepared to inform the faculty of the projected program clarification, which he knew would not be welcomed. Before the 3:15 P.M. faculty meeting on April 25, while visiting with his spiritual director, Father Richard Rice, S.J., Froehle had a heart attack and was rushed to St. Joseph Hospital where an angioplasty saved his life.

Shortly before the April 25 faculty meeting, Victor Klimoski, who was also assistant to the rector, learned that Father Froehle had been taken to the hospital. He announced this to the faculty and indicated that everything was under control. Father Moudry then presented the program clarification plan for what seemed to some the "undoing" of the programmatic part of the affiliation by the separation of the lay and seminary programs. The faculty were troubled both for the health of the rector and for the future of the programs. Four days later, Father Froehle had successful bypass surgery. It was an unsettling time for faculty, staff, and students. Father Moudry became the acting rector during Father Froehle's recuperation and brought leadership and competence to that role during those difficult months.

Program clarification moved slowly. Faculty spirits were at a low ebb. Some felt they had been "sandbagged"—that the vision they had hoped for had been snatched from them. The archbishop might well have felt "sandbagged" as well.[93] What was happening was not what he had envisioned or anticipated. Archbishop Roach came to a dinner with the faculty in May 1988 and explained that he wanted two separate faculties. Those who would be appointed to the seminary faculty would require a mandate from the archbishop. Those appointed to the pastoral studies division would not. Faculty could be appointed to both divisions. He had no objection to seminarians taking courses from faculty in the pastoral studies division, but his goal was to ensure that the oversight of the seminary curriculum and policy and the evaluation process for seminarians would be committed to a faculty with the ecclesiastical mandate under the direction of the rector. This, he believed, would establish the clarity that was needed.

Part of the affiliation agreement indicated that faculty and staff would be retained in the same or a similar position for a period of time. The result was that the School of Divinity from 1986 to 1994 had two academic deans: Victor Klimoski, dean of the Master of Divinity and Master of Theology programs, and Gene Scapanski, dean of the Master of Arts in Pastoral Studies and Continuing Education programs.

Gene Scapanski recalls returning to St. Paul from Rome with his doctorate in August 1988 to resume his role. On the first day in his new office, September 1, 1988, he received a call from Msgr. Murphy inviting him to a meeting with Dr. Charles Keffer and Dr. James Reid, vice-president for academic affairs of the College of St. Thomas. Msgr. Murphy told Scapanski of the archbishop's concern about the direction and the publicity of the new School of Divinity, and said that something had to be done. Scapanski reflected:

> Having left with this wonderful affiliation and all of the momentum that was building up to the actual event, and then to come back to hear that perhaps this needs to be taken apart . . . perhaps we have to have program separation. . . . It seemed to me we needed to clarify the programs rather than take them

> apart. I did not want to see the programs separated. Whether Father Murphy felt that they needed to be separated at this point, I can't say. But I do know that this was one of three options we were considering. It just seemed to me that it had not been given the time to really prove itself. I was really taken aback by what I was hearing in terms of initial reaction to the affiliation. By the end of the meeting, we, as a group, had a consensus that it was not program separation but clarification that was needed. It stands out in my memory because that was my welcome back.

Scapanski emphasized that the affiliation itself would not be dismantled, but that the programs had to be separated. "I think one of the things we talked about was just having the lay programs over at the College. That seemed to be one of the implications." He remembers program clarification as a very painful time.[94]

Victor Klimoski acknowledged that the differences in the culture and ethos of the two groups merging into the School of Divinity made facing the program clarification even more difficult.

> I respected the Center people's concern for this entity—they had really created a community among themselves. . . . They had created this very, very fine relationship as a small staff and they had no notion of what our culture was going to be. . . . We were more conservative. We had to be more cautious. They had done some creative, edgy things. And now that was going to change. They were very much attuned to inclusiveness before it became a concern for us.

Klimoski added that it might have been helpful to have had more organizational consulting. Perhaps then everyone would have been better prepared for program clarification. "We simply had no notion of what that was going to do to us emotionally as an institution."[95]

The focus for 1988–1989 was to construct models for program clarification. The dialogue, discussion, debate, and sometimes dissension among the faculty took place during the era of physical dislocation that enhanced the sense of being fractured. Some faculty tried to find a way around the realities, and even maneuvered to try to avoid the clarification. It was almost impossible to reach a consensus. Father Froehle finally decided he had to design a plan and put the final form together. He remembers it as a period when he felt alone and unsupported by many of the faculty but he knew what had to be done.[96]

Program clarification was implemented in the fall of 1989 at the very time the new buildings were dedicated. To finally be in one place was an invitation to a new relationship. There were opportunities to share despite the "separation," which—to many people—seemed to be more on paper than in reality.

The mechanics of the clarification were a particular challenge for the faculty. The School of Divinity, as described above, now had two divisions with two separate but overlapping faculties. To make this evident, there would be several faculty meetings at which appropriate matters would be discussed and decisions made. Some meetings would be for the entire School of Divinity faculty; others would be for the Seminary Division faculty; a third group would be for the Pastoral Studies Division faculty, which now had responsibility for the master of arts in pastoral studies, the master of arts in theology, and the Continuing Education program. For those who had a joint appointment, that meant at least three faculty meetings per month. There was enormous repetition. New approaches were suggested. In time, the first hour of a faculty meeting was devoted to School of Divinity business and all faculty were expected to attend. The second hour was devoted alternately to the Seminary Division or the Pastoral Studies Division, so those not involved in that group could leave.

Adaptations were made over the years and program clarification was finally written into the amended Affiliation Agreement in 1991. Of particular note is the statement: "The Pastoral Studies Division shall be under the direction of the [now] University, as set forth in the 'Affiliation Handbook.'"[97] The amended Affiliation Handbook of November 1993 described the structure of the School of Divinity as follows:

> The Seminary Division is under the direction of the Rector/Vice President. The Division has its own faculty who hold their positions upon the appointment of the President of the University and the concurrent ecclesiastical appointment of the Archbishop of Saint Paul and Minneapolis. The academic degrees of the Seminary Division are awarded by the University of St.

> Thomas. The Pastoral Studies Division is under the direction of the Rector/Vice President. The Division has its own faculty who hold their positions upon appointment by the President of the University. The total program of the Pastoral Studies Division is under the direction of the University of St. Thomas.[98]

There was some ambiguity in the arrangement for the Pastoral Studies Division; that, too, would be adapted in the future.

Despite the logistical and scheduling challenges and the efforts to implement program clarification, the first year in the new buildings allowed for a new sense of community. The rector wrote in his *Annual Report* for 1989–1990:

> Perhaps the most remarkable change during the past year is that we have spent the entire year in our new facilities. The effect of working and living together in the new facility has been very positive for the whole community of the Saint Paul Seminary School of Divinity. In particular it has assisted us in developing a sense of community which was very difficult to manage when students, faculty, and staff were scattered throughout the campus. The centrality of the chapel and its ease of access make the surroundings even more beneficial for our programs. This past academic year is a very important one in the history of this institution. It marks a kind of new beginning reflected in the external sign of the building.[99]

Relationship to the University

It became clear throughout the various negotiations that a committee to monitor the ongoing implementation of the Affiliation Agreement would be helpful. In the spring of 1990 Archbishop Roach asked Msgr. Pates and Father Froehle to prepare a resolution regarding the establishment of a School of Divinity Committee of the board of the Saint Paul Seminary which would meet jointly with the School of Divinity Committee of the College of St. Thomas board on a regular basis. One of the major goals of this committee would be to carry out a joint review and interpretation of the documents. The resolution was passed at the Saint

Paul Seminary board meeting on May 22, 1990. Archbishop Roach appointed Bishop Joseph L. Charron, Msgr. Richard E. Pates, Kenneth Schoen, Dr. Virginia Schubert, and J. Thomas Simonet to the committee. Father Froehle served as staff.[100] This committee also recommended amendments to the Affiliation Agreement and the Affiliation Handbook.

At the same time, the board of trustees of the College of St. Thomas voted to officially change the name of the college to "University of St. Thomas" effective September 1, 1990, thereby changing the name of the Saint Paul Seminary School of Divinity as well.[101] Shortly thereafter, the first four members of the faculty of the Saint Paul Seminary School of Divinity received tenure from the University of St. Thomas: Sister M. Christine Athans, B.V.M., Ph.D.; Reverend Ronald J. Bowers, J.C.D.; Dr. Thomas Fisch; and Ms. Sue Seid-Martin, M.M. Other faculty members had received tenure at the time of the affiliation because of their longevity: Father Charles Froehle, Father James Moudry, Msgr. Jerome Quinn, Father Jerome Dittberner, and Father Bernard Yetzer.

In the fall of 1990, Msgr. Murphy indicated that he would resign as president of St. Thomas, and a search commenced for a new executive for the university. In March 1991, the University of St. Thomas board of trustees selected Father Dennis Dease to fill that position. As an alumnus of the Saint Paul Seminary and a member of the faculty for six years, Dease was in an excellent position to understand the new School of Divinity and its relationship to the university.[102]

Faculty Departures and Arrivals

Scripture scholar Msgr. Jerome D. Quinn, ill with a heart condition for many years, died on September 13, 1988. With pontifical degrees from Rome—in theology from the Gregorian University, and in scripture from the Pontifical Biblical Institute—he had served since 1961 as professor of Old and New Testament and Hebrew at the Saint Paul Seminary where he transformed scripture studies.[103]

The academic world recognized Quinn's solid scholarship in his many lectures and publications. He was an editor of the *Catholic Biblical Quarterly,* regularly reviewed books, and participated in the preparation of the *New American Bible* (1970), translating and writing introductions and annotations for the books of James, Jude, and 1–2 Peter. In 1971 he was elected president of the Catholic Biblical Association. Twice he was welcomed as a guest professor at the Pontifical Biblical Institute in Rome (1971–1972; 1979–1980), and was also scholar-in-residence at the North American College in Rome (1979–1980). In 1978 he was appointed to the International Pontifical Biblical Commission—which generally had only one American member. Active ecumenically, he served on the Lutheran-Catholic Dialogue for seventeen years.

In 1984, because of ill health, Quinn resigned from organizational activities and focused on the Pastoral Epistles—the letters of Paul to Titus and Timothy in the New Testament which are concerned with pastoring or shepherding the church. In 1965, Quinn had been invited by Doubleday Publishing Company to contribute the volumes on Titus and 1 and 2 Timothy to *The Anchor Bible* series. His life-long work, *The Letter to Titus,* was published posthumously, although he had received the imprimatur from Archbishop John R. Roach on February 29, 1988, seven months before his death.[104] Michael Patrick O'Connor, one of his successors at the Saint Paul Seminary School of Divinity, read, corrected, and annotated the first draft of the work for Doubleday. Quinn had written the first draft of a second volume, *The First and Second Letters to Timothy,* which was completed and prepared for publication after his death by his last student, William C. Wacker.[105] The Quinn Endowment Fund has been established to raise funds for a Jerome D. Quinn Chair of Biblical Studies at the School of Divinity.

Other faculty changes marked the transition from seminary to School of Divinity. Patrick Quinn, T.O.R., began doctoral studies in Paris, and Samuel Torvend, O.P., accepted a position at Aquinas Institute in St. Louis. Two liturgists were added to the faculty: Father Dominic Serra of the Archdiocese of New York, who had recently completed his doctorate at the Pontificio Istituto Liturgico at the Collegio Sant' Anselmo in Rome, and David Stosur, a doctoral candidate at the University of Notre Dame. Father Thomas Krenik, pursuing a second master's degree in spirituality at the University of San Francisco, joined the spiritual formation faculty. The following year, Sister Diane Kennedy, O.P., was appointed academic dean at Aquinas Institute, and Father John Szarke became pastor of the Church of St. Michael in Stillwater, Minnesota.

Joining the ranks of the faculty in 1990 were Father William McDonough, who had just completed his doctoral degree at the Alphonsiaum University in Rome, and Father Michael Papesh, with a doctor of ministry degree from Luther Northwestern Seminary, who became a part-time member of the spiritual formation faculty.

In 1991, Father Robert Schwartz, dean of spiritual formation since 1987, became pastor of St. John Neumann Parish in Eagan, Minnesota. Arthur Zannoni, assistant professor of scripture, who had been acting dean of the Pastoral Studies Division and the assistant director of the Center for Jewish-Christian Learning of the University of St. Thomas, also resigned. Sister Katarina Schuth, O.S.F., the first person to hold the Chair for the Social Scientific Study of Religion at the University of St. Thomas, joined the faculty with her primary appointment in the School of Divinity, and a secondary appointment in the undergraduate sociology department. Father Jan Michael Joncas, having also recently completed his doctorate in liturgy at Sant'Anselmo in Rome, was appointed to the faculty of the University of St. Thomas with a secondary appointment at the School of Divinity.

In 1991–1992 Dr. Michael Patrick O'Connor, well known in the field of biblical studies and with a Ph.D. from the University of Michigan, became assistant professor of Hebrew scriptures. Sister Valerie Lesniak, C.S.J., replaced Barbara Bohrer as coordinator of Lay Spiritual Formation and was also adjunct faculty in spirituality. Carole Kastigar, who had part-time responsibilities in teaching speech, left the faculty in 1991, as did David Stosur, who accepted a position at St. Thomas Seminary in Denver. Father Paul Feela resumed his position in the department of liturgy and sacramental theology.

Father Michael Papesh, who had been appointed spiritual director in 1991, resigned in January 1993 to become pastor at Holy Spirit Parish, and was succeeded by Father Thomas Krenik. Father Douglas Dandurand of the Sioux City Diocese joined the formation faculty. Dr. David Jenkins, who had served as interim director of music ministry due to the illness of Sue Seid-Martin, was formally appointed liturgical music director in 1993.

In May 1993 Msgr. William Baumgaertner and Msgr. John Sweeney were awarded faculty emeritus status by Father Dennis Dease, president of the university. They joined Msgr. Ellsworth Kneal as professors emeriti.

Rectors of the Saint Paul Seminary from 1968 to 2002 (from left): William L. Baumgaertner (1968–1980), Phillip J. Rask (1993–), and Charles L. Froehle (1980–1993)

Departure of the Rector

While all of the above changes were noteworthy, none had as much impact as the announcement of Father Charles Froehle on December 2, 1992 that he would resign as rector effective June 30, 1993. He had served on the faculty for twenty-five years, thirteen of them as rector, and he believed it was time to move on.

In May 1993 he was honored at a Sunday liturgy at which Archbishop Roach presided, followed by a celebratory brunch, and later that day at a special Evening Prayer and dinner. He received a variety of awards during those last weeks, including an honorary doctorate of humane letters from the University of St. Thomas at the May commencement. The faculty also prepared a *festschrift* in his honor entitled *In Service of the Church: Essays on Theology and Ministry Honoring Reverend Charles L. Froehle,* edited by Victor Klimoski and Mary Christine Athans, B.V.M.[106] In the bound volume of essays, past and present faculty members thanked Froehle for "his learning, his leadership and his love." The volume was published in the fall with proceeds directed to the Father Charles Froehle Scholarship Fund. Students offered tributes, perhaps none as telling as the one addressed "To Charlie, our pastor, our leader and our friend."

Phillip Rask—the New Rector

A search committee for a new rector/vice-president had been established by Archbishop Roach with Auxiliary Bishop Joseph Charron as chair. Ten applications were received, and five candidates were identified. Each had a full day of interviews. Late in May, Archbishop Roach announced that, as a result of the search process and interviews in conjunction with the recommendations he had received, he was appointing Father Phillip Rask rector of the Saint Paul Seminary School of Divinity effective July 1, 1993. Father Dennis Dease simultaneously appointed Rask vice-president of the University of St. Thomas for the School of Divinity.

Seven months after Father Rask took office, Archbishop Harry Flynn was appointed coadjutor to Archbishop Roach. Although Flynn did not become ordinary until September 8, 1995, the shift in leadership began. Archbishop Flynn and Father Rask had a "new" institution to lead, largely because of the innovative leadership of Archbishop Roach and Father Froehle.

Some institutions and religious congregations have what is referred to as a "second founder"—one who revitalizes and reconstitutes a project or community in such a way that it has a new beginning. If John Ireland and James J. and Mary Hill are the "first founders" of the Saint Paul Seminary, it can be argued that John Roach, Terrence Murphy, and Charles Froehle may well be the "second founders" who brought to birth the Saint Paul Seminary School of Divinity of the University of St. Thomas prepared to move into the new millennium.

CHAPTER 15

Harry Joseph Flynn

Beginning the Second Century

> What is the clear identity of the man preparing for priesthood? What does he need? Why does he need all these things? What about the human dimensions when he's going to be living a celibate life? How does he live this out in a warm and loving way? Then there are those who are preparing for lay ministry. There is a difference sacramentally and theologically. I think it is a matter of understanding the identity of each, respecting the identity, and knowing that different is not bad. We are living in an age and culture in which "different is bad." And different is not bad. It's two ways of approaching the mystery of life. And it is all right.[1]
>
> Interview, Archbishop Harry J. Flynn
> December 30, 1999

When the appointment of Bishop Harry J. Flynn as coadjutor archbishop of the Archdiocese of St. Paul and Minneapolis was announced in February 1994, Archbishop Roach explained, "I decided last fall that the greatest contribution I could make for the future of this archdiocese was to ensure an orderly transition from my tenure to that of my successor." As requested, he submitted five names as nominees, and Harry J. Flynn, bishop of Lafayette, Louisiana, was at or near the top of the list. Roach added: "I am grateful to almighty God and to the Holy Father that my request was respected."[2]

Harry J. Flynn was born in Schenectady, New York on May 2, 1933. He was the youngest of six children of William Henry and Margaret Mahoney Flynn, Irish-Americans whose parents were born in County Cork,

Ireland. Harry's father died when he was only six years old, and his mother when he was twelve. In 1945 he went to live with his father's family and was educated by the Sisters of St. Joseph of Carondelet at St. Columba Elementary and High School in Schenectady.

Flynn then attended Siena College in Loudenville, New York, where he received a B.A. in English Literature in 1956. Although he had been attracted to the priesthood early on, he did not make up his mind regarding seminary until after college. Flynn attended Mount Saint Mary's Seminary in Emmitsburg, Maryland, from 1956 to 1960, and was ordained to the priesthood May 28, 1960, for the Diocese of Albany by Bishop William A. Scully. From 1960 to 1965 he taught English at Catholic Central High School in Troy, New York, and helped out at St. Peter's Parish. During that time he pursued a master's degree in English, which he completed at Siena College in 1966.

In 1965, Bishop Scully "loaned" Flynn to Mount Saint Mary's Seminary to be dean of men and to teach homiletics and ethics. In 1968 he was appointed vice-rector and became rector in 1970, serving in that position for nine years during a turbulent decade. Flynn reflected that the growth of a seminarian's humanity was a very important part of his development for priestly ministry:

> When I was rector of the seminary I always considered academics important for the men, and, of course, their spiritual development. But I was also very aware of their need to be able to laugh at themselves and the human situation sometimes. It would frighten me if someone preparing for the priesthood was not able to laugh at the human situation. It *is* funny at times. And I think we were able to do that to an extent at the Mount when I was rector.[3]

When he left the seminary in 1979, the Harry J. Flynn Chair of Christian Ethics was established in his honor.

Flynn then returned to his home diocese to become director of continuing education for the clergy. In 1981 he was appointed pastor of St. Ambrose Church, Latham, New York. He described "five gloriously happy years as a pastor." Flynn added: "There's something about being a pastor. . . . One has the possibility of assisting and forming a community and can experience the direction that a community is taking. You're with people in pain and sorrow and joy. You become one of them. The most comfortable I've ever felt were in my years as a pastor."[4]

Harry Joseph Flynn, archbishop of St. Paul and Minneapolis since 1995

In the spring of 1986 Flynn was named coadjutor bishop of the Diocese of Lafayette, Louisiana, and ordained bishop on June 24, 1986, in Albany, New York. Moving south into a different culture proved to be both a challenge and a joy. He came to know and love Cajun Catholics and the large African-American community. He took strong stands against racism and the death penalty. He had to deal with clergy sexual abuse and provided healing and a sense of compassion to many people.[5]

During his years as bishop and archbishop, Flynn has served on the NCCB committees on Priestly Formation, on Black Catholics, on Priestly Life and Ministry, on Sexual Abuse, and on Charismatic Renewal. He was elected to a three-year term as secretary of the NCCB/ USCC Administrative Board in 1997. Flynn was a papal appointee to the Eighth General Assembly of the Synod of Bishops in Rome in October 1995 on formation for priesthood. "An international synod is an eye-opener," he admitted:

> Sometimes, in the United States especially, we might have a tendency to magnify a difficulty. At a synod we hear how in the Ukraine or another place they don't even have enough money to feed the seminarians. Nor do they have books in the library.

These broader experiences were clearly helpful when Flynn arrived in the archdiocese where he serves as chair of the Saint Paul Seminary Board of Trustees.

The Twelfth Rector

Six months prior to Flynn's becoming coadjutor archbishop, Father Phillip Rask had been appointed the twelfth rector of the Saint Paul Seminary. His doctoral dissertation written for the Catholic University of America in Washington D.C. was titled "The Lists of the Twelve Tribes of Israel."[6] The irony was not lost on his friends.

Rask was born on September 14, 1946, the eldest of four sons of a Swedish father and a Polish mother in Minneapolis, Minnesota. He attended elementary school at St. Stephen's Parish and graduated from De La Salle High School in Minneapolis in 1964. He studied at Nazareth Hall from 1964 to 1966 and continued at the Saint Paul Seminary for six years. He was ordained to the priesthood in 1972.

After five years at Immaculate Conception Parish in Columbia Heights, Minnesota, Rask anticipated transferring to another parish when he met with a member of the Archdiocesan Personnel Board in

Phillip J. Rask, rector of the Saint Paul Seminary since 1993

January of 1977. After Easter, when he still had not received an assignment, he phoned the director, only to learn that Msgr. Baumgaertner was going to offer him a position on the Saint Paul Seminary faculty. Rask recalls being flabbergasted.[7]

In 1977 Rask began doctoral courses in the Department of Biblical Studies at the Catholic University of America and lived at nearby Divine Word College. By 1982 he had received his licentiate in sacred theology, and began work on his Ph.D. dissertation under the direction of Father Joseph Fitzmyer, S.J. Rask returned to the Saint Paul Seminary to teach and continue work on his dissertation, which he defended in 1990 under the chairmanship of Father John P. Meier.

After about ten years of seminary service, Rask anticipated returning to parish life. With the resignation of Father Froehle, however, he was encouraged to apply for the rectorship. Rask had very little administrative experience other than as special assistant to the rector for finances, so he worked with consultant James Nichols in preparation for the position, and continued to consult with Nichols after his appointment in May 1993.

Rask's background in biblical studies served him well. The theme of his years as rector has been forming "a community of disciples." That scriptural imagery explicated in his first orientation address to the seminarians and rector's conferences in the fall of 1993 became an important model for the Saint Paul Seminary School of Divinity. Rask discussed this theme in relationship to John Paul II's document *Pastores Dabo Vobis.* He has often quoted the following statement from the document: "The seminary is called to be, in its own way, a continuation in the church of the apostolic community gathered about Jesus, listening to his word, proceeding toward the Easter experience, awaiting the gift of the Spirit for the mission."[8] *Building a Community of Disciples* has been the title of the catalogues of the School of Divinity since 1996.

Reaccreditation

The preparation for the North Central Association/Association of Theological Schools (NCA/ATS) reaccreditation visit scheduled for October 1993 was largely completed the previous spring under the direction of self-study coordinators Dr. Victor Klimoski and Father Bernard Yetzer.

They stated in the introduction:

> We believe that this systematic effort at self-criticism has been successful in raising up the achievements that have occurred over the course of a decade filled with dramatic change and restructuring. It has also alerted us to challenges we need to address to insure the steady progress of this School in fulfilling its educational mission in service of the Gospel.[9]

Father Vincent Cushing, O.F.M., of the Washington Theological Union, chair of the visiting team, in his oral report to the faculty and staff suggested that the Saint Paul Seminary School of Divinity was "the best kept secret among seminaries" and "you should not be afraid to toot your own horn." He added that he believed the institution was "poised for greatness."[10] The final report applauded the affiliation, the new building complex, the faculty, staff, and library. It commended student programs in academics, spiritual life, and pastoral education.

In January 1994, the ATS Commission on Accrediting met and reaffirmed the accreditation of the Saint Paul Seminary School of Divinity without notation for a period of ten years, approving the doctor of ministry degree by virtue of affiliation with the Minnesota D.Min. Consortium, and gave preliminary approval to the master of arts in religious education.[11] In January 1994, Dean Klimoski reported to the board of trustees:

> The report notes that the school has in place a clear mission, well-organized programs of study, a superior library operation, competent, engaged faculty and committed professional support staff, and demonstrated commitment to its students. ...There is need for Board development, review of the role of academic officers, on-going curriculum revision, and a consistent, focused financial plan to insure stability.

Klimoski also noted that the report recognized that the affiliation is an "idea in process" and that the ATS team was respectful of the challenge the school had undertaken.[12]

Institutional Development and Administrative Reorganization

Several of the ATS recommendations had already been addressed. The school had received a $30,000 grant from the Lilly Endowment for board development during Father Froehle's tenure. The grant enabled the seminary to hire Dr. Jeanne McLean, who interviewed all board members as she helped the board review its structure, composition, and functioning.

Early in his term, Father Rask appointed Thomas Keefe, a young and enthusiastic lawyer from Iowa, as director of development to succeed Donald Taylor. Rask also hired Cal Meland as financial officer to replace Sharon Nyman. Both of these appointments helped to ensure the financial viability of the seminary in the post-affiliation period. Keefe set high goals for fundraising that were consistently met. In addition, he proposed that debts of active priests in the archdiocese for their seminary education be "forgiven" as a part of the millennium celebration. An archdiocesan appeal to fund this initiative raised almost a million dollars in the spring of 1999.

At the time of the affiliation, the administrative structure was left unchanged with the understanding that it would be reviewed after about five years. In its 1994 reaccreditation report, the NCA/ATS Committee encouraged in particular "the need for restructuring the positions of two deans."[13] As a result, a committee chaired by Msgr. William Baumgaertner (who had been appointed to the board in 1992), including Sister Katarina Schuth, O.S.F., Dr. Victor Klimoski, Dr. Gene Scapanski, and James Nichols examined the structure. Nichols interviewed faculty and staff members. The committee recommended to Father Rask, and the board approved effective July 1, 1994, the appointment of Dr. Victor Klimoski as the sole academic dean of the School of Divinity.

Dr. Gene Scapanski received a year-long sabbatical and continued on the faculty as associate professor of dogmatic and pastoral theology until he was appointed interim dean (1998–2000) and dean (2000–) of the School of Continuing Studies at the University of St. Thomas. Scapanski was recognized as "a highly skilled, talented, and distinguished professional in the field of lay education and formation for ministry."[14]

The restructuring also included the appointment of Jan Viktora as assistant dean for academic affairs and admissions, and Sister Carol Rennie, O.S.B., as director of the Teaching Parish program, a position she held in addition to her role as director of student services. Joan Chandler continued her work under the new title of registration specialist, and Catherine Slight was named secretary for academic affairs.

Father Bernard Yetzer died unexpectedly on February 11, 1995. He had been appointed to the seminary faculty to teach dogmatic theology

Registration specialist Joan Chandler, dean of pastoral studies Gene Scapanski, secretary Mary Asher, and associate director of BeFriender Ministry Sandra Skach

in 1976 and was remembered for his slow, methodical, and careful presentations, his earthy approach to life, and his concern for students in need. He had received his S.T.L. from the University of Fribourg in 1975 and completed his S.T.D. at the Catholic University of America in 1988. In 1989 he was named vice-rector and served as director of seminarians and director of admissions.

With Father Yetzer's death, Father Ronald Bowers was appointed to fill the three positions that he had held. Bowers, who had received his J.C.D. from the Catholic University of America in 1990, also headed the Archdiocesan Tribunal, taught canon law at the seminary, and served on the spiritual formation faculty. In June 1996, he resigned from the tribunal to serve full-time at the seminary.

Clarifying the Clarification

The Affiliation Agreement had gone through two generations. The original document was put in place in 1986. The 1991 revisions established the two divisions within the school and made it clear that the academic studies program and the spiritual formation program of the Pastoral

Studies Division were both under the direction of the University. In the era of "program clarification," this division of the authority seemed to establish more clearly the separate identity of the seminary.

By 1994 there was a question as to whether the seminary board should assume responsibility for the Pastoral Studies Division. On May 5, 1994, Archbishop Roach appointed a task force to examine this question. The task force included the Long Range Planning Committee of the board (Dr. Frank Indihar, chair, Bishop Lawrence Welsh, Patricia Gries, and Michael Sullivan), plus Coadjutor Archbishop Harry Flynn, Father Charles Froehle, Msgr. Richard Pates, Father Phillip Rask, and Father Ronald Bowers who was chair of the Long-Range Planning Committee of the school. Michael Ciresi and Guy Schoenecker of the University of St. Thomas Board of Trustees were also included.[15]

The task force met eight times beginning June 29, 1994, and concluded its work on April 26, 1995, by formulating a statement on the governance of the School of Divinity which it presented to the seminary board on May 4, 1995. The document described the interrelationship of the two boards of trustees in the light of the affiliation:

> As a result of the affiliation, the University of St. Thomas has assumed final responsibility for the academic programs of the School of Divinity and has assumed final financial responsibility for the parts of the School of Divinity except for the spiritual formation program for seminarians. This means that the School of Divinity functions within the academic program development and review procedures and the budget development and review procedures of the University. In addition, the School of Divinity has certain unique procedures related to academic development and budget development which have been approved by the University and are consistent with its policies.

The statement then continued:

> At the same time, the University looks to the Rector/Vice President of the School of Divinity and to the Board of Trustees of The Saint Paul Seminary to exercise stewardship, leadership, and oversight of the School of Divinity from both an academic and budgetary perspective. In this regard the Board of Trustees is concerned with and promotes academic and formational pro-

> grams and activities of both the Seminary Division and the Pastoral Studies Division of the School of Divinity.[16]

Dr. Indihar then offered the resolutions that formalized expanding the seminary board's responsibilities to review the programs of the Pastoral Studies Division of the School of Divinity. The board approved the resolution and forwarded it to the board of trustees of the University of St. Thomas.[17] After editing and revisions by the School of Divinity committees of both institutions, the document received final approval from the University of St. Thomas board on February 22, 1996, and by the seminary board on May 9, 1996.[18] To some it seemed that "program clarification" had come full circle.

Faculty Changes

In 1995 Dr. Michael Patrick O'Connor accepted an appointment at Union Theological Seminary in New York, and Sister Valerie Lesniak, C.S.J., took a teaching position at Heythrop College in England. In 1998, Father William McDonough returned to parish work and taught part-time at the University of St. Thomas and at United Theological Seminary in the Twin Cities. In the spring of 2000 Father Dominic Serra received an appointment to the theology faculty of the Catholic University of America in Washington, D.C. All of these faculty members had made creative contributions to the life of the school in teaching, lectures, and publications.

The "next generation" of priests who would serve on the seminary faculty had completed their formation since the affiliation. John Echert, ordained in 1987, earned a licentiate in sacred scripture from the Pontifical Biblical Institute in Rome in 1994. His classmate, Peter Feldmeier, received his Ph.D. in spirituality from the Graduate Theological Union in Berkeley in 1996. J. Michael Byron, ordained in 1989, earned an S.T.D. in systematic theology at Weston Jesuit School of Theology in 2000. David Kohner, ordained in 1990, was appointed spiritual director in 1999 and will complete his M.A. in spirituality at Creighton University in Omaha, Nebraska, in 2002. Douglas Dandurand, ordained in 1982 for the Diocese of Sioux City, Iowa, and who served in the spiritual formation department from 1993 to 1998, completed studies in

2001 for a Ph.D. in pastoral psychology at the Institute of Transpersonal Psychology in Palo Alto, California. Peter Laird, ordained in 1997, began work on a doctorate in moral theology at the Lateran University in Rome in the fall of 2000.

In addition to these alumni, other new academic faculty included Father J. Patrick Quinn, T.O.R., who returned to teach systematic theology in 1995, having completed his S.T.D. at the Gregorian University in Rome in January 1997. Dr. Seung Ai Yang, who holds a Ph.D. in scripture from the University of Chicago, was appointed to the faculty in 1998, having taught previously at Sogang University and the Catholic Spiritual Seminary in Seoul and at the Jesuit School of Theology in Berkeley.

Academic Formation

In 1990 Dr. Gene Scapanski, then a member of the executive committee of the Minnesota Consortium of Theological Schools and dean of the Pastoral Studies Division, explored the feasibility of the School of Divinity joining with Luther Northwestern Seminary and United Theological Seminary of the Twin Cities as an active member of the consortium in offering the doctor of ministry degree. After eighteen months of study, the faculty voted to become a full sponsor of the D.Min. degree on November 5, 1991. After subsequent approval by the seminary and university boards, the University of St. Thomas became the first Catholic institution in the Upper Midwest to offer the D.Min. Approval for the degree was granted by the ATS in January 1994.[19]

Ongoing revision of curricula was a regular feature of seminary life. The redesign of the Master of Arts in Pastoral Studies (MAPS) curriculum in 1991 included a move to a cohort model, in which a group of candidates completes a curriculum as a unit. The Master of Arts in Religious Education (MARE) was developed in cooperation with the Murray Institute of the School of Education of St. Thomas and the Archdiocese of St. Paul and Minneapolis. It particularly benefited Catholic school teachers and ecclesial ministers involved in catechetical ministries in the archdiocese.

In 1995, the Master of Arts in Theology was reorganized as a joint program of the School of Divinity and the undergraduate Department of Theology of the university. Father Arthur Kennedy of the latter faculty became director of that program in 1995. In 1999, co-chairs were appointed—Dr. Corrine Patton of the theology department and Father Patrick Quinn of the School of Divinity—and began coordinating the review and revision of the requirements for that degree.

The School of Divinity faculty voted to revise the M.Div. curriculum in January 2000, armed with important information generated by the Keystone Project, which will be described below.

Grants from the Lilly Endowment

Two important grants received in the late 1990s gave the Saint Paul Seminary the opportunity to move into the future with even greater confidence. The Saint Paul Seminary was one of twenty Catholic seminaries invited to participate in a program funded by the Lilly Endowment, Inc., and the Bonfils-Stanton Trust in 1997, designed to help schools strengthen the quality and effectiveness of theological teaching. This "Keystone Project"—known by the title of the location in Colorado where the seminars were held—invited faculty to identify a project that would benefit teaching and learning in their school. Under the leadership of Dean Victor Klimoski, the faculty decided to study the changing needs and expectations in the dioceses served by the seminary formation program. This information would be part of the data used to determine whether and how to revise the Master of Divinity curriculum.[20]

In addition to funding the participation of a seminary team in two summer seminars, the Keystone Project provided a grant of $15,000 that was used in part to send teams of administrators and faculty members to six of the seminary's eighteen supporting dioceses to interview bishops, parish leaders, vocation directors, pastors, and priest alumni.[21] Dr. Christa Klein, dean of the Center for Continuing Formation, St. Mary's Seminary and University in Baltimore, and Dr. James Davidson of Purdue University were invited to share their expertise with faculty regarding the differing backgrounds of incoming students and the changing face of the American church. Sister Katarina Schuth also developed a "profile sheet" to assess the religious, intellectual, and human profiles of students at the point of admission. All of these experiences contributed to the decision of the faculty in January 2000 to revise the M.Div. curriculum. A steering committee was established and, according to Jan Viktora: "As a result of our Keystone project, the revision of the degree will include not only what content we need to teach and in what order to conform to the standards and guidelines of our accrediting bodies and sponsoring dioceses, but also how our students will most effectively engage in learning."[22]

In 1997, the Saint Paul Seminary School of Divinity was once more invited by the Lilly Endowment to participate in an innovative initiative exploring how educational technology might enhance the effectiveness of theological teaching. The invitation was extended to the other three Twin Cities seminaries (Luther Seminary, Bethel Seminary, and United Theological Seminary) to encourage a collaborative approach to the issues involved. St. John's School of Theology joined the project in September 2000. Dr. Gene Scapanski provided energetic leadership in forming a committee at the School of Divinity preparing a plan of action for using the $300,000 each of the consortium schools eventually received.

The seminaries jointly hired James Rafferty as resource administrator in instructional design/technology. He spends one day a week at each seminary, attends some faculty meetings, and offers workshops and individual consultation to faculty in developing web pages and multi-media presentations.[23] With the expertise Rafferty provides, the seminary and its consortium partners have put in place a process that both equips faculty to use technology as a resource for teaching and engages the larger questions of what it means to teach and what it means to learn in today's seminary. The project has also encouraged dialogue and team teaching across seminary lines.

Spiritual Formation

Father Michael Papesh became spiritual director and dean of formation in 1991, but in January 1993 was appointed pastor of Holy Spirit Parish in St. Paul. Father Thomas Krenik, who had been assigned to the spiritual formation department in 1989, and who earned an M.A. in applied spirituality from the University of San Francisco, was appointed spiritual director and continued in that role until 1999. Although the rector's and spiritual director's conference had been rescheduled to Wednesday mornings in the late 1980s, Krenik brought a new vision to the department. Major elements of the spiritual formation program were also transferred to Wednesday mornings and divided into four levels. Eucharist was scheduled at 8:00 A.M. on Wednesdays, followed by a simple breakfast in the gathering space to accent community life among students, faculty, and staff. The rector's conference (9:15–10:15) and the spiritual director's conference (10:30–11:30) were scheduled for the first Wednesday of the month. The other Wednesdays, however, the students met as classes around particular themes: Theology I—"Priests as Men of Prayer"; Theology II—"Priests as Leaders: Common Mission and Personal Style"; Theology III—"Celibacy and the Commitment to Priesthood"; and Theology IV—"Transitional Issues into Presbyteral Ministry." Guest speakers attended some sessions to dialogue with the students on pertinent issues. In addition, seminarians in Theology I continued to have a special three-credit course in the January term titled "Spirituality of the Diocesan Priesthood" that includes a retreat off campus. All seminarians complete their annual retreats in January.

Seminarians have individual spiritual directors whom they can choose from a list compiled by the Formation Department. Formation directors, however, are assigned by the rector. The program has been administered by Sister Paul Therese Saiko, S.S.N.D., who has been on the department staff since 1984. The continuity she has provided has been a stabilizing factor, since she has worked with six spiritual directors in her tenure at the seminary.[24]

The evaluation process, now coordinated by vice-rector Father Ronald Bowers, invites input from all of the faculty. A team that includes the seminarian's formation advisor, academic advisor, and supervisor from the Teaching Parish journeys with each student through the four years of preparation for priesthood. This accompaniment team meets with the student each spring to evaluate his progress.[25]

During his years as spiritual director and director of spiritual formation, Krenik also pursued through the Minnesota Consortium of Theological Schools a doctor of ministry degree that he received from the University of St. Thomas in December 1996. His dissertation, titled *Formation for Priestly Celibacy: A Resource Book,* was published by the National Catholic Educational Association in 1998.[26] Krenik was also active in the National Federation of Spiritual Directors and served as president from 1995 to 1997.

Field Education

Sister Carol Rennie, O.S.B. was appointed director of the Teaching Parish program in 1995 when Jan Viktora became assistant academic dean. She served in that role until she resigned in 1999 to accept a position in her religious congregation. Together with Mary Martin, director of the Archbishop Ireland Memorial Library, who also has master's degrees in theology and counseling psychology, Sister Carol Rennie reactivated a limited program of ministerial reflection with a new emphasis.

During Sister Carol's tenure, some bishops, particularly those in the west, determined that their seminarians would benefit from a pastoral year rather than the four-year Teaching Parish program. Sister Carol worked with faculty to accommodate this need. Dr. Charlotte Berres, who had earned both an M.Div. and a D.Min. degree from the School of Divinity of the University of St. Thomas, joined the faculty as the director of field education in the fall of 1999. She further developed the process of theological reflection and closely monitored the participation of the seminarians in their teaching parishes.

NCCB Seminary Visitation

In 1997 Archbishop Harry Flynn invited the National Conference of Catholic Bishop Committee on Priestly Formation to send a Seminary Visitation Team to review the "history, personnel, organization, courses, programs, practices and procedures" of the Saint Paul Seminary School of Divinity. As in previous visitations, a year-long self-study was conducted by the faculty under the leadership of Dean Victor Klimoski. The team, chaired by Bishop Robert W. Muench, indicated that it appreciated the seminary community for its "gracious hospitality and complete cooperation" during the October 26–28, 1998, visit.

The report of the visiting team stated, "The general tone of the program is very positive, with faculty and student morale being rated quite high." The team added that the stability of the faculty had contributed to a solid program of formation and thus provided "continuity and acquired expertise." The report noted the seminary's long history of educating priests for the archdiocese and the region, adding that, "the faculty is committed, hard-working, competent, generous with its time and willing to help students in whatever way possible. The priests, religious and lay people on the faculty are qualified and fully dedicated to the seminary's mission."

The recommendations the team offered cited the "Program of Priestly Formation" (PPF #250) on the necessity for "distinguishing ministerial priesthood from the priesthood of all the baptized." This would require revision of the seminary's mission statement "to incorporate this understanding and delineate it in all aspects of its programs." Another recommendation indicated that the seminary "needs to examine ways to foster a greater appreciation of priesthood as the central focus of its mission" so that students "receive unambiguous encouragement to respect the priesthood and honor its appropriate place in the life of the Church" (PPF #10-12). The report hastened to add, "At the same time, the seminary must continue to foster collaborative ministry in a fashion that supports the value of ecclesial lay ministry" (PPF #408). Lastly, in keeping with the vision of the PPF, the team urged that progress be made in "advancing sensitivity to and skills for ministry in a multicultural society."[27] The report seemed to imply that the challenge of the affiliation and "program clarification" had not yet been put to rest.

Jerusalem Program

Perhaps one of the most exciting developments over the years was the introduction of the Jerusalem Program. Father Paul Lafontaine recalls reading a notice on the seminary bulletin board in the fall of 1969 announcing that students could sign up for an Interseminary Holy Land Tour January 6–17, 1970. The total cost, including hotels, meals, and tours, was $500. Approximately ten seminaries were involved, including all the seminaries of the Minnesota Consortium. Twenty-one Saint Paul Seminary students, accompanied by Fathers Stanley Srnec and William Hunt, joined a group totaling 326 members. For the first part of the trip, they were based in Nahariya in the Galilee; later they stayed in a hotel operated by a Christian Arab family on the Mount of Olives. Tour members agreed that there could be no better way for a seminarian to spend $500.[28]

The first time Saint Paul seminarians participated in a semester program in Jerusalem was in 1978. Two third-year seminarians—John M. Bauer and James Wolnik—joined a program based at Ein Kerem near Jerusalem and sponsored by St. John's University. It proved to be a successful venture, so the Saint Paul Seminary continued offering this opportunity to a limited number of third-year seminarians.[29]

An unexpected opportunity arose with the deaths of Harold and Helen Shapira, owners of the Highland Drug Company in nearby Highland Village area of St. Paul, in the late 1980s. According to Msgr. Baumgaertner, Shapira—known as "the unofficial mayor of Highland Park"—recounted periodically how favorably impressed he was with the St. Thomas students who worked there and the faculty members from the college and the seminary who came in regularly for service.[30] The Shapiras died without heirs and designated that their estate be allocated for higher education in the city of St. Paul with the largest amount, about half a million dollars, contributed to the College of St. Thomas. This substantial contribution to St. Thomas was to be used at the discretion of the president of the college.

The executor of the Shapira estate, Joseph Selzer, contacted Rabbi Max Shapiro, director of the new Center for Jewish-Christian Learning at St. Thomas, and suggested that some of the money might be used for the center. Rabbi Shapiro phoned St. Thomas College President Msgr. Terrence Murphy and recommended that a portion of the Shapira estate might well be used to establish scholarships for some seminarians to study in Israel. Msgr. Murphy agreed. Rabbi Max Shapiro had always hoped that Catholic seminarians preparing to be priests and American Jewish students preparing to be rabbis could study together in the Holy Land.[31]

The Shapira estate became an endowment enabling the Saint Paul Seminary School of Divinity to establish its own program in Jerusalem. After discussion with Father Froehle, Shapiro phoned the dean at Hebrew Union College-Jewish Institute of Religion in Cincinnati and also the dean at the Jerusalem campus to inquire about the possibility of Catholic seminarians taking a course there while they were in Israel. He described his hope that the interaction of Jewish and Catholic students would give all of them new insights into Jewish-Christian relations. Both deans agreed.[32]

The Shapira endowment enables all third-year seminarians at the Saint Paul Seminary to study in Israel if they so choose. Fathers Charles Froehle and Phillip Rask traveled to the Holy Land in the spring of 1989 to explore possible sites. They met with Dr. Michael Klein, dean of Hebrew Union College in Jerusalem, and arranged for the Saint Paul seminarians to take a course there. They made arrangements to base the program at the Ecumenical Institute at Tantur near Bethlehem.[33] Father Rask accompanied the students in the fall of 1989 and 1990, establishing the program on a sound basis.

Thereafter a different faculty member accompanied the seminarians each year, and offered one course depending on his or her specialization. Three other courses were offered by the faculty at Tantur, in biblical archeology, one of the synoptic gospels, and ecumenism. A course on the Hebrew prophets was offered at Hebrew Union College. Additional tours and lectures were widely available. An addendum to the Israel experience was often a trip to Egypt and an opportunity to travel to Mount Sinai.

In 1995 the program moved to the Ratisbonne Monastery in Jerusalem, and in 1997 to the Coptic Patriarchate in the Old City. Despite the challenges, students have appreciated being in the "holy but troubled land."[34] Some have traveled to Jordan instead of Egypt after classes were completed. Many have toured Rome, Greece, or other parts of Europe en route to or from the Holy Land. All seminarians report that the experience has broadened their vision, deepened their spirituality, and enriched their preaching.

The dialogue of the Saint Paul seminarians with the students at Hebrew Union College-Jewish Institute of Religion in Jerusalem varied each year. The following letter from Jonah D. Pesner, now a rabbi at Temple Israel in the Boston area, articulates the response of one rabbinical student to the opportunities to share in the fall of 1992:

December 15, 1992

Dear Sister Christine,

I am writing to thank you for bringing together the students of the St. Paul Seminary and HUC-JIR. I will always treasure our experiences together.

The connection we have formed is one that I hope will last forever. In our short time together, I learned so much from the thoughtful seminarians of St. Paul's. I found them exceptionally sensitive, willing to share thoughts from their hearts, and true role models. As a first-year student and only 24, I found them to be true "teachers of the way." In my lifetime quest for God, I am comforted that people like my colleagues at St. Paul's will be there to share with me.

Please accept my good wishes for a Merry Christmas and a Happy New Year. I hope you will share this note with your students, my new friends and colleagues.

With Shalom,
Jonah D. Pesner
New York, N.Y.[35]

Rabbi Adam Stock-Spilker and his wife, Cantor Rachel Stock-Spilker, who were classmates of Pesner and friends of the Saint Paul seminarians in 1992, now serve Temple Mount Zion on Summit Avenue, only a few miles from the Saint Paul Seminary School of Divinity, and are involved in interfaith activities.

Completion of the Campus: Gardens, Cross, Organ, Portrait

Although no campus is ever complete, one of Father Rask's goals when he became rector was to beautify the campus with gardens. In an article in the *St. Thomas* magazine, he observed, "I wanted people to look out their office windows and see something beautiful." With the assistance of Cal Meland and Fathers Paul Feela and Dominic Serra, Rask oversaw landscaping the area around the chapel and near the buildings. Although the area is now made up largely of flower gardens, one plot was designated for spices and vegetables. Rask admitted, "It's very therapeutic. I like to come out here and relax. I can move plants wherever I want—without a committee meeting—until they thrive in the right place."[36] The whole community has benefited from his therapy.

For almost one hundred years, the fifteen-foot gilded cross on top of the original administration building had been visible for blocks around the seminary, particularly from the Grand Avenue entrance. The new seminary complex did not have a similar exterior symbol. On September 13, 1998, a new metropolitan cross was dedicated in front of the seminary building by Archbishop Flynn. The new cross, designed by Brother Frank Kacmarcik, O.S.B., is black anodized aluminum, ten feet high, and sits on a twenty-inch gold-plated orb symbolizing the world over which Jesus Christ was lifted up. Cross and orb stand atop a twenty-seven-foot obelisk of Mankato stone. Highly visible in the day, and illuminated at night, it is a focal point designating the goal of Christian ministry—to lift up the cross and invite others to follow the Risen Christ while living out his precepts in the world.[37] The monument is a gift of John and Mary Michel of St. Paul, William Coughlan of Mankato-Kasota Stone Company, and the McGough Construction Company.

When the plans for the renovation of St. Mary's Chapel were laid, they called for the eventual installation of a new pipe organ whose quality would support the liturgy of the seminary. Father Charles Froehle appointed an organ committee in 1988, chaired by Sue Seid-Martin, to begin the selection process for an organ builder.[38] The committee worked closely with Dr. Thomas Fisch, chair of the chapel renovation committee, Brother Frank Kazmarcik, liturgical designer, and Richard Clements and Clifford Olson who oversaw the entire building project. The committee recommended to the board of trustees that a tracker organ be built by Fritz Noack of the Noack Organ Company, Inc., Georgetown, Massachusetts.[39] In 1991, the board approved a budget of approximately $400,000, provided the funds could be raised separately.[40]

Father Phillip Rask and Msgr. William Baumgaertner, working with Thomas Keefe, vice-president for institutional advancement, completed the fundraising needed for the organ. The generosity of major donor Cyril F. Rotter and others made the new organ possible. In late April 2000, when a crew from Noack and Company arrived to install the organ, excitement was literally "in the air" as organ tones emanated throughout the complex. Archbishop Harry Flynn presided over the dedication of the new organ at a special Evening Prayer on May 7, 2000—one more celebration of the millennium. The commissioning of new liturgical music for the Vespers Service was supported in part by a bequest from Sue Seid-Martin and conducted by her successor Dr. David Jenkins. The stunning organ, which frames the rose window enhanced by specially designed molding, would clearly serve the liturgical life of the school for years to come.

Less imposing, but no less beautiful, was the addition of a portrait of Mary Mehegan Hill as a companion piece to the portraits of James J.

Hill and John Ireland in the central conference room of the administration building. This resulted in part from the September 7, 1995, centennial presentation of Sister M. Christine Athans, B.V.M., on the founding of the seminary, in which she suggested that without Mary Hill the school might never have come into existence. Peggy Carter Baumgaertner, a nationally known portrait artist, was selected by the board to undertake the challenge. Drawing on many photographs of Mary Hill, she created a composite portrait that is simple, elegant, and inspiring. A gift of Msgr. William Baumgaertner and others, it is a gentle reminder of the role of women at the seminary from the beginning.[41]

Departures and Arrivals

The late 1990s saw multiple departures from the board of trustees. The deaths of board members Father Patrick Lannan, pastor of Nativity of Our Lord Parish in St. Paul, and the Most Reverend Lawrence Welch, auxiliary bishop of the archdiocese, saddened the seminary community. Long-time board members Bishop Raymond Lucker, Patricia Gries, Kenneth Schoen, Dr. Frank J. Indihar, Bernice Johnson, Msgr. Richard E. Pates, and Mr. F. L. Spanier retired from the board after years of dedicated service. The following year, Dr. Virginia Schubert, Sister Mary Heinen, C.S.J., Michael Sullivan, and Cecile Muehlbauer completed their terms.

Msgr. Pates was named auxiliary bishop for the Archdiocese of Saint Paul and Minneapolis in December 2000 and resumed a position on the board, bringing his many years of seminary expertise.[42] Elected to the board during Archbishop Flynn's tenure were Father William Baer, Bishop Raymond Burke, Father Peter Christensen, Kevin Conneely, Bishop Blase Cupich, Sister Fran Donnelly, B.V.M., Father Donald Dunn, Bishop Bernard Harrington, Father Kevin Kenney, Robert Lannan, Teresa Mardenborough, Walter D. McFarland, Sr., Michael McGovern, Joseph Micallef, William Reiling, (Arch)bishop Roger Schwietz, Norma Swanson, and Deacon Carl Valdez.

Two deans who had provided substantive leadership for faculty, staff, and students resigned from the faculty in spring 1999. Dr. Victor Klimoski, after seventeen years as academic dean, accepted the position of director of Lifelong Learning at St. John's University in Collegeville.

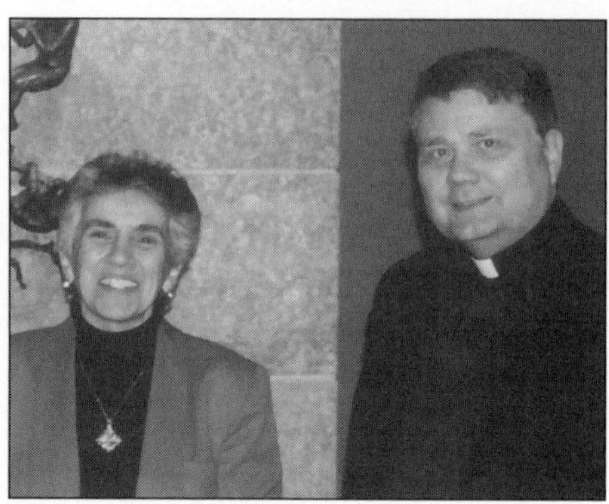

Dean Jeanne McLean and rector Father Phillip Rask

Father Thomas Krenik, having served ten years in the spiritual formation department—six years as dean of spiritual formation—was appointed pastor of St. Richard Parish in Richfield, Minnesota.

A formal farewell took place on May 16, 1999, beginning with a Eucharistic celebration and followed by a dinner and festive program. Father Charles Froehle, who had hired Klimoski, described his creativity, humor, clarity, and integrity, noting:

> Preparation for ministry demands hard work, commitment, good judgment and loyalty. Vic walks that path. In working with Vic I never worried whether he was able to take on a new task; he always was. I never wondered if he would work to accomplish the project; he always did. Vic was always ready to speak his mind on a topic, sometimes with deep passion and a rhetorical eloquence to match.[43]

Sister Paul Therese Saiko, S.S.N.D., spoke on behalf of the faculty, praising Father Krenik's charism as a preacher and spiritual leader.

Archbishop Flynn assigned Father David Kohner as spiritual director to succeed Father Krenik. Dr. Jeanne McLean became acting academic dean in July 1999 and was appointed permanently to the position in January 2000. She was the first woman academic dean of the School of Divinity. Having recently published *Leading from the Center: The Emerging Role of the Chief Academic Office in Theological Schools,*[44] she brought valuable expertise to that position.

The End of the Transition

The adjustments required by the affiliation were many, but in the late 1990s, it became clear that the relationship had solidified and the transition was complete. Evidence of this was that the School of Divinity Committee of the University of St. Thomas board of trustees, whose purpose was to monitor the affiliation, had not met for two years for lack of an agenda. University president Dennis Dease observed: "We are recommending here on our side that the academic responsibilities of the committee be transferred to our Academic Affairs Committee, and that any other day-to-day issues regarding the affiliation be transferred to our Executive Committee. I would foresee the approval of that recommendation on both sides."[45] Father Rask also agreed that the transition was finally over.[46] At the Saint Paul Seminary board meeting on January 20, 2000, the seminary was asked to agree to an amendment to the Affiliation Agreement that would permit the University board to dissolve its School of Divinity Committee. The motion was passed and subsequently approved by the trustees of the university.[47]

At the same meeting, the *Affiliation Handbook* was also amended to state that the archdiocese would no longer be responsible for the financial support of the priestly formation program, and that that responsibility would be assumed by the Saint Paul Seminary Corporation. Should there be a deficit, "no general college funds" would be used for that program. If necessary, the endowment could be used. This was, in one way, a testament to the financial stability of the seminary; fundraising had progressed exceedingly well and financial support from the archdiocese was not required.[48] The bishops sending students to the Saint Paul Seminary were assured, however, that the seminary board, chaired by the archbishop, would ultimately be responsible for the spiritual formation program for candidates for the priesthood.

In evaluating the affiliation, faculty member Sister Katarina Schuth, O.S.F., offered some insightful comments. As one who has an in-depth knowledge of American seminaries and who has authored *Seminaries, Theologates, and the Future of Church Ministry: An Analysis of Trends and Transitions* (1999) as a follow-up to her volume *Reason for the Hope: The Futures of Roman Catholic Theologates* (1989), Schuth provides an important perspective.[49]

> I think we have benefitted enormously from our affiliation with the university. We have access to resources that only those schools with thriving universities have, and that's only a handful. . . . I suppose ours and Seton Hall would be the most alike in that they are both diocesan schools. I think the other thing that is to our advantage is that we have our own building. We also have distinction from the university. It's not just another part of the university. We have our own board. We've retained enough of our separateness and at the same time are fully part of the university. The wonderful administration of the university is in our favor.

Regarding the strengths and weaknesses of the Saint Paul Seminary at this point in its history, Schuth admitted that, as with many seminaries today, the school is struggling to adjust to the need to prepare students for multicultural ministry. There is also need for ongoing development in ecumenism in the curriculum, and the necessity for orienting students to collaboration in pastoral ministry. She reflected:

Seminarians Michael Reding and David Barrett with faculty member Sister Katarina Schuth, O.S.F.

> Certainly in terms of strengths I think our location and our relationship with the university are enormously strong. Our history is strong. We have a good reputation. The context in which we find ourselves in terms of the type of diocese has a lot of respect widely across the country. This place has always been in some type of leadership role starting with Archbishop Ireland.

She added that the focus on liturgy has been helpful. Students seem to be very capable in carrying out their liturgical and preaching responsibilities in the parish. Schuth also noted that the spiritual formation program is well developed. "It is carefully thought through in terms of a developmental model. I think it pays attention to the issues that are of great concern right now—celibacy, and pastoral relationships with people."[50]

Although the seminary could be a little larger, she believes that it is a good size. "The advantage is that you can really focus in on the needs of the students from particular dioceses." In addition, the faculty is of a reasonable size to give attention to students in personal, academic, and pastoral formation.

Schuth reiterated what she has stated in her books and articles:

> There is need for constant adaptation. We are always transitioning into another phase. And I think seminary faculty are amazingly flexible people who try to respond to what's happening in the larger church, try to respond to the bishops, try to respond to the types of students they have. We are constantly reading the signs of the times. And in an effort to do that I think we've done a decent job with very limited resources. The faculty has had to adapt to all of these changes—ecclesiological changes—a half dozen times, as well as to different types of students and different social contexts.

At the Saint Paul Seminary, she added, there are faculty who are also involved on the national scene. They are willing to be creative in experimental ventures such as the Keystone Project, programs in technology, and cooperative opportunities with the consortium.[51] The Saint Paul Seminary has indeed adapted many times and in many ways for more than one hundred years.

Celebrating the Centennial

One of the highlights of the 1990s was the celebration of the seminary's centennial. A committee, responsible to the board, was appointed by Father Froehle in the spring of 1993 to plan a year-long celebration. Msgr. William Baumgaertner served as chair and Dr. Celeste Raspanti accepted the role of events coordinator, working with the development office under the leadership of Thomas Keefe. Activities and events extended from September 1994 through October 1995.

The opening event included a liturgy celebrated by Archbishop Roach in St. Mary's Chapel on September 8, 1994, followed by a dinner and a lecture by Father Marvin O'Connell. Ordained from the Saint Paul Seminary in 1956, and recently retired as professor of history at the University of Notre Dame, O'Connell is the author of *John Ireland and the American Catholic Church.* His presentation "Meximieux and Mr. Hill: John Ireland's Dream Come True" was a substantive and poetic beginning to the centennial year.

Other lectures during the year described the contributions made by the seminary to the history of the Catholic Church. They included: Bishop Raymond Lucker on "Archbishop Edwin O'Hara: Man with a Vision for the Church in the Twentieth Century"; Msgr. John Sweeney and Father Jan Michael Joncas on "Leadership in the Liturgical Revival and in Sacred Music"; Dr. Joseph White on "The Changing Image of the Priest and Its Impact After the Third Plenary Council of Baltimore"; Sister Karen Kennelly, C.S.J., on "Archbishop Ireland, the Saint Paul Seminary, and 'the New Woman'"; Sister Mary Christine Athans, B.V.M., on "Snapshots in the History of the Saint Paul Seminary: The Challenge of Writing Down the Story"; and a Centennial Symposium co-sponsored with the University of St. Thomas and the Archdiocese of St. Paul and Minneapolis on "Religion and Public Life: The Legacy of Msgr. John A. Ryan." A concluding event featured a eucharistic liturgy celebrated by Archbishop John R. Roach with the homily by Archbishop Harry Flynn, followed by dinner and a lecture by Archbishop Roach on "The Challenge of the Future."

Interspersed with these lectures were open houses targeted to special groups, a centennial concert titled "Agape" by alumnus Marty Haugen, and a "Centennial Processional" hymn by alumnus Father Jan Michael Joncas. There were special issues of the "Centennial Chronicle" to ac-

St. Mary's Chapel, the Saint Paul Seminary

company the *Saint Paul Seminary School of Divinity Quarterly Newsletter* with articles on the history of the seminary. A video presentation titled "The Saint Paul Seminary: A Century of Leadership and Vision" was produced and directed by alumnus Scott L. Hippert with Celeste Raspanti as associate producer/writer and Thomas Keefe as executive producer.

The Saint Paul Seminary Distinguished Alumnus Award was inaugurated during the centennial celebration. The first recipient was Msgr. Francis Fleming (ordained in 1942), retired pastor of St. Olaf's Parish in Minneapolis. In 1996 a Lifetime Achievement Award was presented to Archbishop John R. Roach, who retired as archbishop in 1995. On that occasion, special awards were also presented in four categories: Father Michael Arms (ordained in 1968) in pastoral ministry; Father Edward Flahavan (ordained in 1957) in social justice; Msgr. Ambrose Hayden (ordained in 1944) in administration; and Msgr. Gregory T. Schaffer (ordained in 1960) of the New Ulm Diocese, currently serving in Guatemala, for missionary work. Msgr. Hayden was not able to be present due to illness and died shortly thereafter. Msgr. Baumgaertner accepted the award on his behalf.

The Distinguished Alumnus (Alumni) of the Year award has continued to be presented in succeeding years.[52] By means of this honor the celebration of the centennial continues. In these alumni, and in all the other alumni/ae, the Saint Paul Seminary School of Divinity lives on.

CHAPTER 16

"To Work for the Whole People"

> The influence radiating from the Seminary will reach more immediately the people of its own religious faith. They are a large part of the general population of the northwest. Beyond them, however, will its influences go. Its spirit will be *to work for the whole people,* offering its strength to uphold every noble cause, and willing to cooperate with all men [and women] who labor to serve God, humanity and country. No narrowing lines, holding back from doing good wherever, for whomsoever and with whomsoever, will ever be drawn around St. Paul's Seminary. *Allies will ever be here for those who heal the wounds of suffering humanity, or strengthen the social bonds, and the institutions of the country.*[1]
>
> Archbishop John Ireland
> Address at the Dedication of the Saint Paul Seminary
> September 4, 1895

The Saint Paul Seminary has responded in significant ways to John Ireland's challenge "to work for the whole people" in at least four areas under the leadership of distinguished alumni: social justice (Msgr. John A. Ryan), liturgy (Msgr. William Busch), rural ministry and catechetics (Archbishop Edwin O'Hara), and preaching and teaching the Gospel (Archbishop Fulton Sheen). A reflection on their accomplishments highlights the unsung contributions of alumni/ae of the Saint Paul Seminary School of Divinity to the life of the church and society. That tradition of service was embedded in the cornerstone of the seminary by its first archbishop. Ireland's sense of the transforming role of the church rested on his understanding of the priest. At the same time, before collaboration became a fashionable word, Ireland knew that the work of the mission could not be advanced without an empowered laity. John Ireland stated clearly that the diocesan seminary would be "the principal work of our episcopate."[2] Ireland knew, however, that priests alone do not constitute the church. In an immigrant church in particular, the people needed to be educated to provide leadership. A knowledgeable and competent laity became essential to the church's mission.

John Ireland spoke strongly on the role of the laity. When Henry Brownson, the son of Ireland's friend, Catholic convert and intellectual Orestes Brownson, helped to initiate the First Lay Congress in Baltimore in 1889, he invited Cardinal Gibbons and Archbishop Ireland to give plenary addresses. That same year, at the celebration of the centennial of the Catholic hierarchy in the United States in Baltimore, Ireland addressed his brother bishops and others as well on the role of the laity: "Laymen need not wait for priests nor priests for bishops nor bishops for Pope. The timid move in crowds, the brave in single file."[3] Later in the speech he elaborated his point:

> Laymen are not anointed in confirmation to the end that they merely save their own souls, and pay their pew rent. They must think, work, organize, read, speak, act as circumstances demand, ever anxious to serve the Church and to do good to their fellowmen. There is on the part of the Catholic laymen, too much dependence on priests. If priests work, laymen imagine that they themselves may rest. In Protestantism, where there is no firmly constituted ministerial organization, the layman is more keenly alive to his responsibility, and lay action is more common and more earnest. Lay action is to-day particularly needed in the Church. Laymen have in this age a special vocation.[4]

Ireland knew that educating lay people in the church was the only way that the Catholic Church in the United States would come into its own in American society. The "reunion" of the Saint Paul Seminary with the College of St. Thomas in 1986 which produced the School of Divinity to train both priests and lay ministers was clearly congruent with Ireland's vision. Although the leaders of the four movements described below are clergy, the impact they have had on lay programs and the development of lay leaders is unquestioned.

Social Justice

In Ireland's address at the celebration of the centennial of the American hierarchy in the United States, he issued a challenge regarding the place of social justice in the church's mission: "To sing lovely anthems in cathedral stalls, wear coats of embroidered gold . . . while the world outside is dying of spiritual and moral starvation, that is not the religion we need today."[5] Ireland's words and commitment to social justice found an able response from one of the first seminarians to study at the Saint Paul Seminary, John Augustine Ryan. Born in Vermillion, Minnesota, in 1869 of Irish immigrant parents, he attended the St. Thomas Aquinas Seminary and in the fall of 1894 was among the first students to move across the street to the newly completed buildings of the Saint Paul Seminary.

In addition to being influenced by Archbishop Ireland, Ryan was also inspired by political figures such as populist leader Ignatius Donnelly to consider the questions of social justice in America. The publication of Leo XIII's encyclical *Rerum Novarum* ("On the Condition of the Working Classes") in 1891 stoked his passion for justice. After his ordi-

Msgr. John A. Ryan

nation in 1898 and a brief experience in a parish, Ryan was sent by Archbishop Ireland to the Catholic University of America in Washington, D.C., where he completed a licentiate in sacred theology in 1900. As it happened, Archbishop Ireland was in Europe at that time and had neglected to give Ryan an assignment. Taking the initiative, the young scholar returned to Catholic University in the fall and began doctoral studies in moral theology.[6]

In 1902, after completing his doctoral course work, Ryan was assigned to teach at the Saint Paul Seminary. During those early years he prepared new courses and worked on his dissertation. Titled *A Living Wage,* it was completed in 1905 and published in 1906. Ryan continued teaching at the seminary until 1915, during which time he wrote his classic, *Distributive Justice.* Protestant scholar Martin Marty, in *A Short History of American Catholicism,* claims that the Catholic social justice movement in the United States was born in the library and the dormitories of the Saint Paul Seminary in St. Paul, Minnesota in the writings of John A. Ryan.[7]

Although Ryan had an open invitation to return to Catholic University as a member of the faculty, Archbishop Ireland did not want to lose him from the seminary faculty. Finally, in 1915, Ireland relented. While teaching at the Catholic University, Ryan was also appointed to head the Social Action Department of the National Catholic Welfare Conference in the aftermath of World War I. In that position he authored the brief but important document, "Social Reconstruction: A General Review of the Problems and a Survey of Remedies," popularly known as the "Bishops' Program of Social Reconstruction." Protestant church historian Sydney E. Ahlstrom has described it as "the first expression of Catholic social progressivism to be given at least semi-official status in America."[8]

Ryan's commitment to issues of social concern was confirmed with the promulgation of Pope Pius XI's encyclical *Quadragesimo Anno* ("On the Reconstruction of the Social Order") in 1931. Perhaps as a result of his having been an advisor to Catholic Al Smith on issues of church and state when Smith made his unsuccessful bid for the presidency of the United States in 1928, Ryan became a consultant to Franklin D. Roosevelt on his New Deal legislation. Twice he was invited by President Roosevelt to present a benediction at the inaugural ceremonies. Ryan was the first Catholic to receive that honor. On the occasion of Ryan's seventieth birthday, President Roosevelt wrote to him:

> Because of your perennially youthful spirit and your zest for service on behalf of your fellowmen—particularly the under-privileged—it is difficult to realize that you have attained the scriptural age of three score and ten.... With voice and pen, you have pleaded the cause of social justice and the right of the individual to happiness through economic security, a living wage, and an opportunity to share in the things that enrich and ennoble human life. Happily at 70 you are unwearied in your labors.[9]

It was not accidental that Francis L. Broderick titled his Ryan biography, *The Right Reverend New Dealer: John A. Ryan.*[10]

After retirement from Catholic University, Ryan continued teaching and involvement in social justice issues. With the onset of serious illness he returned to Minnesota where he died in 1945. Historians and social ethicists consider Ryan one of the towering figures among pre-Vatican II American Catholic theologians.

One of Ryan's doctoral students at the Catholic University of America was Francis Gilligan. He was born on April 26, 1898, in Fall River, Massachusetts. Both his parents died when he was young, and he entered the seminary as a teenager. He did his classical studies at Jesuit Holy Cross College in Worcester, Massachusetts, his philosophy at St. Mary's Seminary in Baltimore, and his theology at the Sulpician Seminary in Washington, D.C. During the summers he worked as a crewman for the Fall River Steamship Line ferrying passengers "in elegant style" between Boston and New York. During those trips Gilligan became friends with many of the black crew members and learned about their struggle for civil rights. During the layovers in New York, he wandered the parks and listened to soapbox orators make impassioned pleas for a more just society. "Some of their ideas stayed with me," he recalled.[11]

As mentioned above, Gilligan was one of three seminarians, along with William O. Brady and James Connolly, to accept the invitation of Archbishop Austin Dowling to join the Archdiocese of St. Paul and prepare to teach on the seminary faculty. Gilligan was ordained in 1924, began graduate studies at the Catholic University shortly after, and was incardinated into the Archdiocese of St. Paul in 1926. The young priest was challenged by his mentor, John A. Ryan, to apply the principles of Pope Leo XIII on labor to matters of racial equality in the United States. Ryan, according to one source, said, "Have you any guts? Will you work and write on the morality of the color line?"[12] Gilligan accepted the challenge and outlined concerns that people of color were not getting access to jobs, decent housing, and public accommodations. Ryan wrote to Archbishop Dowling regarding Gilligan's research, "I believe that the work will be a valuable contribution to the study of a long neglected subject."[13] Gilligan defended his dissertation, titled *The Morality of the Color Line,* in 1928. In it he stated:

> The Negroes constitute approximately one-tenth of the population of the United States. Against them flourish strong prejudices and numerous discriminations which isolate them from the other inhabitants and partially thwart their progress. Those discriminations have been inaugurated and are now perpetuated by white persons who, to a large extent, profess Christianity. Obviously, such conditions have occasioned a moral problem which is deserving of serious and immediate attention.[14]

The young moral theologian then traveled west and began his twenty-nine-year career as professor of moral theology and economics at the Saint Paul Seminary. In 1950, his good friend William O. Brady, by then bishop of Sioux Falls, wrote of him:

> The Catholic University and Monsignor John A. Ryan gave him more than a doctor's degree. They gave him a passion for social justice and a love for the underprivileged, often called the underdog. The first he has consistently promoted and the second he has doggedly (no pun intended), fostered the while he initiated many a September's class of bewildered philosophers or theologians into the mysteries of metaphysics, or into the sound judgments of moral difficulties.[15]

Gilligan is remembered as an excellent teacher ahead of his time.

The young priest did not limit his energy to the classroom. From 1937 to 1954 he was the director of the Catholic Labor Schools of the Archdiocese of St. Paul. He helped laboring persons learn how to organize for fair wages and safe working conditions, and he introduced them to Catholic social justice principles. Labor leaders learned the facts of economic life and captains of industry were taught the principles of the social encyclicals. He served as a mediator in negotiations, most notably the 1938 Duluth newspaper strike that had simmered for seven weeks and that he brought to closure in twenty-four hours.

In 1943 Gilligan was named the first chair of the Governor's Interracial Commission and received successive appointments from Governors Edward Thye, Luther Youngdahl, C. Elmer Anderson, and Orville Freeman. He served on the board of the St. Paul Urban League, and in 1947 was the only clergyman appointed to the newly established Labor Committee of the National Association for the Advancement of Colored People (NAACP). Gilligan was also instrumental in establishing the Our Lady of Good Counsel Free Cancer Home in St. Paul, under the direction of the Sisters of St. Dominic, Servants of Relief for Incurable Cancer, and the St. Paul-Ramsey Medical Center (now Regions Hospital) in St. Paul.[16]

A practical person, as well as an academic and an administrator, Gilligan often told the story of how he would make room reservations at the St. Paul Hotel for the visits of good friends who were black, such as Clarence Mitchell of the civil rights movement. The black guest would arrive at the desk to discover that his reservation was "lost" or all the rooms were "filled." Gilligan would then step forward and insist that he had made the reservation and had been assured there was space. Room was always found.[17]

After almost three decades of teaching at the seminary, Gilligan was appointed pastor of St. Mark's Parish in St. Paul (1957–1972) where he continued to fight for social justice issues. He was then asked to serve as archdiocesan director of the Society for the Propagation of the Faith, a position which he held for twenty years. Gilligan was honored by the North Central Region of the National Conference of Christians and Jews with their Brotherhood Award in February 1953, with an honorary doctorate from the College of St. Thomas in 1974, and with the Archbishop John Ireland Award from the Archdiocesan Urban Affairs Commission in 1980.

His friend, Archbishop Brady, noted that Gilligan traveled three paths: (1) the formation of the clergy, whose call to be "other Christs" found dynamic expression in Christ among the poor; (2) practical promotion of the welfare of the Negro people and related broader racial questions; and (3) concern for the economic needs of all—especially the laboring classes. He promoted dialogue and advanced these causes by his "priestliness and practicality."[18] Gilligan died April 6, 1997, just three weeks shy of his ninety-ninth birthday.

Many seminarians took Gilligan's message to heart and saw him as a role model. Edward Grzeskowiak, who was born January 4, 1910, in Silver Lake, Minnesota, came from a poor family whom he saw treated unjustly by some priests. He decided at an early age that he would do all that he could to bring justice to the poor.[19] Grzeskowiak studied at the Saint Paul Seminary from 1930 to 1936 and, after ordination in 1936, was appointed to teach at Nazareth Hall, where he remained on the faculty for twenty-seven years. Grzeskowiak had hoped to teach mathematics or classics, but was eventually assigned to teach physics and chemistry. He had no passion for these subjects and recalled, "I was often being told that we needed priest-chemists. I could never find anything in the Old Testament that linked priests with chemists."[20]

Grzeskowiak admired Gilligan as a seminarian, and the latter shared with him concerns about race relations and labor unions. After he was ordained, Gilligan would call Grzeskowiak and invite him to meetings, at first as a chauffeur. "I attended a lot of meetings with great men." The result was that he got involved with labor relations. "Gilligan knew, too, that if I was a little on the wrong side, it was the side of labor. And he thought that was okay." Grzeskowiak remembered the labor schools:

> We had an attorney teaching parliamentary law, and another priest teaching social thought. I think I was sort of like a librarian who got things done that had to be done to cement things. . . . Gilligan gave [the tasks] to me and told me what to do. We all followed his directions very specifically because we admired him so much.

During his years at Nazareth Hall, Grzeskowiak was appointed by Governor Orville Freeman (1955–1961) to serve on the Governor's Commission on Human Rights and was assigned to the subcommittee dealing with migrant farmers and Native Americans. It was very difficult trying to stimulate interest in parishes about the concerns of migrant workers, and on one occasion he was called a Communist by the editor of *The Wanderer*.[21]

In 1963 Grzeskowiak decided it was time to leave Nazareth Hall. Archbishop Binz wanted to assign him to a large parish in Minneapolis as a reward for his years at the seminary. Grzeskowiak told the archbishop that he did not have administrative experience. Binz asked him to serve as pastor of Immaculate Heart of Mary Parish in Minnetonka. Grzeskowiak said he would go wherever he was assigned but he preferred St. Peter Claver, the predominantly African-American parish in St. Paul. Binz suggested that St. Peter's was not an influential parish. The priest replied: "Bishop, what makes a parish 'big'—money or people?"[22]

Grzeskowiak served Immaculate Heart of Mary Parish in Minnetonka, but his heart was not in it. Archbishop Binz finally appointed him pastor of St. Peter Claver effective January 1965. Grzeskowiak approached Father Edward Flahavan, ordained in 1957 from the Saint Paul Seminary, who was teaching English and American history at Nazareth Hall. He asked Flahavan if he would be interested in being his assistant. Flahavan agreed to having his name submitted and was appointed in the summer of 1965. Flahavan, who was also influenced by Gilligan, recalled:

> Working with Ed Grzeskowiak was a great boon. He gave me my in-service training in about five sentences. He helped me unpack my car and haul my stuff up the steps. Basically he said to me: "We are living in a poverty pocket here in this neighborhood. These people do not enjoy power from anybody. Not the church, not the government. Our place is to be on their side of the table in any fight they enter against the government or the church. We're going to always be on their side of the table. That's where we belong. And if we get in trouble and have to break the law, it's not likely to make much difference. Our letters of complaint to the Chancery are not going to have any weight." It was very liberating for me.[23]

Mentored by Grzeskowiak, Flahavan became more deeply involved in social justice. A group of inner-city priests began meeting at the cathedral under Father John Brandes's direction. After a minor riot in one area of Minneapolis, Archbishop Binz wrote to one of the priests and asked, "What advice do you have for me and how can the church respond?" That was how the idea of the Urban Affairs Commission was born, as an effort to examine the root causes of civil unrest, under-employment, under-housing, and discrimination. When the proposal was made to Archbishop Binz, his response, according to Flahavan, was, "If that's a good idea, then take it to the new Senate of Priests, and get the endorsement of the Senate because you are going to need broad support." It was approved, and its current successor is the Archdiocesan Commission on Social Justice under the direction of Ron Krietemeyer.

As executive director of the Office of Urban Affairs from 1968 to 1977, Flahavan lived and worked out of the archdiocesan offices in the Hill House and served as chaplain to the Little Sisters of the Poor in St. Paul. He helped to initiate projects such as the Christian Sharing Fund that predated the Campaign for Human Development, and the Joint Religious Legislative Coalition in which Protestant, Catholic, and Jewish leadership became a voice for the poor. The CommonBond Communities, an arm of the archdiocese, was also a spin-off of the Urban Affairs Commission and helps to provide low-income housing for those in need.

In 1976 Archbishop Roach asked Flahavan to become pastor of St. Stephen's Parish in Minneapolis and continue working in the Urban Affairs Office. After a year it became clear that it was not possible to do both. Flahavan stayed at St. Stephen's for twelve years, during which time he "contributed to a vitality and an emerging sense of common obligation and support of all peoples: the newly visible street people; the influx of Native Americans into the ghettos of Minneapolis; the appalling unemployment rate among his African-American youth."[24] Among other accomplishments, he established St. Stephen's Shelter where homeless men can come at night for a hot meal and a bed. For many years, students, faculty, and staff from the Saint Paul Seminary School of Divinity have continued to cook and serve a hot meal at the shelter on the first Sunday of each month.

Following his years at St. Stephen's, Flahavan became involved in prison ministry and has been the recipient of a variety of awards. In reflecting back on the roots of his involvement in social justice, Flahavan noted that he wrote his master's thesis in church history in 1956 under the direction of Father Patrick Ahern at the Saint Paul Seminary. It was titled *A Quarter Century of Alms: The Aid Given to the Diocese of Saint Paul by the Society for the Propagation of the Faith, 1850–1873.*[25] The

Society for the Propagation of the Faith helped Bishop Joseph Cretin establish the new Diocese of St. Paul. Flahavan stated, "That was the only source of money he had. So we got the profits of that generosity and now we have the obligation to help those who are poor."[26]

Another advocate for social justice who was also a student of Msgr. Gilligan was J. Jerome Boxleitner, ordained in 1956. After five years of pastoral work, Boxleitner studied at the Catholic University of America from 1961 to 1963 and received a master's degree in social work. Upon returning from Catholic University, "Box," as he is known by his friends, was appointed assistant, associate, and finally archdiocesan director of Catholic Charities in 1966. By 1975, however, there were four Catholic social service corporations in the Twin Cities presided over by Archbishop John Roach: Catholic Welfare Services of Minneapolis, Catholic Social Service of St. Paul, Seton Center, and St. Joseph's Home for Children—the first of the four institutions founded in 1869. It became clear to Roach that there was need for consolidation with a new comprehensive agency and one strong governing board. Msgr. Boxleitner created the new Catholic Charities of the Archdiocese of St. Paul and Minneapolis in 1977 and served as its director until 1999.[27] Now under the direction of Father Larry J. Snyder (ordained in 1988), Catholic Charities of the Archdiocese serves 170,000 people each year. With a staff of eight hundred, assisted by twelve thousand volunteers, it is the largest provider of social services in the Twin Cities committed to the poorest of the poor.[28]

Social justice was always a priority for Archbishop John R. Roach. While president of the NCCB/USCC, he provided national leadership in the issuance of the United States Bishops' peace pastoral, *The Challenge of Peace,* and was instrumental in the commitment to the letter of the bishops on the economy, *Economic Justice for All.* In 1991 he issued *Reviving the Common Good: A Pastoral Letter on Social Justice* in the archdiocese. A substantive and user-friendly document with a discussion guide, it was welcomed in the parishes and used for instructing people on Catholic social teaching and raising consciousness about the needs in society, particularly children in poverty, and racism.

Social justice ministry has taken a variety of forms in recent years. For some it meant involvement in politics. Father Leo Tibesar (ordained in 1968), a faculty member at the Saint Paul Seminary and director of the Archbishop Ireland Memorial Library from 1977 to 1987, was elected in 1980 and in 1984 as a delegate from Minnesota to the Democratic National Convention. He was strongly committed to the pro-life movement, to gay rights, and to ministry to those with AIDS. In the fall of 1984, with Sister Joanne Lucid, B.V.M., Paul O'Hara, Charles Ceronsky, and others, Tibesar worked for the establishment of an Office for AIDS Ministry in the archdiocese. Their proposal was finally approved by Archbishop Roach in September 1985 and the Office for AIDS Ministry was established in 1986, the first in any diocese in the United States.[29]

Other alumni of the Saint Paul Seminary School of Divinity have also made outstanding contributions in social justice. Among them are Father David Macauley (ordained in 1963), director of the Minnesota Catholic Conference; Father James Notebaart (ordained in 1971) for his ministry with Native Americans; and Father Stephen Adrian (ordained in 1968), a leader in the development of SPEAC (St. Paul Ecumenical Alliance of Congregations).

More recently, Father John Estrem (ordained in 1986), Father Michael Reding (ordained in 1997), and others, in an effort to broaden the work of SPEAC to other areas, have helped to develop an umbrella group called ISAIAH. Reding was honored in the spring of 1999 by Catholic Charities with the Archbishop's Award for helping to organize a coalition of Catholic churches and other Christian churches to advocate for moving a shelter for the homeless owned by Ramsey County but operated by Catholic Charities to Maplewood. Opposition was strong and adamant in the suburban community which several years earlier had rejected a proposal for an AIDS house. This time, a prayer rally and the presence of over six hundred people at the final public hearing resulted in a decision of the City Council to accept the challenge. Transfiguration Parish, where Father James Smith is pastor and Reding was then an associate pastor, received the John Ireland Award from the Social Justice Commission of the archdiocese for its initiative in this undertaking.

Finally, recognition is due to the many alumni who continue to serve the archdiocesan mission in Venezuela and the mission of the Diocese of New Ulm in Guatemala; innumerable priests in inner-city parishes and in prison ministry; and alumni of every age committed to Hispanic, Asian, and Native American ministry. The tradition of John Ireland, John A. Ryan, and John R. Roach continues into the twenty-first century.

Liturgy and Sacred Music

In 1919, while he was engaged in a series of instructions on the Mass at the College of St. Catherine in St. Paul, Father William Busch, a professor at the Saint Paul Seminary, became distinctly aware of the need for a general liturgical movement.[30] He discovered Romano Guardini's book *The Spirit of the Liturgy,* and began to share his excitement with others, including Alcuin Deutsch, O.S.B, of St. John's Abbey in Collegeville, Minnesota. In that same year the *Ecclesiastical Review* published Busch's article on "Construction of an Altar." He was hardly subtle:

> When will the Catholic Church in the United States rid itself of the kind of altar which Ralph Adams Cram has well called a "glorified soda-fountain"? Will things actually go from bad to worse until we have added mirrors for additional glittering effect? Are we convinced once and for all that a beautiful church can only be secured through the use of polished marbles (or imitations thereof)? The lobbies of theatres and hotels are beginning to break away from the rule, leaving the white marbles for barber-shops, moving-picture houses—and Catholic churches.

Busch suggested that competent architects be consulted, and that "a simple table of good, solid wood, with four substantial columns actually forming 'legs' of the table" would be preferable. He recommended simplicity of decor in the altar area.[31]

William Busch would become a major figure in the liturgical movement in the United States. Born on October 6, 1882, in Red Wing, Minnesota,[32] he completed priesthood studies at the Saint Paul Seminary and was ordained in 1907 by Archbishop Ireland. From 1908 to 1911 Busch served as a curate at St. Luke's Parish in St. Paul, after which he was assigned to do graduate studies at Louvain, where he earned his licentiate in the science of ecclesiastical history. While there he eventually became aware of the European liturgical movement in its new form that was developing under the leadership of Father Lambert Beauduin, O.S.B., at Mount Caser outside of Louvain. Busch returned to the United States in 1913 reflecting on this new liturgical movement in Europe and gradually was converted to it. Busch was in regular contact with Alcuin Deutsch, O.S.B., knowing that St. John's Abbey in Collegeville had a liturgical tradition and "manpower" to implement any initiatives. As Busch was laying the foundation for the American liturgical renewal, Abbot Alcuin Deutsch sent a young Benedictine priest, Virgil Michel, to Rome to study with Lambert Beauduin, O.S.B., at the Pontifical Institute at Sant' Anselmo.

On July 2, 1925, Busch gave an address at the Seminary Division of the Catholic Educational Association on "The Liturgical Movement," laying out in detail the historical and theological roots of the liturgical revival in Europe. He discussed its beginnings in the United States and the importance of a solid program in seminaries preparing future clergy for liturgical ministry. He stated:

> For the heart of the liturgical movement is the right understanding first of all, and then the right celebration of the holy Sacrifice, not by the priest alone, but by all who are present, in the fullest possible expression of the *Ecclesia Orans,* by the general participation which Pope Pius X has said is "the primary and indispensable source of the true Christian spirit."[33]

Msgr. William Busch

The directive of Pius X for general participation in the liturgy was the driving force in Busch's life.

Michel returned to the United States in the fall of 1925 not long after Busch's address to the Catholic Educational Association. He was convinced of the need for a popular liturgical movement in America and had written Abbot Deutsch extensively, pleading with him to look beyond liturgy in the monastic setting to the broader needs of the people. William Busch was making similar requests of the abbot at the same time, as is evident in a letter of Busch to Michel in September 28, 1925:

> During the past months while you were in Europe I had taken up with Abbot Alcuin both by letter and conversation the subject of the presentation to priests and people in this country of some of the excellent European literature on the liturgical movement.... The abbot told me that my first suggestion to him in this regard came to him just at the time when a similar one was made to him by yourself.[34]

Michel responded to Busch immediately and outlined two projects—the liturgical review *Orate Fratres* (now titled *Worship*), and the Popular Liturgical Library whereby important works in the liturgy would be made accessible in America. Busch and Michel mutually agreed on the proposal and Abbot Deutsch gave his approval. *Orate Fratres* was established in the summer of 1926 with Virgil Michel as editor. Busch was named one of the associate editors, a position he held for twenty years.[35]

Michel, Busch, and their colleagues dreamed of establishing a program whereby a national Liturgical Day would be held regularly in the United States. Hopefully it would expand to a celebration of a Liturgical Week similar to the European model. At these events scholars and others committed to the liturgical movement would assemble to hear papers, share ideas and perspectives, and pray. The first Liturgical Day was held at St. John's Abbey on July 25, 1929. Busch wrote later about reflecting with Michel when the day was done:

> When the day was over and he had attended to the guests who were staying at the Abbey, he came at last to my room and in-

> vited me for a stroll under the sky before retiring. As we paced to and fro in the soft night air, with the lake beneath us and at every turn facing against the lighted windows of the Abbey, I observed his subdued feeling of joyous satisfaction. The Liturgical Day had exceeded our expectations, and we knew that something memorable had been done.[36]

In the early 1930s, while recuperating from illness, Michel spent a period of time at one of the Indian missions in northern Minnesota. It was there that he became keenly aware of the linkage between liturgy and social justice and promoted that aspect of the liturgical movement. With Michel's death in 1938 at the age of forty-eight, Godfrey Diekmann, O.S.B., became editor of *Orate Fratres* and continued the commitment of St. John's to the movement.

The First National Liturgical Week was held in Chicago in 1940. Busch was asked to give a major address. In it he stated, "The liturgical movement is not a fad such as springs up suddenly and flourishes a short time. The pace of its growth has been not unlike that of previous liturgical movements." Church historian that he was, he then recounted the various liturgical movements from the time of the primitive church to the twentieth century. He concluded:

> We are called to do our part in it, and let us not lose time. Let us be prompt in corresponding to the grace of the Holy Spirit. But let us not be hasty. None of these movements in the church's history was wrought out in a short time. Let us know well what we are about; let us understand well the meaning of this great event. It is not merely a matter of our personal efforts; it is a movement in the life of the church of which we are members.[37]

Busch also emphasized the relationship between liturgy and Catholic Action—or, in today's terms, social justice:

> For if current notions about Catholic Action are not yet sufficiently clear, I think it is because we have not considered carefully in what way Catholic Action is based on the Liturgy. The apostolate of the laity in Catholic Action follows from the general priesthood of the laity in the Liturgy. On the other hand, if

> we do not recognize the proper outlet or purpose of the Liturgy, it will continue to mean, as it does at present to many, only a matter of better order and greater beauty in Church services. The Liturgy has a double outlet; first, Godward in love and worship and obedience, and second, manward in Catholic Action.[38]

Father Thomas Conroy, a student of Busch's ordained in 1948, taught at Nazareth Hall from 1948 to 1968. He was encouraged by the rector, Louis McCarthy, who was influenced by Busch, to explore the new liturgy program at the University of Notre Dame. Conroy enrolled in its master's program in 1948 and studied during the summers through 1952. When it was time to write his thesis, Conroy asked that Father William Busch be his thesis advisor. Busch's reputation in liturgy was so well known that Notre Dame granted the request. Conroy recalls attending the Twelfth National Liturgical Week in Dubuque in 1951, where Busch was introduced to the assembly as "the father of the Liturgical Movement in the United States."[39]

Busch was indeed the proto-evangelist of the liturgical movement in the United States. He worked closely with his colleagues, Fathers Virgil Michel, O.S.B.; Martin Hellriegel; Gerald Ellard, S.J.; Godfrey Diekmann, O.S.B.; and others. His translation of Joseph Kramp's volume *Eucharistia: Essays on Eucharistic Liturgy and Devotion*[40] from German into English, and authorship of scholarly articles in *Orate Fratres,* some of which were published in book form under the title *The Mass-Drama, An Outline of Its Structure,*[41] were major contributions to the movement.

A contemporary of Busch's, ordained just one year after him, was Francis A. Missia—a larger-than-life figure who was in charge of music at the Saint Paul Seminary for forty-eight years. Missia was born on January 26, 1884, in what is now Slovenia, then part of the Austro-Hungarian Empire. He learned German as well as his native Slovenian, and at the invitation of his uncle, Msgr. Jakob Missia, he studied at the Jesuit gymnasium at Kalkburg near Vienna for his classical and musical studies. In 1884 Missia's uncle was named bishop of Ljubljana (Laibach in German), and was chaplain to the Austrian empress. Later he was appointed archbishop of Gorizia (Gorz), and during that time he received a visit from Archbishop John Ireland who was in search of young priests and students for his Archdiocese of St. Paul. Young Francis Missia was intrigued with the American archbishop and the possibility of adventure and opportunity in America.[42]

In June 1899, Archbishop Missia was elevated to the College of Cardinals but died unexpectedly in 1900. His nephew and protégé, only sixteen years old, was devastated and unsure of his future. He decided to accept the invitation of Archbishop Ireland, arriving in America on August 15, 1903. In later years Missia reflected on the fact that while he was on board ship, Cardinal Giuseppe Sarto was elected pope and took the name Pius X. The new pope issued his *motu proprio* on sacred music the following November calling for the reinstatement of Gregorian chant. That was to be Missia's guiding document for his lifetime.

When the young Slovenian arrived in St. Paul he had very little money and could speak no English. Archbishop Ireland welcomed him and enrolled him in the seminary. Missia's strong, rich voice was impressive and his musical ability was evident. In his last year of studies he was named choirmaster at the seminary. Upon ordination in 1908 he was assigned to the faculty as professor of sacred music and spent his entire priestly life in that role.

As the enrollment of the seminary grew, he built up the choir and began implementing the directives of the *motu proprio* with regard to the use of Gregorian chant, Renaissance polyphony, and other appropriate music. With the seminarians' choir and various parish choirs that he directed, he began to coordinate and conduct music for the major events in the archdiocese, such as the consecration of the six bishops in Saint Mary's Chapel in 1910.

When Archbishop Murray arrived in 1932, he established a Sacred Music Commission with Father Missia in charge. Summer schools were conducted at St. Thomas for all choir directors and organists, and every person with responsibility for church music was required to attend in order to be authorized to work in that field in the archdiocese. Certificates were awarded to those who attended three-week courses. The Saint Paul Catholic Choral Society was organized in 1937, and the Guild of Catholic Choirmasters and Organists was established soon thereafter.

The Ninth National Eucharistic Congress was held June 23–26, 1941, at the Minnesota State Fairgrounds. The event was the largest gathering of people under the sponsorship of the Catholic Church in Minnesota before or since that time. Father Missia was in charge of the music. The Sisters in the Catholic schools taught the children in the upper grades the Gregorian chant Mass *Orbis Factor.* The children were drilled by their teachers in the schools and visited by Father Missia for large rehearsals in different areas. The Mass was sung by almost twenty thousand children at the fairgrounds.

Another massed choir of one thousand voices from adult choirs in the area and the Catholic Choral Society sang a Mass composed by Pietro Yon, choirmaster and organist at St. Patrick's Cathedral in New York. The seminarians were drilled over a period of months in the Gregorian chant for all the Masses celebrated at the fairgrounds. Missia conducted the music at all the main events of the Congress. Msgr. John Sweeney recalled:

> Father Missia assembled a new and special hymnal for the occasion containing hymns and chants to be sung especially by large congregations. The entire proceedings of the Congress were audio-recorded, and a copy of these recordings on the old 78 disks were supplied by the archdiocese to all the parishes and institutions in the area.

The importance of the event was not just the impressive size and the publicity for the Catholic Church, but the effect it had on liturgical music in the archdiocese. The children were schooled in chant. Choirs learned from the event. Congregational singing was given a boost. The music for the Congress was accomplished by a united effort of teachers in schools, choir directors, choirs, and organists throughout the archdiocese. "But the name which everyone remembered in this connection was that of Father Francis Missia."[43]

Missia was killed in an automobile accident on Saturday evening, May 21, 1955, while returning from a visit to his cabin in Wisconsin—a place where he sought solitude and enjoyed the beauty of God. It was presumed that he had had a heart attack because he hit a truck from the rear and died on the highway.

This overpowering man with his strong Slavic accent is remembered for his malapropisms such as "Vell, therefore, a prophet is not born in his own country!" Father Francis Schmitt, a 1941 alumnus of the seminary, recalled, "I think of him [Missia] whenever I see or hear Luciano Pavarotti: about the same build, facial features, and receding hairline—amazingly alike, equally suave in manner, equally something of a ham. And, of course, both tenors."[44] Sweeney agreed with the comparison: "Take a look at Pavarotti when he's performing. Missia was a tenor like Pavarotti, and he was built like Pavarotti, and he had a voice like Pavarotti, and he played to the gallery like Pavarotti."[45]

Missia trained seminarians to love the liturgy and to carry out their roles appropriately. In his forty-seven years on the seminary faculty he had an enormous influence not only on the music of the archdiocese but also on the many dioceses of the Midwest and beyond where alumni of the Saint Paul Seminary—pastors as well as diocesan directors or teachers of church music—introduced both clergy and laity to the revival of church music so desired by Pope Pius X.[46]

After Missia's death, Father John Sweeney, ordained in 1941, who was on the faculty part-time teaching catechetics as well as directing the Catholic Youth Center in St. Paul, was appointed to teach music at the seminary and to direct the Catholic Choral Society. Sweeney noted that he did not take Missia's place—he only succeeded him! He inherited a good seminary choir of about 110 voices and built on the liturgical achievements of the past.

Few appreciated the fact that vast changes in the liturgy would be instituted by the Second Vatican Council. Sweeney was also chair of the Music Commission of the archdiocese and recalls receiving a handwritten letter from Archbishop Binz from Rome in the fall of 1964 asking if Sweeney could assure him that there was enough good music available so that he could give the directive for the implementation of the English liturgy in the archdiocese on the First Sunday of Advent. Sweeney assured him that there was. Although there had been little time to prepare, the English liturgy began at the seminary on that day. Sweeney recalled, "We worked very hard to prepare the first Christmas in the vernacular. The Midnight Mass at the seminary was broadcast that year. There were very few churches that used the English liturgy that first Christmas, so we were news!"[47]

In 1977 Sweeney left the seminary to become pastor at Our Lady of the Lake Parish in Mound, Minnesota, after an exciting decade of transition in liturgy and music after Vatican II. The approach to music was broadened and the daily liturgy of the hours was developed. Singing was introduced into daily Mass. The tradition of the Christmas Carol Service—now known as "Lessons and Carols"—continues. Father David Steinle of the Diocese of Davenport briefly succeeded Sweeney.

He was joined by Elizabeth Stodola on a part-time basis. She then served full-time as music director from 1978 to 1982 and instituted the singing of Morning and Evening Prayer. She also brought in speakers to acquaint the students with the needs of liturgical music in the parishes.[48]

Msgr. Richard J. Schuler, a contemporary of Sweeney's who was ordained in 1945, was also influenced by Missia. He was assigned to Nazareth Hall to teach Latin and music and studied at the Eastman School of Music of the University of Rochester, New York where he earned his M.A. in 1950. In 1954 Schuler was the recipient of a Fulbright scholarship and spent a year studying Renaissance music manuscripts at the Vatican Library. He then taught music at the College of St. Thomas for fifteen years during which time he earned a Ph.D. in musicology from the University of Minnesota.[49]

In 1969, Schuler succeeded Msgr. Bandas as pastor of the Church of St. Agnes. That fall he introduced the *Leaflet Missal* into the parish to increase participation of the congregation in the liturgy. In the post-Vatican II period, Schuler enhanced the traditional liturgy with a Sunday Mass that included sung polyphonic Mass with orchestra, *a capella* compositions, and the propers of the Mass sung in Gregorian chant. He continues to direct the Twin Cities Catholic Chorale and for twenty-two years has served as editor of *Sacred Music,* the longest-published music magazine in the United States. Schuler's commitment to a traditional style of church music is unquestioned.[50]

Two priests who first learned about the liturgy from Father Thomas Conroy at Nazareth Hall and later joined the seminary faculty to teach liturgy were James Moudry and Charles Froehle. Moudry studied philosophy at the Saint Paul Seminary from 1950 to 1952 during the era of Busch and Missia. He was then sent to study theology at Louvain, and was ordained to the priesthood in 1956. After a year at Presentation Parish in Maplewood, Moudry was assigned to teach history at Nazareth Hall, and in 1959 he was sent to Rome for doctoral studies at the Angelicum. He wrote his dissertation on the use of patristic sources by Thomas Aquinas in his development of the doctrine of penance in the *Summa Theologica.* Moudry was able to integrate the emphasis on historical studies that he had imbibed at Louvain with his interest in sacraments and liturgy. He returned to teach at the Saint Paul Seminary in 1962, bringing new life to the study of the liturgy, although he taught moral theology as well.[51]

Charles Froehle took one liturgy course under an elderly Msgr. Busch. He was also in Moudry's first class and became intrigued by the new approach to the liturgy. After ordination in 1963 he served for two years at the Basilica of St. Mary in Minneapolis and was then asked to pursue a doctorate in Rome—the first future faculty member to be specifically assigned to liturgical studies.[52] Msgr. Louis McCarthy wrote to Archbishop Binz early in 1965: "In response to Your Excellency's proposal, I am now making formal application for the appointment of a young priest to be prepared to teach LITURGY in this Seminary in carrying out the directive of the CONSTITUTION ON THE LITURGY (II, #15)." McCarthy added that he had written to pontifical institutes that were established in recent years at existing universities where the candidate would earn both the licentiate and doctorate in theology but "would have a very thorough specialization in the Liturgy."

McCarthy then specifically requested that Father Charles Froehle be named for that preparation. He offered the following assessment of Froehle: "He is a solid, balanced man, an excellent student and, I think, he would do admirable work in both Theology and Liturgy on his return to this Seminary. He is well thought of by all of our priests here and judged competent by them. He would be a very welcome addition to our group."[53]

Froehle was appointed by Binz and began doctoral studies at the Angelicum, taking some courses at the Liturgical Institute at Sant' Anselmo as well. He defended his dissertation in 1968.

Moudry and Froehle, both well qualified in liturgy and both in positions of leadership at the Saint Paul Seminary in the post-Vatican II period, made every effort to develop a sound liturgical program. They were also invited by the archbishop to present workshops to the priests of the archdiocese regarding the liturgical changes. Moudry was director of worship during most of his tenure on the seminary faculty (1962–1989); his expertise in liturgy served more than one generation of priests well. Froehle's years of teaching (1968–1980) also impacted the seminarians in liturgical and sacramental theology, and his subsequent role as rector (1980–1993) ensured that good liturgy would always be a priority at the seminary. Others who continued the tradition of excellence in liturgy and sacramental theology are Thomas Fisch, David Stosur, Walter Ray, and Fathers Thomas Sieg; James Motl, O.P.; Samuel Torvend, O.P.; Dominic Serra; and Paul Feela.

In 1982 Sue Seid-Martin was appointed music director at the Saint Paul Seminary. It was initially a joint appointment with her husband, Larry Martin. She had taught liturgical music and directed the liturgical choir at the University of Notre Dame for seven years and came to St. Paul in the early 1980s to teach at the College of St. Catherine. Seid-Martin developed a music program at the seminary based upon the following principles: (1) music is for the assembly; (2) music is an expressive tool—it both forms and expresses our faith; (3) music is contextual in worship—it must fit the context rather than exemplifying a life of its own.[54] In 1984 she stated: "Our prayer is an expression of who we are as God's people. By being immersed in prayer we also become aware of who we are. Each day we respond to God's call, offering praise and thanksgiving for the gifts He has given us and rediscovering Christ's presence in our midst."[55] During Seid-Martin's ten years on the faculty she brought competence, creativity, and *joie de vivre* to the liturgy. With Father James Moudry, she established a program of liturgy preparation for students and staff and mentored many students and colleagues in creative liturgical expressions. She went on sick leave in 1991 due to multiple health problems, and died in August of 1998.

Sue Seid-Martin was an important influence on a new generation of church musicians. David Haas served as "musician in residence" at the Saint Paul Seminary from 1986 to 1988. During that period Haas composed the album titled "Light and Peace: Morning Praise and Evensong." Seid-Martin directed the Saint Paul Seminary School of Divinity Chorale in the recorded version. Marty Haugen, also an impressive composer, enrolled in the Master of Arts in Pastoral Studies program at the Saint Paul Seminary School of Divinity in 1986 and worked in large part with Seid-Martin. He completed the degree in 1991. In May 1995 he directed a presentation of his musical and dramatic composition "Agape" for the seminary centennial.

Jan Michael Joncas, ordained from the seminary in 1980, came to know Seid-Martin while studying for his M.A. in liturgical studies that he received in 1978 from the University of Notre Dame. During seven years of pastoral assignments, Joncas composed popular church music, including the well-known "On Eagles' Wings." He was then assigned to doctoral studies and received an S.L.D. from the Pontificio Istituto Liturgico at the Collegio Sant'Anselmo summa cum laude in 1991. Upon his return, he received a joint appointment at the University of St.

Thomas on the faculties of the department of theology and the Saint Paul Seminary School of Divinity. Joncas is well known for both his scholarly contributions and his musical compositions.

In 1988, David Jenkins, who had a doctorate from the Eastman School of Music at the University of Rochester in New York, became the professional specialist in pastoral music at the Saint Paul Seminary School of Divinity, assisting Seid-Martin. In 1991, with Seid-Martin's illness, he became acting director of liturgical music. In 1992 he was appointed full-time to that position. Jenkins considered Seid-Martin a mentor, sharing her vision and building on her work. He has given particular attention to increasing the emphasis on a multicultural perspective in worship and making music integral to the liturgy.[56] From William Busch to the present, the Saint Paul Seminary has continued its strong tradition in liturgy and sacred music.

Rural Ministry and Catechetics

While Archbishop Edwin V. O'Hara gained recognition as a major figure in the formation of the National Catholic Rural Life Conference, his commitments were broad and far-reaching. He admired Archbishop Ireland and imbibed some of his progressive stance on justice issues, his exuberant approach to life, and his conviction regarding the compatibility of Catholic truths and American ideals. Born September 6, 1881, on his family farm near Lanesboro, Minnesota, the youngest of eight children of Irish immigrants, he enrolled at the College of St. Thomas in January 1898, and entered the Saint Paul Seminary in September 1900 studying for the Diocese of Winona.

An excellent student, he not only published two articles in the *Catholic University Bulletin* in 1903, but in the following year translated *At the Deathbed of Darwinism* by Eberhard Dennert from German to English. It was reviewed in the *New York Times.* The seminary professor who decidedly influenced him was Father John A. Ryan, recently returned from the Catholic University of America, who was writing his dissertation *A Living Wage.* O'Hara's commitment to social justice was solidified at the seminary. On the recommendation of a priest friend, and of his own brother who edited Oregon City's diocesan newspaper, *The Catholic Sentinel,* O'Hara transferred his affiliation to the Archdio-

Archbishop Edwin O'Hara

cese of Oregon City (now Portland) in 1904, convinced of the need for Catholic clergy in the Northwest. He was ordained a priest by Archbishop Ireland in the recently consecrated Saint Mary's Chapel on June 10, 1905.[57]

Archbishop Alexander Christie appointed O'Hara assistant pastor at the cathedral in Oregon City. The young priest also taught in the local high school and in 1907 formed the Catholic Educational Association of Oregon. He served as archdiocesan superintendent of schools from 1906 to 1920, during which time he wrote *Pioneer History of Oregon* which described the role of Catholics in the early history of the state. He studied for a period of time at the Catholic University of America and at the University of Notre Dame. On May 18, 1914, O'Hara gave a conference to the students in the *aula maxima* of the Saint Paul Seminary on the early history of the church in Oregon.[58]

In 1912, O'Hara helped to author Oregon's minimum wage law for women. Although the law was challenged, the United States Supreme Court upheld its constitutionality on April 9, 1917. The following June, the University of Notre Dame awarded the thirty-five-year-old O'Hara an honorary degree of doctor of laws. During that time O'Hara was also appointed chair of the Oregon Industrial Welfare Commission.

Serving as a chaplain in France during World War I broadened O'Hara's vision of the church as well as his concerns for rural life and the working classes. He extended his time in Paris after the war and audited lectures in sociology at the Institut Catholique. He then traveled to London where he visited English sociologist Father Bernard Vaughn. Returning to the United States in 1919, he toured the east coast and met with the staff of the National Catholic Educational Association (NCEA) to discuss the church and rural life. They asked him to prepare a study for the 1920 NCEA meeting on rural Catholic education.

Once again in Oregon, O'Hara asked to be assigned to a rural area and the archbishop appointed him to St. Mary's Parish in Eugene. Timothy M. Dolan states: "On O'Hara's return from France several incidents rekindled his yearning for the setting of his childhood. For one, reflection on his months as a chaplain reminded him again of the value of the land, the struggles of the farmer, and the dependence of all nations on the fruits of the harvest."[59] O'Hara's report to the NCEA in 1920 became the basis for the establishment of the Rural Life Bureau of the National Catholic Welfare Conference (NCWC) in 1921. Its goal was to provide dioceses with information and suggestions concerning rural economic and social concerns. O'Hara became the first chair of the bureau. In 1922 he published *A Program of Catholic Rural Action.*

His activities with the Rural Life Bureau and his expertise as a rural sociologist put him in a unique position to propose the founding of the National Catholic Rural Life Conference (NCRLC) in 1923. His commitment was deep. He made his own the words of Bishop Vincent Wehrle of Bismarck, North Dakota, at the first meeting of the NCRLC, "There is something sacramental about country life."[60] For O'Hara, rural life not only had a sacramental quality, but was also a vocation, a sacred profession, and a way of living. He knew that rural pastors needed an understanding of rural issues, rural families, and the dynamic of living in rural communities. In 1927 he authored *The Catholic Church and the Rural Community.*

The link between rural ministry and catechetics was always primary for O'Hara. While in Eugene he worked to provide religious education for children who lived in remote areas and could not attend parochial school. O'Hara adopted the concept of the religious vacation school from his own experience of attending Lutheran summer school with his Norwegian boyhood friends in Minnesota. He opened summer religious vacation schools where children who attended public school could have two weeks of intensive religious instruction, usually offered by religious sisters or seminarians.

During the regular school year, especially in the winter, some families in remote areas often could not attend church. O'Hara adopted the correspondence course plan of Msgr. Victor Day from Helena, Montana. He experimented with it in Eugene and eventually made it a staple in his national program. Fifteen illustrated catechism lessons were composed for the children with exercises and tests to be completed and returned by mail. The pastor or his catechist would correct the material and send it back to the families with the next lesson enclosed. Parents as well as children benefited from the program.[61]

For a decade beginning in 1923, O'Hara came to the Saint Paul Seminary almost every year to recruit students for the Summer Vacation School Movement. In the 1930 *Register,* O'Hara was described in the "Chronicle of the Year":

> Rev. Edwin O'Hara, apostle of the Catholic rural life movement, made an appeal for a greater number of Seminarians to act as summer catechists. Last year, he and his associates established a group of vacation catechism schools in the South and Southwest which have won the warm approval of the Bishops in whose diocese the work was undertaken.[62]

The following year an extended description was given in the report of The Saint Paul Seminary Mission Society:

> In 1925 the Mission Society interested the seminarians in the Summer Vacation-School Movement, and an increasing number of seminarians has been engaged in it each succeeding year. At present forty students of The Saint Paul Seminary are enrolled as Summer Vacation School Catechists, and they will teach in eight states: Minnesota, Wisconsin, the Dakotas, Illinois, Montana, Iowa and Michigan. The seminarians engage in other missionary work by correspondence.[63]

In the 1920s, with nativism again on the rise in the activities of the Ku Klux Klan and some Scottish Rite Masons, a bill was proposed in Oregon requiring all children to attend public schools. It was placed on the ballot as a referendum in November 1922. O'Hara organized the Catholic Civil Rights Association to fight it and several Protestant denominations opposed it as well. It passed by a majority of fourteen thousand votes, but O'Hara was convinced that it was unconstitutional. Archbishop Christie agreed that it was a denial of basic American rights, and that it should be challenged in court. A team of attorneys with O'Hara as priest-counselor filed suit in the case titled *Pierce vs. Society of Sisters* in the United States District Court in Oregon in June 1923. In April 1924 the court declared the Oregon State Compulsory School Law unconstitutional. The governor of Oregon appealed the decision to the United States Supreme Court, which upheld the lower court's decision. This has been referred to as the "Magna Carta" of private schools. The conclusion was that "the child is not the mere creature of the state."[64] Parochial schools were thus protected.

In the process of winning the battle for private schools, O'Hara realized that many Catholic children in rural areas could not attend Catholic schools. As a result he became more involved with the Confraternity of Christian Doctrine (CCD). The confraternity had been established at the time of the Council of Trent, but it had received new impetus with the encyclical *Acerbo Nimis* of Pope Pius X in 1905 and had been written into the Code of Canon Law of 1917. In 1923, O'Hara invited the CCD to meet annually with the NCRLC. In Timothy Dolan's words, "O'Hara's romance with the CCD knew no bounds. What the rural crusade was for him in the 1920s the confraternity was in the 1930s."[65] O'Hara was realistic enough to know that wonderful as it would be to have every Catholic child in a Catholic school, at best only half would likely have the opportunity. He also believed that the CCD could be a vehicle for apologetics that he preferred to call "Catholic evidence work." He saw it as a means of carrying out the call to Catholic Action and promoting the involvement of the laity. The CCD was not only a means to educate children and young adults, but also an important opportunity for adult education.

The role of parents as educators of their children, O'Hara believed, was too often overlooked. Parents were "the protocatechists of their children." His words were strong:

> There are those who think that lay people can never teach. *Lay people can teach!* Their apostolate is a teaching office! The diffusion of doctrine is in the hands of lay people, and parents are teachers of religion par excellence. They receive graces to teach religion to their children, graces not given to the pope, bishops, priests, sisters, or brothers.[66]

This fiery statement echoes John Ireland's regarding the role of the laity in the church. Finally, O'Hara appreciated the "cradle-to-grave" coverage which the CCD offered, as well as the opportunity it provided for inquiry classes for non-Catholics.

O'Hara was a pioneer in recognizing the role of women in the church. For many years women were allowed to be only "auxiliary members," not full and active members, of the CCD. O'Hara considered this unjust because the majority of the workers were women. He wrote to the Sacred Confraternity of the Council to protest the rule and in July 1936 received a response that full active membership would from that time be open to women, and that Pius XI himself approved of the leadership roles for women in O'Hara's organization of the CCD in America. O'Hara's appreciation of the role of women in the church was remarkable at a time when few other bishops recognized the contribution of women in the church.[67]

In 1930, O'Hara was appointed bishop of Great Falls, Montana. He wanted his diocese to be a model for rural ministry and the implementation of the confraternity. In time, O'Hara realized that an independent center for the CCD under the auspices of the NCWC was necessary. At the national convention of the NCRLC and the CCD in St. Paul, Minnesota, November 1934, the delegates passed a proposal requesting the host, Archbishop John Gregory Murray, to petition that an Episcopal Committee be established for the CCD. On November 14, 1934, the hierarchy of the United States so voted, and the following day the administrative committee appointed O'Hara chair of the Episcopal Committee. Establishing the headquarters in Washington, D.C., clarified the nature of the CCD as a national program.

Archbishop Murray himself had become an enthusiast regarding the CCD. He invited the priests and people of the archdiocese to attend the convention in St. Paul.[68] As noted in the seminary *Register* that year: "November 7th. Students attend afternoon sessions of the Rural Life Conference and the Confraternity of Christian Doctrine exhibit at the

Lowry Hotel."[69] Permission to go to a hotel downtown was extraordinary for seminarians in the 1930s.

O'Hara realized that the old Douay-Rheims translation of the Bible was not user-friendly for CCD programs, and that a new translation was required. He invited a group of scripture professors to meet in 1935 to set the process in motion. In 1936, under O'Hara's leadership, seventy-eight scripture scholars at the CCD meeting in New York formed the Catholic Biblical Association. The Confraternity Edition of the Bible was the result. O'Hara was also instrumental in the founding of the *Catholic Biblical Quarterly* in 1939. That same year he was elected president of the Catholic Association for International Peace. O'Hara was convinced that the renewal of the church was multi-faceted, and he became a link connecting many of the movements. In 1939, O'Hara was installed as bishop of Kansas City, Missouri. He continued his efforts in rural ministry, catechetics, scripture studies, the liturgical movement, and international peace. In the mid-1950s, he opened the first racially integrated health facility in Kansas City.

O'Hara, however, never lost his concern for the importance of rural ministry. In January 24, 1954, he visited the Saint Paul Seminary for the last time, addressing the student body on "Catholic Rural Life" and on "The Lay Apostolate." The next day he preached at the Pontifical High Mass on the Feast of the Conversion of St. Paul on the "Life and Work of Blessed Pius X."[70]

The following June, O'Hara was appointed archbishop *ad personam*—an honor bestowed on a bishop who, although not the head of an archdiocese, is named an archbishop as a personal honor for all the work he has done. He died unexpectedly on September 11, 1956, in Milan, Italy, en route to a meeting of the International Congress of the Restored Liturgy in Assisi, Italy. O'Hara was an organizational genius, and instrumental in the spread of the CCD to almost every parish in every diocese in the United States.[71] Because he was something of a "Renaissance man" his contributions are significant not only for rural ministry and catechetics, but in all of the areas discussed in this chapter. Bishop Raymond Lucker, retired bishop of New Ulm, Minnesota, knew O'Hara, admired him, and offered the following reflection:

> He was an extraordinary person. He was very involved in almost every major renewal movement touching the life of the Church during the fifty years of his active ministry and was a

> personal and major player in them. He was instrumental in preparing the Church in this country for the renewal that took flesh during the Second Vatican Council.[72]

Lucker concluded, "He was gifted, and he used those gifts in a brilliant and remarkable way. We in this archdiocese and millions through the country have been blessed by his ministry. We are proud that he was an alumnus of the Saint Paul Seminary."[73] Lucker was one of many bishops and priests influenced by O'Hara who themselves helped to develop ministries in rural areas. Lucker's contribution to religious education will be discussed later.

Another alumnus of the Saint Paul Seminary, Bishop Vincent J. Ryan of Bismarck, North Dakota (ordained in 1912), became national president of the NCRLC in 1941. He co-authored the book *Manifesto of Rural Life* emphasizing the dignity of the farmer. He was an advocate of scientific methods of farming.[74]

Concern for rural ministry and religious education was viewed from a broader perspective with the advent of ecumenism in the 1960s. The six seminaries in Minnesota—Bethel Seminary, Luther Theological Seminary, Northwestern Lutheran Theological Seminary, St. John's University Theological Faculty, Saint Paul Seminary, and United Seminary of the Twin Cities—began working together on an informal basis. In 1971 a formal agreement was signed with the title "Consortium of Minnesota Seminary Faculties," an important step for the purpose of applying for grants.[75]

An early project in which this group was involved that was especially welcome in rural areas was "An Interseminary Audio-Visual Project in Continuing Education." It was an effort to provide what would today be labeled "distance learning" to pastors in the five-state area who would not have lectures or courses available to them locally. The audio-visual facility at the Saint Paul Seminary in the new Brady Educational Center offered state-of-the-art television and radio recording services. A package of video or audio tapes of lectures of professors from the various seminaries was made available to clergy—a new approach to continuing education for clergy and religious educators.

In May 1973, President Malcom Moos of the University of Minnesota invited Msgr. William Baumgaertner to chair the university's newly-constituted Task Force on Religion. As a land grant institution, the university was required to offer a program or course annually on rural life for the benefit of the clergy. The purpose of the task force was to address issues that arose from the relationship of the university to the religious denominations in Minnesota. The Annual Report in 1972–1973 stated: "The University of Minnesota through the Agricultural Extension Division continues to cooperate generously with the seminaries in offering an annual course on ministry in rural areas." Baumgaertner recalls that the first sessions which he attended were well received. In retrospect he believes that because the consortium designed the programs without first surveying the people in the field and inviting suggestions, it probably did not have as much success as had been hoped.[76]

Consortium courses in rural ministry continued to be offered in the 1980s, but a resurgence of interest evolved in the early 1990s. With an initial grant from the Lilly Endowment a committee was formed[77] that heeded Msgr. Baumgaertner's advice to listen to the needs of the people on the local level. They developed a proposal titled "Northland Ministry Partnership: Theological Education for Town and Country Renewal." As of 1996, over $140,000 in grants was received from the Otto Bremer Foundation for courses, topical conferences, faculty development, and program support. The objectives of the Northland Ministry Partnership are: (1) strengthening the church's witness to justice in agriculture, the treatment of the land, and justice in the community; (2) strengthening the church's contribution to the renewal of the community and the health of the land; (3) strengthening the church's witness to sustainable, and therefore just, futures.[78]

The Northland Ministry Partnership of the Minnesota Consortium continues to offer a rural immersion seminar annually. Although only a small number of students from the Saint Paul Seminary have availed themselves of the opportunity, those who have speak highly of it. Father James Golka, ordained for the Grand Island Diocese in Nebraska in 1994, reflected:

> The experiential aspect of going to a rural setting was important. . . . People ask different questions when they are sitting in a different setting. The course helped me to understand the financial and emotional struggles confronting people in rural areas and understand their questions from a vantage point I otherwise could not have known. Significant themes like "Bigger isn't better" and "It's in the small and insignificant places that God

can do extraordinary things" have stayed with me and have had a lasting impact on my preaching and ministry.[79]

A particular focus project was woman in rural ministry. A conference offered in three locations, titled "The Land and the People: Journeys of Women in Rural Ministry," was planned by a committee composed of five Protestant and three Catholic women—most of them active in pastoral ministry in rural areas. They developed a day of lecture, prayer, and sharing at Blue Cloud Abbey in Marvin, South Dakota, at Mount St. Benedict Center in Crookston, Minnesota, and at Assisi Heights Retreat Center in Rochester, Minnesota. The search for new programs to raise consciousness on rural ministry continues.

Preaching and Teaching the Gospel

One of the best known among the alumni of the Saint Paul Seminary, Archbishop Fulton J. Sheen, was born May 8, 1895, in El Paso, Illinois, the son of Newton and Delia Fulton Sheen. He was baptized "Peter," but adopted his mother's maiden name, "Fulton," and added "John" as his confirmation name.

Sheen began his studies for the priesthood at St. Viator's College and Seminary in Bourbonnais, Illinois, where he received a B.A. in 1916 and an M.A. in 1917. He completed his preparation for the priesthood at the Saint Paul Seminary from 1917 to 1919. Interestingly, he is "John F. Sheen" from the Diocese of Peoria on the official list in the *Register,* but where he is listed as a member of a seminar or recipient of a prize he is "Fulton J. Sheen."[80] He was ordained to the priesthood in Peoria, Illinois on September 20, 1919. Sheen recalled his seminary experience in his autobiography: "Bishop Edward Dunne sent me to St. Paul's Seminary in St. Paul, Minnesota, to finish my studies for the priesthood. These were the days of World War I; food was meager and I developed an ulcer which required an operation. The courses were extremely good, especially in sacred scripture, history, and moral theology." Sheen particularly remembered Father Missia:

> The music teacher of Gregorian chant had to train all of us, whether we had singing voices or not. I was among those who

Archbishop Fulton J. Sheen

> could hardly carry a key on a ring. . . . About twenty years later, however, when I returned to give a lecture in the auditorium in St. Paul, I was introduced by my music teacher, who praised me for my singing. I am sure the good man did not purposely lie; he just had a bad memory. They say that singing is everyman's birthright but it certainly never was mine. I didn't even sound good in the shower.[81]

After ordination Sheen was sent to the Catholic University of America where he earned the S.T.L. and the J.C.B. in 1920. He completed his Ph.D. at the University of Louvain in 1923 and studied in Rome in 1923 and 1924. He received the prestigious *Agrégé en Philosophie* for his doctoral dissertation, *God and Intelligence in Modern Philosophy: A Critical Study in the Light of the Philosophy of St.*

Thomas from Louvain in 1925. After only a year in pastoral ministry in the Diocese of Peoria, he joined the faculty of the Catholic University of America where he taught from 1926 to 1950.

In 1930 Sheen began a Sunday afternoon radio broadcast on NBC, the "Catholic Hour," which eventually had an audience of four million people. Some letters from the papal duchess Genevieve Brady to Archbishop John Gregory Murray provide insights into Sheen's life in this period and a further link to St. Paul.[82] American millionaires Nicholas and Genevieve Brady exerted great influence at the Vatican in the 1920s, contributing $12,000,000 to the Catholic Church over the years. Nicholas F. Brady died in 1930, and in 1937, Genevieve Brady married William J. Babington Macaulay, Irish ambassador to the Holy See. During the 1930s, she was a star on the social scene in Rome. Cardinals Pacelli, Bonzano, Gasparri, and Pizzardo, and Msgr. Spellman were regulars at her elegant dinners, as were Archbishop Murray and Father Sheen when they were in Italy.

Mrs. Brady wrote to Archbishop Murray on more than one occasion asking him to meet with Sheen. "Bishop Murray, will you be a good friend to Dr. Sheen? He needs an older priest so much, I think. You already are such a good friend, how wonderful your counsel would be."[83] Genevieve Brady Macaulay confided regularly in Archbishop Murray. This may explain why, upon her death in 1938, she bequeathed $68,824 each to Cardinal Eugenio Pacelli, later Pope Pius XII, and to the Right Reverend Fulton J. Sheen, and more than twice that much—$172,061—to Archbishop John Gregory Murray. Sheen traveled to St. Paul periodically and very probably visited with Murray at those times.

Sheen sometimes spoke to the students at the Saint Paul Seminary when in the Twin Cities.[84] Msgr. John Sweeney recalls one time in the 1960s when Bishop Sheen called the rector, Msgr. McCarthy, and asked if he could come and visit the seminary and speak to the faculty. McCarthy's task was to assemble the faculty for the occasion on very short notice.[85] In the spring of 1978, Archbishop Sheen was invited to give a lecture at the College of St. Thomas. Chauffeured by Father Vincent Yzermans, Sheen arrived at the seminary unannounced. The rector, Msgr. Baumgaertner, welcomed him and offered to open the chapel, which was closed for repair, but Sheen said there was no need. Yzermans recalls the story differently, but then describes how he and Sheen walked along the side of the chapel facing the Mississippi River and prayed the rosary together.[86]

A gifted orator, Sheen preached regularly at St. Patrick's Cathedral in New York. He was appointed auxiliary bishop of New York in 1951 and that year inaugurated a television series titled "Life is Worth Living," which reached about thirty million people weekly. As the first "Catholic televangelist," he became a popular figure with Catholics and non-Catholics alike in the post-World War II era. John Tracy Ellis reports that Sheen "consciously abandoned the life of a scholar for that of a preacher, realizing in a realistic way that it is impossible to serve both simultaneously." Ellis added that Sheen's "contribution . . . to the Catholic Church and to the general American public was incalculable."[87]

Sheen was known as one who was instrumental in the conversion to Catholicism of famous people, such as Claire Booth Luce, the wife of Henry Luce of *Time-Life,* who was U.S. ambassador to Italy from 1953 to 1957. Although she was a staunch Republican, when she introduced Archbishop Sheen to an audience in Phoenix, Arizona, in the 1970s she conjectured that very likely he was partly responsible for the election of John F. Kennedy to the presidency in 1960. She believed that Sheen's television programs, which were warm, inspiring, and intelligible, had broken down the hostility that many Americans had felt toward Catholics in the United States for more than two hundred years, and dispelled their fears regarding a Catholic in the White House.[88]

After serving as the national director of the Society for the Propagation of the Faith from 1950 to 1966, Sheen was appointed bishop of Rochester, New York, at the age of seventy-one. Three years later he resigned his see, was named a titular archbishop, and retired to New York City where he continued his preaching and writing until his death in 1979. He authored more than seventy books. Although Sheen was criticized on occasion for his dramatic techniques and his sometimes superficial approach to theology, he clearly had an impact on American culture as one who educated the United States regarding Catholicism—making it acceptable to be Catholic in the post-World War II era.

Thomas Edward Shields preceded Sheen at the Saint Paul Seminary, and—although not widely known—was an academic and an activist in developing methods for teaching the Gospel. Ordained from the Saint Thomas Aquinas Seminary in 1891, he joined the faculty of the Saint Paul Seminary in 1895 after receiving his Ph.D. in biology at Johns Hopkins University. His contribution to teaching grew out of his own unhappy experience as a young person of being perceived as a "dullard."[89] His analysis of the difficulties he faced led him, as professor of physiological psychology at the Catholic University of America from 1902, to make extraordinary contributions in the field of education.

Shields headed the Department of Education at the Catholic University, organized a Catholic Educational News Service, a Correspondence School for Catholic Teachers, founded and edited the *Catholic Educational Review,* wrote articles and books—including *Philosophy of Education,* founded and managed a publishing house, and produced a series of textbooks for primary schools. He is perhaps best known as founder and dean of the Catholic Teachers College, known as Sisters College, at Catholic University in 1911, an effort to provide quality college education to the many Catholic sisters who staffed the parochial schools in the United States.

Undergirding these many activities was his conviction regarding the relationship of biology to educational development, and the importance of the arts in education. He wrote perceptively:

> The first task of education is to bring the emotional life of the child... into subjection to law and under the control of the intelligence. Reading, writing and arithmetic are only tools, the skilled use of which will be helpful throughout life, but it is utterly absurd to think of them as fundamental. It is music and art which constitute the enduring foundation of education, and not the three R's. When this truth is forgotten it is not surprising that the effects of education are seen to be superficial and unsatisfactory.
>
> ...Next to the teaching of religion, the teaching of music and art constitutes the most important work in the elementary school....The real foundations of character are not found in the intellect but in the emotions and the will properly enlightened through the intellect, and it is through music and art that imagination and the emotions may be reached and effectively developed.[90]

Shield's friend and colleague, Dr. Justine Ward, applied his psychological and pedagogical principles to the teaching of music, and developed a method of teaching Gregorian chant to children which greatly enhanced the liturgy.

One of his successors stated that although his ideas may have seemed bizarre and impracticable when first presented, they had far-reaching effects. "Any future historian of Catholic education in the United States must view his [Shields] career and his labors as the turning point in the progress of our schools."[91] Shields died in 1921 at the age of fifty-nine.

Rudolph Bandas was ordained in 1921, the year Shields died. His many years of service at the seminary as professor and rector (1925–1958) have been described earlier. Noteworthy here are his contributions in the area of catechetics. Bandas was appointed archdiocesan director of the Confraternity of Christian Doctrine by Archbishop Murray in 1934 and organized the CCD in the archdiocese while also teaching theology and catechetics at the Saint Paul Seminary. This allowed for an integration of the theoretical and the practical in the lives of seminarians who were given opportunities to teach CCD and summer religious vacation school. Bandas was invited to teach a course on catechetical methods for high school teachers at the Catholic University of America and became internationally known for his publications, which were translated into European and Oriental languages.[92]

Raymond Lucker was assigned as an assistant to Bandas at the Confraternity of Christian Doctrine after ordination to the priesthood in 1952.[93] During his years at the Saint Paul Seminary he had earned a teaching certificate and an M.A. in church history, writing his thesis on Archbishop Thomas Langdon Grace, O.P., under the direction of Father Hugh Nolan, a historian on loan from the Archdiocese of Philadelphia.[94]

From 1952 to 1957, Lucker was assistant director of the CCD, resided at the seminary, and celebrated the daily Eucharist for the sisters at the seminary convent. In the fall of 1957, Lucker was appointed professor of catechetics at the seminary, and in January 1958, with the assignment of Msgr. Bandas to St. Agnes, Lucker was also appointed archdiocesan director of the CCD. Lucker had been taking courses in education at St. Thomas, and in 1957 was asked to begin a Ph.D. in education at the University of Minnesota. In the midst of his other obligations, he completed his doctoral courses in 1963 and began his dissertation on the church/state controversy regarding released time for the religious education of students in public schools.

Before he could complete the dissertation, however, Archbishop Binz sent him to the Angelicum in Rome to pursue a doctorate in theology. From 1964 to 1966, immersed in the excitement of the Vatican

Council, he completed his S.T.D., writing his dissertation on "The Aims of Religious Education in the Early Church and in the American Catechetical Movement." It was published by the Catholic Book Agency in Rome in 1966. Lucker wrote later, "That experience in Rome touched me to the core of my being."[95]

Returning to the faculty of the Saint Paul Seminary and still serving as director of the CCD, Lucker hoped he would be more involved in teaching theology. However, because Superintendent of Schools Msgr. Roger Connole's health was deteriorating, Lucker served as superintendent of education from 1966 to 1969. The 1960s was a crucial period for the Catholic schools because of the departure of many priests, sisters, and brothers and the influx of lay teachers and administrators who needed training in religious education. Finally, in the summer of 1968, Lucker returned to work on his Ph.D. dissertation.

In 1969, however, Lucker was asked by Cardinal John F. Deardon, first president of the National Conference of Catholic Bishops, and Bishop Joseph Bernardin to come to Washington, D.C., and head up a new Department of Education of the NCCB/USCC that would coordinate all education programs, not just the Catholic school system. This was, of course, Lucker's vision. In later years he reflected:

> For twenty years I was intimately associated with religious education. In particular, I was involved with the recruitment, training and formation of lay people who generously responded to the call of "handing on the faith" to children, youth, and adults in their parishes. Nothing is closer to my heart than this.[96]

During his years in Washington, Lucker received his Ph.D. from the University of Minnesota in 1969. Among other endeavors, he promoted the nationwide development of the CCD and the National Conference of Diocesan Directors of Religious Education.

In July 1971, Lucker was recalled to the archdiocese by Archbishop Byrne and subsequently appointed auxiliary bishop. With John Roach, he was ordained to the episcopacy on September 8, 1971. In December 1975, he was installed as bishop of the Diocese of New Ulm. For twenty-five years in New Ulm, Lucker continued his service to people both within and outside the diocese. In 1971 he was a delegate to the International Catechetical Congress in Rome. In 1977, he was elected by the bishops of the United States as a delegate to the Synod in Rome and as an alternate delegate in 1987.

Lucker was a regular attendee at the Catholic Theological Society of America conventions and an unofficial liaison to the NCCB on issues regarding the relationship between bishops and theologians. He was honored by them at their annual convention in Milwaukee in June 2001. Lucker never feared to raise controversial questions. He co-authored, with Bishop Victor Balke of the Crookston, Minnesota, diocese, a pastoral letter on the role of women in the church titled *Male and Female God Created Them* (1981), and challenged the Catholic Church to reconsider its age-old practice of the ordination of married men to the priesthood.[97] He served as president of Pax Christi in Minnesota and as episcopal advisor to the National Conference of Catechetical Leadership and to the National Association of Lay Ministry. His commitment to the church, his continuing theological study and research, the simplicity of his living in community, and his spirituality—especially in time of illness—illustrate how his promotion of religious education and evangelization were integrated into a life of service that continued to his death, September 19, 2001.

John Forliti was ordained and received an M.A. in education from the Saint Paul Seminary in 1962, just ten years after Raymond Lucker. In 1970, after eight years of pastoral work, he was assigned to the Archdiocesan Office of Religious Education, and served as director from 1973 to 1981. During that time he did a study on archdiocesan high school students (in Catholic schools and in the CCD programs), examining their values toward life, beliefs, and family. The inventory included questions regarding drugs, alcohol, and sex, plus attitudes toward parents and school. In 1976, Archbishop Roach approved a policy whereby sex education would be included in religion classes in Catholic schools. This required a solid curriculum, and Forliti began work with a pilot group in the archdiocese. It was values-based, video-assisted, and parent-involved. Video presentations, a valuable resource for teachers, were provided for the students. They also allowed parents to understand both the philosophy and content of what was being presented to the students.

Forliti also began work on a doctor of ministry degree at Luther Northwestern Seminary, and his research was integrated into that program. He received his D.Min. degree in 1980, having completed his dissertation titled "Reverence for Life and Family: Catechesis in Sexuality."[98] The video series titled "Reverence for Life and Family," consisting of fifteen one-hour sessions with three sessions for parents, was published by William C. Brown and Company. It became one of the most popular Catholic programs on sex education in the United States, Canada, and Australia. It was protested by some small but vocal groups of conservative Catholics.

In 1981, Forliti moved to the Search Institute in Minneapolis. He became director of programs and participated in national studies of high school and junior high school students in the public schools. The challenge was to translate data into programs. One of the programs that was developed was titled "Values and Choices." It focused on seven values, including equality, honesty, and promise-keeping. Forliti became involved in training public school teachers for the program. It was used in two thousand public school districts in the United States.

In 1985, Forliti was appointed vice-president of student affairs of the then College of St. Thomas and continued to exercise leadership in religious education by support of the Murray Institute and teaching in the MAPS program. In 1991 he was appointed pastor of St. Olaf in Minneapolis where he has encouraged the implementation of multimedia programs for religious education and evangelization. St. Olaf's provides television access to Sunday liturgies and produces "Generation Cross," a program aimed at young adults.

Gene Scapanski was a seminarian at Nazareth Hall while John Forliti was a student at the Saint Paul Seminary, but their paths did not cross for many years, except on the hockey field. Scapanski completed two years of study at the Saint Paul Seminary and received his B.A. in philosophy in 1964. Archbishop Binz then sent him to the Catholic University of America from 1964 to 1968 for his S.T.L. The documents of Vatican II had a profound impact on him, and Scapanski finally decided that he wanted to serve the church as a lay person and do further study on the role of the laity and the blossoming of ecumenism in the post-Vatican II period.

Scapanski then went to the Diocese of Richmond where he served as a parish religious education director; later he was appointed to the staff of the bishop of Richmond. During those years he collaborated with the Catechetical Office at the NCCB/USCC in Washington, D.C., where he came to know Msgr. Raymond Lucker. Scapanski had known of Lucker in St. Paul, and had always admired the history of the Archdiocese of St. Paul in the area of catechetics, beginning with Father Thomas Edward Shields. Scapanski was proud of that heritage.[99]

In the 1970s, the College of St. Thomas decided to establish a Center for Religious Education. Father Berard Marthaler, O.F.M. Conv., at the Catholic University of America recommended Scapanski, who was hired as the first director in 1975. The program began with non-credit courses and eventually developed a graduate program offering an M.A. in Catechetics and Liturgy with six areas of specialization. In 1983, the name of the degree was changed to the M.A. in Pastoral Studies (MAPS), and in that same year Scapanski was appointed dean of the MAPS degree program and continuing religious education.

In the early years of the center, Scapanski worked closely with Father John Forliti who was director of religious education for the archdiocese, and who believed it was to the advantage of all for the center to offer courses that were helpful for lay ministers in the area and beyond. Scapanski also collaborated with Father Robert Schwartz who was director of continuing education for priests in the archdiocese; together they developed and coordinated clergy institutes. At the celebration of the tenth anniversary of the founding of the center in 1985, fifty thousand people had participated in the various programs.

From 1986 to 1988, Scapanski and his family lived in Rome where he wrote his doctoral dissertation at the Angelicum, titled *The Role of the Laity in the Context of COMMUNIO and Mission in Selected Vatican and World Council of Churches Documents, 1967–1987.* In addition to an S.T.D., Scapanski received an award from the Pontifical Council for Promoting Christian Unity in Vatican City citing his thesis as the best doctoral thesis on an ecumenical topic written at a Roman university during the years 1988–1990.[100] During Scapanski's absence, Arthur Zannoni served as acting dean.

With the 1987 affiliation of the seminary to the College of St. Thomas and the formation of the School of Divinity, the MAPS degree and the Continuing Education programs were challenged by "program clarification" and financial constraints. In the early 1990s, the decision was reached that the School of Divinity would do only what other institutions were *not* doing regarding education of the laity. In addition to the MAPS degree, the three areas that were maintained were Be-Friender Ministry, "clergy institutes" (some expanded to include others in ministry) in collaboration with the archdiocese, and the National Association of Church Business Administrators (NACBA) certification program.

With the decision for administrative restructuring and the appointment of only one dean, Scapanski returned to full time teaching. In his current appointment as dean of the School of Continuing Studies at the University of St. Thomas, he continues in his tenured appointment at the School of Divinity, teaches courses occasionally, administers NACBA and works with clergy education.

Others have contributed to the commitment of the Saint Paul Seminary in religious education, including former dean Victor Klimoski whose expertise is in adult continuing education for the clergy, assistant dean Jan Viktora who is completing a doctoral dissertation on the qualities of leadership for ministry, and Sister Carol Rennie, O.S.B., certified with the National Teacher Education Program, who taught religious education in the M.Div. program. Graduates of the MAPS program now staff many of the parishes of the archdiocese and throughout the region, extending the enduring commitment of the Saint Paul Seminary School of Divinity to the theological formation of the people of God.

Building on Well-Laid Foundations—Institutes and Centers

The activity reported under the headings of social justice, liturgy, rural ministry and catechetics, and preaching and teaching the Gospel, is not the account of deeds done but of processes begun. The innovative and creative work done in these four areas of the Saint Paul Seminary tradition finds its reflection in more recent initiatives.

In 1992, the School of Divinity joined with the Graduate School of Education, Professional Psychology and Social Work of the University of St. Thomas, and the Catholic Education and Formation Ministries of the archdiocese, to establish the new Murray Institute. A $1,500,000 endowment established in the 1960s to honor Archbishop Murray enabled Catholic school teachers to receive scholarships to defray tuition at the (then) College of St. Thomas. The program was viewed as a way to cultivate the professional development of those staffing the extensive archdiocesan Catholic school system.

By the 1990s, the increase in graduate tuition did not allow sufficient financial support and few teachers were taking advantage of the opportunity. Thomas McCarver, dean of the School of Education, Professional Psychology and Social Work, recommended that the scholarship fund be refashioned into the Murray Institute. The endowment funds would be used to pay teachers' salaries and absorb tuition costs for the students, who would study in cohorts of thirty, and offer courses off campus when possible to eliminate overhead. Two cohorts commenced, leading to a Master of Arts in Curriculum and Instruction (MACI), a tuition-free degree offered to qualified teachers who had a track record of service in Catholic schools and who were willing to commit at least three years of continued teaching in these schools after graduation.

Many teachers and principals requested more theology. Some already had master's degrees in education. In 1995, a forty-five-credit program leading to a Master of Arts in Religious Education (MARE) and an Education Specialist certificate were developed. Administered by the Murray Institute, it is offered in conjunction with the School of Divinity and the archdiocese. The collaborative venture offers an integrated approach to the professional and spiritual development of the many teachers, volunteer catechists, and youth ministers in archdiocesan institutions.[101] Sister Mary Katherine Hamilton, I.H.M., served as director of the Murray Institute from 1993 to 2000, and was succeeded by Dr. Margaret Reif.

In addition to its degree programs, the School of Divinity also houses two important centers for study and pastoral care. BeFriender Ministry is an ecumenical program of pastoral formation that prepares people to provide the church's care and compassion in a variety of settings, such as parish, hospital, nursing home, or other community groupings. It is a ministry of listening presence, offering people spiritual and emotional support during times of need and transition in their lives.[102]

Unique to BeFriender Ministry is its undergirding model of mutuality that is a respectful recognition of gifts between people. BeFriender Ministry also provides a model for peer supervision. The thirty-five-hour foundational training program, focus courses, and ongoing support and consultation include a well-honed method of faith reflection that flows from the BeFriender's spiritual roots, adding depth and meaning to the BeFriending experience. With the leadership of director Mary Robinson (1985–2000) and associate director Sandra Skach (1989-1996), the program expanded to become a national center for training Protestant and

Catholic leaders in dioceses, judicatories, and parishes throughout the United States.[103] Gail Dekker, interim director, assisted by Barbara Schwery, Barbara Botger, and Joanne Hansen, continues this important outreach of the School of Divinity and also provides some internal programming for seminary students with workshops on domestic violence.

The Center for Jewish-Christian Learning was established at St. Thomas in 1985. It evolved following a trip to Jerusalem and Rome which Rabbi Max Shapiro and Msgr. Terrence Murphy took in 1983 accompanied by St. Thomas board members, the late Sidney R. Cohen, president of Norstan Corporation, and the late Thomas Coughlan, president of the Mankato Stone Company, and their wives. They shared a dream: They envisioned a special place where Jews and Christians could come together to understand and respect each other's traditions and points of view. It would be a place devoted to interfaith dialogue, a place where ethical, moral, and social issues could be discussed in frank and open exchange.[104] Rabbi Max A. Shapiro, rabbi emeritus of Temple Israel in Minneapolis, who holds a doctorate in education from the University of Cincinnati, became the first director of the center, which has succeeded far beyond expectations. Arthur Zannoni served as associate director from 1988 to 1991. Sandra Skach offered program assistance in the early years. Since 1989, the offices of the center have been located in the new School of Divinity complex.

In addition to offering courses, the center has presented major programs each fall and spring with lecturers such as the Hon. Abba Eban, Cardinal Joseph Bernardin, Elie Wiesel, and Rabbi Harold S. Kushner. Dialogues featured, among others, Dr. Eugene Borowitz and Father John Pawlikowski, Rabbi Chaim Potok and Father Andrew Greeley, Rabbi David Sapperstein and Father Robert Drinan, S.J., Dr. Paula Fredriksen and Father John R. Donohue, S.J. Numerous panel presentations included lecturers such as Dr. Clark Williamson; Father Edward Flannery; Rabbi Michael J. Cook; Sister Mary Boys, S.N.J.M.; Dr. Eugene Fisher; and Rabbi Lawrence Hoffman. From 1985 to 1996, the major presentations were published and were disseminated internationally. These *Proceedings of the Center for Jewish-Christian Learning* were edited by Arthur Zannoni (1985–1992, 1994) and Sister Mary Christine Athans, B.V.M. (1993, 1995–1996) with her assistant editor, Karen Schierman.[105]

A dialogue began in the early 1990s as to how the Jay Phillips Chair of Jewish Studies at Saint John's University in Collegeville,

Minnesota, and the Center for Jewish-Christian Learning at the University of St. Thomas could collaborate. In 1996, an agreement joined the two. Rabbi Shapiro retired and became director emeritus of the center. Rabbi Barry Cytron was appointed director of the new Jay Phillips Center for Jewish-Christian Learning of Saint John's University and the University of St. Thomas, and occupant of the Jay Phillips Chair. Cytron, who holds a Ph.D. in Jewish-Christian Relations from Iowa State University, was senior rabbi of Adath Jeshurun Synagogue in Minnetonka, and also taught in the theology departments of the two schools. Dr. John Merkle, professor in the theology department of the College of Saint Benedict/Saint John's University and a scholar in the Jewish-Christian dialogue, is associate director, and Karen Schierman, who came to the center in 1989, is program coordinator. The new center has continued to offer stimulating programs such as the series of five programs, "Exploring Questions of Life and Death," in 1999–2000.

In 1988 the School of Divinity of the University of St. Thomas became the first Catholic institution accredited by the National Association of Church Business Administrators (NACBA) to offer certification to church business administrators, and the first school north of the Mason-Dixon line to be so accredited. Dr. Gene Scapanski administers the program, one of six in the nation. NACBA is an interdenominational professional development organization dedicated to the professional development of church business administrators. Two ten-day seminars focus on topics such as personnel management, staff development, stewardship and financial management, legal and tax matters, theology and strategic planning.[106] In addition, certification candidates need to complete an approved parish-based project.

Although not directly connected to the School of Divinity, the Institute for Christian Life and Ministry (ICLM), an archdiocesan certificate program for lay ministry founded in 1997, is housed in the school. ICLM also coordinates the education component of the permanent deacon program of the archdiocese. The first program coordinator, Scott Hippert, an alumnus of the Saint Paul Seminary School of Divinity (M.Div., 1995), drew upon faculty of the school as institute teachers. Hippert was succeeded by another alumnus, Joseph Michalak (M.A. in theology, 1996) in 2000. The tradition of religious education, beginning with Fulton Sheen, lives on.

Conclusion

Social justice, liturgy, rural ministry and catechetics, and preaching and teaching the Gospel might be portrayed as colored threads that have been woven together to form a strong cord—the tradition of the Saint Paul Seminary School of Divinity. A cord, however, is only as strong as the threads that intertwine and support each other. The cord can provide for stability, but it must also allow for creativity. The roles played by Archbishop Ireland and James J. Hill, by Mary Mehegan Hill and Msgr. Louis Caillet were nothing short of creative in the founding of the institution.

Throughout these more than one hundred years, the seminary has enjoyed significant financial stability grounded in the wise management and endowment of the Hills. From the very start, the seminary has been the beneficiary of the spiritual and intellectual stability growing out of the vision of Archbishop John Ireland. Upon these foundations, the leadership of archbishops and rectors, of faculty, staff, and students, of lay benefactors who have given support in multiple ways, have all extended Archbishop Ireland's eloquent belief that those associated with the Saint Paul Seminary would be *"allies...for those who heal the wounds of suffering humanity, or strengthen the social bonds, and the institutions of the country."*

With the help of the Spirit, new chapters will be added to the history of the Saint Paul Seminary School of Divinity. While their content will recount new challenges, they will undoubtedly invite future generations to reflect on the question which Jesus asked the apostles and all who prepare for ministry that is depicted in the mural in the apse of the chapel: "Do you love me?"

Epilogue

Archbishop Dowling spoke eloquently about "the rhetoric of architecture" and of how buildings often represent the spirit of an age. The relationship of architecture to ecclesiology as it relates to the Saint Paul Seminary illuminates its history.

When giving a tour of the renamed "South Campus" of the University of St. Thomas that includes the Saint Paul Seminary School of Divinity, we often explain that the three red brick dormitories now used by the university were known as "Jim Hill's boxcars." The power house and one-time gymnasium that still stands and is now the service center of the university is reminiscent of an "engine house." The original administration building, razed to make way for the new Saint Paul Seminary complex, looked like a train station. How did these buildings make the Saint Paul Seminary unique?

They were built in the late nineteenth century in an era when almost all Catholic seminaries and motherhouses of religious congregations were constructed not as separate buildings but as one huge edifice. They often had multiple wings for the various groups being served, usually with the chapel extending back from the center entrance. In that setting, all of life could be lived under one roof. The complex was generally self-sufficient—social historians referred to it as a "total" institution. Other than ordering in necessities, there was little need to have contact with "the outside world." One need only look at St. Bernard's Seminary in Rochester, New York (1893–1981), St. Joseph's Seminary at Dunwoodie in New York (1896–), or St. Patrick's Seminary in Menlo Park, California (1898–), to have a sense of how these immense structures contributed to the "fortress mentality" of the church in that era. "Freestanding" seminaries, as they came to be known, were built on the presupposition that education for priesthood should take place in isolation, in a more monastic environment, rather than at the episcopal residence next to the cathedral as in the earlier days.

"Ultramontanism"—the centralization of the Catholic Church in Rome—had been on the increase since 1815. As the pope lost his temporal power, his spiritual power increased. By 1870, with the definition of papal infallibility at Vatican I and the loss of the papal states, the pope became known as "the prisoner of the Vatican." Catholics built bigger and better edifices in order to "defend themselves" by living in a self-contained world.

Archbishop John Ireland and James J. Hill had another vision of the church—an American frontier vision. They believed there was something healthy about the wide open spaces for one's physical, intellectual, and spiritual well-being. Although the seminary rules required a cloistered atmosphere not dissimilar to that in other seminaries, at the Saint Paul Seminary one had to go outside, move from building to building, appreciate the "fresh air," not only of the Minnesota seasons but of new approaches and new ideas. Archbishop Ireland believed the seminarians should study science and literature as well as philosophy and theology.

John Ireland's ecclesiology, influenced by Isaac Hecker and Orestes Brownson, envisioned the church in terms of organism and incarnation, growth and change, the relationship of the human and the divine. Ireland's emphasis was more on what the church "does" than on what it "is." He was an activist who believed that there should be "space" for activity. James J. Hill saw the seminarians as "bearers of salvation to human society on earth, as well as souls for life to come." Together Ireland and Hill built an institution which enjoyed a sense of intellectual curiosity and mission to a larger world.

As additional buildings were added to the Saint Paul Seminary—the Archbishop Ireland Memorial Library in 1950, Brady Educational Center and the McCarthy Recreation Building in 1968, and Binz Refectory in 1977—the "separate building" approach was maintained. When the old classroom building and dining hall were demolished, the mall was enlarged, providing for more space and openness.

With the affiliation to the University of St. Thomas, however, the architecture of the seminary took a somewhat different turn. The decision to replace the original administration building with a new residence hall and new administration center linked to the chapel by a central gathering space is reminiscent of the single edifice approach. The fact that it was sometimes called "Fort Froehle" in honor of the then rector,

Father Charles Froehle, and the courtyard referred to as "Froehle Field" may have inadvertently reflected this. The rector's office at a key location on the courtyard was affectionately referred to as "Checkpoint Charlie," but it also denoted a certain centralization.

Students, staff, and faculty all enjoy the new complex where the chapel is the center of the life of the school and there is ready access to offices, meeting rooms, and the residence. The seminarians hardly live in a "cloister." Classes in Brady Center, research in the library, meals in "the Binz," and sports in McCarthy Gym help them to fulfill John Ireland's injunction to get fresh air and exercise. Father Froehle has reflected, however, that it may be significant that in earlier years the chapel entrance opened to Summit Avenue—a symbol of preparing priests and lay ministers to "go out into the world." Today the entrance is into the gathering space.

This new, more self-contained seminary complex is not the isolated institution of years gone by. The seminary is an integral part of the larger University of St. Thomas with all the advantages and opportunities that offers, not the least of which is the financial safety net the university provides. The Teaching Parish program requires the students to be involved weekly in the local parish. Lay students, both in the School of Divinity programs and from the Minnesota Consortium of Theological Schools, bring diversity to the classroom.

Yet, in the later 1980s, as the search for priestly identity became more urgent for some, there was fear that the line between ordained and

Lay students Lincoln Wood, Julie McCarty, and Terry McCarty at social justice meeting

lay ministry could be blurred if formation for the ministries of the church was fully integrated. Although the permanent diaconate offices, vocation offices, BeFriender Ministry, and the Jay Philips Center for Jewish-Christian Learning are located at the Saint Paul Seminary School of Divinity, and lay students are welcomed in all of the programs, the increased number of seminarians—for whom the building is "home"—leaves no doubt as to the priority.

Is the new seminary building reminiscent to some degree of the more closed system of a century ago, reflective of the highly centralized church of the late twentieth century? The answer, I would suggest, is both "yes" and "no." The new complex is indicative of a modified Vatican II ecclesiology. In the past ten years there has been a movement to shore up the emphasis on centralized authority in the church. This has influenced how seminarians are educated in programs separate from those for lay formation, with an emphasis on priestly identity. At the same time, the welcoming atmosphere of the school to lay and religious faculty, staff and students, and the relationships within the larger university, remind one and all that a theology of the laity as well as a theology of priesthood undergird the mission of the school. John Ireland's injunction still holds true. The call to those preparing for both priestly and lay ministry is "to work for the whole people."

Appendix A

The Rectors of the Saint Paul Seminary

Louis Eugene Caillet	1894–1897
Patrick R. Heffron, D.D., J.U.D.	1897–1910
Francis J. Schaefer, D.D., Ph.D.	1910–1921
Humphrey Moynihan, S.T.D.	1921–1933
William O. Brady, S.T.D.	1933–1939
Lawrence O. Wolf, Ph.D.	1939–1943
James L. Connolly, Dr. Sc. Hist.	1943–1945
Rudolph G. Bandas, Ph.D. Agg., S.T.D. et M.	1945–1958
Most Rev. William O. Brady, S.T.D.	1958
Louis J. McCarthy, Ph.D.	1958–1968
William L. Baumgaertner, Ph.D.	1968–1980
Charles L. Froehle, S.T.D.	1980–1993
Phillip J. Rask, Ph.D.	1993–

Appendix B

The Faculty of the Saint Paul Seminary

Patrick H. Ahern, Ph.D.	1949–1965
Mary Christine Athans, B.V.M., Ph.D.	1984–
Rudolph G. Bandas, Ph.D. Agg., S.T.D. et M.	1925–1958
Joseph T. Barron, S.T.L.	1917–1926
Gerald Baskfield, S.T.D.	1933–1963
William L. Baumgaertner, Ph.D.	1949–1981
Ronald J. Bowers, J.C.D.	1983–
William O. Brady, S.T.D.	1926–1939
Eugene Bunnell, O.F.M. Conv., M.A.	1977–1983
Francis T. J. Burns, Ph.D., S.T.D.	1922–1935
William Busch, L.Sc. M. H.	1913–1938, 1945–1971
James J. Byrne, S.T.D.	1945–1946
James A. Byrnes, B.Ph.	1914–1919
J. Michael Byron, S.T.D.	1995–
Louis Eugene Caillet	1894–1897
Joseph Campbell	1896–1906
James F. Cecka, S.T.L.	1966–1969
P. Chareyre	1895–1896
Roger Connole, Ph.D.	1943–1949

James L. Connolly, Dr. Sc. Hist.	1928–1940, 1943–1945
Kevin Connor, S.T.L.	1996–1997
James J. Conry	1919–1921
Richard J. Cotter, D.D.	1897–1899
Thomas E. Crane, S.T.L., S.S.L.	1981–1984
Cornelius F. Cremin, S.T.L.	1909–1924
William Curtis, M.A.	1951–1956, 1958–1984
Douglas Dandurand, Ph.D.	1993–
Patrick Danehy	1895–1901
Alvin Daul	1935–1937
Dennis J. Dease, Ph.D.	1979–1985
Donald Dietz, O.M.I., S.T.D.	1979–1981
David A. Dillon, S.T.D.	1945–1946, 1949–1970
Jerome M. Dittberner, S.T.D.	1970–
Richard T. Doherty, S.T.D.	1938–1968
Richard A. Dorr, M.Div.	1977–1983
Mark B. Dosh, Ph.D.	1963–1979
Judith Dwyer, Ph.D.	1998–
John Echert, S.S.L.	1990–
Clyde E. Eddy, B.A.	1968–1977
James Englert, M.A.	1984–1985
Paul Feela, M.A.	1983–
Bernard Feeney	1902–1917
Peter Feldmeier, Ph.D.	1990–
Thomas Fisch, Ph.D.	1981–
Bernard M. Flynn, Ph.L.	1940–1945

Charles L. Froehle, S.T.D.	1968–1993
Leo Gans, J.C.D.	1905–1907
Patrick W. Gearty, Ph.D.	1966–1968
Francis J. Gilligan, S.T.D.	1928–1957
Patrick E. Griffin, B.A.	1972–1973
John C. Gruden, S.T.L.	1910–1938
Francis Hammang, D.Sc.Hist.	1938–1945
Jeremiah C. Harrington, S.T.B.	1918–1926
Mary Daniel Hartnett, C.S.J., M.A.	1977–1987
Ambrose B. Hayden, M.A.	1944–1951
Albert Heer, B.Ph.	1914–1921
Patrick R. Heffron, D.D., J.U.D.	1897–1910
Martin J. Hogan, D.D.	1904–1908
Daniel Hughes, Ph.D.	1904–1909
William C. Hunt, S.T.D.	1967–1981
William D. Jamieson, Litt. B.	1909–1924
David Jenkins, D.M.A.	1992–
Jan Michael Joncas, S.L.D.	1991–1998
Hilary Jordan, J.C.D.	1914–1919
T. E. Judge	1895–1897
Carole Kastigar, M.A.	1985–1986
Gerald Keefe, B.A.	1970–1979, 1991–1994
Diane Kennedy, O.P., D.Min.	1987–1990
Patrick Kennedy, M.Div.	1984–1994
John Kiebooms	1906–1910
Victor Klimoski, Ph.D.	1983–1999

Ellsworth Kneal, J.C.D.	1961–1983
David Kohner, M.Div.	1998–
Merle Kollasch, M.A.	1985–1987
Thomas Krenik, D.Min.	1989–1999
Valerie Lesniak, C.S.J., Ph.D.	1992–1995
Paul Lewis, Ph.D.	1999–2000
Andrew J. Loeffen	1912–1914
Raymond A. Lucker, S.T.D., Ph.D.	1957–1969
Charles R. Maloy	1909–1910
Lawrence Martin, M.A.	1983–1984
Mary Martin, M.A.	1987–
Louis J. McCarthy, Ph.D.	1936–1948, 1958–1968
William McDonough, S.T.D.	1986–1998
Thomas McKenna, M.A.	1975–1985
Jeanne McLean, Ph.D.	1999–
Francis S. Mingo, Ph.D.	1939–1943
Francis Missia, B.A.	1907–1955
Eugene J. Moriarty, J.C.D.	1942–1961
James Motl, O.P., Ph.D.	1985–
James W. Moudry, S.T.D.	1961–1989
Humphrey Moynihan, S.T.D.	1895–1904, 1921–1933
James H. Moynihan, Ph.D.	1932–1933
Peter Nickels, O.F.M. Conv., S.T.L., S.S.L.	1969–1983
Hugh J. Nolan, Ph.D.	1946–1949
Patrick F. O'Brien, A.M.	1915–1918, 1921–1927
Michael Patrick O'Connor, Ph.D.	1992–1995

Anatole Oster	1897–1902
John J. O'Sullivan, S.T.D.	1957–1971
Michael Papesh, D.Min.	1987–1988
Paul Perigord, M. A.	1907–1914
Garrett Pierse, D.D.	1910–1914
Stephen Pope, Ph.D.	1984–1988
James H. Prendergast	1921–1933
Jerome D. Quinn, S.T.L., S.S.L.	1963–1987
Patrick Quinn, T.O.R., S.T.D.	1986–1989, 1996–
Philip J. Rask, Ph.D.	1977–
James Reardon	1899–1909
George B. Reid, S.T.L.	1901–1906
Carol Rennie, O.S.B., M.A.	1986–2000
John A. Ryan, S.T.D.	1902–1915
Lawrence F. Ryan	1945–1964
Patrick J. Ryan, S.T.D.	1964–1977
Leonard Sagenbrecht, M.A.	1985–1986
Paul Therese Saiko, S.S.N.D., M.A.	1986–
John P. Sankovitz, M.A.	1965–1975
Gene Scapanski, S.T.D.	1979–
Francis J. Schaefer, D.D., Ph.D.	1895–1921
Francis J. Schenk, J.C.D.	1934–1942
Katarina Schuth, O.S.F., Ph.D.	1991–
Robert Schwartz, S.T.D.	1986–1991
Sue Seid-Martin, M.A.	1987–1994
John Seliskar, Ph.D.	1901–1932

Dominic Serra, S.L.D.	1989–2000
Thomas J. Shanahan, M.A.	1931–1943,1947–1969
William Henry Sheran	1899–1909
Thomas Edward Shields, Ph.D.	1895–1898
Thomas Sieg, S.T.L.	1979–1985
Louis Simon	1895–1898
Ladislaus S. Sledz, Ph.D.	1947–1957
Mark Smith, Ph.D.	1984–1986
Joseph Soentgerath, D.D.	1895–1896
Stanley Srnec, B.A.	1964–1970
Elizabeth Abeler Stodola, M.A.	1979–1983
David Stosur, M.A.	1989–1992
Nicholas Stubinitzky	1901–1908
Patrick A. Sullivan	1908–1913
John A. Sweeney, B.A.	1945–1977, 1987–1999
John Szarke, M.A.	1985–1990
Leo J. Tibesar, M.A.	1977–1987
Patrick J. Toner, S.T.L.	1899–1904
Samuel Torvend, O.P., Ph.D. (cand.)	1987–1989
William Turner, D.D.	1895–1904
Jan Viktora, Ed.D.	1985–
Paul Waldron, Ph.L., J.C.B.	1915–1918
Lawrence O. Wolf, Ph.D.	1926–1928, 1929–1975
John Wolfe, D.D.	1919–1922
Seung Ai Yang, Ph.D.	1998–
Bernard Yetzer, S.T.D.	1977–1996

Arthur Zannoni, M.A.	1986–1991
Aloysius Ziskovsky, S.T.B.	1904–1932
George Ziskovsky, S.T.D.	1932–1963

Reverend Robert Hart (ordained 2000), who served as my research assistant from 1998 to 2000, compiled this list of full-time faculty from the catalogues of the Saint Paul Seminary and the Saint Paul Seminary School of Divinity from 1895 to the present. Included are the years of service and highest degree(s) that each faculty member had while teaching at the seminary. We apologize for any errors or omissions.

Notes

Chapter 1—Laying the Foundation: Joseph Cretin

1. Thomas O'Gorman, "Laying of the Corner Stone of Seminary Chapel," The Saint Paul Seminary, St. Paul, Minnesota, July 2, 1901, in *The Diocese of St. Paul: The Golden Jubilee 1851–1901* (St. Paul: The Pioneer Press [1901]), p. 90. See also *The Saint Paul Seminary Register* (1902), p. 45. (Hereafter *Register.*)

2. Roger Aubert, *The Church in a Secularized Society* (New York: Paulist Press, 1978), p. 26. Pius IX was beatified by Pope John Paul II on September 3, 2000.

3. James Reardon, *The Catholic Church in the Diocese of St. Paul* (St. Paul, Minnesota: North Central Publishing Company, 1952), p. 66.

4. John Ireland, "Life of Bishop Cretin," *Acta et Dicta: A Collection of Historical Data Regarding the Origin and Growth of the Catholic Church in the Northwest* (St. Paul, Minnesota: The Catholic Historical Society of St. Paul), Vol. IV, No. 2 (July 1916): 216. (Hereafter, *Acta et Dicta.*)

5. William M. Thompson, introduction, *Bérulle and the French School: Selected Writings,* ed. William Thompson (New York: Paulist Press, 1989), pp. 3–26.

6. Susan A. Muto, preface to *Bérulle and the French School: Selected Writings,* ed. with intro. by William M. Thompson, xvi.

7. Joseph M. White, *The Diocesan Seminary in the United States: A History from the 1780s to the Present* (Notre Dame, Indiana: University of Notre Dame Press, 1989), p. 14.

8. Eugene A. Walsh, *The Priesthood in the Writings of the French School: Bérulle, De Condren, and Olier* (Washington, D.C.: Catholic University of America Press, 1949), p. 114, as quoted in White, p. 15.

9. White, p. 15.

10. Ireland, *Acta et Dicta,* Vol. V, No. 1 (1917): 7.

11. Ireland, *Acta et Dicta,* Vol. V, No. 1 (1917): 7–8.

12. Joseph Connors, *Journey Toward Fulfillment* (St. Paul, Minnesota: College of St. Thomas, 1986), p. 2. In 1883 it was merged into the College of Bourg.

13. Ireland, *Acta et Dicta,* Vol. V, No. 1 (1917): 46.

14. Ireland, *Acta et Dicta,* Vol. V, No. 2 (July 1918): 181–189.

15. M. M. Hoffman, *The Church Founders of the Northwest* (Milwaukee: Bruce Publishing Company, 1937). See especially Chapter 2, pp. 6–20.

16. From the *Northwestern Chronicle* as quoted in J. Fletcher Williams, *A History of the City of Saint Paul to 1875* (St. Paul: Minnesota Historical Society Press, 1983), p. 115. First published in 1876. (Hereafter, *NC.*)

17. Hoffman, pp. 246–247.

18. Virginia Brainard Kunz, *Saint Paul: The First 150 Years* (St. Paul: The St. Paul Foundation, 1991), pp. 18–20.

19. J. Fletcher Williams, *A History of the City of Saint Paul and the County of Ramsey, Minnesota* (St. Paul: Minnesota Historical Society, 1876), pp. 312–313.

20. M. Jane Coogan, B.V.M., *The Price of Our Heritage* (Dubuque, Iowa: Mount Carmel Press, 1975), p. 258. The "B.V.M.s" were invited one hundred years later in 1951 by Archbishop John Gregory Murray to staff Our Lady of Peace High School (1951–1973) and continue to serve in the archdiocese.

21. Helen Angela Hurley, *On Good Ground: The Story of the Sisters of St. Joseph in St. Paul* (Minneapolis: University of Minnesota Press, 1951), pp. 19–20. See also Reardon, pp. 77–78.

22. Reardon quotes J. M. Newson in "Pen Pictures of St. Paul and Biographical Sketches of Old Settlers" published in 1886, p. 269. See also Connors, p. 2. Ireland mentions in his "Life of Bishop Cretin" that Ravoux used to refer to Cretin's concern about his girth.

23. A[natole] Oster, "Personal Reminiscences of Bishop Cretin," *Acta et Dicta,* Vol. I, No. 1 (1907): 73.

24. White, p. 6.

25. Connors, p. 4.

26. "Letters of Daniel J. Fisher—A Seminarian in St. Paul," *Acta et Dicta,* Vol. I, No. 1 (July 1907): 45–46, 48.

27. Reardon, p. 90.

28. O'Gorman, p. 90.

29. Ireland, *Acta et Dicta,* Vol. V, No. 1 (1917): 14.

30. Oster, *Acta et Dicta,* Vol. I, No. 1 (1917): 74–75, 77, 81.

31. H. Moynihan, "Father Caillet," in *Some Letters of Monsignor Louis E. Caillet and August N. Chemidlin,* ed. Clara Hill Lindley (Saint Paul 1922), pp 6, 7. Published for private circulation. (Hereafter, Lindley, ed., *Letters.*)

32. Reardon, p. 111.

33. Marvin O'Connell, *John Ireland and the American Catholic Church* (St. Paul: Minnesota Historical Society Press, 1988), pp. 35–36. (Hereafter, "O'Connell" refers to this volume. Other works by Marvin O'Connell cited will be identified as such.)

2. Dreams for the Future: Thomas Langdon Grace, O.P.

1. Reardon, p. 167.

2. Raymond A. Lucker, "Some Aspects of the Life of Thomas Langdon Grace, Second Bishop of St. Paul." Unpublished M.A. thesis, the Saint Paul Seminary, 1952, p. 21. See also Hoffman, p. 361.

3. Johann Fayolle to Joseph Fayolle, Vicar of Le Puy, France, November 9, 1858, as quoted in Lucker, p. 21.

4. Victor Francis O'Daniel, *The Dominican Province of St. Joseph* (New York: Holy Name Society, 1942), p. 210. His mother's maiden name was also "Grace."

5. O'Daniel, pp. 210–211. Lucker gives the date of his reception of the Dominican habit as June 13, 1830, whereas Reardon lists it as June 10, 1830.

6. Reardon, p. 139.

7. Lucker, p. 16.

8. Reardon, p. 119.

9. Connors, p. 7.

10. As quoted in Reardon, p. 158.

11. O'Connell, pp. 68–69.

12. *Minnesotian and Times,* February 26, 1860, as quoted in Lucker, p. 76.

13. Lucker, pp. 77–78.

14. Reginald M. Coffey, O.P., *The American Dominicans: A History of St. Joseph's Province* (New York: Saint Martin de Porres Guild, 1970), p. 510.

15. O'Connell, p. 66.

16. Reardon, p. 159.

17. Reardon, pp. 159–160.

18. Ann Thomasine Sampson, C.S.J., *Seeds on Good Ground* (St. Paul: Sisters of St. Joseph of Carondelet, St. Paul Province, 2000), p. 349.

19. Connors, p. 9.

20. Reardon, p. 167.

21. O'Connell, p. 200.

22. Ralston J. Markoe, "Some Reminiscences of Old St. Paul's Seminary in the Early Days," October 18, 1908. Ralston Markoe Papers, Archives of the Archdiocese of St. Paul and Minneapolis (AASPM), as quoted in Connors, p. 9.

23. See Connors, pp. 11–17.

24. Connors, p. 16.

25. *NC,* December 13, 1873.

26. Connors, p. 25.

27. Reardon, p. 184.

28. O'Connell, pp. 132–133.

29. Reardon, p. 187.

Chapter 3—From Vision to Reality: John Ireland

1. Marvin O'Connell's *John Ireland and the American Catholic Church* is a thorough presentation of Ireland's life and career.

2. Reardon states (p. 213) that the baptismal record indicates that John Ireland was baptized on September 11, 1838, but the certificate gives no date of

birth. O'Connell presumes (p. 9) that Ireland was baptized the day he was born, as was the custom, because no other date is given.

3. O'Connell, p. 8.

4. O'Connell, p. 8.

5. O'Connell, p. 17. William Quarter, the first bishop of Chicago, had established the fledgling institution in 1844. It closed in 1870 but was reopened in Mundelein, Illinois, in 1921. See Philip Gleason, "Chicago and Milwaukee: Contrasting Experiences in Seminary Planting," in *Studies in Catholic History in Honor of John Tracy Ellis,* ed. Nelson H. Minnich, Robert B. Eno, and Robert F. Trisco (Wilmington: Michael Glazier, 1985), pp. 150–151.

6. See O'Connell, p. 18.

7. O'Connell, p. 42.

8. O'Connell, pp. 42–43.

9. Marvin O'Connell, "Meximieux and Mr. Hill: John Ireland's Dream Come True," Centennial Address, The Saint Paul Seminary School of Divinity of the University of St. Thomas, September 8, 1994, p. 5. Hereafter, O'Connell, Centennial Address.

10. O'Connell, p. 52.

11. O'Connell, pp. 49–50.

12. O'Connell, p. 52.

13. Ireland, *Acta et Dicta,* Vol. IV, No. 2 (July 1916): 207.

14. O'Connell, p. 56.

15. O'Connell, pp. 58–59.

16. "The Education of a Priest: Archbishop Ireland's Talks to Seminarians," compiled and with introduction by John F. Duggan, *The Ecclesiastical Review,* Vol. 101 (October 1939): 395. (Hereafter, Ireland, "The Education of a Priest.")

17. James P. Shannon, ed., "Archbishop Ireland's Experiences as a Civil War Chaplain," *Catholic Historical Review* 39 (1953): 302.

18. Shannon, p. 305.

19. O'Connell, pp. 88–114.

20. See James P. Shannon, *Catholic Colonization and the Western Frontier* (New Haven: Yale University Press, 1957). See also O'Connell, pp. 135–161.

21. Reardon, pp. 193–197.

22. Gerald P. Fogarty, S.J., *The Vatican and the American Hierarchy from 1870 to 1965* (Collegeville, Minnesota: The Liturgical Press, 1982), pp. 27–32.

23. Fogarty, p. 31.

24. Fogarty, p. 33.

25. John Ireland, "The Church—The Support of Just Government," *A History of the Third Plenary Council of Baltimore: November 9–December 7, 1884* (Baltimore: The Baltimore Publishing Company, 1885), p. 32. See also John Ireland, "The Church and Civil Society," *The Church and Modern Society* (New York: D.W. McBride and Company, 1903), I: 27–65.

26. Ireland, "The Church—The Support of Just Government," p. 19.

27. John Lancaster Spalding, "University Education," *A History of the Third Plenary Council of Baltimore* (Baltimore: The Baltimore Publishing Company, 1885), p. 81.

28. Spalding, p. 99.

29. *NC* (December 4, 1884), p. 4.

30. Connors; see especially pp. 1–88.

31. O'Connell, p. 206.

32. Connors, p. 35.

33. Connors, p. 36.

Chapter 4—If It Hadn't Been for a Woman . . .

1. James J. Hill, Address at the Dedication of the Saint Paul Seminary, September 4, 1895. (Hereafter, James J. Hill, Dedication Address.) James J. Hill Papers, Hill Reference Library, St. Paul (JJHP).

2. James J. Hill, Dedication Address.

3. The biographical sketches of James J. Hill and Mary Theresa Mehegan Hill presented here are based on material in the James J. Hill Reference Library, St. Paul, Minnesota, and in Clara Hill Lindley, *James J. Hill and Mary T. Hill: An Unfinished Chronicle by Their Daughter* (New York: The North River

Press, 1948); Albro Martin, *James J. Hill and the Opening of the Northwest* (New York: Oxford University Press, 1976); Joseph Gilpin Pyle, *The Life of James J. Hill* (New York: Doubleday, Page and Company, 1917), 2 vols.; and Michael P. Malone, *James J. Hill: Empire Builder of the Northwest* (Norman, Oklahoma: University of Oklahoma Press, 1996).

4. Lindley, p. 46

5 Lindley, pp. 49–50.

6. Martin, p. 61.

7. Pyle, I: 61.

8. Martin, p. 61.

9. Lindley, p. 79.

10. Lindley, p. 80.

11. Lindley, p. 80.

12. Martin, pp. 63–64. See also Lindley, p. 84.

13. Lindley, p. 14.

14. Martin, p. 16.

15. Pyle, I: 15.

16. Martin, p. 11, #14.

17. Lindley, pp. 18–21.

18. Malone, p. 12.

19. Howard Leigh Dickman, *James Jerome Hill and the Agricultural Development of the Northwest.* Unpublished Ph.D. dissertation, University of Michigan, 1977, ix–x.

20. *Midway News,* September 6, 1890, p. 3.

21. Lindley, ed., *Letters,* p. 23.

22. As quoted in Martin, p. 84.

23. Lindley, ed., *Letters,* pp. 29–36.

24. "Called Home by His Master," St. Paul *Pioneer Press,* Nov. 29, 1897.

25. Lindley, ed., *Letters,* pp. 116–117. Emphasis mine.

26. James J. Hill, Dedication Address.

Chapter 5—"The Hill Seminary"

1. *Midway News,* September 6, 1890, p. 3.

2. Reardon, p. 309.

3. Patrick Danehy, "The New Seminary of St. Paul," *Catholic University of America Bulletin,* Vol. 1, No. 2 (April 1895): p. 219. (Hereafter, *CUA Bulletin.*)

4. Building Permit No. 28435 issued to James J. Hill, September 13, 1892.

5. John Ireland to Louis Caillet, March 30, 1892, John Ireland Papers (JIP), AASPM.

6. John Ireland to James J. Hill, May 15, 1892. Seminary Papers, JJHP.

7. In the same letter, Ireland wrote to Hill: "I have been most successful in all matters. An American character is impressed to-day as never before upon the church in the United States. I know your convictions in this regard, and I am sure that you will hear this news with pleasure."

8. O'Connell, p. 383.

9. O'Connell, p. 384.

10. Copy of the original bid. Seminary Papers, JJHP.

11. Unsigned memo, Cass Gilbert Papers (CGP), Minnesota Historical Society (MHS).

12. Sharon Irish, "West Hails East: Cass Gilbert in Minnesota," *Minnesota History* 53, 5 (Spring 1993): 199.

13. James J. Hill to Cass Gilbert, December 12, 1892. CGP, MHS.

14. W. A. Stephens to Cass Gilbert, December 20, 1892. Seminary Papers, JJHP.

15. Cass Gilbert to James J. Hill, September 29, 1894. CGP, MHS.

16. Cass Gilbert to James J. Hill, December 31, 1894. Seminary Papers, JJHP.

17. F. E. Ward to Cass Gilbert, February 5, 1895. CGP, MHS. Handwritten note on bottom of letter reads: "Jany [unclear] 5th 1895. Rec'd by hand. Receipt handed me with check stated that this am't [500.00] was in full 'to date.' I declined to sign it—and the clerk took it back and returned in a few minutes with the words 'to date' omitted."

18. Cass Gilbert to James J. Hill, February 6, 1895. Seminary Papers, JJHP.

19. John Talbot Smith, *Our Seminaries: An Essay on Clerical Training* (New York: William A. Young and Company, 1896), p. 66.

20. Danehy, *CUA Bulletin* (April 1895), pp. 217–218.

21. *Register* (1896), pp. 9–10.

22. Danehy, *CUA Bulletin* (April 1895), p. 219.

23. *Register* (1896) [n.p.]. Described under "The Buildings."

24. Danehy, *CUA Bulletin* (April 1895), p. 219.

25. Frank Martin, et. al, "The St. Paul Seminary Campus: Building on Its Distinctive Past," Proposal, Hammel Green and Abrahamson, Inc.

26. As quoted in Danehy, *CUA Bulletin* (April 1895), p. 219.

27. Reardon, p. 310.

28. Vincent A. Yzermans, *Journeys: People and Places* (Waite Park, Minnesota: Park Press, 1994), p. 51.

Chapter 6—The Dedication

1. O'Connell, Centennial Address, September 8, 1994.

2. See Patrick H. Ahern, "A History of the Saint Paul Seminary," unpublished ms., n.d. [c.1944], p. 26, AASPM. This history was apparently written at the request of the then rector, James L. Connolly, for the fiftieth anniversary of the seminary. See also *Register* (1896), p. 37.

3. St. Paul *Pioneer Press,* September 6, 1894, p. 1.

4. John Ireland to James J. Hill, February 2, 1895. Seminary Papers, JJHP.

5. F. E. Ward to James J. Hill, August 20, 1895. JJHP, MHS.

6. James J. Hill to John Gordon, August 28, 1895. JJHP, MHS.

7. James J. Hill to W. C. Parrington, September 2, 1895. JJHP, MHS.

8. *NC,* September 6, 1895, p. 1.

9. See Ahern, p. 26, and *Register* (1896), p. 37.

10. "Hill Seminary Open," *Chicago Times,* September 4, 1895. Clipping in the JJHP.

11. *NC,* September 6, 1895, p. 1. See also Reardon, pp. 310–311.

12. Danehy, *CUA Bulletin,* p. 40.

13. Danehy, *CUA Bulletin,* p. 44.

14. Danehy, *CUA Bulletin,* p. 44.

15. Danehy, *CUA Bulletin,* pp. 44–45.

16. Danehy, *CUA Bulletin,* p. 45.

17. Cablegram, Mariano Rampolla to John Ireland, September 2, 1895. JIP, AASPM.

18. See James Gibbons correspondence in JIP, AASPM.

19. James Gibbons to John Ireland, September 4, 1895. JIP, AASPM.

20. *Register* (1896), p. 49.

21. *Register* (1896), p. 49.

22. *Register* (1896), p. 49.

23. *Register* (1896), p. 50.

24. *Register* (1896), p. 50.

25. *Register* (1896), p. 50.

26. *Register* (1896), p. 56. See also original, JJPH.

27. Malone, p. 19.

28. *Register* (1896), p. 57.

29. J. R. B. Kelley to James J. Hill, September 24, 1895. Seminary Papers, JJHP.

30. D. Willis James to James J. Hill, September 1895. Seminary Papers, JJHP.

31. Malone, p. 115.

32. D. Willis James to James J. Hill, September 1895. Seminary Papers, JJHP.

33. There is a typed notation at the end of this letter which states: "Mr. Hill directs that the above copy be sent to Archbishop Ireland."

Chapter 7—The Saint Paul Seminary: The Early Years

1. Ireland, "The Education of a Priest," p. 294. (Emphasis mine.)

2. John A. Ryan, *Social Doctrine in Action: A Personal History* (New York: Harper and Brothers, 1941), p. 45. Ryan stated: "My own economic views differed very considerably from those of a railroad president; nevertheless, I taught them for thirteen years in the seminary that Mr. Hill founded, without any objection from him or in his name."

3. James Gibbons, *Ambassadors of Christ* (Baltimore: John Murphy and Company, 1896).

4. Smith, *Our Seminaries: An Essay on Clerical Training.*

5. John Hogan, *Clerical Studies* (Boston: Marlier, Callanan and Company, 1898).

6. Gibbons, p. 170.

7. Smith, pp. 16–23.

8. Hogan, vi.

9. As quoted in White, p. 219.

10. Ireland, "The Education of a Priest." Three of Ireland's conferences were published in *Ecclesiastical Review,* Vol. 101 (1939): 289–300; 385–398; 494–504.

11. Ireland, "Education of a Priest," p. 294.

12. Ireland, "Education of a Priest," p. 295.

13. Ireland, "Education of a Priest," pp. 386–387.

14. Ireland, "Education of a Priest," p. 295. (Emphasis mine.)

15. See Dennis Dease, "The Theological Influence of Orestes Brownson and Isaac Hecker on John Ireland's Americanist Ecclesiology." Unpublished Ph.D. dissertation, Catholic University of America, 1978.

16. John Ireland, *The Church and Modern Society* (New York: D. H. McBride and Company, 1903) I: ix–x.

17. Dease, p. 64.

18. As quoted in Thomas E. Wangler, "The Ecclesiology of Archbishop John Ireland: Its Nature, Development, and Influence." Unpublished Ph.D. dissertation, Marquette University, 1968, p. 87.

19. Sermon by John Ireland at the episcopal consecration of Thomas O'Gorman, April 19, 1896, *Western Watchman* (St. Louis, Missouri), April 23, 1896, p. 1. AASPM. (Hereafter, Ireland, Consecration of O'Gorman.)

20. Ireland, Consecration of O'Gorman.

21. Ireland, Consecration of O'Gorman.

22. Daniel P. O'Neill, "The Development of an American Priesthood: Archbishop John Ireland and the Saint Paul Diocesan Clergy, 1884–1918," *Journal of American Ethnic History* (Spring 1985): 47–49.

23. John Ireland to Louis Caillet, February 14, 1892. JIP, AASPM.

24. John Ireland to Louis Caillet, March 14, 1892. JIP, AASPM.

25. Reardon, p. 312.

26. Lindley, ed., *Letters,* p. 115.

27. Lindley, ed., *Letters,* p. 22.

28. As quoted in James Moynihan, *The Life of Archbishop Ireland* (New York: Harper and Brothers, 1953), p. 244. The North American College was known as the American College in Rome in the nineteenth century.

29. Alfred Loisy to John Ireland, December 8, 1893, AASPM. As much as Ireland might have been intrigued with the idea of Loisy teaching at his seminary, it is unlikely that at that point he would have become immersed in yet another controversy with Rome.

30. Connors, p. 50.

31. See Ahern, pp. 63–67 on the first faculty.

32. Ahern, p. 66; see also Connors, p. 50.

33. Connors, pp. 104, 122.

34. See eulogy given at the funeral of Humphrey Moynihan, by James M. Reardon, Church of the Incarnation, Minneapolis, December 28, 1943. Copy on file in "Necrology of the Priests of the Archdiocese of St. Paul and Minneapolis," compiled by Leonard Leander and Jean Kimber, AASPM. (Hereafter NPASPM.) Reardon described Moynihan's role in the early days of the seminary: "He was assigned to the Chair of Apologetics, appointed prefect of studies to map out and correlate the curriculum, and became the virtual Rector of the Seminary in the formative years when it was nominally in charge of the beloved Msgr. Caillet." Reardon is conspicuously silent about Heffron in *The*

Catholic Church in the Diocese of St. Paul. Humphrey Moynihan was one of his teachers and apparently one of his heroes.

35. Connors, p. 122. See eulogy for H. Moynihan, NPASPM.

36. Ahern, p. 60; see also "Francis J. Schaefer," NPASPM. John Sweeney and William Baumgaertner still refer to him as "Germany Schaefer."

37. See "Patrick James Danehy," NPASPM. The material in this file differs from Ahern, who claims that Danehy did his post-graduate work in Paris.

38. Reardon, p. 320.

39. Connors, pp. 51, 129.

40. John A. Ryan, *Social Doctrine in Action,* p. 45.

41. Raymond A. Lucker, "Archbishop O'Hara: A Man of Vision for the Church," Centennial Lecture, the Saint Paul Seminary, November 10, 1994. Lucker shared stories about the early years of the seminary that he had been told by Anthony Kaesen, who had been a student from 1894 to 1901.

42. See Ahern, p. 23.

43. John A. Ryan, Diary, November 13, 1894, JARP, Archives of the Catholic University of America (ACUA).

44. Interview, Ambrose Hayden, August 20, 1993.

45. *Rules of the Saint Paul Seminary.* Approved by John Ireland, Archbishop of St. Paul, November 15, 1908, pp. 7–8. File, Rector's Office, Saint Paul Seminary (SPS). This is the earliest rule book available, although previous versions may have existed. (Hereafter, *Rules.*)

46. *Rules* (1908), p. 4.

47. *Rules* (1908), p. 9.

48. *Rules* (1908), p. 11.

49. *Rules* (1908), p. 11.

50. Ahern, p. 42.

51. *Register* (1919), p. 59.

52. *Register* (1897), p. 44; (1898), p. 29.

53. *Register* (1900), pp. 34–39.

54. White, pp. 237–239.

55. *Register* (1906), p. 59.

56. *Register* (1908), pp. 30–31.

57. Ahern, p. 24.

58. Emmet Henry Weber, "The Diocesan Seminary in St. Paul, Minnesota." Unpublished M.A. thesis, The Saint Paul Seminary, 1952, p. 98. See also *Register* (1897), p. 32.

59. Interviews with John Sweeney, January 20, 1998, and William Baumgaertner, September 16, 1998.

60. *Register* (1902), pp. 14–17.

61. *Register* (1908), pp. 16–18. See also White, p. 249.

62. Weber, pp. 107–113.

63. Danehy, *CUA Bulletin,* p. 221.

64. See John Ireland, Dedication Speech, AASPM, pp. 4–5, and Thomas O'Gorman, Dedication Sermon, *The Register (1896), The Saint Paul Seminary,* St. Paul, Minnesota, p. 42. JJHP.

65. John A. Ryan, *Social Doctrine in Action,* p. 58.

66. Weber, p. 87.

67. *Register* (1897), p. 40.

68. Ryan, *Social Doctrine in Action,* p. 58.

69. *Register* (1905), p. 45.

70. See *Registers,* 1897–1923.

71. *Register* (1898).

72. *Register* (1899).

73. Ahern, p. 50.

74. Bernard Feeney, *The Ideal Seminary,* ed. Jeremiah C. Harrington, intro. Austin Dowling (New York: Macmillan Company, 1923). Feeney died September 7, 1919.

75. Feeney, p. 16.

76. Feeney, p. 16.

77. F. A. Gasquet, "Some Impressions of Catholic America," *Dublin Review* CXXXVIII (April 1906): 87.

78. Gasquet, p. 87.

79. *Register* (1919), p. 61.

80. *Register* (1896), p. 32.

81. Minutes of the Meetings of the Board of Trustees and The Corporation of the St. Paul Seminary (September 17, 1895–October 12, 1955), May 12, 1897, p. 23. (Hereafter, Trustees, I.) A second ledger includes minutes from October 12, 1956, to January 26, 1970. (Hereafter, Trustees, II.) A third ledger includes minutes from June 17, 1970, to April 5, 2001. (Hereafter, Trustees, III.)

82. Trustees, I, p. 30.

83. Trustees, I, p. 24.

84. Trustees, I, p. 24.

85. Gasquet, pp. 86–87.

86. Volumes described are in the Rare Book Room of the Archbishop Ireland Memorial Library of the University of St. Thomas.

87. Trustees, I, p. 24.

88. O'Connell, pp. 154, 274–275.

89. *Register* (1897), p. 45.

90. Rita Watrin, *The Founding and Development of the Program of Affiliation of the Catholic University of America: 1912 to 1939* (Washington, D.C.: The Catholic University of America Press, n.d.), p. 6. ACUA.

91. From the Annual [CUA] Rector's Report, September 1895 (1895), p. 6, as quoted in Watrin. Keane was present at the dedication of the Saint Paul Seminary on September 4, 1995, and announced the affiliation in his speech on that occasion.

92. Danehy, *CUA Bulletin* (April 1895), p. 225.

93. *Register* (1912), p. 57.

94. Reardon, p. 313.

95. John Ireland to James J. Hill, February 5, 1895. Seminary Papers, JJHP.

96. *Register* (1897), p. 39.

97. *Register* (1901), pp. 39–40. See also Weber, p. 118.

98. *Register* (1901), pp. 39–40.

99. *NC,* June 18, 1904, as quoted in Weber, p. 118.

100. As quoted in Timothy Michael Dolan, *"Some Seed Fall on Good Ground": The Life of Edwin Vincent O'Hara* (Washington, D.C.: The Catholic University of America, 1992), p. 11.

101. Reardon, p. 315.

102. Reardon, p. 313.

103. John Ireland, "Education of a Priest," p. 295.

104. Interview with Patrick Keany, *Catholic Bulletin,* September 8, 1988, p. 14.

Chapter 8—Becoming Rooted in a Changing Church

1. John Ireland to Pastor of St. Peter's in Mendota, January 13, 1895. JIP, AASPM. This may have been a type of form letter because the "$59.00" and "Mendota" are written in different script and the ink seems to match the signature of Archbishop Ireland.

2. Weber, pp. 69–71.

3. Trustees, I, p. 3.

4. See Charter, JJHP.

5. Weber, p. 89.

6. Trustees, I, pp. 7, 12, 15.

7. Trustees, I, p. 11–12. See also Weber, p. 101, n. 110. Caillet accepted no salary for himself while he was rector. The first four months he accepted his salary so that he could donate it to the library; in the years that followed, he turned his salary back to the seminary.

8. T. J. Fortune to James J. Hill, December 18, 1894. JJHP.

9. Trustees, I, pp. 25, 74, 104.

10. *Register* (1896), pp. 34–36; (1898), n.p. [p. 2].

11. Trustees, I, pp. 14, 16.

12. *Register* (1896), p. 10.

13. Trustees, I, pp. 18–19.

14. Weber, p. 93. See clippings, Winona newspaper, and the *NC* at time of his death. AASPM.

15. Connors, p. 47.

16. Trustees, I, pp. 29–30, 33.

17. Malone, p. 188.

18. John J. Toomey to William C. Toomey, July 27, 1903. JJHP.

19. John J. Toomey to William C. Toomey, August 21, 1903. JJHP.

20. John J. Toomey to Patrick R. Heffron, August 8, 1904. JJHP.

21. John J. Toomey to Patrick R. Heffron, August 8, 1904. JJHP.

22. Patrick R. Heffron to John J. Toomey, August 17, 1904. JJHP.

23. Clara Graham, C.S.J., *Works to the King: Reminiscences of Mother Seraphine Ireland* (St. Paul, Minnesota: North Central Publishing Company, 1950), p. 51.

24. "1903—The St. Paul Seminary Domestic Department," Archives of the Sisters of St. Joseph of Carondelet, St. Paul Province, St. Paul, Minnesota. I am grateful to Mary Kraft, C.S.J., for locating this document for me. See also Weber, pp. 122–123, especially interview with Sebastian Cronin, C.S.J., n. 53: "Another task that the Sisters had was cleaning all the students' rooms during vacation: airing the mattresses and blankets, scrubbing the floors, and so on. They had twelve or fourteen women helping them."

25. Graham, p. 52.

26. Ahern, p. 34.

27. *Register* (1902), p. 45.

28. Mary Hill, Diary, July 2, 1901. JJHP.

29. "Jubilee of a Church," St. Paul *Dispatch,* July 2, 1901.

30. St. Paul *Pioneer Press,* February 17, 1997, 1B.

31. Paul Clifford Larson, *Minnesota Architect: The Life and Work of Clarence H. Johnston* (Afton, Minnesota: Afton Historical Society Press, 1996), p. xi.

32. Larson, p. 3.

33. Trustees, I, p. 45.

34. Trustees, I, p. 49.

35. Trustees, I, p. 51.

36. Trustees, I, pp. 54–55.

37. From E. C. Cecha, Pres. of the Minneapolis Trust Company to John J. Toomey, November 1, 1904. JJHP. Signature unclear.

38. *NC,* April 30, 1904, as quoted in Larson, p. 107.

39. *NC,* June 3, 1905, as quoted in Larson, p. 107.

40. Ahern, pp. 34–35. The cost of the chapel as of November 10, 1905, was $60,546.90. Trustees I, p. 64.

41. Sermon Delivered by Thomas O'Gorman, Bishop of Sioux Falls, on Occasion of the Consecration of St. Mary's Chapel, *Register* (1905), p. 68.

42. Trustees, I, p. 56.

43. Ahern, p. 42.

44. The bishops-elect in the order of their appointment were James O'Reilly for Fargo, J. J. Lawlor as auxiliary of St. Paul, Patrick R. Heffron for Winona, Timothy Corbett for Crookston, Abbot Vincent Wehrle, O.S.B. for Bismarck, and Joseph Busch for Lead (now Rapid City, South Dakota).

45. See *Acta et Dicta,* Vol. II, No. 2 (1910): 283–308; *Register* (1910), pp. 51–56; Reardon, pp. 389–392; and Ahern, pp. 37–40.

46. P. A. Sullivan, *Acta et Dicta,* Vol. II, No. 2 (1910): 297. A shorter version of this article was published in the *Register* (1910), pp. 51–56. Sullivan states that twelve hundred invitations were extended. Ahern, p. 39, states that: "In spite of the fact that admittance to the chapel was by invitation there were about 1,500 people assembled in addition to the crowds gathered outside, about 3,000 all told."

47. Reardon, p. 391.

48. *Register* (1910), p. 55.

49. *Register* (1910), p. 55.

50. Weber, pp. 104–105.

51. Weber, p. 130. See *NC,* July 23, 1904, and October 1, 1904, regarding his hospitalization.

52. *NC,* April 9, 1910.

53. Trustees, I, p. 77.

54. Trustees, I, pp. 83–84. See also "The St. Paul Seminary—Statement of Endowment Funds, June 1, 1911" and letter of John J. Toomey to John Ireland, August 17, 1911. JJHP.

55. Eric C. Hansen, *The Cathedral of Saint Paul: An Architectural Biography* (St. Paul, Minnesota: The Cathedral of Saint Paul, 1990), p. 128.

56. Alan K. Lathrop, "A French Architect in Minnesota: E. L. Masqueray," *Minnesota History,* Vol. 47, No. 2 (Summer 1980): 50–51.

57. Ahern, pp. 41–42.

58. Trustees, I, p. 91.

59. Trustees, I, p. 88.

60. Trustees, I, p. 92. The exact amount of the donation received was $14,664.00.

61. *Register* (1914), p. 52.

62. *Register* (1898), p. 13.

63. Trustees, I, p. 41.

64. Weber, p. 106, n. 8, from interview with Sebastian Cronin, C.S.J.

65. *Register* (1913), p. 16.

66. Trustees, I, p. 91.

67. Trustees, I, pp. 99, 101–102.

68. Connors, pp. 40–45.

69. I am grateful to Joseph Maguire, of the maintenance staff at the Saint Paul Seminary School of Divinity, and his aunt Catherine Tsuruoka, for information on Barron's relationship to Fitzgerald. Joseph Maguire is Father Joseph Barron's first cousin twice removed.

70. Andrew Turnbull, *Scott Fitzgerald: A Biography* (New York: Ballantine Books, 1962), pp. 100–101. See also pp. 133, 260.

71. Turnbull, p. 133. See also Joan M. Allan, *Candles and Carnival Lights: The Catholic Sensibility of F. Scott Fitzgerald* (New York: New York University Press, 1978), p. 92: "Even though he was about to leave the Church, Fitzgerald arranged, at his mother's suggestion, to have his daughter baptized, and Father Barron was both the celebrating priest and Scottie's godfather." See also Andre Le Vot, *F. Scott Fitzgerald: A Biography* (New York: Doubleday, 1983), p. 112: "The baby girl was named Frances Scott and was christened in November, with

Father Joe Barron, a McQuillan family familiar whom Fitzgerald had befriended, acting as godfather."

72. Turnbull, p. 260.

73. See obituaries, *Minneapolis Journal,* April 16, 1939, and *The St. Paul Daily News,* n.d.

74. Daniel Patrick O'Neill, "St. Paul's Priests, 1851–1930: Recruitment, Formation and Mobility." Unpublished Ph.D. dissertation, University of Minnesota, 1979. (Hereafter, "Priests.")

75. O'Neill, "Priests," p. 41.

76. O'Neill, "Priests," p. 43.

77. O'Neill, "Priests," p. 135.

78. Hurley, p. 103.

79. Stephen J. Ochs, *Desegregating the Altar: The Josephites and the Struggle for Black Priests 1871–1960* (Baton Rouge, La.: Louisiana State University Press, 1990), p. 64.

80. As quoted in Sharon M. Howell, "'The Consecrated Blizzard of the Northwest'—Archbishop John Ireland and His Relationship with the Black Community," *Many Rains Ago: A Historical and Theological Reflection on the Role of the Episcopate in the Evangelization of African American Catholics* (Washington, D.C.: Secretariat for Black Catholics, NCCB, 1990), p. 42.

81. Cyprian Davis, O.S.B., *Black Catholics in the United States* (New York: Crossroad, 1992), pp. 161–162.

82. Albert Foley, S.J., *God's Men of Color* (New York: Farrar, Straus and Co., 1955), p. 97, as quoted in Howell, p. 41.

83. As quoted in Connors, p. 81. See John R. Slattery, "The Seminary for the Colored Missions," *Catholic World* 46 (1888): 541–550; *NC,* January 20, 1888.

84. Ochs, p. 76. During Dorsey's year at St. Thomas he received no grade lower than a 90 in Christian doctrine, Latin, Greek, English, history, and arithmetic.

85. Connors, pp. 81–83. See Howell, pp. 35–48, and Ochs, pp. 4, 276–277. Dorsey's life was ultimately a sad one. He was one of the few black priests who were active in the first quarter of the twentieth century. They were hounded by southern bishops, who demanded their removal from parishes, and experienced a "living martyrdom." In September 1924 he was hit over the head with a

heavy block of wood by an ex-convict. His skull was fractured and he never recovered. Dorsey died at Mount Hope Sanitarium on June 30, 1926.

86. Ochs, pp. 310, 318.

87. See Marvin O'Connell, *Critics on Trial: An Introduction to the Catholic Modernist Crisis* (Washington, D.C.: The Catholic University of America Press, 1994).

88. Pope Leo XIII in his encyclical *Aeterni Patris* (1879) had required Catholic institutions to teach Thomistic philosophy and theology.

89. As quoted in White, p. 260.

90. See Thomas J. Shelley, *Dunwoodie: The History of St. Joseph's Seminary, Yonkers, New York* (Westminster, Maryland: Christian Classics, 1993).

91. Archbishop Ireland invited the bishops of the province to organize the St. Paul Catholic Historical Society in 1905. They chose the Saint Paul Seminary as the headquarters. John Ireland was the honorary president, and Father Francis J. Schaefer, later rector of the seminary, was president. *Acta et Dicta* was first published in 1907 and became an important resource for understanding the Catholic Church in the Upper Midwest. John Ireland's love of history was contagious. It is noteworthy that when the North Central Association accredited the Saint Paul Seminary in the 1940s, the M.A. degree in church history was the first one offered to the seminarians.

92. Reardon, p. 344.

93. John Ireland, "The Dogmatic Authority of the Papacy: The Encyclical on Modernism," *North American Review* DCXXIX (April 1908): 486–497. See especially pp. 491–492.

94. Reardon, p. 345.

95. Fogarty, p. 193.

96. See Scott Appleby, *"Church and Age Unite!": The Modernist Impulse in American Catholicism* (Notre Dame: University of Notre Dame Press, 1992).

97. See Thomas O'Dea, *American Catholic Dilemma: An Inquiry into the Intellectual Life* (New York: Sheed and Ward, 1958).

98. As quoted in White, pp. 263–264.

99. White, p. 264.

100. Ahern, p. 40.

101. *Register* (1897), p. 44.

102. *Register* (1913), p. 58.

103. Malone, pp. 280, 109.

104. *Register* (1915), p. 62.

105. O'Connell, pp. 284, 518.

106. See Mary Mehegan Hill, Diaries. JJHP.

107. Diary, Mary Mehegan Hill, May 29, 1920, and June 8, 1920. JJHP.

108. Trustees, I, pp. 113–114. Mary Hill established a trust with the Northwestern Trust Co., St. Paul. Deposited therein was $100,000 in cash and $100,000 in Anglo-French bonds with a face value of $100,000. She made a similar $200,000 donation to the College of St. Thomas at the same time. Voucher in the Hill Papers dated July 1920.

109. *Register* (1922), p. 51.

Chapter 9—Austin Dowling: "The Rhetoric of Architecture"

1. Austin Dowling, "Consecration of the Seminary Chapel, Cleveland, Ohio" (Sermon preached October 2, 1925), *Occasional Sermons and Addresses of Archbishop Dowling* (Paterson, New Jersey: St. Anthony Guild Press, 1940), p. 145. (Hereafter, *Sermons*.)

2. Reardon, p. 438.

3. Connors, p. 179.

4. Marvin O'Connell, "The Dowling Decade in Saint Paul." Unpublished M.A. dissertation, the Saint Paul Seminary, 1955, p. 53. (Hereafter, "Dowling.")

5. Connors, p. 193.

6. O'Connell, "Dowling," p. 5.

7. As quoted in Reardon, p. 442. Frances Boardman, in a eulogy written in *Commonweal* shortly after Dowling's death, describes her interview with the archbishop-elect of St. Paul shortly after he received the appointment. His first response was: "You see . . . I don't know anything about Minnesota; I only know I'm dismayed at having to succeed so great a personage as Archbishop Ireland." (January 7, 1931), n.p.

8. Interview with T. Kenneth Ryan, January 19, 1998, New Hope, Minnesota. Ryan attended Nazareth Hall the year it opened, and was a student at the Saint Paul Seminary from 1924 to 1930.

9. The statue of John Ireland on the campus of the University of St. Thomas by Michael Price captures something of the spirit of the archbishop. The sculpture depicts him in a neat frock coat typical of the time, but his pants are rumpled and his boats seem disheveled. One interpretation for this depiction is that Ireland would sometimes visit the poor at the docks in the morning or afternoon, but always wanted to be appropriately dressed to sit down to dinner at the Hill mansion or the home of some other prestigious citizen in the evening.

10. *Le Petit Journal,* June 19, 1892, as quoted in James H. Moynihan, *The Life of Archbishop Ireland* (New York: Harper and Brothers, 1953), p. 143.

11. O'Connell, "Dowling," pp. 3–4, based on pictures in the *Catholic Bulletin.* According to Dowling's passport he was 5'5" tall (n. 15, p. 4).

12. Dowling, "Dedication of Sulpician Seminary, Washington, D.C.," sermon preached September 23, 1919, *Sermons,* p. 12. Emphasis mine.

13. *Ad Limina Report* (Draft 1923), Austin Dowling Papers (DP), AASPM.

14. Gibbons to Dowling (General letter to the American hierarchy), May 24, 1919, DP, AASPM.

15. The Vatican did not approve of the word "council" in the title. A council is a singular event and has legislative authority. It was renamed the "National Catholic Welfare Conference" because a conference is ongoing and has an advisory rather than a legislative role.

16. Reardon, pp. 448–449.

17. Reardon, pp. 451–452.

18. Reardon, p. 452.

19. As quoted in White, p. 272.

20. Austin Dowling, "To the Clergy and Faithful of the Archdiocese," August 15, 1923. DP, AASPM.

21. Austin Dowling, "To the Clergy...," August 15, 1923. DP, AASPM.

22. Austin Dowling, "To the Clergy...," August 15, 1923. In his letter, Dowling cites the desire of the Holy See for separate preparatory seminaries, and the need to establish a "parochial burse, or by an annual collection, to provide funds for the purpose of meeting the deficit of poor boys."

23. Reardon, p. 452.

24. Connors, p. 187.

25. See the excellent account in Connors, Parts VI and VII.

26. Connors, pp. 258–259.

27. Austin Dowling to the priests of the archdiocese, August 13, 1928. DP, AASPM. This letter, sent out after the press had released the information, attempts to put a positive spin on the transfer of administration and control of St. Thomas to the Holy Cross Fathers. Dowling recognized that St. Thomas was "the Alma Mater of so many of our priests" and he invited their cooperation in the new venture.

28. Dowling, *Sermons,* pp. 6, 8. Emphasis mine.

29. Eulogy of Austin Dowling in *A Garland of Affectionate Tributes to the Memory of the Very Rev. John Baptist Hogan, D.D., S.S.* (Boston: Alumni Saint John's Seminary, 1906), pp. 32–35, as quoted in John Tracy Ellis, *Essays in Seminary Education* (Notre Dame, Indiana: Fides Publishers, Inc., 1967), p. 202.

30. Connors, p. 181.

31. Interview with Charles Eggert, January 20, 1998, St. Paul, Minnesota. Eggert attended Nazareth Hall from 1926 to 1932 and the Saint Paul Seminary from 1932 to 1938. His recollections of Humphrey Moynihan concur with those of T. Kenneth Ryan, although Ryan was stronger in his descriptions referring to Moynihan's "fixation about table manners" and being "fanatic about punctuation." Interview, January 19, 1998.

32. Interviews with T. Kenneth Ryan, January 19, 1998; Ambrose Hayden, August 20, 1993; and Charles Eggert, January 20, 1998.

33. Interview, T. Kenneth Ryan, January 19, 1998.

34. This statement was signed by Paul C. Bussard, Joseph E. Law, Bernard H. Murray, William A. Brand, and Joseph A. Ettel, and dated April 29, 1926. No addressee is given, but—along with two similar statements—it can be found in the Seminary Papers, AASPM.

35. Humphrey Moynihan to Mrs. E. C. [Clara Hill] Lindley, St. Paul, December 18, 1927. DP, AASPM.

36. O'Connell, "Dowling," p. 36.

37. Humphrey Moynihan to Clara Hill Lindley, December 20, 1930. DP, AASPM.

38. Interview, T. Kenneth Ryan, January 19, 1998.

39. Interview, T. Kenneth Ryan, January 19, 1998.

40. Austin Dowling to James H. Prendergast, December 22, 1920. DP, AASPM.

41. Austin Dowling to James H. Prendergast, August 9, 1921. DP, AASPM.

42. Interview, T. Kenneth Ryan, January 19, 1998.

43. Interview, T. Kenneth Ryan, January 19, 1998.

44. "Rules of the St. Paul Seminary," 1908, p. 11. Copy is hand-dated 1920. Archives of the Saint Paul Seminary (ASPS).

45. Interview, T. Kenneth Ryan, January 19, 1998.

46. *Register* (1923), p. 46.

47. See *Registers,* 1919–1930.

48. *Register* (1931), p. 37.

49. *Register* (1928), p. 2.

50. White, pp. 272–273.

51. White, p. 273.

52. White, p. 273.

53. Pietro Fumasoni-Biondi, "Copy of Letter Addressed to All the Ordinaries of the United States by Order of the Sacred Congregation of Seminaries and Universities," *American Ecclesiastical Review* 79 (July-December 1928): 74–83.

54. Pietro Fumasoni-Biondi to Austin Dowling, November 25, 1925. DP, AASPM.

55. Interview, T. Kenneth Ryan, January 19, 1998.

56. Interview with John Sweeney, January 20, 1998. He was told the story by Lawrence O. Wolf.

57. *Register* (1929), p. 67.

58. Humphrey Moynihan to Clara Hill Lindley, March 15, n.y. [1927]. DP, AASPM.

59. Humphrey Moynihan to Clara Hill Lindley, June 26, n.y. [1927 or 1928]. DP, AASPM.

60. Trustees, I, pp. 113, 115 for minutes regarding the endowment from Mary Hill. See p. 114 for note on garage.

61. Trustees, I, p. 119.

62. In a letter to the priests of the archdiocese dated December 28, 1923, Austin Dowling indicated that he would sail for Rome on January 8, 1924, and expected to be back by Easter. DP, AASPM.

63. St. Paul *Dispatch,* August 4, 1925.

64. St. Paul *Dispatch,* August 5, 1925. According to this article, "An offering of the home was made previously to Archbishop Austin Dowling, but the offer was temporarily rejected at the time." This arrangement allowed for a substantial trust fund for the maintenance and upkeep of the property.

65. St. Paul *Dispatch,* August 22/23, 1925. Clipping in JJHP. Date unclear.

66. Austin Dowling to Clara Hill Lindley, December 11, 1926. DP, AASPM.

67. *Pioneer Press,* January [n.d.] 1927. Clipping in the JJHP.

68. Humphrey Moynihan to Clara Hill Lindley, March 15, n.d. [1927]. DP, AASPM.

69. Maginnis and Walsh to Clarence H. Johnston, June 2, 1925. DP, AASPM.

70. Trustees, I, p. 122.

71. Austin Dowling to Clara Hill Lindley, December 11, 1926, DP, AASPM. In 1919 the tuition, room, and board per student was increased to $250; in 1920, to $300; and by 1926, to $400, where it remained until the end of the decade.

72. Humphrey Moynihan to Clara Hill Lindley, December 18, 1926. DP, AASPM.

73. Austin Dowling to Maginnis and Walsh, March 29, 1927. DP, AASPM. For a description of the decoration of St. Mary's Chapel, see "St. Mary's Chapel of The St. Paul Seminary School of Divinity: A Historic and Artistic Guide" (St. Paul, Minnesota: University of St. Thomas, 1998). For the carving of the capitals see pp. 6–8. (Hereafter, "Chapel Guide.")

74. Austin Dowling to Clara Hill Lindley, December 2, 1927. DP, AASPM.

75. Austin Dowling to Maginnis and Walsh, January 25, 1928. DP, AASPM.

76. Austin Dowling to Priests of the Archdiocese, March 7, 1928. See also Dowling to Clara Hill Lindley, March 15, 1928. DP, AASPM.

77. Austin Dowling to Priests of the Archdiocese, July 26, 1928. DP, AASPM.

78. Trustees, I, p. 124.

79. Henry Adams, *The Education of Henry Adams* (Boston: Houghton Mifflin Company, 1918), p. 371.

80. See John La Farge, S.J., *The Manner is Ordinary* (New York: Harcourt, Brace and Company, 1954).

81. John La Farge, S.J., p. 234.

82. Hansen, p. 83.

83. Austin Dowling to Maginnis and Walsh, September 8, 1928. DP, AASPM.

84. Austin Dowling to Maginnis and Walsh, September 8, 1928. DP, AASPM.

85. Austin Dowling to Maginnis and Walsh, November 6, 1928. DP, AASPM.

86. Austin Dowling to Maginnis and Walsh, November 6, 1928. DP, AASPM.

87. Austin Dowling to Maginnis and Walsh, November 10, 1928. DP, AASPM.

88. Austin Dowling to Maginnis and Walsh, June 13, 1929. DP, AASPM.

89. Austin Dowling to Maginnis and Walsh, February 7, 1930. DP, AASPM.

90. Austin Dowling to Maginnis and Walsh, February 18, 1929. DP, AASPM.

91. Austin Dowling to Maginnis and Walsh, May 11, 1929. DP, AASPM.

92. Austin Dowling to Maginnis and Walsh, June 13, 1929. DP, AASPM.

93. Austin Dowling to Maginnis and Walsh, July 9, 1929. DP, AASPM.

94. Interview, T. Kenneth Ryan, January 19, 1998.

95. Austin Dowling to Bancel La Farge, June 13, 1929. DP, AASPM.

96. Hansen, p. 82.

97. Bancel La Farge to Austin Dowling, July 8, 1928. DP, AASPM.

98. See "Chapel Guide," pp. 13–16.

99. Austin Dowling to Bancel La Farge, January 29, 1929. DP, AASPM.

100. Austin Dowling to Maginnis and Walsh, March 26, 1929. DP, AASPM.

101. In a most un-Dowlinglike statement, the archbishop wrote to Clara Hill Lindley on December 29, 1928: "Mr. Bancel La Farge or more likely his son Tom will do a painting on the wall of the apse just over the High Altar. The whole thing will be quite 'scrumptious' to use a time honored word." DP, AASPM.

102. Bancel La Farge to Austin Dowling, February 13, 1929. DP, AASPM.

103. Austin Dowling to Bancel La Farge, n.d. DP, AASPM.

104. Bancel La Farge to Austin Dowling, January 23, 1929. DP, AASPM.

105. Bancel La Farge to Austin Dowling, February 13, 1929. DP, AASPM.

106. Austin Dowling to Maginnis and Walsh, May 11, 1929. DP, AASPM.

107. Austin Dowling to Bancel La Farge, June 13, 1929. DP, AASPM.

108. Bancel La Farge to Austin Dowling, August 25, 1929. DP, AASPM.

109. Trustees, I, p. 126.

110. Trustees, I, p. 129.

111. Bancel La Farge to Austin Dowling, August 9, 1930. DP, AASPM. "The suggestion of the figure of Christ standing straight as in No. 1 would not, I think, express the idea as well as the turning movement as suggested in the others."

112. Francis Schenck to Bancel La Farge, November 13, 1930. DP, AASPM.

113. Francis Schenck to Bancel La Farge, November 13, 1930. DP, AASPM. Emphasis mine.

114. Austin Dowling to Clara Hill Lindley, March 15, 1928. DP, AASPM.

115. Austin Dowling to Clara Hill Lindley, March 31, 1927. DP, AASPM. The archbishop expresses his gratitude: "The three sets of beautiful vestments you were so good to send us have arrived in good condition and I hasten to thank you for them—for them and the constant evidence of your thoughtfulness which we receive at the Seminary and Nazareth. Your pictures are everywhere in evidence making bright beautiful walls."

116. Austin Dowling to Clara Hill Lindley, April 11, 1928. DP, AASPM.

117. Austin Dowling to Clara Hill Lindley, December 29, 1928. DP, AASPM.

118. Bancel La Farge to Francis Schenck, December 14 [unclear], 1930. DP, AASPM.

119. Humphrey Moynihan to Clara Hill Lindley, December 20, 1930. DP, AASPM.

120. Humphrey Moynihan to Clara Hill Lindley, n.d. DP, AASPM.

121. *Register* (1931), p. 46.

Chapter 10—John Gregory Murray: Priesthood in the Era of "Catholic Action"

1. John Gregory Murray to priests of the Archdiocese of St. Paul, December 14, 1937. John Gregory Murray Papers (JGMP), AASPM.

2. Connors, p. 252.

3. *Time,* February 8, 1932, pp. 32–33.

4. Reardon, p. 507.

5. James P. Shannon, *Reluctant Dissenter* (New York: Crossroad Publishing Company, 1998), p. 50. (Hereafter, Shannon, *Reluctant Dissenter.*)

6. Reardon, pp. 508–509.

7. I am grateful to Joseph M. White for this vignette, which he describes in an unpublished manuscript of the life of Archbishop Peter L. Geraty of Newark, New Jersey, who was also a former bishop of Portland, Maine. Murray's relationship to Genevieve Brady is discussed in chapter 16.

8. John Gregory Murray to priests of the Archdiocese of St. Paul, November 8, 1932. JGMP, AASPM.

9. Humphrey Moynihan to Clara Hill Lindley, December 20, 1930. DP, AASPM.

10. See Connors, pp. 252–265, for an excellent account of this dilemma.

11. Connors, p. 257.

12. Interviews with John Sweeney, January 20, 1998; and Thomas Conroy, July 29, 1998. Conroy reported that in one version Brady responded: "Where are the keys?"

13. Interview, Edward Grzeskowiak, July 29, 1998.

14. Interview, John Sweeney, January 20, 1998.

15. Interview, Ambrose Hayden, August 20, 1993. Sweeney agreed regarding Brady: "He *was* sure of himself. But I don't think it was lilacs; I think it was bridal wreath." Interview, January 20, 1998.

16. See *Register* (1934).

17. Interview, John Sweeney, August 20, 1998.

18. Ahern, pp. 54–55. See also *Register* (1930), p. 26–27, and (1934), pp. 8, 14.

19. Interview, Charles Eggert, January 20, 1998.

20. As quoted in White, pp. 280–281.

21. *Rules,* 1945 and 1954. File, Rector's Office, SPS.

22. Interview, Charles Eggert, January 20, 1998.

23. *Register* (1939), p. 17.

24. White, p. 281–283.

25. Ahern, p. 62.

26. Yzermans, p. 55. Thomas Conroy agreed that Wolf was a good teacher.

27. Interview, John R. Roach, October 15, 1998.

28. Interview, Terrence J. Murphy, September 28, 1998.

29. Interview, John R. Roach, October 15, 1998.

30. Shannon, *Reluctant Dissenter,* p. 30. The author described the incident but does not refer to Missia by name. The story was recounted to me, however, by John Sweeney and Thomas Conroy.

31. Interview, John R. Roach, October 15, 1998.

32. Connors, p. 309.

33. Interview, William Baumgaertner, July 23, 1998.

34. Interview, Thomas Conroy, July 29, 1998.

35. Interview, William Baumgaertner, July 23, 1998.

36. Interviews with John R. Roach, October 15, 1998; Alfred Wagner, July 13, 1998; Thomas Conroy, July 29, 1998; and Terrence Murphy, September 28, 1998.

37. John Gregory Murray to priests of the Archdiocese of St. Paul, June 5, 1942. JGMP, AASPM.

38. Ahern, p. 47.

39. Interview, Thomas Conroy, July 29, 1998.

40. Interview, William Baumgaertner, July 23, 1998.

41. "Anniversary Reflections," Thomas Conroy, Golden Jubilee Booklet, The Saint Paul Seminary, Class of 1948.

42. Interview, Alfred Wagner, July 13, 1998.

43. Interview, John R. Roach, October 15, 1998.

44. Trustees, I, 183. Copy of invitation in JGMP, AASPM.

45. Reardon, p. 552.

46. Reardon, p. 552.

47. John O'Sullivan, "Remembering a Bishop," *Catholic Bulletin,* September 21, 1986, p. 27. Interviews with John R. Roach, October 15, 1998 and Thomas Conroy, July 29, 1998.

48. Richard J. Schuler, *History of the Church of Saint Agnes of Saint Paul, Minnesota (1887–1987)* (Saint Paul, Minnesota: 1987), p. 123.

49. Interview, John Sweeney, January 20, 1998.

50. Interview, John R. Roach, October 15, 1998.

51. John Gregory Murray to the priests of the Archdiocese of St. Paul, August 20, 1934. JGMP, AASPM.

52. Interview, Eugene Abbott, August 31, 1998.

53. Interview, Richard J. Wolter, October 16, 1998.

54. *Register* (1955), p. 21.

55. *Register* (1955), pp. 26–27.

56. White, p. 392.

57. Interview, William Baumgaertner, August 21, 1998.

58. White, pp. 393–394.

59. White, p. 395.

60. White, p. 396.

61. *Register* (1947), p. 45.

62. *Register* (1946), p. 9.

63. *Register* (1946), p. 9.

64. *Register* (1952), p. 13.

65. Trustees, I, p. 201. Although the accreditation of the Saint Paul Seminary by the North Central Association was approved at the N.C.A. meeting in March, the letter of accreditation was very likely not sent until April.

66. Trustees, I, p. 202.

67. According to William Baumgaertner, in the 1950s the Catholic University of America offered to reinstate the affiliation with CUA to offer the S.T.B. which had been discontinued in the 1930s. The Saint Paul Seminary faculty voted against that option on more than one occasion. Interview, August 21, 1998.

68. *NC* (April 4, 1903), p. 1. File, Archbishop Ireland Memorial Library.

69. Rudolph Bandas to John Gregory Murray, December 18, 1948. File, Archbishop Ireland Memorial Library.

70. Thomas J. Shanahan, "The John Ireland Library of the Saint Paul Seminary," May 19, 1949, pp. 1–2. File, Archbishop Ireland Memorial Library.

71. Shanahan, pp. 2–3.

72. Interviews with Ambrose Hayden, August 20, 1993, and Thomas Conroy, July 29, 1998.

73. Trustees, I, p. 193.

74. Trustees, I, p. 204.

75. Trustees, I, p. 207.

76. Rudolph Bandas to John Gregory Murray, December 18, 1948. File, Archbishop Ireland Memorial Library.

77. Rudolph Bandas to John Gregory Murray, December 18, 1948. File, Archbishop Ireland Memorial Library.

78. John Gregory Murray to alumni of the Saint Paul Seminary, February 10, 1949. JGMP, AASPM.

79. Reardon, p. 553.

80. St. Paul *Dispatch* (December 9, 1948), p. 1, ff. File, Archbishop Ireland Memorial Library.

81. Shanahan, p. 3. There is no indication in Shanahan's account as to who laid the cornerstone. Presumably it was Archbishop Murray. The board minutes indicate that the construction had begun on December 11, 1948. See Trustees, I, p. 211.

82. *Register* (1950), p. 21.

83. Reardon, p. 553.

84. Reardon, p. 575. The five were: Richard Moudry, John Liebert, and Leo Goblirsch of St. Paul, and Edward Baumann and Henry Tenhundfeld of the Diocese of Covington.

85. In the *Register* (1956), pp. 16–17, the recipients of the M.A. degree from 1949 to 1956 are listed along with the titles of their dissertations and the dioceses for which the students were studying. At the annual meeting of the board of trustees each October, the list of candidates for the B.A. and M.A. degrees was presented and approved. After the meeting, the archbishop conferred the degrees on the seminarians for the B.A. degree, and the newly ordained for the M.A. degree.

86. Trustees, I, p. 237.

87. Interview, Eugene Abbott, August 31, 1998.

88. Trustees, I, p. 213.

89. Trustees, I, p. 215.

90. Interview, Hattie Klisch Karpinski, January 20, 2000. I am grateful to Mary Payne for putting me in contact with her.

91. Trustees, I, p. 215.

92. Trustees, I, p. 217.

93. *Register* (1952), p. 21.

94. *Register* (1951), p. 10.

95. *Register* (1950), p. 20.

96. *Register* (1954), p. 23.

97. See Martin E. Marty, *The New Shape of American Religion* (New York: Harper and Brothers, 1958).

98. Trustees, I, pp. 189–190.

99. Trustees, I, p. 210.

100. Trustees, I, p. 213.

101. Trustees, I, p. 215.

102. See *Register* (1951), p. 11; (1952), p. 12.

103. John Gregory Murray to priests of the Archdiocese of St. Paul, October 25, 1934. JGMP, AASPM.

104. The *Register* for each year offers a "Chronicle" of the activities of the previous year from which the following lists have been constructed.

105. *Register* (1947), pp. 17, 19.

106. *Register* (1947), p, 23.

107. *Register* (1946), p. 23.

108. *Register* (1947), p. 23.

109. Interview, Thomas Conroy, July 29, 1998.

110. Shannon, *Reluctant Dissenter,* pp. 31–32.

111. Interview, John R. Roach, October 15, 1998.

112. Lawrence F. Ryan, ed., *The Ryan Family* (St. Paul, Minnesota: 1971), pp. 134–135.

113. Interview, Eugene Abbott, August 31, 1998.

114. Lawrence Ryan, ed., p. 142. Spiritual conferences were on Monday, Wednesday, Friday, and Saturday evenings. The rector's conference was on Thursday. Tuesday evening was reserved for confessions.

115. Interview, Thomas Conroy, July 29, 1998.

116. Interview, John R. Roach, October 15, 1998.

117. Interview, John F. Kinney, October 9, 1999.

118. Yzermans, pp. 62–68.

119. Fred Mertz, *The Ore and the Dross* (St. Paul, Minnesota: Rickshaw Publications, 1992).

120. The priest who shared this incident with me prefers to remain anonymous.

121. *Rules,* 1954, p. 4.

122. *Rules,* 1954, p. 7.

123. *Rules,* 1954, p. 9.

124. *Rules,* 1954, pp. 14–15.

125. Interview, John R. Roach, October 15, 1998.

126. Interview, Thomas Conroy, July 29, 1998.

127. Interview, William Baumgaertner, July 23, 1998.

128. Interview, T. Kenneth Ryan, January 18, 1998.

129. Interview, Eugene Abbott, August 31, 1998.

130. Shannon, *Reluctant Dissenter,* p. 47.

131. James M. Reardon, "The End of a Glorious Era: The Last Six Years of the Life of John Gregory Murray, Archbishop of St. Paul (1951–1956)." Unpublished manuscript, 1961, pp. 51–52. JGMP, AASPM.

Chapter 11—William O. Brady: Professor, Rector, Trustee, Archbishop

1. William O. Brady, "Champions for Social Rights," *The Voice* (Baltimore: St. Mary's Seminary, February 1950), pp. 12–13. (Hereafter, *The Voice.*)

2. Archbishop Ireland served for thirty-four years as ordinary from 1884 to 1918. Murray served for twenty-four years from 1932 to 1956.

3. *The Durfee Record* (1916), p. 16.

4. William O. Brady to Austin Dowling, February 11, 1923. William O. Brady Papers (WOBP), AASPM.

5. William O. Brady to Austin Dowling, February 11, 1923. WOBP, AASPM.

6. William O. Brady to Austin Dowling, April 29, 1923. WOBP, AASPM.

7. William O. Brady to Austin Dowling, August 6, 1924. WOBP, AASPM.

8. William O. Brady to Austin Dowling, August 20, 1924. WOBP, AASPM.

9. William O. Brady to Austin Dowling, December 26, 1925. WOBP, AASPM.

10. William O. Brady to Austin Dowling, April 23, 1926. WOBP, AASPM. Walter Peters described Brady's dissertation as "a searching examination of the question of what happens if a person receives the sacraments unworthily, under duress, or out of a desire to ridicule. Later the person has a change of mind and wishes with all his heart to be a fervent and practicing Catholic. Three of the sacraments can be received only once. In other words, in the state of true conversion can that grace be received retroactively?" WOBP, AASPM.

11. William O. Brady to Austin Dowling, July 13, 1926. WOBP, AASPM.

12. William O. Brady to Austin Dowling, July 24, 1926. WOBP, AASPM.

13. Biographical sketch of William O. Brady by Walter Peters, August 1956. WOBP, AASPM.

14. Interview, Mary William Brady, C.S.J., October 9, 1998. See also Rosalie Ryan, C.S.J., and John Christine Wolkerstorfer, C.S.J., *More Than a Dream: Eighty-Five Years at the College of St. Catherine* (St. Paul, Minnesota: The College of St. Catherine, 1992), pp. 63–64.

15. Interview, Mary William Brady, C.S.J., October 9, 1998.

16. John Gregory Murray to William O. Brady, June 26, 1933. WOBP, AASPM.

17. *Catholic Bulletin,* June 17, 1939, pp. 1, 6.

18. William O. Brady, "Why I Am A Catholic," Address given at the Methodist Episcopal Church, Red Wing, Minnesota, November 23, 1933. WOBP, AASPM.

19. William O. Brady, "The Seminarians Vacation," Address, Seminary Department, Catholic Educational Association, Chicago, 1934. WOBP, AASM.

20. Interview, Gerald O'Keefe, October 4, 1998.

21. Shannon, *Reluctant Dissenter,* p. 66.

22. Interview, Gerald O'Keefe, October 4, 1998.

23. See photograph albums in the WOBP, AASPM. Not long after Brady was appointed to Sioux Falls, Mary William began doctoral studies at the University of Chicago. Mrs. Brady found herself alone again—this time in St. Paul. She moved to Sioux Falls to be with her son William and died there in 1948. Interview, Mary William Brady, C.S.J., October 9, 1998.

24. Trustees, I, pp. 165, 167.

25. Trustees, I, pp. 171–172.

26. William O. Brady, untitled five-page sermon preached at the Saint Paul Cathedral, August 21, 1956. WOBP, AASPM.

27. Interview, Mary William Brady, C.S.J., October 9, 1998. See Ryan and Wolkerstorfer, pp. 63–64.

28. William O. Brady to John Gregory Murray, June 25, 1956. WOBP, AASPM.

29. Interview, Charles Froehle, October 2, 1998.

30. Interviews with Charles Froehle, October 2, 1998; Thomas Hunstiger, October 11, 1998; James Whalen, October 13, 1998; and Richard Wolter, October 16, 1998.

31. Interview, Richard Wolter, October 16, 1998.

32. Interviews with James Whalen, October 13, 1998, and Richard Wolter, October 16, 1998.

33. Interview, John F. Kinney, October 6, 1999.

34. John Tracy Ellis, "American Catholics and the Intellectual Life," *Thought* 30 (Autumn 1955): 351–388.

35. Gustave Weigel, S.J., "American Catholic Intellectualism—A Theologian's Reflection," *Review of Politics* 19 (July 1957): 275–307.

36. Thomas F. O'Dea, *American Catholic Dilemma: An Inquiry into the Intellectual Life* (New York: Sheed and Ward, 1958), Chapter VIII.

37. O'Dea, p. 166.

38. "Address of Welcome Given By Archbishop William O. Brady to the Catholic Theological Society of America in Convention at Saint Paul, Minnesota, June 24, 1958." WOBP, AASPM. (Hereafter, Brady, CTSA.)

39. Brady, CTSA.

40. Brady, CTSA.

41. Joseph Connors described a lecture that Bandas was invited to give on the evils of communism at a conference on Catholic social thought for the Catholic colleges in the area at St. Thomas. During the lecture a bat swooped down on the stage and flew a figure eight around Bandas's head several times. Instead of acknowledging the creature and introducing a little humor, the lecturer focused intently on his manuscript and tried to ignore the situation. Interview, September 9, 1998. This lack of humor and almost rigid stance was reiterated by others who were interviewed as well.

42. The descriptions of Brady and Bandas are based on the multiple interviews undertaken for this volume.

43. Interview, John Sweeney, January 20, 1998. Sweeney also remembered Holy Thursday in 1957 when the seminary choir was to sing for Brady's first Chrism Mass at 9:00 A.M. in the cathedral. As choir director, Sweeney drove down early with a few students. At almost 9:00 A.M. when the others had not arrived, someone phoned the seminary to discover that the buses had not been ordered. An announcement had to be made that the Mass would be postponed to 10:00 A.M. Brady was not a happy person. Sweeney wondered if that incident was just one more irritant in the disaffection between Brady and Bandas.

44. Interview, Ellsworth Kneal, September 30, 1998. Some have suggested that Brady engineered the creation of the diocese of New Ulm in an effort to move Bandas to St. Agnes, but Bishop Gerald O'Keefe recalled Brady returning from a visit with the apostolic delegate after being told that he would get only one auxiliary and not two because New Ulm was being established as a diocese. Interview, October 4, 1998.

45. Interview, David McCauley, October 19, 1998.

46. Interview, Charles Froehle, October 2, 1998.

47. It should be noted that Bandas served as pastor of St. Agnes from 1958 until his death in 1969. He served as a peritus at Vatican II in the area of seminary education. See Schuler, Chapter 11.

48. Gerald O'Keefe, Chancellor, "Archbishop Brady Announces Changes . . . ," *Catholic Bulletin,* February 8, 1958.

49. Gerald O'Keefe, Chancellor, "Archbishop Announces Seminary Top Posts," *Catholic Bulletin,* March 1, 1958.

50. Interview, James Whalen, October 13, 1998.

51. Interviews with Raymond Lucker, September 15, 1998; and Charles Froehle, October 2, 1998.

52. Interviews with James Whalen, October 13, 1998; and Charles Froehle, October 2, 1998.

53. Interview, David McCauley, October 19, 1998.

54. Interview, David McCauley, October 19, 1998.

55. Interview, Raymond Lucker, September 15, 1998.

56. Interview, Ellsworth Kneal, September 30, 1998.

57. Interview, Ellsworth Kneal, September 24, 1998.

58. Pierre Teilhard de Chardin, S.J., "The Mass on the World," *Hymn of the Universe* (New York: Harper & Row, 1965), p. 20.

59. Interview, John F. Kinney, October 6, 1999.

60. Interview, Raymond Lucker, September 15, 1998. Lucker was present at the breakfast when Brady made the announcement.

61. Interview, Mark Dosh, October 16, 1998.

62. Interview, Charles Froehle, October 2, 1998.

63. Interview, Thomas Conroy, July 29, 1998.

64. Interview, Charles Froehle, October 2, 1998. William Baumgaertner recalled that when Brady would "lay down the law" and expect McCarthy to implement it, some of the faculty felt he was treating the rector like "an errand boy." The result was that the faculty supported McCarthy even more strongly. Interview, August 30, 1999.

65. Interview, Gerald O'Keefe, October 4, 1998. Raymond Lucker, on September 15, 1998, shared an incident about another Easterner, Francis Gilligan, while both were members of the Saint Paul Seminary faculty. On one very hot summer day, as they were leaving the refectory in their long black cassocks, Lucker suggested that there should be a rule that when the temperature rose above a certain point, they should be allowed to come to the faculty dining room in their shirt sleeves. Gilligan was not persuaded and replied: "Ought to have a little dignity around here."

66. John Sweeney recalls that after the noon and evening meals, the students would go in small groups to the chapel for brief prayers.

67. Interview, Ronald Bowers, October 16, 1998.

68. Interview, John Sweeney, January 20, 1998.

69. See "Chronicle of the Year" section in *Saint Paul Seminary Register* for the years 1956–1962.

70. Interview, James Whalen, October 13, 1998.

71. Shannon, *Reluctant Dissenter,* p. 75.

72. Interview, Raymond Lucker, September 15, 1998.

73. Trustees, II, p. 5.

74. Trustees, II, p. 7.

75. Trustees, II, p. 7.

76. Interview, Raymond Lucker, September 15, 1998. Lucker noted that Brady was treasurer of the National Catholic Welfare Conference in the late 1950s. He was very helpful when the North American College in Rome was built after World War II in terms of transferring American money to lira at a profitable rate to the American bishops.

77. Trustees, II, p. 21.

78. Trustees, II, pp. 37–39.

79. Interview, Mary William Brady, C.S.J., October 9, 1998.

80. Martin O'Connor to Gerald O'Keefe, September 23, 1961. WOBP, AASPM.

81. Interview, Mary William Brady, C.S.J., October 9, 1998.

82. Charles Rea, M.D., to "Your Excellency" in St. Paul from Rome, October 2, 1961. It is presumed that this was written to Bishop O'Keefe, as the initial cablegram and other correspondence was addressed to him. However, Auxiliary Bishop Leonard Cowley was named administrator of the archdiocese upon Brady's death.

83. There are letters of sympathy from both Rabbi Bernard Raskas of Temple of Aaron and Rabbi Bernard Martin of Mount Zion Temple, both in St. Paul, as well as others in the Protestant and Jewish communities.

84. Interview, Thomas Conroy, July 29, 1998.

85. William O. Brady, "The Spiritual Opportunity of Seminary Faculty Life," n.d., n.p. WOBP, AASPM. The reference to the prominent author was very likely Father John C. Gruden who was on the faculty at the Saint Paul Seminary at the same time as Brady and whose volume *The Mystical Christ* was published in 1936. In 1937, while Brady was rector, Gruden was appointed pastor of St. Agnes Parish in St. Paul. One wonders if Brady was in any way responsible for Gruden's reassignment.

86. Trustees, II, pp. 43–49.

87. As quoted in William Busch, "In Memoriam: Archbishop Brady," *Worship* (January 1962): 87.

Chapter 12—The Binz-Byrne Era: Vatican II and a New Vision of Priesthood

1. "Address Delivered by His Excellency, Archbishop Leo Binz, at the St. Paul Seminary on March 9, to a Meeting of the District Chairmen of the Opus Sancti Petri," *Register* (1966), p. 51. Emphasis his. (Hereafter, Binz, OSP.)

2. *Catholic Bulletin,* March 2, 1962, p. B 5.

3. Albert Cardinal Meyer of Chicago presided at the funeral and did the final prayers at the cemetery. Bishop William Cousins of Milwaukee preached the sermon. From "Death and Obsequies of Archbishop Brady," James Reardon (not signed), March 14, 1962. Leo Binz Papers (LBP), AASPM.

4. Margaret McEachern, "Leo Binz Was Industrious Farm Boy, Sister Recalls," *Catholic Bulletin,* March 2, 1962, B 17. I am grateful to David A. Hoffman for an unpublished paper written in spring semester 1996 at the Saint Paul Seminary School of Divinity titled "Archbishop Binz and His Role in Implementing the Liturgical Reforms of Vatican II."

5. McEachern, B 17.

6. See biographical sketch and *curriculum vitae* of Leo Binz, LBP, AASPM.

7. Leo Binz to James P. Shannon, September 22, 1966. LBP, AASPM.

8. *Catholic Bulletin,* March 2, 1962, p. 1.

9. Leo Binz, Episcopal Letter to Archdiocese of St. Paul, "Council Seeks to Remake World," *Catholic Bulletin,* October 11, 1963, p. 1.

10. "Information to the International Catholic Documentary—Archdiocese of St. Paul in Minnesota," n.d. Letters accompanying the document are dated: to Archbishop D. Petro Palazzini, February 28, 1963, and to Archbishop Egidio Vagnozzi, Apostolic Delegate, February 28, 1963.

11. Leo Binz, "Vatican Council Success Depends Especially on Youth of the World," *Catholic Bulletin,* January 3, 1964, p. 1.

12. Interview with Ambrose Hayden, April 9, 1996, as quoted in Hoffman paper.

13. Interview, James Moudry, September 15, 1999.

14. Janet Grant, "'Austere' to national magazine, Abp Binz known as 'very warm person' to those who work close to him," *Catholic Bulletin,* December 15, 1967, p. 3.

15. Interview with Thomas Conroy, April 10, 1996, as quoted in Hoffman paper, p. 9.

16. Grant, p. 3.

17. Trustees, II, pp. 51–55.

18. Trustees, II, p. 55.

19. See chapter 10, p. 196 for biographical sketch of McCarthy and his time as spiritual director, and chapter 11, p. 220 for his tenure as rector under Brady.

20. Interview, James Moudry, September 15, 1999.

21. *Register* (1961–1962), pp. 43–44.

22. Interviews with Michael Arms, July 14, 1999; John Malone, July 19, 1999; and Ronald Bowers, July 21, 1999.

23. Saint Paul Seminary Annual Report, 1964–1965, p. 2. (Hereafter, "Annual Report.")

24. *Register* (1964–1965), p. 12.

25. Annual Report (1964–1965), p. 3. Msgr. James Cecka was temporarily appointed to teach American church history, and the Reverend Marvin O'Connell, assistant professor of history at the College of St. Thomas, agreed to be the reader for several M.A. theses that were all but completed at the time of Ahern's death.

26. See *Register* (1938–1945). Busch was replaced by the Reverend Francis Hammang who had earned a D. Sc. Hist. at the University of Louvain in Belgium and was appointed "Professor of Church History, Patrology, Archaeology and Breviary Studies." Hammang died unexpectedly in 1945, and Busch—then in residence at the seminary—was invited to return to the faculty.

27. Interview, Ronald Bowers, July 21, 1999. This story has been corroborated by many former seminarians over the years.

28. Interview, William Baumgaertner, August 30, 1999.

29. Trustees, II, p. 65. See also Annual Report, 1965–1966, pp. 8–9 regarding arrangements for seminarians to do their practice teaching.

30. Trustees, II, p. 65.

31. Interview, William Baumgaertner, August 30, 1999.

32. Interview, William Baumgaertner, August 30, 1999. This responsibility was later shifted to the rector's office.

33. Interview, William Baumgaertner, August 30, 1999.

34. "Institutional Survey: The Saint Paul Seminary" (St. Paul, Minnesota: October 1, 1967). ASPS.

35. Annual Report (1966–1967), p. 3.

36. Annual Report (1967–1968), pp. 1, 7.

37. Interviews with John Malone, July 19, 1999; and Michael Arms, July 14, 1999.

38. Annual Report (1965–1966), Documentation—"Diaconate Summer Program." Interview with Ronald Bowers, July 21, 1999.

39. Annual Report (1966–1967), Section I, p. 8.

40. Interviews with Michael Arms, July 14, 1999; and John Malone, July 19, 1999.

41. Interview, John Malone, July 19, 1999.

42. Interview, John Sweeney, February 2, 2000.

43. Interview, Gerald Milske, January 21, 2000.

44. Interview, Thomas Fisch, September 19, 1999.

45. Interviews with Michael Arms, July 14, 1999; John Malone, July 19, 1999; and Phillip Rask, September 19, 1999.

46. Interview, John Malone, July 19, 1999.

47. Interview, John Malone, July 19, 1999.

48. Interview, Thomas Hunstiger, July 25, 1999. John Malone alerted me to this event, July 19, 1999, and it was confirmed by John F. Kinney, October 6, 1999.

49. Interview, John Malone, July 19, 1999.

50. Interview, Stephen Adrian, November 24, 1999. See also "Saint Paul Seminary Faculty-Student Conference Constitution." Seminary Papers, AASPM.

51. White, p. 415.

52. White, pp. 416–417.

53. Louis J. McCarthy to Leo Binz, March 8, 1963, and April 8, 1963. Louis W. Hill, the last of James J. and Mary Hill's sons, died on April 21, 1948. The twenty-one-year mandate for the continuance of Hill surveillance of the endowment would expire in April 1969.

54. Trustees, II, p. 59. At the board meeting on April 15, 1963, the date for the termination of the trust was incorrectly given as April 27, 1967.

55. Louis McCarthy to Leo Binz, June 2, 1964. LBP, AASPM.

56. Trustees, II, pp. 63–67.

57. Annual Report (1964–1965), p. 11.

58. Binz, OSP, p. 49.

59. Binz, OSP, p. 50.

60. Copies in LBP, AASPM.

61. Binz, OSP, p. 50.

62. Binz, OSP, p. 51.

63. Binz, OSP, pp. 51–52.

64. Trustees, II, p. 81. Emphasis mine. As of 1966 the name of the metropolitan see was changed to the "Archdiocese of St. Paul and Minneapolis."

65. Interview, William Baumgaertner, September 2, 1999.

66. Trustees, III (October 17, 1972), p. 4. Dates are included in trustee minutes in Volume III because each meeting has its own pagination.

67. See articles and clippings, Leo C. Byrne Papers (LCBP), AASPM.

68. Interview, Max Shapiro, October 28, 1999. Rabbi Shapiro recalls Byrne's participation at Temple Israel, Minneapolis, in a service for Russian Jewry in the early 1970s.

69. See *Catholic Bulletin,* October 25, 1974.

70. Intervention of Archbishop Leo C. Byrne at the 1971 World Synod of Bishops, "The Rights of Women, Especially in the Church," October 22, 1971. LCBP, AASPM.

71. Trustees, III (October 17, 1972), p. 2.

72. Interview with William Baumgaertner, August 30, 1999. Both John Sweeney and Charles Froehle recall hearing of Byrne's less-than-supportive approach to the Saint Paul Seminary.

73. Interview, John Sweeney, September 20, 1999.

74. Interview, William Baumgaertner, August 30, 1999.

75. Leo Binz to Leo Byrne, November 4, 1968. LBP, AASPM.

76. Interview, William Baumgaertner, August 30, 1999.

77. Annual Report (1967–1968), p. 12.

78. James P. Shannon, "Report to Archbishop Brady On the Subject of Training Seminarians at the College of St. Thomas," November 23, 1959. ASPS.

79. Report of the Seminary Planning Commission, Section II, May 21, 1963. AASPM.

80. M. V. Seymour of Seymour and O'Connor, Attorneys at Law, to William Baumgaertner, March 25, 1963. See also Appendix A attached. LBP, AASPM.

81. Rachel Boeckmann to Leo Binz, December 26, 1963. Signed letters from many of the grandchildren are also in the file. LBP, AASPM.

82. Louis J. McCarthy to Leo Binz, January 10, 1966. LBP, AASPM.

83. Interview, Jerome Dittberner, November 18, 1999.

84. Report on the Voting and Opinions Expressed in the Questionnaire Submitted to the Clergy of the Archdiocese of St. Paul and Minneapolis, February 12, 1968. Baumgaertner File.

85. Annual Report (1967–1968), pp. 12–13.

86. Interview, Timothy Nolan, September 21, 1999.

87. Trustees, III (June 17, 1970), p. 2.

88. Executive Committee, Board of Trustees (June 17, 1970), III, n.p. and Trustees (October 6, 1970), III, p. 1.

89. John A. Sweeney, Jerome D. Quinn, and Patrick J. Ryan to William Baumgaertner, January 27, 1971, Seminary Papers, AASPM.

90. Trustees, III (January 27, 1971), p. 1.

91. Trustees, III (January 27, 1971), p. 5.

92. Trustees, III (March 1, 1971), pp. 2–3. This meeting was held in conjunction with the Saint Paul Seminary faculty.

93. Trustees, III (March 1, 1971), pp. 1–2.

94. Interview, Timothy Nolan, September 21, 1999.

95. Interview, John R. Roach, November 17, 1999.

96. As quoted in White, p. 413. From the introduction to Stafford Poole, *Seminary in Crisis* (New York: Herder and Herder, 1966), p. 14.

97. John Tracy Ellis, ed., *The Catholic Priest in the United States: Historical Investigations* (Collegeville, Minnesota: St. John's University Press, 1971), vii.

98. Greeley, Andrew M., ed. *The Catholic Priest in the United States: Sociological Investigations,* National Opinion Research Center, University of Chicago (Washington, D.C.: United States Catholic Conference, 1972).

99. Gerard Sloyan, ed., *Secular Priest in the New Church* (New York: Herder and Herder, 1967).

100. James Kavanaugh, *A Modern Priest Looks at His Outdated Church* (New York: Trident Press, 1967). Kavanaugh had written an article the year before in *The Saturday Evening Post* (March 12, 1966), titled "I Am a Priest—I Want to Marry," under the pseudonym "Father Stephen Nash."

101. Interview, Charles Froehle, September 16, 1999.

102. Interviews with Paul LaFontaine, September 14, 1999; Thomas Fisch, September 19, 1999; Phillip Rask, September 19, 1999; and Eugene Tiffany, October 14, 1999.

103. Interviews with Charles Froehle, September 16, 1999; and Thomas Fisch, September 19, 1999.

104. Interview, Charles Froehle, September 16, 1999.

105. Shannon, *Reluctant Dissenter,* p. 174.

106. William Baumgaertner, Prayer offered on the Summit Avenue Mall at the entrance of the Saint Paul Seminary at the conclusion of the "Save Our Shannon" march from the Cathedral of St. Paul, June 8, 1969. Baumgaertner File.

107. Interview, Paul LaFontaine, September 14, 1999.

108. Annual Report (1968–1969), "Programs." This segment is in a discussion of the spiritual formation program.

109. Interview, Stanley Srnec, July 26, 1999.

110. Interview, Gerald E. Keefe, September 23, 1999.

111. Gerald E. Keefe, *Formation Models in a Seminary Community* (St. Paul Seminary: 1973). ASPS.

112. Interview, Charles Froehle, September 16, 1999.

113. One visitor stated: "If a program is as good as its director, then this spiritual formation program has to be good since the students are in overwhelming agreement that there is just nobody as good as their spiritual director, Father Keefe. He is lovingly referred to as 'Pastor of our Seminary.'" Report of the Bishops' Committee on Priestly Formation: Concerning Visitation—St. Paul Seminary and St. John Vianney Seminary, March 25–27, 1974, p. 9. ASPS.

114. "Final Report to the American Association of Theological Schools and the North Central Association Regarding the Accreditation of the St. Paul Seminary, St. Paul, Minnesota," November 27, 1973. Included as an appendix to the Annual Report (1974–1975).

115. NCA/AATS Report, November 27, 1973. ASPS.

116. Report of the Bishops' Committee on Priestly Formation on the Saint Paul Seminary, March 25–27, 1974, pp. 1–3. ASPS.

117. Clearly, many of them had "deaconitis" when they were on the campus. Thomas Sieg, ordained a priest in 1971, recalls that when the class returned for spring semester they did a parody on the Lipton's soup advertisement "Is it soup yet?" Tom ordered buttons, which the deacons faithfully wore, that read: "Is it May yet?" The faculty was not amused. Interview, Thomas Sieg, September 23, 1999.

118. Interview, Kathleen Marie Shields, C.S.J., July 9, 1996.

119. "Interim means on-the-job training for seminarians," *Catholic Bulletin,* n.d., n.p. I am grateful to Kathleen Marie Shields, C.S.J., for this clipping. Robert Rolfes, ordained in 1977 for the Diocese of St. Cloud, was one of the Theology II students quoted, so it was very likely published in winter 1975.

120. Interview, William Baumgaertner, December 2, 1999.

121. Interview, John F. Kinney, October 6, 1999.

122. John R. Roach, "Homily for Archbishop Binz's Funeral," LBP, AASPM.

123. Interview, Gerald O'Keefe, September 27, 1999. Bishop O'Keefe described a plane trip to a meeting with Binz and Byrne. Byrne had brought along a briefcase of papers and spent the better part of the trip briefing Binz and getting his "approval."

Chapter 13—John R. Roach: Facing the Seminary Challenge

1. Confidential Minutes, Meeting of the Representatives of the Boards of Trustees of the College of St. Thomas and the Saint Paul Seminary, December 16, 1983. I am very grateful to Thomas Dolan, member of the Saint Paul Seminary Board of Trustees from 1980 to 1993, for giving me his file of material from his years on the board. (Hereafter, Dolan Papers.)

2. Thomas Reese, *Archbishop: Inside the Power Structure of the American Catholic Church* (San Francisco: Harper and Row, 1989), pp. 27, 29.

3. *Catholic Bulletin,* Special Section: "Legacy of an Archbishop," September 28, 1995, pp. 4, 10–11.

4. Martha Sawyer Allen, "Each dawn, new hope: Archbishop Roach, 65, finds it in his faith, in his life," Minneapolis *Star and Tribune,* December 25, 1986, Section A: 1, 8.

5 *Catholic Bulletin,* September 28, 1995, pp. 10–11.

6. *Catholic Bulletin,* September 28, 1995, Special Section, pp. 10–11. Roach was appointed archbishop on May 21, 1975.

7. Trustees, III (October 7, 1975), p. 2.

8. Trustees, III (October 7, 1975), p. 5.

9. Interview, W. Charles Henry, January 4, 2000. Henry was invited to supervise the food service at the newly constructed Minneapolis campus of the University of St. Thomas, and did so for a year (1992–1993), but returned to his previous position in Binz Refectory after that interim and retired in May 2001. See also Annual Report (1975–1976), p. 10, and Annual Report (1976–1977), p. 9.

10. Timothy P. Quinn to William Baumgaertner, March 24, 1977. Included with board minutes, Trustees, III (June 15, 1977).

11. Interview, J. Thomas Simonet, September 14, 1999.

12. Trustees, III (October 3, 1978), p. 4.

13. Trustees, III (October 2, 1979), p. 2.

14. Interview, John Sondag, October 28, 1999.

15. Annual Report (1972–1973), p. 4a.

16. See Seminary Directory, 1974–1975, and 1975–1976. Seminary Papers, AASPM.

17. Annual Report (1972–1973), p. 1, and letter of announcement from Msgr. William Baumgaertner, May 22, 1973 in appendix. See also brochure, "A Priestly Call—For All Seasons," LBP, AASPM.

18. Interview, Kevin McDonough, November 19, 1999.

19. Interview, James Moudry, November 11, 1999.

20. Admissions Report, 1982–1983 (September 3, 1982), p. 2. Dolan Papers.

21. Interview, John Bauer, November 23, 1999.

22. Interview, William Baumgaertner, October 24, 1999.

23. Trustees, III (January 21, 1980), p. 3.

24. Interview, Charles Froehle, November 16, 1999.

25. Louis McCarthy to Leo Binz, February 20, 1965. LBP, AASPM.

26. Charles Froehle, *The Idea of Sacred Sign According to Abbot Anscar Vonier* (Rome: Catholic Book Agency, 1971).

27. Trustees, III (October 14, 1980), p. 3.

28. Interview, John R. Roach, November 17, 1999.

29. Trustees, I (September 19, 1895), p. 8.

30. Trustees, III (January 28, 1983), p. 4.

31. Trustees, III (October 6, 1981), pp. 3–4. Emphasis mine.

32. Interview, Charles Froehle, November 16, 1999.

33. Interview, John Forliti, September 27, 2000.

34. Interview, James Moudry, November 11, 1999.

35. Trustees, III (December 1, 1981), pp. 3–4. Emphasis mine.

36. Interview, John R. Roach, November 17, 1999.

37. Summary of Meeting with John R. Roach, January 13, 1982. Dolan Papers.

38. Interview, Charles Froehle, November 16, 1999. Trustees, III (June 15, 1977), p. 3.

39. Interview, Thomas Sieg, September 23, 1999.

40. Minutes, Faculty Workshop, January 20, 1982.

41. Strategic Plan, "Goals," The Saint Paul Seminary, September 1, 1982.

42. Trustees, III (June 8, 1982), pp. 2–4.

43. Trustees, III (January 28, 1983), pp. 2–3.

44. Interview, Victor Klimoski, November 11, 1999. See also Annual Report (1981–1982), p. 2.

45. Interview, Thomas J. Fisch, November 23, 1999.

46. Annual Report (1981–1982), pp. 2–3.

47. Interview, William Bullock, November 27, 1999. See also Trustees, III (October 5, 1982), p. 3.

48. Memorandum to File, Charles Froehle, "Committee for Future Directions" (Bullock Committee), December 3, 1982. Dolan Papers.

49. John Gilbert to Charles Froehle, December 1, 1982. Seminary Papers, AASPM.

50. Long-Range Planning Committee, Resolution (Tennis Courts), January 28, 1983. Msgr. Terrence J. Murphy to Father Charles Froehle, February 17, 1983. Cover letter with copy, James Fennell to Thomas E. Dolan, February 24, 1983. John B. Burke, Jr. to James Fennell, March 3, 1983. Memo on "Tennis Courts: St. Thomas Proposal," March 14, 1983. Father Charles Froehle to Msgr. Terrence J. Murphy, March 18, 1983. Dolan Papers.

51. Charles Froehle to Terrence J. Murphy, March 18, 1983. Dolan Papers.

52. James J. Fennell to J. Thomas Simonet, April 5, 1983. Dolan Papers.

53. Tom Hauser, "Committee to Study Integration of Seminaries, College," *Catholic Bulletin,* June 9, 1983, p. 8.

54. Future Directions Committee, Summary of Meeting, June 24, 1983. Letter and document of appraisal, E. Vincent Dolan to Msgr. Terrence J. Murphy, July 11, 1983. Dolan Papers.

55. Memo, James Fennell to Charles Froehle, Summary of Long-Range Planning Committee Meeting, July 18, 1983. Dolan Papers.

56. Present were Bishop Bullock, Msgr. Murphy, Father Froehle, Msgr. Pates, Dr. Patrick Barrett, Donald Moorhead, Father John Gilbert, Thomas Dolan, and David Koch.

57. Future Directions Committee, Summary of Meeting, July 22, 1983; memo, William Bullock to Committee for Future Directions, July 28, 1983. Dolan Papers.

58. Charles Froehle to Thomas E. Dolan, August 26, 1983. Dolan Papers.

59. Interview, Thomas Brioschi, February 16, 2000.

60. Trustees, III (October 6, 1981), p. 4.

61. Annual Report (1982–1983), p. 7.

62. Confidential Memo, Charles Froehle, Summary of October 11 Meeting for Long-Range Planning, October 21, 1983. Dolan Papers.

63. William Bullock, Memo to Committee on Future Directions, October 28, 1983.

64. Thomas E. Dolan to Charles Froehle, November 7, 1983. Dolan Papers.

65. Brady Educational Center, Binz Refectory, McCarthy Recreation Building, the seminary convent, Grace Residence, Cretin Residence, Loras Residence, the heating plant, and the free-standing garages.

66. Confidential Memo—Draft #4: The Saint Paul Seminary Board of Trustees Long Range Planning Committee, November 16, 1983. Dolan Papers.

67. Trustees, III (November 29, 1983), pp. 2–3.

68. Interview, Charles Froehle, January 5, 2000.

69. Interview, Thomas Dolan, November 19, 1999.

70. Minutes of the Board of Trustees of the College of St. Thomas, October 7, 1983, and March 6, 1984. President's Office, University of St. Thomas.

71. Interview, Charles Froehle, January 5, 2000.

72. Confidential Notes, Meeting of the Representatives of the Boards of Trustees of the College of St. Thomas and The Saint Paul Seminary, December 16, 1983. Dolan Papers.

73. Appraisal attached to Confidential Memo regarding Budget Projections, April 30, 1984. Dolan Papers.

74. Father Charles Froehle to Board Members, January 5, 1984. Dolan Papers.

75. Interviews with Charles Froehle, March 15, 2001; and Victor Klimoski, March 23, 2001.

76. Bishop Matthew H. Clark to Archbishop John R. Roach, n.d. A copy of a memo from Bishop Matthew Clark to Bishop John Marshall accompanying the letter to Archbishop Roach and the Report of the Visitation Team of the Saint Paul Seminary, St. Paul, Minnesota, February 13–17, 1984, is dated Sep-

tember 18, 1984. Rector's File, Saint Paul Seminary School of Divinity of the University of St. Thomas (SPSSOD). (Hereafter, the report will be referred to as "Vatican Report, 1984.")

77. Vatican Report, 1984, p. 21.

78. Vatican Report, 1984, pp. 23, 25, 34, 43, 59 and beyond.

79. Interview, Charles Froehle, March 15, 2001.

80. Vatican Report, 1984, p. 24.

81. NCA/ATS Reaccreditation Report, March 1984, p. 24. SPSSOD Rector's Files. (Hereafter, "NCA/ATS Report 1984.")

82. NCA/ATS Report 1984, p. 28.

83. NCA/ATS Report 1984, p. 2.

84. Interview, James Moudry, November 11, 1999.

85. Interview, Charles Froehle, October 29, 1999.

86. Interview, Thomas Holloran, February 25, 2000.

87. "College of St. Thomas/Saint Paul Seminary Discussions—February 1984," initialed by CJK (Charles J. Keffer), February 7, 1984. A second proposal is stapled to it which appears to be the work of the seminary team. Dolan Papers.

88. Charles Froehle to Thomas Dolan, March 5, 1984. Dolan Papers.

89. Confidential Memo, Long-Range Planning Committee, April 9, 1984. Dolan Papers.

90. Confidential Memo of Clarification: Proposal by the Saint Paul Seminary regarding Land and Buildings, April 9, 1984. Dolan Papers.

91. Charles Froehle, Confidential Memorandum for Board of Trustees Meeting (May 23, 1984), May 15, 1984, p. 3. Dolan Papers.

92. Affiliation Agreement, effective July 1, 1986. The documents were formally signed in a ceremony on May 3, 1987.

93. Trustees, III (May 23, 1984), p. 4.

94. Charles Froehle to Thomas E. Dolan, May 1, 1984. Dolan Papers.

95. Thomas E. Dolan, "Remarks to the Saint Paul Seminary Board of Trustees," May 23, 1984. Dolan Papers. Dolan's commitment to the seminary and to the archdiocese was explicit in more than his effort and energy regarding the affiliation. His son, Timothy Dolan, who had been a student at Saint Paul

Seminary, was ordained to the priesthood in 1983. Dolan himself was ordained a permanent deacon for the archdiocese the same year. Interview, Thomas E. Dolan, November 19, 1999.

96. Trustees, III (May 23, 1984), pp. 1, 5.

97. Charles Froehle, Confidential Memorandum, Board of Trustees Meeting, May 23, 1984, p. 5. Dolan Papers.

98. Charles Froehle, Confidential Memorandum, Board of Trustees Meeting, May 23, 1984. Dolan Papers.

99. Annual Report (1983–1984), p. 9.

100. Charles Froehle, "To the Planning Committee of the Board of Trustees," August 20, 1984. See also Donald R. LaMagdeleine, "Summary of the Archdiocesan Priests' Responses to the St. Thomas-Seminary Affiliation," September 20, 1984. Dolan Papers.

101. Interview, John R. Roach, October 15, 1998.

102. Interview, Michael O'Connell, November 9, 1999.

103. Charles Froehle to The Saint Paul Seminary Board of Trustees, "Consultation on Affiliation," September 19, 1984. Dolan Papers.

104. In addition to the agreement on governance and administration, land and buildings, and finances, there was a section titled "Clarifications" composed by Father Froehle and Dr. Keffer. Although attached to the document, these were not definitive but were intended to shed light on areas that were not yet clarified in the document submitted above. These included the transfer of the Religious Education Center and the Master of Arts in Pastoral Studies program to the School of Divinity, budget procedures as they would function under the affiliation, and library services—particularly the position of the Archbishop Ireland Memorial Library within the larger St. Thomas library system. There were recommendations regarding the seminary maintaining a business office and a development office but transferring the responsibility for coordinating use of facilities to the college, with the exception of the seminary buildings. The clarifications also addressed maintenance, food service, and arrangements for the residence of seminarians and offices in Cretin and Grace while the new building was under construction and the administration building was renovated.

105. Trustees, III (October 2, 1984), p. 2.

106. Trustees, III (October 2, 1984), pp. 3–4.

107. Annual Report (1984–1985), p. 1.

108. Interview, Richard Banker, January 12, 2000.

109. Interview, Thomas Brioschi, February 16, 2000.

110. Minutes of the Meeting of the Faculty of the Saint Paul Seminary, November 12, 1984. Athans File.

Chapter 14—The Seminary Within the University: Crisis, Consolidation, Clarification (1985–1995)

1. Transcription of Archbishop Roach's comments at the conclusion of the Presbytery Day, September 18, 1985. Minutes of the Presbyteral Council, Chancery, ASPM. (Hereafter, Presbyteral Council.)

2. Trustees, III (February 22, 1985), pp. 1–4.

3. Interview, Michael O'Connell, November 9, 1999.

4. "Support Pours in While Archbishop Awaits Court Date," *Catholic Bulletin,* February 28, 1985, p. 1.

5. Presbyteral Council, February 26, 1985.

6. "Resolution," *Catholic Bulletin*, February 28, 1985, pp. 3, 10.

7. Interview, Michael O'Connell, November 9, 1999.

8. Allen, *Star and Tribune*, December 25, 1986, pp. 1A, 8A.

9. Interview, Edward Flahavan, November 15, 1999.

10. Presbyteral Council, March 26, 1985.

11. Presbyteral Council, April 23, 1985.

12. Interview, Edward Flahavan, November 15, 1999.

13. Presbyteral Council, April 23, 1985.

14. Interview, Charles Froehle, January 5, 2000.

15. Presbyteral Council, April 23, 1985.

16. Interview, Frederick Campbell, February 10, 2000.

17. Interviews with Edward Flahavan, November 15, 1999; John M. Bauer, November 23, 1999; and Frederick Campbell, February 10, 2000.

18. Interview, Thomas Fisch, August 23, 2000. This is also the recollection of the author.

19. Interview, John R. Roach, November 17, 1999.

20. Fathers Stephen Adrian, Michael Kennedy, William Kenny, Frederick Campbell, Charles Froehle, John Sweeney, Walter Sochacki, Arnold Weber, and Michael O'Connell, and college provost Dr. Charles Keffer.

21. Michael Kennedy to priests, n.d., but fact sheet is dated May 28, 1985. These documents, plus the "Analysis of the Presbyteral Council Survey" by Donald LaMagdeleine, are with the Minutes of the Presbyteral Council, Chancery, ASPM.

22. Presbyteral Council, July 23, 1985.

23. Trustees, III (May 29, 1985), p. 3.

24. Michael J. Kennedy to Mary Christine Athans, B.V.M., September 10, 1985. Athans File.

25. The author had a brief telephone conversation with Msgr. Richard Schuler, November 15, 1999. He declined to be interviewed but agreed that he had a major role in composing the proposal. He stated: "I don't want to discuss it [the affiliation] except that I am against it."

26. Interview, John M. Bauer, November 23, 1999.

27. Interview, Kenneth Pierre, November 19, 1999.

28. Minutes of the Presbytery Day, September 18, 1985. See also John Sweeney's introduction to the first issue for discussion. Presbyteral Council.

29. Kenneth Pierre, Journal (unpublished), September 18, 1985. I am very grateful to Father Pierre for sharing his written reflections with me. Over three hundred priests were in attendance for most of the day.

30. From a transcription of Archbishop John Roach's comments at the conclusion of the Presbytery Day, September 18, 1985. Presbyteral Council.

31. Material from Presbytery Day, September 18, 1985, Athans File. The specific percentages were calculated by Donald LaMagdeleine for the final report to the Presbyteral Council.

32. Interview, James Motl, O.P., January 14, 2000.

33. Presbyteral Council, October 15, 1985.

34. Minutes of the Board of Trustees of the College of St. Thomas, October 29, 1985.

35. Clark Morphew, "Plan for Seminary Affiliation with St. Thomas," Saint Paul *Pioneer Press,* October 16, 1985.

36. Annual Report (1983–1984), pp. 9–10.

37. Interview, Charles Froehle, January 5, 2000.

38. Annual Report (1985–1986), p. 9.

39. Kenneth Pierre, Journal, September 5, 1987.

40. Trustees, III (November 4, 1987), pp. 3–4. John Rauma, the architect, noted that City Council member Sonnen would take architectural data to the other council members to see that all the approved conditions intended by the council were included in the final council plans.

41. Interview, Charles Froehle, February 28, 2000.

42. Interview, Charles Froehle, November 16, 1999.

43. Interview, Gerald Anderley, February 25, 2000.

44. Annual Report (1986–1987), p. 13.

45. *Catholic Bulletin*, October 13, 1985, p. 2.

46. Annual Report (1986–1987), p. 13.

47. Interview, Richard Pates, November 8, 1999.

48. Trustees, III (January 23, 1990), p. 5.

49. Charles Froehle to Christine Athans, B.V.M., November 12, 1984. Correspondence, plus minutes of meetings and other data in Athans File.

50. The membership included faculty members James Moudry, Thomas Fisch, and Sue Seid-Martin, plus student Rick Banker, from the chapel committee; faculty member Christine Athans, B.V.M.; board member John Burke, Jr.; director of ministry for the archdiocese Patricia Gries; acting dean of the Pastoral Studies program Arthur Zannoni; associate director of vocations Kathleen Storms, S.S.N.D.; associate director of BeFriender Ministry Sandra Skach; business manager Lois Nyman from the Administration Building Committee; faculty member Jerome Dittberner; board member Patrick Lannan; and students Gregory Baxter and Thomas Strapp from the Residence Hall Committee.

51. James W. Moudry to Christine Athans, B.V.M., May 6, 1986. This letter and other material from the Program Design Committee are in Athans File.

52. James Moudry to Building Committee, June 19, 1986. Athans File.

53. The Summary Report of the Building Committee, St. Paul Seminary School of Divinity, College of St. Thomas, September 17, 1986. This document is expanded in the Report of the Program Design Committee—Progress Report to the Board of Trustees, November 7, 1986. Athans File.

54. Interview, Thomas Dolan, March 1, 2001.

55. Trustees, III (November 19, 1986), pp. 3–4.

56. Charles Froehle to Building Committee and Program Design Committee, December 8, 1986. Athans File.

57. Trustees, III (April 14, 1987), pp. 4, 7.

58. Charles Froehle to Program Design Committee Members, September 21, 1987. Athans File.

59. Annual Report (1986–1987), p. 6.

60. Katarina Schuth, *Reason for the Hope: The Futures of Roman Catholic Theologates* (Wilmington, Delaware: Michael Glazier, Inc., 1989), p. 196.

61. Interview, Robert G. Kennedy, May 9, 2000.

62. Interview, Jan Viktora, April 25, 2000. She inquired of Martin Shallbetter, the vocation director, as to the possibility of beginning the M.A. program in theology at the seminary in May 1974. He asked the rector and the archbishop at a meeting shortly thereafter. They indicated that if she met the requirements, she could be accepted. She began in the fall of 1974 and completed her course work in 1978. She finished her thesis in 1985 shortly before joining the staff at the seminary.

63. Annual Report (1986–1987), p. 8. According to this report there were fifty-three registered in the fall semester, sixty-one in the spring semester, and seventy-five in the summer session. In the 1986–1987 academic year there were four lay students studying for the M.Div. degree, seven lay students in the M.A. in theology, and 189 registrants for MAPS courses in the fall, spring, and summer semesters.

64. See Saint Paul *Pioneer Press,* February 4–5, 1987; Minneapolis *Star and Tribune,* February 4–5, 1987; *Catholic Bulletin,* February 15–22, 1987.

65. Minneapolis *Star and Tribune,* February 4, 1987.

66. Saint Paul *Pioneer Press,* February 5, 1987.

67. Pat Norby, "Archdiocese was national leader in addressing sex abuse," *The Catholic Spirit*, June 22, 2000, p. 56A.

68. Interview, William McDonough, April 11, 2001.

69. Archbishop Harry J. Flynn published a revision of the statement titled *A Time to Heal: Preventing and Responding to Ministry-Related Sexual Misconduct* (St. Paul, Minnesota: Archdiocese of St. Paul and Minneapolis, 1998).

70. "NCCB Establishes Committee on Sexual Abuse," *Origins* 23 (1993): 104–105.

71. Interview, William S. Fallon, May 2, 2001. The amount of punitive damages was reduced, and the Diocese of Winona was held liable for $187,000. The $855,000 in compensatory damages was covered by insurance.

72. Charles Froehle, "Father Adamson and Child Abuse," Rector's Conference, Saint Paul Seminary, December 12, 1990. Froehle File.

73. Charles Froehle, "Ceremony Marking the Demolition of the Ad. Bldg.," December 14, 1987. ASPS.

74. Interview, Stephen Adrian, November 24, 1999.

75 Charles Froehle to Christine Athans, B.V.M., March 18, 1988. The author was invited to participate as a representative of the Program Design Committee, and as a representative of the faculty. Athans File.

76. Annual Report (1987–1988), p. 18.

77. Annual Report (1988–1989), p. 15.

78. See Dedication File 1989. ASPS.

79. Interview, James Moudry, November 16, 1999.

80. Material prepared for the Saint Paul Seminary Board of Trustees by the Building Committee, April 29, 1986. This quotation is from a draft dated April 10, 1985. Athans File.

81 Interview, Thomas Dolan, March 1, 2001.

82. Interview, John R. Roach, November 17, 1999.

83. Interviews with Charles Froehle, March 25, 2000; and Patricia Gries, January 24, 2000.

84. Interview, John R. Roach, November 17, 1999.

85. Kenneth Pierre, Journal, May 25, 1985.

86. Interview, John R. Roach, October 15, 1998.

87. Richard E. Pates to John R. Roach, November 12, 1986. ASPS.

88. Interview, John R. Roach, November 15, 1998.

89. Interview, Richard E. Pates, November 8, 1999.

90. Rector's File, SPSSOD.

91. Interview, John R. Roach, November 17, 1999.

92. Interview, Charles Froehle, March 25, 2000.

93. Interviews with James Moudry, November 11, 1999; and Charles Froehle, November 16, 1999.

94. Interview, Gene Scapanski, November 22, 1999.

95. Interview, Victor Klimoski, November 11, 1999.

96. Interview, Charles Froehle, November 16, 1999.

97. See Affiliation Agreement, July 1, 1986, Article VI, p. 9, and Amended Affiliation Agreement, October 29, 1991, pp. 9–10.

98. Amended Affiliation Handbook, November 11, 1993, p. 7.

99. Annual Report (1989–1990), p. 1.

100. Trustees, III (May 22, 1990), pp. 5–6.

101. Annual Report (1989–1990), p. 21.

102. Annual Report (1990–1991), p. 23.

103. See Jerome D. Quinn, *The Early Church: Two Studies* (St. Paul, Minnesota: University of St. Thomas, 1996). This booklet, prepared by Michael Patrick O'Connor, contains a bibliography of Quinn's work and an article by O'Connor and includes a preface with biographical material on Quinn by Phillip J. Rask.

104. Jerome D. Quinn, *The Letter to Titus: A New Translation with Notes and Commentary and An Introduction to Titus, I and II Timothy, The Pastoral Epistles,* The Anchor Bible, v. 35 (New York: Doubleday, 1990), xi–xiv.

105. Jerome D. Quinn and William C. Wacker, *The First and Second Letters to Timothy* (Grand Rapids, Michigan: William B. Erdmans Publishing Company, 2000).

106. Victor Klimoski and Mary Christine Athans, B.V.M., eds., *In Service of the Church: Essays on Theology and Ministry Honoring Reverend Charles L. Froehle* (St. Paul, Minnesota: University of St. Thomas, 1993).

Chapter 15—Harry Joseph Flynn: Beginning the Second Century

1. Interview, Harry J. Flynn, December 30, 1999.

2. See *Catholic Bulletin,* February 24, 1994, p. 1, and March 3, 1994, p. 1.

3. Interview, Harry J. Flynn, December 30, 1999.

4. Bob Zyskowski, "So, What's the New Archbishop Like Anyway?" *Catholic Bulletin,* February 24, 1994, p. 3.

5. See articles by Bob Zyskowski and Pat Norby, *Catholic Bulletin,* February 24, 1994, p. 3.

6. Phillip J. Rask, "The List of the Twelve Tribes of Israel." Unpublished Ph.D. Dissertation, Catholic University of America, Washington, D.C., 1990.

7. Interview, Phillip Rask, September 27, 2000.

8. John Paul II, *Pastores Dabo Vobis,* #60. Phillip Rask, "Orientation for New Students," September 1993, and "Rector's Conference," October 27, 1993. Rector's Office, SPSSOD.

9. "Institutional Self-Study for the Association of Theological Schools and the North Central Association: The Saint Paul Seminary School of Divinity of the University of St. Thomas," October 1993. See also "Appendices."

10. Cushing made these comments at the oral report delivered to faculty and staff on October 20, 1993, at the conclusion of the visitation.

11. Daniel O. Aleshire, Associate Director of the ATS, to Father Phillip Rask, January 28, 1994. Rector's Office, SPSSOD.

12. Trustees, III (January 27, 1994), p. 6.

13. Final Report of the ATS Visiting Team, November 29, 1993, p. 19.

14. Annual Report (1993–1994), p. 4.

15. "Summary of the Work of the Task Force on Governance of the School of Divinity," submitted to the Saint Paul Seminary Board of Trustees, May 4,

1995. Kindness of Janet Gould, executive secretary to the rector/vice-president. (Hereafter, "Summary.")

16. "Governance of the School of Divinity" (Draft Statement), April 27, 1995, submitted to the board May 4, 1995.

17. Trustees, III (May 4, 1995), pp. 4–5.

18. Trustees, III (May 9, 1996), p. 5. See also Affiliation Agreement (1996 edition), p. 10 on the role of the rector in the administration of the School of Divinity.

19. Annual Report (1990–1991), pp. 9–10.

20. Annual Report (1996–1997), p. 26.

21. Annual Report (1998–1999), p. 26.

22. Jan Viktora, "Theological Teaching for the Church's Ministries," Report of the St. Paul Seminary School of Divinity of the University of St. Thomas to the Keystone Project, June 2000.

23. Interview, Jan Viktora, November 2, 2000.

24. Interview, Sister Paul Therese Saiko, S.S.N.D., October 20, 2000. Initially Sister Paul Therese joined the spiritual formation faculty part-time as a spiritual director, but she has also been coordinator of evaluations and administrator of the spiritual formation program.

25. The rector and the student's vocation director may also participate. (The rector attends all third-year reviews.) At the conclusion of each review, the accompaniment team offers commendations and areas for growth and makes a recommendation to the rector for continuance or non-continuance in the program. This approach has allowed the seminarian to be both supported and challenged in his discernment for priesthood.

26. Thomas W. Krenik, *Formation for Priestly Celibacy: A Resource Book* (Washington, D.C.: NCEA, 1999). Introduction and Epilogue ("Celibacy: A Way to Love") by Archbishop Harry J. Flynn.

27. "Seminary Visitation Team Report: The Saint Paul Seminary School of Divinity, University of Saint Thomas, Saint Paul, Minnesota, October 26–30, 1998," p. 6. Rector's Office, SPSSOD.

28. Interview, Paul Lafontaine, November 17, 2000.

29. Interview, John M. Bauer, December 7, 2000. On average, only five students could be accepted each year.

30. Interview, William Baumgaertner, November 21, 2000.

31. Interview, Max Shapiro, November 1, 2000.

32. Interview, Charles Froehle, November 4, 2000.

33. Interview, Charles Froehle, November 4, 2000.

34. An expression used frequently by Father Thomas Stransky, C.S.P., director emeritus of the Tantur Ecumenical Institute in Jerusalem.

35. As quoted in Max A. Shapiro, "Introduction," *Proceedings of the Center for Jewish-Christian Learning,* ed. Mary Christine Athans, B.V.M., Vol. 8 (Spring 1993), p. 7.

36. "In a Seminary Garden," *St. Thomas: The Magazine of the University of St. Thomas* (St. Paul, Minnesota: University of St. Thomas, Winter 1999), p. 28. Photos by Roger Rich.

37. This type of cross signifies the archbishop's jurisdiction over the ecclesiastical province, emphasizing the school as a seminary that serves the larger region. See also Annual Report (1997–1998), p. 26. In that year the seminary served nineteen dioceses.

38. Others on the committee were Dr. David Jenkins, Dr. James Callahan of the music department of the (then) College of St. Thomas, and James Frazier, then music director of the archdiocese.

39. Dedication Booklet, "Cyril F. Rotter Memorial Organ, May 7, 2000, Saint Mary's Chapel."

40. Trustees, III (January 24, 1991), p. 6.

41. See Trustees, III (January 18, 1996), p. 5; May 9, 1996, p. 3; and October 17, 1996, p. 5. Msgr. William Baumgaertner contributed $2,000, one-third the cost of the commission.

42. Martha Sawyer Allen, "Woodbury Priest Named Auxiliary Bishop," *Star Tribune,* December 23, 2000.

43. Annual Report (1998–1999), pp. 2–4.

44. Jeanne P. McLean, *Leading from the Center: The Emerging Role of the Chief Academic Officer in Theological Schools* (Atlanta, Georgia: Scholars Press, 1999).

45. Interview, Dennis Dease, October 29, 1999.

46. Interview, Phillip Rask, September 27, 2000.

47. Trustees, III (January 20, 2000), pp. 5–6.

48. Trustees, III (January 20, 2000), pp. 4–5. Interview, Phillip Rask, September 27, 2000. One reason for the financing of the spiritual formation program by the archdiocese at the time of the affiliation was so that the tax-exempt status of the university would not be jeopardized. Hence, the clarification that university funds would not be used for that program.

49. Katarina Schuth, *Seminaries, Theologates and the Future of Church Ministry: An Analysis of Trends and Transitions* (Collegeville, Minnesota: Liturgical Press, 1999).

50. Interview, Katarina Schuth, O.S.F., October 24, 2000.

51. Interview, Katarina Schuth, O.S.F., October 24, 2000.

52. Recipients have been: Father Bernard Reiser (ordained in 1949) in 1998; Father John Forliti (ordained in 1962), and Father Damian Zuerlein (ordained in 1981) of the Omaha Archdiocese in 1999; Msgr. John Sweeney (ordained in 1941) and Father Raymond Monsour (ordained in 1963) in 2000; Father William Fahnlander (ordained in 1946) of the Bismarck Diocese, Mr. Richard Leahy (class of 1957), and Father Gregory Tolaas (ordained in 1983) in 2001. Father Fahnlander received the award posthumously.

Chapter 16—"To Work for the Whole People"

1. "Address of Archbishop Ireland at the Dedication of the Saint Paul Seminary on 4 September 1895." Original copy used by the archbishop on the occasion in JIP, AASPM. Emphasis mine.

2. See above, chapter 3, p. 27.

3. John Ireland, *The Church and Modern Society,* I, 90.

4. John Ireland, *The Church and Modern Society,* I, 99.

5. John Ireland, *The Church and Modern Society,* I, 95.

6. John A. Ryan, *Social Doctrine in Action,* pp. 69–70.

7. Martin E. Marty, *A Short History of American Catholicism* (Allen, Texas: Thomas More—Tabor Publishing, 1995), p. 150. An earlier version of this work was titled *An Invitation to American Catholic History.*

8. Sydney E. Ahlstrom, *A Religious History of the American People* (New Haven: Yale University Press, 1972), p. 1005.

9. Franklin D. Roosevelt to John A. Ryan in "Testimonial to Right Reverend John A. Ryan, D.D. on Occasion of His Seventieth Birthday Anniversary May 25, 1939," p. 16. JARP, ACUA.

10. Francis L. Broderick, *Right Reverend New Dealer: John A. Ryan* (New York: Macmillan, 1963).

11. "Francis Gilligan, 'labor priest' during the 1930s and 1940s, dies at 98," *Pioneer Press* (April 7, 1997).

12. Bob Zyskowski, "You build up a lot of stories during 65 years as a priest," *Catholic Bulletin* (January 4, 1991). See also "Father Timeless," *Star Tribune* (July 5, 1991).

13. John A. Ryan to Austin Dowling, June 20, 1926. DP, AASPM.

14. As quoted in "Monsignor Gilligan Blessed Us Thrice," eulogy preached by Msgr. Richard Pates at the funeral of Msgr. Gilligan April 10, 1997, *The Catholic Spirit*, April 24, 1997.

15. Brady, *The Voice,* p. 12.

16. I am grateful to Father Edward Flahavan for the notes he prepared for the panel "A Catholic Vision of Social Justice: Monsignor Francis J. Gilligan" at the University of St. Thomas, October 16, 2000. Other panelists included Fathers Frederick Mertz and Austin Ward.

17. Pates, p. 17.

18. Brady, *The Voice,* p. 13.

19. Interview, Edward Grzeskowiak, July 29, 1998.

20. Interview, Edward Grzeskowiak, July 29, 1998.

21. Interview, Edward Grzeskowiak, July 29, 1998.

22. Interview, Edward Grzeskowiak, July 29, 1998.

23. Interview, Edward Flahavan, November 15, 1999.

24. From the speech delivered at the presentation of the Distinguished Alumni Award to Father Edward J. Flahavan from the Saint Paul Seminary School of Divinity, Fall 1996.

25. Edward J. Flahavan, "A Quarter Century of Alms: The Aid Given to the Diocese of Saint Paul by the Society for the Propagation of the Faith, 1850–1873." Unpublished M.A. thesis, Saint Paul Seminary, 1956.

26. Interview, Edward Flahavan, November 15, 1999.

27. Interview, J. Jerome Boxleitner, May 30, 2001. See also John S. Swanholm, *Caring Beyond Belief: A History of Catholic Charities of the Archdiocese of St. Paul and Minneapolis* (Minneapolis: Catholic Charities, 1995).

28. J. Jerome Boxleitner, "Catholic Charities: First of Many Programs began in 1869," *The Catholic Spirit,* June 22, 2000, p. 45A. Boxleitner is now director emeritus.

29. Interview, Leo Tibesar, October 5, 2000.

30. William Busch, "An Apostle of Liturgical Life," *Orate Fratres* (1938–1939) 13: 103. See also William Busch, "Past, Present, Future," *Orate Fratres* (1951) 25: 482.

31. William A. Busch, "Construction of an Altar," *Ecclesiastical Review* 61 (1919): 439–440.

32. See Jan Michael Joncas, "Leadership in the Liturgical Revival and Sacred Music at the Saint Paul Seminary: A Centennial Reflection." Lecture presented at the Saint Paul Seminary, January 25, 1995. Copy in University of St. Thomas Archives. I am also grateful to Thomas Fisch, associate professor of liturgy and sacramental theology at the Saint Paul Seminary, who has done extensive research on Busch and has lectured about him.

33. William Busch, "The Liturgical Movement," *Proceedings of the Catholic Educational Association* (1925), p. 680.

34. As quoted in Paul B. Marx, O.S.B., *Virgil Michel and the Liturgical Movement* (Collegeville, Minnesota: The Liturgical Press, 1957), p. 38. See pp. 36–40 for correspondence in which Michel urges Deutsch to implement the liturgical movement, and reference to Busch's role.

35. William Busch, "An Apostle of the Liturgical Life," *Orate Frates* 13 (1938–1939): 103. A tribute written by Busch at the time of Michel's death.

36. Busch, "An Apostle of the Liturgical Life," p. 104.

37. William Busch, "The Living Parish," *National Liturgical Week* (Newark: Benedictine Liturgical Conference, 1941): 224.

38. Busch, *National Liturgical Week,* p. 227.

39. Interview, Thomas Conroy, December 14, 2000. Busch took the opportunity to make the radical announcement that he did not intend to celebrate [a private] Mass, but instead would *attend* Mass with the congregation. In the days before concelebration was restored, those were indeed challenging words.

40. Joseph Kramp, S.J., *Eucharistia: Essays on Eucharistic Liturgy and Devotion,* trans. William Busch (St. Paul: E.M. Lohmann Company, 1926).

41. William Busch, "The Eucharist as Means and End," *Orate Fratres* 5 (1930–1931): 221–228. See also *The Mass-Drama: Outline of the Structure of the Mass* (Collegeville, Minnesota: The Liturgical Press, 1930).

42. For information on the life of Missia, see Richard J. Schuler, "Father Francis A. Missia (1884–1955)," reprinted from *The Catholic Choirmaster,* Vol. XLVI, No. IV (Winter 1960), and Frances Boardman, "Father Missia." The source of the latter is unidentified, but the author is described as music critic and editorial writer for the St. Paul *Pioneer Press-Dispatch.*

43. John A. Sweeney, "Leadership in Liturgical Revival and Sacred Music at the Saint Paul Seminary: A Centennial Reflection," January 25, 1995, pp. 5–7. (Hereafter, "Leadership in the Liturgical Revival.")

44. Sweeney, "Leadership in the Liturgical Revival," p. 8.

45. Interview, John Sweeney, January 20, 1998.

46. See Schuler, "Father Francis A. Missia," and also "Discourse Pronounced by the Most Reverend Francis J. Schenk, D.D., Bishop of Crookston, at the Funeral of Rev. Francis A. Missia, St. Paul Cathedral, May 26, 1955."

47. Interview, John A. Sweeney, July 4, 1999.

48. Sweeney, "Leadership in the Liturgical Revival," p. 18.

49. Schuler, *The Church of Saint Agnes,* pp. 149–150.

50. See also Schuler, *The Church of Saint Agnes,* Chapter 10, and Terry Kolb, "Liturgical Music Lifetime Love of Msgr. Richard Schuler," *The Catholic Spirit* (June 22, 2000): 42 A.

51. Interview, James Moudry, September 15, 1999.

52. Interview, Charles Froehle, March 15, 2001.

53. Louis McCarthy to Leo Binz, February 20, 1965. LBP, AASPM.

54. Sweeney, "Leadership in the Liturgical Revival," p. 19.

55. "The Experience of Prayer Grows Richer," *The Saint Paul Seminary MIDYEAR REPORT* (Spring 1984), p. 1.

56. Sweeney, "Leadership in the Liturgical Revival," pp. 19–20.

57. See Dolan, *"Some Seed Fell on Good Ground": The Life of Edwin V. O'Hara.* See also Raymond A. Lucker, "Archbishop O'Hara: A Man of Vision for the Church," Centennial Lecture, The Saint Paul Seminary, November 10,

1994 (hereafter, Lucker, "O'Hara"), and Kevin J. O'Reilly, "O'Hara, Edwin (1881–1956)," *Encyclopedia of American Catholic History* (Collegeville, Minnesota: Liturgical Press, 1999), pp. 1080–1082.

58. *Register* (1913–1914), p. 58.

59. Dolan, p. 50.

60. Dolan, p. 58.

61. O'Reilly, p. 1081. See also Dolan, pp. 74–75.

62. *Register* (1929–1930), p. 62. See also *Registers* for 1913–1914, 1923–1924, 1924–1925, 1925–1926, 1930–1931, and 1932–1933.

63. *Register* (1930–1931), p. 37.

64. Dolan, pp. 41–46.

65. Dolan, p. 129.

66. Dolan, p. 138.

67. Dolan, pp. 130–139.

68. John Gregory Murray to Priests of the Archdiocese of St. Paul, October 25, 1934. JGMP, AASPM.

69. *Register* (1934–1935), p. 20.

70. *Register* (1953–1954), p. 25.

71. Interview, Raymond Lucker, March 2, 2001.

72. Lucker, "O'Hara," p. 8.

73. Lucker, "O'Hara," p. 24.

74. "Vincent J. Ryan, Second Bishop of Bismarck—1940–1951," *Dakota Catholic Action* (March 9, 1999), p. 16.

75. See "Articles of Agreement," Annual Report (1969–1970) signed by William Baumgaertner, Rector, and Patrick J. Ryan, Dean, and revision in Annual Report (1970–1971) signed by representatives of all six seminaries.

76. Annual Report (1972–1973), p. 6. Interview, William Baumgaertner, January 10, 2001.

77. The committee included Dr. Lance Barker of United Theological Seminary of the Twin Cities, Dr. Bernard Evans of the School of Theology of St. John's University, Dr. C. Dean Freudenberger of Luther Seminary, Dr. Victor Klimoski and Ms. Mary Martin of the Saint Paul Seminary School of Divinity, and Dr. James Mason of Bethel Theological Seminary.

78. "Board of Directors, Minnesota Consortium of Theological Schools, Resolution: Northland Ministry Partnership," December 12, 1996. I am grateful to Mary Martin for sharing her files with me.

79. Mary Martin to SPSSOD Faculty, Memo on Rural Ministry Course for Spring 2000, November 1, 1999.

80. See *Register* (1917–1918), pp. 11, 68–70, 72, and *Register* (1918–1919), pp. 8, 35, 45.

81. Fulton J. Sheen, *Treasure in Clay: The Autobiography of Fulton J. Sheen* (New York: Doubleday and Company, 1980), p. 20.

82. In the early 1930s she wrote from her estate in Rome: "Father Sheen was here for a week with the Farrells. I have had my talk with Archbishop Bernardini. . . . I think he does not give Father Sheen any spiritual motives at all. He says his preaching is getting poor and he needs much more profound study. What do you think? . . . B.[ernardini] advises Sheen not to preach for a year. I am telling you all this so you will know why Dr. Sheen is coming to you for advice. I think B. is very harsh on him and does not understand him at all. . . . Dr. Sheen is coming to talk over his plans for the future with you and says he will take your advice. . . . I had him meet Cardinal Pacelli here at dinner and [he] talked quite a little with the Cardinal afterwards. He said his first duty was to his classes. That if he felt he conscientiously prepared his class work, he thought he should go on preaching. You see Cardinal Pacelli likes preaching himself and so appreciates what good can be done. They have all heard of Dr. Sheen's preaching here. Of course the Cardinal said no one should preach without much preparation." JGMP, AASPM.

83. Genevieve Brady to John Gregory Murray, n.d., JGMP, AASPM.

84. See *Register* (1939–1940), p. 16, and (1957–1958), p. 23. See also Yzermans, pp. 68–69.

85. Interview, John Sweeney, January 11, 2001.

86. Interview, William Baumgaertner, January 10, 2001. See Yzermans, pp. 68–69.

87. As quoted in Thomas J. McSweeney, "Sheen, Fulton John (1895–1979)," *Encyclopedia of American Catholic History* (Collegeville, Minnesota: Liturgical Press, 1999), p. 1286.

88. The author was present at two lectures that Archbishop Sheen gave at the Dell Webb Town House Auditorium in Phoenix, Arizona, and remembers Luce's introduction.

89. *Dullard* (Washington, D.C.: The Catholic Education Press, 1909).

90. As quoted in Justine Ward, *Thomas Edward Shields—Biologist, Psychologist, Educator* (New York: Charles Scribner's Sons, 1947), p. 249.

91. George Johnson, *The Sisters College Messenger* (January 1929), as quoted in Ward, p. vii.

92. Schuler, *The Church of St. Agnes,* p. 123.

93. The material in this section is based on interviews with Bishop Raymond A. Lucker, September 15–16, 1998 and October 29, 1999, as well as on his own writings.

94. See Lucker, "Some Aspects in the Life of Thomas Langdon Grace."

95. Raymond A. Lucker, *Prairie Views: Twenty-Five Years of Pastoral Letters* (New Ulm, Minnesota: Diocese of New Ulm, 2000), p. 562.

96. Lucker, *My Experience: Reflections on Pastoring* (Kansas City, Missouri: Sheed and Ward, 1988), p. 13.

97. Raymond A. Lucker, *The Prairie Catholic: Pastoral News from Across the Diocese of New Ulm,* October, November 1998.

98. Interview, John Forliti, January 11, 2001. See "Reverence for Life and Family: Catechesis in Sexuality." Unpublished D.Min. dissertation, Luther Northwestern Seminary, 1980.

99. Interview, Gene Scapanski, January 12, 2001.

100. Interview, Gene Scapanski, January 18, 2001.

101. Mary Katherine Hamilton, I.H.M., Donald R. LaMagdeleine and Thomas McCarver, "The Murray Institute: One Model of University/Diocesan Cooperation for Enriching Catholic K-12 Schools," *Current Issues in Catholic Higher Education* 14, 1 (Summer 1993): 31–33.

102. *Building a Community of Disciples: The Saint Paul Seminary School of Divinity of the University of St. Thomas,* 1998–2000 Catalogue, p. 35. (Hereafter, Catalogue.)

103. Interview, Sandra Skach, January 17, 2001.

104. Brochure, Center for Jewish-Christian Learning, "Giving Substance to a Dream," 1995.

105. The series for 1994 was in book form, *Jews and Christians Speak of Jesus,* ed. Arthur Zannoni (Minneapolis: Fortress Press, 1994).

106. Catalogue, 1998–2000, p. 34.

Bibliography

Books

Adams, Henry. *The Education of Henry Adams.* Boston: Houghton Mifflin Company, 1918.

Ahlstrom, Sydney E. *A Religious History of the American People.* New Haven: Yale University Press, 1972.

Allan, Joan M. *Candles and Carnival Lights: The Catholic Sensibility of F. Scott Fitzgerald.* New York: New York University Press, 1978.

Appleby, Scott. *Church and Age Unite! The Modernist Impulse in American Catholicism.* Notre Dame, Indiana: University of Notre Dame Press, 1992.

Aubert, Roger. *The Church in a Secularized Society.* New York: Paulist Press, 1978.

Broderick, Francis L. *Right Reverend New Dealer: John A. Ryan.* New York: Macmillan, 1963.

Coffey, Reginald M., O.P. *The American Dominicans: A History of St. Joseph's Province.* New York: Saint Martin de Porres Guild, 1970.

Connors, Joseph. *Journey Toward Fulfillment: A History of the College of St. Thomas.* St. Paul: College of St. Thomas, 1986.

Davis, Cyprian, O.S.B. *Black Catholics in the United States.* New York: Crossroad Publishing Company, 1992.

Dolan, Timothy Michael. *"Some Seed Fell on Good Ground": The Life of Edwin Vincent O'Hara.* Washington, D.C.: Catholic University of America, 1992.

Dowling, Austin. "Consecration of the Seminary Chapel, Cleveland, Ohio." October 2, 1925. *Occasional Sermons and Addresses of Archbishop Dowling.* Patterson, New Jersey: St. Anthony Guild Press, 1940.

———. "Dedication of Sulpician Seminary, Washington, D.C." September 23, 1919. *Sermons.*

———. "Eulogy." *A Garland of Affectionate Tributes to the Memory of the Very Rev. John Baptist Hogan, D.D., S.S.* Boston: Alumni of Saint John's Seminary, 1906, pp. 32–35.

Ellis, John Tracy, ed. *The Catholic Priest in the United States: Historical Investigations.* Collegeville, Minnesota: St. John's University Press, 1971.

———. *Essays in Seminary Education.* Notre Dame, Indiana: Fides Publishers, 1967.

Feeney, Bernard. *The Ideal Seminary.* Ed. Jeremiah C. Harrington, intro. Austin Dowling. New York: Macmillan Company, 1923.

Flynn, Harry J. *A Time to Heal: Preventing and Responding to Ministry-Related Sexual Misconduct.* St. Paul, Minnesota: Archdiocese of St. Paul and Minneapolis, 1998.

Fogarty, Gerald P. *The Vatican and the American Hierarchy from 1870 to 1965.* Collegeville, Minnesota: The Liturgical Press, 1982.

Foley, Albert, S.J. *God's Men of Color.* New York: Farrar, Straus and Co., 1955.

Froehle, Charles. *The Idea of Sacred Sign According to Abbot Anscar Vonier.* Rome: Catholic Book Agency, 1971.

Gibbons, James. *Ambassadors of Christ.* Baltimore: John Murphy and Company, 1896.

Gleason, Philip. "Chicago and Milwaukee: Contrasting Experiences in Seminary Planting." *Studies in Catholic History in Honor of John Tracy Ellis* Ed. Nelson H. Minnich, Robert B. Eno, and Robert F. Trisco. Wilmington, Delaware: Michael Glazier, 1985.

Graham, Clara, C.S.J. *Works to the King: Reminiscences of Mother Seraphine Ireland.* St. Paul: North Central Publishing Company, 1950.

Greeley, Andrew M., ed. *The Catholic Priest in the United States: Sociological Investigations.* National Opinion Research Center, University of Chicago. Washington, D.C.: United States Catholic Conference, 1972.

Hansen, Eric C. *The Cathedral of Saint Paul: An Architectural Biography.* St. Paul: The Cathedral of Saint Paul, 1990.

Hoffman, M. M. *The Church Founders of the Northwest.* Milwaukee: Bruce Publishing Company, 1937.

Hogan, John. *Clerical Studies.* Boston: Marlier, Callanan and Company, 1898.

Howell, Sharon M. "'The Consecrated Blizzard of the Northwest'—Archbishop John Ireland and His Relationship with the Black Community." *Many Rains Ago: A Historical and Theological Reflection on the Role of the Episcopate in the Evangelization of African American Catholics.* Washington, D.C.: Secretariat for Black Catholics, NCCB, 1990, pp. 35–48.

Hurley, Helen Angela. *On Good Ground: The Story of the Sisters of St. Joseph in St. Paul.* Minneapolis: University of Minnesota Press, 1951.

Ireland, John. "The Church and Civil Society." *The Church and Modern Society.* New York: D. W. McBride and Company, 1903.

———. "The Church—The Support of Just Government." *A History of the Third Plenary Council of Baltimore: November 9–December 7, 1884.* Baltimore: The Baltimore Publishing Company, 1885.

John Paul II. *Pastores Dabo Vobis.* See *Origins* 21: April 16, 1992.

Kavanaugh, James. *A Modern Priest Looks at His Outdated Church.* New York: Trident Press, 1967.

Keefe, Gerald E. *Formation Models in a Seminary Community.* St. Paul: St. Paul Seminary: 1973.

Kramp, Joseph, S.J. *Eucharistia: Essays on Eucharistic Liturgy and Devotion.* Trans. William Busch. St. Paul: E. M. Lohmann Company, 1926.

Krenik, Thomas W. *Formation for Priestly Celibacy: A Resource Book.* Introduction and Epilogue by Archbishop Harry J. Flynn. Washington, D.C.: NCEA, 1999.

Kunz, Virginia Brainard. *Saint Paul: The First 150 Years.* St. Paul: The St. Paul Foundation, 1991.

LaFarge, John, S.J. *The Manner Is Ordinary.* New York: Harcourt, Brace and Company, 1954.

Larson, Paul Clifford. *Minnesota Architect: The Life and Work of Clarence H. Johnston.* Afton, Minn.: Afton Historical Society Press, 1996.

Le Vot, Andre. *F. Scott Fitzgerald: A Biography.* New York: Doubleday, 1983.

Lindley, Clara Hill. *James J. Hill and Mary T. Hill: An Unfinished Chronicle by Their Daughter.* New York: The North River Press, 1948.

———, ed. *Some Letters of Monsignor Louis E. Caillet and August N. Chemidlin 1868–1899.* St. Paul: 1922. Published for private circulation.

Lucker, Raymond A. *My Experience: Reflections on Pastoring.* Kansas City, Missouri: Sheed and Ward, 1988.

———. *Prairie Views: Twenty-Five Years of Pastoral Letters.* New Ulm, Minnesota: Diocese of New Ulm, 2000.

Malone, Michael P. *James J. Hill: Empire Builder of the Northwest.* Norman, Oklahoma: University of Oklahoma Press, 1996.

Martin, Albro. *James J. Hill and the Opening of the Northwest.* New York: Oxford University Press, 1976.

Marty, Martin E. *The New Shape of American Religion.* New York: Harper and Brothers, 1958.

———. *A Short History of American Catholicism.* Allen, Texas: Thomas More—Tabor Publishing, 1995.

McLean, Jeanne P. *Leading from the Center: The Emerging Role of the Chief Academic Officer in Theological Schools.* Atlanta, Georgia: Scholars Press, 1999.

McSweeney, Thomas J. "Sheen, Fulton John (1895–1979)." *Encyclopedia of American Catholic History.* Collegeville, Minnesota: Liturgical Press, 1999, pp. 1285–1288.

Mertz, Fred. *The Ore and the Dross.* St. Paul: Rickshaw Publications, 1992.

Moynihan, James. *The Life of Archbishop Ireland.* New York: Harper and Brothers, 1953.

Newson, J. M. *Pen Pictures of St. Paul and Biographical Sketches of Old Settlers.* n.c., n.p., 1886. Quoted in James Reardon, *The Catholic Church in the Diocese of St. Paul.* St. Paul: North Central Publishing Company, 1952.

Ochs, Stephen J. *Desegregating the Altar: The Josephites and the Struggle for Black Priests 1871–1960.* Baton Rouge, Louisiana: Louisiana State University Press, 1990.

O'Connell, Marvin. *Critics on Trial: An Introduction to the Catholic Modernist Crisis.* Washington, D.C.: The Catholic University of America Press, 1994.

———. *John Ireland and the American Catholic Church.* St. Paul: Minnesota Historical Society Press, 1988.

O'Daniel, Victor Francis. *The Dominican Province of St. Joseph.* New York: Holy Name Society, 1942.

O'Dea, Thomas. *The American Catholic Dilemma: An Inquiry into the Intellectual Life.* New York: Sheed and Ward, 1958.

O'Gorman, Thomas. "Laying of the Corner Stone of Seminary Chapel." *The Diocese of St. Paul: The Golden Jubilee 1851–1901.* St. Paul: The Pioneer Press, 1901.

O'Reilly, Kevin J. "O'Hara, Edwin (1881–1956)." *Encyclopedia of American Catholic History.* Collegeville, Minnesota: Liturgical Press, 1997, pp. 1080–1082.

Poole, Stafford. *Seminary in Crisis.* New York: Herder and Herder, 1966.

Program of Priestly Formation. Washington, D.C.: NCCB/USCC, 1971. Revisions, 1981, 1993.

Pyle, Joseph Gilpin. *The Life of James J. Hill.* 2 vols. New York: Doubleday, Page and Company, 1917.

Quinn, Jerome D., *The Early Church: Two Studies With a Bibliography of His Work.* St. Paul, Minnesota: The Saint Paul Seminary School of Divinity of the University of St. Thomas, 1996.

———. *The Letter to Titus.* The Anchor Bible, Vol. 35. New York: Doubleday, 1990.

Quinn, Jerome D., and William C. Wacker. *The First and Second Letter to Timothy.* Grand Rapids, Michigan: William B. Eerdmans Publishing Co., 2000.

Reardon, James. *The Catholic Church in the Diocese of St. Paul.* St. Paul: North Central Publishing Company, 1952.

Reese, Thomas. *Archbishop: Inside the Power Structure of the American Catholic Church.* San Francisco: Harper and Row, 1989.

Ryan, John A. *Social Doctrine in Action: A Personal History.* New York: Harper and Brothers, 1941.

Ryan, Lawrence F., ed. *The Ryan Family*. St. Paul: 1971. Privately published.

Ryan, Rosalie, C.S.J., and John Christine Wolkerstorfer, C.S.J. *More Than a Dream: Eighty-Five Years at the College of St. Catherine.* St. Paul: The College of St. Catherine, 1992.

Sampson, Ann Thomasine, C.S.J. *Seeds on Good Ground.* St. Paul: Sisters of St. Joseph of Carondelet, 2000.

Schuler, Richard J. *History of the Church of Saint Agnes of Saint Paul, Minnesota (1887–1987).* Saint Paul: 1987. Privately published.

Schuth, Katarina, O.S.F. *Reason for the Hope: The Futures of Roman Catholic Theologates.* Wilmington, Delaware: Michael Glazier, Inc., 1989.

———. *Seminaries, Theologates and the Future of Church Ministry: An Analysis of Trends and Transitions.* Collegeville, Minnesota: Liturgical Press, 1999.

Shannon, James P. *Catholic Colonization and the Western Frontier.* New Haven: Yale University Press, 1957.

———. *Reluctant Dissenter.* New York: Crossroad Publishing Company, 1998.

Sheen, Fulton J. *Treasure in Clay: The Autobiography of Fulton J. Sheen.* New York: Doubleday and Company, 1980.

Shelley, Thomas J. *Dunwoodie: The History of St. Joseph's Seminary, Yonkers, New York.* Westminster, Maryland: Christian Classics, 1993.

Shields, Thomas E. *The Making and Unmaking of a Dullard.* Washington, D.C.: The Catholic Education Press, 1909.

Sloyan, Gerard, ed. *Secular Priest in the New Church.* New York: Herder and Herder, 1967.

Smith, John Talbot. *Our Seminaries: An Essay on Clerical Training*. New York: William A. Young and Company, 1896.

Spalding, John Lancaster. "University Education." *A History of the Third Plenary Council of Baltimore.* Baltimore: The Baltimore Publishing Company, 1885.

Swanholm, John S. *Caring Beyond Belief: A History of Catholic Charities of the Archdiocese of St. Paul and Minneapolis.* Minneapolis: Catholic Charities, 1995.

Teilhard de Chardin, Pierre, S.J. *Hymn of the Universe.* New York: Harper and Row, 1965.

Thompson, William M., ed. *Bérulle and the French School: Selected Writings.* Trans. Lowell M. Glendon. New York: Paulist Press, 1989.

Walsh, Eugene A. *The Priesthood in the Writings of the French School: Bérulle, De Condren, and Olier.* Washington, D.C.: Catholic University of America Press, 1949.

Ward, Justine. *Thomas Edward Shields—Biologist, Psychologist, Educator.* New York: Charles Scribner's Sons, 1947.

Watrin, Rita. *The Founding and Development of the Program of Affiliation of the Catholic University of America: 1912 to 1939.* Washington, D.C.: The Catholic University of America Press, n.d.

White, Joseph M. *The Diocesan Seminary in the United States.* Notre Dame, Indiana: University of Notre Dame Press, 1989.

Williams, J. Fletcher. *A History of the City of Saint Paul to 1875.* St. Paul: Minnesota Historical Society Press, 1983. First published in 1876.

Yzermans, Vincent A. *Journeys: People and Places.* Waite Park, Minnesota: Park Press, 1994.

Zannoni, Arthur, ed. *Jews and Christians Speak of Jesus.* Minneapolis: Fortress Press, 1994.

Journal and Periodical Articles, Catalogues, and Pamphlets

Boardman, Frances. "Father Missia." N.d., n.p. AASPM.

———. Interview with Archbishop-elect Austin Dowling. *Commonweal* (January 7, 1931), n.p.

Brady, William O. "Champions for Social Rights." *The Voice.* Baltimore: St. Mary's Seminary, February 1950, pp. 12–13.

Busch, William. "An Apostle of Liturgical Life." *Orate Fratres* 13 (1938–1939): 103.

———. "Construction of an Altar." *Ecclesiastical Review* 61 (1919): 439–440.

———. "The Eucharist as Means and End." *Orate Fratres* 5 (1930–1931): 221–228.

———. "In Memoriam: Archbishop Brady." *Worship* (January 1962): 87.

———. "The Liturgical Movement." *Proceedings of the Catholic Education Association* (1925), p. 680.

———. "The Living Parish." *National Liturgical Week.* Newark: Benedictine Liturgical Conference, 1941, p. 224.

———. "Past, Present, Future." *Orate Fratres* 25 (1951): 482.

Danehy, Patrick. "The New Seminary of St. Paul." *Catholic University of America Bulletin,* Vol. 1, No. 2 (April 1895): 213–226.

Duggan, John F., compiler. "The Education of a Priest: Archbishop Ireland's Talks to Seminarians." *The Ecclesiastical Review,* Vol. 101 (October 1939): 289–300; 385–398; 494–504.

Ellis, John Tracy. "American Catholics and the Intellectual Life." *Thought* 30 (Autumn 1955): 351–388.

Fisher, Daniel J. "Letters of Daniel J. Fisher—A Seminarian in St. Paul." *Acta et Dicta,* Vol. I, No. 1 (July 1907).

Fumasoni-Biondi, Pietro. "Copy of Letter Addressed to All the Ordinaries of the United States by Order of the Sacred Congregation of Seminaries and Universities." *Ecclesiastical Review* 79 (July–December 1928): 74–83.

Gasquet, F. A. "Some Impressions of Catholic America." *Dublin Review* CXXXVIII (April 1906): 79–98.

Hamilton, Mary Katherine, I.H.M., Donald R. LaMagdeleine, and Thomas McCarver. "The Murray Institute: One Model of University/Diocesan Cooperation for Enriching Catholic K-12 Schools." *Current Issues in Catholic Higher Education* 14, 1 (Summer 1993): 31–33.

"In a Seminary Garden." *St. Thomas: The Magazine of the University of St. Thomas.* St. Paul: University of St. Thomas (Winter 1999): 28. Photographs by Roger Rich.

Ireland, John. "The Dogmatic Authority of the Papacy: The Encyclical on Modernism." *North American Review* DCXXIX (April 1908): 486–497.

———. "Life of Bishop Cretin." *Acta et Dicta: A Collection of Historical Data Regarding the Origin and Growth of the Catholic Church in the Northwest,* Vol. IV, No. 2 (July 1916); Vol. V, No. 1 (1917); Vol. V, No. 2 (July 1916). St. Paul: The Catholic Historical Society of St. Paul.

Irish, Sharon. "West Hails East: Cass Gilbert in Minnesota." *Minnesota History* 53 (Spring 1993): 5.

Lathrop, Alan K. "A French Architect in Minnesota: E. L. Masqueray." *Minnesota History,* Vol. 47, No. 2 (Summer 1980): 50–51.

O'Neill, Daniel P. "The Development of an American Priesthood: Archbishop John Ireland and the Saint Paul Diocesan Clergy, 1884–1918." *Journal of American Ethnic History,* Spring 1985: 33–52.

Oster, A[natole]. "Personal reminiscences of Bishop Cretin." *Acta et Dicta,* Vol. I, No. 1 (1907).

Saint Paul Seminary Annual Report. 1964–1965 through 1976–1977; 1981–1982 through 2000–2001.

Saint Paul Seminary Bulletin. 1961–1986. (Renamed *Catalogue* in 1988.)

Saint Paul Seminary Catalogue. 1998–2000. (Earlier versions listed as *Register* and *Bulletin).*

Saint Paul Seminary Register. 1896–1960. (Renamed *Bulletin* in 1961.)

Schuler, Richard J. "Father Francis A. Missia (1884–1955)." *The Catholic Choirmaster,* Vol. XLVI, No. IV (Winter 1960): 1–6.

Seid-Martin, Sue. "The Experience of Prayer Grows Richer." *The Saint Paul Seminary Midyear Report* (Spring 1984): 1.

Shapiro, Max A. "Introduction." *Proceedings of the Center for Jewish-Christian Learning.* Ed. Mary Christine Athans, B.V.M. Vol. 8 (Spring 1993), p. 7.

Slattery, John R. "The Seminary for the Colored Missions." *Catholic World* 46 (1888): 541–550.

"St. Mary's Chapel of the St. Paul Seminary School of Divinity: A Historic and Artistic Guide." St. Paul: University of St. Thomas, 1998.

Time, February 8, 1932, pp. 32–33.

Weigel, Gustave, S.J. "American Catholic Intellectualism—A Theologian's Reflection." *Review of Politics* 19 (July 1957): 275–307.

White, Joseph M. "The Diocesan Seminary and the Community of Faith: Reflections from the Catholic Experience." *U.S. Catholic Historian* (Winter 1993): 1–20.

Unpublished Works

Ahern, Patrick H. "A History of the Saint Paul Seminary." Unpublished manuscript. The Saint Paul Seminary, 1945. AASPM.

Dease, Dennis. "The Theological Influence of Orestes Brownson and Isaac Hecker on John Ireland's Americanist Ecclesiology." Unpublished Ph.D. dissertation. Catholic University of America, 1978.

Dickman, Howard Leigh. "James Jerome Hill and the Agricultural Development of the Northwest." Unpublished Ph.D. dissertation. University of Michigan, 1977.

Flahavan, Edward J. "A Quarter Century of Alms: The Aid Given to the Diocese of Saint Paul by the Society for the Propagation of the Faith, 1850–1973." Unpublished M.A. thesis. Saint Paul Seminary, 1956.

Forliti, John. "Reverence for Life and Family: Catechesis in Sexuality." Unpublished D.Min. dissertation. Luther Northwestern Seminary, 1980.

Hoffman, David A. "Archbishop Binz and His Role in Implementing the Liturgical Reforms of Vatican II." Unpublished paper. The Saint Paul Seminary, 1996.

Lucker, Raymond A. "Some Aspects of the Life of Thomas Langdon Grace, Second Bishop of St. Paul." Unpublished M.A. thesis. The Saint Paul Seminary, 1952.

O'Connell, Marvin. "The Dowling Decade in Saint Paul." Unpublished M.A. thesis. The Saint Paul Seminary, 1955.

O'Neill, Daniel Patrick. "St. Paul's Priests, 1851–1930: Recruitment, Formation and Mobility." Unpublished Ph.D. dissertation. University of Minnesota, 1979.

Pierre, Kenneth. Journal. 1985; 1987.

Rask, Phillip J. "The List of the Twelve Tribes." Unpublished Ph.D. dissertation. Catholic University of America, 1990.

Wangler, Thomas E. "The Ecclesiology of Archbishop John Ireland: Its Nature, Development, and Influence." Unpublished Ph.D. dissertation. Milwaukee, Wisconsin: Marquette University, 1968.

Weber, Emmet Henry. "The Diocesan Seminary in St. Paul, Minnesota." Unpublished M.A. thesis. The Saint Paul Seminary, 1952.

Newspaper Articles

Allen, Martha Sawyer. "Each dawn, new hope: Archbishop Roach, 65, finds it in his faith, in his life." Minneapolis *Star Tribune,* December 25, 1986, Section A: 1, 8.

———. "Woodbury Priest Named Auxiliary Bishop." Minneapolis *Star Tribune,* December 23, 2000.

Binz, Leo. Episcopal Letter to Archdiocese of St. Paul, "Council Seeks to Remake World." *Catholic Bulletin,* October 11, 1963, p. 1.

———. "Vatican Council Success Depends Especially on Youth of the World." *Catholic Bulletin,* January 3, 1964, p. 1.

"Called Home by His Master." St. Paul *Pioneer Press,* November 29, 1897.

Catholic Bulletin, June 17, 1939, pp. 1, 6; March 2, 1962, pp. 1, B5; October 25, 1974; October 13, 1985; February 15–22, 1987; February 24, 1994, p. 1; March 3, 1994, p. 1; September 28, 1995.

"Francis Gilligan, 'labor priest' during the 1930s and 1940s, dies at 98." St. Paul *Pioneer Press,* April 7, 1997.

Grant, Janet. "'Austere' to national magazine, Abp Binz known as 'very warm person' to those who work close to him." *Catholic Bulletin,* December 15, 1967, p. 3.

Hauser, Tom. "Committee to Study Integration of Seminaries, College." *Catholic Bulletin,* June 9, 1983, p. 8.

"Hill Seminary Open." *The Chicago Times,* September 4, 1895. Clipping in the Hill Papers.

"Hill Seminary Opens Today: Another Great Educational Institution in St. Paul." Saint Paul *Pioneer Press,* September 6, 1894.

"Jubilee of a Church." St. Paul *Dispatch,* July 2, 1901.

Keany, Father Patrick. Quoted in *Catholic Bulletin,* September 8, 1998.

Le Petit Journal, June 19, 1892. Quoted in James H. Moynihan, *The Life of Archbishop Ireland.* New York: Harper and Brothers, 1953.

Lucker, Raymond A. *The Prairie Catholic: Pastoral News from Across the Diocese of New Ulm.* October–November 1998.

McEachern, Margaret. "Leo Binz Was Industrious Farm Boy, Sister Recalls." *Catholic Bulletin,* March 2, 1962, B17.

Midway News, September 6, 1890.

Minneapolis *Star Tribune,* February 4–5, 1987; July 5, 1991.

Morphew, Clark. "Plan for Seminary Affiliation with St. Thomas." Saint Paul *Pioneer Press,* October 16, 1985.

New York *Herald Tribune,* January 29, 1941.

New York *Times,* January 29, 1941.

Northwestern Chronicle, December 13, 1873; January 20, 1888; September 6, 1895; April 4, 1903; June 18, 1904; July 23, 1904; October 1, 1904; April 10, 1910.

O'Keefe, Gerald. "Archbishop Announces Seminary Top Posts." *Catholic Bulletin,* March 1, 1958.

———. "Archbishop Brady Announces Changes…" *Catholic Bulletin,* February 8, 1958.

O'Sullivan, Msgr. John. "Remembering a Bishop." *Catholic Bulletin,* September 21, 1986, p. 27.

Pates, Richard. "Monsignor Gilligan Blessed Us Thrice." Eulogy preached at the funeral of Msgr. Francis Gilligan, April 10, 1997. *The Catholic Spirit,* April 24, 1997.

"Resolution." *Catholic Bulletin,* February 28, 1985, pp. 3, 10.

St. Paul *Dispatch,* August 4, 1925; August 5, 1925; August 22/23, 1925.

St. Paul *Dispatch,* December 9, 1948.

St. Paul *Pioneer Press,* January 19, 1927; February 4–5, 1987; February 17, 1997.

"Support Pours in While Archbishop Awaits Court Date." *Catholic Bulletin,* February 28, 1985, p. 1.

"Vincent J. Ryan, Second Bishop of Bismarck—1940–1951." *Dakota Catholic Action,* March 9, 1999, p. 16.

Zyskowski, Bob. "So, What's the New Archbishop Like Anyway?" *Catholic Bulletin,* February 24, 1994, p. 3.

———. "You build up a lot of stories during 65 years as a priest." *Catholic Bulletin,* January 4, 1991.

Archival Materials

Affiliation Agreement between the College of St. Thomas and the Saint Paul Seminary. Effective July 1, 1986; formally signed May 3, 1987.

Aleshire, Daniel O., to Rev. Phillip Rask. January 28, 1994. Rector's Office, Saint Paul Seminary School of Divinity.

Amended Affiliation Agreement. October 29, 1991.

Amended Affiliation Handbook. November 11, 1993.

Archbishop Ireland Memorial Library correspondence files.

Association of Theological Schools. Final Report to the American Association of Theological Schools and the North Central Association Regarding the Accreditation of the St. Paul Seminary, St. Paul, Minnesota. November 27, 1973. Included as an appendix to the Annual Report (1974–1975).

———. Final Report of the ATS Visiting Team. March 30, 1984.

———. Final Report of the ATS Visiting Team. November 29, 1993.

Athans, Mary Christine, B.V.M. Personal files: Presbytery Day, Building Committee, and Program Design Committee.

Baumgaertner, William. Personal files.

Binz, Leo. Papers. AASPM.

Brady, William O. Papers. AASPM.

Byrne, Leo C. Intervention of Archbishop Leo C. Byrne at the 1971 World Synod of Bishops. "The Rights of Women, Especially in the Church." October 22, 1971. AASPM.

Conroy, Rev. Thomas. "Anniversary Reflections." *Golden Jubilee Booklet.* The Saint Paul Seminary, Class of 1948.

Dedication Booklet, "Cyril F. Rotter Memorial Organ, May 7, 2000, Saint Mary's Chapel."

Dedication File 1989. ASPS.

Dolan, Thomas. Papers, 1980–1993. Personal files.

Dowling, Austin. Papers. AASPM.

Faculty Workshop Minutes. January 20, 1982.

Flahavan, Edward. Notes for panel discussion "A Catholic Vision of Social Justice: Monsignor Francis J. Gilligan." University of St. Thomas. October 16, 2000.

Froehle, Charles. Personal files.

Gilbert, Cass. Papers. Minnesota Historical Society.

"Giving Substance to a Dream." Brochure of the Center for Jewish-Christian Learning, 1995.

Hill, James J. and Mary. Papers. James J. Hill Reference Library. St. Paul, Minnesota.

"Information to the International Catholic Documentary—Archdiocese of St. Paul in Minnesota." N.d. Letters accompanying the document: to Archbishop D. Petro Palazzini, February 28, 1963; to Archbishop Egidio Vagnozzi, Apostolic Delegate, February 28, 1963.

"Institutional Self-Study for the Association of Theological Schools and the North Central Association: The Saint Paul Seminary School of Divinity of the University of St. Thomas." October 1993.

"Institutional Survey: The Saint Paul Seminary." St. Paul: October 1, 1967. Saint Paul Seminary Archives.

Ireland, John. Papers. AASPM.

Leander, Leonard, and Jean Kimber, compilers. "Necrology of the Priests of the Archdiocese of St. Paul and Minneapolis." AASPM.

Markoe, Ralston J. "Some Reminiscences of Old St. Paul's Seminary in the Early Days." October 18, 1908. Ralston Markoe Papers, ACHS. Quoted in Joseph Connors, *Journey Toward Fulfillment.* St. Paul: College of St. Thomas, 1986.

Martin, Frank, et al. "The St. Paul Seminary Campus: Building on Its Distinctive Past." Proposal, Hammel Green and Abrahamson, Inc.

Martin, Mary. Memo to Saint Paul Seminary School of Divinity Faculty on Rural Ministry Course for Spring 2000. November 1, 1999. Personal files.

Minnesota Consortium of Theological Schools. Board of Directors Resolution: Northland Ministry Partnership. December 12, 1996. Mary Martin files.

Minutes of the Meetings of the Board of Trustees and The Corporation of the St. Paul Seminary. ASPS.

Minutes of the Meetings of the Board of Trustees of the College of St. Thomas. President's Office, University of St. Thomas.

Murray, John Gregory. Papers, AASPM.

"1903—The St. Paul Seminary Domestic Department." Archives of the Sisters of St. Joseph of Carondelet, St. Paul Province, St. Paul, Minnesota.

Pates, Msgr. Richard E. to Archbishop John R. Roach. November 12, 1986. ASPS.

Presbyteral Council Minutes. Presbyteral Council. Chancery, Archdiocese of Saint Paul and Minneapolis.

Rare Book Room, Archbishop Ireland Theological Library, University of St. Thomas. (Several rare volumes described in chapter 7.)

Rask, Phillip. "Orientation for New Students." September 1993. Rector's Office, Saint Paul Seminary School of Divinity.

———. "Rector's Conference." October 27, 1993. Rector's Office, Saint Paul Seminary School of Divinity.

Reardon, James J. "The End of a Glorious Era: The Last Six Years of the Life of John Gregory Murray, Archbishop of St. Paul (1951–1956)." Midsummer 1961, pp. 51–52. Murray Papers, AASPM.

Report of the Bishops' Committee on Priestly Formation: Concerning Visitation—St. Paul Seminary and St. John Vianney Seminary, March 25–27, 1974. ASPS.

Report of NCCB Seminary Visitation Team: The Saint Paul Seminary School of Divinity, University of Saint Thomas, Saint Paul, Minnesota, October 26–30, 1998. Rector's Office, Saint Paul Seminary School of Divinity.

Report of Papal Visitation of the St. Paul Seminary. February 13–17, 1984. ASPS.

Report of the Seminary Planning Commission, Section II, May 21, 1963. AASPM.

Report on "The Interim Term—1972." ASPS.

Rules of the Saint Paul Seminary. Approved by John Ireland, Archbishop of St. Paul. November 15, 1908. ASPS.

Rules of the Saint Paul Seminary. Approved by John Gregory Murray, Archbishop of St. Paul. 1945; 1954. ASPS.

Ryan, John A. "Diary." Catholic University of America Archives.

Saint Paul Seminary Faculty Meeting Minutes. ASPS.

"Saint Paul Seminary Faculty-Student Conference Constitution." Seminary Papers, AASPM.

Saint Paul Seminary School of Divinity public relations brochure. Autumn 1987.

Seminary Directory, 1974–1975; 1975–1976. Seminary Papers, AASPM.

Seminary Papers. AASPM.

Shanahan, Thomas J. "The John Ireland Library of the Saint Paul Seminary." May 19, 1949, pp. 1–2. File, Archbishop Ireland Memorial Library.

Shannon, James P. "Report to Archbishop Brady on the Subject of Training Seminarians at the College of St. Thomas." November 23, 1959. ASPS.

Strategic Plan, "Goals." The Saint Paul Seminary. September 1, 1982. ASPS.

"Summary of the Work of the Task Force on Governance of the School of Divinity." Submitted to the Saint Paul Seminary Board of Trustees, May 4, 1995. ASPS.

"Testimonial to Right Reverend John A. Ryan, D.D. on Occasion of His Seventieth Birthday Anniversary May 25, 1939." Ryan Papers, ACUA.

Viktora, Janet. "Theological Teaching for the Church's Ministries." Report of the Saint Paul Seminary School of Divinity of the University of St. Thomas to the Keystone Project. June 2000.

Speeches and Sermons

Binz, Leo. "Address Delivered by His Excellency, Archbishop Leo Binz, at the St. Paul Seminary on March 9, to a Meeting of the District Chairmen of the Opus Sancti Petri." *Register* (1966).

Brady, William O. "Address of Welcome Given by Archbishop William O. Brady to the Catholic Theological Society of America in Convention at Saint Paul, Minnesota, June 24, 1958." Brady Papers, AASPM.

———. "The Seminarians' Vacation." Address given at the Seminary Department, Catholic Education Association, Chicago, 1934. Brady Papers, AASPM.

———. "The Spiritual Opportunity of Seminary Faculty Life." N.d., n.p. Brady Papers, AASPM.

———. Untitled five-page sermon preached at the Saint Paul Cathedral, August 21, 1956. Brady Papers, AASPM.

Cushing, Rev. Vincent, O.F.M. Oral report to faculty and staff of the Saint Paul Seminary School of Divinity at the conclusion of the Association of Theological Schools/North Central Association visitation. October 20, 1993.

Froehle, Charles. "Ceremony Marking the Demolition of the Administration Building." December 14, 1987.

———. "Father Adamson and Child Abuse." Rector's Conference, Saint Paul Seminary, December 12, 1990. Froehle file.

Hill, James J. "Speech at the Dedication of the Saint Paul Seminary." September 4, 1895.

Ireland, John. "Address of Archbishop Ireland at the Dedication of the Saint Paul Seminary on 4 September 1895." *Register* (1896). The Saint Paul Seminary.

———. Sermon at the Episcopal Consecration of Thomas O'Gorman, April 19, 1896. *Western Watchman* (St. Louis, Missouri), April 23, 1896.

Joncas, Jan Michael. "Leadership in the Liturgical Revival and Sacred Music at the Saint Paul Seminary: A Centennial Reflection." Centennial Lecture, the Saint Paul Seminary School of Divinity of the University of St. Thomas, January 25, 1995. Copy in University of St. Thomas archives.

Kennelly, Karen, C.S.J. "Archbishop Ireland, the Saint Paul Seminary, and 'The New Woman.'" Centennial Lecture, the Saint Paul Seminary School of Divinity of the University of St. Thomas, May 1, 1995.

Lucker, Raymond A. "Archbishop O'Hara: A Man of Vision for the Church." Centennial Lecture, the Saint Paul Seminary School of Divinity of the University of St. Thomas, November 10, 1994.

O'Connell, Marvin. "Meximieux and Mr. Hill: John Ireland's Dream Come True." Centennial Lecture, the Saint Paul Seminary School of Divinity of the University of St. Thomas, September 8, 1994.

O'Gorman, Thomas. Dedication Sermon. *Register* (1896). The Saint Paul Seminary.

———. Sermon Delivered by Rt. Rev. Thomas O'Gorman, Bishop of Sioux Falls, on Occasion of the Consecration of St. Mary's Chapel. *Register* (1905). The Saint Paul Seminary.

Roach, John R. "Homily for Archbishop Binz's Funeral." Binz Papers, AASPM.

Schenk, Francis J. "Discourse Pronounced by the Most Reverend Francis J. Schenk, D.D., Bishop of Crookston, at the Funeral of Rev. Francis A. Missia, St. Paul Cathedral, May 26, 1955."

Sweeney, John A. "Leadership in Liturgical Revival and Sacred Music at the Saint Paul Seminary: A Centennial Reflection." Centennial Lecture, the Saint Paul Seminary School of Divinity of the University of St. Thomas, January 25, 1995.

Interviews

Abbott, Rev. Eugene. August 31, 1998.

Adrian, Rev. Stephen. November 24, 1999.

Anderley, Gerald. February 25, 2000.

Arms, Rev. Michael. July 14, 1999.

Banker, Rev. Richard. January 5, 2000.

Bauer, Rev. John. November 23, 1999; December 7, 2000.

Baumgaertner, Msgr. William. July 23, 1998; August 21, 1998; August 30, 1999; September 2, 1999; October 24, 1999; December 2, 1999; November 21, 2000; January 10, 2001.

Bowers, Rev. Ronald. October 16, 1998; July 21, 1999.

Boxleitner, Msgr. J. Jerome. May 30, 2001.

Brady, Sister Mary William, C.S.J. October 9, 1998.

Brioschi, Rev. Thomas. February 16, 2000.

Bullock, Bishop William. November 27, 1999.

Campbell, Bishop Frederick. February 10, 2000.

Carlson, Bishop Robert. November 2, 1999.

Connors, Joseph B. September 9, 1998.

Conroy, Rev. Thomas. April 10, 1996; July 29, 1998; December 14, 2000.

Dease, Rev. Dennis. October 29, 1999.

Dittberner, Rev. Jerome. November 18, 1999.

Dolan, Thomas. November 19, 1999.

Dosh, Rev. Mark. October 16, 1998.

DuLac, Msgr. Henri J. September 11, 1998.

Eggert, Rev. Charles. January 20, 1998.

Fallon, William. May 2, 2001.

Fennell, James. October 9, 2000.

Fisch, Thomas. September 19, 1999; November 23, 1999; August 23, 2000.

Flahavan, Rev. Edward. November 15, 1999.

Forliti, Rev. John. September 27, 2000.

Froehle, Rev. Charles. October 2, 1998; September 16, 1999; October 29, 1999; November 16, 1999; January 5, 2000; February 28, 2000; March 25, 2000; May 30, 2000; November 4, 2000.

Gould, Janet. November 3, 2000.

Gries, Patricia. January 24, 2000.

Grzeskowiak, Rev. Edward. July 29, 1998.

Hartnett, Sister Mary Daniel, C.S.J. November 11, 1999.

Hayden, Msgr. Ambrose. August 20, 1993; April 9, 1996.

Henry, William Charles. January 4, 2000.

Holloran, Thomas. February 25, 2000.

Hunstiger, Rev. Thomas. October 11, 1998; July 25, 1999.

Joncas, Rev. Jan Michael. December 22, 2000.

Karpinski, Hatti Klisch. January 20, 2000.

Keefe, Rev. Gerald E. September 23, 1999.

Keefe, Thomas. December 1, 2000; January 2, 2001.

Keffer, Charles. October 14, 1999.

Kennedy, Robert G. May 9, 2000.

Kennelly, Sister Karen, C.S.J. December 17, 1999.

Kinney, Bishop John F. October 6, 1999.

Klimoski, Victor. November 11, 1999.

Kneal, Msgr. Ellsworth. September 24, 1998; September 30, 1998.

LaFontaine, Rev. Paul. September 14, 1999; November 17, 2000.

Lucker, Bishop Raymond. September 15–16, 1998; October 29, 1999; March 2, 2001.

Malone, Rev. John. July 19, 1999.

McCauley, Rev. David. October 19, 1998.

McDonough, Rev. Kevin. November 19, 1999.

Mertz, Rev. Frederick. September 25, 2000.

Milske, Gerald. January 21, 2000.

Motl, Rev. James, O.P. January 14, 2000.

Moudry, James. September 15, 1999; November 11, 1999; November 16, 1999.

Moudry, Msgr. Richard. September 15, 1998.

Murphy, Msgr. Terrence J. September 28, 1998.

Nolan, Rev. Timothy. September 21, 1999.

O'Connell, Rev. Michael. November 9, 1999.

O'Keefe, Bishop Gerald. October 4, 1998; September 27, 1999.

Pates, Bishop Richard. November 8, 1999.

Pierre, Rev. Kenneth. November 19, 1999.

Rask, Rev. Phillip. September 19, 1999; September 27, 2000.

Reding, Rev. Michael. January 16, 2001.

Roach, Archbishop John R. October 15, 1998; November 15, 1998; November 17, 1999.

Ryan, Rev. T. Kenneth. January 18, 1998; January 19, 1998.

Saiko, Sister Paul Therese, S.S.N.D. October 20, 2000.

Sankowitz, Msgr. John. November 1, 1999.

Scapanski, Gene. November 22, 1999; January 12, 2001; January 18, 2001.

Schuler, Msgr. Richard. November 15, 1999.

Schuth, Sister Katarina, O.S.F. October 24, 2000.

Schwartz, Rev. Robert. November 2, 1999.

Shannon, James P. November 1, 1999; January 17, 2001.

Shapiro, Rabbi Max. October 28, 1999; November 1, 2000.

Shields, Sister Kathleen Marie, C.S.J. July 9, 1996.

Sieg, Rev. Thomas. September 23, 1999.

Simonet, J. Thomas. September 14, 1999.

Skach, Sandra. January 17, 2001.

Sondag, John. October 28, 1999.

Srnec, Msgr. Stanley. July 26, 1999.

Sweeney, Msgr. John. January 20, 1998; July 4, 1999; September 20, 1999; February 2, 2000; January 11, 2001.

Tibesar, Rev. Leo. October 5, 2000.

Tiffany, Rev. Eugene. October 14, 1999.

Viktora, Janet. April 25, 2000; November 2, 2000.

Wagner, Rev. Alfred. July 13, 1998.

Whalen, Rev. James. October 13, 1998.

Wolter, Rev. Richard J. October 16, 1998.

Index

Ad limina visits and papal audiences, 23, 54

Adamson, Thomas, 338–39

Adrian, Stephen, 314, 316, 321, 341–42, 397

Affiliation with College of St. Thomas, 278–82, 286–308, 311–12, 315–26, 332, 344, 351–54, 366–68, 381, 387, 434

Ahern, Patrick J., 218, 239–40, 395

Alumni Day, 180, 192, 255

American Association of Theological Schools, 266–67, 292, 297, 299, 308, 363–65, 369

American Ecclesiastical Review, 73–75

Americanism, 92, 102, 125–27, 139–40, 151

Anderley, Gerald, 308, 326, 330

Archbishop Ireland Educational Fund, 140, 152

Arms, Michael, 385

Asher, Mary, 366

Athans, M. Christine, 308–9, 324, 354, 357, 379

Authority, 35, 37, 213–14, 217, 434, 436

Balke, Victor, 425

Baltimore III, 35–38, 73, 86–87, 138, 140

Bandas, Rudolph, 149, 172–73, 180–84, 186–88, 191, 193–94, 205–6, 215–16, 225, 237, 406, 423

Barron, Joseph T., 120–21

Baumgaertner, William, 177, 179, 200, 218, 228, 237, 241, 251–52, 254–55, 257–58, 261, 263–64, 266, 268, 274, 276, 336, 356–57, 363, 365, 375, 378–79, 384–85, 416–17, 420

Beauduin, Lambert, 398–99

BeFriender Ministry, 333, 336, 427, 429–30, 436

Bell, Minnie, 191, 225

Belly, Diocese of, 9, 30, 32

Benedictines, 19, 22, 122

Berres, Charlotte, 373

Bérulle, Pierre de, 7

Binz, Leo, 218, 233–39, 241, 244, 247–53, 255–57, 263, 268–69, 271–72, 277, 394–95, 405, 407, 423

Board of Trustees, 104–6, 111, 152–53, 157, 187–88, 193, 211,

224–26, 237, 247–48, 250–51, 259, 277–78, 280–81, 283–84, 292–95, 297, 307–8, 312–13, 321, 328, 367, 379

Boeckmann, Rachel Hill, 256

Bohrer, Barbara, 336, 356

Bowers, Ronald, 240, 285, 310, 313, 354, 366, 372

Boxleitner, J. Jerome, 396

Brady, Genevieve, 420

Brady, Mary William, 207, 211, 226–27

Brady, William O., 145, 172–75, 186, 193, 201–22, 224–27, 229–30, 233–34, 237, 248, 256, 390–93

Brothers of the Holy Family, 19

Brownson, Orestes, 77, 387, 434

Buildings, 59–61, 83, 95, 104, 110–13, 116–19, 135, 153, 190–92, 212, 225, 247, 248–50, 255–56, 273, 282, 293–95, 301, 303, 323–24, 329–34, 341–44, 352–53, 434–36

Bullock, William, 286, 288–90, 293, 328–29

Bunnell, Eugene (Adam), 284

Burke, John, Jr., 329

Busch, William, 146–47, 163, 191, 195, 197, 215, 228, 230, 238, 240, 386, 398–402, 409

Byrne, James J., 200

Byrne, Leo C., 237, 251–54, 259, 263–64, 268–69, 272

Byrne Residence, 294, 322

Byron, J. Michael, 348, 368

Caillet, Louis, 13, 14, 34, 42–45, 49–52, 70, 80, 82, 104, 106

Campbell, Frederick, 275, 316

Carlson, Robert, 328

Catholic colonization movement, 35

Catholic/Non-Catholic relations, 21, 55, 69, 208, 355

Catholic University of America, 21, 38–39, 67, 97–99, 119–21, 126, 183, 186, 422

Cestelli, Alessandro, 81

Chancellor, Archdiocesan, 104, 216, 263

Chandler, Joan, 365–66

Chareyre, John, 81

Charron, Joseph L., 354, 358

Chemidlin, August N., 50–52

Church property transactions, 11, 24–25, 53, 141, 163, 256, 288, 293, 295

Cicognani, Amleto, 174, 234

Civil War, U.S., 20, 34

Conferences (Archbishop's), 75–77, 100

Conferences (Rector's), 174, 209, 216–17, 243, 371

Confraternity of Christian Doctrine, 182, 194, 224, 242, 413–15, 423–24

Conlin, Daniel, 348
Connolly, James L., 145, 173–74, 177–78, 180, 187, 189, 390
Conroy, Thomas, 402, 406
Cotter, Joseph B., 99, 104–5, 113–14
Cowley, Leonard, 227, 229, 237, 245
Cretin, Joseph, 3–15, 16, 30, 66, 111, 119, 396
Curriculum, 86–91, 147, 150, 239–40, 242, 266, 282–83, 290–91, 308, 349–53, 369–70
Curtis, William, 242, 285, 308
Cytron, Barry, 431

Dandurand, Douglas, 356, 368–69
Danehy, Patrick, 82, 89
Deacon internship, 267
Dease, Dennis, 285, 291, 310, 334, 354, 381
Dekker, Gail, 430
Deutsch, Alcuin, 398–400
Devie, Alexander Raymond, 9, 11, 32
Devotions, 148, 221–23
Diekmann, Godfrey, 401–2
Dillon, David, 216–17, 220, 225, 237, 241
Distinguished Alumnus Award, 385
Dittberner, Jerome, 257, 309, 336, 354
Doctor of Ministry degree, 364, 369
Doherty, Richard T., 195, 222, 228, 238
Dolan, Daniel, 289
Dolan, E. Vincent, 288–89
Dolan, Thomas, 281, 289, 293–95, 301, 303, 307, 312, 330
Dominicans, 17
Dorsey, John Henry (Harry), 124
Dosh, Mark, 218, 220, 238
Dowling, Austin, 113, 135–48, 150–68, 172, 178, 181, 203–6, 278, 390–91, 433
Dress code, 84, 199, 221, 242, 244, 261
Duggan, John F., 75

Ecclesiology, 75, 77–79, 130, 434, 436
Echert, John, 368
Europe: Enlightenment, 4, 6; Church history, 5–6, 18; Romanticism, 6
Extracurricular activities (On-campus), 86–87, 91–92, 146–49, 192, 194–95, 220–21, 223, 238, 309–10, 340–41, 384–85

Faculty, 80–83, 89–90, 101, 104, 108, 119, 145–46, 213, 218, 227, 229, 238, 242, 249, 254, 280, 282–83, 285, 298–99, 308–9, 334–36, 350, 354–56,

365–66, 368–69, 373–74, 379–80

Fayolle, Johann, 17

Feela, Paul, 276, 285, 356, 377, 407

Feeney, Bernard, 93

Feldmeier, Peter, 368

Fennell, James, 274, 287–88, 291

Field education, 242–43, 266–67, 282–83, 285, 290, 335, 373

Finances, 103–9, 116–18, 140–41, 156–57, 187–89, 193–94, 211, 224–26, 247, 250–51, 266, 274, 277–78, 295–97, 302, 312–13, 323, 328

Fisch, Thomas, 285, 354, 378, 407

Fisher, Daniel J., 12–13

Fitzgerald, F. Scott, 120

Flahavan, Edward, 314–16, 385, 394–96

Flynn, Harry, 339, 358–62, 373, 378–79

Forliti, John, 342, 425–27

France: Church history, 5–6; French School of Spirituality, 7–8, 14

Franciscans, Conventual, 256–57

Franciscans, Third Order, 25

Froehle, Charles, 216, 260–61, 264–65, 268, 277, 280–81, 283–85, 287–89, 291–93, 295–98, 300–6, 311, 315, 322–30, 332–33, 338–43, 345, 347, 349–50, 352–54, 357–58, 363, 375–76, 378, 384, 406–7, 434–35

Fumasoni-Biondi, Pietro, 150–52

Galtier, Lucien, 11

Gasquet, Francis Aidan, 93–95

Gaudeamus, 245, 291–92, 309, 324

Gibbons, James, 36, 38, 68, 74, 125–26, 131, 140, 387

Gilbert, Cass, 56–58, 111

Gilbert, John, 218, 289–90

Gilligan, Francis J., 145, 173–74, 178, 218, 227, 313, 390–94, 396

Gould, Janet, 308

Grace, Thomas Langdon, 16–27, 35, 37, 50, 66, 119, 423

Great Northern Railway, 48

Grzeskowiak, Edward, 393–94

Haas, David, 408

Ham, Richard, 349

Harrington, Jeremiah C., 146, 206

Hartnett, Mary Daniel, 285, 290, 310, 334–35

Haugen, Marty, 408

Hayden, Ambrose, 173, 187, 236, 319, 385

Hecker, Isaac, 77, 92, 125, 157, 434

Heffron, Patrick, 75, 80, 92, 94, 99, 106–9, 114–16, 118

Henry, W. Charles (Chuck), 273
Hill, James J., 41–58, 61–72, 96, 103–7, 109, 112, 116–18, 129–30, 153, 157, 434
Hill, Mary Theresa Mehegan, 41–45, 49–52, 54, 65, 67, 70, 72, 96, 111, 131–32, 152–53, 378
Hogan, John B., 74–75, 143–44
Holloran, Thomas, 300
Holy Cross Congregation, 142, 171

Institute for Christian Life and Ministry, 431
Interim Term, 267
Ireland, John, 13, 20, 22–23, 25–40, 45, 53–55, 59, 61–73, 75–83, 86, 89–107, 111, 113–14, 117, 121–24, 126–31, 135, 137–38, 142, 144, 151, 171, 187, 257, 278, 386–89, 402–3, 409–10, 432, 434–36

James, D. Willis, 71–72
Jay Philips Center for Jewish-Christian Learning, 375, 430–31, 436
Jenkins, David, 356, 378, 409
Jerusalem Program, 374–77
Jesuits, 23, 79, 94, 257
Jewish-Christian relations, 375, 430–31
John Paul II, 292
Johnston, Clarence E., 111–12, 154
Joncas, Jan Michael, 275–76, 356, 408–9
Jubilee celebrations, 111, 180, 384–85
Jubilemus, 309

Kacmarcik, Frank, 331, 378
Kastigar, Carole, 308, 310
Keane, John J., 39, 97–99
Keefe, Gerald, 265
Keefe, Thomas, 365, 378, 34
Keffer, Charles, 287, 301, 305–6, 323, 350
Kelly, Anthony, 104–5, 107
Kennedy, Arthur, 369–70
Kennedy, Diane, 310, 335, 355
Kennedy, Patrick, 308, 335
Kennedy, Robert G., 336
"Kentucky Press," 213
Keystone Project, 370–71
Kinney, John F., 197, 213, 219, 268, 278–79, 281, 317–18, 339
Klein, Felix, 92
Klimoski, Victor, 284, 297, 349–51, 357, 363–65, 370, 373, 379–80, 428
Kneal, Ellsworth, 218, 264, 356
Kohner, David, 368, 380

Kollasch, Merle, 335
Krenik, Thomas, 355–56, 371–72, 380

La Farge, Bancel, xii, 157–58, 160–66, 331
La Farge, S.J., John J., 124, 158, 194
Laird, Peter, 369
Lannan, Patrick, 329, 379
Leo XIII, 125, 388, 391
Lesniak, Valerie, 356, 368
Leyden, Donald, 287–88
Library, 94–96, 110, 116, 180, 186–90, 224, 293–94, 299, 301, 434
Lindley, Clara Hill, 152, 154–55, 165–66, 171, 190, 226
Liturgical Movement, 398–402
Liturgies, 84, 101, 110–11, 114–15, 147, 174, 191–92, 212, 221, 244–45, 299, 310, 342–43, 405–8
Loisy, Alfred, 81, 126
Loras, Mathias, 9–10, 119
Lucker, Raymond, 217–18, 224, 228, 272, 284, 379, 415–16, 423–26

Markoe, James C., 118
Marshall, John, 292, 298, 348
Martin, Larry, 285, 408
Martin, Mary, 336, 348, 373
Marty, Elaine, 309
Masqueray, Emmanuel Louis, 117
Master of Arts in Pastoral Studies, 304, 333–34, 337, 352–53, 366–69, 426–28
Master of Arts in Religious Education, 369, 429
Master of Arts in Theology, 242, 266, 299, 336–37, 369–70
Master of Divinity, 266, 299, 337, 370–71
Mathew, Theobald, 28, 35
McCarthy, Louis J., 196, 220–21, 225, 228, 237–38, 240–43, 247, 249–52, 254, 257, 277, 402, 407, 420
McDonough, Kevin, 275, 339, 347
McDonough, William, 339, 356, 368
McGolrick, James, 96, 99, 104, 106, 111, 113, 118, 144
McGrade, Patricia, 309
McKenna, Thomas, 285, 334
McLean, Jeanne, 365, 380
McQuaid, Bernard, 91
Medical care, 118, 195, 309
Meland, Cal, 365, 377
Merkle, John, 431
Mertz, Fred, 197
Metropolitan Cross, 377–78
Meximieux (France), *petit seminaire*, 4, 9–10, 13, 30–33

Michel, Virgil, 399–402
Milske, Gerald, 244, 343
Minnesota Consortium of Theological Schools, 364, 369, 374, 416–18, 435
Missia, Francis A., 115, 158, 176, 179, 191, 402–5, 418–19
Missia, Jakob, 402–3
Mission Society, 149, 412
Mission statement, 283–84
Modernism, 126–28
Moriarty, Eugene J., 218, 228, 241
Motl, James, 321, 334–35, 407
Moudry, James, 218, 238, 268, 275, 280, 292, 324, 329–32, 344, 349–50, 354, 406–8
Moynihan, Humphrey, 80–82, 107, 144–46, 148, 151–52, 154–55, 159–60, 166, 168, 171–72, 187
Mulcahy, Leroy, 326
Murphy, Terrence, 176, 178, 254, 276, 278, 280–81, 283, 287–91, 295–96, 301, 304–5, 325–27, 349–51, 354, 358, 430
Murray Institute, 369, 426, 428–29
Murray, John Gregory, 168–72, 174–75, 177–78, 180, 182–83, 188–89, 192–94, 198–202, 207–8, 211, 218, 224, 271, 278, 403, 414, 420, 423

National Association of Church Business Administrators, 427–28, 431
National Catholic Educational Association, 183–84, 208–9, 411
National Catholic Rural Life Conference, 409, 411, 413–14, 416
National Catholic War Council, 139
National Catholic Welfare Conference, 140, 170, 178–79, 389, 411, 414
Native American ministry, 10, 23
Nazareth Hall, 24, 39, 140–42, 146, 152–54, 159, 167, 256, 259, 273, 303, 316, 393, 402, 406
Neighborhood relations, 323–25
New Ulm, Diocese of, 215
Nichols, James, 365
Nickels, Peter, 280, 284
North Central Association of Colleges and Universities, 183–86, 193, 241–42, 266–67, 292, 297, 299, 308, 363–65
Nyman, Lois, 308
Nyman, Sharon, 365

O'Brien, John D., 104
O'Connell, Denis, 81, 92, 98, 124
O'Connell, Marvin, 384
O'Connor, Michael Patrick, 121, 355–56, 368
O'Dea, Thomas F., 213–14
O'Gorman, Thomas, 13, 30, 38–39, 65–66, 70, 78, 89, 99, 107, 111, 113–15, 119, 121, 136
O'Hara, Edwin, 386, 409–16

Olier, Jean-Jacques, 7–8
Onahan, William James, 96
O'Neill, James H., 130
Orate fratres, 146, 400–401
Oster, Anatole, 12–14, 22, 34, 45, 92
O'Sullivan, John, 217–18, 228, 244

Palen, Rose, 272, 345
Papesh, Michael, 356, 371
Pates, Richard, 281, 289–90, 329–30, 347–49, 353–54, 379
Patton, Corrine, 370
Pedophilia, 338–40
Pierre, Kenneth, 318, 320, 324, 346
Pius IX, 3–4, 16, 35
Pius X, 126–28, 399–400, 403, 413, 415
Pius XI, 141, 149–50, 174–75, 235, 389, 414
Pius XII, 183, 218–19, 235, 420
Pope, Stephen, 308
Prendergast, James H. (Harry), 147–48
Presbyteral Council, 304–5, 313–23, 325
Pre-theology program, 275
Program of Priestly Formation, 246–47, 268, 299, 374

Quinn, J. Patrick, 334, 355, 369–70
Quinn, Jerome D., 213, 218, 238, 258, 354–55
Racial integration, 122–24, 391–93
Rafferty, James, 371
Ramsey, Alexander, 20
Rask, Phillip, 285, 357–58, 362–63, 365, 376–78, 380–81
Raspanti, Celeste, 384
Ravoux, Augustine, 10–11, 13, 16–17, 19, 30, 34, 42, 49
Ray, Walter, 407
Reardon, James, 90
Recreation (Off-campus), 85–86, 148, 194, 208–9, 223, 262
Rennie, Carol, 334, 343, 365, 373, 428
Riley, Marion, 308
Roach, John R., 176–78, 180–81, 196–97, 199, 254, 257–59, 268–73, 276–78, 281–82, 285, 292, 294–96, 298, 301, 303, 305, 307–8, 312–17, 320–22, 326–28, 330, 332, 339, 342–43, 345–50, 353–54, 357–59, 367, 384–85, 395–97, 424–25
Robinson, Mary, 429
Rogge, Leonard, 308
Rotter, Cyril F., 378
Rural ministry, 409, 411–12, 415–18
Ryan, John Augustine, 83, 90–91, 120–21, 146, 196, 386, 388–91, 409
Ryan, Lawrence F., 195–97, 215, 223, 228, 243

Ryan, Patrick J., 218, 258, 262, 266–68
Ryan, Vincent J., 416

Sacred Congregation for Catholic Education, 246–47
Sacred Congregation of Propaganda, 36, 87–88, 138, 395–96, 421
Sacred Congregation of Seminaries and Universities, 138, 149–51, 182–83, 215, 246
Saiko, Paul Therese, 310, 334, 372, 380
Saint Cloud, Diocese of, 26
Saint John Vianney College Seminary, 256–59, 271–72, 279, 281, 347
Saint Mary's Chapel, 110–14, 154–66, 294, 301, 303, 326, 329–32, 343–44, 378, 385
Saint Paul Diocesan Normal Institute, 153–54
Saint-Sulpice, Seminary (of Paris), 7, 8, 9
Saint Thomas Aquinas Seminary (St. Paul, Minn.), 38–40, 53
Saint Thomas, College/University of, 24, 39, 142, 171–72, 177, 240–241, 256–58, 278–82, 286–90, 293–307, 311–12, 316–26, 342, 350–54, 366–69, 375, 381
Sankowitz, John, 240
Satolli, Francesco, 64–67, 72
Scapanski, Gene, 334, 348, 350–51, 365–66, 369, 371, 426–28, 431
Schaefer, Francis J., 82, 116–17, 144
Schaffer, Gregory T., 385
Schedule, 84–85, 147, 173–74, 179, 209, 239
Schierman, Karen, 431
Schladweiler, Alphonse J., 151, 215
School Sisters of Notre Dame, 43
Schools (elementary and secondary), 12, 22–23, 30, 39, 42, 413, 425–26
Schuler, Richard J., 318, 406
Schuth, Katarina, 356, 365, 370, 381–83
Schwartz, Robert, 310, 336, 356, 427
Seid-Martin, Sue, 285, 310, 354, 356, 378, 408–9
Seliskar, John, 90
Seminarians, 13, 121–23, 260–61, 274
Seminaries: France, 4, 7–10, 32–33; Iowa, 10; Rome, 18, 81, 107, 205–6, 234; U.S., 58, 136, 145, 204; Louvain, 218
Serra, Dominic, 121, 355, 368, 377, 407
Sevenich, Roman, 193
Shanahan, Thomas J., 151, 187, 189–90, 228, 238
Shanahan, William, 90
Shanley, John, 99, 114

Shannon, James P., 176, 196, 210, 224, 254, 256, 262–64, 268
Shapira, Harold and Helen, 375–76
Shapiro, Max, 375, 430–31
Sheen, Fulton J., 192, 223, 386, 418–21
Shields, Thomas Edward, 119, 421–23, 427
Sieg, Thomas, 334, 407
Simonet, J. Thomas, 287, 300, 354
Sisters of Charity of the Blessed Virgin Mary, 11
Sisters of the Good Shepherd, 109
Sisters of St. Joseph of Carondelet, 11–12, 19, 30, 42, 109–10, 118, 190–92, 207, 211, 333
Skach, Sandra, 366, 429–30
Slattery, John R., 123
Sledz, Ladislaus, 212
Slight, Catherine, 365
Smith, John Talbot, 74
Smith, Mark, 308
Snyder, Larry J., 396
Social justice, 20–21, 123, 139–40, 170, 252–53, 388–97, 401–2, 409–11, 415
Soentgerath, John, 81
Sondag, John, 274
Spiritual formation and direction, 92–94, 150, 173–74, 196–97, 243–44, 264–65, 282–83, 290, 310, 319–20, 322, 336, 338–39, 371–72
Srnec, Stanley, 243, 264
Stariha, John, 104, 118
Steinle, David, 405
Stodola, Elizabeth, 285, 406
Stosur, David, 355–56, 407
Summer placement of seminarians, 209, 242–43
Summer Vacation School Movement, 149, 412
Sweeney, John, 173, 181, 196, 218, 222–23, 228, 243–44, 254, 258, 266, 336, 356, 404–5
Szarke, John, 334, 355

Tanqueray, Adolph, 89
Taylor, Donald, 365
Teaching Parish program, 290, 335, 337, 373, 435
Temperance, 28, 35, 86
Theobald, Stephen, 124–25
Tibesar, Leo, 335, 396–97
Tonsure, 245
Toomey, John J., 107–9, 112
Toomey, William C., 107, 112
Torvend, Samuel, 336, 348, 355, 407
Trobec, James, 99, 111
Turner, Thomas, 124
Tyrell, George, 126

Vatican Council II, 219, 223, 226, 233, 236–38, 244–46, 262, 264

Visitations, U.S. Bishops', 265–67, 373–74
Visitations, Vatican, 150–52, 174–75, 292, 297–99, 308
Viktora, Jan, 334–37, 365, 371, 373, 428

Wetherald, William, 46–47
Wolf, Lawrence O., 151, 175–78, 183, 211, 215–16, 228, 238

Yang, Seung-Ai, 369
Yetzer, Bernard, 354, 363–66

Zannoni, Arthur, 334, 356, 427, 430